D1596709

NINTH—HEAVEN—TO—NINTH—HELL

NINTH HEAVEN TO NINTH HELL

THE HISTORY OF A NOBLE CHINESE EXPERIMENT

QIN HUAILU

EDITED BY WILLIAM HINTON
Translation by Dusanka Miscevic

BARRICADE BOOKS INC.
New York

Published by Barricade Books Inc.
150 Fifth Avenue
New York, NY 10011

Book design by LaBreacht Design.

Printed in the United States of America.

Library of Congress Cataloging-in-Publication Data

Ch' in, Huai-lu.
Ninth heaven to ninth hell: history of a noble Chinese experiment / Qin Huailu; edited by William Hinton.
p. cm.
ISBN 1-56980-041-3
1. Ch' en, Yung-kuei. 2. Vice prime ministers—China—Biography. 3. Agriculture—China—Ta-chai (Shansi Province) I. Hinton, William. II. Title.
DS778.C59157N56 1995
338.1'851'092—dc20
[B] 95-15361
CIP

First printing

CONTENTS

PREFACE

Vice-Premier Chen Yonggui's rough-hewn face, craggy as the rock on Tigerhead Mountain, was completely mobile, changing expression swiftly and completely as his mood changed. It reminded me of the face of Fernandel, the great French comedian, so serious, even tragic, at one moment, yet creased with laughter the next. On his head he always wore a white hand towel tied behind in typical Taihang Mountain fashion. He wore this towel even in Beijing, even while attending the National People's Congress. When this peasant leader went to the city, the countryside held its own, no doubt about that. Chen Yonggui enjoyed meeting people, particularly people who were interested in the Chinese countryside. He had much to say, it rolled out in a flood of stories, self-criticisms, exclamations, philosophical musings. He acted out each part, bracketing ideas with his swiftly moving hands.

Chen's voice was deep and gravelly, his vocal cords no doubt as stained with nicotine as his fingers from smoking too many cigarettes and lighting one from the other. He spoke as if he had called too often to the people breaking rock in the next ravine. His accent was pure Xiyang, broad yet angular. Not too many tones. Shanxi people don't speak in the tones of Beijing. And his vocabulary—it was as rich as any vocabulary I ever heard, not only rich in words but rich in images and colloquialisms, in imitative sounds; a knock on the door—ka tsa, ka tsa; depression—hui liu liu de; dismay—ai ya, ai ya; empty-handed—like a tall sorghum stalk, nothing but pith inside; glory—the whiskers of Jiang Fei (legendary hero) all over our faces; pride—a tail in the air that nobody dares touch; plot—the weasel says Happy New Year to the chicken. No English translation could ever be more than a pale reflection of a conversation with Chen Yonggui of Dazhai. [Description of Chen Yonggui from William Hinton's *Shenfan*, page 236.]

Today, from in front of the impressive stone stele marking Chen Yonggui's tomb, looking north toward Tiananmen as Chen, seeing that palace gate in his mind's eye, so often did, the view is breathtaking—rock-walled step-terraces, tier-on-tier, hold firm the sides of gullies plugged with arch-shaped dams also laid up with rock; small Dazhai plains surround nestling villages fashioned from cut-stone designed to last, they say, two thousand years; orchard-covered ridges overhang irrigation channels that wind snakelike across ravine-serrated slopes. Raising the eyes brings into view jumbled hilltops, distant mountain summits, wave on wave, beneath an azure, overarching sky. Chen always said the North could outproduce the South because the North, unlike the overcast warmer regions, has sunlight all day most days. Who could avoid sitting quietly on Tigerhead, taking in the full sweep of the spectacle below and marveling at the human ingenuity, skill, long hours and endless travail that went into its creation? Not many landscapes in the world are so much a product of natural force and human counter-force as this one.

Looking at a deep slot cut by storm waters through solid rock, Premier Zhou Enlai once asked Guo Fenglian, the leader of Dazhai's "Iron Girls," what was stronger, water or people.

"People," said Guo Fenglian.

"But water cut right through that rock," said the Premier, skeptical.

"Water took thousands of years to do it. My team could do that in a few days!" Guo exclaimed.

Premier Zhou Enlai had no answer for that.

As for the village itself, it nestles, virtually out of sight from any vantage point, in a deep cleft in the mantle of loess soil that overlies the bedrock under Tigerhead Mountain. Before the return to privatization in the eighties, the elongated courtyard at the bottom of the cleft retained the ambience of a quiet nurturing ground for family life. Double- and triple-storied tiers of stone-lined caves surrounded it on three sides. Close to the middle, jutting rakishly from the base of a high masonry retaining wall, the mighty, ancient willow so beloved of Dazhai residents, at once a tree of joy and a tree of sorrow, survived, more or less intact, generations of benign neglect. Under its spreading branches many a long meeting convened of a summer evening to hammer out consensus of thought and action. A few small one-story buildings crowded the upper end of the gully. Brick-walled and tile-roofed, they served as cookhouses and spare sleeping quarters for families living in the first tier of caves. Since the community maintained most livestock, fuel supplies (both stalks and coal), communal privies, and staple stores outside the confines of the gully itself, the spacious yard, swept clean daily, appeared as well kept as a public park, and like any popular urban park, was always alive with children playing, women chatting, sewing, or simply sunning themselves. Chickens clucking, scratching and pecking beneath the feet of a stray dog or two added an extra rural touch to the scene.

This book constitutes an unusual biography. It is not so much the life story of Chen Yonggui, an outstanding common man turned statesman, as it is a defense brief, a polemic riposte, a vindication, and an exoneration, a call for justice and a cry of pain for a person, a community and a world outlook grievously distorted and wronged in the maelstrom of sudden historical reversal that struck China in 1978.

Throughout the book the author, Qin Huailu, puts emphasis beyond a well-rounded, conventional portrait of the subject in question—Chen Yonggui and his village base, Dazhai. He sets the record straight vis-a-vis the various trumped-up charges and slanders that Deng Xiaoping's media confederates launched against the peasant Vice-Premier, his village, his County and above all his life work. The attack began on October 17, 1980, with the publication in the *Shanxi Daily*, the official voice of Shanxi Province, of the first critical diatribe entitled "Dazhai's Departure From the Spirit of Dazhai," then expanded, at many levels and in a plethora of forms, into an all-out, general offensive. This attack elicited very little by way of defense until Qin Huailu, many years later, dared to take up the task with a counter-polemic.

In some ways the defensive warp of Qin's book is detrimental to the dramatic unfolding of Chen Yonggui's life story, but overall the polemical intensity of Qin's treatment is what gives his writing its emotional depth, its urgency, its vitality, its bite. Had Chen Yonggui never suffered attack, there would have been no need to rally in his defense, to pore through all the records, to interview all the people whose lives touched his, and to examine all the issues as the author Qin Huailu has done. Without the unfair repudiation inflicted on Chen Yonggui, who would have felt compelled to compile this remarkable story of a near miraculous rise and an undeserved and ignominious fall?

Chen Yonggui's career formed the heart of a seminal controversy in China's modern history. By joining battle on the issues, Qin Huailu has done the world a great service. Everyone pays lip service to "seeking truth from facts," a slogan misused by Deng Xiaoping to elbow his way to supreme power, after having twice been set aside. But unless people have a chance to hear all sides, how can they ascertain the facts? A slanderous re-condemnation of Chen Yonggui, entitled *The Rise and Fall of the Red Flag of Dazhai*, was published in Honan in 1990, in the same year that the Communist Party Central Committee banned Qin Huailu's book on the grounds that the Party had not yet passed a final verdict on Chen Yonggui. So much for reason and fair play in the age of "reform."

I will have more to say about Chen Yonggui and Dazhai in an Afterword to this volume. But first, here is Qin Huailu's candid, vital story of the peasant statesman who transformed his own life, his village, his County, his Province, and at least for a time influenced the course of human affairs in all of China.

William H. Hinton

PART ONE

THE MAKING OF CHEN YONGGUI

INTRODUCTION

He started out as a plain, down-to-earth, average peasant. Like many generations of Chinese peasants before him who carried the weight of the "clear heavens" on their backs while their feet trod the yellow earth, Chen Yonggui toted wicker baskets on shoulder poles, wielded pickaxes and grub hoes, ploughed and weeded in the terraced fields, and nursed along crop after crop. He staged his battles over many years along the narrow foot-trails that wind amid the rocks and caves of the Taihang Mountains and the gullies and ridges of the loess plateau.

Forty years ago, beyond the confines of his village, hardly anybody even knew him. But as history entered the second half of the twentieth century, this simple peasant became a "star," known throughout the vast land of China. His small, multi-level hamlet of a mere 110 households became the red banner on China's agricultural front. State leaders propagated the experiences of the little village among 800 million Chinese peasants, and its fame spread well beyond the borders of the nation.

On the map of China, which covers some three million six hundred and ninety thousand square miles, the village of Dazhai is a tiny dot—

albeit a dot on which many an admiring eye has focused attention. Yet Chen Yonggui and a few other ordinary down-to-earth peasants of his circle, all of whom hailed from that dot, rode the crest of the tide of history straight into the County Party Committee, into the Yingze Guesthouse in the Provincial Capital, into the Great Hall of the People in Beijing, into the seat of the central government at Zhongnanhai, and well beyond the boundaries of China on travels to foreign lands. For a relatively long time Chen Yonggui was one of a handful of dynamic figures on the Chinese political scene. In his later years the hoe-wielding farmer made an enormous leap by "ascending the throne" as a member of the Political Bureau of the Central Committee of the Chinese Communist Party and as a Vice-Premier of the State Council.

Learn from Dazhai! Hey!
Catch up with Dazhai!
Red flowers of Dazhai
Blossom low and high.

The surging melody of the opening song on the Village Broadcast of the People's Central Radio used to reverberate over the mountains, rivers and lakes, reaching all corners of the motherland. It moistened many a singing throat, and touched many a heart. It aroused multitudes to action, and led them to take their destiny into their own hands. It drove millions of people to transform barren mountains, fill in forbidding ravines, and tame unruly rivers. It confused others into committing foolish deeds that defy the logic of objective laws. Nature, in turn, while punishing those who abused the land, offered bounteous gifts to those who learned well from Dazhai. There are people, endlessly stirred by this song, who have fought selflessly because of it. Some have even laid down their lives.

The Dazhai song was the agricultural battle hymn of the 1960s and 1970s. Even the high tides and lapses of Chinese agriculture seem to have followed its tune. From the time when people first learned the song in the mid-1960s, through many tireless campaigns and lively struggles, the "Learn from Dazhai" mass movement in agriculture unfolded on a grand and spectacular scale throughout China's far-flung domain.

During those twelve or more years, over seven million pilgrims embarked on strenuous journeys from the far corners of the motherland and descended on Xiyang County, crossed the Songxi River, and converged on Tigerhead Mountain. They brought along their devotion for the Great Leader, Chairman Mao, and when they raised their red books and shouted "Learn from Dazhai, catch up with Dazhai," their voices seemed to shake the earth and echo back from the sky. Central regional and local leaders held more than twenty meetings in Xiyang County and Dazhai, all rooted in the momentous mass movement initiated there. The sheer number of these meetings, their high level, and the scope of the government departments involved were truly something seldom seen in a small County like Xiyang, and a tiny hamlet like Dazhai.

How could Dazhai's influence stop at China's borders? From the 1960s onward, the fame of the little village started spreading overseas and, indeed, it seems as though its name made the rounds of the entire globe.

When I looked at the records of two decades ago, I found that 2,288 international groups and 25,478 individual foreign guests of varying skin color, nationality and creed from 134 countries and regions had visited Tigerhead Mountain. On one occasion, the village received guests from 35 countries in a single day. What's more, the enormous, mind-boggling influence of Dazhai aroused the interest of the heads of State of more than twenty nations, and a vast assortment of lesser leaders. They all climbed Tigerhead Mountain in person to find out what gave this little village such magical powers. The late President of Mozambique Samora Moises Machel came to Dazhai twice in search of a way to promote agriculture in his country. Albania's Political Bureau member and First Vice-Chairman of the Council of Ministers Spiro Koleka, Mexico's President Luis Echeverria Alvarez, Mali's President Moussa Traore, Cambodia's Prime Minister Prince Norodom Sihanouk, Singapore's President Lee Kuan Yew, General Secretary of the United Nations Kurt Waldheim, General Secretary of the Communist Party of Kampuchea Pol Pot, American friends of the People's Republic of China Edgar Snow and William Hinton, and the famous Sino-Belgian writer Han Suyin, among others, all paid visits to Dazhai. Dazhai received high praise for its amazing achievements from several international organizations and won the Italian International "Expert in Agriculture Award."

Although that momentous age is now gone, many enthusiastic people still ask to this day: "Why did Chairman Mao Zedong bring forth the slogan 'In agriculture, learn from Dazhai' in 1968, and how did he empower it to sweep across the entire land? What is it that propelled Chen Yonggui, a mere dirt farmer who raised corn, to 'ascend the throne' as a member of the Political Bureau of the Central Committee of the Chinese Communist Party and as a Vice-Premier of the State Council, and to preside over the fate of China's agriculture for almost a decade? And why is it that, even after his precipitous fall from favor, many people still tenaciously honor his memory and undertake investigations on his behalf?"

Chen Yonggui took part in a series of sweeping, soul-stirring social dramas that occurred on the stage of Chinese history. Some played out as comedies, some as tragedies, others as sheer farce. There may be unknowing people who think these dramas strange. But nobody who lived during the 1960s and 1970s and knew the facts would find them absurd, though tragic they surely were.

Chen Yonggui's rise and fall may seem an anomaly of history and yet, in truth, it was no miracle. The real story leaves a puzzling, poignant aftertaste. Today, as history has ostensibly dropped the final curtain on this drama and the story can be told, many of the fascinating "myths" and object lessons that had remained in people's memories and among their stored documents cannot but enhance the allure of the name: Chen Yonggui.

CHAPTER 1

THE PERVERSE CHEN FAMILY GRAVEYARD

Through the ages Dazhai has occupied hotly contested territory. Tradition has it that the armies of the Northern Song, when they attempted to stop the invading Jin troops, garrisoned the Hongqiao Pass at the back of Tigerhead Mountain. Since they pitched their camp and stored their grain and fodder in Dazhai, they made Dazhai's name well known. Yet, during the next thousand and more years, history recorded no further mention of this place. Not until Dazhai, having reared the rustic hero Chen Yonggui, changed beyond recognition and entered the twentieth century through the big door of revolution did the hamlet elbow its way once more into history.

Our modern age has added new content to an ancient area of contention: seemingly endless debate about Chen Yonggui, an endless debate even over the simple facts of Chen Yonggui's origin and personal history to add to similar controversies originating in ages past that have escalated from dynasty to dynasty.

I don't know why the circumstances surrounding Chen's arrival in Dazhai managed to give birth to such an array of fraudulent explanations. Is it mere coincidence that the sources of the fraud display such distinctly human features? Some say that Chen Yonggui came to Dazhai fleeing famine in Shaanxi Province—people have even written logically coherent articles about this. Others claim that he was a runaway landlord from Shandong; or a secret agent from Hebei, who was later recognized somewhere by somebody from his hometown; or that his place in history is such and such.... According to Liang Bianliang[1], when the author of *Dazhai's Place in the World*, Zhang Zhenglong, went to Dazhai in 1983 to gather material for this book of creative nonfiction, in the process of clarifying Chen Yonggui's personal history he asked Liang Bianliang: "Where is good old Chen from, after all?"

"There you go!" Liang Bianliang answered in all earnestness. "But, I suppose, it's just as well that you get it clear. Why don't you get a car at the County town and go to look at his old house yourself? That would be good enough to convince you, wouldn't it?"

Faced with facts, I could find no justification to inquire further.

What I find intolerable is that after the Central Committee investigated, clarified and reached a conclusion regarding Chen Yonggui's personal history, Sun Qitai and Xiong Zhiyong, in their book entitled *The Rise and Fall of the Red Flag of Dazhai* published in 1990, mentioned several times how "Chen Yonggui, during the Resistance War Against Japanese Occupation, participated in a meeting of the 'New Asia Society' which was organized by Japanese officials." They planted the personal history of some other Chen Yonggui onto the head of Chen Yonggui from Dazhai. Once again, the much maligned man was treated unjustly without an opportunity to right the wrong.

But, let's begin with the story of the real Chen Yonggui.

In Xiyang County there is a hamlet called Shishan or Rock Mount, about 30 Chinese *li* from Dazhai.[2] This is the place Chen Yonggui hails from. Several generations of Chens have found their final resting place in the old graveyard, just outside the village. A lone pine, gnarled and ancient, dominates the graves. The Chens like to think of it as a symbol of the timeless glory of their clan, yet the pine has let them down

1. Liang Bianliang, a Dazhai peasant, was a colleague and staunch supporter of Chen Yonggui.
2. Shishan literally means "rock mount," which illustrates the nature of terrain in Xiyang County. One Chinese *li* equals 0.5 kilometers or 0.3107 English miles.

time and again by extending its branches all too readily to those who wish to die.

One of the Chens who hung himself from the old pine was Chen Zhiru, whose childhood name was Chen Keni. It happened sometime during the Tenth Year of the Republic.[1] Men of all ages, white sashes around their waists and long-stemmed pipes hanging on strings from their necks, gathered around the body, but no one was in the mood to smoke. As a stifling mist enshrouded the entire graveyard, the sound of muffled sighing mingled with heart-wrenching sobs.

Probably because of the legacy of *I Ching*, Chinese people like to fuss over graves in order to make them auspicious. They spare no expenses when it comes to inviting a geomancer to select a good site for the family's grave mound. The geomancer who selected the Chen family graveyard pronounced the position of the mountains auspicious, and announced that the family would flourish, produce a person of high rank, and achieve riches and honor. Alas, his invocation did not seem to be efficacious! For several generations, the fate of the Chens was nothing but miserable. Chen Keni and his four brothers all had to leave home to make a living. Only one of them died at home, but little comfort can be gleaned from that. It was not a natural death.

In the winter of 1914, Chen Keni took his entire family to Little South Mount at the back of Tigerhead Mountain. On the first day of the lunar New Year, Chen Keni's wife gave birth to a son in a cave[2] dug out of the ground. They called him Jinxiao, but in order to bring him good luck, they also gave him an official name, which they chose carefully from the old family genealogy: Yonggui (Forever Precious). Before him his mother bore a girl, after him another boy.

One year somebody must have offended the old Dragon King[3] because for twelve long months he didn't send us humans a good ground-soaking rain. Peasant families did not harvest a single kernel of

1. 1921.

2. The caves of the loess plateau are manmade, high-ceilinged long vaults, usually dug into perpendicular, standing faces of loess soil. They are roomy, light at the front due to paper windows, warm in winter, cool in summer—in other words attractive, comfortable, affordable peasant housing. Modern Dazhai cave vaults are lined with cut-stone masonry to make them flood- and earthquake-proof. (W.H.H.)

3. The God of Rain in Chinese mythology.

grain, and I'm not talking just about grain to eat—I mean grain for seed too. In order to survive, all Chen Keni could do was pick up a carrying pole with a sigh, load the cooking pan, eating bowls, gourd ladle and washbasin on one end of the pole, his infant child on the other, and head back to his old home in Rock Mount. Unfortunately poor people, no matter where they ran or how far they hid, could not escape the old society's wide-open bloodthirsty mouth. Chen Keni reclaimed a field from wasteland but still found himself working for a rich landlord. When the land lay wasting nobody claimed ownership, but once some desperate peasant reclaimed a piece and started growing crops, some landlord always claimed it as his own. Hard as Chen Keni tried he could not make enough to pay high rent and still support his wife and children.

Chen Yonggui remembers one completely moonless night before the family left Rock Mount when his father hugged his wife tightly and cried like a wounded animal. Although, when the year is bad, nobody is to blame, the husband's head drooped while he searched for caring words with which to console his wife. In order to keep his family alive he had no choice but to sell his wife and two of his three children to buyers in other places, while he himself with his oldest son moved on, hoping to change their fortunes.

When a couple parts, it's never easy. "If our fate is not to live, no matter how far we go, we'll still die," the wife pleaded. "It looks like Heaven will not bypass our entire family, so why don't we just all die here? At least our bones will be gathered in one place."

"If fate spares others, why wouldn't it spare you and me?" the husband argued, trying to persuade her to accept the tragic deal. "I'm only suggesting what's best for everybody. I've arranged to sell you and the little son into Heshun County. You go along with him and try to make it. I'll keep the big son. We should be able to get enough to eat and drink when we sell our labor. As for the girl, she's a maiden. There's no shortage of people who want her. I've sold her into Yagou Village in Xizhai Township. For better or worse, she won't be single at least, so she won't turn into a vengeful ghost."

The husband and wife tried to console each other, sobbing intermittently. They longed for the night to never end, so they could speak out their minds and pour out all their tears. People were coming to get the wife and the girl as soon as the curtain of darkness lifted. The marriage that had lasted many years was about to break up. She, who had been until that moment a Chen bride and a Chen family daughter-in-law, was to become the bride of a Yang.

The following day, a Heshun County peasant surnamed Yang came to take Chen Yonggu's mother and younger brother away. Another peasant from Yagou village in Xizhai Township, at the western end of Xiyang County, fetched the older sister to serve as a child bride.

One would expect that Chen Keni would have been able make ends meet easily after he sold his wife, his son and his daughter, but fate had just the opposite in store for him. He settled in Dazhai, on the other side of the mountain range. But a year or two in that barren place so impoverished him that he could no longer survive. The skin on the cheeks of his son Chen Yonggui had nothing to stick to but bare bones, so he turned him over to two old peasant women, Old Lady Xiang and Old Lady Meng, who were somewhat better off and happy to have another son to raise.

Chen Keni himself, in return for something to eat, went off to work in Wujiaping[1] or Five Family Flat, for a landlord surnamed Wang. For an entire year the landlord provided only food and drink, paying him nothing for his services. He even hinted that the elder Chen should have been happy for something in his stomach in a bad year like that one. Then, at the end of the tenth month of the lunar calendar,[2] when most landlords no longer needed any temporary farm hands, Chen Keni saw that he had reached the end of the road. For several days he sighed, without uttering a word, then finally accepted his fate. On a pitch-dark night, when it was hard to see the tip of your own nose, without a word to anybody he returned to his native village, Rock Mount. Once there, he spilled his last tears on his ancestors' graves, and then hung his useless body from the pine tree, which had never been good at answering human wishes and seems perversely to have utterly disregarded the geomancer's prophesy. Thus a snap of the rope put an end to the life of Old Man Chen.

---

1. Wujiaping, literally Five Family Flat, was a large village on the flat land next to Dazhai.
2. Beginning of winter, when the farming season is over.

When the great tragedy of Keni's death reached the Chens, the family members had long since gone their separate ways. The only one who could have paid his last respects to the deceased was the son left behind in Dazhai, Chen Yonggui. Old Lady Xiang and Old Lady Meng tried to comfort the boy, who was only six at the time. There was not much the two widows could do for him but sigh as their eyes swelled with tears. The emaciated little boy kept crying, "Daddy! My daddy!" until his voice went hoarse. Finally, Old Lady Meng overcame her penury and brought out the few chicken eggs she had collected in the rice jar. She used them to buy a foot of white cloth at the village supply store, which she then tied around Chen Yonggui's waist by way of a mourning dress. She pushed him around to face in the direction of Rock Mount and instructed him, visibly pained: "Jinxiao! Let's kowtow to your father. Aunty is not sure what's the proper way to do it, but let us try."

Chen Yonggui, his face smudged with tears, faithfully followed the movements of Old Lady Meng.

The adults in Dazhai who were there at the time made sympathetic comments. They all felt saddened by Chen Yonggui's fate. Several women, having sighed profusely, asked him: "Jinxiao, what do you think should be done for your dad?"

According to several who witnessed the scene, Chen Yonggui did not utter a word. Perhaps he was too young to adjust to the sudden catastrophe. Or perhaps the cruel stratagems so far inflicted by fate had already toughened his character.

Although they were a family belonging to the Jia clan, the paternal sisters Xiang and Meng treated Chen as one of their own. Chen Yonggui had no blood relatives in Dazhai. The Chens of Rock Mount, on the other hand, were very numerous. At that particular time, however, they were all struggling to keep themselves alive, and were in no position to help a destitute child who was wandering far from home. Chen Yonggui kept hoping that someone from Rock Mount would at least come to take him back to the ancestral burial ground to look at his father's grave. Meanwhile, the resentment of the older villagers toward his father's death reverberated in his ears.

"That geomancer sure fooled your family, one generation after another."

"What did he have to go back to that old graveyard for? To have his soul return to earth there?"

"What good could have come to him from returning to that place?"

And yet several decades later, when Chen Yonggui became "a person of high rank," the geomancer's words seemed miraculously to have come true. Due to the honor associated with the post of Vice-Premier, people suddenly recalled the story of the Chen family graveyard and that old, gnarled pine tree. Indeed, it was quite an extraordinary coincidence. Thanks to this coincidence, if indeed that's what it was, the old pine tree remains standing in Rock Mount to this day, its roots unharmed. There is even a patch of wild grass in the shape of a human figure spreading around it that nobody dares touch.

After Chen Keni went back to the old family grave site in Rock Mount to release his soul, Chen Yonggui became, in Chinese eyes, an orphan even though his mother was still alive. Old Lady Xiang and Old Lady Meng continued to care for him in Dazhai. They treated him as their own grandson. After these two died, Old Lady Meng's widowed daughter-in-law, the not-so-old Old Lady Wenzhou, took on the responsibility. This is how the unique "combined household" of widow Meng and the stripling Chen emerged in benighted Dazhai.

CHAPTER — 2

A UNIQUE "COMBINED HOUSEHOLD"

I don't care whether one speaks of ancient times or of today, of China or abroad—a woman's capacity for kindness is always great.

Old Lady Wenzhou's kindness to Chen Yonggui was obvious to all in Dazhai. The widow had a son of her own, but she never made a distinction in the way she treated the two boys. If anything, she lavished extra care on Chen Yonggui.

Later in life, Chen Yonggui often talked about the tender care he had received from Old Lady Wenzhou as a child. Every time Chen Yonggui returned from the field shouldering his grub hoe and dripping with sweat, Old Lady Wenzhou called out to him affectionately to put down his hoe and wash his face. Then she swung around painfully on her "golden lotus" feet,[1] which feudal etiquette had bequeathed her as a reminder of its courtesy, and brought him the bran pancakes that she had cooked especially for him.

---

1. In those days almost all of Shanxi's older women had bound feet, which their mothers formed by binding doubled-under toes beneath the arch of the foot with strips of cotton cloth—an extremely painful and drawn-out procedure that crippled the women so bound, and condemned them to walk on their heels, as if on stilts. (W.H.H.)

"Look Auntie," Chen Yonggui protested with a frown whenever this happened. "It's been a bad year. Why don't you just feed me the wild root curd?[1] If you let me eat my fill of grain, you will really have to tighten your belt."

"Ayiiiya! If I tell you to eat it, just eat it," Old Lady Wenzhou would reproach him, pulling a long face. "There's always something an old woman can eat."

The affection between Old Lady Wenzhou and Chen Yonggui was truly extraordinary. Although he was not her natural son, she alone had pretty much brought him up. When he turned eleven, Old Lady Wenzhou felt the time had come to commemorate the fifth anniversary of his father's death. She urged him to go back to the family graveyard and burn paper money for his father. Having given him detailed instructions, she saw him off to the edge of the village with tears in her eyes.

He left Dazhai in the early morning. Chen Yonggui had hardly ever gone past Dazhai's village gate since early childhood. He knew nothing of the roads and paths around Rock Mount. He had no choice but to ask his way whenever he ran across someone. Thus delayed, he arrived at his ancestral home at dusk.

He stayed the night in the house of one of the Chen clan elders. On the following day, this elder took him to the ancestral graveyard for the paper-burning ritual. Later in his life Chen Yonggui recalled the unspeakable grief that overwhelmed his heart the moment he set his eyes on the old pine tree where his father's life had ebbed away. He examined the tree closely, then followed his guide to his father's grave. There he burned some paper money, knelt down and bowed his head low. He had trouble regaining his feet because he could no longer control his emotions and in the end he broke down, wailing loudly. His sorrow moved even the clan elder and he too began to sob.

Chen Yonggui longed for his father, but he missed his mother even more. The one thing he never imagined was that he might some day be able to reunite with his mother and younger brother, who had been sold off to the peasant Yang in Heshun County, or with his older sister, who had been sold off as a child-bride to Xizhai. But sometimes even a cruel fate relents. During that trip to his father's grave he had the good for-

1. "Fake beancurd"—the consistency of tofu but it was made from rhizomes found in the wilderness.

tune to learn of his mother's whereabouts. Tempered by his family's tragic experience Chen Yonggui had always had to be brave and keep his chin up. Now the eleven-year-old decided to make the long trip to Heshun County and look up Old Yang, who had bought her. He was determined to find his mother, whatever the effort.

The road from Rock Mount to Heshun went over a formidable highland, passing across the ridges and gorges of Zhanling Mountain. It was then a barely passable mountain trail, overgrown with nettles and thorn-studded shrubbery. As he followed the trail, the undergrowth pierced and stung him from head to toe, but he was so eager to find his mother he barely noticed the pain. He greeted other travelers along the way, addressing each politely as "Uncle," and asked for directions to Heshun County. Around noon, completely exhausted and hungry, he stopped to eat the bran pancake Old Woman Wenzhou had given him for the trip to Rock Mount.

He walked the entire day. The sun had already set behind the mountains in the west when he finally arrived at his destination—the home of the Yangs. There he found his mother.

When Chen's mother realized the little boy who now appeared in front of her was the son whom she, heartbroken, had left behind five years earlier, her grief overwhelmed her. She took him into her arms and, as they held each other tightly, neither could say a thing. Only streaming tears communicated their feelings. Now that she knew her husband had committed suicide, and now that her son had gone through the trouble of finding her, her mother's heart almost broke a second time. The thought of letting her son leave again overwhelmed her. But in a society where "men eat men" to survive, and where adding an extra mouth can mean starvation for all, people cannot avoid the cruelest of choices.

On the night Chen Yonggui found his mother, the master of the house, Yang, was not at home. Chen Yonggui slept comfortably with his mother and younger brother on a warm brick-bed *kang*.[1] Early the next morning, following his mother's instructions, he left the Yang

---

1. A kang is a mud-brick bed taking up one entire wall of a room and heated by the kitchen fire in a mud-brick stove built into the side of the kang. Under the surface layer of the kang the bricks are laid on edge to form a front-to-back series of horizontal flues that heat the whole kang surface before the smoke and fumes reach the vertical updraft provided by the hollow chimney, which, in the case of a loess cave, exhausts them from the ground surface, often many feet above the living space. (W.H.H.)

household and traveled far along Zhanling Mountain back to Xizhai township, this time in search of his older sister, who had been sold to be the wife of a man in Yagou Village nearly six years earlier.

After trudging another half-day Chen Yonggui reached Yagou Village and found his sister. When they met they wept in each other's arms and sobbed out recollections of the past. Years later Chen Yonggui told an audience interested in his personal history that his sister's husband had welcomed him warmly during that visit, but that the husband and wife had such a difficult time keeping themselves alive, there was no way they could take in this younger brother and feed him. Thus his sister had no choice but to send him back to Dazhai to be cared for by the old woman who had adopted him as her own.

Old Lady Wenzhou, who was waiting for him at the village gate, started sobbing as he approached. His eyes also filled with tears.

"You'll be the death of me," sighed the old woman. "I worried about you so much. I wondered whether you were still alive."

Tugging at him, she burst into tears.

Early experiences leave lasting impressions. The longer Chen Yonggui's separation from his mother and sister lasted, the more he thought about his dead father and his younger brother, who had been sold off along with his mother. He waited for the day when he could be reunited with those still alive. But the reunion of the family never took place. A few years later his mother passed away, and Chen Yonggui only heard about her death after the founding of the People's Republic. It was then, also, that he was told that his younger brother, born under an unlucky star, had lost his life as well. The story was that this brother had died working as a hired hand when he was only thirty years old. In later years the story was proved false in a most surprising way.

Because she was so fond of Chen Yonggui, Old Lady Wenzhou looked after him with great solicitude. At the age of eight Chen Yonggui had gone to work herding cows and sheep for a rich man. The rich man was only interested in using people and never even gave Chen Yonggui a pair of pants to cover his private parts or enough money to buy a pair. Old Lady Wenzhou cut down a new pair of her own pants and gave them to Chen Yonggui to cover himself and shield his limbs from cold. At the age of ten Chen Yonggui, as the saying went, "found what he was looking for." That is he became a long-term hired hand for the rich man. When he didn't get enough to fill his stomach at the boss's place, Old Lady Wenzhou always fed him something, even if the only food she had was thin gruel flavored with bitter wild herbs.

Under the old woman's tender care Chen Yonggui slowly grew into a young lad over five feet in height who was well trained in a score of skills needed on a peasant homestead. Not only did his peers among the poor admire him, even landlords looked upon him with special respect because he shouldered a double load of work. For several years he worked as a hired hand for a landlord in Five Family Flat, while also tending the few *mu* of sorry fields Old Lady Wenzhou owned. Even the landlord treated Chen Yonggui as though he was a native of Dazhai, just as though he was not separated by clan and family name from the woman who cared for him.

Old Lady Wenzhou had a big enough holding to be self-supporting, but fate had dealt her a heavy blow. Her son died just a few days after he got married, leaving his poor bride behind. Widowed in the prime of her youth, Bulky was bound by feudal norms and moral codes—"the three duties and the five constant virtues"—not to remarry after the death of her husband. Because of this, Old Lady Wenzhou placed her hopes more than ever before on her adopted son. "Don't worry about anything," the old woman instructed her dependent daughter-in-law. "You just slowly clear the way with the Jia family in this courtyard. Jinxiao will take care of the few *mu* that we have. He'll make sure we don't go hungry. You should cook for him and mend his clothes. In any event, you'll still be able to face people."

Widow Bulky showed great respect and obedience to her mother-in-law and took proper care of Chen Yonggui. She accepted his presence as legitimate. She used the same pot and ladle to serve his food as she used to serve her own. She used the same needle and thread to mend his clothes as she used to mend her own. As a result, they were able to resolve whatever frictions may have arisen between them.

People return measure for measure, kindness for kindness. Chen Yonggui did his very best to farm the land well and provide for all their material needs. As the days passed, Bulky, on her part, started treating Chen Yonggui as a true and beloved brother-in-law.

"Ayyaaa! Look at that coat!" she chided, expressing pity when she saw him wearing dirty clothes. "If you wear it a few days longer, you will choke from the stench of sweat and soil. Take it off and let me wash it!"

"Hng! If you want to master the land, how can you avoid getting stained with soil and mud? Ah?" Chen Yonggui would chide back, brushing her off as he shook the dirt from his garments.

The way things were in the countryside back then, however, it was extremely difficult for a person with an outsider's surname to find a place to stay in a village inhabited by families bearing a local patronym. If one clan monopolized an entire village, other "miscellaneous" surnames simply could not live there. Beneath it all lay a common fear that the outsider might seize some property.

In Dazhai it was the Jias who occupied the dominant position. Chen Yonggui had to use the Jia family gate at all times and, naturally, he suffered their disapproval and censure. They knew of Chen Yonggui's formidable reputation as a worker and were ill at ease facing him directly, so they looked for opportunities to express their misgivings through Old Lady Wenzhou and Jia Siyuan, who lived in the same compound.

On one occasion this Jia Siyuan, having noticed that Chen Yonggui had left the village, closed the compound gate at night before Chen Yonggui returned. When Chen Yonggui arrived home and found the gate closed he simmered with rage. He started pounding loudly on the heavy planks. Widow Bulky felt each "bang" as a pang in her heart because it not only announced that Jinxiao was unable to come in—it also clearly demonstrated how patriarchal neighbors could bully two powerless widowed women. Bulky never used vicious or abusive language with people, but this time her anger exploded, giving her spittle the sharpness of nails, and she used the moment when the gate finally opened to curse out the culprit.

"Whose fingers itched so badly that they closed the gate before everybody came home?" Widow Bulky screamed.

Jia Siyuan couldn't abide any such abuse. He was just about to make a vicious retort when he remembered that he was an elder, being Old Lady Wenzhou's brother-in-law, and that he was supposed to set an example of propriety. So he curbed his response.

"I closed the door! What about it? Two families live in this compound, yours and mine. So you tell me, who else is missing? If someone from elsewhere shows up, even if his surname is Jia, are you telling me that we can't close this gate any longer?"

"Never you mind whether it's my family or not!" retorted Widow Bulky. What Jia Siyuan was hinting at made her so angery her jaw dropped, and her voice grew coarse. "The man lives here, and if he hasn't come back you can't close the gate."

Jia Siyuan realized that the young widow was no pushover. His tone softened a little: "This doorway has one handle, and that's me. I have the right to close the gate."

Chen Yonggui strode into the courtyard as though he heard nothing. He stretched out on the warmer end of the brick-bed *kang* and went to sleep.

But Old Lady Wenzhou couldn't keep out of the fray. She, too, appeared in the main room facing the courtyard to yell her support for her daughter-in-law and stepson: "Old Number Four![1] What rights are you talking about? It's one compound and two families. Half of the rights are yours, but half are mine. When you feel like closing the gate in the future, close your half. Leave the other half to me."

There was nothing Jia Siyuan could come up with in response. But that didn't mean he got used to the idea of having someone of a different surname in his own yard, coming and going as he pleased. He kept looking for an opportunity to vent his discontent. One year on New Year's Eve Chen Yonggui went back to his home village of Rock Mount to celebrate the holiday. Jia Siyuan dusted the road in front of the compound gate with lime, which, according to feudal custom, meant that the household was engaged in a "grand sweep" to rid itself of all impurities, and that from then on "miscellaneous surnames would not be welcome to visit the house."

---

1. The "Si" in Jia Siyuan's name implies that he was the fourth son. He was Old Woman Wenzhou's deceased husband's younger brother.

Chen Yonggui, on his part, was not concerned with any kind of feudal symbol. When he returned from the New Year's holiday in Rock Mount, he stepped on the line drawn in lime dust with both feet, and went on to eat from the same pot with the two women and chat with them in the same courtyard, just as he had done before.

At the age of twenty-five, Chen Yonggui became a junior shop assistant in a pancake shop at the County seat. Carrying his merchandise on a shoulder pole, he went to hawk the pancakes in the streets. One day a group of beggars accosted him and pleaded with him in every possible way to save their lives by letting them eat a few pancakes. Chen Yonggui, moved by their suffering, gave in and handed them his whole consignment. Since a salesman who takes no money for his goods cannot square accounts with his boss, Chen Yonggui decided not to go back to the shop. He quickly dropped the baskets in front of it and, as a way out of the fix he was in, headed for the Provincial capital, Taiyuan. Who could have foreseen that he would only be able to drift aimlessly around Taiyuan for a while before hunger forced him to return on foot to Dazhai?

On his way home he walked through Shouyang, and somewhere in the countryside around Bazhou, in one of the corn fields of Double Mountain Head village, he spotted a chit of a girl, not more than twelve or thirteen, in tattered clothes and thin as a stick. All by herself, she gnawed at an ear of green corn.

"Why are you eating raw corn?" Chen Yonggui asked. "Don't you know you are not supposed to eat it raw?"

"Hungry," replied the girl, squeezing a single word out of her stomach.

Then she ran over and wrapped herself around Chen Yonggui's thigh, pleading: "Take me with you, brother. Save me. I'll go wherever you go."

The girl's heartbreaking cries moved Chen Yonggui. He gripped her hand tightly. But, not in any position to provide for himself, how could he take on a young girl? With kind words he tried to persuade her to let him out of her grip. He didn't expect that she would hang onto him like that. But for her, nothing would do except some promise of aid. If he couldn't help her on the spot he must help her later. In the end he agreed. He promised to come back for her in two years. No certain salvation that would seem, but Chen Yonggui meant what he said.

Two years later, he went back to Double Mountain Head to take the girl, Li Huni, as his wife. To celebrate his wedding his clansmen in Rock Mount put on a "feast" consisting of creamy wheat noodles. Then he took Li Huni with him to Dazhai. Since nobody from the Chen clan owned a strip of land or even a single roof tile in the village, Chen Yonggui and Li Huni continued to live in Old Lady Wenzhou's house. Widow Bulky took to Li Huni as though she were her younger sister.

"Jinxiao," she warned Chen Yonggui, "now that Huni sits on our bed, you better not be rude to people. If you get in some argument, we cannot take the blame for your bad reputation."

Unfortunately, Widow Bulky's fate was as bad as her husband's. That very year she fell gravely ill and before long the King of Hell took her soul away. Since she was the widow of a Jia, Chen Yonggui took her body to the Jia family graveyard. A few years later, Old Lady Wenzhou also died. Chen Yonggui wrapped himself in sack cloth and went into deep mourning for her. He buried her, fulfilling his obligation as her stepson. After the funeral, he turned all her inheritance over to the Jia family, allaying their fears and demonstrating that he was a man of unyielding integrity. Before land reform he never owned any land. After land reform he soon pooled what he had. A true proletarian,[1] Chen Yonggui devoted his whole life to making a success of cooperative production without asking one bit more for himself than the collective provided to all. In him this commitment to "public first, self second," apparently innate, manifested itself full blown. It was a faith capable of moving mountains.

People should take good note of the old women who took Chen Yonggui in, for if the two of them had not helped Chen, with his "miscellaneous" surname, settle in Dazhai, Dazhai's later history would almost certainly have been quite different. If one wants to consider the factors that shaped Chen Yonggui's disposition, one should not overlook his experience with foster mothers in an alien courtyard. If we

1. In Chinese, "proletariat" is wu chan jie ji—literally "class without property." (W.H.H.)

assume that his tragic childhood helped forge his unyielding character, having to fight for a place in the courtyard helped shape his headstrong will to resist fate, however merciless. At the same time the love and support he got from three unrelated "mothers" and a "sister" surely instilled faith in the potential of humankind for mutual support.

CHAPTER — 3

FROM MUTINEER TO BOGUS REPRESENTATIVE

Chen Yonggui was an "exposed pole"[1] of his time.

During the Warring States Period some two thousand years ago, a man recommended himself for a post. His story contains a celebrated maxim about "the point of an awl sticking out through a sack," meaning that talent will out regardless of circumstances. When a man of ability enters a common crowd, his "cutting edge," his exceptional nature, will automatically reveal itself, just as the tip of an awl pierces a sack without the slightest hindrance. There is some truth to the old maxim.

Chen Yonggui not only managed to settle down in Dazhai; before long he showed his gifts and revealed the power of his character. The point of the awl pierced the enveloping sack. Two incidents stick out in the memory of most fellow villagers: One is his manipulation of the lantern procession during the Lantern Festival, on the fifteenth of the first lunar month; the other is his service as a bogus "representative"

1. An "exposed pole" is the door prop that holds half a swinging front door open. Since it runs from door to ground outside the house, it is insecure, "exposed." Anyone passing can easily kick it away. Yet it also stands as a symbol for someone stout and brave. Cowards don't take exposed positions. (W.H.H.)

doing liaison work with the Japanese conquerors as a means of gathering intelligence for the resistance movement.

There is an old saying in Xiyang: "If you are looking for a dragon or a tiger, wait for the fifteenth of the first moon." The fifteenth of the first lunar month was considered to be an auspicious day by both the rich and the poor of the old society. On that date many went to Wudao Shrine to offer sacrifices, kneel, bow their heads and pray for good luck.

Dazhai did not get the crowds and bustling activities that the County seat, Xiyang, enjoyed on the fifteenth of the first month, but it had its own time-honored customs. Every year, following the instructions of the few rich families in the village, poor men would ascend Dragon Mountain and then Tigerhead Mountain in the dark of night, beating drums, clapping prongs, and carrying dragon and tiger lanterns. Having completed the long winding route around and over the two mountains, they would return to the village guiding the Lucky Dragon Star and the Lucky Tiger Star back to their homes.

In the beginning of one particular year, things seemed no different. The landlord who held real power in the village, Jia Cunyuan, planned the procession. He strutted about arrogantly, issuing special instructions to his poor fellow villagers who were readying the musical instruments and lanterns. He told them how to carry the potent lantern symbols this year; to go to Dragon Mountain first, then on to Tigerhead Mountain; to pass through Kang Family Ridge on their way down from the Tigerhead; and, finally, to guide the Lucky Dragon and Tiger Stars to his own house so as to bring him good weather and a bumper harvest in the coming year.

"If the year turns out bountiful, you folks will be able to eat your fill too," he added, to win their cooperation. "But make sure you don't change the route!"

In the end, he even promised to feed them some holiday cake when they came back.

The poor villagers did not particularly care for the holiday cake, but they wouldn't turn it down either. Basically, they were under the sway of the man who had all the power in the village. All they wanted was a little respect.

The lantern-carrying contingent started out amidst much excitement and merrymaking. No one expected that they would start cursing halfway up the mountain. But, on that particular night of the lantern festival it just so happened that Heaven was in no mood to cooperate. From an overcast sky fine snowflakes started swirling downward.

"Curse be on his ancestors!" said one. "He wants us to bring him the lucky stars!"

"Even if he gets luckier, we won't get richer," said another.

"What's in it for poor folks like us?" asked a third.

"What we eat is the landlord's. We live off the landlord. There's nothing we can do about it," responded a fourth.

"Nothing we can do? Hah!" retorted Chen Yonggui, who was carrying the bass drum. "I'll tell you what we can do!" he said, looking the men over.

The moment they heard his brash talk, they all felt how upset Chen Yonggui must be. Chen Yonggui, they knew, was one of those rough-edged young bloods who feared nothing, who could stand up to any kind of challenge or danger. What other people didn't even risk trying, he managed to carry out with ease. But, as the saying goes: "A dragon is no match for a snake in its own lair!" so no one believed this young outsider would dare provoke the landlord.

Nevertheless, someone challenged him.

"If you dare give the landlord a lesson, I'll treat you as my elder and kowtow to you," said a voice from the crowd.

Chen Yonggui accepted the challenge on the spot, halfway through the Lantern Procession. A word spoken goes faster than a team of four horses. Not a single person present had any idea what action Chen would propose. But, since all knew there was no reason to question his brashness or his ability, the whole group waited to see what would develop as the day grew dark.

Landlord Jia Cunyuan believed the snow falling around the lanterns on the night of the Lantern Festival was a good omen, so he dressed up in new clothes, his face content and aglow. But just as he surrendered to feelings of complete self-satisfaction, he realized that something was going wrong. He could no longer hear the sound of beating drums. Were there no people on the mountain? As he waited for the procession to return, it dawned on him that it had never ascended Dragon Mountain, that it had never climbed Tigerhead Mountain. The lantern bearers had quietly traced a small circle on the mountainside and come back.

"A tiger that eats the Mountain God! Now that's a little too brazen!"

Jia Cunyuan's anger shook him from head to toe so severely that he had trouble keeping his feet. Not only had they not guided the Dragon and Tiger Stars to gather in good fortune—they had led away whatever luck and good fortune might have blessed his household previously! He broke into a furious rage.

"Who is the ringleader of this conspiracy? Who told you not to climb Tigerhead Mountain, ah? It's an old custom, handed down by our ancestors. Who dares to break it?"

He was intent on ferreting out the perpetrator of the scheme, but none of the participants uttered a sound. They just stared back, looking him in the eye, as though hoping to find in their mutually locked gaze some counter-measure for his attack.

"If you don't bring out the culprit, I won't let any of you off the hook!" Jia shouted.

In order to shed more light on what happened next the author of the present work sought out an old man who was a contemporary of Chen Yonggui, one Li Xiqing. Old Li Xiqing was seventy-six when I caught up with him and he had lost the sight of both eyes. His answers to my first questions were guarded. Quite a few of the journalists who came to visit Dazhai had taken sides against the village in the political struggle of the seventies, so the locals learned to be extremely cautious with their answers.

After carefully reviewing his recollections, the old man told me: "Jia Cunyuan pursued his target with a burst of energy. We could see that Chen Yonggui had trouble remaining silent. He sneered ever so slightly when, unable to hold back any longer, he finally blurted out: 'Whatever the landlord has to say, let him say it to me. No need to drag everybody else into this.'

"Jia Cunyuan took the cue and, 'Pooh,' he spat in Chen Yonggui's face. 'Fuck your mother!' he cursed him. 'This poor devil comes from

Shishan with only his mouth and two scrawny shoulders. He eats on me, he drinks on me, and now he shits on me! You don't want to climb Tigerhead Mountain, fine. Don't ever come knocking on my door again either! Pooh! Poooh!'"

The old folks from Dazhai will readily admit that Chen Yonggui was a have-not in the old society, but in the eyes of many he was nevertheless a real man, a hero. He was a good companion, a smart talker, and an able worker. In regular circumstances even the landlord would be hard put to make things difficult for him. But this time Jia Cunyuan, at long last, found something to rage about. Chen Yonggui had to endure some cursing. From the landlord's point of view the curses were well awarded. On Chen's side, strange to say, the few hard words suffered were well worth their cost. Chen Yonggui thought changing the route of the lantern procession might well put an end to the good fortunes of the Jia family. Thus, he could punish the landlord and force unaccountable losses upon him. And yet, because he himself was robust, strong and a skilled hand at growing crops, the landlord would not want to part with him just yet—not on account of this one incident anyway. That is why Chen Yonggui dared behave the way he did. And he proved to be right.

The second incident that the villagers remember best is related to a controversy regarding Chen Yonggui's personal history stirred up by the two factions during the Cultural Revolution. It is the story of how Chen Yonggui became a bogus puppet representative for the Japanese and how he went in and out of the enemy blockhouse unscathed.

Once, after the victory of the War of Resistance Against Japan, the village of Dazhai did hold a mass rally to publicly accuse and denounce traitors. And in this instance the person denounced was indeed Chen Yonggui.

Chen Yonggui was tied by a motley crowd and pushed onto the stage of the rally. His accusers and denouncers were the poor and hired peasants with whom he had associated for years. These fellow have-nots simply asked him, "Chen Jinxiao, be frank. How many bad things did you do while you were the bogus representative? Lower your head, you dog! Confess!"

His poor-and-hired peasant compatriots ordered him to raise his hands, and once they had untied him, he obediently folded his two callused hands, as rough as pine-bark, on the top of his head. When the crowd of poor tenants and hired laborers ordered him to lower that "dog-head," he lowered his head.

There was something extraordinary about this particular denunciation rally. On the surface it looked as if the whole crowd was denouncing Chen Yonggui, but in fact the beating his tormenters gave him was only nominal and their hearts cried out in sympathy. They knew Chen Yonggui inside and out, and they knew he was serving as a scapegoat. The man who still held all levers of power in Dazhai was landlord Jia Taiyuan, old Cunyuan's brother. Jia Taiyuan organized the denunciation rally in order to gratify the Communist Party and carry out the revolutionary call to "oppose local despots and weed out enemy agents" that was the order of the day. Denouncing Chen Yonggui was his cunning scheme. The rest of the citizenry, like it or not, had to oblige.

At that time the Eighth Route Army had just liberated Xiyang County. Not a single Communist Party member lived in Dazhai. The "Reduce Rent and Interest" campaign was therefore left in the control of people who wielded power locally. Jia Taiyuan became aware of this campaign early on. If he didn't make himself out to be an activist who sang profuse praises of the Revolution, there was a danger that he himself might be denounced. As a result, trying to downplay his own role as a bogus puppet village head, he jumped at the opportunity to turn Chen Yonggui into a scapegoat for having served as a puppet representative during the Anti-Japanese War.

"Chen Jinxiao, make a sincere confession! How did it come about that you became Dazhai's representative?"

In the midst of his fellow have-nots' interrogation, someone raised a fist. The fist rose high, clenched firmly, and came down fast. But when it hit Chen Yonggui's body, it didn't hurt. Chen Yonggui confessed that he wasn't sure himself how he became a representative. But in reality, both Chen Yonggui and his dispossessed fellows knew at the bottom of their hearts how the thing had come to pass.

Barely a few days after the July 7th Incident in 1937 when, after the armed clash at Lugou Bridge, the Japanese invaded north China, they occupied the city of Xiyang. They divided Xiyang County into an eastern and western part. Some big-time traitors to China emerged in Xiyang, under the foreign name of "Black Devils." They committed even worse atrocities than the Japanese. They organized themselves into a riffraff-type gang called "The Truncheon." There was no hideous crime they would not commit, thus bringing the County into double jeopardy.

The village of Dazhai lies just over three miles from the County seat.[1] The arrival of the Japanese to conduct village mop-up operations was quite a common occurrence and before they withdrew for good they killed several dozen people of Dazhai. The Communist Party-led Anti-Japanese Government of the Border Region, based on its conviction that the only way to counter Japanese mop-up operations was to establish a "Peace Preservation Association,"[2] adopted a policy of selecting bogus representatives who dealt overtly with the Japanese, placating them with gifts, and interceding on behalf of the Chinese, while covertly providing the Eighth Route Army with information and organizing support for the underground resistance movement. The gong-beating village head from the *Guerrilla Detachment on the Plains*[3] was one such bogus representative. Bogus representatives had to enjoy the esteem and trust of the people, be smart talkers, and have good relations all around, that is, they had to be acceptable to the Japanese while actually working clandestinely for the Eighth Route Army. In Dazhai the question was: Who was the right person for this dangerous and complex task?

There was a senior officer in the Independent Battalion of the Eighth Route Army, who fought at that time in the Taihang Mountain area under the alias "Storehouse." He designated Chen Yonggui for the assignment and secretly did some work to promote Chen's candidacy. In the end, after a lot of picking and choosing, the poor peasants of the area settled on Chen Yonggui and enthusiastically recommended him to the village head, Jia Taiyuan. Jia Taiyuan was in fact more panic-

1. The distance is only ten Chinese li, which equals roughly three English miles.
2. A local puppet organization during the War of Resistance Against Japan (1937-1945).
3. A popular film in the People's Republic of China.

stricken than anybody else in the village because he knew what would befall his family's grain and property as soon as the Japanese devils arrived. His first and oldest brother Jia Zengyuan had already died under the Japanese sword. If somebody could maintain peace with the Japanese, he believed, it would certainly benefit both himself and the village. So he wholeheartedly endorsed the appointment of Chen Yonggui as a bogus representative.

Consequently, Jia Taiyuan threw a banquet at his house and invited Chen Yonggui to enjoy a few cups of sorghum liquor.

"Drink up, Jinxiao! In the name of all the men in Dazhai, I congratulate you on becoming the Peace Preservation representative."

A man with no guts would not have dared take on the challenge of acting as double agent. Chen Yonggui had the guts and he dared. Moreover, he didn't mince words regarding the nitty-gritty issues. "Let me set all accounts straight. If you ask me to trick and deceive on behalf of my countrymen, so that Japanese dogs don't kill us all and plunder our grain, that I will do, that's no problem. I am a daredevil anyway, so I can pretty much do whatever needs doing. But, there is one thing I cannot handle: If they come to the village for material rewards my empty words will be totally useless. Their mouths are going to be wide open and they will be looking for things to eat and drink. But, you tell me, where am I going to get that food and those drinks?"

Jia Taiyuan nodded after each word, appearing very generous, which was quite unusual. "Oh, that! I'll get the food! If the landlord doesn't feed them, who else will?"

Thereafter Chen Yonggui acted as the bogus representative in the true sense of the word. With his daredevil courage and his glib and tireless tongue, with liquor, meat and vegetables provided by the two Jia brothers, Taiyuan and Cunyuan, he handled whoever showed up at the village gate. Thus Dazhai escaped several major disasters.

Chen Yonggui, however, paid a price for success. Twice he almost lost his life. Once the enemy locked him up for half a month and came within a hair of cutting off his head. A Japanese sentry caught him when he entered the County seat in 1943 to deliver grain. He won release only after his wife Li Huni and some friends and relatives bought off the Japanese with presents and cash. On another occasion Chen Yonggui gave protection to an underground Communist Party cadre, and ended up in some surprising and dangerous deal-making with the chief of the traitors, Liu Suoyuan. Liu Suoyuan entered the village and, wasting no words, put his sword to Chen Yonggui's neck. In this situation, where both advance and retreat meant a sure death, Chen Yonggui acted as though he had nothing to lose. He tossed his head and moved his neck closer to the blade. Liu Suoyuan had intended only to intimidate with a big show of force so when he realized his ploy wasn't working he drew back his sword.

Liu Suoyuan asked Chen Yonggui why he was not afraid to die. Chen Yonggui answered that he had never been able to do anything that might trouble his conscience, so he was not afraid that ghosts would come calling on him in the middle of the night. "Had I been sheltering the Communist Party, I would have broken out in cold sweat a long time ago, right in front of your eyes."

Chen Yonggui's ability to react in this emergency confused his enemy so thoroughly that his answer tricked Liu Suoyuan into thinking that perhaps, after all, Chen Yonggui was not concealing a Party member.

Several years later, after the Japanese surrendered, landlord Jia Taiyuan wanted to strike first before any challengers smoked him out. So he turned on Chen Yonggui at the denunciation rally. But Chen's poor fellow villagers knew that Chen Yonggui had committed no crimes, so the rally never picked up steam. In the end, it was Jia Taiyuan himself who had to endure denunciation. But that occurred later during the Land Reform Movement.

Serving as bogus representative was useful, but Chen Yonggui wanted to take a more direct part in the Armageddon then in progress. After repeated demands that he be allowed to join the War of Resistance Against Japan he picked up arms and went off to Yangquan to enlist in 1940. He joined in the middle of the war along with another People's Militiaman, Jia Chengwei. He started out as a squad leader of thirteen fighters in charge of transporting ammunition, medicine, and weapons to the front and of rescuing and evacuating the wounded.

One night heavy shellfire enveloped Yangquan. Smoke from exploding gunpowder choked the air. Time for several meals had come and gone, but Chen Yonggui hung on amidst heavy enemy fire without so much as a drop of water or a grain of millet. Jia Chengwei's stomach started grumbling and he wanted to look for something to eat, but there was nothing in sight except for bullets and artillery shells flying in every direction. Our soldiers kept falling under the artillery bombardment into wretched pools of blood. As Chen Yonggui watched the comrades suffer wounds and die, his heart seethed with hatred. He turned toward Jia Chengwei and the other fighters of his squad and shouted at the top of his voice, "Whoever is a hero, follow me."

While his voice still carried he jumped up and charged toward the front line, picked up a blood-covered soldier and ran back. Shells fell all around him.

Through the continued hail of shells and bullets Chen Yonggui looked at the fallen comrades in the trenches ahead. Suddenly an idea struck him. He quickly undid his trouser belt and, holding his pants with one hand and his belt with the other, he braved the incoming fire. Using his belt as a sling he rescued several badly wounded men and inspired others of his unit to do the same.

Chen's bravery earned him a commendation for meritorious service from the Eighth Route Army Command to Dazhai Village. The commendation letter fell into the hands of Jia Zhiyuan, who started teaching school in the village about that time. Jia Zhiyuan, evidently counting on the fact that there were no literate peasants in Dazhai, blotted out Chen Yonggui's name in the letter and substituted his own. When he sent the report on to the higher authorities it looked as if the merit earned was his. Chen Yonggui found out about this only much later. He had long wondered how a letter that clearly stated his merit turned up to Jia Zhiyuan's credit.

CHAPTER 4

LEADING THE WAY WITH YOUNGSTERS AND HAS-BEENS

In 1945, after a turbulent line storm, Tigerhead Mountain emerged from clouds and mists with the red sun rising above it. The trials of battle experienced by all those living on its flanks paved the road for Chen Yonggui to assume a leading role.

In 1946, party organizations on various levels appealed to the peasants of the Border Regions of Shaanxi, Gansu and Ningxia, Shanxi, Chahar and Hebei, as well as all the other Liberated Areas, to act upon Chairman Mao Zedong's earlier call to "organize yourselves" by establishing labor exchange and mutual aid groups. In response, several advanced model organizations emerged on the territory of Xiyang County, such as the mutual aid teams in "Knife Handle Gateway" and "White Lamb Ravine." The peasants of Dazhai were eager to have a go at it, too.

The first person to organize a mutual aid group in Dazhai was the first Party Branch Secretary of the hamlet, Jia Jincai. Every morning, just as the day was beginning to break, Jia Jincai, the leader of the "Stalwart Group," woke up early. He would get dressed and start going from door to door, knocking on gates, calling people by name, pressing the members of his group to hurry into the fields. He seems to have done this every day before dawn.

Jia Jincai pressed his group members hard because: one, he wanted to gain some extra time for farm work; two, he wanted to challenge the rival "Feeble Group." Ever since Chen Yonggui planted his own flag by establishing a "Feeble Group," members of Jia Jincai's "Stalwarts" felt they had come under some pressure which they could not fully grasp. Everything under their group's control was good: the land, the livestock, the farming tools. Furthermore they were all able-bodied and strong. People used to say of them "Poplar goes where the willow thrives; good soldiers follow a good general." Why, then, were they worried about a challenge? Who could outdo them anyway? Apparently only Chen's Feeble Group, which seemed to do well against all odds.

The Stalwart Group decided to stage a year-long competition with Chen Yonggui's "Feebles." People would learn the outcome after all the farm work wound up in the autumn. The pressure of this decision caused Jia Jincai to go around in the morning, banging on doors, calling on people, and urging them time and again to get going. As they were about to depart for the fields, he even yelled out for those still missing, giving them instructions as to what tools and implements to bring along.

Several front gates would open and Jia Jincai could see his group members taking off in the direction of the fields, toting heavy loads of compost on shoulder poles. But when they reached the halfway point in the road, he would look back and see that Chen Yonggui and his group had already carried off half their compost pile. And all the while he had thought they were sound asleep!

Not even the first battle of the planned yearlong war went smoothly for Jia Jincai. Naturally, he couldn't prevent people from poking fun at him: "Jincai, you sure got here early!" The best thing for him would be to grant them the point: "OK, OK, I'm late." He just couldn't figure out where the Feeble Group, composed mainly of old folks and children, got so much drive.

After a few of these incidents he realized that some people had methods more ingenious than his own. Chen Yonggui, when he summoned the folks from his group, never shouted at the top of his lungs as Jia Jincai did.

Looking for ways to stay on top, Chen Yonggui's group members showed even more enthusiasm and vigilance than Chen Yonggui himself. They all agreed on the following time signal: No shouting to announce the start of work; only a stone thrown at the front gate or into the yard. As soon as the team members heard the sound, they put on clothes, grabbed their tools, and took off for the field with military discipline.

There was a history behind all this, including the military style. Two years earlier Jia Jincai had decided to level his piece of land, and he shoveled and shoveled for a good while, without much visible progress. While he was busy shoveling, three men from his extended family—two with the name of Jia Chengfu, and one Jia Chenglu—along with one Zhao Qifa, came down the mountain. When they saw Jincai straining away by himself, they offered to join him.

"Look," they asked, "how much can a man do by himself?"

"Not much, not much," Jincai agreed.

"If the four of us get down to work with you, why, it'll be done in less time than it takes to smoke a pipe."

"No, thanks. I'll do it myself. You've got your own land to worry about."

"Well, that's not what we came for. We want to see you because you are in charge of political work. There's that government call to organize into labor exchange and mutual aid groups. How come you are not organizing us? They're a good thing, those groups, aren't they?"

People were used to bringing whatever problems they had to Jia Jincai. They wanted to talk them over with him because Party leaders had earlier groomed him as a Party member in Dazhai, and though the Party Branch was still underground,[1] he was now responsible for political work. Jia Jincai had to admit that he didn't dare make the final decision on organizing a group. Besides, his mind had not yet set in favor of collective work in whatever form.

Several months went by. The New Year came, and with it the boisterous festivities that are supposed to induce prosperity. Jia Jincai was

1. With civil war impending, the Communist Party knew it was not safe for village Communists to go public.

just entering the village on his way back from a Regional Party meeting, when a group of villagers, the two Jia Chengfus and Jia Chenglu among them, surrounded him. They wanted to find out if the higher authorities had any plans for mutual aid groups.

Jia Jincai passed on the instructions he had received from the Regional Committee. He told the assembled group that the authorities were calling for major efforts in building mutual aid and labor exchange groups. They stressed, however, that the groups should be formed voluntarily, and they should be based on the principle of mutual benefit. Whoever wanted to join was welcome.

Everybody in that group turned to Jia Jincai to organize them. They wanted a person who could take charge and who had the ear of people higher up. But Jia Jincai, on his part, realized that Chen Yonggui had not been seen in the village for several days, neither had he dropped by to consult. Jia suspected that he might have some objections.

Although Chen Yonggui was not yet a Communist Party member, he was already head of production in the village. A word from him could influence many people, Jia thought. So he smiled vacuously at the people surrounding him and put them off.

Let's wait till Jinxiao comes back. We'll talk it over with him," Jia Jincai said.

"Hey," some people reacted, "what kind of Party Secretary is it that can't control the head of production? Isn't this, perhaps, too flattering to Jinxiao?"

Actually, the group, now trying to form its own "cabinet," had earlier set its sights on attracting Chen Yonggui into its midst. Knowing Chen Yonggui as a real work-horse, they felt they couldn't lose by having him on their team.

"It's not that I can't control him," Jia Jincai answered. "I just want to talk it over with him, that's all."

This conversation showed that Jia Jincai could have led the way right then and there in organizing labor exchange and mutual aid groups in accordance with the spirit of the Regional Party Committee directive. Yet he hesitated, because he was still unclear as to the rate of Chen Yonggui's pulse—that is, as to Chen's stand on the matter.

Chen Yonggui, in the meantime, was overwhelmed with New Year festival activities. According to local custom, several villages always got together to organize a big yangko[1] dance. They took turns hosting the get-together. The Eighth Route Army had liberated Xiyang County just that year, so the villagers no longer feared mop-up operations by the Japanese. Naturally, they were all for organizing a big show, moving from village to village, making merry up and down the valley. Chen Yonggui was just a twenty-year-old youth at the time. He was renowned far and wide as an excellent yangko dancer: He would tie the white hand towel, popularly known as "the lamb-stomach weave," around his head with a knot and make his face up in the "three-flower" style.[2] Then when he started moving with the yangko rhythm one and all found him irresistible. Naturally, he wouldn't have wanted to miss the village-to-village romp that particular season. As a result, he hadn't shown up at home for several days and nights in a row.

On the day Chen finally did return to Dazhai after touring the villages with the yangko team, Jia Jincai stopped him in his tracks hoping to get a line on his thoughts.

"Jinxiao, I have something to discuss with you. Everybody's organizing labor exchange groups. We...."

"Discuss what?" retorted Chen Yonggui hoarsely, cutting him off in mid-sentence. He walked on with barely a sidelong glance at Jia Jincai. "Let's just do it."

"I wanted to talk to you about...."

"What's there to talk about? If you are organizing right now, I'll join."

This seems to have given Jia Jincai the necessary jolt. Then and there he made a decision to take the lead in organizing a labor exchange group.

By the time Chen Yonggui got to his house, as several people who were there that day recall, he had no time to rest his backside before a crowd

1. A popular rural folk dance, related to spring and summer sowing activities.
2. The make-up design used in theatrical productions to depict a comical character.

squeezed in behind him. As he took in the sizable group at a glance, he noticed that it was made up entirely of old folks and youngsters.

After asking a few questions about the yangko tour the group settled down. Then the old men pulled at their long pipes, made a few smacking sounds, and came straight to the point.

"Jinxiao, the government calls on us to cooperate through mutual aid. Those few stalwarts from Liangshan have already organized. All that's left now is the few of us old men, and these youngsters."

Chen Yonggui took a drag at his pipe. Then he too let out a smacking sound from his spot on the earthen sleeping platform.

"What do you have in mind?" he asked, frowning slightly.

"Everybody's organizing," said the sixteen-year-old Liang Bianliang, taking the question head on. "We want to organize, too. But who's going to take the lead in organizing such folks as you see here?"

Chen Yonggui understood at once. Liang Bianliang's words reminded him that he had seen Liang Bianliang crying the previous year as he labored in the field, because he was too small to lift the heavy loads. His best efforts were pitiful.

"Bianliang, good intentions are not enough to get our organization going," Chen Yonggui responded thoughtfully. "Why don't you look for some others?"

"I don't know if any others want me," Liang Bianliang answered, rubbing his eyes.

"Right," Chen Yonggui said to himself. "Who would want him if he can't even use a shoulder pole?"

Then he went on to consider how he could help Liang Bianliang promote himself more successfully.

"Poor kid," he mused. "He's really got a problem. What can I do to help him? How about letting him join Jincai's group along with me? I could let him work at my side."

But he didn't voice the idea at the time. He just politely waved his hand at the group to acknowledge its plea, then proceeded to light his pipe, which he had already filled with tobacco. His guests were embarrassed to bother him any more. They murmured thanks and left, one by one.

Right after Chen Yonggui's return from the New Year celebration, Jia Chengfu, Jia Chenglu, Zhao Qifa and their friends formally organized a labor exchange group, headed by Jia Jincai. But, they knew if they were to be unbeatable, they couldn't pass up on a robust worker like Chen Yonggui. They resolved to drag him onto their team at all cost, and even went to his house more than once to persuade him. Their arguments posed a great dilemma for Chen Yonggui. Two groups: one strong, one weak both sought him out. Even if the latter, whose members had come knocking on his door first, were to organize without his help, he still had a big problem. The strong group included many rich and well-to-do middle peasants; the weak ended up with poor and lower-middle peasants, many of whom were war orphans whose parents had been Chen's old comrades-in-arms before they lost their lives. Which group was he supposed to go with?

After a few days Liang Bianliang, Li Xiqing, and some others from the weak side came to his house again. Chen Yonggui waited for all of them to be seated before he turned on the kerosene lamp and laid out his views. "Everybody in this room is a poor or a lower-middle peasant. The land we've acquired is the fruit of revolution. If we don't sow it properly, if we fail to harvest the crop, it will be the same as renouncing revolution. I've made up my mind to lead this group of the too old and the too young, so that we can plant the land as it should be. I had already told Jia Jincai that I would join his group. In the last few days his group members, too, came to see me several times. I thought about it, back and forth, and in the end I pulled out of it. You can relax. You can all come to work with me."

As soon as Chen Yonggui made clear where he stood, the people assembled in his room began to feel somewhat ill at ease. To put the one man whose reputation as the top worker went well beyond the village into their group, wouldn't that be a losing proposition for him? But he was quite emphatic about it. "Let's not talk about who's a loser. When I herded cows for other people, I couldn't even earn enough to buy a pair of pants. Was I a loser, or what? Chairman Mao gave us the land to plant: That's our biggest gain. Let's leave it at that. But there is one condition: You must work closely with me, so we can be of one heart. If we are of one heart, we won't be second to anyone—not even the other group."

This is how the Stalwart Group and the Feeble Group came into being. Nobody called them that at the time. It was only after Dazhai became famous and the villagers started to recollect their experiences that they came up with the two names. Back then, as soon as the Feeble Group unfurled its banner, it got reviled by the opposing Stalwart Group. The Stalwarts said that the oldsters among the Feebles were "too feeble to mount a horse," and that the youngsters were "too feeble to stretch a bow." But Chen Yonggui, as the leader of the Feeble Group, had his own way of assessing the situation:

"The so-called old have experience; the young will grow up. So long as we listen to the Party, we won't have anything to worry about," Chen asserted.

This was a simple way of putting it, but it was brimming with genuine dialectics. These words, in fact, decided the future of the Feeble Group.

At the time when they first formed, both the Stalwart Group and the Feeble Group had only nine households each, which was quite a coincidence, but as things developed the two groups matured as sharply contrasting entities. Although the Stalwart Group could match the other group exactly, soldier for soldier, General for General, and despite the fact that it was led by Jia Jincai, who was a Communist Party member, its members each had a mind of his own and frequently did not apply themselves unsparingly to the common task. When they worked together, disputes erupted. When Jia Jincai was present they were at least able to go on working, but as soon as he was gone all their contradictions came into the open.

Disputes broke out particularly frequently over the issue of job assignments. Some opportunists even tried to profit from their work allotments. After they finished threshing the allotted grain, they went to Jia Jincai asking for more shocks to thresh and thus get a disproportionate share. Meanwhile, members of the Feeble Group were at ease no matter what they did, because they agreed on joint priorities before they set out to work. Whether it was the question of soil preparation in winter or planting in spring, all work was organized personally by Chen Yonggui, who kept score of every activity past and present.

I took to heart the stories that I heard from the few old group members who are still alive, and I feel endlessly grateful to them. Dazhai's Old Man Jia Chenglian told me the following:

> I was the smallest of the Feebles—even a couple of years younger than Liang Bianliang. My father passed away when I was very small, and I was left alone with my mother, but we were still cultivating the twelve mu of land allotted us by the land reform. At the time I joined the Feeble Group I felt that I was too small and that it wasn't right that I should be working that much land. But Old Chen told me to work beside him and everything would be fine.
>
> "This way," he said, "I guarantee you that not only your twelve mu but my twenty-two mu will not go to waste."
>
> From that time on I planted my feet firmly on the ground and worked along with Old Chen. He'd be in front working with the hoe, and I'd be following him close behind. Whatever he loaded on the shoulder poles to carry, I carried too. I was so afraid Old Chen would scold me for not working hard enough, that in the end I got scolded for not obeying him. When we carried millet to the threshing ground in autumn, for instance, Old Chen used to prepare our loads ahead of time. He decided who should carry how much. But when we lifted the poles to our shoulders, we always felt that he loaded our slings too lightly, so we always secretly added a few handfuls of extra stalks. The moment he found out about it, he gave us a big lecture on how we shouldn't be doing things like that.
>
> "We don't just stress hard work," he said. "We have to protect our labor force."

He was afraid that we teen-agers would injure ourselves carrying too much. When he was at the helm, although we were not yet mature, we worked as hard as the grown-ups. To give you an example: We didn't need Old Chen to call us in the morning; we were able to get up on our own and carry manure from the village to Wolf Den Ravine, then under reclamation. We made the round trip six times before daybreak. In the morning it wasn't us, it was always Old Chen who got up late. He usually had meetings in the evening and went to bed very late. In the morning he couldn't get up unless somebody woke him up. Consequently, he made a rule: We were to call him as we left in the morning. Once we deliberately didn't call him because we wanted to let him get some more sleep. By the time he showed up for work the sky was already bright. The moment he arrived at the field he gave me an earful:

"How come you didn't call me? Was it intentional, so you could earn extra work points?"

"You'll make all the points you need to make," I said.

This got Old Chen angry.

"You all made five trips carrying manure, while I had time for only one. How do you think I'll earn my points?" he protested.

"You had a meeting in the evening," I said. "You get points for that too."

This made Old Chen even angrier.

"Whoever ruled that attending meetings would count for work points?" he replied, scolding me for counting that way.

That week, when the time came to allot work points, he himself said that I wouldn't get any for that morning. It was a lesson for me.

Chen Yonggui put into effect an excellent scoring system for the allotment of work and work points. He was able to arouse the enthusi asm of his entire group not only because he was skillful at everything, but even more because he always set an excellent example for others. Chen Yonggui was the only strong able-bodied person in his group. People used to call him a "donkey and a half." But when time came to distribute the work points he only got two more than an average worker. Everybody said that he scored himself too low, but he insisted.

"It's enough. I still got more points than the others," he would say.

He also insisted on giving youngsters like Liang Bianliang and Jia Chenglian as many as eight points. Those favored complained that their score was too high, but Chen Yonggui countered: "If I score you a little higher, you'll work that much better!"

It was in this way that the Feeble Group forged itself into a "tightly woven rope," and, along the way, defeated the Stalwart Group at its own game—production.

Before long, the membership of the Feebles grew from nine to forty-nine households. The Stalwart Group readily acknowledged defeat in the face of the Feeble Group, yet, when judged against others in the County or the region, it too was an advanced work unit. When the higher authorities awarded prizes on several occasions they honored both groups as County and Regional models. After word of the Feeble Group's prowess spread far and wide, many outsiders doubted what they heard of the group's success. Then the Regional authorities organized a visit to Dazhai for all the village-level Party Branch Secretaries. Even after that, however, some people remained skeptical. So the authorities organized visits for production leaders and village representatives. Dazhai's fame spread farther and wider with each of these visits.

What all these people got to know, as they studied Dazhai, was an interpretation of history that accorded with the theory of "continuous revolution" prevalent at the time—the story of how a collective made up of poor and lower-middle peasants defeated the power of the rich and middle peasants. In all fairness, this interpretation did not entirely tally with the facts. People of different class backgrounds made up the Stalwart Group, not just former rich and middle peasants. Jia Jincai by original intent never weighted it in the latter direction. Its composition was a result of the original distribution of plots according to specific land use during land reform. People with neighboring plots tended to get together.

As for why the Feeble Group surpassed the Stalwart Group in production, the answer lies in the realm of unity of mind and purpose. Precisely because all Stalwart Group members were stalwarts, they pulled the group in different directions and were unable to avoid disagreements, which, in the absence of a powerful leader, tended to cancel out their strength. The Feeble Group, on the other hand, was an association of the weak, who, precisely because of their individual weaknesses, had no way out but to help each other and rely on their collective strength. Most importantly, also, they had a daring and knowledgeable leader in Chen Yonggui, who organized their strengths in the most effective way, enabling the group to succeed. Beyond that and more important still, they based their success on a common life philosophy summed up as "Public First, Self Second." This philosophy served as a backbone to the Feeble Group. It created the "ten heroes" of Dazhai some years later, and proved the most reliable aid to Chen Yonggui. One cannot deny that Chen Yonggui was farsighted as a peasant-hero in the making.

Jia Jincai, who was on the losing end of the competition, knew this all too well. He saw in the whole episode Chen Yonggui's emerging talent for leadership. Being diligent and conscientious, honest and kind as he was, Jia Jincai did not approach the situation with any personal gain in mind. He expressed only wholehearted good will toward his colleague and rival, Chen Yonggui.

In 1947, the District of Xiyang County to which Dazhai belonged was preparing to recruit new Party members in order to expand and strengthen the Party organization. The District leaders were considering Chen Yonggui as one of their candidates. After several years of the training and toughening that he experienced on his return from the War of Resistance Against Japan, Chen Yonggui was equipped with the basic qualifications for Party membership. On a previous occasion when the higher authorities went to Dazhai to draft conscripts, Chen Yonggui had volunteered to join the Peoples Liberation Army, but the leaders took into consideration the fact that he was the top production expert in the village and decided he should stay in the village to head up production. They did not allow him to enlist in the armed forces. He was thus even more qualified to join the Party.

According to Jia Jincai's recollection, this is how it all happened:

One day, Chen Yonggui trudged across Jia Jincai's doorstep, went straight for the brick-bed kang, and seated himself on the edge. After clicking his tongue a few times, he spoke with visible anxiety:

"I've already come twice. It's quite something, waiting for you to return!" After this brief comment, he knitted his brows and waited for a reply.

"What happened? Speak up!" said Jia Jincai, sensing his anxiety.

Chen Yonggui puckered his lips and clicked his tongue again, then stuttered: "I...I...want to join the Party. You wouldn't be able to sponsor me, would you?"

The Party organization in Dazhai developed rather late. From the time when Jia Jincai joined in 1946, the local branch admitted only six new members in three years. In the past, Dazhai and its neighboring village, Five Family Flat, had merged into one Party Branch. In 1947, due to the slow progress of recruitment in Dazhai, the Regional Committee decided to establish an independent Party branch in Dazhai, and appointed Jia Jincai as the Party Branch Secretary. His immediate task was to recruit new members.

"You want to join the Party? That's great. I'll sponsor you," Jia responded immediately to Chen Yonggui's request. Afterward, Jia Jincai submitted a special report to the Regional Committee.

This experience with Jia Jincai took a heavy load off Chen Yonggui's mind. But a later turn of events caused him some distress. Just as the Regional Committee got around to considering his candidacy, a directive from the higher authorities called for dissolving all the old Party organizations. It said the Regional Committee had discovered a serious problem of "impurity" within the Party organization, that bad elements had infiltrated the Party and that, as a result, many villages had not carried out land reform thoroughly. The directive called for removing these stumbling blocks. Consequently, the directive announced that the Party should stop all organizing activities. For the time being this put off Chen Yonggui's candidacy for Party membership.

When the Party leaders got to the heart of the problem in July of 1948, they clearly stipulated that new applicants for Party membership should submit to rigorous investigation. In the past the whole procedure consisted of the local Party Branch admitting a candidate and reporting it to the Regional Committee. From this time on, two full Party members had to recommend and sponsor every new member, and a general membership of the Party Branch had to approve the candidacy, then report it to the Regional Committee by filing a standard form. The admission was complete only after the Regional Party Secretary put his Consequently, the directive announced that the Party should stop all organizing activities. For the time being this put off Chen Yonggui's candidacy.

When the Party leaders got to the heart of the problem in July of 1948, they clearly stipulated that new applicants for Party membership should submit to rigorous investigation. In the past the whole procedure consisted of the local Party Branch admitting a candidate and reporting it to the Regional Committee. From this time on, two full Party members had to recommend and sponsor every new member, and a general membership of the Party Branch had to approve the candidacy, then report it to the Regional Committee by filing a standard form. The admission was complete only after the Regional Party Secretary put his signature on it. This meant that this time around Chen Yonggui's candidacy for Party membership had to be handled with much greater stringency.

When the issue of Chen Yonggui's candidacy for Party membership came on the agenda again, some people in the Regional Committee pointed out the problem of his acting as a double agent during the War of Resistance Against Japan. The Regional Party Secretary, Zhang Huaiying, had known Chen Yonggui since 1946, and was well familiar with his situation. Moreover, he had already made some investigations into the circumstances surrounding Chen Yonggui's double role. But faced with the issue of Chen Yonggui's candidacy for Party membership, he maintained an extremely cautious attitude. He personally dispatched the Regional Organizing Secretary, Yan Weizhou, to Dazhai to look into it.

After Yan Weizhou arrived in Dazhai, he called together all Party members—Jia Jincai, Jia Chengcai, Jia Chengfu, Xing Yuqing and Song Liying among them—and talked to each one of them individually. After these individual encounters, the impression of the Party members was that Yan Weizhou had found their accounts to be in perfect agreement.

Meanwhile, Chen Yonggui was losing appetite and sleep over the problem. He guessed that the delay was rooted in the old bogus puppet representative problem. He went twice to see the Regional Committee Secretary, Zhang Huaiying, in order to remind him:

"I became the bogus representative because the people elected me and because of what the Independent Battalion's Old 'Storehouse' told me, but I can't speak openly about that. To many people it ended up looking as though Jia Taiyuan had caught a big fish. He may have caught a fish, but I still didn't do anything bad...."

Each time, Zhang Huaiying comforted him: "Comrade Chen Yonggui, relax about your personal history. The organization will clarify it all for you."

In order to treat Chen Yonggui's case responsibly, Zhang Huaiying used every opportunity to sound things out and examine it from as many angles as possible. Zhang found a man who had worked underground in a neighboring village and had had numerous contacts with Chen Yonggui during the War of Resistance Against Japan. He was well acquainted with the circumstances surrounding Chen Yonggui's wartime role. His account confirmed all the details previously revealed: the role the Eighth Route Army senior officer "Old Storehouse" played in recruiting Chen for the job, Jia Taiyuan's attempted frame-up, and all the other circumstances surrounding the case. In the end, with full confidence in Chen, Zhang Huaiying signed his application to join the Party, adding his personal observations and comments to the document.

Sponsored by Jia Jincai and Yan Weizhou, and approved by he Regional Secretary Zhang Huaiying, Chen Yonggui finally became a full Party member in good standing.

Chen Yonggui's morale soared very high in those days. He took the initiative in whatever work he set himself to do, and gained the trust of the people in the Feeble Group. Under the bright red flag of the Party, with his fist raised high, Chen Yonggui took the oath: "I will dedicate my life to the struggle for Communism."

Once Chen Yonggui entered the gate of the Communist Party, his affection for the Party grew deeper with time and his faith in revolution grew firmer. His knowledge of Party fundamentals grew as he learned, his experience in leadership waxed richer, and his prestige in the Feeble Group rose as time passed. In the eyes of Jia Jincai, Chen Yonggui, after two years, seemed like a completely different person. Jia realized Chen Yonggui's talents, particularly when it came to debates on various issues raised during Party meetings. He was truly at a loss when he had to counter Chen Yonggui's arguments.

On several occasions Chen Yonggui criticized him. His main complaint was that Jia Jincai was too meek, that he didn't deal with issues forcefully enough. Whenever Jia Jincai had to listen to such criticism he grumbled to himself, but afterward he was always able to overcome any hard feelings. He knew he deserved this kind of scrutiny. He was no match for Chen Yonggui in the way he talked and the way he handled issues. He began to feel that it would indeed be a blessing if he were to let Chen Yonggui take responsibility for Dazhai's affairs, so that they might be well taken care of.

And so Jia Jincai conceived the idea of recommending Chen Yonggui for the post of Party Branch Vice-Secretary. That's when Chen Yonggui first rose from obscurity. At a Party Branch meeting he was elected Vice-Secretary of the Branch. What Jia Jincai intended was to let Chen Yonggui assume the office of Branch Secretary by arranging to switch duties with him. The trouble was, the switch could not be made so easily. This was the time, not so long after Lberation, when the Party organization took extreme care about whom it elected to positions of Branch Secretary. Changes in appointments could not be made at will, or without the approval of the higher authorities. Jia Jincai understood the reasons behind this policy, but he nevertheless made up his mind to do just as he intended.

One day, after the Party meeting disbanded, Jia Jincai asked Chen Yonggui to stay behind at his house and he made the following suggestion: "Jinxiao, I have an idea, but I don't know whether you will agree with it. I'm thinking of letting you take over the duty of Branch Secretary...."

The moment Chen Yonggui heard this, he exploded in a fit of temper, as though he felt there was a hidden meaning behind Jia Jincai's words:

"Isn't it just fine as it is, with you doing it? You are resentful because of what I said about you, aren't you?"

Jia Jincai didn't find it easy to swallow Chen's comment but he kept saying: "No! No! I mean it honestly...."

"Is it because we used your kerosene to light the meeting? Because the higher-placed comrades who came to the village for the meeting boarded at your house? If you think you are getting a worse deal, OK, I'll pay for the kerosene...."

"Look at you! Where are you leading this conversation? The more you say, the more it goes astray. I'm proposing this without any selfish considerations whatsoever. You are more capable than I am—if you become the Secretary, I'll be able to relax. What I have in mind is switching duties with you: You become the Secretary, I become the Vice-Secretary. I've never opposed you. I've never been halfhearted. When you criticized me, I did not object. I'll be happy to follow your lead diligently. You'll take charge of the meetings. If two meetings take place at the same time, you chair one of them, I'll chair the other. As for the kerosene for the lighting, we'll take turns to provide it. All I care about is coming up with an able man to put Dazhai's affairs in order."

Both faces under the kerosene lamp looked glum. Although Jia Jincai's words revealed that he had been misunderstood, Chen Yonggui still couldn't accept it: "No, no, no. I'm not going to be the Secretary. Don't tell me you can't perform your duties well because you are the Secretary."

But Jia Jincai went on, doing his best to persuade him. Chen Yonggui sat there for what seemed like ages in silence, until he finally spat out a mouthful of tobacco. "Well, then, what about the leadership?"

"The leadership I'll take care of."

Jia Jincai kept his word. The previous evening he had gone to speak about this with Song Liying.[1] The following morning he got on his feet right after breakfast and took off for the County capital. The Regional Committee Secretary in those days was still Zhang Huaiying. When Jia Jincai walked into the Regional Committee office, Zhang Huaiying thought that he had come to make a report on production and the state of affairs in Dazhai. As he discovered that Jia Jincai's purpose was to talk about swapping duties, he wasn't entirely clear on what was behind the suggestion, so he couldn't take a position rashly. To Zhang Huaiying's mind, Chen Yonggui would indeed make a good young successor to the post of Branch Secretary, but such matters could not be taken casually. Cadres could be appointed only after careful observation. So in the end, despite Jia Jincai's candid persuasion, a protocol-conscious Zhang Huaiying declined.

Jia Jincai returned to Dazhai quietly, but since he had firmly made up his own mind about what should be done, he insisted on seeing it through. Only a few days later, he again went to see the Regional Committee Secretary. Zhang Huaiying, who was in the midst of reading documents, pulled up a chair for him and heard out his earnest plea. After long deliberation, although he did not offer a reply, his attitude changed: "This suggestion of yours has to be seriously thought out. Why don't you talk with Zhang Yongshun and find out what his position is?" At the time Zhang Yongshun was a Section Chief, in charge of organizational work. He received Jia Jincai, considered carefully Zhang Huaiying's opinion, and declared that the swap of duties could be made provided the two people involved had nothing against it.

As soon as Jia Jincai won this concession he returned to Dazhai and went to see Chen Yonggui. It was already time for the evening meal.

"Jinxiao, we can do it! The Regional Committee Secretary didn't agree at first, but he sent me to discuss it with Zhang Yongshun and Old Zhang agreed to it. So, we're all set!"

Chen Yonggui hesitated. He was still holding his enormous dinner bowl in his hands, but he had stopped eating."So, are you still going to be in charge of things?"

---

1. Song Liying was the first female member of the Dazhai Branch. She became head of all women's work and served as Vice-Secretary to the Branch after her husband retired.

"Look now, Jinxiao!" said Jia Jincai. "What did I tell you the other day, in the middle of the night? If you still think I'm not playing fair with you, go ahead and find out."

Jia Jincai and Chen Yonggui exchanged their posts through a new election, conducted at the general membership meeting of the Party Branch. The next time Jia saw Zhang Huaiying he exclaimed happily: "Old Zhang, Jinxiao and I have exchanged posts."

For several days Zhang Huaiying had had the Dazhai matter constantly on his mind. He was very much inclined to start using Chen Yonggui but he was afraid of Jia Jincai's misgivings. He planned to work on the idea a while longer. This kind of candid spirit on Jia Jincai's part moved him greatly, but caught him up in amazement just the same.

"Changed?"

"Changed," Jia Jincai repeated. "I assure you I have no second thoughts about it."

The value of "yielding to the worthier person" was reflected very soon in the productivity of Dazhai. Had Jia Jincai not yielded his position to the worthier person, Chen Yonggui could not have brought his talents into full play, and the Red Flag of Dazhai would most likely not have risen with such speed to fly in the skies of our motherland.

In 1952, only one year after Jia Jincai yielded his position, Chen Yonggui became a Model Worker of the Province of Shanxi. He went with the Delegation of Shanxi Model Workers, organized by the Shanxi Provincial Government, to study the experiences of the villages on the outskirts of the city of Tianjin in setting up agricultural Cooperatives. It was the first time he ever set foot beyond Shanxi's Niangzi Pass, the first time he had a chance to "see the world." The train passed through Yangquan and emerged on the other side of the Niangzi Pass. Through the window, wherever he looked, waves of green surged from the boundless plain, making him feel envious. Who could have foreseen beyond mountains what other heights there were to scale and conquer! He had been quite pleased with Dazhai's production, but now he realized that, in comparison with the plains, Dazhai left a lot to be desired. If only they could turn Dazhai's slopes, her gullies and ridges into this kind of flat land, and make them green twice a year!

On the train Chen Yonggui met another Model Peasant Worker from Shanxi. His name was Li Shunda.

Li Shunda was already famous nationwide at that time: "In 1943 Li Shunda started a mutual aid group with six neighbors," William Hinton wrote in *Shenfan*. "They hitched themselves to a plow and opened up wasteland in an abandoned ravine high in the mountains of Pingxun County. Some of this land they planted to cotton. Li Shunda's mother cut down a tree, fashioned a spinning wheel, and taught the women of the group how to spin cotton thread. Cooperative effort led to high yields on the land and high productivity in cottage industry." The mutual aid group developed into a village-wide Cooperative that received the personal attention of Chairman Mao. After that the State awarded Li Shunda the title of Gold Star Hero. He and Wang Chonglun were the two earliest worker- and peasant-heroes in New China. When Li Shunda got on the podium to deliver his speech at the Congress of Model Workers, the entire auditorium broke into applause. Provincial leaders invited him for a banquet. They say that later he even visited the Soviet Union.

When Chen Yonggui saw Li Shunda on the train, Model Workers from his Province completely surrounded him. Chen Yonggui could see very clearly what Li Shunda's social status was. In order to strike up a conversation with him and learn something from him, Chen Yonggui got up from his seat, took off his long-stemmed pipe, which had been fastened around his neck, and very deliberately drew closer: "Master Li, let's have a smoke together."

Li Shunda had never seen Chen Yonggui before but he had been in similar situations countless times. So he received Chen Yonggui in a familiar fashion—neither imperious nor fawning. Li Shunda was a peasant, but he wore nothing resembling the short button-front peasant-style jacket and the white towel-turban that Chen Yonggui often wore after he became famous. Li Shunda was fond of Chinese tunic suits named after the founder of the Chinese Republic, Sun Yatsen, and "forge-ahead"-style caps. He was not really a pipe smoker either.

"Please, could Master Li tell me what it is that makes your Xigou village so well organized and successful?" Chen Yonggui asked.

Li Shunda's vocabulary had already been enriched with the new phraseology of the time. "There are two aspects to it," he answered. "One is the activism of the masses; the other is appeals by the leadership. The Communist Party has led the poor in their struggle against the landlords, defeating feudalism and distributing the land to the peasants. Once the peasants get their own land, if they don't seed it they can't reap anything from it, so they have to get organized and cooperate. I decided early on that forming Cooperatives was the right thing to do. In that I happened to be ahead of just about everybody else in the country."

"Xigou's conditions are good," Chen Yonggui continued. "It has the potential to develop both agriculture and forestry. All we have are worn-out gullies and barren ridges. A fistful of soil here, a dustpan there—how are we to develop it?"

"Didn't Chairman Mao say the Foolish Old Man could move mountains?" Li Shunda asked. "You have to believe strongly in everything you do. The question is not whether you have the conditions or not, the question is will you do it?"

People say Chen Yonggui was struck with reverence and awe during his first meeting with the hero from West Gully. Of course, he had no idea that some dozen years later he would replace Master Li as the national representative of the peasantry. He could have guessed even less that in the midst of the Cultural Revolution he and Master Li would each become "tiger skins," pulled by the hands of two opposing factional organizations, and that they would engage in many unhappy disputes.

At the time of their first encounter, Chen Yonggui was truly inspired by Li Shunda, and he determined to bring Dazhai's barren mountains and unruly ravines under control. After the living example of the villages around Tianjin unfolded in front of his mind's eye, no storm could break his resolution.

CHAPTER—5

STAND ON TIGERHEAD MOUNTAIN AND LOOK AT TIANANMEN

In 1952, the Agriculture Cooperative Movement was on the rise throughout the country. Following the policies of the Party Central Committee, Xiyang County set up pilot primary agricultural Cooperatives in the villages of White Lamb Ravine and Zhao Shelter. By 1953, the Secretary of the Xiyang County Communist Party Committee, Zhang Huaiying, established additional primary Cooperatives in Lower Fourth Happiness, Clear Pestle Head, and Dazhai. At various times he dispatched Zhang Laotai, Wang Dianjun, Chen Yonggui, and other Model Workers and progressive individuals to the Central Shanxi region for training. They went to hear experiences and learn techniques for establishing primary agricultural Cooperatives. As Chen Yonggui underwent the training, his desire to organize a Cooperative grew even more intense. The moment he came back to Dazhai and walked through the village gate, he started advocating to the people he chanced upon, the benefits of collectivization and explaining what he knew about how Cooperatives should be run.

Under Chen Yonggui's leadership, organizing a Cooperative had become an urgent need for the Feeble Group even before he went for training. The group had already discussed in private the prospects of setting up a Cooperative. So it was inevitable that the group members should surround him when he came back. Even Jia Jincai and a few other members of the Stalwart Group rushed over to hear the news and find out about the thinking of the higher authorities. Chen Yonggui estimated that the time for setting up a Cooperative was ripe, and he rushed back to the County capital the following day to apply for permission to organize one.

But, in view of the fact that the entire country lacked experience in Cooperatives, the County leadership approached the issue rather cautiously. An attitude prevailed at the time that in principle no Cooperative in its primary stage of development should consist of more than thirty households. The authorities soon approved Chen Yonggui's request, provided that he upheld the principle of thirty households. But Chen Yonggui had decided, based on the concrete situation in Dazhai, that only a Cooperative based on the Feeble Group would be sound enough organizationally, and the Feeble Group already comprised forty-nine households. If he were to set up a Cooperative of thirty households, some members would have to withdraw and go to work on their own. In the minds of the members of the Feeble Group at the time, Cooperatives had become the symbol of the glorious road to progress. Individuals who could not take the road would end up feeling somehow inferior to others, not to mention poorer.

Not surprisingly, even before the County approved the request, quite a few people dropped in on Chen Yonggui to let him know they wanted to enter the Cooperative. This pushed the households who were not able to make up their minds at first to follow the mainstream. At the very beginning of the Party Branch meeting convened to examine the prospects of establishing a Cooperative, Chen Yonggui laid out the problem of household numbers and asked everybody to come up with a viable solution. After individuals voiced their views, it became apparent that everybody was of the same mind: Since their mutual aid group had grown to forty-nine households, there was no way they would reduce their number to thirty households when they organized an agricultural Cooperative.

In the circumstances, it remained to be seen how skillfully their helmsman would deal with the situation. Chen Yonggui decided on an innovative method of a sort rarely proposed by a laboring peasant. His proposal was: On the one hand, take into account the spirit of the policy, but on the other, take care of the concrete situation. This is how he planned to work it: He would report the number of households to the higher authorities as thirty, and those peasants who were not too keen on joining the Cooperative would at first not be entered into the records. Once the members established the Cooperative firmly, those who still wanted to join would be accepted as the occasion allowed. He called it "the inside outside Cooperative."

After they settled this issue, they started examining concrete ways of setting up their organization. They discussed the relative value of labor and land shares, the allotment of labor and livestock, and the distribution of bonuses to the members of the Cooperative. They came up with the formula: 55 percent of all earnings would be distributed based on work points earned, 40 percent on land shares held, while 5 percent would go into the collectively held accumulation and welfare fund. Finally, the gathering addressed the issue of the peasant households who would not, at first, join the Cooperative. Chen Yonggui suggested that, in order for the Party Branch to lead the households who were not in the Cooperative, the Vice-Secretary of the Party Branch, Jia Jincai, should assume responsibility for work with them. After he made the suggestion, Chen Yonggui asked Jia if he had any objections. Jia Jincai originally wanted to join the Cooperative, but since Chen Yonggui wanted him to work with people who would not be in the Cooperative, he declared: "I'll do whatever the Party Branch assigns me to do."

From then on Jia Jincai assumed responsibility for all matters involving the three mutual aid groups and four households of individual farmers that remained outside the Cooperative.

Through the beginning stages of organizing into an Agricultural Producers' Cooperative some people maintained a negative, spoilsport attitude. "If mutual aid groups operate by turning the grain over to individuals, and the agricultural Cooperative turns it over to the collective, isn't it obvious which organization will win the people's trust and which will not?"

The people who were saying this were the well-to-do middle peasants who owned houses and land and who could not bear to part with the advantages they enjoyed in the old society. Chen Yonggui refused to take into consideration their views, believing that those interested should set up their Cooperative following the prescribed rules, rather than letting everybody do as they please. But, whenever the opportunity presented itself he did criticize such destructive opinions.

One time, he countered the the dissidents at the meeting of the Cooperative Council as it made plans for the spring sowing.

"Is the collective or the individual better after all?" Chen asked. "I say, the key factor is the leadership. When the leader is good, the fire burns high because everybody adds firewood to it. This year we've worked out how to seed the good land as well as the bad, the sunny slopes as well as the shady side. Come autumn, we'll see whether we'll reap a harvest. Don't they say the mutual aid groups operate by turning the grain over to individuals, while the Agricultural Cooperative turns it over to the collective? That's right, we'll see whether the rivulets run dry while there's still water in the big river. I believe that, with a well-led collective like ours, our Cooperative is bound to succeed."

These words bolstered morale among the peasant households who had joined the Cooperative. Consequently, for a period of time after the meeting, not only did the men throw themselves enthusiastically into hard work but women did, too—all showed up on the edge of the fields in order to earn a few extra points, which would give them a bigger share of the harvest in the fall. There was a woman called Jia Tianhuan who, in those days, took part in the soil-building project with five other women that she brought along, and although they got only five work points for a day's work, they felt well content. The number of women who participated in field labor later increased to twenty-three. This caused a headache for some members of the Cooperative, who complained that if so many women went to work in the fields the farm work could not be properly planned and more work points would have to be awarded. "There is no way our collective can award that many work points," they insisted.

Chen Yonggui was sensitive enough to know he had a problem on his hands. He had already heard of the problems posed by surplus women's labor at some other Cooperatives. The others all limited the right of women to participate in agricultural labor to varying degrees. In the end would there turn out to be a problem of surplus labor, or of a severe shortage of labor? Chen Yonggui brought the question forth at another Cooperative Council meeting. He spoke under the light of a kerosene lamp, gesticulating freely.

"If we maintain our land as is, now that we have the Cooperative, planting a plot here, a plot there, what kind of future do we have?" he asked. "I saw the land in the villages around Tianjin. They are going to use big machinery to cultivate it. And we here? We have some plots that aren't big enough to lead an ox onto. Can we afford not to transform them? If you ask me, we have to join all the land in Dazhai that can be consolidated into connected flat fields that will be easy to work and plant. That will also shake out the unwanted dregs of the old society. If we want to transform the land we need a big labor force. Twenty-three women? Two hundred and thirty will not be enough. And some are saying we can't even take care of these we have at the moment! The first thing to do is let women take part in soil building!"

Once again, Chen Yonggui's words got through to the Cooperative Council members. That year, the women worked 120 tons of manure and compost into the soil, improving the quality of over 140 *mu* of land. When May came around and with it the time to thin out the millet seedlings, women alone thinned out 155 *mu* of the total of 205 *mu* that the Cooperative had planted to millet. They took care of 75 percent of the millet seedlings. This exemplary accomplishment educated all Communist Party members in the village and the entire membership of the Cooperative Council.

"Do you believe me or not?" Chen Yonggui asked them publicly at the edge of the field. "If not for our womenfolk who hold up half the sky, we'd still be thinning the millet. And for quite some days to come!"

Thereafter, Chen Yonggui began to value Dazhai's labor even more. By July of the same year, in order to let people develop their talents to the limit, and to use their energies to the utmost, Chen Yonggui decided to rebuild White Camel Gully. He figured on using the slack farming season to turn the little plot of land there into a huge field.

Actually, that year of various broken records was also a year of competition between the new Agricultural Producers' Cooperative on one side, and mutual aid groups and individual farmers on the other. Due to Chen Yonggui's leadership, the households that had joined the Cooperative put forth a united effort and invested an enormous number of man-hours into soil enrichment and land-building activities. That year they used pesticides and chemical fertilizers for the first time, and achieved a grain yield per *mu* of over 360 *jin*. That same year, the *per-mu* yield of the three mutual aid groups was just over 230 *jin*, while the average *per-mu* yield of the four individual farmers came to only 204 *jin*. The *per-mu* yield for the village of Dazhai as a whole increased to 250 *jin*—an increase of 5 percent from the previous year.

After the autumn harvest, the Agricultural Cooperative held a big meeting to sum up the results of its first year. The Committee rewarded members of the Cooperative who did well throughout the year with diaries, fountain pens, and six-foot- long pieces of the hydron-blue cloth. Chen Yonggui read out their names: Liang Bianliang, Li Xiqing, Zhao Dahe, Jia Chengqing.... They climbed onto the stage. Chen Yonggui handed out their awards, while the people below congratulated them with thunderous hand clapping. The event had a great impact on farmers from the entire village. Those who did not belong to the Cooperative envied the ones who did. Those who did not get a prize envied the ones who did.

Right after the event, Chen Yonggui organized the entire labor force of the Cooperative, male and female alike, to harness White Camel Gully. The Xiyang County Party Committee attached great importance to his actions. At the end of the year the leaders chose Chen Yonggui to attend the Conference of Model Workers of the Central Shanxi Region, where he delivered a hard- hitting speech. Regional Party leaders asked him to talk about his experiences in giving free reign to labor and expanding production. He displayed unusual creative ability on this occasion. Not only did he speak objectively and honestly, he was eloquent and logical. In his summary remarks at the end of the conference Regional Secretary Wu Zhongtai said, "Chen Yonggui from Dazhai is a very smart person of great ability. I hope that the other Cooperatives will be like Dazhai: not just completing their yearly production plans successfully but also engaging in the capital construction of farmland. Only if we do so can our collective economy gradually grow, and only then will the advantages of socialism gradually be brought into play."

Although Chen Yonggui became a celebrity elsewhere, some people in Dazhai were still not convinced of the merit of his methods and kept looking for excuses to disrupt his plans. The following is a story of how one man, proven to be a counterrevolutionary in the past, "slapped himself in the face."

The incident happened during the first winter after the Cooperative was set up. Just as the people present at the meeting, overwhelmed with joy, busily discussed various aspects of the Cooperative's bumper harvest, this man suddenly butted in sarcastically: "All right already! Don't tell us again about the advantages of the Agricultural Cooperative! A yield of 250 *jin* per *mu* is something to make a fuss about, too. And I, as an individual farmer, even got over 300 *jin*!"

This was like pouring cold water on the Cooperative. The *per-mu* yield of the village was just over 250 *jin*, while this individual farmer got over 300 *jin*! So where were the advantages of collectivization? Farmers who had joined the Cooperative were puzzled. Their arguments lost force. Chen Yonggui, however, knew exactly how things stood and was fully prepared to handle it. He had been hoping that someone would jump out to challenge them all.

Being the convener of the meeting, Chen Yonggui decided to change the order of proceedings and announce the new policy of a State monopoly on the purchase and marketing of grain right there and then. Since he people were still not aware of this policy, which had just been put nto effect nationally, he knew that the moment he announced it, it was ound to cause a great uproar. Consequently, he addressed the gathering peaking softly and mildly. "Our Agricultural Cooperative, the mutual id groups and the individual farmers all had a bumper harvest this year. hat's great! The Party Branch trusts that our village will be able to meet nd even surpass the purchase quotas, which were set for us for the first ime this year. And now, let's have every household sell their surplus rain to the State, according to the yield they reported themselves."

The proposal almost scared out of his wits the man who had boasted earlier. His yield was not as high as he had claimed, so now, in a manner of speaking, he had to reap a whirlwind of his own sowing. As Chen Yonggui later remembered it, what followed resembled a scene from a movie. The man squatted in a corner, hitting himself on the cheeks with both hands and letting his mouth fall wide open. "Ayaa, this mouth of mine is a bad mouth," he said as he struck himself. "It's a wind-breaking mouth. This fart-mouth of mine is worthless. It drops nothing but drivel. My *per-mu* yield wouldn't amount to 300 *jin* even if I were to add all the straw left after threshing onto the scales."

People were at once annoyed and amused by his behavior. They spoke in concert, although without previous agreement: "You reported the yield yourself. How could it be sham? Just calculate the amount of grain to be purchased by the State based on your own figures!"

The man begged for mercy with every fiber in his body. People asked him why he had lied? Unable to advance any arguments to defend himself, he stammered and stuttered out a confession: "I wouldn't join the Cooperative. I was even opposed to the idea of others doing it. I was afraid I would suffer losses if I entered the Cooperative. That's why I made trouble."

Chen Yonggui estimated that the drama had been played out pretty much to its conclusion, so he ended it up by saying: "The Communist Party has always stressed seeking truth from facts and has been opposed to telling lies. Don't you think your fellow villagers will know how much grain you actually reaped just by looking at it? If you think you need to lower your yields, you'll have to go from door to door admitting that you were at fault, and let the people discuss how to deal with you."

This particular disturbance may have run its course, but the work on State purchase and marketing of grain was just beginning. Wher the State first started implementing the policy of a State monopoly or the purchase and marketing of grain, farmers were very apprehensive Their grain output was still not very high at the time, while the State purchase price looked low[1] If they sold too much grain, they could enc

1. State grain prices might have seemed low to the producers but over the years the followed very closely world market prices. As a grain producer myself in America, I wa able to make realistic comparisons during many trips to China in the seventies an eighties. (W.H.H.)

up short of it themselves, in any case the low price was bound to depress their income. In order to assure grain deliveries from producers, the higher authorities began to mobilize from level to level until the task of meeting community quotas came down to each Party Branch at the basic level.

Chen Yonggui, being the Provincial Model Worker that he was, carried out the grain collection task without the slightest reservation. Both times when he returned from meetings of Model Workers, one in Taiyuan, the other in Yuci, County leaders invited him to attend "banquets." Although both banquets consisted merely of some stir-fried sweet potatoes and a glass of liquor distilled from sorghum, still they were a "special treatment" in a manner of speaking. People who were assigned to entertain the guest of honor always came from a certain rank. For instance, the County Magistrate and Party Secretary hosted Zhang Laotai and Wang Dianjun, while the Vice-Magistrate entertained Chen Yonggui. Even so this banquet provided great encouragement to Chen Yonggui. What kind of Party Branch Secretary would hc be if he couldn't even handle the people while implementing the State's policy on the purchasing and marketing of grain?

He spoke repeatedly at the meetings on people's livelihood organized by the Party Branch. Old regional Communist Party members were all highly disciplined ideologically. If the higher authorities called for something to be done, they would not come out to oppose it publicly even if they disagreed with it at the time. They all concentrated on the common objective as implemented by Chen Yonggui. If he could deliver, they'd be able to make it too.

Chen Yonggui had no misgivings on this score. Most people, even if they wanted to turn over more grain, would always be handicapped by wives who dragged their feet and held them back. But Chen Yonggui's wife, Li Huni, was a Communist Party member who had been very active in the Party for the past few years. Even in the most straitened circumstances Li Huni would never be a hindrance to Chen Yonggui. Even though Chen Yonggui didn't get much grain as his share that year, he sold off over 5,000 *jin* without blinking. Jia Jincai also turned over his family's quota grain at that same time, so there was nothing other

Party members could say—they all raced each other to the grain collection station to deliver their due.

According to the recollection of an old Communist Party member from Dazhai, there were only two Dazhai families who resisted turning over their quota grain that year: One was the family of Jia Siyuan, registered as a farming household; the other was a Communist Party member who had just returned from Army service. This Party member, in particular, put up a big show of not turning his grain over while venting his resentment. He jumped on some shortcomings in the way the leadership carried out the work, and he wouldn't let up. Chen Yonggui had to go an extra mile to modify this man's stance. In the end, he was able to do this because of excellent work at the grass-roots level. That year Dazhai sold the State over 40,000 *jin* (20 netric tons) of grain that year.

The task of turning over the required grain for the State was accomplished, but before spring of the following year was over, Dazhai faced a grain shortage. People had very little grain to eat, so they focused all their resentment on Chen Yonggui.

"Say, how are we to live through these dog days? How much grain have you got, anyway?" they asked.

Chen Yonggui, on his part, had sold off many times more grain than the average peasant household, and was now faced with the most severe shortage in the entire village. But he couldn't tell anybody about the misery of his own stomach, because he was supposed to anticipate and lead. If he didn't, he risked turning Dazhai upside down.

Other parts of Xiyang County experienced the same problem with the State grain purchasing quotas that year. The County had to hand out stored grain three times in order to solve the practical problem of survival, and it still did not meet the people's needs. One of the County Committee leaders remembered Dazhai, wondering how it was that Chen Yonggui did not show up when all the other Branch Secretaries paid him a visit asking for grain. So he took the long ten-Chinese-mile walk to Dazhai and paid Chen Yonggui a visit.

When he saw the straits Chen Yonggui's family was in, the leader sat down with him on the edge of his brick-bed *kang* for a heart-to-heart talk.

"It seems that I'll be left with no resources this year," Chen Yonggui told him straight out.

"You'll be left with no resources! I'll be left with even fewer than you!" answered the leader. "To allay, at least for a while, the pending disaster, should I give some of the stored grain back to Dazhai? If I don't, and they get nothing to eat, how will they produce?"

"No need. No need for that," said Chen Yonggui, waving the suggestion off. "To tell you the truth, although the people of Dazhai are a bit short of grain to eat, they can all still pretty much feed themselves. It is my grain that's become a problem, and I've had two visits in three days by comrades who have come down to the countryside and needed to be fed! However, squash and beans are almost here. We won't have cereals, but we'll have vegetables. How could we possibly go hungry? Think of other places that could better use that grain before you give it to us."

During the visit Chen Yonggui treated the County leader to squash leaf soup at his home. Chen's act of self-denial moved the cadre deeply, but since Chen Yonggui turned down the County's relief assistance, he wasn't sure how to help him. When he returned to the County seat he learned that Chen Yonggui's wife, Li Huni, often went to the town's East Gate Vegetable Garden to buy vegetables. The news upset him very much. If Chen Yonggui had to rely on purchased vegetables to survive, what a burden this must put on his purse! He notified Chen Yonggui the same day that he wanted to see him in his office.

Chen Yonggui went as soon as he received the word. He entered the leader's office like someone about to receive a difficult assignment and sat down, positioning himself on the old-fashioned chair facing his host. The County leader did not say a word, just stared at him. Then he took two packs of cigarettes from his drawer and handed them to Chen.

"Here. Take these two packs of cigarettes," he said.

This gesture puzzled Chen Yonggui. "Whenever this Party Secretary called for me in the past," he mused, "he offered me a cup of tea at the most—never 'gifts.' Besides, he doesn't even smoke. What is he getting at with these two packs of cigarettes?"

Chen Yonggui figured that there must be some special assignment awaiting him, so he blurted out, "Just give me the task you have in mind. I've got my own pipe tobacco, which is good enough for me. Save the cigarettes for your guests."

"I have not prepared any assignment for you today," the County leader explained cordially. "I called you in to help you solve the emergency you are facing. Take those two packs of cigarettes, and...." As he spoke, he handed Chen some grain coupons, which he had saved up over the last few months, enough to buy some forty or fifty *jin* of grain.

"Old Chen, take these coupons and swap them for flour at the grain distribution station. Our comrades who visit the village often eat at your house. You accept neither grain nor money from them, so you should take this to supplement your own supplies."

"You are something else!" exclaimed Chen, breaking into loud laughter. "Here I was, thinking you had some special assignment for me, and this is what it's all about? Forget it! I'll hold onto these cigarettes, but the grain coupons—I don't want any, not even for one *jin*. You must be pretty hard up for grain yourself. I'm finding things a little tight this year, but next year everything will be fine. Even though now she has a baby, my wife doesn't mind it because she is a Party member. If she blames me for selling too much grain, I'll remind her of the old society. Whatever we have to face now, it's better than gnawing at raw corn the way she was the day I found her!"

One man was pushing, the other refusing. In the end, the County leader had to yield to Chen Yonggui, who took the cigarettes, but did not touch a single grain coupon. That's how harmonious relations were then between different levels of authority in the Old Liberated Area.

Chen Yonggui's respect for the County Committee cadre, who was twelve years younger than he, increased greatly after that trip to the County seat. If the leaders could discover his personal difficulties so promptly and take so much trouble to help him solve them, nothing was too hard for him to handle! He knew that so long as his outlook on the world was clear he'd find the strength to overcome even greater difficulties. To buy vegetables in East Gate he'd been borrowing money from a relative in Yangquan, but he didn't care. "What's borrowing some money?" thought Chen Yonggui. "You break into a sweat a few times, then you can break clean." But that difficult year taught him a lesson. When the time came to sell grain the following year, he made a careful plan. Not only did he leave the village enough grain for food, he left some stored up as a collective reserve. Even with that much set aside Dazhai was able to satisfy in full the whole task set by the State Grain Bureau for that year's deliveries.

Accomplishing such a feat, however, didn't mean that everybody understood or supported their leader. More often than not, Chen Yonggui's activities cast clouds of worry over the faces of those involved in the consequences. His enthusiastic grain sale invited more than a little cursing in the village. Some people went so far as to compare him to a dog.

"Other dogs bite outsiders, but this dog from our village bites our own people," they said. Depending on who they came from and what their purpose was, Chen Yonggui had his own way of dealing with these slanders. Such words, spoken by certain people, called for a ruthless counterattack on his part. Spoken by others, they elicited reasoned argument. Chen Yonggui spent long hours pondering how to explain everything to people who were honestly puzzled. People from Dazhai itself were not the only ones who cursed the activist village leader for selling too much grain. Quite a few outsiders cursed him even more crudely, because Chen Yonggui, in their eyes, had visited on them many an unrighted wrong. Dazhai had sold a lot of grain, and the higher authorities frequently brought Dazhai's figures out for comparison.

"Dazhai was able to sell this much grain," they pointed out, "so how come you can't sell anything like as much?"

Chen and Dazhai were only trying to lead the way by setting a good example, but due to the situation at the time the pressure to sell so much grain impinged on many vital interests of the peasants generally, so it was very easy for Chen Yonggui to end up in opposition to the majority. Finally, not just the rank-and-file, but some village cadres also complained that they could never surpass Dazhai in the amount of grain delivered. Incidentally, all their grumbling added greatly to the enormous pressure Chen was already feeling.

There was a time when Chen Yonggui delivered speeches and received awards at the County seat, accompanied to and from the stage by boisterous applause. But the moment he set out on the road back to Dazhai, he had to worry about which route to take. If he passed through the villages of Liu Settlement and Five Family Flat on his way back and ran into peasants there, they were bound to taunt him fiercely.

"He went to the County seat to eat steamed buns," some said.

"The people are starving, but he's wearing a red flower,"[1] taunted others.

Chen Yonggui didn't want to listen to such taunts, but people kept up their attacks, leaving him no place to hide. After the State-established monopoly to purchase and market grain had been in operation for a year or two, County leaders, at a year-end evaluation meeting, awarded Chen Yonggui a silk banner. He didn't dare carry it back from the meeting in the open so that people could see it; instead, he tucked it into his jacket above his heart. As he passed through the village of Five family Flat some people who were working outdoors spotted him and decided to amuse themselves at his expense.

"Jinxiao, come over here! Have a seat," said one man.

"I can't. I have some work to do back home," said Chen Yonggui, trying not to look at them.

"What's the thing you are hiding over your heart?"

Thus questioned, Chen Yonggui's face turned slightly red, but he bluffed his way past with a quip.

"I'm hiding a silver ingot! Can you believe it?" he laughed.

Over time Chen Yonggui got used to this kind of sarcastic exchange. After all, could such idle talk really blow away the truth about Dazhai's integrity and commitment to national well being? From then on, when he left the village to attend meetings, he would simply inform everybody that he was going off to eat steamed buns made of white flour free of charge. Then, as he followed the road back home, he would hang his red silk trophy around his neck, stand tall and walk straight. Chen Yonggui understood clearly that genuine concern for the people did not mean selling less grain, it meant finding a way to stimulate their initiative to increase the amount of grain raised. Reaching a common understanding with the people was crucial to accomplishing his goal. He called a general meeting of all Cooperative members in the village. There he placed a grub hoe on the table and asked everybody:

"What do you think, where did this hoe come from?"

"It was made by workers," answered a member of the Cooperative.

1. A red flower was often awarded for outstanding work.

"What do you think," Chen Yonggui went on, "these brother-workers of ours who make our machines and tools, do they eat grain or not?"

The meeting hall began to buzz with comments.

Chen Yonggui continued: "The workers who make our farm tools eat grain; the Liberation Army soldiers who defend our country eat grain; if we don't sell them the grain, what are they going to eat?"

After these last words, Liang Bianliang and some other Communist Party members spoke too. "We cannot only think of ourselves, we must think of the country. If we have the grain that we don't need and we don't sell it, are we really heeding the Party's call? If we have surplus grain to bring forth, we should sell it!"

Chen Yonggui guided the members of the Dazhai Cooperative into accepting the idea that they should always take the interests of the whole into account. So they didn't just fulfill the State purchase quotas year after year, they kept increasing their grain output too. Once the people had enough grain, the surfeit dispelled their misgivings.

Gradually, people from neighboring villages saw what Dazhai was really doing. They stopped reviling Chen Yonggui and turned to reproach their own village cadres.

"Nothing is wrong with Cooperatives," they started to say with conviction. "If there are problems, it's the fault of the cadres."

People are prone to equate victory with honor and glory. Dazhai won a big battle on the road to the cooperative transformation of agriculture, which thereby became the "glorious road."

CHAPTER 6

THREE BATTLES WITH WOLF DEN RAVINE

Dazhai is located in a mountainous region subject to serious soil erosion and other ecological damage. The area is rather densely populated, the average per capita holding being just over 1 *mu*[1] of non-irrigated farmland. Moreover, these holdings are divided into myriad small plots perched atop rock outcroppings that are both infertile and hard to reach, sustaining only with extreme effort the elementary needs of the people. History bears proof that the manual labor of individual peasants going it alone cannot change these conditions.

In order to steer clear of the trap of hunger set for them by the evil spirits of the netherworld, and in order to rid themselves once and for all of harassment from natural calamities, the people of Dazhai resolved to transform the landscape and wrest new land from the mountain together as a well-organized collective. The very terrain, coupled with the indigent condition of those who tilled it, forced this decision upon them. It also forced them, at times, to go without sleep, work through the night, and eat porridge that had frozen over in the bowl on the way to the field.

1. One *mu* is one-sixth of an acre or one-fifteenth of a hectare. (W.H.H.)

Chen Yonggui may be said to have been a hero molded by these circumstances, and he proved himself well worthy of the title.

Chen Yonggui never intended the transformation of White Camel Gully, with the use of female as well as male labor, as described in Chapter 5, to be the terminal point of Dazhai's struggle for security and plenty. Neither was he content with being a Model Worker and eating steamed buns at the County seat. From the very beginning, right after he had organized the Agricultural Producers' Cooperative, Chen Yonggui began drawing up a blueprint for his life's grand enterprise: Turning Dazhai's rock and yellow loess overlay into the foundation for a new socialist community. He talked about his vision often with cadres on the Cooperative Council, with Party members, with members of his village Cooperative. In the end, he drafted a ten-year plan for the transformation of Dazhai. The objectives of the plan were as follows: Turn all uncultivated ridges and gullies into fertile farmland, turn all hillside plots into terraced fields, turn "running" or washed out fields into "retained" or consolidated fields, turn all cultivated soil into "Dazhai-sponge" soil and thus ensure stable yields and good harvests every year despite drought or excessive rainfall. The first, most crucial task was to turn the "running" fields into "retained" fields.

Traditionally even terraced fields in Dazhai sloped steeply and did not have enclosing barriers or confining walls. Since they were just earth terraces they turned into "running" fields the moment it rained. Such fields generated "Three-Runoffs": runoff water, runoff nutrients, and runoff soil. As a result, the size of the fields, the depth of the topsoil, its fertility and its yield, kept decreasing no matter how hard people worked, so Chen Yonggui designed his ten-year plan to contain the "Three Runoffs" and turn "running" fields into "retained" fields. In consultation with many others he mapped the course of the action: block gullies by building dams; protect slopes by building terrace walls of laid-up stone; bring in topsoil where the topsoil is too thin; fill in and level off land that slopes too steeply; remove earth from the high ends or sides of fields to build up the lower ends or sides, making the surface of all fields slant down and inward toward the uphill side, thus catching and holding water.

Dazhai cooperators determined to take the above steps in the following order: Tackle easy and small plots first; tackle difficult and large plots later. The village Party Committee, with Chen at its head, having created a comprehensive plan, decided to administer it centrally according to the following timetable: Every year, after the completion of farm work in the autumn, the labor force would focus on the reconstruction of gullies. In the period from the Spring Festival up to spring plowing, the labor force would focus on leveling land. During the summer and fall seasons, whenever there was time left after farm work, all labor would focus on building terrace walls. These projects would take priority over all others.

Chen first put this ten-year plan to the Party Branch Committee and then to the general membership of the Branch to discuss. After the Party Branch approved it, he announced it to the general meeting of the members of the Cooperative. There Chen Yonggui countered various wavering and negative opinions by exercising his vocal cords and giving free rein to his inborn powers of persuasion.

"A ten-year plan is a long-term plan," he said. "But each period within the ten years has its own objectives. For instance, we presently want to wage a grand battle with Wolf Den Ravine. Although it is a big area of deep ravines, the mountain side is dead, inert, lifeless, while the people are an active, living force. Every dam we erect is one more dam, every terrace is one more terrace. We'll tackle them one at a time. Why shouldn't that be enough? I admit this project is rather big, but the bigger the project, the sooner we should start attacking it. Only if we work at all will we ever change the mountain around us. If we don't dare take action and just sit around on our butts, Dazhai will remain the same for generations to come. Therefore, I say, we should not have any illusions—be prepared to wage long- term war. We will prevail, if not in three years then in five, if not in five years then in ten, if not in ten then twenty. If we don't succeed in our lifetime, we have children and grandchildren to carry on the battle. So long as we keep digging into the mountain like the Foolish Old Man in the fable, there will come a day when Dazhai is transformed."

In an attempt to persuade his audience and stir people into action Chen Yonggui followed up his big arguments with talk about some concrete hows and whys. He cited the example of two brothers from Dazhai, Jia Juyaun and Jia Shengyuan, who, in pre-revolutionary times, cultivated three *mu* of land. They spent an entire year, month after month, reclaiming the barren slopes surrounding their three-*mu* field. They built dams, laid terrace walls and leveled land into fields. In the end, by dint of hard work, they created ten *mu* of good land. He also brought up the example of White Camel Gully, which they had put under control the year before. In the past, under individual ownership, each person had a piece of it, but not a single family was able to harness the gully. Now, with their collective strength, they had completed this task in one season. Thus Chen reasoned with the impoverished mountain folk and, overcoming all doubts and hesitation, he convinced them. Even those who loved to slip in a cynical remark or complaint here and there had to acknowledge that Chen Yonggui was onto something big.

In the first two years that followed the establishment of the Agricultural Producers' Cooperative, Dazhai engaged in a series of gully-harnessing projects aimed at turning "running" fields into "retained" fields. White Camel Gully was only the first of several. They also succeeded in harnessing Back Side Draw and in harnessing Leech Gulch, but could they, after all, harness Wolf Den Ravine? Since Chen Yonggui was determined to do it, they were waiting to see the temper of his determination and, what was more important, his plan of action.

Wolf Den Ravine was called "evil," the "evil old mountain gully." The largest of the seven major fissures in the rock and loess of Dazhai, it tore a ragged gash down the mountainside almost a mile long, as many as twenty yards wide, and well over thirty yards deep. It cut through a steeply pitched high knoll of barely accessible terrain. During the rainy season water converged on it from all directions. The mountain torrents raged through it like ferocious wild beasts, rolling along rocks too big for a pair of men to lift, as if they were marbles. Building dams to create fields in a gully like this was no easy task. No wonder some people ridiculed the effort.

"Can those picks you clutch in your fists, those shovels you hold high, those worn-out carrying baskets and stiff shoulder poles really hope to tame the barren hilltops and unruly flash floods of Dazhai?" they asked.

And yet it was by using these very tools, together with some cleverly placed dynamite, by rising before daybreak, and working long after sun down under the moon and the stars, that the people of Dazhai built stone dams and filled the hollows behind them with countless tons of rich yellow loess.

The boom of explosions, the crash of hammers, the rhythm of work-songs synchronizing the movement of bodies as they cut into the mountain breaking stone, the rise and fall of human shouts and greetings—all these combined to create the symphony orchestrated by Dazhai's unique undertaking. That symphony filled the air at Wolf Den Ravine as the first great battle with the formidable canyon began.

In the dead of winter a piercing cold wind from the Northwest whistled as it swept up flakes from the snow-covered ground. The cold people felt on their hands when they extended them out of their sleeves cut through the skin like a knife. Yet Wolf Den Ravine seethed with enthusiasm. The new masters of Dazhai were attacking this sinister, unconquered old mountain gully with the radiant spirit of the Celestial Maiden scattering flowers.[1] Everybody sweat profusely: those with hammers who were breaking stone or drilling holes in hard rock for sticks of dynamite and setting them off; those who were fastening steel cables to lift rocks out of the gully; and those who were wielding pickaxes to crack the frozen topsoil. The vigorous effort of all dispelled both fatigue and cold.

For several days and nights in a row Chen had been working hard on the rock in the gully by day, then attending endless meetings night after night. For one thing, he had needed to make several trips to the village of Five Family Flat to negotiate the disposition of a few parcels of land that residents there cultivated in Wolf Den Ravine. Failure to arrange a friendly trade of these few parcels would disrupt his plans for harnessing the canyon. After several setbacks in the prolonged negotiations he managed to reach an agreement to swap a piece of land just outside the village of Dazhai for those few plots cultivated by the village of Five Family Flat in Wolf Den Ravine.

1. The Celestial Maiden, Xian Nu, is a mythical goddess in the sky who scatters flowers to express her joy. Her radiant form and joyous gestures are embedded in the culture. Every child knows about the Xian Nu, but few can tell you how she got there or why she is so happy.

Now his body just couldn't take it any longer. Too dizzy to stand, he sat down on a nearby boulder, reached for the long-stemmed pipe that always hung round his neck on a string and, smacking his lips, filled its small brass bowl with tobacco, struck flint on the steel striker he always carried at his waist, caught the sparks on some tinder, and lit up. He took a few drags on the pipe and felt some strength slowly return to his body.

Truly there was no end to unavoidable meetings. During the past few days Chen had also convened a series of get-togethers with the Branch Party Committee, the full Party Branch, the Cooperative Council, and the general membership of the Cooperative. There he had explained the tasks to come, decided on concrete measures, examined how the work was being carried out that week, and discussed how to deal with the problems that kept arising with each stage of the "battle." This last meeting continued well into dawn. When Chen Yonggui heard the rooster crowing his expression turned grave.

"That will be it for now," he announced. "But that doesn't mean the meeting is over. It will only be over when we solve all our problems. When we break up, don't go home and sleep. Pick up your tools and get out to Old Wolf Den."

Right after the meeting Chen Yonggui picked up his tools and groped his way through the pre-dawn gloom to the work site. The members of the Branch Committee and all the Party members followed. Some of them grumbled, others frowned, yet in the end they individually decided they could do it if the others could. In the minds of the people of Dazhai, waging a battle against Wolf Den Ravine was like going to war. War knows no difference between night and day—you can't say you'll fight the enemy only after a good night's sleep! When a train runs fast it relies on the locomotive to pull the whole contrivance. If the leader can do it but his followers cannot, this war will be hard to fight. With that spirit they conquered Wolf Den Ravine and added three dozen level fields to their ancestral domain.

The following year, after a gully washing rain, runoff water broke through all thirty-eight dams, tearing gaps big and small in the stone work. Chen Yonggui, the Party members and all the rank-and-file watched in horror as their winter's hard toil poured down the mountain.

They rushed to Wolf Den Ravine in the midst of the downpour and tried to use their bare hands wherever possible to keep the dams from breaking. This was when Zhao Xiaohe, with his ulcerated leg, jumped into a waist-deep mud pit to plug the gap and lost his life.

Despite all their efforts, Dazhai's first great battle with Wolf Den Ravine ended in defeat. The defeat brought discontent, which emerged in the form of pithy sayings like: "People choose their course, but water carves its own channel." That is why, many years later, some so-called liberal, but nevertheless small-minded individuals, called this experience "the least glorious page" of Dazhai's history.

But, in a situation like that, should one bow to difficulties or should one continue the battle? In Chen Yonggui's mind the answer was unpleasant but clear. When announcing his ten-year plan for rebuilding Dazhai he had stated his readiness to engage Wolf Den Ravine in one, two, even ten hard battles, if need be. He had made a commitment and he intended to honor it. Accepting one defeat he never looked back but proceeded to throw his hardened troops into a second battle in the winter of 1956. During that battle the practice of getting up in the dark before dawn, staying on after dark, and sometimes eating frozen food in the field re-emerged.

In 1955, when they waged their first battle against the ravine, Chen Yonggui and his comrades had the full support of the Chinese Communist Party of Xiyang County and the Xiyang County Government. During the second attempt to harness Wolf Den Ravine, the County leadership again backed them up at crucial moments, bolstering their confidence that all difficulties could be overcome.

The winter sun hung over Tigerhead Mountain, its weak rays dispensing a wan, cold light over the gullies and ridges of Wolf Den Ravine. The wind, blowing in from the far Northeast, dried the sweat on every face at the work site. These mountain folk did not feel cold; they felt rather as though they were allaying a fever. Just as their work picked up speed, someone shouted, "Look, Comrade Huaiying is here."

Everybody looked down the path toward the village. In the distance they saw a man jump off his horse and walk toward them on foot. He had several people in tow. All the members of the Dazhai Cooperative who were working in the ravine at the time rushed to shake his hand and greet him. Zhang Huaiying was not very good at flattery or small talk. He usually only asked a question or two aimed at helping him understand the whole situation. When he saw Chen Yonggui he asked, "What method are you using this time to construct the dams?"

Chen Yonggui introduced his plan for the second construction drive. Zhang Huaiying expressed his support for the project, then picked up a carrying pole and proceeded to carry earth along with those members of Dazhai Cooperative who were building up a level field. Zhang Huaiying was not yet old at the time. He had no trouble carrying loads that equaled those of the Dazhai peasants. The purpose of his visit was to back up Chen Yonggui with concrete action and encourage him to carry the second Wolf Den Ravine project to completion.

At noon that day the members of the Dazhai Cooperative ate their food at the edge of the field. Chen Yonggui grasped a huge, fired-clay bowl and started munching with delight what people had dubbed "frozen food." Addressing Zhang Huaiying he said, "This is how we do it for now. I don't know when we'll be labeled as criminals for it."

Zhang Huaiying, aware of the snide complaints made by some contemporary journalists regarding "frozen food," urged Chen Yonggui not to be upset. "Don't worry about them. They don't understand. I understand. If you asked them to eat food in this condition, they couldn't swallow it. If they could swallow it they couldn't digest it. But I have eaten plain ice, which is even worse than this frozen food. If you asked me to eat it today, I couldn't, but back then I simply had to gulp it down."

Zhang Huaiying was referring to the time in 1944 when he led the people's militia in a battle to shake off an enemy attack and give cover to the troops in the rear. His unit had to run almost five miles in formation.[1] After they had gone some three miles he could no longer stand his thirst, so he picked pieces of ice from the river to suck. The ice relieved him, cooled him off, and boosted his energy for the remaining miles.[2] After he told the story to the Dazhai cooperators he added: "You eat in

1. Fifteen Chinese li in the original.
2. Ordinarily Chinese never drink cold liquids, much less cool anything off with ice. (W.H.H.)

the evening, but when you get up in the morning and start working you get hungry right away. Before long your body is covered with sweat. The frozen food can, very conveniently, cool you off. This is the dialectics of frozen food. Ask certain cadres and journalists to eat it, and I'm afraid they won't even dare look at it. But if they can't stomach it, I can."

This wasn't just empty talk. What Zhang Huaiying said was reasonable and justified. Chen Yonggui found Zhang's interpretation convincing, but he was already thinking ahead.

"Ayaah! When they want to give you a hard time though, it all turns into a big problem," he sighed.

"Don't pay any attention to them," Zhang Huaiying said, trying to comfort him. "If they intend to give you a hard time it doesn't have to be frozen food. They'll find any number of things like that to attack."

"Why don't they come around and look into it? Those who have never given birth can't know what a real stomach ache is," replied Chen in anger.

"That's precisely the problem," Zhang Huaiying said. "It's the question of contrasting class attitudes that Chairman Mao has been talking about. People of different professions, status, and experience are bound to look at things with different eyes."

In the second battle of Wolf Den Ravine, Dazhai's "men and women of steel" again tempered themselves with hard work, lack of sleep, cold food and unjustified criticism from hostile observers. However, they still could not satisfy fickle fate. It could not help fooling around with Chen Yonggui and his comrades once more. The following summer Wolf Den Ravine swallowed all the structures the members of the Cooperative had rebuilt during the second winter, when the dragon opened its mouth and sent down a torrent that destroyed stone dams, terrace walls, sponge soil fields and crops alike. Chen Yonggui's opponents seized yet another opportunity to poke fun at him and, sure enough, they addressed their new sarcastic remarks and satirical ditties at Dazhai once more. One of them went:

The wood you gather
In a thousand days
Can go up in smoke overnight

A whole winter's toil and trouble
One summer storm
Can wash from sight.

As floods washed the arduous toil of a second winter eastward, Chen Yonggui had trouble sleeping at night. He kept pondering: "We placed such huge stones in the dams, how come they couldn't withstand the thrust of the water?"

Then one day at dusk, while he stared dejectedly at the ceiling of his cave dwelling, a thought crept up somewhere from the depths of Chen Yonggui's cerebral cortex. "There's a whole mountain of earth above my arched ceiling. It puts enormous pressure on it, so how come the ceiling hasn't collapsed after all these years?"

Then he remembered the arched stone bridge in Back Side Draw that remained serenely undisturbed despite the generations of people and vehicles that constantly trekked over it. At that moment a seminal idea emerged from the tangle of his thoughts: "The key word in building stone dams is 'arch.'"

It was not a part of Chen Yonggui's character to yield in the face of difficulties. He had tempered himself amidst adversity by confronting tough tasks with tough responses. Now his obstinacy once more welled to the surface. With a new method he simply had to challenge fate again. That's when he issued a call for a third battle with Wolf Den Ravine.

Before the third battle unfolded, however, Chen Yonggui spent some time reviewing the lessons of the previous two battles with his comrades and with the higher cadres concerned. Together they decided to adopt the new dam construction design that he had devised. Instead of straight-line barriers they would build structures that bowed arch-like toward the upstream side. Then when the flood water rushed down the mountain, virtually liquefying the loess fields, all the pressure would load against the back of the stone arch, driving each rock ever more tightly against the other. This design would help the dams endure the assault of the flood waters and the terrible lateral pressure of the mud slurry they created in each field. Once he determined on this new design, Chen Yonggui relaxed.

In preparation for launching his third offensive against Wolf Den Ravine, Chen Yonggui convened a meeting of the Dazhai Party Branch to solicit pledges of mass support. Bitter experience had made Chen Yonggui an expert at propaganda and advocacy. He delivered his impassioned speech from behind a raised table, all the while dragging on his pipe even though the tobacco had long since burned out of it. Speechmaking is an art form, but if you want to raise the morale of hill-country villagers you can't just be a smooth and expressive talker—you have to find ways to move the audience and open channels of enlightenment.

Chen Yonggui started out bravely, using rational analysis: "Our dams caved in twice, but we are changing our formula this time. We will build arch-shaped dams that curve in toward the mountain. They'll be wide at the bottom and narrow at the top—five feet[1] at the base, two at the top—like a native carpenter's ladder. The last two times we piled up large rocks without binding them. This time we'll fill all the gaps with pebbles and pour mortar into the cracks so the water can't find any weak spots. As long as the rocks stay put the arch will force them together. Let's see who's tougher, the floods or the people of Dazhai!"

Chen Yonggui's clear strategy and forceful words inspired genuine enthusiasm. Their applause left no room for doubt that the people of Dazhai trusted their leader. It also demonstrated their will to strike another blow against their destiny, although all knew they would have to pay a high price for doing so.

Chen Yonggui pressed on with the season's assignments.

"We'll need large quantities of stone for the dams. Let's have Old Jincai shoulder the responsibility for this again."

As the sound of his words sank in, the slight figure of the over-fifty-year-old hero, Jia Jincai, stood up from amidst the crowd. The deep wrinkles on his diminutive face were unable to conceal his smile.

Chen Yonggui nodded toward him, as if to acknowledge that he had faith in him, and went on to say: "We have to use horse-drawn carts to transport the broken stone. Liang Bianliang will be in charge of that. I and Laiheng will take charge of laying up the dams, and we'll make Jia

Five chi in the text. One chi equals 1.0936 English foot.

Chengrang responsible for digging the foundations. Carrying mortar and bringing in the soil needed to level the fields takes quite an effort, too, but it's somewhat easier than the other jobs. Song Liying has been instructing women to 'hold up half the sky,' so let's have her shoulder this 'half of the task.'"

On the first day of construction everything proceeded smoothly. Everybody went about their preassigned chores. In the morning, and again at noon, everybody ate food that had frozen on top. Wolf Den Ravine resounded with a hubbub of human voices throughout the day, although no more than five to six people came there at any one time. Still, the atmosphere was invigorating. An arch-shaped dome, almost fifteen yards long, eight yards high[1] and two yards wide at the bottom, was all but finished while the sun still hung a bamboo stick high above the mountain top in the West.

History is not likely to forget the contribution of Jia Jincai to the construction of this particular dam. Daybreak had hardly arrived when Jia lifted an iron hammer that weighed over thirty pounds[2] onto his shoulder and hurriedly left home for the construction site. He was surprised when his feet sank into deep snow the moment he stepped out of his door. Lifting his head, he noticed that the fields were shrouded in a foot or more of white powder. He hesitated for a moment about going to work in such weather but, as a Communist Party member and the former first Party Secretary of the Dazhai Branch, he was used to making heavy demands on himself. He added a big broom to his load and proceeded to the quarry to sweep the ground. He swept a work pit clean and started banging at the rocks all by himself. By the time other members of the Cooperative showed up on the job, he had already carved out a pile of slate-blue stones.

This is how Jia Jincai described for me what happened that day: "'I've sure run into a peck of trouble today,' I said to myself. As I swept snow at the quarry, enormous, solid, oil-blue rocks appeared in front of my eyes, finely grained and smooth. There's no better kind of stone i

1. Over four zhang long and over two zhang high in the original. One zhang equal 3.3333 meters or 3.6454 English yards.
2. Thirty jin in the original. One jin equals 1.1023 pounds.

you want to construct a dam or build a house. Unfortunately, the rocks were free of any cracks, which made them extremely hard to break. 'But rocks are dead things,' I thought, 'while we humans are a living force. If we heed the words of Chairman Mao and approach solid obstacles in the spirit of the Foolish Old Man who moved mountains, I don't care how firm the rock is, it will never surpass the firmness of my human will!' So I lifted my iron hammer and with one deep breath hit forty-nine times at one spot.[1] The rock barely showed a dent when...Bang! All of a sudden the thirty-pound iron hammer split in two against that smooth, oil-blue surface. Oh, you bastard rock!

"Just at that time Jia Laile and another youth came bouncing down the road making a hell of a racket. They brought along an enormous iron hammer, which they took turns carrying. I grabbed the hammer from them and again pounded forty-nine times with one breath, but this time, when the hammer descended for the forty-ninth time, I let out a howl: 'Split!' And then, 'Crrrrrr,' a long crack appeared on the surface of that mother-fucking rock."

As I listened to the recollections of Old Jia and other villagers, I was reminded of the documentary footage in the film *The Fields of Dazhai* and I felt how very well made the film was. I had seen such scenes with my own eyes when I visited Dazhai and they matched the film frame for frame. But when, much later, I paid my second visit to the heroic old man he was no longer young by any means. Although at eighty he was neither blind nor deaf, he showed many signs of advanced age. On one occasion, when I went to inquire about the details of the third battle of Wolf Den Ravine he thoughtfully brought out the watermelon that he had bought with funds from his local government pension. At the sight of his deformed, liver-spotted hands offering the watermelon, I felt tears welling up in the corners of my eyes. What hands those were! It is because of deformed hands like these, I thought, that the Dazhai of today exists. These two gnarled hands have caressed almost every stone in every dam and every cave dwelling in Dazhai. Back then, when he brandished the thirty-pound iron hammer as if it were made of pumice, under his hands nine-hundred-pound rocks did as he commanded. The

1. This is probably impossible but serves as a metaphor for intense hard work. (W.H.H.)

small slice of watermelon which he now placed in my hands weighed heavily on my heart.

I once saw a poem in some book, which described the people of Dazhai:

The stonemason knows
How to manipulate stone,
On the stone his fate rests,
Stone, heavier than paper.

I can guess what the poet was getting at with this artful comparison, but when I think of the past and present of the old hero Jia Jincai I have no idea how to balance his stone against my words on paper.

Many other members of Dazhai Cooperative followed Jia Jincai into the snow-covered quarry pit that morning. They too brought brooms and swept the snow away, clearing space for the beginning of an orderly work day.

As the number of hands in the pit increased, cut stone began to emerge. Now the transporting of stone became the principal problem. Dazhai did not have many horse-drawn carts at that time, and it had absolutely no cables rigged to hoist the stone to higher altitudes. The community had to rely on its people alone to carry all the stone used in dam construction, piece by piece, along mountain trails and into the gully. Transporting material this way was all the more difficult on a snowy day, so the people of Dazhai have told me.

On this day, Liang Bianliang and Zhao Dahe teamed up, pledging to match each other's strength and knock each other out of competition. Liang Bianliang was not exactly tall; in fact, he measured barely a meter and a half, and didn't look robust to anyone at first glance. Zhao Dahe was not much taller than Liang Bianliang, but he was very thickset. The two walked up to a big rock, which Zhao Dahe tapped lightly and asked, "How about this one?" Liang Bianliang agreed without hesitation, so they threw a steel cable around the rock and attached it to a carrying pole.

"Lift," the men shouted simultaneously from both ends of the stick. Crrra—-ck, the elmwood pole, as big around as a teacup, broke in two under the pressure. After the two men found a tough new pole, they finally lifted the rock. Their feet scraped and slipped as they carried it. By the time they arrived at the construction site, cold white flakes, falling from the sky, had transformed them into snowmen.

When my great curiosity led me to interview Liang Bianliang some twenty years later, I found a man whose hair was peppered with gray. As an old Communist Party member, he had held the position of a Deputy Party Secretary of Dazhai all those years. A thick wall of caution, built by the change in attitude of some members of the press who swung overnight from excessive praise to tactless criticism, stood between us. Liang Bianliang sat on a wooden block and ate his food while we talked.

"You ask me where we got the strength to do it back then?" he said. "Let me ask you, instead: Where did Chairman Mao and the Communist Party find their strength to carry out the Revolution? We went along with the tide. Battling Wolf Den Ravine was just like waging a war. If you don't win it, what are you going to do? Without that war Zhao Dahe and Zhao Xiaohe would never have become martyrs. Like Old Chen said, Dazhai did not drop from the sky, nor was it made by journalists. The people of Dazhai created it themselves."

In those days of hard work and perseverance, Chen Yonggui was the one who first made the strategic decision to conquer Dazhai's forbidding landscape. He also led the people into each and every phase of the battle. He was an expert dam builder. Whether big or small, square or round, in his hands every stone behaved exactly the way he wanted it to. Wherever he put it, it stuck. And he was fast as well as skillful, too! At times Chen Yonggui had a feeling that he was aided by some supernatural power. He enjoyed the trust of the people because he was well acquainted with all the members of his Cooperative. Nobody ever refused to follow his directions when working under his leadership.

Northern winter. People could hardly bear the morning chill. Snow ay heavy on the ground, but gusts of cold wind turned the skin dry and rittle. If attention slipped for only a moment, the rough edges of the tone just brought to the construction site split it open. The injured ands of Chen Yonggui and members of the Cooperative bled slowly. Vorking in pairs and disregarding their lesions, they moved huge three-to-four-hundred-pound stones onto the dike. When they poured the mortar on, the stones looked as though they had grown in place. By the time most of the people arrived for work, the heads of those who had arrived a step ahead were already steaming. Then, the steam turned into frost on their eyelashes and brows. The new arrivals could see that the arch-shaped dam had already grown by a foot or two since the previous day.

When Chen Yonggui forged ahead, nobody wanted to retreat. When Chen Yonggui worked, he boosted collective morale: "The weather is cold, but it can't chill our enthusiasm! The ground is frozen, but it can't freeze our resolution! The icy wind bites but can't topple our confidence! Winter can never break the will of the people of Dazhai!"

Chen Yonggui had barely finished his pep talk when Old Man Jia Gengyun, who was over seventy, came to the site. Aware of the old man's age, Chen Yonggui tried to persuade him to go home and take it easy, but the more he urged, the heartier the old man's effort became. Who is to say that back in those days, when people in Dazhai feared falling behind in their struggle to get ahead, they were not blessed with some magical power?

Where did such magical power come from? No one has been able to come up with a precise answer, but human psychology has awarded everybody a yardstick with which to measure it. Naturally, the actions of Chen Yonggui and the people of Dazhai reflect things like Chairman Mao's appeals and the directives of Party Committees on various levels. Regional and County Party leaders showed up in Dazhai at all times to inspect and instruct; they summed up Dazhai's experiences and popularized them time and again. All this activity exerted invisible pressure on Chen Yonggui himself, but it also gave him extra motivation. In order not to let the higher authorities down, at various stages of each project Chen Yonggui always tried to bring the Party members and people together to review and appraise each other's work. They compared notes, praised and rewarded the good, criticized and penalized the bad and thus propelled everything forward.

Chen Yonggui convened one meeting especially for the purpose of reasoning with and denouncing the cynicism which certain individuals were spreading with their pessimistic rhymes, including the devastating

The wood you gather
In a thousand days
Can go up in smoke overnight,
A whole winter's toil and trouble,
One summer storm
Can wash from sight.

The meeting collectively rebutted the rhymes, whereupon all those present engaged in self-criticism. The chair called up by name and criticized several Party members who did not quite measure up to their vanguard role, after which they took the initiative and criticized themselves. As the dim kerosene light shone on Chen Yonggui's heavily creased, awe-inspiring face, the whole meeting turned serious and tense. Here was a Party Branch Secretary of peasant stock, a Communist peasant cadre, his style a typical country style, straightforward, spontaneous, and unconstrained, giving to the whole gathering an unmistakably peasant air. The effect of the meeting could hardly be imagined by someone divorced from the peasantry. Nevertheless it was highly visible to one and all in the sphere of production.

The original plan was to complete the third battle of Wolf Den Ravine in one month. In the end it took only twenty-seven days. The terraced fields, which fanned out from the sides of cliffs slightly sloping toward the inner edges, turned into a rich granary that produced over 1,000 *jin* of grain per *mu*, over 100 bushels of grain per acre. By 1962, Dazhai had successfully completed its ambitious ten-year plan. During those ten years, Dazhai erected 180 rock dams and hewed out 130,000 cubic meters of cut stone. On the average, each able-bodied person carried more than 880 loads of stone a year. As a whole, the Cooperative put over 210,000 man-days into basic construction projects; on the average, each able-bodied person put in 120 man-days a year. Dazhai Cooperative members put every piece of cultivable land on Tigerhead Mountain's ridges and ravines under control, thus turning more than 4,700 small sloping fields into 1,700 level terraced fields, each capable of ensuring stable yields regardless of drought or excessive rain.

Nowadays, these stone dams and terraces, built with such great courage, vision, and sacrifice, lie backed up by tier upon tier of yellow loess soil. I wonder whether anybody will ever make an attempt to excavate that period of Dazhai's history?

CHAPTER 7

SEIZE THE TIME, SERVE THE PEOPLE

In the 1960s, in order to achieve the Communist Party's general goal for the transitional period by consolidating and advancing the position of socialism, Chairman Mao Zedong issued a call to all members of the Central and Provincial Committees of the Communist Party and to the heads of various departments that fall directly under the Central Committee to go down to the grass-roots level and look for the truth. The truth, he said, could be found among the peasants, or perhaps among the kitchen staff, or among the animal grooms, or even among the grass-roots-level Party cadres. He asked them to submit written reports on their findings.

This was the historical background of the visit by Li Xuefeng, Secretary of the North China Bureau of the Chinese Communist Party to Wenshui County in Shanxi Province in the month of May, 1961. He was accompanied by the Secretary of the Shanxi Provincial Committee, Tao Lujia. Zhang Huaiying received them at the guesthouse, where Tao Lujia introduced him to Li Xuefeng as "the newly appointed County Secretary, sent down from Xiyang less than a month ago." The moment Li Xuefeng heard the word "Xiyang" he inquired cheerfully: "I've heard that Dazhai has some good things going. Can you give me a report on Dazhai tonight?"

In the evening, Zhang Huaiying spoke to Li Xuefeng about various aspects of Dazhai's experiment, especially mentioning the experiences of the four levels of cadres from Xiyang County who had gone to Dazhai and other villages to take part in physical labor. I should mention that the Xiyang cadres, while participating in collective production, could not avoid the pervasive influence and leadership of Chen Yonggui.

In the beginning stages of the Agricultural Cooperative movement, nobody in Xiyang had paid much attention to the call for cadres to participate in physical labor. The proportion of cadres was very high back then: Each production team had a team leader, a vice-team leader, an accountant, a storeroom keeper, a work point recorder, and sometimes more. This created two sets of consequences: One, ordinary members of the community were responsible for too much work and paid too little for what they did. Two, the cadres were not immersed in and familiar with production, so they were psychologically unprepared and unable to direct it.

A jingle made the rounds of society:
Top-ranked cadres
Beyond the fields circulate.
Second-ranked ones
On abacuses calculate.
Third-ranked ones
Have all to Yangquan gone.
Only fourth-ranked ones
On flooded lands work on.

And another:

Work hard, seven-to-eight points
Is all you'll ever get;
Amuse yourself, stroll about,
Ten points are a sure bet!

People were saying: "In the past, four people used to carry one person sitting in the sedan chair. Today a bunch still rides, and another bunch still carries." And also: "Agriculture has produced a new phenomenon: the cadres who are taking a great leap away from production!"

The case of Panzhang Village in Hongshui Township was typical: When the time for autumn harvest came, people discovered that one whole tract of land remained unplanted. The cadres had failed to notice it, because they had never gone near the fields. It is because of situations like this one that the decision requiring cadre participation in physical labor became the key issue of the effort to consolidate the results of the collectivization of agriculture.

In regard to this question Dazhai was already an entirely different world. From the very establishment of the first mutual aid groups, Chen Yonggui insisted on going to work in the fields, just as Jia Jincai did. In the end he became the Model Worker of the mutual-aid group era. After they set up their Agricultural Producers' Cooperative, Chen Yonggui, Jia Jincai, Liang Bianliang, and Jia Chengrang always took the lead, regardless of what the work at hand might be. At the end of each work day, when the members of the Cooperative picked up their tools and went back to the village, Chen Yonggui and the other cadres stayed behind to inspect what had been done. Chen Yonggui was good at instructing people, but he was also good at leading them into action. On account of his raw strength and his skill at finding ad hoc solutions, nobody dared idle about when he worked, and when he worked so did the other cadres.

The Dazhai Cooperative was planning to work on the mountain peak exposed to freezing western winds. People were afraid they would turn numb with cold. But if they did the job quickly, moved fast, and made an effort, they were bound to generate some warm sweat. Only the ones who failed to exert themselves to the utmost would come to grief for it. On the appointed day the members of the Cooperative brought their pickaxes and grub hoes. The task was to dig holes and then plant trees in them. Everybody scrambled to do the digging because that took a lot of effort and made them warm, even sweat-soaked. Of course,in the circumstances, the work had its difficulties.

People's hands got so cold the skin cracked and bled; then their feet grew numb, making their discomfort almost unbearable. It wasn't just the ordinary members of the Cooperative who couldn't take it; even the cadres found it hard to go on. It was the most unbearable experience Song Liying ever had. She was wearing only a pair of unlined cloth shoes and her feet hurt as though somebody was stabbing them with sharp knives, but she couldn't leave the scene to look for a place to warm up. For one, she was afraid that she would leave a bad impression on other members of the Cooperative; for another, she feared that Chen Yonggui would notice and the Party Branch would give her a hard time for failing to go through with the ordeal. Since Chen Yonggui was not far from her, she worked faster than anybody else. Noticing her predicament, some other members quietly pressed her to take a break and find a way to get warm. Several women made her sit on the ground, created a shield around her with their bodies, and then let her stick her feet under their jackets. When she felt a little better, she went back to work.

I'm afraid such practices look too harsh when seen through the eyes of the young people today. They may even suggest an aura of slave-like labor. In reality, however, they only reflected the readiness of the rural cadres to pass the stiffest tests when it came to physical labor. Only because Dazhai's cadres were truly up to the mark were they able to conceive, express and execute Dazhai's achievements.

At the first Party Branch meeting after the establishment of the Cooperative, Chen Yonggui proclaimed: "Those who become cadres in Dazhai have to take the lead in speaking and doing. Those who do not engage in physical labor cannot become cadres; those whose labor leaves something to be desired are not good cadres."

In the course of time this became an integral part of Chen Yonggui's personnel credo. He adhered to this philosophy, and the cadres whose physical labor was not up to the mark could not pass muster with Chen Yonggui.

In Dazhai, people still remember an autumn in the 1950s, right after Dazhai and a few neighboring villages had established the "New Victory Advanced Agricultural Production Cooperative," when Chen Yonggui, busy with work in other villages, arranged for another Communist Party member to take charge of production in the village o

Dazhai. For three months this Party member did not take part in productive labor. The first thing Chen Yonggui noticed when he came back to the village was that Dazhai had not properly carried out "three autumn duties" he had planned. His dissatisfaction grew when he heard that the Party member in charge rarely went into the fields. Right away, Chen Yonggui convened a meeting of the Party Branch. At the meeting, he called on this Party member to report on his most recent work. Chen Yonggui cut off his long-winded report midway: "How many days did you do physical labor during the last three months?"

The Party member tried to find an excuse by saying that he had been too busy to get into the field, but Chen Yonggui jumped right in: "Let's see here. Who's busy, you or I? How many times did you do physical work in three months? How many times did I? No wonder nothing has been accomplished here! If you don't even get near the edge of the field, how can you carry out your work?"

On account of this incident Chen Yonggui announced at the end of the meeting that the man would no longer act on his behalf as the head of production.

In Chen Yonggui's words, "Cadres always lead the troops—whether they make only one step, or go all the way and then some." In other words, as mentioned before, "If a train runs fast, it's because the locomotive that pulls it is good."

At the Party Branch meeting that day Chen Yonggui set down the "Three Nos" rule for the cadre participation in physical labor: One, short of an extraordinarily grave situation, no cadre was allowed to hold meetings in the village during farm-work hours. Two, cadres were not to do office work while farm work was in progress. Three, no cadre should summon any member of the Cooperative away from the fields for talk.

In addition, Chen Yonggui put into place a system of "three assemblies": the "head assembly," the "food assembly," and the "field assembly." Every night, rain or shine, the Party Branch Committee members got together to discuss their work. They exchanged experiences gained in the course of the day at this "head assembly," and made plans for the following day. They announced these plans to the members of the Cooperative the next morning at the "food assembly." Work assignments, study sessions, and discussions took place during breakfast.

When they finished their meal, the cadres went into the fields with other members of the Cooperative. If they found a problem they would use the rest break to gather at the field's edge for the so called "field assembly." There they talked things over while having a smoke. Putting it briefly, Chen Yonggui said that the system was a way to "make work planning rational and the labor participation regular." He also summed it up as "full-time work, no-time for talk."

After Chen Yonggui passed away, the people of Dazhai, who had been struggling along beside him for many years, recalled how he used to carry the seed corn for the spring sowing and bury the seeds one by one in the soil, using his feet to press them into the layer that contained moisture. They also remembered him during the millet-sowing season, pushing the small two-legged seed drill through field after field, back and forth, thousands of times, until he had planted all the seeds. But what everybody remembered most vividly was the time when Chen Yonggui picked up some rocks at the stone pit on the way back from work and brought them to the village.

This happened soon after the establishment of the Cooperative, when its members decided they wanted to build new houses. When the issue was discussed at the Cooperative Committee meeting, some people brought up the question of where the stone would come from and how it would be transported to the village. After quite a bit of talk, nobody agreed on anything. That's when Chen Yonggui spoke up.

"Forget it. Let's not waste time on this. When the time comes, we'll come up with something," he declared.

The discussion took place just days before they were to start breaking the ground and building. Everybody wondered why he wouldn't discuss it. Not a single person could guess what was on his mind.

The following day they were all back in the fields. When the tim came for the noon break, Chen Yonggui deliberately walked out ahea of the others. He spotted a stone, put his grub hoe down, and called member of the Cooperative.

"Lift it onto my shoulder," he said, pointing at the stone.

The man did as he was told. Chen Yonggui picked up his grub hc with one hand while he steadied the stone with the other, and starte off. When the man realized that Chen Yonggui was taking the stor back to the village, he couldn't very well go back empty-handed himself, so he too grabbed a stone and put it on his shoulder. Then the Cooperative Committee cadres noticed what was going on. As if waking from a dream, they realized why Chen Yonggui had refused to discuss the transportation of stones. He had already planned to do this! Needless to say they too, one by one, raised stones onto their shoulders and carried them toward the village. Now that the cadres were carrying stones, what were the people supposed to do? They followed suit. Even the few villagers who had left the work site before Chen Yonggui, when they saw what was going on, had to turn back and get a few stones themselves.

In these circumstances the leaders of the local branch of the Communist Youth League organized a "youth shock brigade" and set the temporary regulation: "Don't waste time! Don't travel the road empty-handed!" On the way to the fields the youngsters carried manure or compost, on the way back they carried stone. At the meeting of the Party Branch that evening Chen Yonggui was full of praise: "The kids caught up with us all right. And how about the old? As the saying goes, 'When an old General mounts a horse, he equals two young ones.'"

From that day on everybody carried a stone on the way back from work, two stones per person a day. It took them just a few days to bring back enough to build new houses. Looking at the huge pile of stones, Chen Yonggui chuckled, "Had we gone on discussing this at the meeting, I suspect we still wouldn't have figured it out. This way we neither had to assign people to do the labor, nor did we issue any work points. And we got all the stone we need in just a few days!"

When the County leaders heard of this experience, they summed it up in one phrase: "Doing teaches better than talking." In the West one could say, "One act is worth a thousand words."

From the launching of the Feeble Group up to the Cultural Revolution, Chen Yonggui by and large managed "not to waste time, and not to travel the road empty-handed." Even when he went to attend meetings at the Regional or County level he brought along some bean-flour noodles to sell at the Tobacco and Wine Company, or pulled along a cart of fruit which he would first put up for sale at the market. After the meetings he either went to have the sales calculated at the consignment shop and get a receipt, or he bought a head or two of livestock to take back with him to the Cooperative. At one meeting, some County Committee leaders brought up the issue of "serving the people wholeheartedly," and asked what "wholehearted service" might be?

"When Comrade Chen Yonggui comes to the County to attend meetings, yet takes care of some business on behalf of his village on the way—that indeed amounts to 'serving the people wholeheartedly,'" they explained.

After the meeting, the leaders of other Cooperatives started paying close attention to what Chen Yonggui would take back to his village this time. It so happened that Chen Yonggui was driving back a pig that he had bought earlier. The Dazhai Cooperative Committee had decided to start a cottage industry to make bean noodles and to fatten a pen of pigs on the by-products, so as soon as he got to town Chen bought a pregnant sow due to farrow in few days.

Chen Yonggui's attitude moved the Communist Party County Committee Secretary, Zhang Huaiying. He saw the cadres in Dazhai taking part in physical labor, and he noticed during a tour of inspection in Daobakou and Baiyangyu that the cadres there, too, led the villagers both in words and in deeds. The experiences here stood in clear contrast to other places, where the way cadres ran Cooperatives left a lot to be desired. Wherever the results of the Cooperative movement lagged, it was inevitably because the cadres strutted about without participating in the physical labor, issuing arbitrary orders from the comfort of their homes. He came to the conclusion that the places where the Cooperative movement succeeded were the ones where the cadres led other members in physical labor and where, having penetrated into the realities of life and production, they issued their directives right on the spot.

Consequently, the County Committee decided that all four levels of cadres in the County should follow the example of cadres in Dazhai, Daobakou and Baiyangyu and take the lead by participating in collective production. In the interest of finding a complete solution to the problem, Zhang Huaiying himself, along with Wang Guike, Tian Gendong and Wang Fuyuan from his office, took up tools and agricultural implements and headed for the bare slopes along the Main Street just out of the Western City Gate to help the members of the local

Cooperative turn them into arable land. "Here come our seventh-rank officials to reform themselves through farm work!" commented a woman, joking as she saw them.

"Right you are," Zhang Huaiying, who never joked around, said laughing. "We have to reform through farm work. If we don't, if we just sit around the house all day long indulging in creature comforts, are we any different from the Nationalists? Chen Yonggui kept doing farm work from the very beginnings of the Feeble Group all the way to his Advanced Agricultural Producers' Cooperative, and directing every undertaking personally. Nobody dares make fun of him!"

Because Xiyang County had promoted the experiences of the cadres in Dazhai, Daobakou and Baiyangyu, who took part in the collective productive labor, by 1960 this practice became a general trend among all four levels of cadres in Xiyang County. From that time on, Chen Yonggui's fame grew by the day but he never divorced himself from production. According to the annual work attendance figures, during the period from 1966 to 1973 Chen Yonggui turned up for work on average 234.5 days a year; Guo Fenglian, 288 days; Jia Chengrang, 351 days; Liang Bianliang, 350.5 days. During that period Chen Yonggui often attended conferences and entertained guests, but he made every possible attempt to take part in labor.

Some old cadres from Xiyang County remember that Chen Yonggui used to get headaches when he was not able to get to the fields to work. He mentioned once, while the participants of a County meeting engaged in chitchat: "Ayaaah! I haven't been able to eat lunch at home in three months, not even once—ever since Minister Liao left Dazhai!"

He was referring to the period in 1964, following the tour of inspection that brought the Minister of Agriculture, Liao Luyan, to Dazhai. Because of the great importance that the Party Central Committee and Chairman Mao attached to Dazhai, crowds of journalists were descending on Dazhai, demanding interviews with Chen Yonggui. If Chen Yonggui were to consent to all those demands, even thinking about going to work would be pointless. Yet when the reporters showed up at his door, he had a hard time turning them away. What he came up with was a hiding scheme. He hid in the fields working. He didn't even dare come home for lunch, so he ended up eating out on the work site every day.

When the County leaders asked him why that was the case, Chen Yonggui answered cautiously, while pulling at his pipe: "Ayaaah! I'm a Model Worker! I'm not like you County cadres, divorced from production. If the Model Worker doesn't work, what kind of model is he?"

He blurted this out from the top of his head, unaware of the profound significance of the theory hidden in his words.

All this Zhang Huaiying related to Li Xuefeng in Wenshui. When Zhang finished his report, Li Xuefeng said to Tao Lujia emotionally: "This is it! The whole truth lies right here! Whether the cadres are capable of participating in collective productive labor relates directly to the larger question of whether our Party can stay true to its ideals or whether it will change color—to the ultimate question of whether or not we'll be able to consolidate our socialist system. They have been able to solve a whole lot of problems in Dazhai because they've got Chen Yonggui there. That bunch of cadres, able to mingle with the masses, have done the same for Xiyang County."

"Huaiying, write it up! I'll make sure it gets published," he said, turning to Zhang.

When Li Xuefeng left Shanxi Province, he wrote a report to Chairman Mao about how all four levels of cadres in Xiyang County participated in collective productive labor. The matter immediately received Chairman Mao's full attention, because it confirmed his prediction that the truth would ultimately be found among the peasants, and he prepared an important memorandum, well known to everybody, about the participation of the cadres of all four ranks in collective productive labor in seven provinces, including Zhejiang Province.

At the time very few people who probed into the problem of cadre participation in collective production had any idea of Chen Yonggui's impact on it. He was therefore able to stand on undisputed ground, while continuing to perform physical labor up to the mark. Thus he immersed himself continuously among the common people and developed superb skills both physical and political.

CHAPTER 8

WHICH SIDE ARE YOU ON?

Whenever Chen Yonggui's position as Commander-in-Chief of Dazhai comes up, enthusiasts make a painstaking effort to scan it from all possible angles and sides. They are particularly interested in Chen Yonggui's work in educating people and transforming their world outlook and in his ability to work with and remold all kinds of people. Chen Yonggui's entire life was spent working with and educating others. People's memories retain three striking examples: How he reformed Zhao Xiaohe, how he pried open the rusty lock to the past under the big willow tree, and how he handled the rightists. These three interesting stories more than illustrate Chen Yonggui's outlook, feelings and nature. They also reveal some of the recesses of his mind and heart.

In the old society pain and hardship overflowed Zhao Xiaohe's childhood. He lost both parents as an infant and worked as a shepherd for a landlord from an early age. The landlord then sold him to buyers in another County. He was only able to take shelter in Dazhai after the land reform. Once in Dazhai, however, Zhao Xiaohe started to act very selfishly. For example, he bought a sick sheep for the collective, but when he applied for reimbursement he pretended the sheep had been a healthy one. There were many other examples of his attitude.

Chen Yonggui watched his behavior and worried.

"Are you in some kind of trouble, Xiaohe?" Chen Yonggui asked when he saw him. "Are you short of cash?"

"No trouble at all," Zhao Xiaohe answered.

"Why, then, are you acting so selfishly?"

"I'm just making a few bucks to spend as I like," Zhao Xiaohe answered casually, without blinking.

"You should be ashamed of yourself! We all know about making a few bucks to spend as one likes—it's the rich man's golden rule. All the landlords and rich peasants are dying to squeeze some oil out of the bones of poor folks, just so they can make a few extra bucks. Don't you remember the bitter taste of the old society, or is it that you haven't had enough of it?"

Chen Yonggui's words did make Zhao Xiaohe feel rather bitter and miserable. He leaped to his feet, charging at Chen Yonggui: "Who says I don't remember the old society? Everybody in Dazhai knows what shape I was in under the old society!"

Noticing that he had stirred up Zhao Xiaohe's feelings, Chen Yonggui decided to strike while the iron was hot and straighten him out once for all: "You don't want to live like you did in the old society? So why are you treating the collective that way? What would happen to our economy if everybody acted like you? When the river overflows, the water in canals is high. When there's no water in the riverbed, the irrigation ditches run dry. If we bring our collective economy down, what do you think people like you and me are going to do? You can't only think about yourself at the expense of others!"

This time Chen's words moved Zhao deeply. People say that he broke into tears. He determined to embrace the collective wholeheartedly, so much so that people began calling him a "collective-freak." After that he took on whatever duties the Cooperative assigned him and carried them out rather well. He took upon himself the kind of work that nobody else would do. One doesn't know whether to laugh or cry over some of the stories about his "good deeds" for the benefit of the collective.

One time when he was in charge of driving the cart, the Cooperative sent him to deliver grain to the County Grain Bureau. He dropped the grain off and returned from the Bureau with four gunny sacks "for the collective."

When Chen Yonggui found out about it, he inquired, "Why did you bring those sacks back?"

"I brought them back for our collective," Zhao Xiaohe answered grimacing. "A collective is a collective. Theirs or ours —what difference does it make?"

Chen Yonggui got very upset. He criticized him for acting to the detriment of the other collective, and ordered him to take the sacks back immediately.

The second time, the Cooperative dispatched Zhao Xiaohe to haul rolled steel for the County ironworks. Just as he was delivering the steel to the ironworks with his horse-drawn cart he suddenly remembered that right at that moment his Cooperative's farm-tool workshop needed steel for making some implements. He loaded a roll from the ironworks yard and brought it back as a present to the Coop.

When he discovered what Xiaohe had done, Chen Yonggui reprimanded him firmly, "Who told you to steal other people's things?" Chen Yonggui asked.

"We need it for our Cooperative. They've got so much rolled steel—how would they ever notice a roll or two was missing?" Zhao Xiaohe answered.

"You dug into somebody else's flesh to fatten yourself!" protested Chen Yonggui. "You can't go around cheating other people's collectives to serve your own. If nothing else, consider what kind of an impression people will have about us when they find out!"

Chen Yonggui brought up every argument and principle he could think of while trying to beat some sense into Zhao Xiaohe. He talked for an entire evening. In the end, he decided to remove Zhao Xiaohe as a cart driver.

Zhao Xiaohe no longer drove the cart, but his "red heart" continued to beat "for the collective." Before long, the Cooperative sent him to Heshun County to buy four cows. He came back with five. When people asked him why he had bought five, he informed them, glowing with satisfaction: "I didn't buy the fifth one. This one followed me all by itself. If a pig shows up at the temple door, who wouldn't let it in?"

This made Chen Yonggui angry again.

"You think that's OK, just because it followed you?" Chen Yonggui scolded. "Don't you think people count their cows? If they come knocking on our door, what are we going to tell them?"

Chen Yonggui wanted to change Zhao Xiaohe's way of thinking. He recalled a time in the past when he himself sold an ox. Dazhai had been using this ox to till the land, but it strained its back badly in an accident and put on a lot of weight. It looked nice and fat, but it couldn't do any work. Chen Yonggui took it to the Foodstuffs Company to sell, but as he passed through the County market some people who were determined to buy it held him back. Someone offered fifty, then sixty *yuan*; somebody raised the offer to seventy, even eighty—the more they haggled, the higher the price rose. But Chen Yonggui told them the ox was crippled, and he couldn't sell it to them. Yet the more he insisted he couldn't sell it, the more they were determined to buy it—only now, since Chen Yonggui felt so bad about selling them faulty merchandise, they were waiting for the price to drop. This is the way the street peddlers make a profit: They listen for the counterpart's tone of voice to clinch a deal. In the end, somebody from the Foodstuffs Company came by. Chen Yonggui explained what it was all about and sold the ox for twenty-seven *yuan* to the company. The event caused different reactions in the market. Some people praised Chen Yonggui's fair play, others said that only a fool would go about selling an ox that way.

"If you were asked to sell this ox, who would you sell it to? What kind of price would you ask for it?" Chen Yonggui asked Zhao Xiaohe.

Then Chen Yonggui summoned all the Party members in Dazhai to a meeting with Zhao Xiaohe's cow purchase the sole topic on the agenda. They discussed for an entire evening before they finally decided that Chen Yonggui would personally take the cow back to Heshun, with an explanation and an apology. The following morning Chen Yonggui had just finished his breakfast and was getting ready to take the cow back when somebody from Heshun came knocking at his door looking for the missing cow, and it was restored to its rightful owners. This only confirmed Chen Yonggui's belief that people like Zhao Xiaohe have to be re-educated to show ardent concern not only for their own collective but for other collectives as well.

Eventually, by dint of Chen Yonggui's great patience and effort, Zhao Xiaohe accepted re-education and adopted a new outlook. Once again he drove the horse cart. And then a strange thing happened. Zhao Xiaohe fell and broke his leg. But he was so anxious to get back to work, despite the great pain, that he ended up having to ask the doctor to reset his fracture. Later, he tragically lost his life hauling stone during a flood. Trying to save his horse, he himself drowned. Chen Yonggui praised him as a "fighter for Communism."

The second story revolved around the big willow tree, but before we relate how Chen Yonggui opened the rusty lock of the past under its spreading branches, we have to mention an earlier, "August 1st" incident, when the folks from Dazhai went to a temple fair.

By 1963, year after year of soil-building projects had greatly improved the fertility of land in Dazhai. This, combined with good field management, produced, for several years in a row, yields far higher than they had been in the past. On the eve of the "August 1st" festival, Chen Yonggui wanted to do something to warm the people's hearts. He pushed two decisions through the Party Branch meeting. The first was to distribute a few pounds of white flour from accumulated stores to each member of the Cooperative during the holiday. With it, they could make steamed buns of white flour to bring with them to town for the traditional celebration—a great improvement over the corn meal buns that they had been taking for years. The second was a decision to undercut the market with more reasonable prices. In view of the inflationary upsurge caused by the implementation of the "Four Freedoms,"[1] raging through society, Chen Yonggui decided to have several people sell food

1. These "Four Freedoms" adopted with the land reform were: freedom to rent land out and in, to buy and sell on the open market, to hire labor for wages and to lend out money at interest. The Government had restricted such activities for many years, but the debacle of the "hard years," 1959-1961, brought a plethora of free market reforms inspired by Deng Xiaoping's "black cat, white cat" aphorism: "It doesn't matter if the cat is black or white so long as it can catch mice." (W.H.H.)

at a uniformly low price and thus drive food prices down in favor of the majority who had no grain to sell.

On the day following the two decisions, all members of the Dazhai Cooperative received white flour, and several of them set out to destabilize the market. At their stalls a bowl of bean-flour noodles in broth sold for twenty cents, while elsewhere everybody was asking for thirty or forty cents. All the customers crowded the Dazhai stalls. At one point the people who were lining up could no longer get service because the stalls ran out of bowls. According to Liang Bianliang, even after he bought additional bowls for use at the stalls, they remained short of them. In addition, Dazhai Brigade dispatched people to sell sweet buns on the main street. Others were selling sweet buns for twenty cents a piece, but Chen's peddlers sold them for only five. Actually they were only calling out to advertise their wares without necessarily making a sale because they had just a limited quantity of sweet buns in their baskets. But as soon as the people on the street heard the sales pitch, "Hot buns, plump and sweet, for five cents you can eat," they rushed forward to buy. The Brigade members were not really prepared to deal with all the demand, so they sold only one here, two there, and wrestled their way out of the crowd to continue advertising elsewhere. The confusion they created naturally drove market prices down. The other stall keepers cursed them without letup, but they achieved their goal.

Insofar as the white flour was concerned, Chen Yonggui thought the members of the Cooperative would be happy to receive the few pounds he issued per person, but quite a few people disappointed him with expressions of resentment, and even a few Party Branch cadres complained. The problem was that Dazhai issued only a few pounds of white flour, while the cadres in some neighboring villages also handed out cash to spend at the temple festival to the members of their Cooperatives, saying: "This is for a taste of something different. You can buy watermelons or bean jelly in town."

Here we see the contrasting experience of an "advanced unit" and a "regular unit." Dazhai was "advanced," and its economic foundation was sound, but the remuneration its members received for the temple festival did not measure up to that distributed to less "advanced" units.

The difference, of course, was due to Dazhai's greater determination to save and invest.

Dazhai Cooperative members experienced another disparity in the food-for-the-road that the women brought to the festival. Women from other villages prepared steamed buns and deep-fried dough cakes for the trip to town, while Song Liying and other women from Dazhai, reluctant to use up the white flour they had been issued, made only sugar-glazed steamed corn bread.

That's how the trouble started.

When the Dazhai contingent took out their food at noon, a woman from a neighboring village saw Song Liying's corn bread and, without really meaning to be sarcastic, mocked her.

"Ayaah! You guys are a red-banner unit! How come you eat corn? We here are nothing of the sort, we're backward as hell, but we have white steamed buns!"

The faces of Song Liying and other women from Dazhai turned red. They felt they had somehow lost face by eating corn bread. They went back to Dazhai looking for Chen Yonggui. How would he deal with the situation? Song Liying, assuming a neutral stance, made a full report to Chen Yonggui. Having heard her out, Chen Yonggui felt this was not an incident he could belittle—he saw it as a good opportunity to engage in class education.

The education session took place under the willow tree, and it demonstrated perhaps better than any other incident Chen Yonggui's special ability to engage in ideological work to help others remold their world outlook.

The willow tree in question grew in the center of Dazhai. By the time Chen Yonggui came around to stressing education for class consciousness the tree was already known both as the "tree of misery" and as the "tree of joy." Its fame had spread far and wide. On this day Chen focused on how the name "tree of misery" came about.

The way the tree grew was in itself special. The tree trunk stood no higher than five feet. It didn't grow upward; it stretched, instead, in the direction of the northwest, twisting and turning as though to show its arduous and tortuous life. The four main branches varied in size and angle, but each one of them stretched desperately in its own direction, as though it had taken a lot of hard work to manage to strike out on its own. Twisted twigs of irregular length drooped in dense clusters from the branch-tips, winding around and drifting through the air like the fine, unkempt hair of a young maiden.

Only history knew the age of this willow tree. There was a tale, handed down by earlier generations, that the tree had once been hollow at the center and that a person could crawl into it. The treetop grew to an enormous size, sporting unusually luxuriant foliage. One year, however, because the tree trunk was no longer able to support the weight of its heavy top, a strong wind "decapitated" the venerable giant. Villagers cut it down with a saw, thinking that would be the end of its long life. Nobody guessed that only a few days later the tree would once again send forth the tips of new branches, and that in only a few generations it would grow to its present size and shape. It almost seems as though its struggle for life was meant to serve as a reminder of Dazhai's own painful history. The past and present life of the tree became a symbol of the contrast between the old society and the new.

After all members of the Dazhai Cooperative, young and old, assembled under the willow tree, Chen Yonggui asked Li Youlu a question: "How did your mother die?"

Li Youlu choked with emotion, was unable to speak. Li Xiqing and a few other poor peasants put together the story out of the past.

Li Youlu's mother had been born to a Liu family in another village. Her parents named her Liu Eni. Right after she turned ten, a poor peasant bought her and brought her home to Dazhai as his child bride. In order to eke out a living, her young husband had to go to Gold Rock Slope to do odd jobs for a landlord. Liu Eni stayed at home to cook for her in-laws. Once she went to their field to pick a handful of kidney beans. On the way back she noticed an ear of corn lying in the middle of the road. She picked it up and brought it home with her. As luck would have it, the landlord, Jia Taiyuan, saw her carrying the corn. He cursed her viciously.

"You damned little bastard! Don't you dare walk away! Let me see that corn!"

Looking up, Liu Eni found herself staring at Jia Taiyuan's terrifying face. She broke into cold sweat.

"I...I...I picked it up from the middle of the road," she stuttered, her words almost inaudible.

"Picked it up in the middle of the road," Jia Taiyuan mimicked her. "That's quite a picking! Why didn't you pick one for me too?"

"I really did pick it up," said Liu Eni making a trembling effort to defend herself.

To no avail. The twisting top-heavy willow tree became an accomplice in Liu Eni's persecution. Jia Taiyuan, unleashing his terrible temper, suspended the woman from a branch of the tree and pounded her whole body with a wooden stick. Bystanders found it sickening to watch but dared not lift a hand to save her.

That's how Landlord Jia drove the life out of Liu Eni. Li Youlu was barely five months old when Jia beat his mother to death.

Li Youlu's behavior was generally quite good. It was only during a period of time when he started frequenting restaurants for his meals that his behavior contrasted sharply with the conduct of the women, headed by Song Liying, who ate corn bread on their trip to the township temple festival. When he staged his "living theater of class education." Chen Yonggui specifically aimed at these two divergent situations

After Chen so vividly reminded the formerly poor peasants of the story behind the name "tree of misery," he delivered an emotional speech: "Liu Eni is dead, but the willow tree is still alive—as a living reminder left behind by the old society! Let's not look at Li Youlu's visits to restaurants too simplistically. He who doesn't know the past, cannot understand the present! So, what is the present like, now that we've recalled the past? My intention today is not to criticize Li Youlu at all. With the exception of those restaurant visits, he is really quite OK. I'm targeting this new preoccupation with pleasure-seeking that is taking hold over our society. I want to sound an alarm for the benefit of our young people.

"This is how I feel: Even if you don't support the idea of Song Liying and other women taking corn bread to the temple festival on "August 1st," I stand by it. You may frown upon it, but I like the sight of it! You don't like getting only white flour, you say, because all the neighbors got money too. How much money do they have? Let them get their money—let them get twice and three times what they got this time! Our country is poor. Our economic base is fragile. This is not the time to feast and celebrate! Even if we become rich one day, we are likely to end up in poverty if we don't act prudently. Think of the past! Look at today! Compare, and you'll understand what I mean. A Red Banner village eats corn bread! Regular village eats deep-fried dough cakes! Let them eat, I say! Let them eat white flour all three hundred sixty-five days of the year! Let's see who can out-eat whom!"

Chen Yonggui's speech grew more moving with each word. In the end, Li Xiqing and some other formerly poor peasants were shedding tears. When the people started to scatter after the meeting, he announced solemnly: "As for the big willow—we'll keep it. There may be some future use for it."

And so the two names, "the tree of misery" and the "tree of joy," entered Dazhai's records. After that the willow tree also served as a symbol of Chen Yonggui's class education in Dazhai.

In the second half of 1957, some disturbing events occurred on China's political scene. Individual well-to-do middle peasants showed various signs of discontent with the Communist Party throughout the countryside. Their complaint essentially came down to: "Three hundred and sixty pounds of grain to eat, as for cloth, it's eighteen feet!" Someone wrote a couplet for their courtyard front gate which read, on one side, "State grain procurement cleared out our earthen jars." And on the other, "After distribution only one pound of white flour is ours," while across the top, joining the two previous sentiments together, the punch line read "We can't get two square meals out of it." It was easy to see at whom the spearhead of criticism was directed.

Early signs of this critical trend also appeared in Dazhai. The complaints targeted the sale of grain and Chen Yonggui's style of work. People were saying: "Chen Yonggui increases production with corn[1]; he makes his living cursing people out."

1. People looked down on corn as a coarse grain. Chen won his greatest successes raising corn yields. One way to minimize them was to say, "Who wants to eat coarse grain? Show us some results with wheat." Though not so palatable, corn is at least equal to wheat nutritionally. At Dazhai, from one mu of land peasants could harvest four times as much corn as wheat. Even if they had to swap it two jin for one, it paid off handsomely, in a one-crop-a-year climate, to raise corn. (W.H.H.)

People started saying what they never dared say before and doing what they never dared do before. This threw Dazhai's Party cadres into despair. Liang Bianliang, Jia Chengrang and Song Liying—all core Communists in Dazhai—showed up at Chen Yonggui's home, without previous notice, to find out what was going on. They sat around frowning, clicking their tongues, smoking pipe after pipe, and secretly observing Chen Yonggui's expression in silence, all the while wanting to ask just one thing: "Did the policy change?"

They wanted to find out where Chen Yonggui stood. The truth was that Chen Yonggui felt rather confused himself. He still talked tough: "What policy change? You think cursing Chen Yonggui can change policy?" But, in fact, even sleeping it off hadn't put his mind at ease. He recalled the disturbances surrounding the moving of rocks and the shake-up of the old Party organization, which had occurred just as he was joining the Party. Those troubles had come to a head in no time. Then in just a few days things returned to normal. He had encountered similar difficulties before. When he was young, he made his living wandering from place to place. After the revolution, several trials had taught him the meaning of the saying: "When Sima Yi defeated the State of Chen, the horses' hooves no longer ran amok." He would have to get brave himself if he wanted to imbue people under his command with the courage needed to stabilize the situation in Dazhai. So, during and after meetings, he started spreading his philosophy, "Spirits and ghosts alike are afraid of an official who will not be paid off." This was his way of criticizing his colleagues for exhibiting mouselike timidity, which was out of character for the revolutionaries they were supposed to be.

The chorus of curses by the well-to-do middle peasants grew by the day. Every time they ran into Chen Yonggui they showed annoyance. This unsettled him a bit. He was afraid that if he took his next step without fully assessing the strength of his opponents, he might never be able to get out of the bind he saw coming. As a result, his first move was to delegate his duties in the village to other cadres, and set off for the fields, farm implements in hand, a good Model Worker. Only, without telling anybody, he dropped his tools off along the road and secretly went off to the County seat to look for the County leaders. He found them gathered at the gate of the County Committee building—the various secretaries, directors and all—discussing the issue of mass debate. The moment they saw him, they eagerly inquired about the situation in Dazhai.

Chen Yonggui sat down, rolled his sleeves above his elbows and his pants above his knees, took a puff on the cigarette offered by a County director, and started recounting the latest unusual events in Dazhai. "These are your emperors and officials of tomorrow, so they say," explained Chen Yonggui. "If they overturn the realm, I'll be the one that gets hit!"

The County leaders noticed the pained expression on his face and asked him: "Old Chen, are you involved in some corrupt deal?"

"No!"

"Have you taken more than your fair share in food and goods?"

"More than my fair share?" Chen Yonggui said, and laughed. "I've taken on more than my share of work. I've worked more than any one of them, and I've surpassed them all in the small size of my reward."

Hearing this, the County leaders laughed, too. "Don't you remember what the ancients used to say? 'Spirits and ghosts alike are afraid of an official who will not be paid off.' First, you are not corrupt. Second, you haven't taken more for yourself. You always take the lead in work. You transformed the Dazhai of yesteryear into what it is today. What is there to be scared of? They say you sold a lot of grain. You admit to that! Selling a lot of grain can be seen as a sure sign that a lot of grain has been harvested. Ask them how much grain they had to sell in the old society! They say you make your living cursing people out. You admit to that, too. You cursed the landlords, you cursed the rich and well-to-do middle peasants—you didn't curse any ordinary folk. But now they curse you! That's class struggle for you! Chairman Mao has said: 'Heavens will not come tumbling down if you let the people talk. We'll see what to do when they are done talking.' Just tell them: 'When you are all done saying what you have to say, let's talk it over.'"

Different keys open different locks. The moment Chen Yonggui heard the word "class struggle," he felt relief. He admired these County leaders who ranked a notch above him. Although they were all young, still in their twenties and thirties, what they said showed quite a level of understanding! Their words nourished Chen Yonggui's spirits. He felt strong all over again, and he prepared himself to tackle the situation.

Not too long after he came back to Dazhai, Chen perceived a very definite change in the atmosphere. With powerful words he succeeded in putting his attackers on the defensive. But one well-to-do middle peasant, feigning madness, went so far as to threaten: "If we don't get rid of that Chen Yonggui, Dazhai will never pull itself out of misery."

With a knife tucked at his waist at all times, he was looking for an opportunity to kill Chen Yonggui. The sight of him really frightened Chen's wife, Li Huni. She couldn't even talk about her fear—she just spent entire days hiding at home, crying. In the past, Chen Yonggui had often lost his temper with his wife. But now, in the face of real life threats, he showed great concern for her and offered earnest advice. He used every device he could think of to boost her courage. After he came back from East Gate vegetable market he prepared a bowl of noodles especially for her and served it in person, trying to induce her to eat. In order to ward off the unpredictable, Chen Yonggui gave specific instructions to his wife: "Lock the gate after I leave. If anything happens, at least you'll be prepared."

From that time on, Li Huni locked the gate every time Chen Yonggui went out to work. But locking the gate did not solve the problem. The precaution provoked the maddened antagonist to even greater ferocity. He would now pound on the gate screaming bloody murder. He once left a note on the gate, which said: "Give back my land; give back my house." One day he waited until dark, and then, after Chen Yonggui had returned from work, hid in the doorway with a huge kitchen knife in his hand. Zhao Dahe and Liang Bianliang chased him away.

During that period Li Huni was not the only alarmed person. Chen Yonggui, too, remained constantly on guard. Every evening he had a feeling that something was astir outside, but every time he went out to check he found no sign of activity. Li Huni always wanted to lock the door before they went to bed, but Chen Yonggui refused to let her do it. "Leave it," he'd say. "So long as I'm here, damn it, who would dare?"

On the third evening Chen Yonggui again felt that something was wrong outside, but when he got up and looked beyond his courtyard, he didn't see a thing. Only after listening very carefully did he hear the sound of quiet snoring outside his gate. This upset him at first, but he soon calmed down. Walking over to the gate, ears alert, he discovered that somebody was sleeping right in front of it.

"Who's there?" Chen Yonggui shouted.

The snoring stopped. A moment later, however, it resumed as before.

Chen Yonggui opened the gate with great caution. Sticking his head out through the half-opened door he shouted out again: "Who's there? Why don't you answer me?"

The snoring stopped at long last.

"It's me!" the sleeper muttered.

"Who are you?"

"Brother Jin, it's me," said a young man, getting up from the ground.

Only then did Chen Yonggui realize he wasn't facing a potential assassin but the Communist Party member Zhao Dahe. He felt grateful and angry at the same time.

"What are you doing here? Go back home!" Chen ordered.

For the past few nights Chen Yonggui had not taken his clothes off when he went to bed. Zhao Dahe had gone even further. He had spent those long nights lying fully clothed on the ground. When Chen Yonggui reversed himself and invited him into his house, he was forced to reveal his heartfelt concern.

"My good old brother," said Zhao. "If somebody intends to kill you, I cannot sit by without trying to stop him. If I get in his way out there in front of your gate, damn it, he'll have to kill me first, before he can kill you."

At this point Liang Bianliang, who lived in the same courtyard as Chen Yonggui, woke up, aroused by all the commotion.

"Ayaah! You!" he said to Zhao Dahe in reproach. "It's dangerous, sleeping out there by yourself. If you can't handle the attacker, what then? In here, we can all help. Even a mouse makes noise when it steals in to eat, let alone a man! Just because he says he's gonna kill doesn't mean he'll be able to."

"How could I have warned you?" Zhao Dahe clicked his tongue. "If I had let Brother Jin know what I was up to, he wouldn't have let me do it."

Zhao Dahe's nightly guard duty revealed the meaning of "class brotherhood" once more to Chen Yonggui. From then on he put his worries to rest. What could be so terrifying when there were all those poor and lower-middle peasants in Dazhai to set themselves on guard against just one or two troublemakers? Old Xiyang County cadres recall that when Chen Yonggui came to see them again his mood had completely changed. This time, as he submitted his report, he was full of confidence. "Nothing to worry about! There's no problem in Dazhai. We are a multitude; they are but one or two individuals. There's no market for their way of thinking!"

Right after that, the Anti-Rightist Struggle,[1] which criticized bourgeois right-wing views, spread nationwide. At the very beginning of the campaign, I'm told, Chen Yonggui was not too level-headed. He believed that right-wing, bourgeois views existed especially in Dazhai. Some higher-level cadres informed him that Dazhai's problem wasn't all that grave. They advised him to be careful not to make the scope of his counterattack too broad. The struggle should be waged by argument and reasoning, they said. Their words turned on a switch, so to speak. They enlightened Chen Yonggui. As a result, Dazhai conducted the struggle against the bad elements[2] by means of reason. This time the investigative method involved the balancing of all production accounts.

Dazhai called an Anti-Rightist meeting under the curtain of night. Party members Zhao Dahe, Liang Bianliang, Jia Jincai and Song Liying sat amidst poor and lower-middle peasants, facing a bright gasoline mantle lamp as they worked out the sums, using their fingers to count. The comparative figures would show which type of production was bet-

---

1. Cadres in many places carried the Anti-Rightist Campaign to extremes. Mao said real rightists might number several thousand nationwide. Under Deng Xiaoping's direct leadership the campaign targeted some 500,000 people and did great damage, particularly vis-a-vis intellectuals. (W.H.H.)

2. At the time of land reform Party leaders named four "bad elements": landlords, rich peasants, counter-revolutionaries, and "bad apples," criminals of all kinds. This list was later expanded to encompass eight categories that included "rightists" or "bourgeois" rightists. Intellectuals, often targeted for "remolding," called themselves the "stinking ninth" category, but neither Mao nor the Party ever officially designated intellectuals as "bad elements" or even thought of them as such. (W.H.H.)

ter—collective or individual, and which society was better—new or old. Confronting the formerly rich peasant who carried the knife around, Liang Bianliang brought up the issue of the grain Chen Yonggui sold and the curses he used.

"What selling a lot of grain means is that you've harvested a lot of grain. How much land did your families have to plant anything on in the past? How much grain were you able to sell each year? If you didn't starve, you were already happy, right?" asked Liang.

"When Chen Yonggui cursed you, why did he curse?" added another. "It's because he knew exactly what your problem was. If he didn't go after your mistakes, he wouldn't be doing responsible work. It's like the last time you laid rocks to build a terrace wall. When you finished your work the wall collapsed. It would have saved a lot of trouble for all of us if you hadn't laid them up at all."

The plaintiff hung his head in silence.

"You got three hundred sixty pounds of grain to eat," Li Xiqing continued to reason with him. "Has Chen Yonggui eaten a pound more than you? You got coupons to buy eighteen feet of cotton cloth. Did you see Chen Yonggui wearing an inch more cloth than you did? All that Chen Yonggui latched onto more of than you is work, work and work. If he worked for himself, a worker like him would get twice as much grain as you! We've carried out the land reform without killing a single landlord, but you—you want to kill Chen Yonggui. And have you succeeded?"

This meeting, using struggle by reasoning, gave Chen Yonggui a good lesson. He could see that his work earned him the genuine trust of the people, and he was able to appreciate the broad support they gave him. At the end of the meeting he said, "I never imagined that someone would stand on guard for me when I got into trouble. If it weren't for the Communist Party, I'd still be peddling sesame seed cakes on the street. From now on, I'll be even more eager to listen to the Party. I'll staunchly support the socialist road and struggle against all reactionary forces that oppose socialism!"

Owing to the wise leadership of the Communist Party, Chen Yonggui, when he engaged the rightist forces, attacked only with reason.

He didn't stick any labels on people arbitrarily and he didn't turn little issues into big ones, inflating contradictions out of all proportion to their seriousness. This way of leading struggle did him credit and added honor to his image.

CHAPTER 9

TEMPERED BY THE COMMUNIST WIND

We Chinese have a saying, "Repeated tempering makes fine steel." But this is easier repeated than practiced. Producing good-quality steel is not at all easy. In 1958, during the period so many people in China made iron in the backyard furnaces of the Great Leap Forward campaign, the nation already recognized Chen Yonggui as a Model Worker. As to the kind of tempering he actually had to go through in the furnaces of that year—this has already been recorded by history.

Chen Yonggui, once he became famous, committed himself to "public ownership of the means of production." He was constantly on the lookout for newly emerging socialist forms and methods. He showed interest in every novel experience and occurrence. Although he had never been to school and wasn't well educated, he managed to read through most newspaper articles and important documents. When he didn't recognize any word he solved the problem by asking one of the "teachers" for help. He used the "tobacco break" during work hours to look at the newspaper and discuss current affairs; also, he often read the news right before attending evening meetings. As he put it back then: When you till, you must pay attention to the lumps in the soil. If you don't, you'll never till the land properly." This applied, as well, to political leadership, he saw. If you didn't analyze and absorb the documents with their nuggets of theory and practice, you couldn't lead properly.

One evening Chen Yonggui got hold of the *People's Daily*. A news item that caught his eye was the report on Chairman Mao Zedong's inspection of Qiliying in the South New Town district of Henan Province. He could never let go of a newspaper once he saw the words "Chairman Mao" printed on it. Consequently, he grabbed this particular issue and continued to read for all he was worth. The article explained how on August 6, 1958, Chairman Mao saw the People's Commune[1] that had been established in Qiliying, and made a statement during his tour of inspection: "People's Commune seems to be the right name for what you have here, incorporating industry, agriculture, commerce, education and the military." He also said: "The distinguishing features of a Commune are: one, it's larger in size; two, it has a higher degree of public ownership."

Chen Yonggui had gone to the County Party School many times to attend classes. The subject was always "Communism." When it came to things like "abolishing individual ownership and instituting public ownership," Chen Yonggui saw them as guides to action. But when he now saw the words, "The distinguishing features of a Commune are: One, it's larger in size; two, it has a higher degree of public ownership," come out of Chairman Mao's own mouth, he became deeply excited. On the following day he rushed off to Five Family Flat to deliver the news and urge the Party Branch Secretaries of the neighboring villages to set up a People's Commune. His arguments were completely successful. In less than two days they were all ready to spring into action.

Surprisingly, only Dazhai resisted the proposal. Not only did most members of the Cooperative object, even some cadres found it quite unimaginable. Allegedly, they felt anxious about shared property. If all

1. Communes were federations of village-level Cooperatives that coordinated management of agriculture, forestry, animal husbandry, fisheries and such side occupations a[s] trade, education, culture, and military affairs (local militias). While production team[s] or Brigades (villages) continued to keep their own accounts, Communes undertoo[k] such things as high schools, hospitals, bigger industries and large capital constructio[n] projects that were beyond the capacity of the smaller collective units down below t[o] handle. (W.H.H.)

the families in Dazhai put their property on the table, then merged it with more backward villages, wouldn't they be looking to lose out—and of their own free will at that? But Chen Yonggui managed to persuade them, albeit with considerable effort, and finally accomplished his goal. He lined up several dozen cadres from seven villages, who applied to establish a People's Commune. After the County authorities approved, the seven villages established Xiyang County's first People's Commune—the Red Flag Commune—in Five Family Flat, with much celebration and drum-and-gong beating.

There were issues, however, on which Chen Yonggui would never act impetuously if he was not able to make an accurate assessment. As soon as he could see that there was no way out of a certain situation, he would never take another step in that direction. His objection to distorting reality, boasting and exaggeration can easily illustrate this point.

In 1958, Dazhai did not follow the practice, common during the Great Leap Forward, of making back yard iron. The village put its main energy, as always, into developing agricultural production; Dazhai Coop members wisely spent the entire year on solid farm work. The autumn harvest took in 540 *jin* of grain per *mu* of land (64 bushels per acre, 4 metric tons per hectare). This figure, according to the forty provisions of the National Program for Agricultural Development, put Dazhai in the forefront of China's agricultural production. Yet, Chen Yonggui—a special-class Model Worker of the Province of Shanxi—did not get to go to Beijing to attend the All-China Congress of Model Workers. How was that possible? It was due to the distortions made by the boasting and exaggeration wind that was blowing at the time.

That same year Chen Yonggui had attended a conference called "Activists for the Socialist Construction of Shanxi Province," organized by cadres from the provincial capital, Taiyuan. Several well-known Model Workers from Xiyang County attended the rally: Zhang Laotai; Wang Dianjun; and lastly Zhang Yinzhou, who had started as a functionary of the New Forever Cooperative in Knife Handle Gate, later transferred to East Steet Village in the Gaoqian District of Huolu County in Hebei Province, and ended up as an All-China Model Worker. Tian Gendong, the County Committee Deputy Secretary in charge of agriculture led the group. Chen Yonggui and Li Shunda were both members of the steering committee. They sat on the rostrum during each session of the conference. During the discussion sessions many people discussed how they smelted iron, and boasted of astronomical *per-mu* grain yields.

Chen Yonggui so much disliked the tenor of the discussion that he started arguing with some of the participants. According to individuals who attended the conference, Chen Yonggui let his pipe dangle from his mouth while he raised his feet onto an old chair and told people, with what seemed like a smile on his face, although he was not smiling: "I can't get you a yield of ten thousand *jin* on the kind of land I have. Neither do I believe that their land can yield tens of thousands. If they can really get the yields they boast of, let them be my guests in Dazhai. I'll serve them 'drawn noodles'!" Xiyang County people considered "drawn noodles" to be a great delicacy. They served them to guests on special occasions. Undoubtedly, Chen Yonggui was expressing his dissatisfaction when he invited them all for this Shanxi specialty.[1]

No matter what he said he was not able to block the endemic boasting. Before the Congress, the Party Central Committee had convened a meeting in Xian, Shanxi Province, precisely to discuss the ways of increasing grain output. Eight Vice-Premiers gave speeches. The pressure on various Provinces and cities, growing out of that meeting, was great indeed. Shanxi Province was no exception. When the member of the Provincial Committee who had attended the Xian meeting returned to Taiyuan, he started feeling out the situation at a subcommittee meeting. He first asked Li Shunda: "Can you raise your yields?"

Li Shunda bitterly resented the exaggerated boasting. He had seen the reports showing that many places surpassed his West Gully in their grain output by far, but for the sake of honesty and adherence to the facts he was willing to forego his Model Worker status. Consequently, his answer was: "No. My yields can't go up."

---

1. To make drawn noodles the cook first kneaded the dough well. Then he formed it like a piece of rope in his hands and threw the center of the rope at the floor with lightning speed. Just before the loop of dough hit the dirt, he crossed his hands, causing the two strands to wind up on themselves to form a single rope again. This throwing and twisting further kneaded the dough into proper shape to be drawn, that is pulled out, doubled back, pulled out and doubled back again until it formed long strands that could be cut loose and dropped into a waiting pot, as "drawn noodles." (W.H.H.)

The comrade from the Provincial Committee then asked Chen Yonggui: "Can your yields be any higher?"

Chen Yonggui answered with a laugh: If I could raise them, you would have had my report to that effect a long time ago!"

Pressed by the exaggeration wind, the Provincial Committee leader gave in to expediency and said, "You seem to be lagging behind."

After this meeting the two Model Workers, Li Shunda and Chen Yonggui, conferred and agreed that they wouldn't lie and alter production figures for the purpose of going to Beijing. Returning to the guesthouse, Chen Yonggui sought the opinion of the delegation leader Tian Gendong, and other Xiyang County delegates at the Conference—Zhang Laotai, Wang Dianjun and Zhang Yinzhou. They gave him their full support.

That is how Chen Yonggui rejected out of hand all false credentials for attending the Congress of Model Workers. Li Shunda's qualifications for the trip to Beijing also proved to be insufficient. Although neither of them made it to the capital, Chen Yonggui felt very much at ease in his heart.

That year's National Congress of Model Workers, by reporting grossly exaggerated yields, left many people in the dark and the Government in a quandary. The Congress took place at the Beijing Gymnasium. Quite a few of the Congress delegates were Model Workers of "outer space" who "rode on beams of cosmic light." The most typical of this group was a nineteen-year-old woman, head of a Cooperative in Xiaogan County, Hubei Province. Instigated by some misguided delegates, she issued a warning: If the yields from land under her charge didn't rise to ten thousand *jin* per *mu* (75 metric tons per hectare, or 1,100 bushels per acre) she wouldn't get married! This startling news item immediately mobilized the journalists, always sensitive to headline-grabbing opportunities. They flocked to her in droves for interviews. In the end, Premier Zhou Enlai cited this incident in a report in which he criticized the current practice of exaggerating and boasting.He wrote: "Based on the condition of land and the level of scientific knowledge in China today, I conclude that you will not get married in your lifetime."

The Premier's words amounted to a clear indication of national agricultural policy. Naturally, the words of the female delegate lost their credibility, and the journalists' stories vanished without a trace. The journalists, needless to say survived to jump on the next bandwagon. By that time the practice of exaggeration had already spread throughout the expanse of China. It was impossible to put an abrupt stop to it with a single sentence uttered by Premier Zhou Enlai.

At the time when Chen Yonggui attended the conference in Taiyuan, Dazhai, under pressure from this general trend, had entered a trash- and straw-burying contest. Villagers of the Central Shanxi Region were digging holes and pits, packing them with straw and other crop residues, then covering them over with soil. To enliven the scene, a "mobile red banner" traveled from village to village. When a village lost the contest, it sent the banner voluntarily to the village that won, announcing its own defeat with the beating of drums and the striking of gongs as though it were a thing to celebrate.

The contest put a lot of pressure on Dazhai. Cooperative members felt they were very likely to lose the red banner within the following three days. The village cadres, in view of the fact that Chen Yonggui was still in Taiyuan attending the conference, became very anxious. If they were to lose, how would they explain their loss to him when he came back? When they heard that he had stopped over in Yangquan on the way back from Taiyuan to take care of some business, the cadres sent the Branch Secretary of the Dazhai Organization of Production Brigades, Jia Haihe, to look for Chen and give him an account of things back home.

Jia Haihe found Chen Yonggui at the Public Bath Inn in Yangquan. He had just finished eating, and was getting ready to go to the town center to take care of business for the village. Chen Yonggui was surprised when Jia Haihe showed up, but he was not a bit upset when he heard Jia's report. He had already formed his opinion about the whole idea of this contest. He was therefore able to state his position clearly: "First of all, no one is to worry about who will win and who will lose. When you get back, tell everybody to work at rebuilding the terraced fields as we agreed before I left. Take the soil from the inner, hillside edges of the terraces and raise the outer rims. Their second task is to shred straw and stalks for compost. As for the business of delivering the red banner on the third day—leave that to me. I'm strong enough to carry a banner, and besides, there's no need to beat drums and bang gongs. I'll definitely be back within three days. For now, though, please convey to them what I have just said."

Chen Yonggui had planned to spend three days in Yangquan, but he was afraid he'd miss the banner delivery. He ended up staying only two days and left unfinished business behind when he returned to Dazhai. A bus line had just started running between Yangquan and Xiyang, so Chen Yonggui took the bus, passing through Pingding County. On both sides of the highway he could see crowds of people sprinkled across the landscape as though by the hand of the Celestial Maiden, Xian Nu, scattering flowers. They were all digging and filling in pits. The more he looked, the more upset he got. This kind of empty formalism could not benefit socialist construction! But what was one to do about it?

Back in Dazhai, Chen Yonggui rushed straight to the mountainside without even stopping at his own house. When he saw that all the able men and women were in the fields, some busily rebuilding terraces as planned, others shredding straw and making compost, he relaxed. As Jia Jincai, Jia Chengfu and Liang Bianliang approached him to report, he greeted them by calling out what which most occupied his mind.

"Did I miss the delivery of the banner?"

"It's not time yet," all three said, laughing. "Tomorrow."

"So long as I haven't missed it. It's I who told you not to dig those pits, so I should be the one to take the banner away."

And so he did. At dawn the following day he took the red banner and carried it on foot some three miles to the favored village beyond the mountain.

A public controversy erupted at the time regarding the relative merits and faults of Dazhai's performance and Chen Yonggui's maturity as a leader. After Dazhai became famous and many people enthusiastically studied the genesis of its success, the tendency was to attribute its high yields to the use of chemical fertilizer.

Wang Chengwang, the Secretary of the Regional Party Committee, found his answer through hands-on experience. When he received information about Dazhai's high yields he went personally to Dazhai and lived, ate and worked with the members of the Dazhai collective. As they worked in the field one day, Chen Yonggui told him various "tricks of the trade" that produced high yields.

"Can you raise your yields any higher based on your current production conditions?" Wang Chengwang asked.

Chen Yonggui dropped his head, sank into deep thought for a moment, and gave an answer that revealed an attitude entirely different from the one he had expressed in Taiyuan. He wanted to be completely honest with his Regional Committee Secretary. "There is still some potential for increase. If we could feed the land adequate chemical fertilizer, we could get higher yields."

Thus the Regional Party Committee Secretary became familiar with the specifics of Dazhai's sparse use of chemical fertilizers.

He called the County Committee Secretary, Zhang Huaiying, to raise the following issue: "Huaiying, the extent of Dazhai's per unit area yield increase has been so large and its contribution to our country so great, yet they have not been allocated much chemical fertilizer at all. The amount is nowhere near what some people have been saying! Can you give them a break and send them some extra fertilizer?"

Distribution of chemical fertilizer in the County is determined higher up, by the national distribution policy," responded Zhan Huaiying. "Dazhai sold a lot of grain to the State so, naturally, it will get more fertilizer than other places. But I cannot step beyond the parameters set by the policy. I have to treat Dazhai as I do other places, like Knife Handle Gate and White Lamb Ravine."

"And would you supply a little more if that would raise Dazhai's output still further?" Wang Chengwang asked.

"If I give more to Dazhai, it will end up being bad for Dazhai regardless of how others look at my action," said Zhang Huaiying, laughing.

"I see," Wang Chengwang nodded with understanding. "You've given it careful thought. I've heard all those rumors too. But I've discovered that they are all wrong. When weighed against Dazhai's grain deliveries, its chemical fertilizer supplies are actually on the short side. That Chen Yonggui is something. So is that Song Liying. She's shoring up half the sky! They sure have a bundle of talent in Dazhai!"

Later, Tao Lujia[1] went to Dazhai to deal with the issue of chemica fertilizer. He spent a lot of time discussing it with Zhang Huaiying anc

1. Tao Lujia was a member of the Central Committee of the Communist Party of Chin and was Party Secretary of the Shanxi Provincial Committee. (W.H.H.)

Chen Yonggui. He stressed that he wanted Dazhai to maintain its commitment to self-reliance. He was prepared to extend it more political support, but not to give it more economic aid. As a result, everybody in the cCunty received concrete instructions not to give Chen Yonggui any preferential treatment. On public occasions everybody talked about Chen Yonggui's meritorious deeds, but whenever a problem emerged it was dealt with in private conversation and settled quietly, thus leaving lots of room for continued false rumors.

It is really because of the great concern and caring shown by the higher Party authorities that Chen Yonggui didn't run into serious road blocks along his way, and that the steps he took were sound in the main. Although he lost the opportunity to go to the National Congress of Model Workers in Beijing in 1958, in 1959 during the tenth anniversary National Day celebrations in Tiananmen Square, Chen Yonggui played a conspicuous part.

Chen Yonggui's impending trip to Beijing hardly caused a stir in his tiny mountain village prior to his departure. Once Dazhai became famous, the comings and goings of various people, important or otherwise, had become commonplace in the village. Besides, one could hardly expect its citizens, up to their ears in farm work as they were, to engage in speculation about such a trip. As a result, when the time came for Chen Yonggui to depart, the local Party Branch Committee members, Party members and the members of the Cooperative came to his house to see him off quite casually. They staged no special ceremony. But Chen Yonggui sensed keenly that his trip to Beijing would not be an ordinary one. Had not a County official made a special trip to talk to him, and had he not brought forms to fill out? Therefore Chen instructed his "old woman," Li Huni, to wash his head-towel time and again. There was a shortage of soap in China at the time, but Chen Yonggui willingly used up several cakes of white soap for the purpose.

He was born in the hills and grew up in the hills. Had it not been for the road opened for him by the Communist Party, not only would he have never made it to the nation's capital—he would rarely have made it into the homes of local landlords and usurers. That's what he himself thought in any case, and that's what he told everybody after his visit to Beijing. But he didn't pour out his feelings freely at the time. He remained outwardly calm from beginning to end.

Once he set out on the journey the first stop was Yangquan. There he waited for the rest of the Shanxi delegation. True to the ingrained habits of a peasant, he avoided the high-class hotel and stayed instead at the Public Bath Inn. His insistence on practicing frugality and preserving a spirit of hard struggle over many years was central to turning the old Dazhai of barren mountains and unruly gullies into a new village where bumper harvests were commonplace. Now five times as much grain as before the land reform poured from each *mu* of land, and Dazhai's sales of commodity grain to the State kept increasing annually. It was accomplishments like these that made Chen Yonggui's white towel the trademark for an entire era.

Thus when, in China's capital, Chen Yonggui ascended the visitor's stand wearing his trademark white towel around his head he held his chin and his chest high. The "sheep belly weave" hand towel was a common, all but universal, headpiece in the villages of northern China, but it dazzled the eye as something markedly different and intriguing amid the crowds in Beijing. Chen Yonggui's appearance in this headgear on the visitor's stand in Tiananmen could not but create a stir. Standing there, looking at the enormous crowd in the Square, Chen's excitement mounted.

A long-felt wish was coming true.

Beloved Chairman Mao appeared! As Chairman Mao approached, walking with vigorous strides and waving his hand in greeting, a cheerful melody boomed across the great expanse of the Square. Moved Chen Yonggui took the white towel off his head and held it as high as he could, joining the other Model Workers from Shanxi Province in a giant wave and a high-pitched cry: "Long live Chairman Mao! A hundred million years!"

The pressing crowd forced him forward. While he was shouting the slogans, he had a hard time getting a hand free to quietly use his white towel to wipe away the tears streaming down his face.

In the midst of the fervor of the National Tenth Anniversary celebrations Chen Yonggui suddenly remembered the words of Count comrades who congratulated him as he was about to leave. They hoped that he would get to see Chairman Mao and shake his hand. "Give our regards to him," they had said. He now recalled the task they had given him. Of course, he too hoped that Chairman Mao would walk up to him. But such hopes were not to be fulfilled at that time. The visitors' stand was quite far from the gate-tower rostrum. Chen Yonggui had no chance to shake Chairman Mao's hand, let alone to deliver any greetings. Nevertheless, in the eyes of Chen Yonggui and his Dazhai compatriots, this was an unprecedented event.

Chen Yonggui was exceedingly happy each day and night that he spent at the seat of China's government in Zhongnanhai. He was aware of how difficult it had been for him to come to the capital, and that he owed it all to his struggle with that expanse of yellow loess earth back home. There, he couldn't even dream that he would be visiting these famous sights and attending high-level receptions and banquets in Beijing. Premier Zhou Enlai came in person to the place where the Model Workers were staying and asked them, one by one, for their positions and their names. Following the example of other Model Workers Chen Yonggui submitted respectfully: "I am Party Branch Secretary of the New Victory Agricultural Cooperative in the village of Dazhai, Xiyang County, Shanxi Province. My name is Chen Yonggui."

Just as he did with all the other Model Workers, Premier Zhou simply shook his hand and passed by. Yet even that simple act engraved itself in Chen Yonggui's memory.

When Chen Yonggui returned triumphantly from Beijing, the sound of drums and gongs echoing over the mountain wilderness shook the atmosphere. Dazhai peasants lined both sides of narrow village passageways to welcome him. Various members of the local Party Branch Committee, wearing thick padded clothing and white towels like his own on their heads, waited impatiently to greet him. When their gaze met Chen Yonggui's smiling face they hastened forward with affectionate appellations of "Old Chen," "Brother Jin," and the like. They all wanted to hear the story from his own mouth. How did Chairman Mao receive him? What did Premier Zhou Enlai say? Chen did not need to embroider the experience in any way to satisfy the villagers from isolated, back country Dazhai. They were content with his unadorned account. Some even shed tears. They drew inspiration from his words, which acted as drops of high octane fuel poured into a straining motor. They showed themselves ready and willing to suffer and exhaust themselves once more.

Chen Yonggui felt that his compatriots' reaction was the "portent" he had hoped for.

CHAPTER 10

QUALITATIVE CHANGE

No one who evaluates events dialectically can avoid moving from quantitative to qualitative analysis. Likewise, as the spirit of Dazhai slowly evolved and wrought "miracles" of transformation, there were people who moved from superficial admiration of the work performed to a deeper understanding of the ideological force, the philosophy, behind it. As these people's comprehension evolved so did the way in which society viewed Chen Yonggui.

At the very beginning of the movement to organize Agricultural Cooperatives, there were people who didn't understand Chen Yonggui's grain sales policy. But the Dazhai they saw at the end of the 1950s, after many years of Chen's unrelenting struggle and many displays of his growing ability, presented a very different picture from the one they once knew so well. As a result, the views of many people, both from Dazhai and elsewhere, changed. And, yes, many a pipe-smoking peasant with a white towel wrapped around his head came to wish that his own village had a Chen Yonggui, who could lead the transformation at his location! In response to such wishes this was the time when Dazhai started extending a helping hand to the neighboring villages.

Dazhai's grain output had been increasing annually. Not only was it able to meet the quotas set by the State Grain Bureau, its collective grain reserves also grew considerably. On the other hand, the village of Five Family Flat, which was just a third of a mile down the road, could not meet its grain sales quotas. Every year, the peasants of The Flat completely consumed the previous year's harvest before the new crop ripened. Then the members of the Five Family Flat Cooperative went looking for cadres in search of grain to eat. The local cadres pulled on long faces, unable to cope with the problem. Even the cadres higher up in the structure, when asked for help, were not able to provide much grain.

Circumstances thus drew Five Family Flat closer to Dazhai. The Party Branch Secretary of The Flat approached Chen Yonggui testily, and asked to borrow grain. Chen Yonggui had not forgotten the curses that had once been hurled at him as he went in and out of Five Family Flat, but he didn't let the past sour the present. He had been quite aware of the grain shortage in The Flat for some time, and was mentally prepared to help out. So, when asked, he opened up Dazhai's warehouse for the first time and loaned out a portion of the stored-up grain to his neighbors.

No sooner did Chen Yonggui show such generosity than the attitudes of Five Family Flat's residents, both young and old, changed. In the past, Chen Yonggui had met with curses and grumbling every time he passed through their village. Now he was welcomed on the way in and sent out at the other end with warm greetings. Those who had once maligned him and accused him of going to the County seat to eat steamed buns, praised him incessantly. They now claimed that the only thing Five Family Flat needed to turn things around was Chen Yonggui's leadership.

When the people of The Flat saw him leading a donkey laden with two gunnysacks of bean-flour noodles on the way to the County seat, they reproached him affectionately: "Hey, Old Chen, while you run around attending meetings and selling noodles, Dazhai is left without its chief workhorse! Have you ever thought of it that way?"

"They'll just have to work a bit harder," Chen Yonggui answered. "But they have one less worker to pay! I sell the noodles, and still make it to the meeting!"

These days, when Chen Yonggui came back from the County seat carrying an awarded silk banner, the people of Five Family Flat discussed it among themselves very differently from the way they used to in the old days. "See that? Chen Yonggui's made it! True, he had to kick down some fences. But look at these cadres in our village!"

Once Chen opened the stores for Five Family Flat, the village of Gao Family Ridge came asking for grain. When he opened the storehouse for Five Family Ridge, the village of Gold Gash held out a hand. Chen Yonggui not only gave the neighboring villages the grain they needed for food; come spring, he provided them with seed for planting. In the spring of 1959, when the village of Gold Rock Slope, having ploughed its first furrows, discovered it did not have enough seeds to plant, its Party Branch Secretary got hold of Chen Yonggui and begged him for aid. Chen Yonggui found it impossible to turn him away and, in the end, handed out some more seed grain.

When the County Party Committee Secretary and the representative to the County Standing Committee went to Gold Rock Slope to investigate the situation they asked the local Party Branch Secretary what he thought he could learn from Dazhai.

"People in Dazhai are OK," the Secretary replied. "When I went knocking on their village gate, Old Chen gave us the seeds we needed. We would have been in trouble this year."

"You are wrong! You shouldn't start by begging from Dazhai," said the County leaders, cutting him short. "The first thing you should do is learn from their spirit of self-reliance and arduous struggle. The way you are going in your village, you'll all be beggars in a couple of years!"

Between the time Dazhai first set up its Agricultural Producers' Cooperative and 1955, Dazhai was able to reach "four highs" in grain production: high yields, high sales, high reserves and high consumption. As a result, both in Dazhai and elsewhere one kept hearing more and more praise of its success. In 1957, Dazhai began lending grain, selling straw, and distributing seed. If someone, for instance, borrowed 1,000 pounds of grain from Dazhai this year, he would not have to give it back until next year. If he was truly unable to give back grain the next year, he could make a cash payment based on low State purchase prices.

When it came to selling straw, Chen Yonggui refused to sell at the high market price of twenty cents a *jin*. He sold each *jin* instead at the low State price of three cents. All you needed was a letter of introduction from a Commune or a production team to ensure a transaction at the low State price. Within a few years Dazhai had lent out 70,000 pounds of grain and sold 50,000 pounds of straw. As a result, people admired Chen Yonggui more and more. Their attitude toward collectivization also changed. The skeptics now were saying what they heard all around them, that there was nothing wrong with collectivization as such. If there were problems the fault lay with the village cadres in charge.

In 1959 Dazhai experienced two natural disasters in one year. First there was a drought, then it rained so much the fields became waterlogged. Even so, grain yields per *mu* remained somewhere around 600 *jin* (seventy bushels per acre), the average per capita grain consumption reached 450 *jin*, and the Cooperative's grain reserves grew year by year. It is said that at this same time some members of the West Main Street Commune, which was located just outside Xiyang City's West gate, asked the Party Branch Secretary for grain. The Party Secretary declared publicly: "The key to whether we can solve the food problem lies in whether we learn the spirit of Dazhai—whether or not we follow Dazhai's lead. Had we made a concerted effort to learn from Dazhai, we would have had more grain than we can eat this year. I'd be the one lending Chen Yonggui 10,000 *jin*."

The advantages of socialism first made themselves manifest in Dazhai, then went on to influence our entire society.

In 1960, Xiyang County experienced a severe drought that lowered the average yield of grain. In this, the hardest of hard years, the yields in Dazhai continued to grow, reaching 650 *jin* per *mu* (seventy-seven bushels per acre) in spite of the drought. On the average, every household sold the state 3,500 *jin* of grain, while the per capita consumption of grain held at about 400 *jin*, a figure somewhat lower than the year before.

The Regional Party Committee of Central Shanxi called a meeting of all County Party Secretaries. Wang Qian, Vice-Secretary of the Shanxi Provincial Party Committee, also attended. The sole item on the agenda was a discussion of overall production and living conditions that year. The meeting determined that, in view of the hardships the national economy was undergoing at the time, the average per capita consumption of grain should be no lower than 350 *jin* and no higher than 380 *jin*. Wang Qian made a point of stressing this at the meeting. During the discussion period Jia Jun, Prefectural Party Committee Secretary, briefed the delegates on living conditions and production figures in Dazhai. Wang Qian listened, stated his position once again very clearly, and went on to say that Dazhai was an exception. Dazhai's per capita grain consumption of more than 400 *jin*, he said, reflected the policy of distribution according to labor. Dazhai people worked harder, reaped more, hence should get more.

After the close of the meeting, the Xiyang County Party Committee relayed the gist of the decisions to the entire County. It also communicated Wang Qian's statement about Dazhai to Chen Yonggui. When Chen Yonggui heard it, he felt there was something wrong with it. He picked up a lantern one night and walked to town in order to make his position known to the County leaders. "If the whole country is beset with difficulties, if the people live in straitened circumstances—I can't eat that much grain!" Chen told them.

Actually, even the 400 *jin* suggested by Wang Qian represented a decrease compared to the 450 *jin* reached the year before. County leaders insisted on this point and went on to comfort Chen Yonggui by saying that grain consumption nationally would never again fall below 400 *jin* per capita. But Chen Yonggui told them: "Even if we don't get enough grain to eat, we in the country can reinforce our diet with gourds and beans. But what are the workers and soldiers going to do if they don't get enough cereals? What I'm proposing is that we lower the amount of grain set for our consumption."

In the end the County leaders acquiesced, lowering Dazhai's per capita grain allotment to a minimum of 390 *jin*, but keeping it above the County average because they still wanted to implement the policy of distribution according to work performed.

It was after this that the revolutionary call, "I stand here on Tigerhead Mountain, China on my mind, the whole world in my heart," came from Chen Yonggui and the people of Dazhai. They were not merely mouthing fine-sounding words, as the later critics of ultra-leftism would have it. They were actually eating less so they could help out more.

At the time the Xiyang County Party Committee dealt with the issue of Dazhai in a twofold manner. Its internal policy was somewhat different from that which it announced to the outside world. Internally, it was doing its best to prevent Chen Yonggui from selling more grain in order to save him from food shortages before the next harvest came around. All it wanted was for the current year's sales to surpass last year's by a small margin. Toward the outside, however, the Committee actively advocated the spirit of emphasizing general or nationwide interests by selling more grain.

After the news reached the Regional Party Committee of Central Shanxi, the Committee brought all village Party Branch Secretaries, village Chairmen, propaganda committee members and committee members in charge of organizational work together at an ad hoc meeting. The delegates gathered in Xiyang in January 1961. All participants endorsed Chen Yonggui's spirit of arduous struggle and adopted a regional resolution of the Party to study the lessons from Dazhai and its model Branch Secretary, Chen Yonggui. Many people stressed how important it was to encourage and promote the Dazhai spirit during the transition period Chinese society was going through at the time.

As the meeting took place a cold wave swept the region. Most people avoided going outdoors. However, Jia Jun, the Regional Party Secretary, insisted on visiting Dazhai so as to better acquaint himself with the situation there. A car dropped him and a County leader off in the village. There Chen Yonggui joined them for a trek up Tigerhead Mountain to a spot from which they could observe the transformation that various slope-control and water-control projects had imprinted on Dazhai's landscape. Having just heard Chen Yonggui's exposition of his ten-year plan, Jia Jun was visibly pleased.

Jia patted Chen Yonggui on the shoulder and said: "Really, Old Chen! Could you go on working like this for another ten years? Twenty years?"

"Don't worry," Chen Yonggui responded cheerfully, "there's enough work here for another generation or two."

Jia Jun then remarked to the County leader: "Our national economy is experiencing grave difficulties right now. We are under a lot of pressure. Imagine: if every County were to produce a Chen Yonggui—I mean in terms of his contribution only, and assuming that there would be no need for special treatment—and if we reduced the amount of grain used for consumption, what would things look like in the Central Shanxi region?"

Despite the cold wind that cut to the bone, Jia Jun remained on the top of Tigerhead Mountain for quite a while taking a good look around him. When he finally came down he never called for his car. He walked all the way back to the County seat, engaging the accompanying County leader in lively, light-hearted conversation.

The news that the Regional Party Committee of Central Shanxi had held the ad hoc meeting and adopted a resolution to study from Chen Yonggui made a great impact on Tao Lujia, the Shanxi Provincial Party Committee Secretary. Tao Lujia was fascinated to discover that a high-quality Party Branch Secretary like Chen Yonggui could emerge even during the transitional period[1] that China was in, and he was determined to retain this wonderful model regardless of cost. At the beginning of 1960 he summoned a meeting of the Provincial Party Committee, where he conferred with Wei Heng, Wang Qian and other Party Branch Secretaries, then sent out a notice that the entire Province should "Study from the Model Party Branch Secretary, Chen Yonggui." Under Tao Lujia's direction *Shanxi Daily* published a news report and an editorial under the title "Chen Yonggui—Good Model for All Party Branch Secretaries."

With this publicity Chen Yonggui's reputation in Shanxi soared.

Chen's ability was apparent not only in the way he expanded production; the broad scope of his talents could be seen from the way in which he handled the intricate interplay of social contradictions generated by hard times. One good example was his treatment of the thieves

1. What the author calls the "transitional period" was made up of the three hard years that followed the "Great Leap." Bad weather, policy extremes, the withdrawal of Soviet aid, and heavy debt repayments brought on a severe crisis that resulted in a general food shortage and severe famine in some regions of China. (W.H.H.)

who came from Zanhuang and Heshun Counties to steal corn from Dazhai.

Everybody who lived through the transition period remembers that 1960 was the most difficult year for China's national economy. Seven of the northern provinces—Shanxi, Hebei, Shandong, Henan, Shaanxi, Gansu and Qinghai—experienced a severe drought and a major decrease in grain production. The disaster seriously affected Sichuan Province, China's chief producer of commodity grain. At the same time the Soviet Union broke off the Friendship Treaty and unscrupulously chose this very moment of temporary distress for our country to press for the payment of debts. Beset with difficulties at home and pressure from abroad, many Chinese farmers led a life of semi-starvation. Countless people allayed their hunger eating wild herbs and tree leaves, others drifted away from their villages and became beggars. Many starved to death.

Due to a prolonged dry spell most of the crops in Xiyang County could not gather any strength to grow. As leaves withered, ears of corn failed to fill. All that some plots could produce were clumps of desiccated grass. But Dazhai was another world altogether. On Tigerhead Mountain the stalks waxed thick, the foliage unfolded luxuriously, and each ear of grain grew plump. Some people called it "the Jade Emperor's experimental plot." This "heavenly kingdom" on earth made people envious. The eyes of those with empty stomachs fixed on this "ideologically red," model piece of land, and schemed how to stretch out an invisible third hand into the dead of the night and grab a bite or two to quell the pangs of hunger.

As soon as one man in Dazhai found ears missing he informed Chen Yonggui. Considering Dazhai's propitious circumstances, Chen had to give the situation some serious thought. Having visited the scene of the crime, he told one of the Party Branch Secretaries to organize some people to walk the fields for a few nights.

"First we have to catch a few culprits," he said.

For many years prior to this time, in Dazhai, just as in all the other villages in the area, people had not been locking the gates during the day or closing the windows at night. As a rule there were no thefts, so there was no need for special protection of the crops even at harvest time. This year turned out to be different. After the newly appointed harvest guards tailed the thieves for a few nights they finally caught two of them red-handed. They discovered that it was not people from the neighboring villages who were stealing corn but thieves from two adjacent Counties, Zanhuang and Heshun.

"Move it!" shouted the guards as they led their captives off to Chen Yonggui for treatment. "Take the corn to the Production Brigade!"

"Good brothers, let us get away with it this time!" the sallow-cheeked lad from Zanhuang pleaded piteously. "We'll never dare do it again."

"No way! Is stealing a criminal offense or what? It has to be dealt with!" came the angry reply.

The two harvest guards escorted the thieves to the offices of the Production Brigade. As luck would have it, Chen Yonggui was waiting there at the time.

"What happened?" he asked.

"We caught two corn thieves! This one's from Zanhuang. All that stolen corn—it's all his doing!"

"Ayah, my good Branch Secretary!" said the Zanhuang thief, trembling. "I just snapped this fistful of corn, that's all. As for the rest, that's not...."

With a grave expression on his face Chen Yonggui pulled up a stool and dragged the thieves to it. "Sit down!" he ordered.

The two harvest guards were preparing to carry out a major interrogation,[1] but Chen Yonggui waved them back, hinting that it wouldn't be necessary.

"How many nights have you gone without sleep?" Chen asked, looking the thieves in the eye.

"Oooh...one...just one night," they answered reluctantly.

"Have you eaten?" inquired Chen Yonggui.

Without waiting for an answer Chen turned to the two harvest guards. "Go to the little mess hall. Tell them I sent you. Ask them to prepare two bowls of food for the corn thieves."

---

1. It seems likely that if Chen Yonggui hadn't stopped them, the guards would have, as peasants say in Shanxi, "repaired" these two thieves, which means to beat them severely. (W.H.H.)

"They stole from us, and now they get to eat?" protested one of the guards, incredulous.

"The prisoners have to be treated well, don't you know that? Get going!" said Chen darting a look of severe disapproval at him.

After the harvest guards were gone, Chen Yonggui continued to question the man from Zanhuang. "Why did you steal our corn?"

"I'm hungry! I couldn't stand the hunger!" said the Zanhuang thief, breaking into tears.

Chen Yonggui nodded, barely uttering a sound of acknowledgment. "It's the hunger. Of course, it's the hunger," he said. "We've got grain in Dazhai. We can't supply much, but the few of you that came here—the few dozen, actually—we'll be able to take care of you for a while. If you are hungry, come to see me. I'll give you food. Why trample my crops like that? How are we to fix that? Ah? What do you have to say? Am I right or not?"

"Ayah! My Branch Secretary! I...I...I...." The man from Zanhuang was at a loss for words to express his remorse.

"You are hungry, so you'll eat! You won't be hungry once you've eaten, right?"

The thieves were moved by a thousand emotions. How could they ever have expected to encounter a man like Chen Yonggui?

When the food arrived Chen personally placed it in their hands. "No need to worry about anything now," he said. "Eat! Our food is not great. Coarse grain and coarse noodles, that's all. But we give it from the heart! Yes, we have grain in Dazhai, but if the whole country's in trouble, we have to tighten our belts a little, too."

The thief from Zanhuang held back his tears as he swallowed the food. He was waiting for punishment. But Chen Yonggui made no such move. No beating, not even a curse. He just fished a few *yuan* from his pocket, along with some grain coupons good for the purchase of several *jin* of grain, and handed them over to them.

"Here, comrades!" he said. "I'm kind of short of cash too, but you take this and use it to go back home. Take some cooked sorghum noodles for the trip. You'll need some, when you get hungry on the road."

The Zanhuang thief could hardly believe that such a kind Party Secretary existed. He was so moved that his eyes blurred, he could no longer hold back his tears. "No; no, no," he protested. "I stole, Secretary, you should punish me. Not only are you not punishing me, you are even giving me all this. I can't...."

"You were hungry, so you stole," said Chen Yonggui, taking him by the shoulder. "How do you want me to punish that? Ah? If this were the old society and you stole from the landlord, no begging or pleading would save you from being suspended from a willow tree and beaten stiff with a leather whip. But this is a new society, led by Chairman Mao. Our country's in trouble and our people are hard put, so what kind of argument would I use to justify that I should live and you should die? I just hope one thing: When you guys get back home, I wish you would try to find a way to deal with natural disasters. Find a way to fight back and stay on top!"

The Zanhuang thief left Dazhai reluctantly, holding back his tears and firmly clutching the "relief" money, grain coupons and dry provisions for the road that Chen Yonggui had given him.

It is easy to imagine that Chen Yonggui's "special treatment" of petty thieves left some people and some cadres quite unhappy. The men assigned the duty of guarding the autumn harvest were particularly upset. There they were, straining their eyes in the dead of the night, going through all kinds of trouble to catch the thieves, then Chen Yonggui just lets them go! Not only does he let them walk away, he even gives them money and food! How could Brigade members be expected to go on guarding crops and catching thieves?

When Chen Yonggui heard the complaints uttered behind his back, he knew this was not something he could easily dispel by the usual method of lecturing and rebuking. He realized that many people were not able to comprehend the "lesson" of the thieves' case, and that more patient work lay ahead of him. He called together a few Party members, a few cadres and the men assigned to harvest guard duty, and said:

"In the past, when we fought the war, we used to talk of treating the captured prisoners well. Now we are building our country and I say we should treat petty thieves well. You may not understand it now, but you will in due time. Think about it carefully: Why is it that we never lost our autumn harvest before? How come we keep losing it this year? How come the thieves don't steal from anybody else, just from us? Ah? The reason is very simple. In the past their bellies were not empty. They are this year. Nobody else has any grain, only we do! That being the case, we'd be committing a crime if we didn't save them when we see them dying. You too noticed that the thieves are not the people from our neighboring villages but people who came from elsewhere. Why is that so? The neighboring villages have been eating our grain, the grain we let them borrow from us. Why not let those men from Zanhuang and Heshun eat it too? It's a simple principle: The human heart has the capacity to expand—you show someone a little kindness and they have the capacity to respond. Furthermore, when someone comes knocking on your door, you get an excellent opportunity. For the price of a meal you get the chance to teach them about arduous struggle and perseverance, about ways to surmount their difficulties and raise their production. Isn't that an unexpected gain? When they learn from our experience and produce enough grain on their own, do you think they'll come back to steal even if you invite them to? Hah?"

Cut the cloth to fit the torso, you might say. This brief speech did the trick! The harvest guards went on catching thieves in Dazhai, but once they caught them they gave them food, money and provisions for the trip back home. I've heard that these "petty thieves," once gone, became vigorous propagators of the "spirit of Dazhai." Not long thereafter there didn't seem to be any grain thieves any more. Real-life experience had taught these mountain folk a lesson.

That was, indeed, a period of difficulties for the Chinese people. Unfortunately, the kind of spirit exhibited by Chen Yonggui was very rare.

Reliance on Dazhai's "relief," of course, was of no use to the majority of China's population. Before the spirit of Dazhai could reach and be mastered by China's peasantry, the Communist Party's Central Committee announced its "four slogans" for the adjustment of the national economy. It aimed at easing the difficulties of the transition period: "Adjust! Consolidate! Substantiate! Enhance!" It later issued the so-called "Eight Word Charter of Agriculture," which pointed to water, fertilizer, soil, seed, stand, crop protection, capital construction, and management as the key problems to be solved if a way was to be found to increase grain production under drought conditions.

Dazhai was able to withstand the severe test. When time came to sow the fields in the spring, the top three inches of soil contained practically no moisture at all. By the time the summer heat struck, the corn badly needed water. Yet for days not even a shred of a cloud appeared in the sky above Dazhai. The people felt as though they themselves were on fire.

The people of Dazhai deeply cherished their good name. As the model Party Branch Secretary of Xiyang County, Chen Yonggui took part in the grand celebration on the tenth anniversary of the founding of the People's Republic, adding his fame to the list of participants. The whole country started to watch Dazhai closely. Dazhai could not afford to fail in the face of the drought and, in fact, it did not fail. The grain output per *mu* of land in many places dropped from two to three hundred *jin* (22 to 33 bushels per acre) to just over one hundred, or even only ninety jin (less than ten bushels per acre), but that was not the case in Dazhai. Not only did its output increase, Dazhai even managed to sell some 280,000 *jin* commercially. This brought the village a citation from the leadership at various levels. It also spread its fame throughout Xiyang County, reaching eventually the two models, Knife Handle Gate and White Lamb Ravine. A popular song started circulating among the inhabitants of Xiyang County:

> Hills bloom red,
> Blossom after blossom,
> Red all the way.
>
> People love red,
> They love the model Party Sec
> Chen Yonggui.
>
> Xiyang bore him,
> Dazhai raised him,
> Chen Yonggui, Chen Yonggui!

Many people whispered confidentially that an immortal sage had appeared in Dazhai. In droves they poured into the hamlet, as though on a pilgrimage, seeking knowledge from him. At a place some fifty *li* from Dazhai there was a Party Branch Secretary called Jiao Wanyi who did not believe that Chen Yonggui was quite that divine and decided to go and see for himself. One early morning he set out on the journey.

Along the way, he studied the villages that lined the road. He saw beggars in some, private plots in others. Elsewhere he saw people gathering wild fruit for food. But as soon as he crossed the heights of Meng Mountain and came within sight of Tigerhead's bald summit he experienced something entirely fresh and new. That spring the Old Lord of Heaven had not sent down a single drop of rain. In many villages hardly any sprouts had broken through the ground. Even the few that came up here and there were withering away. But in Dazhai the crops grew lush and green, without a single sign of the drought anywhere. Jiao Wanyi looked and looked, unable to go on.

He spotted a few villagers turning a field with grub hoes. This bewildered him.

"Hey-yah, partners," he called out to them. "It's been so dry we don't even dare use our hoes! How come you guys are turning the soil so deep? Aren't you killing the shoots?"

One of Dazhai Brigade's members answered jokingly: "Aaah, it's something you wouldn't know. It's one of those clever methods devised by our Chen Yonggui! He experimented and figured it out: So long as you don't hurt the taproots, the deeper you dig the more grain you'll get."

The visiting Party Secretary didn't quite get it and, having no time to think about it, shifted the topic to the question of planting.

"Everywhere else there are hardly any sprouts. How come all the shoots in your village came up?"

"Aaah, it's no mystery, you know," came the answer. "Those planting seed in our village are all trained. A pinched seed doesn't sprout, so we don't do that. There are some fields on the slopes where the moisture is low—Chen Yonggui personally plants all of those. We only plant seeds in moist ground, you see! What about you? Is that the way you do it?" Jiao Wanyi became very interested in Dazhai's special planting techniques. He decided to sit down and have a heart-to-heart talk with the Brigade members. In the course of conversation he found out about the origins of Dazhai's "spongy fields." He also discovered how Chen Yonggui carried out "three conservations" by lowering the terraced fields on the uphill, or inner edge, and raising them on the downhill, or outside edge, by building dams and sloping the land so it sloped back from them, by increasing the compost content of the soil, and by raking the fields to a near-perfect, fine surface suitable for seeds. He also learned how Chen Yonggui mastered a mysterious quirk of nature. Seeds did not germinate before the dog days of summer heat if planted deep into deeply turned fields. Once the weather got hot they came out suddenly, grew with increased vigor and produced higher yields, especially if deeply hoed between the rows as the crops developed. Unexpectedly, Chen Yonggui had developed a new trick in the high-yield trade: deep-turning with grub hoes.

When Chen Yonggui first decided to try deep inter-row tillage many people were not convinced, although they did not say so. They reacted pretty much the same way as Jiao Wanyi had at first, asking: "If you hoe that deep, won't you kill the shoots?" Under the pressure of such suspicions, some young fellows, born long after Chen Yonggui, decided to show their somewhat vague dissatisfaction. They formed a long line across the corn rows in Backside Draw and all faced East. The youth in charge yelled "One, two, three." The lads struck the ground in unison with their grub hoes so furiously that they ended up sinking the broad blades a foot or more into ground. Chen Yonggui had called for turning it seven inches deep at the most.

By tilling so deep they added Chen Yonggui to the list of those who became nervous. Could such deep stirring have hurt the sprouts? But the result turned out to be miraculous because of a terrible drought. Every normal year, when storms struck during the hot summer days, the peasants would flood Backside Draw with runoff water. But this year not even a small stream turned up on the surface of the land. When the villagers went into the fields to take a look, they discovered that the uneven surface left by deep tillage had produced myriad little reservoirs that trapped the water. The loose soil where the hoes had struck allowed the water to penetrate. That's how they discovered that the deeper one hoed the ground the more water it was able to store. By fall, they could see the results even more clearly: Wherever they had broken up the ground deeply, the ears of grain were larger and the kernels plumper than in previous years. After the harvest, those who went into the fields to till them said the soil was much easier to break up than before. Chen Yonggui observed it all and, mimicking the clapping beat of stage actors, uttered a phrase he had learned from a popular opera: "Heaven is helping me!"

Add a layer of rich top soil, increase the compost content, make it as granular as possible, and you've got yourself a spongy field! Needless to say, having heard all this, Jiao Wanyi did not feel his trip had been in vain. In fact, he rather felt as though he had indeed met the "immortal sage" of Dazhai! Only, since entering the village he had not once caught the sight of Chen Yonggui himself and was now beginning to feel anxious. He hastily took leave of the villagers, and set out to look for their famous leader.

Jiao climbed onto the shoulder of Tigerhead Mountain, entered Wolf Den Ravine and came out through Back Side Draw. He searched every gully and ridge, but Chen Yonggui was nowhere to be seen. When he came back to the village, he just aimlessly strolled about. Suddenly he caught sight of Chen Yonggui emerging from a toilet near the gate of his yard.

"Ayah, Old Chen! Where have you been hiding?"

Chen Yonggui looked pained as he glanced up and saw Jiao Wanyi. His eyes sank deeply into their sockets. "Damn it! You knew to look for me here! OK. C'mon! Come with me."

As he walked in the direction of his house, he staggered and almost fell to the ground. Jiao Wanyi barely caught him by lunging ahead. He propped him under his arm and led him into his cave home.

"I've been busy planting for a month," Chen said. "Working during the day, holding meetings at night. My body couldn't take it. I caught a cold. I had to come back home."

"Ayah, Old Chen, you are such an achiever!" said Jiao with enthusiasm. "All your sprouts came out evenly, and they are growing well! When it comes to the saying "eight *mu* of land produced one sprout," that's typical of Xiyang right now. But you here, what a difference!"

Jiao Wanyi was considered an "advanced" cadre in Xiyang County, but after he saw Dazhai he started to feel there was such a thing as "Heaven beyond Heaven."

Chen Yonggui lit his pipe and, sighing ever so slightly, said, "That's no merit of mine. Practice makes perfect! I just groped and fumbled until I came up with a way to do it. I just followed Chairman Mao's 'Eight Word Charter,' developed 'the three conservations' and came up with a spongy field. When people said that deep hoeing would kill the sprouts, I just dug deeper and waited to see whether they would live or die. Others still plant open-pollinated Golden Queen corn, but I planted a single cross-hybrid and waited to see whether the yield would be higher or not."

"I saw the spongy fields as soon as I entered the village," said Jiao Wanyi.

"Check it out after a rain," said Chen Yonggui, his spirits perking up. "All you need is to grab a handful. Soil from any other field sticks together when you squeeze it, but soil from a sponge field remains loose and breaks up when released, yet it is still dense and heavy. What could you plant in such a soil but grain? But let me knock it off. I've talked enough!"

Chen Yonggui's words set his visitor's mind whirling. Jiao Wanyi could not help but see Chen Yonggui as a standard-bearer, an example. During this terrible dry year Chen Yonggui had managed an unprecedented achievement, yet he went hungry just like everyone else! So hungry, he had eaten steamed dough made of chaff, and then he had fallen sick. When the Government lowered the grain allotment per capita the year before, he too squeezed his belt a little. As Jiao Wanyi scanned Chen Yonggui's sickly face and observed the tattered straw mat on his brick platform bed, he caught a glimpse of the depth of Chen Yonggui's pioneering spirit. Later he swore he clearly saw the image of an "immortal" standing right in front of his eyes.

Jiao Wanyi has been dead for a long time, yet every time I recall his description of those years everything lights up in my mind and the image of Chen Yonggui that emerges with such lucidity moves me all over again.

In 1962 before Dazhai's fame spread beyond Provincial borders, Chen Yonggui had already laid down two more important stepping stones on the path of his unusual career: One, he had helped the village of Five Family Flat transform itself; two, he had formed a lasting bond of friendship and mutual aid with the village of Gold Gash. Chen Yonggui proved to be someone who was not only concerned about the fate of Dazhai, but who was intimately and strongly linked to the success and failure of the surrounding villages. The County Party Committee advocated that Dazhai link up with Five Family Flat, Gold Rock Slope and Gold Gash in a village union, with Chen Yonggui assuming leadership and becoming the Secretary of a General Party Branch, responsible for unified political leadership of all three neighboring communities, and providing concrete aid in their work. That same year County leaders decided to send Li Xishen, who had been working at the Commune level, back to his village of Five Family Flat on salary as Party Branch Secretary. Chen Yonggui helped him in many ways and Li Xishen was able to implement Dazhai's experience there, with the end result that within just one or two years The Flat changed from relying on State-supplied grain for its upkeep to delivering surplus grain to the State.

The other village, Gold Gash, lay close by under the eastern slopes of Tigerhead Mountain. Chen Yonggui linked up with this village too, and he helped the local Branch Secretary, Zhao Yinquan, develop production. The two men were on friendly terms and Zhao Yinquan respected Chen Yonggui tremendously. Seeing that Chen Yonggui had only one child, a son, Zhao sent his five-year-old daughter to Chen Yonggui's house to be raised by him. Thus the two men became "family." Nevertheless, when Chen Yonggui discovered some problem in Gold Gash he did not exactly mince words with Zao. On one occasion he found out that, after the stone cutters hewed out the big stones for a dam with sledge hammers and wedges, the stonemasons did some fine chiseling to bring out the natural texture of the rock and shape each piece to perfection. Angered by what he considered superfluous shaping and styling, Chen scolded Zhao Yinquan.

"What do you think you're doing here? Decorating a fancy monument or building a solid dam? What was on your mind, permanence or art? Not to mention utility! I don't seem to know you at all, my dear in-law," said Chen Yonggui.

The comment sobered Zhao Yinquan up and persuaded him to abandon his labor-wasting excursion into elegance.

With each step he took, Chen Yonggui seemed more assured and firm.

Chen Yonggui's communitywide achievements, added to the original transformation of the home village, brought him and Dazhai such renown in Shanxi that it overflowed Provincial bounds and spread as far as the national capital, Beijing.

CHAPTER 11

LI SHUNDA AT DAZHAI, CHEN YONGGUI AT WEST GULLY

Tigerhead Mountain is not very high as Taihang peaks go. It is not even the highest peak in Xiyang County. Mengshan and Zhanling Mountains overshadow it. But it holds a commanding position on the flank of the West River Valley and provides a panoramic view of all the country to the West, North and East. Standing at its summit you have the feeling that all China stretches out before you and that if only you stood on tiptoe you could indeed see Beijing's Tiananmen.

Symbolically, of course, with the growth of Dazhai's reputation, Tigerhead Mountain loomed higher and higher until it surpassed the famous Wutai, Shanxi's five-peaked highest, and challenged all the renowned summits of old, Mount Tai and Mount Omei included. It was this burgeoning stature of Tigerhead Mountain and the near-legendary exploits of the tillers on its slopes that caught the attention of that other model worker and labor hero of national renown, the Shanxi peasant, Li Shunda. In 1963 Li Shunda decided to visit Dazhai in person. He brought with him Shen Jilan, the famous woman labor hero, model workers Wu Houli, Zhang Juquan, Wang Denghe and several other

West Gully notables. This was an important opportunity for the two Shanxi peasant leaders to meet again and join forces.

Li Shunda's visit to Dazhai not only honored Chen Yonggui but also Xiyang County and the entire Central Shanxi Region. Consequently, Chen Yonggui and the Xiyang County Party Committee took the matter of the West Gully leader's reception very seriously. They made exhaustive preparations for every aspect of his stay. In the village of Dazhai itself this personal visit by a celebrity of great repute naturally turned into a priority event. All Brigade members gathered at the village gate to greet the visitors and invite them to eat hot thorn date pudding, a local delicacy, followed by a savory feast featuring platters of well-browned fat pork and copious toasts with Shanxi's most potent sorghum liquor.

Dazhai's rebuilt landscape now unfolded in front of Li Shunda's eyes. He inspected Tigerhead Mountain, Wolf Den Ravine, and the Brigade's many rock-lined gullies and loess-covered ridges. Years of hard labor had transformed Old Dazhai, which had once consisted of over 4,700 small strip terraces, into a new Dazhai of 1,700 enlarged terraces and "plains"[1] where men with machines could plow and sow scores of medium-sized fields. Human persistence had transformed a place where one *mu* of yellow loess soil produced just over 100 *jin* of grain into a land of "sponge-soil fields" that reached all the yield targets set by the National Program for Agricultural Development and surpassed those set for the Yellow River basin. Li Shunda and Shen Jilan looked, listened and pondered. They recalled the evaluation of Dazhai issued by Tao Lujia, the Shanxi Provincial Committee's circulated dispatch, and the article in *Shanxi Daily*. The more they deliberated the more they felt there was a "Heaven beyond Heaven," and that Chen Yonggui was most certainly not a run-of-the-mill fellow! During his visit to Tianjin, Chen Yonggui had pledged to create "plains" in his hometown, and now in just a few short years, he had made good his promise. Li Shunda had no

1. What Dazhai people called "plains" were not plains in any usual sense, but simply flat fields on the ridges and in the gullies that were big enough for a tractor to turn around on. They boasted areas sized from a third of an acre or less to four acres and fraction at the upper limit. But these were ideal compared to what the peasants started with so they called them with justified pride "plains." (W.H.H.)

idea that Chen Yonggui was so seriously interested in scientific farming, nor had he anticipated that he'd be able to turn these locss knolls, ridges and gullies into the likeness of fertile fields to the south of the Yangtze River.

"Now that I've seen it, I believe it!" Li Shunda exclaimed emotionally to Shen Jilan. "I have no misgivings about Chen Yonggui. No wonder the Secretary praised him like that!"

The two looked over the thirty-eight inward-arching dams in Wolf Den Ravine and Back Side Draw, and the small leveled fields of Leech Gulch. When they compared the growth of the crops in these previously barren arroyos with the crops in the neighboring villages, they ended up with fulsome praise. They walked away feeling that somehow they had learned more from this experience than they were supposed to or had expected.

From what I've heard, Chen Yonggui was planning to host an informal banquet in honor of the guests when they finished their tour of the mountain. This "banquet" was unusually meager, consisting only of some simple home-style dishes like the anise-seed-flavored boiled pork and sliced sweet potatoes. The kitchen staff placed only three or four prepared dishes on the table, along with a glass of hard sorghum liquor for each guest. But back in those days even a meal like this constituted "high-class" treatment. During the banquet Chen Yonggui personally filled the glasses of each one of his guests and then solemnly proposed a toast.

"First, let's drink in honor of my Master, Li Shunda, who came to Dazhai to inspect and guide us!" Chen said, holding out his glass toward Li.

Li Shunda was just about to empty his glass in response when the gist of Chen Yonggui's toast sank in. Instantly his brow knit into a deep frown.

"I can't drink to that!" he protested. "I came to your village today to study your successes. You've already reached the forefront in Shanxi Province. The Provincial Committee has appealed to us all to learn from you. What's more, you've been to Beijing and met with Chairman Mao! The way things go, with the new superseding the old, it is I who should be calling you Master!"

"You became my Master in 1952," said Chen Yonggui with his glass still raised for his own toast. Smiling warmly, he continued, "Wasn't that when Chairman Mao issued a memorandum about your agricultural cooperative? Don't you remember how I apprenticed myself to you during the train ride to Tianjin? The master-student relationship can never be changed! I propose that we all raise our glasses and drink to Master Li, who came to our doorstep to give us guidance!"

The atmosphere was not such that one party looked down on the other. On the contrary: the two acted as equals, speaking out and listening, getting up and sitting down, passing the baton of mutual admiration back and forth.

"O.K. If Master Chen wants to toast me, so be it. In the past it would have been just a toast, but today it means that the pupil has learned from and outdone his teacher. I'm set on calling you Master Chen!"

"Master Li...."

"Master Chen...."

Amidst the candid laughter and clinking of glasses, the hearts of these two peasant heroes of new China were infused with warm liquor, carrying their spirits forward onto China's high, sloped loess fields.

After the liquor had made the rounds three times the two men were ready to speak their minds most frankly. Li Shunda, for one, having talked about Dazhai's outstanding innovations, brought up its lack of attention to irrigation, forestry and fruit growing. Chen Yonggui said he hoped to get a chance to go to West Gully and see how they developed the forests and the orchards there.

"Master Li, I have a task for you!" Chen added. "It's hard to force an esteemed guest into doing something for us, but everybody in Dazhai would love to hear you speak. I've put aside half a day for that."

"Half a day!" Li Shunda responded in shock, laughing modestly. "Do I really have that much to talk about? Why not ask your villagers to speak?"

"Once you unlock the treasure chest, subjects for conversation will pour out," Chen Yonggui assured him. "We'll talk about your West Gully and about your visit to the Soviet Union. Nobody from Dazhai has yet been abroad, so we want you to open up some horizons. Then we'll feel as though we have all been to the Soviet Union too. You just keep on talking. If half a day is not enough, we'll talk a whole day, or two or three—whatever it takes! When you finish your talking, we'll talk about ourselves and you'll tell us what you think."

And so the Brigade members staged a mass rally under the banner "Dazhai Production Brigade Welcomes Li Shunda on His Generous Visit." Chen Yonggui chaired the rally. Shen Jilan spoke first. Then it was Li Shunda's turn. The spirits of the Brigade members ran high and they kept clapping throughout both speeches. Afterward, several of the visiting model workers took to the podium. They talked to their hearts' content about their impressions of Dazhai and made suggestions about Dazhai's future development. When it came time to adjourn, the guests found it hard to take their leave. Showing the greatest enthusiasm, they repeated their invitations to Chen Yonggui to visit West Gully in the fall.

And so it came about that in the fall, after the weather turned cold, Chen Yonggui eagerly set out on his long-awaited journey to West Gully. The green army truck sent from Pingxun County to pick up his party sped across the yellow-tinged southeast Shanxi countryside, plunged into the narrow canyons that threaded the limestone crags of the Taihang Range, and came out finally on the Shangdang Plateau, that famous highland redoubt of warrior kings of old. Several Dazhai villagers, including Chen Yonggui and Sung Liying, sat in the cab. Chen Yonggui's son, Chen Mingzhu, rode in the back of the truck, under the canopy, along with the other Brigade members from Xiyang, and more West Gully visitors returning home. By the standards of the 1960s, this was the highest-level conveyance that Li Shunda, Shen Jilan, and the Pingxun County Committee could accord their guests. Needless to say, Li Shunda and Shen Jilan could not show anything but the greatest warmth toward compatriots who were visiting from that far away. They were anxious to tap Chen Yonggui's rich experience in agricultural development and listen to his impressions and opinions in order to make West Gully more productive and beautiful.

When the truck came to an abrupt stop in West Gully, Li Shunda saw Chen Mingzhu jump off the back, covered in dust from head to foot. He greeted him apologetically: "The youngsters have had it rough, you might say! Why don't you wash up? Then we'll go and eat."

"What kind of rough time is that?" Chen Yonggui protested. "It's nothing compared to what the youth in West Gully go through every day. Our young ones ought to go right to work to toughen themselves up!"

Li Shunda accompanied Chen Yonggui to the Production Brigade offices for a brief conference, while Shen Jilan assumed the role of hostess by rushing about preparing for the promised meal. She served several hot dishes: stir-fried pork, vermicelli, braised celery, cabbage—dishes considered high-class delicacies in those days, but not before a round of toasts with sorghum liquor warmed stomachs and set heads spinning after the long journey.

Chen Yonggui arrived in West Gully as enthusiastic and as eager to learn from its experience as he had once been while battling nature in Wolf Den Ravine. Li Shunda had told him, during his visit to Dazhai, that Dazhai's work with trees, whether for timber or fruit, lagged far behind. On entering West Gully he feasted his eyes on pine-clad mountain slopes and on fruit-bearing apple trees on reclaimed gully land with branches bent to the ground from the weight of their bounteous offerings. The sight thrilled him. "Why couldn't Dazhai develop an apple orchard like this?" he thought.

During dinner Li Shunda and Shen Jilan inquired about an enormous flood that had just washed out Dazhai, and Chen Yonggui elaborated on its course. Li Shunda then asked whether there was any way they could help.

"No, no, no," said Chen with a smile. "We don't need anything from you. We've had offers of relief money, material and food from the Central Government. We definitely don't need anything in addition to that. But if you want to help us, please share with us your experiences in surmounting hardship."

Deeply moved by his attitude, Li Shunda proposed another toast, expressing the hope that Dazhai would not again be victimized by disastrous floods for a hundred years to come. "Clink, clink," the liquor glasses sounded off each other, adding to the resolve of all present from Dazhai to tackle the present calamity head on.

The moment he got off the truck on returning to Dazhai Chen Yonggui went right to the fields to examine the flood repairs then under way. Having determined that all was well on that front he seized the opportunity to call an evening meeting to inform the Brigade members about the trip to West Gully. With his opening remarks he challenged whatever complacency they might have had about past victories.

"Here we are in Dazhai, always thinking how well we are doing," Chen Yonggui said and laughed. "But let me tell you, we are far behind those folks over there! Ayaaah! There is Heaven beyond Heaven! Over there, in Xigou, you can just lie down on the ground with your mouth open and bite into an apple that's still on an apple tree!"

Everyone, and especially his pipe-smoking colleagues, the village cadres, broke into unrestrained laughter. But Chen Yonggui adopted a very serious expression as he continued, "Don't you go laughing! I'm telling you, those folks over there, they pruned those apple trees so well. They kept everything low. The fruit grows so densely that its weight makes the branches almost trail on the ground. Of course you could take a bite out of an apple if you lay down under an apple tree!"

Dazhai learned something important from West Gully: how to develop agriculture, forestry and fruit growing simultaneously, thereby diversifying the village economy. It was indeed after Chen Yonggui's trip to West Gully that groves of apple trees started emerging on the Kang Family Slope of Tower Knoll. The trees produce large fruit, which to this very day remains the most valuable product of Dazhai.

That period was, it must be said, the honeymoon of the two peasant heroes of Shanxi Province. If it weren't for the ten years of turmoil during the Cultural Revolution, the pair might have continued to learn from each other's merits and faults, maintaining and deepening their growing warm friendship. But things don't always happen as one wishes. After that last meeting both men ran into obstacles generated by all-pervading factionalism that proved insurmountable and lasted until the end of their lives.

CHAPTER—12

SEVEN DAYS, SEVEN NIGHTS, THE RAIN KEPT ON FALLING

The small hamlet under Tigerhead Mountain was not destined to rival Li Shunda's West Gully without further trials and tribulations. Even Chen Yonggui was caught by surprise when Dazhai, with its ever-growing fame, suffered a devastating blow.

When the disaster struck, Chen Yonggui didn't know whether to cry or laugh.

"Are the Heavens testing us or are they out to destroy us?" he asked in confusion as fate sent them all crashing through the Gates of Hell.

Nevertheless, in the aftermath, he and Dazhai came through with flying colors.

The event in question was the great flood of September 1963—the kind of flood that comes only once in a hundred years.

Autumn crops grew vigorously that summer, painting the slopes of Dazhai's many gullies and ridges a deep green. Field management also excelled. The crops looked better than ever before. In keeping with custom, the villagers hung up their hoes without a single worry on their minds and, to dispel the fatigue from their back-breaking labor, went to town for the Temple Fair. Out of the blue, drenching rains of a magnitude no one remembered seeing before poured down, numbing everyone with fear. More rain fell in the following week than usually fell in the course of a year. Torrents rolled down Tigerhead Mountain's seven ravines with a roar. Wherever the flood water reached earth, mountains flowed, roads crumbled, dams collapsed, topsoil ran, and crops toppled—in a word, ten years of Dazhai's land reclamation work dissolved with one thunder clap. About 139 *mu* (23 acres) of terraced fields washed out; cave-ins and mud slides buried 41 *mu* (7 acres) of crops under a deep layer of mud: 500 *mu* (83 acres) of corn went down, some stalks at rakish angles, some flat on the ground. No fewer than 190 of the village's 270 cave dwellings caved in from the rain, while 63 more threatened to collapse at any moment; only a dozen or so remained fit for habitation. The storm left 78 of Dazhai's 80 households homeless. Overnight Dazhai had turned into a disaster area. For seven days and seven nights the rain kept on falling. For seven days and seven nights people wrung their hands in worry and despair.

When the rain started Chen Yonggui was attending Xiyang County's People's Congress meeting. He was unable to return to Dazhai. At this critical moment, with their leader absent, the Dazhai Party Branch organized an emergency squad to deal with the crisis. Jia Chengrang, Jia Jincai, Liang Bianliang and Zhao Dahe led some thirty-odd party members, Communist Youth League members, and core members of the people's militia to the worst-hit areas. There they risked their lives rescuing people, livestock, collective and private grain reserves, and other property of the Brigade and its members from collapsing cave dwellings, stock pens and storehouses.

At the County People's Congress, Chen Yonggui, an alternate member of the County Party Committee, raised the question of the natural disaster that had struck the whole County and led the Congress to adopt emergency measures. Despite the active role he played in County affairs, Chen's main interest was Dazhai. With such big rains, such swollen streams and rivers, what was happening with homes, fields and people back there? Unable to go back, due to the flooding, he managed to establish a telephone connection with Jia Chengrang. Jia's report came as a big shock.

"The situation is serious. Homes have caved in. The topsoil has washed away from many fields."

"Is anybody injured?" inquired Chen Yonggui.

"We acted fast. No one is injured."

"No matter what you do, don't let anybody suffer bodily harm," instructed Chen Yonggui. "One more thing: Have you taken care of the families of the revolutionary martyrs and others entitled to special protection?"

"Everything's taken care of. The emergency squad is on patrol day and night. The moment they see danger, they rush to the rescue. There is only one problem," Jia Chengrang went on to explain. "Some families simply refused to move from their homes."

"Better force them to move!" shouted Chen Yonggui, his voice tight with tension. "You must ensure...."

At this point Jia Chengrang could no longer hear him talking at the other end of the line. As the onrushing flood waters snapped electric poles the telephone connection went dead.

Chen Yonggui felt like an ant frying in hot oil. He figuratively spun round and round in the wok, unable to get out—no telephone, no roads across the surging river, no way to get home.

On the eighth day the rain stopped. The County meeting adjourned. Burning with impatience, Chen Yonggui rushed homeward, but surging billows completely submerged the valley road, leaving no way to get across. The swollen Songxi River, which now blocked all access to Dazhai from the County seat, was usually just a dry flood plain strewn with rocks. Now, after the big rain, it was more than a hundred yards wide. Chen Yonggui tried several times, but he couldn't make it across. He recalled that there was a floodgate upstream, near Gao Family Ridge, where the river bed was wider and the water less deep. There, whenever high water came down during the rainy season, several rock and earth barriers divided the flow into several channels. The water in each channel flowed slowly through the shallows. "Maybe I can cross there," Chen Yonggui thought, as he headed for Gao Family Ridge. But he didn't find what he expected. Flood water, having completely submerged the barriers, was pouring in great waves over the entire area. Chen Yonggui was so anxious to cross the river that he completely disregarded what he saw. He rolled up his trousers, jumped into the torrent, and headed for the other side, relying on his memory to find the surest footing.

There were all kinds of things Chen Yonggui could do including cooking, peddling steamed buns and transplanting millet, but swimming was not one of them. Crossing the river given the circumstances was, for him, a great risk. He made his way across the first branch-channel, then the second, but when he came to the third, which was the age-old river's main course, the water gradually deepened. He found himself sinking to his chest, then to his neck. Suddenly, he was unable to move ahead, but neither could he turn back.

At this very moment, fate took Chen Yonggui by the neck, literally. Just as his life fell into mortal danger, a hand grabbed him from behind. He had only enough time to twist his head and catch a glimpse of an unfamiliar young man.

"Aren't you Old Chen from Dazhai?" the youth asked.

"That's right," said Chen Yonggui. "Who are you?"

His rescuer identified himself as a Gao from the Gao Family Ridge Production Brigade—a community that knew Chen Yonggui well. He urged Chen Yonggui not to cross, but Chen insisted on trying one more time. In the end, several young men from Gao Family Ridge joined the first. They jumped into the river, formed a human chain, and passed Chen Yonggui across from hand to hand, propping him under his arms and holding him up from behind in the process. It was an unforgettable transition in Chen Yonggui's life.

"When Heaven failed, men delivered!"

Once Chen Yonggui had crossed the river, the road took him through Five Family Flat. One glance told him that even the mountains were flowing. "This is the end!" he thought. But that grim notion lasted only a moment. Chen Yonggui knew that if he revealed such desperation to the people in Dazhai, he would never again be able to get anything done there. He had to show daring and bold vision if he wanted to act as the steward of his community.

When he appeared in Dazhai, his head still wrapped in a white hand towel and the black pants of his soaked cloth outfit rolled high above his knees, the cadres couldn't bring themselves to ask him how he had crossed the river. Their own predicament dominated their thoughts. A few of the tougher ones among them, usually so unshakable, felt a slight tingling in their noses and almost broke into tears.

"Just look at the mess we're in!" one of them exclaimed in agony. "We ended up with a rock-strewn flood plain instead of our own rich loess fields!"

The occasion produced a peculiar reaction in Chen Yonggui. It worried him to the marrow, but outwardly he displayed high spirits. He acted as though he knew exactly what should be done.

"How are the people?" he asked Jia Chengrang.

"All accounted for," Jia Chengrang replied.

"The livestock?"

"All accounted for."

"The grain?"

"We salvaged most of it."

Knowing that the people, animals and grain were all safe gave Chen Yonggui a reason to stand up straight and tall.

"So long as Blue Mountain stands, we'll never be out of firewood!" he exclaimed proudly, repeating an old saying.

The good news emboldened Chen Yonggui to try to ease the worries of the cadres by distracting them with a scolding. He shocked them by saying they weren't showing enough backbone. The problems presented by the current flood were relatively trivial and not worth losing sleep over. While he spoke, he scanned the situation from the corner of his eye and contemplated the rescue measures that should be taken. Seeing nothing that couldn't be put under control, his first move was to call the Brigade members to a meeting. He, Jia Chengrang, Liang Bianliang and Jia Laiheng headed for the still-standing village club room, to which the now homeless villagers had all been evacuated.

The club room, crowded with people of all ages and filled with thick smoke, exploded as Chen Yonggui stepped into the room. It was as though someone had taken the lid off a hot wok. People jumped from their stacked bedrolls and surrounded their leader from all sides, venting their discontent on his toweled head.

"You left home for eight days! While you were gone, the Heavens collapsed on Dazhai," complained some older men as they tugged at Chen Yonggui's torso and grabbed him by the hand.

"The water stripped our soil away! Our cave homes collapsed! How are we to live from now on?" asked one old woman, crying. "You better think of something!"

As Dazhai's main pillar, Chen Yonggui could not afford to express his own worries. He met everybody else's with a smile on his face. Offended, Li Xiqing spoke words that, for him, were quite out of character.

"Jinxiao," he said, "Dazhai is reeling under a major disaster. Don't you care?"

Life is full of unexpected surprises. Chen Yonggui surmised that the torrent outside had swept everybody's feelings into a common maelstrom of panic and that a word of commiseration might cause them all to fall apart. Because of this insight he decided to confront the tragedy as though it were a comedy, or at least light opera. Chen Yonggui, feigning ease of mind, kept smiling. "Xiqing," he said in response to the younger man's challenge, "this is quite a disaster, but I still intend to convince you that it is a happy occasion!"

Li Xiqing was usually able to follow Chen Yonggui's thought processes without a question, but he certainly could not comprehend the meaning of this "happy occasion." So he mumbled incoherently.

"Our homes have collapsed," he protested, "our terraces have caved in, the topsoil has washed away—there are no more tears left in us from all the grief. What's this 'happy occasion' talk all about?"

This is the point at which Chen Yonggui exhibited the strength of a true hero, self-confident that he was doing the right thing.

"I mean it when I call this a happy occasion," he announced loudly for all Brigade members to hear. "Don't you recognize your good fortune? Number one: despite the enormous disaster, not a single person died! Isn't that fortunate? Number two: despite the enormous disaster, we didn't lose any of our animals. Isn't that fortunate? Number three: despite the enormous disaster we managed to salvage most of our grain. We won't go hungry. Isn't that something to celebrate? The flood washed the soil off some fields. We'll fix them again! Homes caved in. We'll build them anew! Old Dazhai is gone but the New Dazhai is waiting to be born! Isn't that something to celebrate? Isn't this a happy occasion?"

These words finally dispelled Li Xiqing's worries. Biting hard on his pipe, he nodded his approval.

"It's true, isn't it? So long as the people are alive and well, we'll break even," he admitted. "That we're alive and still here today is truly a happy occasion!"

Today's readers may not have much sympathy with such a "happy occasion" as "all being alive." The people of Dazhai were without homes, without some of yesterday's best land, without the half-standing corn or the many acres of crops that now lay flat on the ground buried in mud. But this is exactly the way things happened back then in Dazhai. Somehow Chen Yonggui got away with staging that "happy occasion" charade. It boosted the morale of the rank-and-file and enabled them to face up to reality with greater courage. Words are the key to people's hearts and minds, so it is really up to the leader to say the right things. The outcome depends on how wisely he or she chooses them. As soon as Chen Yonggui shook up Li Xiqing's thought and straightened out his head, the latter's spirits recovered.

"Say, Jinxiao," he asked, looking Chen Yonggui full in the face, "what should we be doing now?"

"Take it easy," said Chen Yonggui. "When the time comes, you'll get your share of doing."

He wasn't ready to lay out the work plan just yet. First he had to visit the Brigade members who hadn't yet moved in spite of the danger to their caves. It was only at this point that he found out that the one person who refused flat out to move was none other than a man from his own clan, one Chen Yongbao. The reason for his obstinacy: His wife was about to give birth.

"Did he move, yet? Where is his wife now?" Chen Yonggui asked.

When he was told they had not been able to find an adequate place for the wife's confinement, he decided to vacate his own home, where he arranged special care for her.

"Get some decent grain for her from the Brigade stores," he instructed. "Start the diesel engine and grind some white flour for her. Let's make her confinement as comfortable as possible."

Only after settling this matter did he attend to other business, making plans for each and every thing that needed doing.

Once he got village affairs under control, Chen Yonggui went up the mountain to "investigate." It didn't take prolonged "investigation" to find out that most of the terraced fields built on the steep slopes had been badly damaged, with rock and soil torn away leaving scores of deep trenches. Parts of the remaining terrace walls had collapsed, so many that he could hardly bear to look. He turned around and made a rough estimate. There would be some 180 *mu* of fields without any crop that year. Not only that, it would be hard to plant those the following year, too. In addition, some six to seven hundred *mu* of crops had either fallen flat or were tilting dangerously. Mud had completely buried many *mu* of the fallen stalks. He walked into a corn field and, squatting down, carefully righted a lodged corn plant. The plant just swung and swayed, unable to stand erect. Chen Yonggui used his foot to collect some dirt and pile it up around the roots of the plant. He then stepped on the pile lightly, tamping it down. The plant stood up! He picked up another fallen plant and stood it up.

After Chen Yonggui looked at the crops, checked out the rubble of the cave homes, and estimated the village's available labor force, he made an important decision. They would take care of the slopes first, then worry about housing. In Chinese this rhymed: *xian shou po, hou shou wo* (first fix up the slopes, then repair the dwellings). He arranged for people to work on the cropland during the day; then on their homes at night. Chen Yonggui divided the entire village into three squads. He assigned the first to prop up the fallen crops, repair fields and prepare vacant land for sowing a catch crop of oats. This squad would comprise 60 percent of the entire labor force. He assigned the second to cut weeds and brush, like the ubiquitous artemisia, and make compost from it. This would provide the basis for the agricultural output of the following year. The second squad would comprise 20 percent of the labor force. He assigned the remaining 20 percent of the labor force to cut stone, bake bricks and burn lime for the repair and construction of new homes.

Faced with the disaster that had struck Dazhai, Chen Yonggui used his old recipe: Hard Work! More Work! Work as Long as it Takes! He didn't give much thought to other aspects of the relief effort—he didn't care to think about them at all. But, just as he was about to climb the mountain to inspect how the work on propping up crops was coming along, a telephone call summoned him back to the Production Brigade offices. When he picked up the receiver, he heard the voice of Dazhai Commune's Party Committee Secretary, Bu Hongyi. Bu informed him that Dazhai Commune had decided to hand over 6,000 *yuan* in relief funds to Dazhai Brigade, and Chen Yonggui should go right away to the Commune headquarters to sign for and pick up the money. The money was part of a fund that the Central Government had allocated for the entire disaster-stricken area.

Chen Yonggui winced at the news. After the disaster, group after group of solicitous politicians had visited Dazhai, and numerous letters expressing sympathy had poured in. Visitors and letters alike all asked for details of Dazhai's difficulties and offered help. One letter even included eighty *yuan* in cash for medical costs. Chen Yonggui had thanked them all, but rejected their help. In regard to the medical contribution of eighty *yuan*, Chen made clear that no one in Dazhai had suffered even a cut, so the Brigade didn't need any medical funds. His reply read: "We thank the higher authorities for their concern, but the flood caused no injuries in Dazhai. Give the sum marked for medical treatment to other villages."

In regard to Bu Hongyi's big 6,000-*yuan* relief fund, Chen Yonggui responded as follows: "Say, Old Bu, why not put that money temporarily into a bank account? I have to consult the others to see whether we want it or not."

As soon as he put down the receiver, Chen Yonggui began mulling over the whole question of aid and relief. His thoughts, according to his own recollection, developed in the following fashion: "We've received group after group of well-wishers and sympathizers, and letter after letter expressing solicitude—all on account of the disaster. Aren't those sentiments the best possible kind of support? If we take material goods and money, once we use them up, we'll have nothing left. But the moral strength accumulated from people of the entire country—that's something we can never use up. The relief fund they are offering us is substantial, but we'll be better off if we don't take it. Still, I had better discuss this issue with the local Party Branch and with all the members of our Brigade."

Chen Yonggui presented the situation to the local Party Branch and to a mass meeting of the Brigade at two separate meetings. He also explained his position, one-on-one, to numerous skeptics. At first some people advocated accepting the relief fund, but after Chen Yonggui made his stand clear they all fell silent. Then Li Xiqing, who had once been a poor peasant, spoke up.

"When disasters struck in the old society," he reminded everyone, "even if Dazhai's entire population died, nobody would have bothered to inquire about it. This time, expressions of sympathy and support have poured in from as high up as the Party Central Committee and Chairman Mao himself, and as low as County and Commune leaders—offering relief to boot. It's like past Hell and current Heaven! But while our entire country is facing difficulties, we here are able to handle the disaster. We don't need the money the Commune is prepared to give us. Let other places use it!"

His reasoning opened the eyes of many villagers. They all began to look on Chen Yonggui as a man of foresight. However, I understand that at that point there was still one man, a horse-cart driver, who insisted that they take the money.

"The higher authorities gave it to us—we didn't ask for it," he argued.

But in the end it was Jia Jincai's counter-argument that prevailed. "Disaster struck our village, for sure," Jia countered, "but we can still get a *yuan* in shared income for a day of labor. There are places where people only get one tenth of that. If you want to send relief, send it to those people over there!"

Chen Yonggui had already used this very same argument several days earlier, when he rejected a shipment of relief supplies. On that day, a loaded horse-cart had pulled into Dazhai. "Aha! There they come!" exclaimed Chen Yonggui in dismay when he saw it.

But instead of welcoming the goods he said to the drivers, "Well, since you are here already, we better invite you to eat something." Whereupon he personally accompanied the drivers to lunch at the Brigade's small mess hall without a word about welcoming the goods they brought.

"You asked us to accept," Chen Yonggui told them after the meal, "and we asked you to lunch. You ate. Your assignment has been completed! Insofar as the things you brought are concerned, take them back. The disaster that struck us here in Dazhai was serious but, serious as it was, nobody died. Is that fortunate or not, what do you say? When we suffered a severe drought during the ninth year of the Republic [1920], dozens of people died, dozens of others left home, while still others were sold for pitiful amounts of cash or grain. It's different now. Our production team still has 10,000 *yuan* saved. Look at some other places! No savings, and low workday earnings! Take Meng Mountain, for example! They are a Production Brigade in Dazhai Commune, too, but their workday is worth only twenty cents. Do you want to help those who work for a dollar, or those who work for twenty cents? That's why we don't want the stuff. You can be sure that we won't be short of anything this year, be it grain for sale to the State, our own consumption, or our accumulated reserve!"

Chen Yonggui managed to send the drivers with their horse-cart away. But, they came right back again. Chen Yonggui sent them off in the same way for the second time. He had two preoccupations: how to execute the "three rejections" (of State relief funds, relief grain and relief goods), and how to prevent the "three shortages" (of grain for sale to the State, grain for personal consumption and grain for Dazhai's reserve).

Dazhai Commune Party Committee Secretary, Bu Hongyi, was quite worried about possible shortages. He sought out Chen Yonggui to discuss that topic thoroughly. He was afraid that no household in Dazhai would be able to meet the State purchase quotas, and he offered to lower them.

"Don't lower them," Chen Yonggui insisted. I guarantee we'll meet them. Moreover, we'll have enough grain to eat and to store, too. Just relax, will you!"

Chen Yonggui was very clear-minded as he spoke, very aware that the success of his pledge depended mainly on whether he would be able to raise and sustain the morale of Dazhai's Party members and rank-and-file. He could put forth the slogans, but that didn't mean that all Party members and the people in general would understand the situation as he did.

Chen Yonggui welcomed the expression of different opinions as an excellent opportunity to educate people and raise their consciousness. In order to clarify the significance of self-reliance, he held a series of discussion sessions seven days in a row, and he spent seven nights reflecting on the topic. On the last night he lay sleepless on the brick-bed *kang*, turning back and forth like a pancake in a hot pan. Finally he came up with a list of ten benefits of self-reliance. As he reviewed them over and over again, he felt quite satisfied. Then he began to fear he might forget them. He thought of asking somebody to write them down.

"If I have them recorded on paper," he thought, "there's no way I can forget them, is there?"

Chen Yonggui suddenly remembered the two cadres in the hamlet sent down from the County for practical experience—Li Jinrong and Kong Qingzhong. He put on his clothes and went to knock on the comrades' door. They had spent a busy day and were sound asleep. Chen Yonggui had a hard time waking them. That accomplished, he recited his ten benefits, one by one, while the two literate cadres wrote them down. When they were sure the ten points were well in order, they laid them out on the office table. It was as if a giant rock had fallen from Chen Yonggui's shoulders. He could finally go to sleep—even if it meant forgetting.

The ten benefits, according to Chen Yonggui, were:

One: Doing whatever you can on your own, without depending on the State, helps the State and all socialist construction everywhere. This benefits the whole nation.

Two: Overcoming difficulties through self-reliance, you demonstrate the great strength of collectivization, and help everybody appreciate the collective. This benefits the collective community, the Commune.

Three: Self-reliance directly challenges individuals to work hard for the prosperity of the country and stimulates them to overcome all difficulties by applying themselves. This benefits every individual in the Commune.

Four: Defeating a natural disaster through self-reliance proves that the collective economy is sound and stable This benefits the growth of working people's aspirations, while wiping out the arrogance of class enemies.

Five: Self-reliance helps train cadres. It develops their reasoning power and problem-solving capacity through hands-on education and practical training, learning by doing. This helps the cadres to mature.

Six: Defeating disaster through self-reliance will encourage our brother Production Brigades to surmount their own difficulties through self-reliance. This will benefit the revolutionary drive to learn, think and act progressively.

Seven: Surmounting difficulties through self-reliance can foster the Commune members' courage to tackle their problems head-on, thus raising their ability to fight natural disasters. This will benefit their future struggle against natural disasters and enable them to reap even better harvests.

Eight: Self-reliance will benefit the consolidation of People's Communes. Dazhai Commune has twenty-three Production Brigades in all. They all suffered from the flood this year. Many of them have far fewer resources than the Dazhai Brigade. Their troubles are much worse. If Dazhai Brigade doesn't take State money or grain, there will be more for those Production Brigades that are facing much more severe difficulties. This will demonstrate the advantage of People's Communes in general, and enhance unity within Dazhai Commune in particular, thus stimulating increased production throughout the Commune.

Nine: Self-reliance will benefit the training of successors for the revolutionary cause. Today's youngsters have all grown up "eating honey." They lack real tempering. If we ask for help whenever we run into difficulties, these youngsters will do the same when they grow up. If we guide them to depend on themselves to solve problems we will help them toughen themselves and turn themselves into dependable successors who can advance the cause of proletarian revolution.

Ten: Self-reliance will benefit the continued progress of Dazhai Production Brigade. It will ensure that Dazhai continues to follow Chairman Mao's revolutionary road.

Chen Yonggui pulled these ten points together under the name "Ten Chief Benefits of Self-Reliance." He first took them to the Party

Branch Committee for discussion. The Committee members all felt that Old Chen had made an excellent summary, that his outlook was lofty and his vision farsighted. They approved all points smoothly. Chen Yonggui then took them for discussion to the general meeting of Production Brigade members.

The large club room quickly filled with smoke and a hubbub of voices. A thick stack of letters of sympathy and support lay piled on the table. Chen Yonggui asked the bookkeeper to read them out, one by one. They came from all over the country.

After the bookkeeper finished his reading, Chen Yonggui started to speak. As might be expected, he did not neglect talking about past events like the sale of millet straw at cost price and the fat ox at salvage rates. But the main point of his speech was how, in the face of the current disaster, to achieve his "three rejections" while not suffering from "three shortages" Chen Yonggui wamted to know if his constituency thought it appropriate or not to reject the 6,000 *yuan* relief fund and the delivered supplies. In the end he presented his "Ten Benefits of Self-Reliance," one by one. Chen Yonggui never learned how to write, but he was literate enough to read the draft in public. He could pretty much read anything, so long as the writing was clear. As he read that day, everybody recognized his "Dazhai style" and the membership started opening up to his ideas.

This is how the "three rejections" took root in the hearts of Dazhai's people.

But, just before the meeting ended, Li Xiqing asked the following question: "We don't want this, we don't want that.... Tell me, though, are we going to rebuild our homes or not? You need money to build a home, you know? Our collective has 10,000 *yuan* saved, but who's gonna foot the bill for the rest?"

"You will!" everybody replied jokingly.

That's exactly what Li Xiqing wanted to hear, and he continued: "I'm prepared to do it, but I only have 800 *yuan*. That won't be enough. We have eighty households in Dazhai; over seventy of them have savings. Why don't we all lend our savings to the Production Brigade?"

People erupted in simultaneous babble.

"Li Xiqing hates to waste his money even on a pair of chopsticks," somebody said. "If he is going to dig up his savings for the construction of cave dwellings, we should do it too!"

The time had come to test Chen Yonggui's leadership skills. If he provided good leadership, everyone would follow; if his leadership faltered, they would all be in trouble. Chen Yonggui, of course, was expert at using an opportunity to advance the cause he favored. All he needed to do was praise Li Xiqing and Zhao Xiaohe, who were advocating that they all contribute money. It was like pouring oil into the fire! That evening the Brigade members crowded in to sign up their contributions of 300, even 500 *yuan*. The smallest contribution was 20 *yuan*. Chen Yonggui could now completely relax about the investment needed for the construction of the New Dazhai.

Once Chen Yonggui accomplished this task, he put down the orderly draft of his "Ten Benefits of Self-Reliance" on the office table. On the following day some well-wishers from the provincial level came to visit Dazhai. With them came several journalists. Seeing the draft, one of the provincial leaders inquired about it. Having heard Chen Yonggui's explanation, the leader handed the draft to one of the journalists, noting its high value as the kind of testimony most needed at that time. The journalist made due note of the comment. A few days later the *Shanxi Daily* published the draft. The *People's Daily* picked it up soon thereafter. Unexpectedly, the news item quickly gained attention country-wide.

Chen Yonggui's "Ten Benefits" rekindled Dazhai villagers' enthusiasm to resume production and rebuild their homes. The old and the young, men and women, all came out to join the battle for propping up flattened crops. The women used their hands to dig out young plants drowned in mud and pressed under rocks. Song Liying's "Women's Team" and Guo Fenglian's "Iron Girls" worked at the foot of the mountain, while Chen Yonggui's and Liang Bianliang's men's teams worked on the higher slopes, each engaging the other in a contest. Not only were they trying to keep up with each other; they were trying to surpass each other! The "Iron Girls" couldn't accept falling behind the men, if even for a day. They immediately rushed to overtake them. This was the time when they gained everybody's respect and became famous outside Xiyang.

After a day in the fields salvaging crops, Dazhai's villagers spent their evenings repairing their homes. At the time the Brigade members hotly debated this order of priorities. It was actually one of the Jia family, so they say, not Chen Yonggui, who first raised the idea. "We'll work in the fields during the day," this Jia said while the storm was still raging. "When night falls, we'll light up the gas lamps and go to level the ground for the foundations of our new homes, move bricks, and carry the stone."

Chen Yonggui readily adopted the suggestion. There was no way that he would want to back away from such an effective measure. As a result, even before dawn Dazhai's peasants rolled up their sleeves and went to work barefoot in the fields propping up young plants. When they came back from work after dark they gathered at locations designated for foundations. There they dug trenches and placed rocks according to blueprints already drafted. They put in three hours every evening toward the construction of the New Dazhai! After that, Chen Yonggui was still wont to meet with the stonemasons and carpenters to draft further plans and inspect the quality of engineering. During this period the sound of Jia Jincai's hammer shook the sky and the earth, while its handle got soaked in blood! Zhao Xiaohe's horse-cart trundled into many a villager's heart! Zhao Xiaohe's final martyrdom became the glorified model for an entire Dazhai generation!

Owing to all that hard work and sacrifice, yet another miracle occurred. In the year of the big flood Dazhai's production did not drop! Not only that—the per *mu* yield surpassed 800 *jin*![1] In the language of the day, Dazhai had accomplished the feat of "crossing Yangtze River."

1. Eight hundred jin per mu was the crop production goal set by the State Council for farmers south of the Yangtze River. For North China, north of the Yellow River, the goal was 400, and for the farmland between the two great rivers the goal was 600. (W.H.H.)

CHAPTER 13

A NATIVE RETURNS

If China was to extricate itself from the difficult predicament it found itself in at that time, its people had to develop a spirit of working together for the prosperity of the country as a whole. The experience of Dazhai was immediately put to use. It caught the attention of the higher authorities, and the media played it up for its propaganda value. History has not forgotten the journalists who first opened the window on Dazhai, as they were the ones who first introduced its "fresh flower" to the world. Two Xinhua Agency reporters, Song Shayin and Fan Yinghuai, published a long dispatch on February 24, 1964, in *People's Daily* entitled "The Dazhai Road" accompanied by an editorial entitled "A Fine Example of How to Build Up Mountainous Areas Through Revolutionary Spirit." Zhang Liquan and Hao Zhanao published a monograph entitled *Dazhai's Spirit, Dazhai's People* with the Shanxi People's Press, dedicating a lot of space to Chen Yonggui's militant career.

Among those who visited Dazhai to give press coverage was also Xinhua Agency's Feng Dongshu. The *Shanxi Daily* truly took pains back then to spread the spirit of Dazhai. On October 19, 1964, it carried an article on the front page under the title "The People of Dazhai Spare No Effort to Save a Desperate Situation: In Terms of Grain Output They Cross Yangtze River." The subtitle read "Dare to Fight, Dare to Win: Bumper Harvest Follows the Great Disaster." In the introduction, the article said:

> The heroic people of Dazhai have raised high the red flag of Mao Zedong's thought, while adhering to the principle of self-reliance. After a year of hard work without respite they have managed to defeat last year's great flood, a flood the scope of which has not been seen in a hundred years, and to obtain a bumper harvest. Their grain output has met the target set for the region to the south of Yangtze River by the National Program for Agricultural Development. The average per-mu-yield of the entire Production Brigade reached 826 jin (97 bushels per acre), which is the highest yield in its history. Total yield was over 620,000 jin (340 metric tons)—an increase of 60,000 jin (30 metric tons) over the previous year. Dazhai made 300,000 jin (150 metric tons) available for State purchase, which is 60,000 jin (30 metric tons) above the State-set target, and is the largest amount of grain ever sold to the State by the village. In addition, 100,000 jin (50 metric tons) were added to the collective reserve, while each Brigade member received an average of 460 jin (506 pounds) of grain for personal consumption.

The rest of the report contained the following figures: "Before the end of this year's spring sowing season Dazhai reclaimed 130 *mu* (22 acres)of its flood-devastated land and revived 500 *mu* of field-damaged crops. By the end of the year 62 old cave dwellings had been repaired and many new homes built: 72 tile-roofed brick houses and 36 cut-stone-lined cave dwellings. The villagers did several years' work in just one year." The article went on to say that some 80,000 people had already visited Dazhai to marvel at the results.

The paper published a relatively large collective picture of Dazhai's residents at the construction site at the bottom of the front page. Chen Yonggui stood in the center; the other Brigade members gathered on either side in two contingents, holding tools and smiling broadly.

One cannot separate Dazhai's and Chen Yonggui's amazing achievements from the propaganda unleashed in the media and, above all, one must not forget the support of many leaders on all levels. There is no way that Dazhai's home province, Shanxi, would easily discard the model that it discovered, reared, and established. Provincial Party Committee Secretary Tao Lujia, Vice-Secretary Wang Qian, and Governor Wei Heng were reluctant to give up on Dazhai and they meticulously watched every step of Chen Yonggui's work. Tao Lujia wracked his brain to find a way to popularize Dazhai's experience. After an extensive exchange of views with members of the Standing Committee, he summarized Dazhai's experience into "One Red Thread" and "Five Key Points." The Red Thread was: Guiding people's thinking and actions with Mao Zedong thought. The Five Key Points were: socialist and Communist lofty ideals; drawing of a clear line between what to love and what to hate, with a firm, wholehearted pro-party stand; strong adherence to self-reliance and joint effort for the good of the country; the heroic spirit of daring to disregard difficulties and remake nature; the noble style of cherishing the country and taking pleasure in helping others. Once newspapers and documents disseminated this ingenious summary it immediately became Shanxi agriculture's "symphony for the 1960s."

In addition to all of the above, another important factor in Dazhai's rise to fame and Chen Yonggui's ascent up the administrative ladder was an intervention by a high-level Central Government cadre who was a native of Xiyang County. Dazhai's social record still contains the true history of this event.

Not long after the big flood, one of the Xiyang County Party Committee Vice-Secretaries, Zhao Mancang, who was the head of the Organizational Department, held a reception for a high-level visitor at the County Guest House. The visitor was Li Yiqing, the head of the Secretariat of the Central Committee's Bureau for South-Central Regional Affairs. Li Yiqing was the first man from Xiyang County ever to join the Communist Party. He became a member during the Anti-Japanese War in the early forties. His return visit to Dazhai came in November, 1963.

Prior to the visit, Li Yiqing attended the meeting of the National Planning Commission in Beijing. Although this was already well past the Plan's three-year transitional period, the economic base of the South-Central Region was still just as weak as that of the entire country. The South-Central Regional Committee Secretary at the time, Tao Zhu, planned to ask for money from the Central Government in order to solve his region's problems, but he didn't think it was appropriate that he should say so directly. He used the opportunity provided by Li Yiqing's trip to Beijing to attend the Planning Commission's meeting to have the latter bring it up with the central authorities. After Li Yiqing made the request, Premier Zhou Enlai posed a critical question to him: "Comrade Li Yiqing, is it possible that the economy could be in bigger trouble in the south than it is in the north?"

Although Zhou Enlai criticized Li Yiqing's demand, he responded to it right after the meeting by allocating part of the requested funds to the South-Central Bureau. It was at this time that the Secretary of the Communist Party Central Committee's Bureau for Northern Regional Affairs, Li Xuefeng, informed Li Yiqing that his very own home region had produced an example of how to cope with a great natural disaster without asking for aid, namely Dazhai. Li Yiqing knew Dazhai well—it was only ten *li* (about three miles) from Xiyang County Town's South Gate, his hometown. He knew it as a dirt-poor place. How could a poor village like Dazhai survive a natural disaster without getting money from the Central Government? It was a mystery to Li Yiqing, so he took the trouble of arranging a visit to his home region to see for himself.

On the way to his hometown Li Yiqing passed through Yangquan and stopped in Taiyuan for a meeting with Provincial Party Committee Secretary, Tao Lujia, who received him enthusiastically and related to him the details of Dazhai's self-reliance and arduous struggle. According to Tao Lujia's plan, Li Yiqing was then to board a special vehicle for a visit to Xiyang County, accompanied by his nephew, Provincial Planning Committee's Deputy Director Li Jinjun.

They say Li Yiqing was already suffering from poor health back then. It wasn't easy for him to make the trip. On the other hand, a home visit by such a high-ranking personality was undoubtedly an event of great joy for Xiyang. Local party and administrative leaders went out of their way to make it memorable. Knowing that Li Yiqing enjoyed Xiyang County's home-cooking, the Guest House prepared a special menu for him. Xiyang County folk eat a kind of pancake made from water-thinned flour lightly fried in a thin layer on a hot griddle. Eaten with hot chili soup, it is truly delicious. It can be made from any kind of flour: white wheat, corn, bean, millet. This is what the Guest House prepared to whet Li Yiqing's appetite when he arrived from thousands of miles away.

As he ate, Li Yiqing reminisced about how, during the war, he had left school to take part in the resistance, then afterward returned to Xiyang to start revolutionary work. He mentioned some outstanding individuals from Xiyang County who took part in the early years of the Revolution, like Ma Guangyuan from Jingyang Village on East Wilderness Hilltop and Zhao Wucheng from West Wind Edge on Zhao Cliff, and several Eighth Route Army officers who fought in Xiyang. But the main subject of his inquiry during the home visit was not a reunion with old comrades, it was Dazhai.

Li Yiqing already knew that Xiyang County cadres of all four levels took part in collective productive labor. The leaders of the Bureau for Northern Regional Affairs and of the Shanxi Provincial Party Committee also told him about recent developments and changes that had taken place in Dazhai. He took a sip of wine and sighed with emotion: "We from Xiyang were famous during the war. Today, Xiyang is known for other things. Xiyang cadres are excellent! So are the people of Dazhai! Elsewhere, everybody keeps talking about them!"

As soon as Li Yiqing returned to his hometown Xitang's South Gate, he found out from local grass-roots-level cadres and old County cadres about the situation surrounding Dazhai's refusal of flood relief funds. The details stirred him deeply. "My country folk sure are good! So honest and sincere! I'm going to take a look at Dazhai. It's just across the river to the south of town. I don't even need a car!" County comrades were hoping that he would spend more time touring and visiting Xiyang, so how could they deny him the chance to take a walk?

Accompanied by Zhao Mancang, Li Yiqing hurried to Dazhai on foot to undertake an on-the-spot investigation.

When Chen Yonggui heard that this leader from the Central Committee's Bureau for South-Central Regional Affairs was about to come knocking on his door, he naturally wanted to greet him warmly by organizing a small reception.

The moment Li Yiqing shook Chen Yonggui's rough, pine-bark hard hands, he felt how exceptional for a Brigade leader they were.

"Do you often do manual work?" he asked.

"If a Model Worker didn't do manual work, what kind of qualifications would he have to be a model worker?" answered Chen Yonggui, laughing. "When I don't work for just a day, my conscience is ill at ease."

"Good! Good! That's exactly the way it should be," exclaimed Li Yiqing.

Having sampled the apples and sweet potatoes brought out by Chen Yonggui, Li Yiqing announced that he wanted to see Dazhai's flood destruction and reconstruction sites. Chen Yonggui took him to the location, talking along the way. The "Iron Girls" were rebuilding fields in the Back Side Draw. "What a pity," Li Yiqing said sympathetically, "that such fine fields should be washed out!"

"No problem," replied Chen Yonggui. "We'll fix what's ruined. We won't allow production to drop."

Chen Yonggui led Li Yiqing along the road that passed in front of the stone-lined cave dwellings. Li Yiqing noticed the incessant sound of Jia Jincai hammering. He shook hands with him and wrested his hammer from him.

"Such a big hammer for such a small man!" said Li Yiqing lifting the thirty-pound maul. "These rocks are hard! You just hit them a few times like that and they split, heheh?" Li asked.

"Look at his hands!" Chen Yonggui urged.

"Oooy!" cried Li Yiqing. "Can you still work with those hands? They are both bleeding! You should lay off of it!"

"I'm used to it," Jia Jincai said simply. "Doesn't hurt."

"Three times we battled Wolf Den Ravine. Somebody suggested we build him a monument," interjected Chen Yonggui. "Building a dam is the best monument for me," was Jia Jincai's reply.

"Oh, right," said Li Yiqing, his memory jogged. There's still that Wolf Den Ravine. Let's go take a look!"

And so Chen Yonggui took Li Yiqing to the famous canyon. Despite the great flood Wolf Den Ravine's many high dams stood rock-firm; only some of the fields behind them had silted up. Li Yiqing was quite surprised.

"How come this ravine didn't wash out?" he asked.

"We lost it twice before we learned our lesson," explained Chen Yonggui. "Each dam is built like an arch and its foundation is broad and deep. You see, man is still more formidable than water! We've harnessed the Wolf; this year we have to harness the Tiger! That will be an even bigger job!"

Li Yiqing had an impression that he had entered an entirely different universe.

"I commend you with enthusiasm for not taking any money from the State after such a big disaster," he exclaimed. "It is not often in China today that one finds such enthusiasm and determination to combat nature as one finds here in the people of Dazhai. They should be accorded the same treatment that Chairman Mao said should be given the four levels of Xiyang County cadres."[1]

Li Yiqing felt that he gained much from his home visit. When the time came to leave, he decided to stop in Taiyuan for further discussions with Shanxi Provincial leaders.

The Provincial capital, Taiyuan, bustled with heavy traffic and bubbled over with high spirits, which conveyed a mood of welcome to Li Yiqing. After he shook hands with Tao Lujia, he told him about his visit home, barely able to contain a big grin. The other Provincial Committee leaders present couldn't refrain from chiming in with an old saying: "An old man sees his native place, tears start streaming down his face!"

And indeed, as Li Yiqing talked about various experiences he had enjoyed during the visit, he admitted he felt like crying at the sight of his native place. Among other things, he pointed out how Xiyang County cadres lived among and struggled along with the ordinary people. But the main issue he wanted to discuss with Tao Lujia was, after

1. Mao favored circulating to the whole nation valuable examples like cadres all joining productive labor and Dazhai recovering from calamity by its own efforts.

all, Dazhai. Specifically, he wanted to discuss Dazhai's leader, Chen Yonggui. He talked about how this remarkable peasant could use a statesman's broad political perspective to assay what benefited the whole collective and beyond that, the whole country, about his eloquence and ability, about his talent for leadership under various complicated circumstances, about how demanding he was of himself, and about how, from beginning to end, he maintained a simple proletarian style. All the things he said were fully in agreement with the Chen Yonggui with whom Tao Lujia was familiar. For that reason, Tao Lujia urged Li Yiqing, when he found a convenient opportunity, to let the Central authorities know about Dazhai and Chen Yonggui.

When he returned to Beijing Li Yiqing spoke to Li Xuefeng very emotionally about his trip to Dazhai. Afterward, he continued to speak glowingly about Dazhai to scores of his old schoolmates, old colleagues, and old comrades-in-arms who were now in Beijing, including Bo Yibo and Li Fuchun. He described the victory over the natural disaster, and how the village surmounted all difficulties and accomplished "three rejections," while avoiding "three shortages." The impact on Beijing was significant. He also used the opportunity, provided by his need for instruction about future work, to make a special visit to Zhongnanhai, the seat of the Central Committee, to inform Premier Zhou Enlai about the situation in Dazhai. This was the first time anyone reported the Dazhai story to a high-ranking figure at the Central level.

Because he felt he had experienced something very special, Li Yiqing conveyed the details of Dazhai's victory over the great flood to many leaders from the Bureau for South-Central Regional Affairs. Upon his return to Guangzhou from Beijing, he ran into a meeting of these regional and other leaders, who were in charge of related matters, at the Chonghua Convalescent Spa. Attending the meeting were Tao Zhu, Li Ruishan, Hua Guofeng, Wang Renzhong, Zhang Pinghua, and the Deputy Director of the State Planning Commission, Wang Guangwei. At the meeting, Li Yiqing made a highly systematic presentation of Dazhai's development with emphasis on the community's victory over the great flood. The presentation created a stir. Li Ruishan and Zhang Pinghua fought for the right to speak, initiating extensive debate on conditions in Dazhai and the state of agriculture in the nation.

When it came to discussing concrete aspects of Dazhai, Tao Lujia expressed more opinions than anyone else. He was also very moved by the achievements of Dazhai's residents in combating nature.

No one was more impressed by Dazhai's record than the Deputy Director of the State Planning Commission, Wang Guangwei. He was supposed to inspect Sichuan Province after he finished inspecting Guangzhou, but after he learned of the changes that took place in Dazhai during the year of the great flood, he deliberately changed his plans and decided to go there first. He met with Chen Yonggui several times during his trip and got to know many details about his life. The reality of Dazhai moved him deeply. When he returned to Beijing he first gave an oral report to Premier Zhou Enlai and later submitted a written report to the State Council and the Central Committee Secretariat. The report caught the attention of Deng Xiaoping and Peng Zhen. People praised it again and again. Thus Dazhai's and Chen Yonggui's reputation gradually started spreading among the highest echelons of the Communist Party Central Committee.

At that time the Central Committee of the Communist Party was concentrating its effort on solving the problem of feeding the nation, publicizing the slogans "Learn From Lei Feng," and "Learn From the People's Liberation Army, and promulgating the "Three Main Rules of Discipline and the Eight Points for Attention of the Chinese People's Liberation Army," and also the "Four Firsts" throughout the mass media. In terms of concrete measures, the government took a bold step in adopting the plan drawn by Chinese scientific and technical experts to produce the atomic bomb, the hydrogen bomb, and the man-made satellite within ten years. It launched a great battle for oil and set up the Petroleum General Headquarters at Daqing, headed by Yu Qiuli, Tang Shi-en and Song Zhenming. This unit started extracting petroleum on the Songliao Plain in Heilongjiang Province and shook off the "oil poor" yoke chained to China's neck by foreigners.

When they came to examining China's broad prospects in agriculture and confronted the fact that millions upon millions in China still went hungry on a regular basis, both the Communist Party Chairman Mao Zedong and the Republic's Premier Zhou Enlai asked that the entire Party membership engage in discussion over how to look for and choose one representative model among the many models of the country-wide agricultural cooperative movement. Thus challenged, the Party turned its attention to Dazhai, with its long-established popular spirit of self-reliance and hard struggle, with its success in putting the State into proper relationship with the collective, and the collective, in turn, into proper relationship with the individual. Somehow this seemed to hold special significance as the embodiment of Party and State practice. Objectively speaking, Dazhai would never have emerged in the forefront of national politics merely on account of being an advanced work unit at the Provincial level had it not been for the difficulties of the 1960s and critical condition of China's agriculture at the time. Conditions being what they were, however, Chen Yonggui became an invaluable asset to China's top leaders and to the nation as a whole.

CHAPTER—14

DAZHAI'S TRUMPET SOUNDS IN HEAVEN

Li Qi, the Director of the Propaganda Department of the Shanxi Provincial Party Committee, telephoned Xiyang County soon after the 1963 flood, inviting Chen Yonggui to give a talk at the Provincial capital. This was an important step in Chen Yonggui's ascent to new heights, and the County leadership was bent on preparing the draft of his speech, to make sure that his appearance in Taiyuan was a success, and that he won honor for Dazhai and Xiyang County. The draft consisted only of a simple outline that laid out the basic structure of the whole speech. All Chen Yonggui wanted were a few key words—anything more would have been too tiresome. Chen Yonggui's idea was: The simpler the better. The people preparing the draft were happy to oblige.

The first of the talks he gave in Taiyuan was chaired by the Director of the Propaganda Department, Li Qi. Before the meeting, Chen Yonggui asked for instructions from Li Qi: "How long do you want me to speak?"

"Speak as long as you want!" Li Qi answered.

Chen Yonggui spoke for more than four hours amidst enthusiastic applause. Except for outbursts of clapping, the auditorium sat in dead silence.

The first time around, the organizers allowed for an intermission. At the lounge, Chen Yonggui asked other leaders: "Is it O.K. the way I'm speaking?"

"Sure. It's great. You made Dazhai's history come alive!" said the leaders, surprised by the quality of his speech.

Nobody expected Chen Yonggui's talk to cause a stir in Taiyuan, but due to the demand of Taiyuan residents, Chen Yonggui went on to talk five times in a row! Many prominent people from Taiyuan heard his words. They particularly moved the famous writer Zhao Shuli and the famous performer of the Shanxi Opera Ding Guoxian.

"I am awed by Chen Yonggui's speaking ability," Zhao Shuli exclaimed in admiration. "What a talent! He never mentioned Mao Zedong, but his entire speech was imbued with Mao Zedong thought! He never studied dialectics, but his entire speech was pure dialectics! That was great! He is terrific!"

Some people were concerned that Chen Yonggui would never be able to leave Taiyuan. It was wrong to hold him up with all those speeches while there was so much work to be done in Dazhai! Finally, their pleas moved the leadership and they dragged him away from the lecture circuit.

For a while after this experience Chen Yonggui strongly opposed writing out systematic summaries of material like one, two, three, a, b, c, etc.

"People can't take that kind of stuff," he said. "They nod off as they listen. If Wang Jinzi were to talk for four hours—even if he could talk that long—nobody could listen! The result of his speeches at the Great Hall of the People is always predictable. And all on account of his early quality preparation!"

Dazhai's growing fame and Chen Yonggui's oratorical talent propelled him right up into clouds. He received, along with several other nationally recognized Model Workers, an official invitation to address over 10,000 people at the Great Hall of the People in Beijing on January 19, 1964. The world seldom sees a peasant speaking from a national government platform. The residents of the capital, expecting a good speech, lost no time spreading the news. They were anxiously awaiting

Chen Yonggui's arrival at the capital in order to evaluate his appearance and his speaking ability. Thunderous applause broke out as Chen Yonggui walked onto the plenary session platform to be seated with the Central Committee leaders who were accompanying him. Chen Yonggui had never before received this kind of high-level treatment. He couldn't help feeling very special. After an introduction by the person chairing the meeting, Chen Yonggui stepped to the center of the stage. This time his peasant clothing captivated the audience. Once again it broke into a stormy applause. People who are in the know say that at first Chen Yonggui appeared to be somewhat bashful. His speech, too, started out in a very low key. As he spoke, however, his timidity gradually disappeared and he became very relaxed, as he always was at home when addressing Dazhai residents. He talked about the Feeble Group and Stalwart Group, about Wolf Den Ravine and about victory over the great flood of 1963. He explained his "Ten Chief Benefits of Self-Reliance"—he went on and on for what seemed like ages, but he never repeated a single sentence. He became cautious as he concluded the speech. "I turned fifty this year," he said. "These days I forget more easily than I remember. I can't guarantee everything I have said. If I was wrong in any way, please feel free to correct me."

What he had to say must have sounded very fresh to city residents, but since the audience constantly interrupted his speech with enthusiastic applause it must also have been very much in tune with how people felt in China in the 1960s. Listening to his eloquent talk, the audience began to feel that this man sporting a white hand towel around his head was no ordinary peasant. I understand that several leading people also received him while he was in Beijing. They all engaged him in cordial conversation, encouraged him to keep up the good work and wished him the successful completion of even achievements in the future. Before he left for Shanxi they invited him to a banquet.

In no time the word of Chen Yonggui's successful speech at the Great Hall of the People spread to all corners of China, to both sides of the Great Wall and both sides of the Yangtze River.

The following story also got around by word of mouth. Somebody leaked the information that Chen Yonggui was riding in a certain passenger car on the way back to Yangquan. Great commotion erupted on the train as all passengers, afraid they might miss the excellent opportunity, rushed to catch a glimpse of this great man who had emerged from some mountain gully. The trainmaster had a hard time maintaining order on the train, so he decided to take Chen Yonggui on a tour of all cars. The train ride ended up as one prolonged acclamation. It was also a rare and elevating political experience for the thousand and some passengers.

People who heard Chen Yonggui's speech, be it reporters or political analysts, all shared one opinion: Chen Yonggui may not be highly educated but he speaks with a flair for philosophical discourse. I have also heard from some no longer active old cadres that Chen Yonggui needed to have somebody organize the material for him before he delivered long speeches on important occasions, but he himself never wanted to have the whole speech written out in typical fashion, word by word.

"I would only get confused," is how Chen Yonggui explained his special demand.

Chen Yonggui, propelled by the march of events, ascended new levels. From this time on, he occupied a very powerful position on China's political stage. The Central People's Broadcasting Station broadcast his speech at the Great Hall of the People live. After the broadcast, it received some one hundred letters from its listeners from thirteen different provinces and municipalities: Heilongjiang, Jilin, Liaoning, Inner Mongolia, Hebei, Shaanxi, Shanxi, Sichuan, Guizhou, Fujian, Shandong, Jiangsu, and Bweijing. Most of the letters were written by Commune members, state farm workers and Production Brigade cadres; others came from an office worker, an electrical worker, a soldier of the People's Liberation Army, a vocational school student, and an elementary school teacher. They all expressed a desire to learn from Dazhai's spirit of self-reliance and hard work for the prosperity of the country. Some two thousand representatives participating in the 1964 Agricultural Production Mobilization meeting on the outskirts of Tianjin also heard Chen Yonggui's speech. Their letter praised Chen Yonggui and Dazhai fulsomely.

A listener from Hebei, Liu Yanfang, wrote: "Comrade Chen Yonggui loves his class brothers profoundly, he never forgets the poor and lower-middle peasants; he leads us all toward prosperity for all."

A listener from Shaanxi, Liu Tianlong, wrote: "Chen Yonggui engages in class education of his Commune members, he is concerned about their weal and woe, he discusses every issue with them—he is a good cadre of the Communist Party."

Having heard of Chen Yonggui's deeds, an electrical worker, He Guitian, wrote a letter to his parents urging them to excel in their village work, learning from Chen Yonggui.

As I leafed through many such letters and documents, I began to understand that at that particular moment "learning from Dazhai" had already become an irreversible trend—a necessity brought on by circumstance which made Dazhai a signpost on the road to the future.

In May 1964, Chairman Mao Zedong and Premier Zhou Enlai instructed China's Minister of Agriculture, Liao Luyan, to travel to Dazhai and undertake an extensive on-the-spot investigation. His trip was destined to be seminal for the future of China's agriculture. It came as the first public move made by China's highest leaders after they took note of Dazhai.

Ever since Li Yiqing's and Wang Guangwei's report to Party and State leadership, an increasing number of people at the top began to pay attention to Dazhai. Chairman Mao's energies at this time were already chiefly devoted to the issue of combating and preventing revisionism, and steering China away from repeating what he saw as the Soviet Union's mistakes. He had already come out with his "We Must Under No Circumstances Forget the Class Struggle" slogan. At the same time, on the economic development front, he was still devoted to solving the problem of feeding China's population. Consequently, the well-being of China's agriculture was an issue of keen interest to him day in and day out. He saw the emergence of Dazhai as the opening of a bright highway along which China's agriculture could advance, but he wasn't too familiar with the real situation in Dazhai. The questions of how to develop China's agriculture and how to choose some models of collectivization in agriculture were always on this Party leader's mind. He decided to visit Hebei, Henan and several locations in China's south himself in order to thoroughly investigate the state of national agriculture, just as he had done at the beginning of the movement to organize agricultural cooperatives.

Chairman Mao's special train entered Handan station in Hebei on March 28, 1964, for a brief stop. The city of Handan falls under the jurisdiction of Hebei Province, but it lies only a mountain's width from Shanxi Province. Chairman Mao made a telephone call to Tao Lujia, Lin Tie and Liu Zihou, asking them for reports on conditions in Shanxi and Hebei. When the Shanxi Provincial Party Committee Secretary, Tao Lujia, received notice of the telephone call, he decided to give Chairman Mao an account of his stay in Dazhai and the firsthand experience he had gained there. He had spent over half a month at the end of February and the beginning of March that year in Dazhai, investigating its operation at the grass-roots level. He had also written a report specifically about that firsthand experience. Now he had a chance to amplify everything with Chairman Mao face to face.

Tao Lujia, Lin Tie and Liu Zihou climbed onto Chairman Mao's train together. When Tao Lujia announced that he intended to make a report on Dazhai and Chen Yonggui, Chairman Mao said: "Chen Yonggui? How do you write his name? I have the impression that I saw an article about him in the *People's Daily* recently."

He had his secretary bring out the article and he read it right then and there. Tao Lujia informed him that he had made three visits to Dazhai and that he was relatively familiar with both Dazhai and Chen Yonggui. He then went into detail about how Chen Yonggui learned to read at the age of forty-three, how he first set up his mutual-aid group and later a cooperative, and finally how he defeated the great flood. He also mentioned Zhao Shuli's evaluation of Chen Yonggui. Chairman Mao was very pleased.

"Good! There's some true talent in Shanxi again!" he exclaimed, adding by way of explanation: "Shanxi is the place where many a talent is born. Wasn't Liu Zongyuan, the famous Tang dynasty philosopher and poet, from Shanxi? He spent some time in the South, as a Jitian County official, where he did some good work. Never look down on an uneducated person! Chen Yonggui may be able to read only a few words, but his deeds are many."

Tao Lujia informed Chairman Mao about labor allocation and payment systems in Dazhai: how the distribution of work points was handled in a simple and convenient, yet effective way. "There must be some differentiation when the work points are awarded," Mao interjected. "They should reflect the quantity and quality of labor performed, but the procedure shouldn't be too complicated. What they're doing sounds right. They've put politics in command, but the politics don't interfere with the time set for labor."

Tao Lujia's report to Chairman Mao lasted two full days. On the second day he reported on the Shanxi Provincial Party Committee's drive to publicize Dazhai's experience, and its call to all grass-roots-level Party Branch Secretaries in the Province to learn from Chen Yonggui. Chairman Mao was very pleased. He added a few words of praise for Chen Yonggui.

After the stopover at Handan train station, where he received those reports, Chairman Mao continued on his tour, ending up in China's southern provinces. At each stop on the tour he spoke to the local cadres and populace about the Dazhai spirit of self-reliance.

"Dazhai is great," he said. "If our agricultural output is to improve, it will have to rely on the Dazhai spirit. To me, Dazhai is truly a standard-bearer. Are you going to learn from it? We will never solve the problem with agriculture without that kind of spirit."

Shortly after Chairman Mao's tour, there was an upsurge in learning from Dazhai throughout China's south.

Tao Lujia's report made Chairman Mao pay close attention to Dazhai. At a meeting convened by the Central Committee in April 1964, he addressed several discussion groups with the call: "Agriculture must rely on the Dazhai spirit." In June 1964 he spoke at the enlarged session of the Political Bureau of the Party Central Committee.

"Agriculture should mainly depend on the Dazhai spirit, on the spirit of self-reliance. It must produce several Dazhais and many Chen Yongguis," Tao said.

In a climate characterized by an all-out international anti-China campaign, the instructions he wrote on a document dealing with the village of Chen Family Settlement in Shandong Province were: "Some people are willing to borrow money from the devil, so long as it's profitable. We are not going to take that road. The devil is not giving us a loan, but even if he did, we wouldn't want it. We'll rely on Chen Yimeis from Chen Family Settlement and Chen Yongguis from Dazhai. So long as we depend on the spirit of self-reliance, there's bound to be change for the better."

While capturing the attention of the highest authorities, the conditions in Dazhai aroused the interest of many in various walks of life. It was time to investigate thoroughly and sum things up. That was the role of Liao Yuyan.

After Minister Liao Luyan accepted the historical mission of further clarifying Dazhai's experience, he spent over twenty days in Dazhai,living and eating with the Commune members, lining up with other visitors at the reception center to buy food, taking the time to go to the fields and work alongside everybody else. During the spring sowing season he even joined Five Family Flat Production Brigade to help with sowing. He carefully read over a lot of material on topics like "Dazhai Commune Launches a Broad Movement to Learn From Dazhai and Do It the Dazhai Way," "Dazhai's Natural Conditions," "Focusing on the Capital Construction of Farmland, Fully Implementing the Eight-Point Charter for Agriculture," "Dazhai Cadres Persist in Participating in Collective Productive Labor," "Chen Yonggui Sows an Experimental Plot," "Comrade Jia Jincai, the Dazhai Production Brigade's Former Party Branch Secretary, Willingly Steps Down to Make Room for the More Able Leader," "How Much External Assistance Does Dazhai Get?" etc. He analyzed them one by one. In order to be sure about the specifics of Dazhai's case, he compared Dazhai's micro-climate, soil quality and land configuration with the same features of comparable pieces of land elsewhere in the County. This way he was able to see Dazhai's remarkable transformation. He then summarized Dazhai's experience during eight back-to-back joint meetings.

Just before the end of his tour of investigation, Minister Liao Luyan called for a conference at the Dazhai Production Brigade on May 21, 1964. Many leaders attended. From the National level there were Zheng Zhong, Xu Yuntian and Zhang Liyun; from the Provincial level there were Liu Kaiji and Li Pengfei; from the Regional level there were Zhang Zhi, Deng Yuxi and Zhang Ziyi; and all the top leaders from the County, the Communes and the Production Brigades.

Minister Liao first gave a summary of his current investigation.

"I've already spent twenty days in Dazhai," he said. "I've seen a lot. When I get back, I'll be reporting on it to the Chairman and the Premier. I'm going to tell you now what I intend to report, so that you can see whether you agree. I'm not going to give you a full account of Dazhai because that has already been said many times, in the press, on the radio. When Comrade Chen Yonggui spoke in Beijing, over ten thousand people heard him in person. All these accounts show that our Party's line, the Great Leap Forward, and the People's Communes are good. Khrushchev says our People's Communes are bad, but he has eaten up all Stalin's grain reserves, and has had no results from his land reclamation effort in Siberia. We are better than Khrushchev!"

Minister Liao went on to stress four issues: one, Dazhai's concrete measures and experiences in the construction of fields that produce consistently high yields; two, the wise implementation of various Party policies and Chairman Mao's directives; three, Dazhai's labor management system; four, how to raise the red flag of Dazhai even higher.

At the end of his speech, Minister Liao added a few words of encouragement. "Dazhai's trumpet has sounded! The entire country is aiming to equal Daqing in industry and learning from Dazhai in agriculture. This is now national policy. The Chairman and the Premier have said so. This is of profound significance for the entire country. We cannot let this red flag fall!"

He exhibited his wit by pointing at Chen Yonggui: "In the past, Wang Dianjun from White Lamb Ravine was your teacher. He now learns from you. If you don't watch out, you may have to learn from somebody else in a few years!"

Chen Yonggui nodded and laughed.

"The Premier devotes much attention to model workers," Minister Liao continued, gesturing at the audience. "Lately, he's been paying attention to Dazhai. He asked me to carry out a thorough investigation, because he wants to make it a model for others to learn from. Being advanced does not necessarily mean being advanced in all respects. Various branches of the Government want Dazhai to be number one in their fields, but that's impossible. It could bring Dazhai down. The Premier is very concerned about Dazhai. He has talked to me about it at length. He doesn't want it to fall. He doesn't want its trademark of self-reliance to break. Several Vice-Premiers have told me we must keep it going according to its own self-proclaimed rules."

Realistically speaking, what Minister Liao said was very objective. He fully affirmed Dazhai's achievements without glorifying them as something divine. He regarded Dazhai experience as positive but he also pointed out its shortcomings. Undoubtedly, he was not expressing only his personal view. His speech reflected the concern and hope for Dazhai held by the highest Party leadership.

Responding to requests from Dazhai residents of all stripes and colors, Minister Liao convened a joint meeting of Communist Party members, Communist Youth League members, and poor and lower-middle peasants in the village that same evening. Fifty people in all attended the meeting: nineteen Party members, sixteen Youth League members, five members of the Poor and Lower-Middle Peasants' Association, and ten rank-and-file activists. In addition to the fifty, the afternoon session was attended by two cadres from the provincial Women's Association and five people from a provincial film studio.

Chen Yonggui presided over the meeting and immediately pointed out that it had been called strictly in response to popular demand. Minister Liao once again addressed Dazhai's residents amidst the enthusiastic applause:

"We've been here for over twenty days, and we still don't seem to be able to leave. We came to accomplish three things: one, to learn from you; two, to see your experience firsthand and find out about your concrete conditions; three, investigate ways to raise the red banner even higher."

Minister Liao summarized his experience in Dazhai in six points. "First," he said, "we've learned from your revolutionary way of thinking. You've changed the look of this place—some people say you've transformed heaven and earth. Chen Yonggui says it will take more than one generation to transform the entire mountain. Second, we've learned from the way you've integrated your revolutionary enthusiasm with a scientific approach. You've managed to integrate your enthusiasm and scientific spirit very successfully. Chen Yonggui has been carrying out his own experimentation, and quite outstandingly at that. Third, your cadres have set an example for us with their selfless conduct in the public interest. According to the press, you are outstanding in this way. Your Chen Yonggui is an excellent leader, which Jia Jincai discovered early on. He stepped down to let Chen take command. This was not an easy thing to do. If Dazhai's affairs are all well taken care of, it seems to me that the initial credit must revert to Jia Jincai. What do you say, Chen Yonggui?"

Chen Yonggui smiled and nodded but made no comment.

"Fourth, we've learned from your spirit of self-reliance and arduous struggle. Fifth, we've learned from your work in reforming people, namely your work on transforming their political thinking, their world outlook. Sixth, we've learned from your communist style of work, with its correct handling of relationships between the State and the collective, between the collective and the individual."

At the end of the speech, in order to encourage Dazhai's grass roots cadres, he said: "Dazhai is well known today. The entire nation is learning from the People's Liberation Army, Daqing, and Dazhai—the banner of workers, peasants and soldiers. The entire nation! It is important that the red flag of Dazhai continues to be red. One red flower does not a spring make. Only when tens of thousands of red flowers begin to bloom will we be sure of the change of season!"

Minister Liao spoke with great ease and poise, all much to the liking of Dazhai villagers. After the speech the participants in the meeting started discussing, looking for areas where they fell short and for ways to continue to improve. The minister was very pleased with the discussion his speech had generated. When he returned to Beijing, he submitted a detailed written report on his investigation to Chairman Mao and Premier Zhou. The report became the basis for Premier Zhou's government work report to the First Session of the Third National People's Congress. Liao Luyan participated in the drafting of that report and provided detailed material for the Premier's praise of Dazhai.

CHAPTER—15

A MEAL WITH CHAIRMAN MAO

Historical materials contain the following record: Chairman Mao Zedong rarely invited anybody to dinner. Even his former subordinates who took care of him were frequently treated only to a plain cup of tea. But on his seventy-first birthday he issued a special invitation to the man from the remote Taihang Mountain ravines—Chen Yonggui. The story of this special invitation begins at the First Session of the Third National People's Congress.

Chen Yonggui went to Peking to attend the Third National People's Congress as a representative from Shanxi Province, along with other Shanxi notables, Li Shunda, Zhao Shuli, Ding Guoxian, and Guo Lanying. Due to his speech at the Great Hall of the People, Chen Yonggui was by this time far better known than the others. During the Congress he was elected to the Presidium and seated at the presidential rostrum. He was also elected Executive Chairman of the Congress and asked to preside over meetings. It was during this Congress that Chairman Mao's idea that people should be the masters emerged as a coherent philosophy. Yet, it is also necessary to recognize Premier Zhou Enlai's "Government Work Report" to the First Session of the Third

National People's Congress cleared the way for Mao Zedong's call "In Agriculture, Learn from Dazhai."

When Chen Yonggui appeared at the Third Congress he entered the Great Hall of the People for the second time. This was the second time he had a chance to see Mao Zedong, Zhou Enlai, Liu Shaoqi and other high-ranking party leaders. But he never expected the high praise accorded Dazhai in Premier Zhou's report, a report which elevated Dazhai to the same level as Daqing and the People's Liberation Army.

The first thing Premier Zhou Enlai said in his "Government Work Report" was that China needed the spirit of self-reliance and arduous struggle. It continued with a concrete analysis of China's national condition at the time.

The three years of the transition period were just over. China's agriculture had suffered tremendously from a series of severe natural disasters. In addition, the nation was facing international challenges. In these difficult economic conditions, however, China did not incur a cent of foreign debt. On the contrary it managed to pay back almost completely the debt incurred previously. Of the various loans and interest payments owed the Soviet Union, totaling 1,406,000,000.00 New Rubles (most of the loans had been used to finance military operations during the War to Resist U.S. Aggression and Aid Korea[1]), the sum of 1,389,000,000.00 New Rubles had already been repaid on schedule. China also proposed that a portion of its 1964 balance of trade surplus with the Soviet Union be used to pay off the remaining debt ahead of time. Of the 500,000 tons of refined sugar borrowed from the Soviet Union 200,000 tons had already been paid back. China returned the remaining 300,000 tons in full, ahead of schedule in 1965. Within those few years China managed to pay back its outstanding trade bills with the Soviet Union and Eastern European socialist countries.

That was not all. Living frugally, China managed during the same period to come up with a substantial amount of money and material support for friendly socialist countries and national liberation movements. By the end of 1964, China's foreign aid totalled 6,670,000,000.00 *yuan*, of which 3,550,000,000.00 *yuan* were expended during the period from 1961 to 1964.

1. Chinese name for the Korean War (1950-1953).

Just at the time when China faced the gravest internal difficulties, and persistently hostile imperialist threats from beyond her borders, the Soviet Union and various reactionary countries joined together to form an anti-China chorus. The Soviet Union withdrew its technical assistance, the United States and Japan dispatched undercover agents to China to engage in sabotage, and Chiang Kai-shek raised a hue and cry about raiding the mainland. Only one course remained for the Chinese people: self-reliance. Without self-reliance there would have been no way out for socialism, no way out for China's Communist Party, and no way out for Chinese people.

Under such immense pressure Premier Zhou's morale remained as high as ever, his vision as grand and daring as before. Ending the first part of his report, he cautiously announced: "And now I want to bring up a few typical examples that will show you what China can achieve through self-reliance.

> Dazhai Commune's Dazhai Production Brigade in Xiyang County, Shanxi Province, is an advanced model of how to proceed with agricultural development and construction based on the spirit of self-reliance and the collective strength of people's Communes. Conditions in this Production Brigade used to be very poor. This was a place of barren mountains and unruly waters, meager soil and steep hill fields dispersed among many ridges and ravines. In the past ten years or so, under Party leadership, this Production Brigade has managed to mobilize and arouse the enthusiasm of its members and rapidly expand its agricultural output by using human labor to create arable land and by fully applying the Eight-Point Charter for Agriculture. They have undertaken formidable large-scale field construction, joining their previous 4,700 original small plots into 2,900[1] today. Moreover, what they've constructed are

1. All other reports say Dazhai cut plot numbers from 4,700 to 1,700. Have not been able to clear up this discrepancy. Perhaps the Premier was reporting an intermediate figure, not the final ten-year plan figure that was accomplished by 1964.

> plots and fields of improved soil that can ensure stable and high yields despite drought or excessive rain. Their per-mu grain output in 1952 was 237 jin; in 1962 it had increased to 774 jin; in 1963, despite severe flooding, they still maintained an output above 700 jin.[1]
>
> All this extensive construction and rapid development of agricultural production relied entirely on their collective strength. They handled the relationship between the collective and the State correctly. They borrowed money from the State only once and repaid it promptly the following year. During the eleven years between 1952 and 1963, while gradually improving the living conditions of its members, this Production Brigade sold the State a total of 1,758,000 jin of grain, which means that each household, on the average, sold 2000 jin a year.

Finally, Premier Zhou made a brilliant summary of the Dazhai spirit: "Everything Dazhai Production Brigade upholds: the principle of putting politics in command and letting ideology play the leading role, the spirit of self-reliance and arduous struggle, and the Communist-style love for the country and the collective, deserves to be encouraged and promoted."

The summary linked together and put into words all Dazhai's past experiences. During the period when China's agriculture learned from Dazhai, State leaders publicized it time and again. Even after Dazhai fell back to earth from "Heaven" nobody denied the last three points of Premier Zhou's summary. Realistically speaking, there is no way to deny them.

After this, Premier Zhou spoke highly of the Daqing Oilfield's mass battle for oil, set by China's second five-year plan. He said that Daqing built the enterprise by relying on Chairman Mao's two essays.[2] By putting Chairman Mao's thought in command, the extraction unit dis-

1. Other reports say that Dazhai crossed the Yangtze that year with a yield of 800 jin. Presumably the Premier was trying to be on the safe side. (W.H.H.)
2. That is, "On Practice" and "On Contradiction."

pelled, once and for all, the myth that China was an oil-poor country. After this assessment, Premier Zhou continued: "Of course, not everything done at Dazhai Production Brigade and Daqing Oilfield, that I just spoke of, is perfect. They are not free of shortcomings. But their achievements are outstanding. On the whole, their experience deserves to be studied."

After concluding the topic of Dazhai and Daqing, Premier Zhou went on to talk about China's achievements in detonating her first nuclear bomb and the build-up of China's national defense. He summed them up with the following: "That our country succeeded in detonating its first nuclear bomb shows in a most succinct way what a powerful force our self-reliance can be as we build up our national economy and defenses. By learning from the People's Liberation Army and by unfolding mass movements on a large scale, through immersion among the people at the grass roots and down-to-earth painstaking work, our construction and production have achieved great results. The Ministry of Petroleum Industry, Daqing Oilfield, and Dazhai Production Brigade are all models in this respect."

Regarding such questions as the Socialist Revolution and the People's Democratic United Front, Premier Zhou said: "Amidst the movement to emulate the advanced, learn from the advanced, catch up to the advanced, and help those who lag behind, which was launched in all China's many trades and industries, there emerged a great mass fervor to learn from the People's Liberation Army, to learn from Daqing, and to learn from Dazhai. Our leading organizations at all levels, various institutions, and vast numbers of cadres should indeed want to learn from the thoroughgoing revolutionary spirit and style of work of the People's Liberation Army, Daqing, and Dazhai which will enable us to take a step forward in our effort to revolutionize all walks of life."

Judging from the written documents, Premier Zhou's report mentioned Dazhai more often than the other two models. As the Congress prepared to hear Chen Yonggui's "The Model Speaks" speech, the auditorium broke into long, thunderous applause, while photographers took shot after shot of him from all possible angles, and scores of people turned on their tape-recorders to record his voice. The rustic with a white towel on his head had become the hottest topic at the People's

Congress. Premier Zhou attended several sessions of the Shanxi discussion group. He ended up talking about Dazhai and Chen Yonggui many times, calling on people to promote the spirit of Dazhai and strive for higher yields in agriculture. Premier Zhou's appeals raised Dazhai's fame a notch or two, perhaps eight or ten notches, higher.

Everybody started treating Chen Yonggui with even more respect. It was during this People's Congress that people began to admire the image of Chen Yonggui, clad in a Chinese peasant-style button-up cloth jacket, with his white towel tied around his head. Li Shunda and other model workers from Shanxi, delegates to the Congress, also became more intimate with Chen Yonggui, often getting together to discuss various issues. Members of literary and art circles like Zhao Shuli, Ding Guoxian and Guo Lanying, who had previously not felt quite at ease with Chen Yonggui, increased their contacts with him during the Congress and even started exchanging occasional jokes. I have seen photographs of Chen Yonggui and Guo Lanying taken together as a memento, and it seems to me that there was some special feeling between them.

The essence of the matter was that Premier Zhou's promotion of the spirit of Dazhai had given expression to Chairman Mao Zedong's guiding ideology. Great slogans didn't easily cross Mao Zedong's lips. Once he settled on one and voiced it, the launching of a new trend was certain. With every uncommon act of the leader, therefore, the arrival of a new trend was certain.

During the People's Congress, Chairman Mao accorded Chen Yonggui very special treatment. At the end of the afternoon session on December 26, 1964, as the delegates filed out of the Great Hall of the People, Chen Yonggui heard a call from behind: "Comrade Yonggui!" When he turned his head he realized it was Premier Zhou calling him.

"You don't have to go to the ordinary mess tonight," Premier Zhou told Chen Yonggui warmly. "Come with me, please."

Where to? Chen Yonggui had no idea, nor did he dare ask. He followed the Premier right to Chairman Mao's quarters in the Great Hall of the People. When he understood where he was, he felt a surge of warmth in his chest, and his deep-set eyes filled with tears—he realized that Chairman Mao was about to receive him personally.

"It's the Chairman's birthday today," Premier Zhou explained simply. "He especially asked that you be invited."

Chen Yonggui had no way of knowing then that Chairman Mao rarely invited guests to dinner. He was fully aware, however, that the treatment he was about to receive was not something one could obtain at will. Premier Zhou told him that even the Chairman's children got to see their father only a few times a year, not to mention a chance to dine with him. There were many things Chen Yonggui wanted to say, but not a single phrase came out. As he explained later, all he could think of at the time was the trouble that various leaders on all levels like the Shanxi Provincial Committee and the Regional Committee for North China had been taking on his behalf, especially their concern after the recent death of his wife Li Huni, and he was overwhelmed by feelings of gratitude intermixed with a sense of heavy obligation. But he never dreamed that Chairman Mao and Premier Zhou would want to receive him personally. He just stood there not knowing whether he should speak, and if so what he should say.

Premier Zhou proceeded to inform him that the other guests invited to Chairman Mao's birthday dinner were the representatives of the workers from Daqing, Iron Man Wang, the famous scientist Qian Xuesen, and two persons representing high school graduates, Xing Yanzi and Dong Jiageng.

They all arrived before the preparations for the banquet were completed, so Premier Zhou took them to visit Liu Shaoqi's quarters. The President of the State, Liu Shaoqi, who had just returned from the last People's Congress session, was writing his comments on a document dealing with the Socialist Education Movement. Premier Zhou introduced Chen Yonggui, Iron Man Wang, Qian Xuesen and the other members of the party to him.

From President Liu Shaoqi's quarters Premier Zhou led them back to Chairman Mao's anteroom. This time the Chairman was on hand and expecting them.

"Ah! Yonggui! Good, good," Chairman Mao greeted Chen Yonggui as soon as he stepped into the room. He shook Chen Yonggui's hand first, then went on to greet the others one by one. After he shook hands and spoke to each one of them, he invited them to sit down, and addressed Chen Yonggui in his heavy Hunan dialect: "You are an expert in agriculture!"

Chen Yonggui didn't fully understand what the Chairman was saying. The only thing he heard clearly was "agriculture," so he nodded at Chairman Mao and uttered, "Uhuh." Chairman Mao repeated his assessment, calling Chen Yonggui an "expert in agriculture," and this time Premier Zhou explained his words to Chen Yonggui, who, suddenly realizing his self-aggrandizing error, turned red in the face.

"Oh! No, no, no. I'm no expert in agriculture," he stammered out.

Chairman Mao laughed, Premier Zhou laughed, Qian Xuesen and the others laughed. As their candid laughter filled the reception hall, Chen Yonggui grew increasingly uncomfortable.

After Chen Yonggui regained his composure, he was able to take in the details of the leader's quarters. The room was so simple that its books were just about the only decoration. It certainly didn't look like the emperor's audience hall he had expected. It had no special facilities for entertaining and dining. He took another look at the man who was the supreme commander of China's hundreds of millions people. He was big, tall, and vigorous. He seemed amiable and accessible, yet also possessed some uncommon quality. Chen Yonggui was not able to figure out just what that special quality was. Consequently, he started thinking about The First Emperor of the Qin and the Han Dynasty's founder, Liu Bang.

Chairman Mao led the guests to the Great Hall Little Dining Room. He and Premier Zhou took their seats at the same table with Chen Yonggui, Wang Tieren, Qian Xuesen, Xing Yanzi and Dong Jiageng. Chairman Mao warmly offered cigarettes and candy to everyone. An ample supply of good sorghum liquor appeared in the middle of the table. Chairman Mao stood up, raising a glass, and proposed a toast to everybody. Then everybody joined in a toast wishing "long life" to the Chairman.

Chairman Mao was not fond of drinking. He was merely wetting his lips with the liquor in his glass, but he urged the others to drink: "You fellows should drink! Go on and drink!"

The attendants filled and refilled the glasses; the liquor went around three times.

"Eat, Yonggui. Eat!" Chairman Mao urged, noticing that Chen Yonggui was somewhat restrained.

"Hmmm. Hmm," uttered Chen Yonggui in response.

He subconsciously picked a bite of food with his chopsticks and stuck it into his mouth in a funk. He swallowed, then put his chopsticks down. He kept staring at Chairman Mao. Afterward he had absolutely no idea what kind of dishes he sampled at that dinner.

Aware of Chen Yonggui's embarrassment, Chairman Mao smiled and placed another plate of food in front of him.

"This one is good. Try this one," Mao said.

Chen Yonggui nodded, but he didn't move his chopsticks. In the past few years he had had some opportunity to sample many delicacies from land and sea, but eating at the same table with the nation's leader! That certainly was unprecedented! He never again received this kind of honor—not even after he became Vice-Premier of the State Council. He just kept looking at Chairman Mao with deep emotion, thinking: "If this food is good, then I really shouldn't eat it. Let Chairman Mao have it, so he can be healthy and live long. That way, the Chinese people can longer enjoy the bounties bestowed by him."

"Eat something, Yonggui," Chairman Mao urged again.

"Don't stand on ceremony, please, Comrade Yonggui," urged Premier Zhou.

Chen Yonggui smiled fatuously, picked up his chopsticks and put them back down again. Premier Zhou knew how to ease the situation. He poured two glasses of liquor and offered to drink with Chen Yonggui. Then he proposed that Chen Yonggui, Iron Man Wang and Qian Xuesen drink together. According to Chen Yonggui's own interpretation of events when he returned to Dazhai, he was quite used to drinking, so no matter how many drinks Premier Zhou proposed, he did not get drunk. In the end, after several toasts, Premier Zhou stopped proposing, and instead went on urging him to eat.

That a peasant from a mountain gully should have a chance to dine with Chairman Mao seems like a fairy tale, but the fairy tale did indeed happen among mortals.[1]

---

1. According to Chinese culture fairies are immortals, which is what the word xien (often translated with dubious accuracy as fairy) means. Xien could be fairies and they could be gods. In any case they are not subject to the biological laws governing human life such as growing old and dying. (W.H.H.).

Chairman Mao talked with Wang Tieren, Qian Xuesen, Xing Yanzi and Dong Jiageng for a while. Then he turned to Chen Yonggui, asking him cordially: "How old are you, Yonggui?"

"Fifty," answered Chen Yonggui.

"Ahah! Fifty, and he knows the will of Heaven!"

Chen Yonggui had no idea whose famous dictum that was, and he was even less aware of its implied meaning. He just pulled his face into a grin.

During the dinner, Chairman Mao struck up conversations with Chen Yonggui time and again. When the subject turned to various Dazhai residents, Chairman Mao sighed with emotion: "Huh, that Jia Jincai should step down so that you could fulfill your promise! It has happened before, but it is a rare thing, surely!"

Chen Yonggui informed Chairman Mao about the situation in the Dazhai Party Branch Committee, and the Chairman, in turn, encouraged him to keep up the good work. "Don't get cocky when you do a job right," Chaiman Mao advised. "Don't get cocky when you do two jobs right. When you've accomplished three or four things, you should be even less cocky. Being cocky is no good, and it's not wise."

Chairman Mao was very pleased with the get-together. After the banquet, the Political Bureau of the Party Central Committee asked the high-school graduate, Dong Jiageng, to write up a memo about the event. This historical document should have some research value to future historians. Ever since the establishment of the People's Republic, Chairman Mao and other highly placed leaders wracked their brains to find a way to build China into a strong socialist country with the beginnings of prosperity; yet time and again, following shifts in the direction and emphasis of Party work, putting their ideas into practice ran into serious difficulties. The Chairman had put forth the slogan,"Catch up with England, overtake the United States," as the vigorous campaign of the Great Leap Forward unfolded across the 9,600,000 square kilometers of China's land. Warped and exaggerated implementation, however, led China's economy off the main road and onto a side street. When Chairman Mao visited the countryside in Hubei during his tour of investigation in 1958, he urged people to tell him the truth. Upon receiving the information that some areas were producing 10,000 *jin* of rice per *mu*, he broke into tears. "I cannot agree with this idea of 60,000,000,000 *jin* from Hubei," he moaned. "That's subjectivism! That's bureaucracy! It's not your fault, though. I, the Chairman of the Party Central Committee, am to blame." Finally, on this day, he found a model for agriculture who had both feet planted solidly on the ground.

People often ask: How did Chairman Mao find Dazhai? The above is a straightforward account of how Dazhai came to such prominence, and how Chairman Mao hoisted the Red Flag of Dazhai as an example. From this time on, under pressure from the outside world and from the demands of domestic economic development, Dazhai and Daqing naturally took their place on the agenda of the Political Bureau of the Central Committee of the Chinese Communist Party. Following Chairman Mao's and Premier Zhou's example all the top leaders of the People's Republic also put Dazhai on their agenda, turning Chen Yonggui into the preeminent model for China's peasantry.

Following the changing demand of the times, during the Cultural Revolution the Red Flag of Dazhai received diverse write-ups. At first one would read: "Dazhai is the Red Flag on China's agricultural front." Then it became: "Dazhai is the Red Flag promoted by Chairman Mao." At the peak of the Learn From Dazhai Campaign, the writing became more specific: "Dazhai is the Red Flag personally hoisted by Chairman Mao." Then the slogan "In Industry, Learn from Daqing; in Agriculture, Learn from Dazhai; Let the Whole Country Learn from the People's Liberation Army" started appearing in the press and on the radio waves. It became one of the often used quotations from Chairman Mao, and a guideline for China's industry, China's agriculture and Chinese society in general.

Chairman Mao's invitation made Chen Yonggui more than ever aware of Dazhai's place and role in the nation. At the same time it placed invisible new pressures on him. Returning to Dazhai he recounted, in a voice filled with emotion, all that he had experienced to Dazhai's cadres and rank-and-file members. In order to turn the pressure he himself felt into a great motivating force for the Dazhai collective, he recited a poem—the only poem he was ever to compose—at a public meeting:

Easy downhill, uphill tough,
Hilltop views are grand. Enough!
This is not the only peak.
Climb on, better views to seek.

His emotion-packed recital brought an enthusiastic response from the audience. After reciting the poem, he added a few sentences.

"Don't laugh," he said. "Tell me, isn't the view from the mountain-top wide? I say it isn't just the view. It's the same as when we shouted that we were gazing at Tiananmen from the top of Tigerhead Mountain. Whether you can see Tiananmen from Tigerhead Mountain or not depends on your aspirations! It is only because of high aspirations that we have the Dazhai of today."

But Heaven has its mishaps in store for everyone. Just when Chen Yonggui enjoyed the highest honor among China's leaders, China's workers and China's peasants, a thick, all-enveloping fog of a kind that is the hardest to escape caught Dazhai's cadres unaware. The indiscriminate "Four Clean" movement made everything obscure and complicated.

CHAPTER 16

DIGGING FOR WORMS IN THE FLAGPOLE

Editor's Note: In 1964 Mao Zedong organized the launching of a nationwide campaign called the Socialist Education Movement, otherwise known as "The Four Clean." Its aim was to reassert the primacy of socialism as the goal of the Revolution after several years of economic and social retreat, and at correcting especially among rural leaders—the village Communists—bourgeois tendencies such as profit-mongering, privilege-seeking and abuse, influence-peddling and advantage-taking of all kinds. Mao saw it as a mass movement arising from below, electing poor and middle peasant delegates to review, criticize and correct mistaken ideology, personal transgressions and corruption. For most individuals participation was to entail a warm immersion where the majority of basically honest peasant cadres could wash their hands and faces, take a bath and start afresh by uniting with the people "to achieve greater, faster and more economical results in building socialism."

But since implementation was in the hands of a Party badly split over ultimate goals, strategy and tactics, it often resulted in an invasion of chosen targets by mass work teams from above who, rather than trying to reform and save errant cadres, focused on finding fault everywhere and punishing culprits severely. The Xiyang County Work Group, five thousand strong, sent 300 cadres to Dazhai alone. Since the total population of the Brigade numbered less than 400, this was almost one functionary per capita.

Even though subjectively Chen Yonggui wanted to follow Chairman Mao's directives closely, charging down new roads and rendering meritorious service, in reality his aspirations lay within the realm of remaking Nature, whereas the main area of the Party Chairman's consideration at this time focused on sorting out the complicated class struggle rending the Party from top to bottom. Guided by his philosophy of "continuing revolution" Mao was starting to apprehend a new and complicated phenomenon, that there were people in power in the Communist Party who were taking the capitalist road. This was something that Chen Yonggui, at the time, was not able to comprehend fully, and it showed acutely in his attitude toward the work team in charge of The Four Clean Movement.

The Xiyang County Party Committee informed Chen Yonggui in October, 1964, that a work team in charge of the "Four Clean" Movement was about to arrive in Dazhai. Having, some time earlier, already received some of the "Double Ten" documents[1] sent down from the top, Chen Yonggui was prepared, this time as ever, to execute Chairman Mao's directives, but he had no idea what to do about this Four Clean Work Team poised to descend like a swarm of locusts on Dazhai.

In keeping with the Central Committee directives, the Regional Committee for Central Shanxi had organized a joint Four Clean Work Group consisting of several thousand members of Xiyang County's twenty People's Communes. The idea was to launch a mass Four Clean campaign, grand in scale. The Work Group first went through special training, which prepared it to enter villages with "one weapon and three

1. In May, 1963 the Central Committee issued the first "Ten Point" document, primarily Maoist in inspiration, which called for mobilization from below. Some months later Deng Xiaoping drafted a "Later Ten Points" that stressed higher Party and Party-led work team intervention. It appeared in September 1963. In September 1964, Liu Shaoqi issued a third "Revised Ten Points" stressing central control. The "Double Ten" document received by Chen Yonggui probably contained the "First" and the revised "Later Ten Points." (W.H.H.)

duties." The "weapon" consisted of the resolutions and stipulations of the Chinese Communist Party's Central Committee regarding the problems of the Socialist Education Movement in the countryside, a twenty-part directive called the Double Ten Document. In reality, the second ten stipulations of the document contradicted the first ten stipulations. Chairman Mao presided over the drafting of the first ten; President Liu Shaoqi presided over the drafting of the second ten. When a Four Clean work team entered a village it ignored the contradictions, voiced the rhetoric of both, but basically implemented Liu's version, a top-down, fierce assault on grass-roots cadres.

Work teams first publicized the Double Ten Document. This was supposed to mobilize the poor and lower-middle peasants to take an active part in the movement. Team members admonishing the village cadres to "drop the burdens on their minds and take part in the movement with nothing on their conscience, stop their malpractices, reform themselves and unite in fighting the enemy." After this initial step the Four Clean work teams tried to "intermingle" with the masses, visit the poor and find out about their hardships, strike root in the countryside and establish contacts with the villagers in order to gather evidence against their leaders who had been prejudged as seriously compromised. Some people even promulgated the necessity of a second land reform. As a result, a feeling of fear enveloped the entire cadre stratum of village society. Initially, there were some village cadres who had transgressed accepted norms, accepted payoffs, even committed various other crimes. Their work and world outlook needed to be rectified, but the way the movement developed, rife with framed-up charges, fierce interrogations, mass suspensions, and heavy punishments, was quite beyond the imagination of most people and came as a painful surprise.

Dazhai, too, had to engage in the Four Clean campaign, but its cadres were full of misgivings about it. When Chen Yonggui left the Committee offices, the worried cadres came up to ask him about the news. Chen Yonggui, who was not in the habit of dispensing comments lightly, explained that the Four Clean Work Team's arrival in the village had been announced by the County Committee. The "Clean-up" campaign was to be executed in accordance with the Double Ten Document. To ensure the success of the campaign everybody—from the members of the Party Branch Committee to the poor and middle-level peasants—had to actively and enthusiastically cooperate with the Four Clean Work Team.

Old man Li Xiqing moved closer to Chen Yonggui and asked in a low voice: "Jinxiao, you don't know how to do this campaign, do you?"

"What do *you* say?" asked Chen Yonggui of Li Xiqing, in turn.

"Definitely rely on our Party Branch poor and lower-middle peasants, I reckon," said Li Xiqing. "Ever since the land reform, what campaign could ever have been carried out without us, the poor and lower-middle peasants? Chairman Mao has always trusted the poor and lower-middle peasants."

"You are right," agreed Chen Yonggui. "That has been Chairman Mao's outlook all along."

How was Chen Yonggui to know that the Four Clean Work Team was coming to expose Dazhai? How was Chen to know that its members had already been briefed to treat Dazhai as a Brigade of the "Third Kind," a Brigade with serious problems of corruption and abuse of privilege.

After the Team entered Dazhai it talked things over with Chen Yonggui. Both sides agreed that Liang Bianliang was to act as the designated liaison person for the Party Branch Committee. He was to report to the Team's office every day for contact work. For the first few days Liang Bianliang went to the office regularly, once a day, but he soon discovered that there were other people from the village talking to the team members: some idlers and drifters, and some perennial "campaign enthusiasts" or "movement specialists."[1]

One day Liang Bianliang showed up at the office only to be told: "Comrade Liang, there's no need for you to come any more."

Liang Bianliang realized that things didn't look too good, so he went to Chen Yonggui's home to let him know about it. Chen Yonggui gave it some thought and said: "If they tell you not to go then don't go."

And so Liang Bianliang stopped going to the Four Clean Team offices.

---

1. "Movement specialists" are people who jump into every campaign and try to earn brownie points by their activism. They often carry things to extremes. (W.H.H.)

From that time on the Team took great pains to find fault with Chen Yonggui's whole record. Team members tried for several days, but with the exception of the few "revelations" surreptitiously furnished by the "movement specialists," they could not pry open the mouth of any Dazhai resident. This worried them a lot because it would be difficult to explain to their superiors why they couldn't find any problems.

One day Chen Yonggui made an appointment to visit the offices of the Four Clean Work Team with other members of the Dazhai Party Branch Committee. The head of the Team strained to appear calm.

"Old Chen, we've already studied the Double Ten Document several times," he said, "and the Team's own cadres have already engaged several times in reforming themselves and exposing and cleaning up their own malpractices, but you fellows have not even made one worthwhile attempt to relieve yourselves of the burdens on your consciences. This raises the question of your attitude toward the Socialist Education Movement!"

"We've been cadres for over a decade," Chen Yonggui responded. "How could we be without the slightest defect? We've all already examined these issues carefully, however...."

"Chen Yonggui!" the head of the Four Clean Team interrupted him, openly displeased, "The poor and lower-middle peasants are quite unhappy with the way you don't subtract anything for the moisture content when you calculate their per capita grain. You cadres don't listen to the masses' point of view at all!"

Chen Yonggui suspected soon after they arrived that the Four Clean Team members might want to stir up the peasants on the issue of per capita grain shares. He watched them "strike roots and establish contact with the villagers" by cultivating relations with some backward elements, well-to-do middle peasants, and "movement specialists," so he was not unprepared for the attack.

"So what do you think? Should the moisture content be subtracted?" he countered with a question without tipping his hand.

"Of course," replied the Team leader.

"In that case I have to ask you," said Chen, switching to the offensive, "where should we find the additional moisture content to subtract, after we've dried the grain thoroughly in the sun? We don't do it the way other places do. They divide everything right out of the field, including the straw and the stalks. Of course they have to make an allowance for high moisture content. We distribute dry grain!"

The Four Clean Work Team leader was at a loss for words.

"We are talking about our own country and our own Commune members," Chen Yonggui continued candidly. "We'd only be practicing deception and tricking our country if we made allowances for moisture content when we distributed perfectly dry grain for personal consumption." At this point the Four Clean Team leader was waiting for an opening that he thought he saw.

"Right. But by not subtracting the moisture content you inflate your real yields per unit area. That's tricking the country, too."

When he heard this Chen Yonggui confirmed his suspicion that the Four Clean Team had come to Dazhai to make a case not only out of Dazhai's grain distribution, but out of its grain output as well.

"I'm listening to you," he said, forcing himself to suppress his anger, "and I get the feeling that you doubt Dazhai's grain output figures. Do you?"

The Four Clean Team leader knew very well—after all he had conducted a ten-day investigation of Dazhai's account books and even made a special trip to the County Grain Bureau to check them against the County record—that Dazhai did not fabricate its grain output figures. The figures set for sales of grain to the State had been met completely, too. So he was ill at ease when Chen Yonggui rebutted him on the issue. Not ready to draw hasty conclusions, he dropped the subject for the time being.

In all honesty, it appears that the Four Clean Team leader pretty much had to do what he was told to do under pressure from "upstairs." Some actions of the Xiyang County Socialist Education Joint Work Group show this quite clearly. Soon after the Socialist Education Movement unfolded in Xiyang County, many Four Clean work teams in Xiyang started sending in lengthy reports on the cadres in the countryside. These piled up to the point where even the man in charge of the Four Clean work, the Joint Group's Political Director, Bu Hongyun, became suspicious about so many long lists of problems. Yet, as the leader of the Four Clean Movement, he could not throw cold water on the enthusiasm of his work teams. He just clenched his fists and went on with the work.

That's exactly what happened in Dazhai. Since the Team could find nothing to expose or even question, in regard to moist grain, it delved into the subject of work points.

"Now, has there ever been a situation when you recorded work points arbitrarily?" the team leader asked Chen Yonggui.

"Everybody in Dazhai, from cadres to common members, earns rewards according to labor," Chen Yonggui managed to answer very calmly. "We have never marked up a single work point arbitrarily."

"I'm holding in my hand at this very moment material evidence to the opposite," the Team leader said. "Do you dare declare there is no such thing?"

Chen Yonggui's mind was completely at rest when it came to work points, so he told the man to produce the evidence. The Team leader pulled out the 1963 account book and threw it on the table in front of Chen Yonggui's face.

"No? Take a look! What work points are these?" he asked, putting his finger on some work-point figures he had already marked.

Chen Yonggui glanced at the place the Four Clean leader had underlined and marked over and over with a red pen. He was annoyed and amused at the same time. Holding back his temper, he prepared to confront his interrogator, come what may. He realized that the Team leader was pushing him into an uncompromising battle.

"Those are work points for sweeping snow," he answered with one laconic sentence.

"Do other teams have work points bearing such a name and description?" the Team leader asked, enraged by Chen Yonggui's carefree attitude and seemingly gratuitous evasion.

"There's only one Dazhai in Xiyang County. Nobody goes to visit the other Production Brigades, of course."

"So why do you put this in your records?" asked the Team leader, ignoring the clear meaning of Chen's reference to the thousands of visitors descending daily on Dazhai.

Liang Bianliang was getting ready to enter the debate, but Chen

Yonggui shot a glance at him. It was snowing outside. The snow fell in big goose-feather flakes, and since there were many visitors in Dazhai at that time, Chen Yonggui had a plan. The Four Clean Team was on his back, and even if Chen Yonggui were to grow three heads and six arms, he still had to pay attention to what that Team leader said. Now that the Team leader had pounced on the work point issue, Chen Yonggui planned to accept his criticism, then look for an effective countermove. Like all the other village cadres, Chen was boiling with anger at those village "movement specialists" who had cut the ground from under their own people's feet by bringing up snow removal to start with. He was waiting for an opportunity to retaliate against them as well.

"If the leaders feel that our allocation of snow-sweeping work points is not appropriate, we won't do it in the future," he said.

The Four Clean Team leader figured that Chen Yonggui was admitting his mistake so he eased up a little on the severity of his tone, but he persisted in asking questions just the same:

"And how about the previous cases?"

Chen Yonggui responded by removing all previously recorded work points in that category from the books.

Since entering Dazhai this snow removal issue was the first result the Four Clean Work Team had achieved in more than twenty days of effort.

As luck would have it, it kept on snowing heavily all day. When the snow stopped falling the following day, a group of visitors arrived from Yangquan. They wanted to climb Dazhai's heights. Tigerhead Mountain lay under a thick blanket of white flakes. The visitors were unable to climb it. So the only thing the Team leader could do was to ask Chen Yonggui to send people up the mountain to clear the snow.

The chicken had come home to roost! Chen Yonggui's turn to speak out had come.

"How could I dare make the same mistake again? I erred so badly with that snow-sweeping last time! I can't do snow-sweeping again. If I did I'd have to enter those work points in the record again."

This ploy of Chen's trapped the Team leader. He had no choice but to plead with Chen Yonggui again and again for a snow removal crew. In the end Chen Yonggui ordered his Dazhai Brigade members to sweep the snow off the trails, but not without promising work points in return. The "Four Clean" Team members never forgave him for making fools out of them.

Chen Yonggui was clearly in a predicament when, in the midst of the Four Clean Movement, he had to leave Dazhai to attend the Third National People's Congress. The local leader's departure did not cause the Four Clean Work Team to call off its offensive. The Team had its own duties and objectives, and it was very clear on what its own position would be should it fail to indict some Dazhai cadres on economic issues. Consequently, the Team leader called a meeting to brief the villagers one more time on the purpose of the whole operation. He minced no words.

"First of all," the Team leader said, "when we came to Dazhai this time we wanted to dig out the worms gnawing at the pole of the Red Flag of Dazhai. We wanted to do this together with all of you. If we don't get rid of these worms, not only will the Red Flag of Dazhai not fly high, there's a danger it may topple. Secondly, we came to help you vent your resentment and raise your objections to your cadres. As for those of you who dare criticize the cadres, we'll support you, help you, unite with you, and rely on you. Third, those who dare oppose the Four Clean Movement are counterrevolutionaries!"

At that meeting the Four Clean Work Team started off in high gear, criticizing Liang Bianliang.

"People say that Liang Bianliang is a good comrade," the Team leader said. If he is a good comrade, why doesn't he bring forth his self-criticism? People say that you, Dazhai, are an advanced Production Brigade. So far as I can see you are not really advanced. Circumstances and connivers rushed you into premature advancement!"

In a word, the Team brazenly treated Dazhai as a "Brigade of the third kind," a Brigade with serious problems. As for the "worm-digging," the Work Team referred to an article published in the *Shanxi Daily* under the title "Dazhai Deviates from the Dazhai Spirit," that had introduced the phrase and attributed it to Jia Jincai's daughter Jia Xiulan. But no Dazhai resident will confirm that calumny. Two old Dazhai Branch

Committee members, Guo Fenglian and Song Liying, say that the "worm-digging" expression first came out of the mouth of a female member of the Four Clean Work Team. The Four Clean Team then used it as their reason for treating Dazhai as a "Brigade of the third kind."

The Double Ten document did not differentiate between "advanced Brigades" and "backward Brigades." It only ranked them: one, two, three. Yet this ranking was precisely the basis for the attacks on Jia Chengrang and Jia Laiheng. It provided the basis for all investigations of Dazhai's cadres, who had to wrack their brains to find some reason for criticism, some reason for a need to justify themselves. They suffered so much in the process that they could no longer eat or sleep properly.

In all fairness, the behavior of the Four Clean work team was closely related to Party policy and the dominant theory of the time, or at least that part of it promoted by Liu Shaoqi. The everyday excessive talk of "class struggle" was made so universal that, even if Dazhai were twice as good, it would still have had to produce a worm for the catching. If none got caught, what use would there be for all the red-ink-titled documents of the Central Committee? Of course, this is not to say that I deny the seriousness of class struggle.

"What hurts a tree is broken roots; what hurts a human is a broken heart." Even the most patient man can endure only so much. After a certain point every extreme turns into its opposite. At one of the meetings a Dazhai Brigade member stood up.

"I've got ten fingers on my body," he said, holding his hand up. "If you bite this one, it hurts all the way to my heart, but if you bite that one, it goes all the way back to my heart too. Our fellow cadres are all close friends of mine. They are not corrupt; they don't embezzle. In fact, they haven't even taken an extra gulp of hot water from the collective. But you insist on forcing the rank-and-file members to press charges, to fabricate crimes and misdemeanors. I don't know what kind of heart you've got! I can't take part in these heartless meetings of yours."

As soon as he finished, he left the meeting hall. Many others followed him out.

In the midst of the cadre-cleansing frenzy in Dazhai, Chen Yonggui returned from the Third National People's Congress. In the past, whenever Chen Yonggui returned to Dazhai from a trip to Beijing or some other place, the cadres and common people would keep coming to his door to ask or tell this and that. The atmosphere was always very friendly. This time, Chen Yonggui could feel that things were very abnormal. His courtyard was completely desolate and the tension in the village was palpable. He paced around his room smoking pipe after pipe but nobody came to his door. The Four Clean Movement was destroying even the regular routines of village life.

Deep in the night, as Chen Yonggui lay on his brick-bed *kang*, he heard a faint knock on the door. When he opened it his colleagues, the Party Branch Committee members filed silently in. Jia Chengrang, Liang Bianliang, Jia Laiheng all looked worried and pained. They refrained from talking and asked no questions, limiting their discourse to just one sentence: "This is our last meeting!"[1]

Chen Yonggui himself was very upset, but seeing his closest comrades-in-arms heading toward self-destruction, he suppressed his own feelings in order to give them both encouragement and stern criticism. He criticized and encouraged in turns, at length dispatching them one by one. In the end he was left alone, hugging himself and hopelessly crying onto his own shoulder. While attending the meeting in Beijing he had told Premier Zhou and various other top leaders that in his view the scope of attack in the Socialist Education Movement was too broad, so broad that the grass-roots-level cadres were unable to go on with their work.

Only Chen Yonggui, after all, was Chen Yonggui. It is only because of his uncommon qualities, so rare among China's cadres, that he turned into the Chen Yonggui capable of functioning well beyond anybody's expectations. On the second day after his return to the village Chen Yonggui stood very cheerfully in front of Dazhai's cadres and Commune members. He talked about the Third People's Congress and passed on Chairman Mao's and Premier Zhou's greetings to all the people of Dazhai.

"Chairman Mao and Premier Zhou send their special regards to you!" he said, turning to Jia Jincai. His pep talk was like an injection of

1. They had actually already decided to commit suicide. (W.H.H.)

strength that hit everybody's heart. It rescued the Brigade members and cadres from the road to ruin and despair. They began to recover slowly their previous energetic outlook and to throw off the burden weighing heavily on their backs.[1]

After Chen Yonggui returned to the village the Four Clean Work Team invited him in to talk. Their attitude during the talk was clearly different from the one presented prior to his trip to Beijing. In addition to a very ceremonious greeting, they formally raised the issue of agricultural production. It was obvious that the Beijing meeting had opened the Team's eyes to Chen Yonggui's status with the Central authorities. They had come to realize the importance of Chen Yonggui's position on the national level and trimmed their sails accordingly. But how could Chen Yonggui easily dispense with his pent-up grievances? He was the leader of his village and he had to take responsibility for the village cadres. His strategy was to confront the Four Clean Team with a challenge.

"Let's talk about your Four Clean methods first, then we'll talk about production," he said.

Chen Yonggui accused the Team of being too rigid, of conducting the movement in a dogmatic manner.

What was the implication of Chen Yonggui's participation in the Third National People's Congress? The Team was hard put to know which way to argue. Still, Team members had a clear premonition regarding it. Based on the turn of events heretofore, they were quite wary of the direction things were likely to take in the future. The only thing they did not foresee was how deeply Chen Yonggui's words might influence Chairman Mao and Premier Zhou. He had already made those leaders aware of what was going on, and they were already taking counter-steps.

A new Chinese Communist Party Central Committee document made up of twenty-three points, entitled "Some Problems Raised in Regard to the Socialist Education Movement in the Countryside," circulated nationally on January 23, 1965. An announcement that accom-

---

1. This makes it sound too easy. Actually the Party cadres met with Chen on the mountain after dark to avoid contact with the work team, and talked all night before Chen Yonggui was able to restore their will to live, and instill a little morale. (W.H.H.)

panied the document said that, should there be any contradictions between the current and the previous document, everyone should regard the current document as the definitive text. The new document went on to refute big sections of the old Double Ten instructions. The Twenty-Three Points of the new document communicated Chairman Mao's own six standards[1] for the successful execution of the Four Clean Movement. It also pointed out that local Party branches and Four Clean teams should jointly lead "Production Brigades of the first kind" and "Production Brigades of the second kind." In response to Chen Yonggui's views expressed to the Central authorities, the Party Committee Secretary of the Bureau for North China, Li Xuefeng, sent Chen Yonggui a word: "Send no report; your critique has reached the very top. No need to worry in future." What he really meant was: "Chairman Mao has spoken."

Had Chen Yonggui not been the Party Branch Secretary of Dazhai, with strong links to "Heaven" in Beijing, I suspect that his open resistance would have led to much greater catastrophes for him personally and for his village. It is only because he was the model chosen by the central authorities that events took a miraculous turn for the better[2].

During the second week of February, 1965, a Joint Work Group composed of seven representatives from the Central Committee, the North China Bureau, the Shanxi Provincial Committee, and the Xiyang County Committee, as arranged by Premier Zhou Enlai, arrived in Dazhai. At the same time the previous Four Clean Work Team withdrew. Nobody from the Central Shanxi Regional level participated in the new Joint Work Group. This Group, under the direct guidance of the Shanxi Provincial Committee and in accordance with the "aid" principle specified by Premier Zhou and Li Xuefeng, engaged in aiding the Dazhai Party Branch to carry out socialist education. The new Twenty-Three Point Document also shook up every other village in the

1. For a review of the conflict between Mao Zedong and Liu Shaoqi over the conduct of the Socialist Education Movement, see William Hinton's *Shenfan*, Chapters 46 and 48. Also Maurice Meisner, *Mao's China and After*, Chapter 17, pp. 288-93. (W.H.H.)
2. On the other hand, had it not been Mao's model Dazhai, the Party, at that time in Liu's hands, would not have assigned three hundred team members to try to find fault and persecute the cadres—even unto death. (W.H.H.)

country, producing a change in the direction of the Four Clean Movement. Even the Political Director of the Four Clean Joint Work Group in Xiyang felt that a heavy chip had fallen from his shoulder. He was now able to say what he previously had not dared say, and to show the kind of attitude he previously dared not show—he was able to deal with the village cadres by seeking truth from the facts instead of "hunting worms in the woodwork."

On May 21, 1965, the Shanxi Provincial Committee received a report addressed to the Central Committee and the North China Bureau bearing three signatures—those of Kang Pilie, Fei Run, and Wei Aimin. The Provincial Committee transmitted it to lower levels as Document No.(65) 138, adding its own comments. The document's title was "Shanxi Province Communist Party Committee Dispatch of the 'Report on the Progress of the Socialist Education Movement at the Dazhai Party Branch' by the Dazhai Joint Work Group." The following is the text of the comments:

> Central Committee and North China Bureau:
>
> The following is the Dazhai Joint Work Group's "Report on Aiding Dazhai's Party Branch Carry Out the Socialist Education Movement."
>
> The Socialist Education Movement at the Dazhai Production Brigade started in November of last year, but it basically failed because the original Four Clean-ups Joint Work Team adopted the method of treating Dazhai as a "Production Brigade of the third kind." The Joint Work Group dispatched in February of this year summarized the experiences and lessons of the Four Clean-ups Work Team and, following instructions issued by Premier Zhou Enlai and Comrade Li Xuefeng, adopted the policy of aiding and the position of advising the host unit in helping the Dazhai Party Branch carry out the Socialist Education Movement. After seventy-eight days of work, in addition to helping the Dazhai Party Branch successfully accomplish the task of socialist education, it has also gained some new

experience in how to carry out the Socialist Education Movement in "Production Brigades of the first kind...."

In their report Kang Pilie, Fei Run and Wei Aimin say: The testing of the Socialist Education Movement has once again proved the Party Branch led by Comrade Chen Yonggui to be a revolutionary unit capable of going through a series of serious trials with class struggle and struggle for production. Our evaluation is as follows:

1. They wholeheartedly embrace socialism, constantly minding the interests of the collective and the nation.

2. They consistently rely on the poor and lower-middle peasants, keeping a very clear dividing line between ourselves and the enemy.

3. They consistently take the lead in the collective productive labor, doing hard and solid work.

4. They are selfless, fair and impartial in their work.

In November of last year, the original Four Clean-ups Work Team sent by the Central Shanxi Regional Committee and the Xiyang County Committee caused antagonism between the Party Branch and the Work Team due to its lack of ideological clarity and experience, to its inability to boldly trust the Party Branch and to rely on it, and to its mechanical implementation of the Four Clean way of dealing with Production Brigades of the third kind. When the Joint Work Group first entered the village, Comrade Chen Yonggui and some of the cadres were still full of resentment. Due to such circumstances, we had to make it clear to the cadres and the masses at the very beginning that Dazhai was the Socialist Red Flag Unit of the entire Chinese countryside, and that we were there in order to "aid," to further strengthen their unity, mobilize their enthusiasm and raise their Red Flag even higher.

The report went on with detailed analyses under the headlines, "Are Dazhai's Cadres After All Honest About Their Economy?" and "Is Dazhai's Cultivated Land Area and Grain Output Reported Factually?" The final conclusion was:

> Through our over-two-months-long work and investigation, we gained an intimate understanding that Dazhai is a clean unit by all four Four Clean standards: politically, economically, organizationally, and ideologically. It conforms to the six standards for the successful accomplishment of the Socialist Education Movement in the countryside set by Chairman Mao. Dazhai is worthy of the title "The Red Flag on China's Agricultural Front."

The East wind blowing from Beijing dispersed the dark clouds that had enveloped the hearts of the people of Dazhai. After the Joint Work Group's fair-minded conclusion, Dazhai felt encouraged once more.

"If we had done anything corrupt, it wouldn't have passed by Chen Yonggui in the first place," the cadres were saying.

"In the past, when we worked for the landlords, we had to do four, even five different jobs every day. We work for ourselves now, all right, so what's the big deal about overtime work?" the people were saying.

And so things went back to where they were for the people of Dazhai, and the relations between the Brigade members and their cadres grew closer than ever before.

The extraordinary course of events left a conundrum to those who came afterward. Fighting for principles is an ideal end in itself. Fabricating principles so you can fight makes a good opening for a farce. If one looks at the effects of policy implementation, the earlier and the later Socialist Education Movement documents achieved two entirely different results. The two work groups held diametrically opposed points of view, which is why at the peak of the "Learn From Dazhai" campaign, talk of the "correct line" and the "erroneous line" emerged. If, however, one only considers the directives sent down for the Socialist Education Movement, although the first Ten Points and the second

Ten Points were drafted by two different people, both were circulated to lower levels in the name of the Central Committee. If one takes the position that Chairman Mao, so solicitous of all the old cadres at the grass roots, represented the correct line, then why did the Great Proletarian Cultural Revolution that he himself set in motion later hurt so many old cadres?

This is a phase of history with significant meaning.
This is also a phase of history hard to evaluate.[1]

In 1964, after the snowstorm showed up the Four Clean work team, things went back to the way they had been for the people of Dazhai. That year's summary appraisal of the early period of Brigade history, 1947-1964, held up for many years. Even after 1978 when Dazhai suddenly came under attack as a false "Red Flag," no one tried to warp the record of Chen Yonggui's first fifteen years. But in 1990 a most damning critical book, *The Rise and Fall of the Red Flag of Dazhai*, came out. Among other things it charged that, at the end of the Socialist Education Movement, the North China Bureau and the Shanxi Provincial Party Committee openly resorted to deception in order to protect that "Red Flag."

Fortunately we have a record of a visit in 1965 made by Li Xuefeng of the North China Bureau and Tao Lujia of the Shanxi Provincial Committee to Dazhai. They came specifically to recheck the area of Dazhai's cultivated land and Dazhai's per *mu* grain output, the key issue being whether Dazhai's yields did or did not equal yields south of the Yangtze River—that is, 800 *jin* per *mu*. They met all the people concerned, they supervised careful land measurements, they checked all the records, and they concluded that:

1. Dazhai's land area was less than reported, not more.
2. Dazhai's yields per unit area crossed the Yangtze and surpassed 800 *jin* per *mu*.
3. Dazhai distributed 490 *jin* of grain to every Brigade member for personal consumption.

---

1. For a discussion of the author's dilemma on this point see my Afterword. (W.H.H.)

The trip to Dazhai gave Li Xuefeng and Tao Lujia a pretty good idea of where things stood in the village. It also brought ease of mind to Chen Yonggui and Dazhai's cadres. After the trip, Tao Lujia said, by way of evaluation: "Quite remarkable, Chen Yonggui is."

The problems that emerged during the Four Clean Movement in Dazhai and Xiyang County, however, still persisted, particularly among some famous Model Workers with heavy mental burdens. Thus, on February 21, 1965, before the leaders left, Chen Yonggui invited Li Xuefeng, Tao Lujia, and their companions to visit White Lamb Ravine, a Brigade famous for its forestry. The persecutions of the Four Clean Movement had driven White Lamb Ravine's model worker Wang Dianjun onto a dead-end road. As the visitors arrived he was contemplating suicide. Li Xuefeng and Tao Lujia had to engage in some concentrated and painstaking ideological work before they were able to bring him around to a commitment to life. Only then did they dare take their leave.

All this is a true record, obtained from public archives. These real-life facts show that the growth of Dazhai did depend on support, aid and guidance of Party organizations on various levels. The blossom of Dazhai could grow more red with the time and Chen Yonggui could be drawn ever closer to the high-level political orbit because the leaders supported and encouraged him. The facts also confirm that without the great lifelong effort by Chen Yonggui and the people of Dazhai, high-placed individuals like Li Xuefeng and Tao Lujia would have never expended such painstaking care on a small hamlet like that, patiently listening to reports and resolving concrete problems.

These astute leaders remind one of Bo Le and his skill at picking out horses that could cover a thousand Chinese miles a day.[1] Bo Le's rules for judging candidates, equine or otherwise, started from the inside out, valuing energy and spirit most highly, while discounting awkwardness and ungainly conformation, such as, say, a man who wore a towel on his head and found reading and writing difficult.

1. Bo Le stands for a man who knows how to appreciate horses. According to one tradition, he was a minister under Duke Mu of Qin. When evaluating horses for the Duke, he said one should appreciate the energy and spirit of a horse and forget its coarseness, value what's within and forget the outside appearance.

The trip of Li Xuefeng and Tao Lujia to Dazhai increased understanding within the highest levels of Chinese Communist Party leadership of what Dazhai was all about. It set the stage for a visit by Premier Zhou Enlai himself.

Since Tao Lujia was still alive and in good health at the moment of this writing, after The Rise and Fall of the Red Flag of Dazhai came out, I approached him with the questions the authors raised about this period and particularly the charge that he practiced "deception" to protect Dazhai.

"I can bear witness to the truth of our conclusions. One cannot distort history," he said.

CHAPTER 17

THE FOUR SEAS ENFOLD ONE NEIGHBORHOOD

From the time the Joint Work Group upheld Dazhai's achievements the village truly opened its heart to everything and everybody from China and abroad. Famous individuals of exceptional ability and multitudes of most ordinary people poured in, longing to take a look at Dazhai's ridges and gullies and find out what kind of model Chen Yonggui had created. These were scenes from a new era!

In the winter of 1965, China's greatest contemporary man of letters, Guo Moruo, made a visit to Dazhai. It must be said that this was quite an honor for both remote Xiyang County and the Dazhai Production Brigade.

Guo Moruo did not make any public announcement about his trip to Dazhai. He was planning to go quietly to Xiyang County by train and car, then stay overnight at the County Guest House as just another visitor. But since it was the Venerable Guo coming, the County and Chen Yonggui naturally wanted to receive him with lavish hospitality. Chen Yonggui and the County leaders organized a discussion session to inform Guo Moruo of the history of Dazhai's development. Chen Yonggui accompanied him up Tigerhead Mountain and into Wolf Den

Ravine. There he gathered firsthand impressions of the outstanding achievements of Dazhai's battle with Nature. Every spot they visited inspired Guo Moruo to compose poems, which he wrote out in his fine handwriting and passed around. Even before he came to Dazhai, Guo Moruo had acquired a deep affection for this model established by Chen Yonggui and affirmed by Chairman Mao, but on-the-spot inspection aroused even more powerful emotions and a new artistic impulse. Two of his poems, entitled "Ode to Dazhai" and "Visit to the Dazhai Exhibition Center," appeared in the *People's Daily* on December 7, 1965. "Ode to Dazhai" reads as follows:

> The nation learns from Dazhai,
> Dazhai learns from the nation.
> People old and young, the lowly and the high
> From a thousand miles away, express their jubilation.
> Wolf's Den vanquished, reborn as fertile land
> Great crops wrested from famine years gone by.
> The Red Flag planted by Mao Zedong's own hand
> Colors a big corner of the overarching sky.

Naturally, this poem is a bit less refined than the "Goddess" he had written in his youth, but it expresses a sincere feeling. His outlook in the lines, "The nation learns from Dazhai, Dazhai learns from the nation," was greatly admired. Just before he passed away, he left behind a testament: He wanted those he left behind to disperse his ashes over Dazhai's land.

In May 1978, respecting his last wish, an airplane brought Guo Moruo's ashes from Beijing to Dazhai and sowed them in the sky above the gullies and ridges of Tigerhead Mountain. Early in the morning workers from the airfield in Shihjiazhuang laid out a red carpet and radar and sound communications equipment on the ground in the village of Dazhai. Then they waited for the plane to arrive. Dazhai and Xiyang County leaders took up key positions and groups of ordinary people bearing wreaths came to take part in the ceremony.

Around nine o'clock in the morning an ordinary plane appeared in the air space over Dazhai. It flew in from the direction of Xiyang

County Town. The workers on the ground immediately called out from below by electronically amplified sound:

"You are in Dazhai airspace now."

"We are starting the job," the plane crew responded in kind.

The plane circled over the gullies and ridges once, then called out again from the sky, "The job is done."

Flying back across the town of Xiyang, the plane returned to Beijing. This vivid scene often reappears in the minds of Dazhai's residents, and they can still hear in their ears a replay of the sky-to-earth dialogue. Guo Moruo's widow, who was on the plane during the drop of the great poet's ashes, wrote to Guo Fenglian several days later, warmly thanking Dazhai's citizens for their concern. She went on to describe some impressions of her husband's visit to Dazhai and stressed his reluctance to leave it.

During the height of the national "Learn from Dazhai" movement in 1965, countless celebrities and prominent groups went to salute Dazhai and pay their respects. The famous novelist Ba Jin, feeling drawn to the wondrous character of Dazhai, insisted on leaving his coastal city of Shanghai to set foot on the yellow loess plateau and take a look at the near-mystical village. He used every detail about the now legendary Chen Yonggui, from the way he looked and behaved to the way he got along with people, as rich literary source material. Chen Yonggui's every word and move became the basis of a draft worked out in his mind. He used the peasant hero's figure to recreate the course of events in Dazhai, and the essay about his trip, written upon his return to Shanghai, became a great favorite among editors and readers, just as his novels *Family*, *Spring*, and *Autumn* had done back in the 1930s.

A few years later, China's famous mathematician Hua Luogeng went to Dazhai from Beijing. His pioneering works, *The Theory of Optimization*, and *The Law of Overall Consideration*, already acknowledged by mathematicians, were gaining wide recognition from people of other disciplines as well, and were clearly beginning to bear on the field of economics. Hua Luogeng had a deformed leg, and had to use a walking stick, but the moment he set foot in Dazhai he climbed tirelessly. He went to the top of Tigerhead Mountain with several specialists to probe into ways of finding broad applications for his theory of optimization in the field of agriculture. He also paid a visit to the County Fertilizer Plant and the Xiyang Cement Plant, inquiring about the industrial use of his theory of optimization in Xiyang County. Finally, in response to requests from Xiyang and Dazhai, he gave a lecture at the County's Grand Auditorium on how he had shaped and popularized his theories of optimization and overall consideration.

Other visitors to Dazhai at that time included groups like the Central Philharmonic Orchestra, the Central Theatrical Company, the Chinese National Table Tennis Team, and the National Motorcycle Team. The first thing they all requested when they came to Dazhai was an audience with Chen Yonggui. They also staged brilliant performances, whether in the field of art or sports.

I remember a summer night in 1965, when a crowd of spectators gathered in front of the makeshift stage at the entrance to the village. It would have been almost impossible to buy tickets for a performance by such top-quality artists in Beijing, but here in Dazhai, given the inadequate facilities, the same artists showed a lot of forbearance as they rehearsed singing in the yard of the County Cultural Center and then performed in Dazhai's homemade "theater." Moreover, the spectators made special note of the fact that there was one Ma Ji in the troupe—a well-known comic dialogue artist second only to the famous Hou Baolin, the nation's most popular. On his account alone, residents of several neighboring villages jammed the hall with the spectators from Dazhai. The crowd below the stage was as dense as the stars in the sky above.

The performance officially started after the head of the troupe and Chen Yonggui sat down in front of the stage holding hands. The vocal and instrumental solos, the chorus and instrumental ensemble numbers were all superb, but the spectators were not really satisfied. They kept waiting for the comic dialogue artist Ma Ji. When the announcer called out his name, the entire auditorium broke into long, enthusiastic applause. After Ma Ji's performance, the spectators kept clapping, asking for him to come back on stage. The performers on the stage applauded, too. They wanted Chen Yonggui and the Dazhai Party Committee members to join them on stage. It was an event to remember as long as one lives.

As mentioned above, the Red Flag in the field of agriculture attracted a number of celebrities from the world of sports. In order to promote friendship between sport circles and Dazhai, the National Table Tennis Team, led by the famous Ping-Pong coach, Li Furong, arrived one fall. Among the members of this high-level team were the gold, silver and bronze medalists at the World Table Tennis Championships. They were in Dazhai to pay respects and exhibit their skills. It was an event of great meaning from their point of view, as they jointly expressed during their meeting with Chen Yonggui. They put on a splendid exhibition, and the people of Dazhai and all Xiyang received them warmly.

Jia Jincai and Song Liying remember receiving two female guests from Beijing, who were scheduled to room and board with Song Liying for a while. Many people had stayed with Song Liying previously—so many that she was not able to distinguish clearly their identity and circumstances. Since the two women were going to lodge and eat with her family, the hostess, naturally, wanted to treat them hospitably. Both women were already advanced in age: one wore a military uniform, the other plain clothes. Song Liying thought that the one wearing the military garb was perhaps the boss, so she consulted with her on every issue that arose during their stay. The two women often asked her about Dazhai, and she in turn asked them about Beijing. After half a month of life together, as they were about to part, Song Liying still didn't know who the two women were.

Only much later somebody at the Reception Center told Song Liying that the woman in plain clothes was Li Xiannian's wife, Lin Jiamei, and that the woman in military uniform was merely the orderly accompanying her! What a blunder! To this day, whenever the topic comes up, Song Liying looks devastated as she blames herself for the mistake. At that time, however, many wives of China's leaders came to take a look at Dazhai. Jiang Qing, Deng Yingchao, Cai Chang, Cai Sumei, and Kang Keqing also came, and it couldn't be expected of the people of Dazhai to know, without some kind of preparation, which one was which.

In those ten years or so, Dazhai received many a politician, revolutionary, military strategist, writer and artist on its ordinary patch of yellow loess. They all inspected Dazhai's ridges, gullies and mountain peaks, while these raw features in turn imparted a sense of security and spiritual comfort to the visitors. Each of them felt honored and proud to have been there. Thus Dazhai left its colorful imprint on society and history.

Of all those who came to visit in that period the most important, the most honored, and the most uexpected was Premier Zhou Enlai. On May 21, 1965, the news ripped like a thunderbolt through Chinese skies. The Premier of the People's Republic of China, Zhou Enlai, was coming to visit Dazhai! The moment they heard the news, Dazhai's residents started happily rushing about talking it over. Premier Zhou was accompanying foreign guests, but in the hearts of Dazhai's residents there was room only for him.

There were many jobs of all kinds to be done before his arrival. The Guest Center had to prepare rooms where the Premier and foreign guests could rest, as well as food for the welcoming banquet. The preparations included such details as choosing the appropriate people to provide services during the visit, and training them in certain things. Various Party Committees on all levels in Shanxi Province, the Central Shanxi Region, and Xiyang County had to prepare what and how to report to the Premier and what kind of arrangements to make for his welcome. People were up to their ears in work, especially in Dazhai. The Premier would be seeing each and every person in Dazhai, from Chen Yonggui and the Party Branch Committee members to regular Party members and ordinary people! His eyes would take in all the scenes from the village and the fields! Journalists would be doing on-the-spot coverage and taking pictures that the press of the world would carry everywhere. Even the slightest oversight would produce a great impact. Not to be left out, Five Family Village and the other neighboring hamlets also made appropriate preparations.

Premier Zhou Enlai, too, worked hard to prepare himself for the visit. His preparatory work focused on one point: Finding out whether Dazhai could be the model for and whether it represented the way forward in China's agriculture.

On the day set for the visit Xinhua News Agency dispatched through domestic and international wires the following announcement: "The Albanian State Delegation for Economic Affairs led by the Albanian Labor Party Central Committee Political Bureau Member and First Vice-Chairman of the Council of Ministers Spiro Koleka, and the

Albanian Labor Party Central Committee Political Bureau Alternate Member and Vice-Chairman of the Council of Ministers Koìo Theodhosi, accompanied by Premier Zhou Enlai, Vice-Premier Li Xiannian and Vice-Premier Luo Ruiqing, arrived at Xiyang County in Shanxi Province for a visit to the Dazhai Production Brigade."

The party flew directly into Xiyang by helicopter.

In Dazhai the sun shines brightly in May. On the day of the visit, no clouds blocked the heavens. The mountains ringed the village, sharply silhouetted against a light blue sky. Dazhai residents gathered early to wait for the arrival of the Premier's helicopters. Provincial Committee leaders Wei Heng and Wang Qian, all chief leaders in the Central Shanxi Region and Xiyang County, and all cadres from Dazhai stood ready for the welcoming ceremony at the makeshift airfield in South River, just one mile from Dazhai.

At nine o'clock in the morning two helicopters and one escort aircraft appeared in the distance, entering Dazhai's air space from northeast. The crowds who were gathered on the ground leaped with joy, waved bouquets and applauded at the sight. Watching the helicopters gradually drop from the heights to the airfield, everybody spontaneously shouted:

"They're here! They're here!"

The crowds, lined up in three prearranged rows, made ready to close in from two sides to form a welcoming corridor. The cars carrying Premier Zhou and the foreign guests from the landing spot slowly entered the clear space in the middle. Premier Zhou jumped from his vehicle to greet everyone warmly and shake hands. Then he and Koleka, escorted by Chen Yonggui, led the group of foreign guests on foot through the corridor formed by the welcoming mass of people.

Back then, the people from Dazhai were not very familiar with welcoming etiquette for foreign guests. Those assembled waved their bouquets and colored ribbons, shouting: "Welcome! Welcome!" The foreign visitors, waving at the masses, shouted: "Mao Zedong! Enver!" The masses responded: "Mao Zedong! Enver!" Premier Zhou, appalled by the blunder, immediately called out loudly: "Enver! Mao Zedong!" The multitudes, taking their cue from the Premier, switched to: "Enver! Mao Zedong! Enver! Mao Zedong!" ["Enver" was Enver Hoxha, First Secretary of the Albanian Labor Party.]

After every few steps Premier Zhou had to stop to exchange greetings with the people. Among Dazhai's residents, in addition to Chen Yonggui, Premier Zhou was most familiar with Chen Yonggui's son Chen Mingzhu. A year earlier Chen Mingzhu had attended the Ninth Conference of the Communist Youth League of China, and had been received by Chairman Mao and Premier Zhou. Mingzhu had left a deep impression on the Premier, who was now very moved as he greeted the young man. Who would have thought the Premier had such a good memory! Following an introduction by Chen Yonggui, Premier Zhou warmly shook hands with Jia Jincai, addressing him affectionately with, "How is the old hero?"

As Premier Zhou's tall frame paused and moved on in the midst of the welcoming crowd, a thousand eyes peered at him intensely. Although already over sixty, his step was firm, his head free of white hair, and his movements energetic. When he spotted Niu Guodong, an old fellow of his own age, standing in the third row, he felt like greeting him. He made his way through the first two rows and offered his outstretched hand to that senior citizen, who shook it firmly. Later, during the visit to the Exhibition Center, he noticed Niu Guodong's photograph, along with the clothes, quilt and pillow he had used in the old society. He asked the photographer to take a picture of the exhibit as a souvenir.

When they entered one of the stone-lined cave dwellings constructed after the flood, Premier Zhou, filled with emotion, told Li Xiannian, "There aren't too many people in Dazhai, but they have certainly accomplished a lot. This indeed is 'transforming heaven and earth'!"

Chen Yonggui led Zhou into Guo Fenglian's house. Guo Fenglian pointed at him and explained to her old mother: "This is our Premier Zhou. He never rests at night!"

"You exaggerate! You exaggerate!" Premier Zhou said, smiling as he waved Guo Fenglian off.

Guo Fenglian's mother brought out some steaming hot corn buns and offered them to the Premier. He gave half of the buns to the other guests and sat down on the brick bed *kang* to eat his half with real gusto, engaging Guo Fenglian's mother in small talk. Some children gathered in the yard to perform a dance called "Looking for a Friend." With one hand the Premier beat time to the music. With the other he held his last steamed bun. When the dance was over he hugged the children and kissed some of them on the cheek.

What impressed Jia Jincai the most was how Premier Zhou, upon entering his stone cave dwelling, set down on the edge of the brick bed *kang*, folded his legs just like any old farmer and started talking about Dazhai's history. Song Liying brought over the freshly steamed thorn date buns she had made for Premier Zhou, but he only ate half a bun. Perhaps he had already eaten too many cornmeal buns at Guo Fenglian's. What surprised Jia Jincai and Song Liying, however, was how much Premier Zhou treasured the food. He wrapped the half he couldn't finish in a handkerchief and put it in his pocket.

"That's it. I'll take it back with me so other Central Committee leaders can try it too," he said, very pleased with the idea.

Having visited the village, Premier Zhou and the foreign guests, led by Chen Yonggui, walked up the flank of Tigerhead Mountain. Part way up the mountain, good soldiers of the famous "Hard Bone" Sixth Company stationed on Nanjing Road were helping Dazhai residents build a reservoir. They sang as they worked: "The army and the common folk, we are all one family...." Premier Zhou stood with them for a photograph while he likened the relationship between the Army and the people to that of fish to the water they swim in. When they had climbed to the top of Tigerhead Mountain, the guests sat down on boulders to rest. Premier Zhou gazed into the distance. Suddenly he noticed a patch of pine trees on the hilltop in front of a village far below.

"What's that place?" he asked.

"That's Five Family flat," said Chen Yonggui. "It's Dazhai's neighboring village."

"Why can't you plant pine trees on Tigerhead Mountain?" asked Premier Zhou.

"Dazhai is planning to do it," answered Chen Yonggui.

Premier Zhou then inquired about the progress of farming in Five Family Flat and asked Chen Yonggui to help it along. Then he asked in some detail about Dazhai's water supplies and level of irrigation.

"You get drought here nine out of every ten years," said Premier Zhou. "You must solve the problem of water conservancy and irrigation!" Turning his face toward the Governor of Shanxi Province, Wei Heng, who was also a member of the group on the Mountain, he added, "There's only one Dazhai in the whole nation. How can a simple problem like that remain unresolved?"

After a rest on the mountainside, Chen Yonggui took Premier Zhou to Wolf Den Ravine. At the sight of the score or more stone dams in Wolf Den Ravine, Premier Zhou explained to the foreign guests: "This is where the three great battles took place."

"It's been four battles by now," Chen Yonggui broke in. "We've increased the height of the dams and the size of the fields."

"You could build drainage canals and water containment vessels to prevent the danger of flooding," remarked Premier Zhou.

On the way back from Wolf Den Ravine Premier Zhou noticed the stalks at the head of a field piled up for composting.

"You should be applying more farmyard manure," he said happily, grabbing a handful of organic material for examination. "It makes the soil easier to work with. Comrade Yonggui, you should also pay attention to the improvement of farm tools. You need to mechanize your labor force."

At four in the afternoon Premier Zhou left Dazhai in a cloud of dust whipped up by the whirling blades of his craft. Dazhai's people, along with her mountains and streams, took leave of him. His helicopter slowly disappeared from the air space above the village, leaving a warm glow in the hearts of all those left behind.

That evening Chen Yonggui convened a meeting of the Dazhai Production Brigade Party Branch, in order to discuss the impressions left by Premier Zhou's visit. The Governor of Shanxi Province, Wei Heng, and some other leaders attended the meeting and delivered important speeches. Chen Yonggui, responding to Premier Zhou's remarks expressed during rest on Tigerhead Mountain, engaged in self-criticism:

"The Premier pointed out that we haven't developed our forestry or our water conservation and irrigation. That's the direction in which we have to work hard from now on. When he criticized Five Family Village the Premier was really criticizing me. I am the General Secretary of our Joint Production Brigades' Party organization. If the work in Five Family Village and other Brigades does not improve, it's my responsibility."

After this, the Party members started a serious discussion. "Just because we saw the Premier and shook hands with him," everybody agreed, "by no means proves that what we do is perfect. If we don't work harder, what will we have to report to him next time?"

Premier Zhou's first visit to Dazhai served as a turning point. The people of the village never forgot the day.

As visitors from far and near grew in number and importance, Chen Yonggui's fame swelled in equal proportion. His status rose accordingly, his presence came into great demand, and he had opportunities to travel. One day in the autumn of 1966 he had found himself enjoying special treatment, political and otherwise, as a member of a high-level Chinese delegation traveling to Albania, because the Chinese Communist Party had chosen Chen Yonggui as one of the seven-member delegation sent to attend the Congress of the Albanian Party of Labor. The group, led by Kang Sheng, included, besides Chen Yonggui, state cadres and worker-peasant-soldier students specializing in international trade. They carried with them a letter from Mao Zedong to Enver Hoxha. The letter used a Tang Dynasty poem to express warm regards from one to the other.

> When you retain as intimates
> People embraced by the Four Seas,
> Even the most remote corners of the earth
> Seem like your own neighborhood.
> China and Albania are separated
> By numerous mountains and rivers
> But our hearts beat in unison.

This trip abroad raised Chen Yonggui's prestige as well as the prestige of Dazhai and Xiyang County. When he returned to Xiyang he stirred new feelings in the hearts of local people. They all spoke glowingly about him, saying that he was an extraordinary person who brought credit to their County. People began to debate whether he had worn his trademark white towel on his head while in Albania. There were also some residents of the County seat who had still never had an opportunity to see him, so they gathered early along the road to wait for him, hoping to enjoy at least a glimpse.

At eight in the morning the rumbling sound of a jeep engine rolled in from the direction of Yangquan. The assembled welcoming ranks started beating drums and gongs, the sound of bamboo firecrackers traveling up to the sky. Chen Yonggui, nodding and smiling at the applauding crowd, jumped from the car and walked through the corridor of well-wishers in the company of the County Magistrate Yang Peichun. People were finally able to verify that, although he still wore a Chinese-style jacket, he had replaced his white towel with a cap. This, they decided, was the result of international influences and pressures. After Chen Yonggui passed through the human corridor, the welcoming crowd followed him to the County Party Committee's big yard. Following Mayor Yang's brief introductory remarks, Chen Yonggui took to the podium. Amidst enthusiastic applause, he said: "I thank everybody for coming out to welcome me despite the bitter cold!"

The Mayor suggested that Chen Yonggui pick a convenient time to inform the public about his visit. Since everybody was dying to hear the story of his trip, Chen Yonggui agreed on the spot to speak the next day.

Cadres from various County organizations and members of various enterprises and institutions packed the Grand Auditorium the following morning. Everybody listened to Chen Yonggui's account of his trip to Albania with rapt attention. Chen Yonggui, dressed once again in his peasant outfit, sat on the presiding platform. He talked about the activities of the Chinese Communist Party Delegation in the country known as the Land of the Mountain Eagle, and about how that nation developed its industry, agriculture and technology. He then compared the situation in the two countries. He also told the audience about the reception hosted by Enver Hoxha, First Secretary of the Albanian Labor Party. Hoxha had asked them whether they were tired. Having run around for several days, they were indeed quite tired, but they did not dare say so in front of the Albanian leader.

"Right. You can't feel tired," Hoxha then said. "Chairman Mao is seventy-three, and he still runs all over the place. Would you say he was tired?"

Chen Yonggui also talked about China's assistance to Albania, Vietnam, and distant colonies and semi-colonies struggling for nationhood—aid given while her own moment of need still plagued the donor. At the end of his speech he emphasized that Spiro Koleka's visit to Dazhai in the company of Premier Zhou had been the beginning of friendship between Albanian people and the people of Dazhai. His own trip to Albania and participation in its Party Congress was yet another step in this growing friendship.

A year later, on October 4, 1967, the then Member of the Political Bureau of the Albanian Labor Party, and currently the Party's First Secretary, Ramiz Alija, led a delegation that visited Dazhai, furthering the friendship with Chen Yonggui. Chen accompanied Alija up Tigerhead Mountain.

"All we have here are big mountains," Chen Yonggui explained to him. "They are suitable for developing forestry. After I saw the tree-clad mountains of your country, I planted pines as soon as I came back."

"One has to admire your spirit of hard struggle," said Alija.

What was quite interesting for Chen Yonggui was that, Albania being very mountainous too, every place he went he saw peasants cultivating fields with walking tractors. He had already talked about this at the National Conference on the Mechanization of Agriculture. As a result, Xiyang County began constructing a tractor factory to manufacture only this kind of small-frame "baby tractor" suitable for tilling mountainous land. But, because of later, perverse changes in the political climate, this dream of Chen Yonggui's never became a reality.

Later on, reflecting his ever-growing fame, Chen Yonggui got other opportunities to travel abroad. By that time, in the eyes of people from foreign lands, Chen was no longer an ordinary Chinese peasant. He was a well-traveled political veteran capable of taking the international spotlight when the occasion demanded.

After the Great Proletarian Cultural Revolution began, however, everything changed. Chen Yonggui's reputation, in spite of many new successes, not only at the village level, but County wide, Province wide and nationwide, suffered serious erosion.

PART TWO

A PEASANT TURNED STATESMAN

CHAPTER 18

A BANNER EVERYONE WANTED TO WAVE

At this time the "Great Proletarian Cultural Revolution" broke out.

The Cultural Revolution was the product of the theory of "continuous revolution." Chen Yonggui was not too familiar with this theory, which can be best seen in the case of Dazhai. Although, later, there was talk of this and that struggle, Dazhai's landlords and rich peasants in fact lived a very peaceful existence in Dazhai. Chen Yonggui treated them with great humanity and without discrimination, letting them enjoy the same benefits as the other Commune members so long as they did not speak out or act irresponsibly. At a time when almost the entire country set its "four elements" to street sweeping and yard cleaning,[1] nothing of the sort occurred in Dazhai.

In Dazhai it was the Party cadres who undertook the cleaning on their own initiative. This is not to say that Chen Yonggui did not draw a clear line of demarcation between class ranks, but simply that he had thought the matter out in his own unique way. When a group of jour-

1. "The four kinds of elements" were the landlords, the rich peasants, the counterrevolutionaries

nalists from Beijing arrived to photograph in Dazhai in 1967, they expressed concern about getting the landlords and rich peasants into their shots.

"Don't worry," Chen Yonggui told them, "they won't get in your way."

He sent the landlords and rich peasants to work in a spot that the journalists were not likely to approach. The chief obstacles Chen Yonggui had to deal with in Dazhai were, in his words, "the well-to-do middle-peasant mentality" and the conservative ideology held by many cadres. When it came to making choices among political targets, he could not escape a certain peasant-generated utilitarian standpoint. Chen Yonggui always saw most Provincial and County cadres as "one of us." He believed that they had discovered Dazhai and nurtured him personally. His simple, peasant-style gratitude made him feel indebted to and protective of them. He could not accept that they be called "capitalist-roaders" lightly, without regard to who they were.

Consequently, as the Cultural Revolution spread and overran the big cities, he at first maintained a kind of perplexed wait-and-see attitude.

Unfortunately Dazhai's fame did not allow him to just wait and look on. The media called on him to express his views regarding the Cultural Revolution. The press and the broadcasting networks wanted to use his name in their coverage. Both factional organizations that had just been formed in the County and Provincial capitals thought it was extremely important to win over Dazhai in their bid for power. In the parlance of the day, it was enormously effective to "use the great banner of revolution as a tiger skin" to impress and intimidate people. Consequently, students from Beijing, Tianjin and Taiyuan coming to Dazhai to "establish contact," kept agitating for Chen Yonggui to join their "group." Chen Yonggui did not approve of this at all. He just smiled indifferently, without stating clearly where he stood. On one occasion, when the County middle school "Red Guards" called on him, he just rubbed his nose and told them scornfully: "It's so easy for you kids to say 'down with this' and 'down with that.' Do you think you will overthrow everything? Go play somewhere else!"

But, whether he participated or not, the flames of the Cultural Revolution raged on just the same. When, at its beginning, self-styled revolutionary rebels criticized and denounced Chen's old County leader, Zhang Huaiying, at a public meeting in Wenshui County and accused many other old cadres in Xiyang County of belonging to an anti-Party clique, he did not understand it at all.

Soon thereafter Red Guards from Beijing's No. 101 Middle School and Xian's Petroleum Institute, pursuing the issue of how Yuan Yaoguang, Secretary of the Xiyang County Party Committee, had entered the Party, physically attacked Yuan at the main entrance to the County's Grand Auditorium. They beat him so severely that his entire body swelled up. Yuan Yaoguang could not endure the humiliation of such a struggle. He jumped from the building and killed himself.

When Chen Yonggui heard the news he sat by the side of a field for a very long time, puffing on his pipe and knitting his brow, completely speechless. He was not able to comprehend how things could have come to such a pass. After the Shanxi Provincial Governor Wei Heng committed suicide he did not utter a word. Only some people who were in the know later revealed that he had retired to his room and cried bitterly for some time. He cried because he could not forget the great consideration Wei Heng had given him over the years. Just a few months earlier, when Wei Heng had come to Dazhai to see him, he had not limited his interest to Dazhai but had also inquired about Chen Yonggui's household. When Chen Yonggui told him about his late wife, his new wife, his only son and heir, and his adopted daughter, Wei Heng said with a sigh: "Hey, my Old Chen, your household is quite something! It sounds like a mini-cooperative!"

Despite the dark clouds that hung heavily over the political scene, Chen Yonggui was not able to distance himself from his pragmatic peasant world-view and make sense of what was happening. The more he thought the more puzzled he was by the tumultuous situation. Yet, as a Model Worker of national and international repute, unlike the immortalized ancients who found refuge from political turmoil in the Utopian land that lay beyond the Peach Blossom Spring, he was not able to carry on untouched by China's raging political turmoil.

What should his attitude toward the Cultural Revolution be? Should he take part in the movement or not? For a long time he was not able to weigh the options clearly. On one occasion some Red Guards from Tianjin came to Dazhai to make trouble. They wanted to seize power from Chen Yonggui. Chen Yonggui took refuge in a hospital. He pretended to be nursing an ailment while he waited out the storm. A Brigade leader from neighboring Five Family Flat by the name of Guo Xiaorong, went through quite some trouble to find him, to give him a piece of his mind.

"You better think of a way to deal with this. Is hiding anyway to do it?" Guo inquired.

"What do you suggest?" asked Chen Yonggui.

"In classical literature and opera important officials always go to the Palace to 'move and shake.' You are a Model Worker of some consequence. Why not go to the Palace and do some 'shaking'? Others don't have access to the Chairman and the Premier, but you do."

"That's right," thought Chen Yonggui, feeling his spirits revive. Even the tobacco smoke he had just inhaled all of a sudden acquired a pleasing taste. "The Premier cares about Dazhai so much and has shown so much concern for me—I'm sure he will not refuse to see me if I go."

And that's how Chen Yonggui went to the capital to 'move and shake.'"

Chen Yonggui's arrival at the capital aroused Premier Zhou Enlai's special attention. He immediately returned Chen Yonggui's telephone call, and received him right away. Premier Zhou and Chen Yonggui shook hands in Zhongnanhai's reception room. There Chen Yonggui presented him with four apples he had personally chosen from the tree. The Premier, happily accepting them, announced that the apples were so good he'd give them to Chairman Mao.

When the Premier asked about recent developments in Dazhai, Chen Yonggui brought up three issues. First, he said, too many people were visiting Dazhai—anywhere from four or five thousand to ten thousand a day—which put too much pressure on him since he could not receive them all. What's more, in search of souvenirs to take back, the visitors even carried off ears of corn from the fields. This kind of visit had a bad effect.

"You think of a way to deal with this and so will I," said Premier Zhou. "We'll work together from the top and from the bottom to bring the number of visitors under control."

The second question raised by Chen Yonggui was whether Central authorities would approve the construction of a chemical fertilizer plant in Xiyang County. Since the cadres in Xiyang were responsible for buying fertilizer it was inevitable that they should make some mistakes even to the point of some unethical dealings, but was it right that forty-six village cadres, some of whom dealt with fertilizer, had been driven to death during the Four Clean Movement on embellished charges of corruption? What the Premier said about the forty-six cadres is not recorded, but in regard to the fertilizer plant, he responded that, since there was coal in Xiyang, the project could be taken under consideration. The third problem raised by Chen Yonggui was the question of the Cultural Revolution. He told the Premier how seven Red Guards had threatened him, wielding small knives. Either he joined them in rebellion or they stripped him of his power. They were also checking the toughness of Dazhais "Iron Girls" by placing huge rocks on their shoulders, thus obstructing normal production in the village.

According to Chen Yonggui's report of the meeting, the Premier gave him three red armbands and said: "They organize their Red Guard, you organize one too. They disrupt your orderly production, you organize your Red Guard to protect your production." He also urged Chen to acquire a better understanding of the movement and change his attitude so as to willingly take an active part in the Cultural Revolution.

The meeting with Premier Zhou eased Chen Yonggui's worries to some extent, but he was still not entirely clear on what kind of attitude to assume toward the Cultural Revolution. That was an unresolved mystery to him. A few days later, returning to Dazhai, he ran into a woman cadre from the Province who told him about an incident in which a rebel faction tried to seize power from the Provincial Party Committee. This was something Chen Yonggui could not fathom: Why seize power? Some outside journalists broke the news to him when he got back to the village: Seizing power from the capitalist-roaders in fact meant seizing power from the leadership on all levels. They even tried to persuade him to participate in the seizures. At that point Chen Yonggui acquired a faint glimmer of what it was all about, but it still didn't add up. In private, he sighed and remarked: "Some people who truly worked hard have been made into counter-revolutionaries; those who didn't work at all are made to look good."

Next, the Central People's Broadcasting Station broadcast an editorial: "Those of you who are true model workers have nothing to fear from the mass movement. You must resolutely stand on the side of the masses and, together with the masses, carry the Great Proletarian Cultural Revolution through to the end." Model workers from all over the country declared their positions with essays on this theme. Papers and magazines published these and circulated them all over China's vast land. Chen Yonggui made up his mind to work according to the "Sixteen Points."[1]

"What Chairman Mao calls us to, we do!" Chen declared.

Just then a Shanxi rebel faction seized power from the Shanxi Provincial Party Committee. Yang Chengxiao packed the looted official seals of various Committee departments into a gunnysack. On January 12, 1967, the Taiyuan Municipal Rebel Army seized and drove from office former provincial leaders Wang Qian, Wang Daren, and colleagues. On the 25th of the same month several hundred people took part in an oath-taking rally at the "May First Stadium," organized by those who had seized power. At the rally, people started seizing cadres they called "capitalist-roaders" and before long began calling for "interrogation through struggle," meaning various forms of violent persuasion. The atmosphere grew extremely tense. Just at that time the Shanxi peasant leader Li Shunda telephoned from a great distance. The purpose of his call was very clear: He wanted to sound out whether Chen Yonggui would join the Shanxi Revolutionary Rebel Army.

Both Chen Yonggui and Li Shunda tried to guess what the other one thought, but neither revealed anything in their conversation. In the end, they both said: "I'll go if you go. I won't if you don't."

As a result, the two men arrived for a meeting in Taiyuan, one from the east the other from the south, to prepare to join in Shanxi's "Cultural Revolution." On February 6, 1967, the *Shanxi Daily* printed a big, bold headline: "Comrade Chen Yonggui Comes Out Screaming

1. The "Sixteen Points" were issued by Mao on August 8, 1966 and served as the Magna Carta of the Cultural Revolution thereafter. They were honored, however, more in the breach than the observance.

'Kill'!"[1] The text declared: "Famous Model Workers Comrades Chen Yonggui, Li Shunda and Jie Yue initiate the establishment of the Shanxi Revolutionary Rebel Liaison Center and join the Shanxi General Revolutionary Rebel Headquarters. This marks a new stage in the grand alliance of workers and peasants in our Province."

The article opened with an editor's note: "The revolutionary situation is getting better and better. A group of Model Workers in agriculture including Chen Yonggui, Li Shunda and Jie Yue came out screaming 'Kill'! Just as Chairman Mao pointed out, the model workers serve as the example, the backbone, and the link with the people. The Model Workers stand in the forefront of the Great Proletarian Cultural Revolution. The fact that they lead in the making of revolution has great significance. With this kind of example to follow, mighty revolutionary rebel contingents are sure to form with greater speed."

As could be expected, the mass organization set up by Chen Yonggui and Li Shunda, made up mainly of workers and peasants, exerted enormous influence. With Chen Yonggui serving as political officer and Li Shunda as his deputy in the role, it swept countless small-scale organizations into its mainstream. But Chen Yonggui and Li Shunda were, after all, peasants, and each had his own business to attend to back home. After just a few days in Taiyuan they both rushed back to their Production Brigades. As soon as they left, their organization and its satellites turned into a rudderless ship unable to agree on compass readings to guide its voyage. It dissolved of itself. Soon thereafter the huge rebel army contingent split into two factions. One of them, the Red General Headquarters of Liu Hao, a student, supported the old Muslim civilian cadre Liu Geping. The other, the Red Liaison Station of Tuan, another student, supported Zhang Riqing, a Long March general who commanded the provincial armed forces. It was impossible for Chen Yonggui and Li Shunda to avoid being swept into the maelstrom.

Back then, however, the antagonistic attitudes of Liu Geping and Zhang Riqing were still not too pronounced. It was not easy to decide which one of them to support and which one to oppose. Later, a direc-

1. The paper may well have said this, but it seems very unlikely that Chen Yonggui ever voiced such sentiments. The Cultural Revolution created factions that engaged in various levels of provocation. (W.H.H.)

tive from Chairman Mao Zedong arrived:[1] "Let me tell the comrades of the 69th Army that they should take the side of Comrade Liu Geping, support Comrade Liu Geping."

Chen Yonggui's attitude became quite clear after that. "Whatever Chairman Mao decides, I just follow, that's all," declared Chen.

Judgments of Chen Yonggui's role in Shanxi's Cultural Revolution differ, which is only normal since that upheaval has moved into the realm of history. Very few of the participants in the events back then escaped being trapped by the biases of this or that faction, and that includes Chen Yonggui. The following can be sketched from the accounts of various people: Chen Yonggui was a straightforward peasant, with all the unsophistication, pigheadedness and limitations that come with the territory. The general principle he pursued was to obey the central authorities, to obey Chairman Mao and Premier Zhou, which was expressed in a simple formula: "So long as I understand that it's a directive from Chairman Mao or Premier Zhou, I don't turn away, I don't hide, I don't flinch even if you put a knife to my neck."

This can best be illustrated by two rather consequential events. One had to do with Chairman Mao's directive to support Liu Geping. The other was Premier Zhou's dispatch of Chen Yonggui to solve the problem of violence that erupted during the factional struggle in Pingyao County.

The first incident occurred during a mass rally organized at Taiyuan's May First Stadium at the very beginning of the Cultural Revolution. Holding mass rallies was the practice back then, whether because Chairman Mao had just issued a "latest" directive or because of some major social event. Needless to say, mass rallies were quite frequent. Although the two factional organizations had already split up their united headquarters, when it came to studying Chairman Mao's

1. My information is that the Central Committee, soon after January 28, 1966, when Liu Geping set up his Shanxi Revolutionary Committee, gave its full support to this new organ of power and held it up as a model. Thus Chen Yonggui was not wrong in thinking that Mao Zedong supported Liu. The grievous split in Shanxi occurred later. By that time Chen Yonggui and Li Shunda had become identified as partisans on opposite sides, and though Chen later pulled back from active involvement in factionalism on the advice of Premier Zhou Enlai, his relations with Li Shunda were already seriously damaged.(W.H.H.)

works or implementing his directives they were completely unanimous. They also maintained a formal unity in respect to Chairman Mao's "grand proletarian revolutionary rebel alliance." Consequently, the two factions had reached a negotiated agreement about the present mass rally and called for it jointly. Each faction had its spokesman and its own slogan-shouting cheerleader present. The agreement permitted only jointly drafted slogans dealing with general principles and did not allow speeches or slogans that represented the positions of either faction separately. The supporters of each faction took their seats in that half of the Stadium reserved for them, thus forming two camps physically as well as politically.[1]

The host of the rally first announced the agenda, which was followed by speeches by the two leading revolutionary cadres—Liu Geping and Zhang Riqing. They both read from prepared drafts. Everything went according to plan, until only a few items of secondary importance remained on the agenda. Chen Yonggui was a great national Model Worker so, out of respect for his position, it naturally seemed appropriate to let him say a few words. How was anybody to know that in his opening remarks he would passionately invoke Chairman Mao's top directive to the 69th Army by uttering just one sentence:

"We should support Comrade Liu Geping!"

This effectively amounted to no less than breaking the agreement reached before the rally. The slogan-shouting cheerleader from the Red General Headquarters, a young woman, was overjoyed. She immediately followed it up by calling out: "Resolutely support Comrade Liu Geping!" This caused great confusion, as supporters of one faction who were seated below the podium responded to her slogan in unison, clapping hands, while the members of the other faction screamed: "Bombard Liu Geping!"

At this point several of the "leading revolutionary cadres" who were seated at the rostrum, including Liu Geping, started casting mournful looks at Chen Yonggui suggesting that he straighten out the things he

1. "Politics" here does not refer to political principles, but merely to personal preferences as to which personalities leading major factions to support. Each group gave support to the aims of the Revolution while condemning the other group as fraudulent. Each thought it alone had the right to carry the Revolution to the end. (W.H.H.)

had said or else stop talking altogether and let somebody else reverse the course of events. But Chen Yonggui remained stubborn as ever, repeating the phrase into the microphone: "We should support Comrade Liu Geping, indeed."

Great disorder enveloped the Stadium. Members of one faction surged forward while the supporters of the other tried to stop them. It seemed as though a large-scale clash was about to break out. Liu Geping promptly announced the end of the rally, ordering the people from his Red General Headquarters to withdraw immediately from the Stadium. Only thus was the massive clash avoided. But people from Zhang Riqing's Military Corps and Red Rebel Liaison Station rushed toward the rostrum to argue with Chen Yonggui when he tried to leave the grounds. They kept him encircled for more than four hours in an underground chamber directly below the Stadium's open-air stage. He somehow didn't seem to object to this at all, smoking as usual and pacing leisurely and contentedly to and fro. After seven o'clock that night the 69th Army Headquarters dispatched several civilian members to the Stadium to talk reason into people amassed around the rostrum, while a small army vehicle fetched Chen Yonggui from their midst. Chen Yonggui had believed that he could stabilize the situation in Shanxi simply by proclaiming Chairman Mao's directives, but the "seize power" situation had already developed into a serious factional standoff. Events took an unexpected turn and the situation in Shanxi grew steadily worse.

Two large diametrically opposed groups, later to be known as "Red" (Liu's) and "United" (Zhang's) came into the open in Shanxi, clearly influencing every region, every county, and every unit at the grass-roots level. Clashes, large and small, became commonplace. Before long things came to a head in Pingyao County, in the Central Shanxi Region.

At the beginning of August 1967, about a year and a half after the factions formed, Zhang's United group in Central Shanxi called a "Learn From Dazhai" rally in Pingyao County Town. While Zhang's contingent paraded in the streets, a serious clash between the two factions broke out. Zhang's United faction lodged a complaint against Liu's Reds for smashing the organizational structure of the gathering and ruining the "Learn From Dazhai" rally. The Central Government sent a helicopter to

Pingyao to distribute leaflets calling on the participants to call off their confrontation, at the same time dispatching the 69th Army and Air Force Units 025 and 027 to march on Pingyao and stop the clashes.

Chou Enlai then asked Chen Yonggui to go to Pingyao to resolve the violent dispute. Chen arived on August 7th. The mass membership of the two Taiyuan factions had already converged on Pingyao, causing such crowding in the streets that it was impossible to locate a single fruit- or noodle-seller. Before long the town ran out of food and water. It was a crisis situation. United had sealed off several of Pingyao's town gates, leaving only one road open for travel. After Chen Yonggui arrived in Pingyao, ringleaders of both factions hoped to receive him in their own encampments. United was the first to act. Getting hold of Chen Yonggui, they took him to a house first, then to their encampment where they had concentrated several thousand adherents. At this point Red forces surrounded the United gathering and blockaded it and Chen as well. An assistant commanding officer of the Provincial Army District came up with a plan for Chen Yonggui to use United's high-pitch loudspeaker to announce that he had come on orders from the Central Government in order to resolve the violent dispute, bearing no arms and hoping that the representatives of the two factions would join him for negotiations. By nightfall the negotiations did not materialize, and the situation grew even grimmer. Since Reds' grand plan to drag Chen Yonggui to their side failed, they too set up their loudspeaker and announced that Chen Yonggui was not in Pingyao at all, that it had all been a rumor created by United.

A violent fight looked imminent.

The heightened antagonism between the two sides meant that by his mere presence in town Chen Yonggui put his life in danger. Some of the Provincial Army District leaders were very worried that they would be held responsible should something happen to Chen Yonggui. They charged a leading cadre of the Central Shanxi Region with sending a telegram to the Central Government, but there was no way to do it since the telecommunications office in town had long ceased operating and the city gates were blocked. They decided to telephone the neighboring County instead, but couldn't get through to it either. In the end they broke through the city gates under the cover of Air Force Units 025 and 027, to send the telegram to the Central Government from the boondocks. No sooner did they finish the dispatch than incessant gunfire broke out. At ten the following morning a cable from Premier Zhou Enlai gave the following order: "First, send in a battalion to bring Chen Yonggui out; second, army troops should enter town and wipe out factional strongholds—but they shouldn't be armed when they go in...."

A large truck under khaki-colored canvas took Chen Yonggui out of the city gates dressed in army fatigues. It drove him to a unit of the 69th Army. The Commander of the 69th Army, Xie Zhenhua, personally directed his troops to suppress both factional strongholds without firing a single bullet. Thus he accomplished the goal of putting down the violent fighting. However, on August 9th, the United faction took control of Pingyao for the second time. After this seizure, because the situation was not dealt with properly and because of the great disparity in manpower between United and Red after United took control of Pingyao, the town remained in constant chaos.[1]

Chen Yonggui's prestige declined after his efforts miscarried in Pingyao. The whole affair caused a big controversy in Shanxi Province. In all truth, given the complexity of the situation, it was impossible to solve such a major incident appropriately unless, of course, the whole political climate changed.

Here is what Chen Yonggui himself had to say about it some years later, in 1971, during a Rectification Meeting to Criticize Chen Yonggui: "According to guidelines issued several times by the Central Government, we were supposed to sum up our experiences. Yet we haven't done it to this day. That nobody died during a big incident like that we owe to the good relations between the Army and the people. They let me wear a military uniform, and then they brought me out under protection. That was the moment of greatest confusion and disorder. People were whipping up public opinion with stories that Chen Yonggui was a runaway landlord and tyrant."

Earlier, when Chen Yonggui faced the crowd in Taiyuan, it was only because of a single sentence uttered by the great leader Chairman

1. For a description of Chen Yonggui in Pingyao see William Hinton's *Shenfan*, Page xxxviii.

Mao, that he publicly expressed support for Liu Geping. Prior to that time Chen Yonggui had only encountered Liu Geping a few times and their relationship was not close at all. On the other hand, Chen Yonggui had worked at various times with the other factional chief, Zhang Riqing. Neither of the two Shanxi chieftains, however, ever took Chen Yonggui seriously. The Provincial Army District commanded by Zhan Riqing had more than once distributed weapons to the people on its side so that they could organize armed battles, then reported to the Central authorities that the people had stolen the weapons. At the time Chen Yonggui reported this and other anomalies in Shanxi to the Central Government. Premier Zhou then requested several times that Chen Yonggui be allowed to come out and solve the problem in the Province. By the time he did so, however, the factional split could hardly be reversed. Regardless of his subjective wishes, Chen Yonggui had already become the banner-bearer of one faction and the thorn in the eye of the other.

Due to the serious antagonism of the two factional organizations in Shanxi, the situation in the Province remained unstable for a long time. In July of 1969, the Central Government released Chairman Mao's Proclamations No. 7 and No. 23 with comments and instructions on the situation. He severely criticized both Liu Geping and Zhang Riqing for their factionalism and grave mistakes in rejecting Party decisions, and he appointed Xie Zhenhua and Chen Yonggui as the new chief "Leading Block" of Shanxi's Revolutionary Committee. After Chairman Mao's proclamation Chen Yonggui enforced his orders and prohibitions strictly, commenting that he'd never be involved in factionalism again. In addition to his participation in the collective leadership of the Shanxi Revolutionary Committee, he concentrated on work in Xiyang County and Dazhai. From that moment on his contacts with Liu Geping and Zhang Riqing became very rare.[1]

Objectively speaking, Chen Yonggui's loves and hates in the Cultural Revolution were plain and simple: He was influenced by the theory of class struggle and he displayed extreme adoration and love for

1. The Shanxi problem continued to fester. As late as 1975 Central authorities had not been able to resolve it completely. For Zhou Enlai's comments in 1971 see William Hinton's *Shenfan*, Page 583. (W.H.H.)

the Great Leader. When Chairman Mao called, "Take power from the clique of capitalist-roaders within the party," Chen Yonggui, although not a direct actor in the fight for power, nevertheless took part in the Provincial Revolutionary Rebel General Headquarters. After he became the Deputy Director of the Shanxi Provincial Revolutionary Committee and Director of the Xiyang County Revolutionary Committee, he was able on his own initiative to criticize and denounce old cadres from the Central Shanxi Region and Xiyang. In the circumstances, compelled by the trend of the times, it was virtually impossible for him to avoid being drawn into the struggle. While he never advocated criticism and denunciation of prestigious old cadres from the Province, because the growth of Dazhai had a lot to do with their support, still, if he refused to participate in the criticism and denunciation at some level, being the well-known Model Worker that he was, he would clearly have to rethink his attitude toward the Cultural Revolution.

Chen Yonggui carried out the Central Committee's Party line of the time 100 percent, saying and doing many things that were contrary to his convictions in the process. In particular, several on-the-spot "Learn From Dazhai" meetings that were supposed to be examining production somehow ended up closely linked to power struggles in progress. Such connections were inevitable. Some of the members of the Provincial Revolutionary Committee used Chen Yonggui's name to drag the old cadres to Xiyang for criticism and denunciations by General Zhang's Provincial Army District leadership. At first, in order to draw a clear line between the cadres and himself, Chen Yonggui looked on as the denunciations destroyed their careers. He did not extend them any protection or show any special consideration for their well-being. In acting thus he was adapting himself to the political climate of the time. Later, however, he did say that he suffered a guilty conscience over his role. When the issue came up during a 1973 meeting of the Provincial Revolutionary Committee's Standing Committee he engaged in self-criticism. After the meeting, the Deputy Provincial Governor Liu Kaiji tapped Chen Yonggui on the shoulder and said in a tone full of understanding: "Oyoyoy, Old Chen! You always want to have this high attitude. How many millstones around people's necks did this one self-criticism remove?"

Objectively speaking, Chen Yonggui's behavior in the Cultural Revolution cannot be summarized in just a few sentences. In addition to the general climate of the times, individual views and standpoints also reflect the interpersonal relations. When a peasant makes real life choices, he is forced to confront common human feelings of gratitude and resentment. On the scale of his conscience he must weigh carefully whom he ought to love and whom to hate. So when Chen Yonggui heard that factionalists were attacking a large number of old Xiyang County cadres as the counter-revolutionary revisionist elements and when he found out that Zhang Huaiying passed out three times during a struggle session in Wenshui County, he began to speak at meetings, and after the meetings. "Zhang Huaiying was my leader for fifteen years," he protested. "Five years as the Regional Committee Secretary, and ten years as the County Committee Secretary. He did many good things for Xiyang County. How could he turn into a counter-revolutionary? That's something beyond my comprehension. Who would want to do this to Xiyang County cadres? And why?"

After one group of rebels denounced Zhang, Chen Yonggui sympathized with the man's predicament and used every possible pretext to insure his safety. When some individuals from the Central Shanxi Region and Xiyang County continued to persecute him, he expressed his unreserved indignation.

Overall, to analyze Chen Yonggui's role in the Cultural Revolution is a complicated matter. In addition to his early passivity as young militants denounced so many old cadres and his failure to bring Shanxi factionalim under control, problems also arose concerning his relationship with Shanxi's other Model Workers. The two cases with the most impact were those of Zhou Mingshan and Li Shunda.

Chen Yonggui paid close attention to Zhou Mingshan, who had been the Party Branch Secretary of the South Fork Production Brigade from Jiang County, and later became the County Committee Secretary there. In the past, Chen Yonggui had some negative impressions of Zhou Mingshan. He, Li Shunda, Wang Dehe and Wu Houli all developed a dislike for the man when they attended the Third National People's Congress in 1964. Zhou Mingshan was not a man without merit, but he liked to show off. During his speech at the Congress, discovering that nobody in the audience applauded him, he cast aside the prepared material and proceeded to talk off the top of his head. He added all kinds of anecdotes and jokes, with the result that many people reproached him. He threw the Congress into confusion because the representatives of various national minorities who were attending the meeting could not follow the translation executed on the spot without previous preparation. Chen Yonggui and Li Shunda criticized him after the meeting. When militants later denounced him during the Cultural Revolution, however, Zhou Mingshan wrote a letter to Chen Yonggui pleading for Master Chen to save him. Even though Chen Yonggui had spoken critically of Zhou Mingshan, he now thought hard to find a way to save his "disciple." In the end, Chen Yonggui advocated that Zhou Mingshan be allowed to re-enter public life and resume a leading post.

The record shows that during the time Chen Yonggui exercised power he had a hard time treating Shanxi's old cadres, other Model Workers and factional opponents impartially and objectively. It was particularly hard for him to handle his relationship with the other Model Workers. Back then, people called it "balancing three bowls of water," but was there a single person able to do that balancing act? Due to the very complicated conflicts of the time, not even Chairman Mao could keep society in proper balance. With the Cultural Revolution "Leading Group" on the Central Committee strapping shackles on a "Leftist" neck here, and slapping a "Rightist" face there—even an experienced acrobat with a natural talent for juggling would have had a hard time maintaining any balance, not to mention staying upright.

Be that as it may, I still ought to say something about Chen Yonggui and Li Shunda during the Cultural Revolution. Chen's friendship with Li Shunda, the other great Model Worker and peasant leader in Shanxi suffered a most complicated set of mishaps. In the chaotic circumstances of the time, with their Province torn by unprincipled factionalism, neither man could break free from early, relatively innocent, or should one say naive, involvement with factions that became sworn enemies as their self-proclaimed leaders contended for high office in Taiyuan, the Provincial Capital.

As the two Model Workers, propelled by their factional connections, parted company, their relations with various Army units played a key role. General Zhang Riqing's Shanxi Regional Army Command was the core of United with which Li Shunda allied. Some airforce and naval units supported Red, with which Chen Yonggui hooked up early, on the strength of Mao's support for Liu Geping. This, incidentally, was before any split occurred and before Red had crystallized out.

Once the identification was made, however, neither man could extricate himself, while each faction, on its part, as a prop to its ambitions, dragged the name of its favorite Model Worker into every arena, up to and including Beijing. In these circumstances discord and conflict between the two peasant dirt farmers who once called each other "Master" was inevitable. In truth, the way assorted activists bandied their names about served more to express the complexity of the struggle in Shanxi than any conflict between them personally.

The stubborn factionalism in Shanxi, in spite of the removal of both General Zhang Riqing and the Muslim functionary Liu Geping from the Province in late 1969, persisted into the middle seventies. Unfortunately Li Shunda's longstanding connection with United drew him and many United leaders and followers into the orbit of the Gang of Four as it rose to prominence and set the stage for is own planned usurpation of power.

In a letter written to Chen Yonggui in 1978, when his relations with the Gang of Four came under scrutiny and he himself was detained for re-education, Li Shunda admitted complicity, or at least passivity, when United activists from all over Shanxi kidnapped, beat and paraded Party Secretary Wang Chien through the streets with a neck-wrenching, heavy-metal dunce cap on his head. This occurred after Wang Chien had been restored to power in the seventies as the Party leader of Shanxi Province. Li Shunda also admitted promoting a film, alleged to be part of a frame-up of Deng Xiaoping, called *The Little Cold River of Rejoicing*, and also taking a hand in the frame-up of a certain prominent physician—all three apparently ultra-left initiatives of Gang of Four supporters in Shanxi. Most serious was the support given by Li himself to the Gang during its final furious drive for national power after Mao's death.

In his letter to Chen Yonggui, Li Shunda made clear how much he respected and admired Dazhai's leader and how much Dazhai's example had meant to him and his village, West Gully.

"Only after Chairman Mao issued the great call 'In Agriculture Learn From Dazhai' in 1964, did we firm up our resolve to learn from you.... During the short six years that followed, Xigou's agricultural development surpassed by far that of the previous fifteen years since liberation. Our grain output increased one and one-half times. I really tasted in practice the sweetness of learning from Dazhai. As for my saying that 'Chen Yonggui has been living off Chairman Mao's five words of praise'—it never occurred to me even to think such thoughts."

Li's emotional account leaves no doubt that no fundamental, serious conflict between Li Shunda and Chen Yonggui ever took place. Both men were earnest and down-to-earth peasants, and both at one time in the history of Chinese agriculture became "men of the day." After factionalism tore a gap between them and after each had gone through a process of political "purification," the two peasant leaders were saying, "Nothing really happened between me and Old Chen." And, "Nothing happened between me and Old Li either!"

At the time, however, neither could extricate himself from the entangling web of connections.

Although, during the Cultural Revolution the central leadership dispatched Chen Yonggui many times to solve concrete problems in Shanxi Province, the severe factionalism rendered him powerless. Since, in addition, this kind of activity was not really what the Dazhai's leader was cut out for and did best, Chen Yonggui withdrew from it as much as possible and, once again, focused his energy on work in Dazhai and Xiyang County.

Once again his work produced remarkable results.

CHAPTER 19

TAKING ON A WAYWARD COUNTY

Once Chen Yonggui became part of the new Provincial Leading Group, the normal tendency would be to put him in control of Xiyang County. The process, however, was not so simple. After the circulation of the "Sixteen Points" one Xiyang County organization of the Red Guards started writing posters and organizing material criticizing cadres. After the January storm in Shanghai and the power takeover in Shanxi on January 12, 1967 a Xiyang Red Guard organization united with an outside organization to detain the chief leader of the County Party Committee and take over the powers held by the people at the County Committee. These youngsters were fully aware that they would not be able to hold onto power by their ability alone. They knew they needed powerful backing. So they asked Chen Yonggui to act as their commander-in-chief, and they immediately announced the news. Chen Yonggui was very angry when he heard this, asking them: "What gave you authority to announce my participation?"

A few days later, Guo Fenglian, acting as a representative of Dazhai, solemnly declared that the above incident had not taken place and that Chen Yonggui had not become their commander-in-chief.

Later, another group of the Red Guards signaled that they were planning to persuade Chen Yonggui to take power. Just at that time some of the old cadres who had been transferred out of Xiyang in 1964 started gradually returning to Xiyang. All these old officials, regardless of what County they had been transferred to, had suffered attacks in the beginning stages of the Cultural Revolution. Insurgent units had paraded some of them through the streets wearing tall dunce hats to instruct the populace, they had put others in isolation and subjected them to severe interrogation, they had locked still others up in prison. Most severe was the case of the Wenshui County Party Committee Secretary Zhang Huaiying. Insurgents beat him until he passed out. He regained consciousness only after several relapses into a life-threatening coma. And he wasn't the only member of his family targeted. His tormenters even went after his five-year-old child.

Chen Yonggui became very anxious about Zhang Huaiying's plight. In the winter of 1966, some natives of the Central Shanxi Region and Xiyang County found out that some Beijing and Taiyuan Red Guards were planning to bring Zhang Huaiying back to Xiyang. As Zhang Huaiying's health was still very weak, Chen Yonggui undertook to protect him and bring him to Dazhai. The route chosen detoured off the main road onto a flank of Tigerhead Mountain. Some individuals bent on laying their hands on Zhang Huaiying surrounded the rescue party on a Tigerhead slope and held it under siege for an entire day. At a critical moment Jia Jincai and several other Dazhai residents armed themselves with rocks and threatened to launch a potentially lethal barrage at their foe.

"Come on, bastards! Come on up and face the rocks!" they yelled.

This scared the would-be attackers and they withdrew. That same night Chen Yonggui sent someone with a bicycle to fetch Zhang Huaiying from Dazhai and take him back to Taiyuan, where in the long run he would be safer.

Those old Xiyang County cadres that returned to the County organized themselves into a number of groups, such as the "Life-and-Death Squad." Then they demanded that Chen Yonggui stand forth and take control. This, combined with a directive received from Premier Zhou Enlai by telephone, convinced Chen Yonggui that he should wrest the power from the rebel faction then in control. On the 10th of February 1967, thirty representatives of various other Xiyang County rebel combat forces assembled at the County Capital Great Auditorium for the ceremony that transferred power to Comrade Chen Yonggui. To a man, the old Xiyang County returnees attended the ceremony. Protocol called for each combat force chieftain to make a statement of his position, declare a firm commitment to follow Comrade Chen Yonggui's commands and play a loyal part in the new leadership group headed by Comrade Chen Yonggui. When Chen Yonggui's turn came to deliver his statement, he raised an issue.

"We are building a general headquarters in the spirit of the Central Committee's policy, with representatives of workers, peasants, cadres, and rebel factions," he said. "That's not enough. Army cadres should be represented too," whereupon he made a motion to that effect.

As the result of Chen Yonggui's motion, the Political Officer of the County Military Unit, Guo Liuwang, became a member of the new leading group. The meeting decided to set up the Xiyang County Revolutionary Rebel General Headquarters with Chen Yonggui as the Commander-in-chief, and a leadership nucleus composed of Chen Yonggui, Wang Guike and Li Chengyuan. On the following day, February 11th, which in 1967 coincided with the Lunar New Year, various Xiyang County Production Brigade Party Committee secretaries, Production Brigade leaders, and other high-ranking cadres staged a mass rally at the South Temple Grounds Square. Chen Yonggui served as Chairman. The rally officially proclaimed the establishment of the new General Headquarters with Chen Yonggui as its Commander-in-Chief. Supporters of the new Headquarters dragged former Chief County Committee leaders Zhang Runhuai and Xiao Gang, and Chief Central Shanxi Regional Committee leaders Wang Xiujin and Xie Zihe onto the stage to be denounced. The event became known as the "February 11th Takeover."

The February 11th Takeover generated several resolutions sponsored by Chen Yonggui: to undertake a thoroughgoing criticism of the "capitalist-roaders," to "grasp revolution, promote production, and finally, to turn Xiyang County into a Dazhai- style County within three to five years."

The first thing Chen Yonggui felt he should do after he assumed power was to report to Premier Zhou Enlai and solicit Premier Zhou's instructions. A three-hundred-mile-long copper wire carried the conversation between the State Premier and the peasant representative.

"Premier, I took power at the County seat!"

"Good! If you are in power, I can put my mind to rest."

"Some of our old County cadres came back. They are acting as my advisers."

"Good. Listen to their opinions, but also follow the mass line."

"After I took power, I made several resolutions. One is to turn Xiyang County into a Dazhai-type County within three to five years."

"Very good, very good. That's exactly what Chairman Mao had in mind when he instructed, 'Grasp revolution, promote production, learn from Dazhai.' Don't be eager to fight; work on a grand revolutionary alliance. Take charge of the construction in Dazhai's home County, and I'll be relieved."

Encouraged by Premier Zhou, Chen Yonggui was careful about the way he handled Xiyang County's past problems. Peasant intuition still guided most of his actions in Xiyang and he tried hard to mesh them well with local conditions. His main rule was still to do whatever Chairman Mao said. The directive from on high was: "Reduce the scale of attacks, expand the range of education." Consequently Chen did not treat County Magistrate Yang Peichun as a capitalist-roader, but listed him among those cadres who had only committed serious mistakes.

There was a County Committee Secretary in Xiyang by the name of Li Qianzhou. He had followed the former County Committee Secretary Zhang Runhuai (not to be confused with Zhang Huaiying) very closely. Li's slogan in a period of difficulty had been merely, "For each slope you plane, a steamed bread you gain!" He had absolutely no ambitious, long-range objectives. He operated on a much lower level of aspiration and attainment than Chen Yonggui. Once, during preparations for a march, many people wanted to bring Li Qianzhou before the public and parade him in the streets. They said that this was the only way to get a mass turnout for the event. Chen Yonggui, however, did not believe that Li Qianzhou was such a bad man. He also needed to reduce the scale of such attacks, so he stated his position: "We can't do that. We have to protect Li Qianzhou."

Later, during a mass rally of active cadres held at the County seat, Chen Yonggui explained his action: "Qianzhou made a mistake, I certainly don't deny that. But do you know what kind of person Li Qianzhou is? Comrades, he is just like me! He grew up bare-assed, labored half his life as a hired hand for whatever period they'd hire him for. He has no schooling. He just blindly follows others. If he has made mistakes, let's investigate them! Chairman Mao says we should unite 95 percent of the people. Only the capitalist-roaders are our enemy! If we push beyond those few, hit or miss, we'll damage our unity!"

After Chen Yonggui took the reins, he concentrated his effort on taking control of and developing the process of learning from Dazhai. To him, it was a question of adherence to a political line. He first set about resolving the issue of the grand revolutionary alliance in Xiyang County Town, and then he focused his problem-solving efforts on the countryside. Due to the nationwide character of agitation to seize power, many villages in Xiyang County were just in the process of seizing power from their Party Branch Secretaries and People's Commune Secretaries. The majority of the power-grabbers were habitual lazy gluttons and addicted office-seekers. Some were not even Party members, yet during the mass rallies they would announce that they were dismissing such-and-such a Party Branch Secretary from his post or expelling so-and-so from the Party. Chen Yonggui was extremely upset by this unusual phenomenon, saying that such people were even worse than the capitalist-roaders.

Was it possible, he asked, that the "Four Clean" Movement did not sufficiently shake up and damage the grass-roots-level cadres, and that the Cultural Revolution was now setting out to wipe them out completely? Even incomprehensible upstarts had targeted many of Xiyang County's Model Workers, like the North Gate Party Branch Secretary Geng Dehua, the South Gate Party Branch Secretary Feng Yan, the Fang Platform Party Branch Secretary Ding Wanfu, and the Rear Settlement Party Branch Secretary Wang Dongzhou, had expelled them from the Party, dismissed them from their posts, seized and denounced them by turn, and even placed them in confinement.

Chen Yonggui used his unique new position of strength to do two things at the same time: One, he transferred a group of errant, faction-prone cadres to several outlying People's Communes to sit it out for a while in the countryside. [2]. He dispatched a forceful Chairman Mao's Thought Propaganda Team to the Settled Peace People's Commune and the Wang Camp People's Commune as a "work team." That is how he implemented the Cultural Revolution in the countryside. At the same time he took steps to resolve the factional conflict that was tearing apart the Cherish Red Middle School in town.

Chen Yonggui wanted to call personally on all the village Party Branch Secretaries who had previously been subjected to particularly severe persecution. He wanted to free them from their predicament, by making his position known. In the case of Party Branch Secretary Wang Dongzhou, from Rear Settlement, who sat locked up in prison, he dispatched somebody to escort him in person back to the County seat. He criticized sharply some rebel faction leaders who opposed this move.

Several Communes had prepared material on these leaders and requested that Chen Yonggui and the County Revolutionary Committee approve dressing them in the dunce hats reserved for bad elements and parading them in the streets. Chen Yonggui glanced at the pile of material spread out on his table and picked up one file. Seated quietly in his chair, he turned the matter over and over in his mind. He then looked at another file, meanwhile asking those present to make their own decision in each case. The more he thought about it the more he felt such matters should be handled with great care. During the collective discussion of the material Chen Yonggui clearly stated his considered position, which was that their mistakes should be treated as policy errors. They should be criticized severely but dealt with lightly. Due to his prudent decisions regarding appropriate treatment, Xiyang County never again witnessed the birth of organizations belonging to the two big opposing factions, never witnessed civil war among the mass of the people, and managed to pursue smoothly its "Learn From Dazhai" campaign. Public opinion strongly favored the way Chen handled the situation. It was hard not to acknowledge the wisdom of it.

However, the quick resolution of one critical situation in Xiyang did not mean that everything was just fine in general. The factionalism unleashed by the Cultural Revolution had plunged the whole country into an abyss of suffering, and the agitation surrounding power takeovers continued to spread through the countryside in several regions, including many in Shanxi. Insurgent groups still continued to hurl unjustified accusations at many village cadres, and production drives could only proceed in fits and starts. Even in Xiyang County itself, although Chen had the situation in the majority of villages under control, there were still some serious problems in several communities and villages that targeted their cadres unreasonably and maintained heavy pressure against them.

On one occasion when Chen Yonggui visited the Wang Camp People's Commune on a purchasing mission, Wang Camp Brigade cadre Zhang Wanchang's aged mother grabbed him by the thigh, pleading: "Others don't get to see Chairman Mao, but you can, can't you? Could you ask Chairman Mao to save our village cadres?"

"Let go, let me go, Granny," Chen Yonggui said, trying to sound comforting. "I'll think of something when I get home."

This experience reminded Chen Yonggui of the four phrases used by the village cadres to sum up their fate:

> Red in the spring.
> Busy all summer.
> Blamed in the fall.
> A criminal by winter!

How could work in the countryside go on without support for the village cadres?

In November, 1967, a newspaper reporter came to Xiyang County and arranged to meet Chen Yonggui. In the lead paragraph of his story the reporter made an emotional summary of the things he had heard and seen while making the rounds of Xiyang. He wanted Chen Yonggui to talk about how he had created such a sound environment for production in Xiyang County when elsewhere in the country workers in the cities stood idle and farmers in the countryside had stopped planting. Suddenly, this topic emerged as the chief subject of the story, something the reporter absolutely had to hear Chen Yonggui talk about. Chen Yonggui said that he was himself a rural cadre, with special feelings for the rural cadres. He said he was not familiar with urban affairs, but when it came to the countryside, how could the villages engage in production when they couldn't even be sure of retaining good cadres?

"In the past," Chen continued, "people in Xiyang County used to say: 'For each batch of field crops there's a batch of cadres.' You'd call people to work, and they'd respond. Whoever says that peasant tillers lack manure must be kidding! It is when the cadres are not up to their task that the people don't get the field work done. How can you expect any grain then? On top of that, when every village is obsessed with 'seizing power,' and every Brigade is busy with 'denunciations,' with all the effort that goes into such turmoil, who still has the energy to go to the fields? During the 'Four Clean' in Xiyang, forty-six cadres died by their own hand in just three months of 'cleaning.' How many more will die in this 'Great Proletarian Cultural Revolution,' if every village tears itself apart with 'power seizures' and disrupts normal life with endless 'denunciations'?"

Chen Yonggui got very excited talking to the reporter. The man wore an army uniform. He was also very congenial. Feeling at ease with him, Chen just said whatever was on his mind. He never suspected that his partner in dialogue might accuse him of opposing the Cultural Revolution. After all that talking, Chen Yonggui even offered a suggestion: "You could do something more useful than just writing about Xiyang. How about taking a chance and helping me out? Could you help me write a document and take it to Chairman Mao, so that he can make some new policies and regulations regarding the Cultural Revolution in the countryside? The main point is: The village cadres should not be subjected to power takeovers. Most of the grass-roots-level cadres are good. Those with problems are really a minority, and the key word in dealing with them is education."

Naturally, Chen Yonggui also ended up repeating those four phrases used by the village cadres:

Red in the spring.
Busy all summer.
Blamed in the fall.
A criminal by winter!

The reporter admired Chen Yonggui's argument. He said Chen Yonggui, despite his lack of higher education, had a quick mind, was astute in assessing problems, truly had the courage to take risks, and was able to speak with great assurance. Furthermore, Chen almost always knew exactly what to say and what not to say. The reporter was glad to risk universal condemnation by acting on Chen Yonggui's behalf. As he worked on the document, he cleverly fused Chen Yonggui's position with the most current, accepted theory. The resulting letter stressed five points:

One, the Cultural Revolution in the countryside must target the group of big capitalist-roaders within the party who hold power, and their sinister lackeys spread throughout the Provinces, Regions and Counties.

Two, the Cultural Revolution in the countryside must steadfastly implement Chairman Mao's directive to "trust and rely on the majority of cadres," by letting them lead the movement and organize production. It must absolutely not turn its spearhead against the grass-roots village cadres, that is, against its own broad base among the people.

Three, in those places which have established revolutionary committees, these committees must accept direct guidance from the County and Commune-level organs of power. Revolutionary leading cadres must go out to the Production Brigades and teams, investigate and learn, engage in policy implementation, and help solve problems at the grass-roots level.

Four, the Cultural Revolution in the countryside must rely on the poor and lower-middle peasants and organize a rural revolutionary force whose main body should be composed mostly of poor and lower-middle peasants. They will liberate themselves, they will educate themselves.

Five, the Cultural Revolution in the countryside must set up study groups for mastering Mao Zedong Thought on a large scale, and use struggle against selfishness and repudiation of revisionism as the guideline to enhance the ideological education of Brigade and team cadres.

The letter said: "I possess an intimate knowledge of rural cadres. Cadres inevitably make mistakes. But we must clearly understand the nature of their mistakes. After all, bad cadres are a minority—we cannot overthrow each and every village cadre."

After the reporter edited the document and sent it up, days went by without any response. Chen Yonggui became somewhat uneasy and sought the opinion of the old cadres around him as to whether anything could have gone wrong. The old cadres analyzed the matter from different angles and assured him that he should relax, that nothing could go wrong. But Chen Yonggui could not set his mind at ease.

When he went on business to Beijing, he thought about paying a personal visit to Chairman Mao, but he did not have enough nerve to do it. While in the capital, he crossed paths with a group of old military officers whom he had known before. They all shook hands with him warmly, but after he took his leave, he heard them talking behind his back. This set him to imagining all sorts of bizarre results. He wondered if they knew about the letter he had sent to Chairman Mao. Then, in Taiyuan, as he was traveling home, he saw some old cadres who couldn't restrain their praise.

"Old Chen," they said, "that was quite something!"

He had no idea what they were talking about. Only after he returned to Xiyang did he see with his own eyes that Chairman Mao had sent back personal comments on his five suggestions. On November 7, 1967, Central Party authorities circulated the five suggestions to all the provincial, metropolitan and regional Revolutionary Committees, with instructions to distribute them to small groups. They also went to the military control commissions, to the greater military areas, and to provincial military area commands as "Central Committee of the Communist Party of China Document No. (67) 339."

The Chairman's comments on the suggestions said, among other things: "The five suggestions that Comrade Chen Yonggui brought up in his discussion of the 'Great Proletarian Cultural Revolution' in the countryside should be used as sound reference in locations with similar circumstances."

Soon thereafter the editorial departments of the *People's Daily, Red Flag* Magazine, and *Liberation Army* carried a piece entitled "The Two Line Struggle in China's Countryside," which spoke highly of Chen Yonggui's five-point suggestion for checking the unhealthy tendency to overthrow power holders throughout the countryside. Once the articles were published, people engaged in extensive discussion of the situation.

"Only Chen Yonggui would have dared write such a report and only Chairman Mao would have dared approve it!" they said.

In the midst of the irresistible general trend for seizing power, no average person could ever have expressed the view that cadres in the villages should not be overthrown, and no average person could have approved of that kind of letter. Later, when Chen Yonggui was criticized and people quibbled about his mistakes during the denunciation of old cadres, many people jumped to his defense.

"Chen Yonggui's clash with the old Shanxi cadres was a mistake, but he protected the grass-roots-level cadres of the entire country by writing that letter to Chairman Mao. That was an enormous service! Chen Yonggui's achievements during the Cultural Revolution outweigh his errors."

With time, Chen Yonggui's undertakings became better known by society at large, and more noticed by public figures from all walks of life. He earned a reputation for unusual resourcefulness. And so, whenever a difficult, insoluble problem arose people flocked to consult him and include him in the search for a solution. Some people admired him for it, others hated him. To some people he was the Saviour, even God. Following in the wake of this reputation, some strange episodes occurred.

In September 1967, the Central Shanxi Region held an "In Agriculture Learn From Dazhai" On-the-Spot Conference in Xiyang County Town's July First Stadium. For several days, delegates listened to speakers from Dazhai, and speakers from several other production units that were outstanding in "Learning from Dazhai," talk about their experiences. In this way they were able to examine and compare their own shortcomings.

One afternoon there was a change in the agenda. A man dressed in army uniform got up in front of the microphone and cautiously began to criticize himself. Along with several other leading cadres of the County and the Region, Chen Yonggui sat in the middle of the rostrum with a dignified expression on his face. The speaker was one of the commanding officers of the Central Shanxi Military Sub-region, Cui Bing. A renowned partisan of United, he talked about how he had made a mistake in not supporting the broad masses of the Left, and how he had become involved in factionalism. He took off his army cap with its red-star insignia, and his two-little-red-flag collar insignia, then read earnestly from the statement of self-criticism he had composed himself.

It might seem that a statement of self-criticism by an army officer did not exactly fit into the context of an "In Agriculture Learn From Dazhai" On-the-Spot Conference, but it was actually very much in keeping with the theoretical framework of the time. The goal of the Cultural Revolution was indeed to solve the problem of incompatibility between the superstructure and the economic base, so as to propel the development of the productive forces forward. The issue was how to launch a thoroughgoing, long-lasting "Learn From Dazhai" movement. The question of foremost importance was how to grasp the Party line. Launching self-criticism, mutual criticism, and mass criticism from below was the way to achieve that. That is how the slogan "Learn From Dazhai, Catch Up With Dazhai—You Can't Learn If You Hold No Power" came into being.

The Conference revealed that at the meeting of the Central Committee, which convened to find ways for the Cultural Revolution to solve the problems of Shanxi Province, leading cadres had criticized this commanding officer of the Central Shanxi Military Sub-region for deliberately singing a different tune from Dazhai when it came to major issues of principle, thereby seriously obstructing the local Cultural Revolution and "Learn From Dazhai" movements. That's why he now stood before them making his self-criticism.

Cui Bing finished his remarks at long last and awaited, somewhat uneasily, the reaction from the audience. The usual practice of the time was for the faction in power not to even accept as passable most of the self-criticism within its own ranks, let alone what came from Cui Bing, whose supporters in the Central Shanxi Region were in absolute opposition to the Xiyang County faction. The few instances when Chen Yonggui found himself in harm's way while traveling from the County on business illustrated the depth of accumulated rancor. Consequently, the stadium, abuzz with discussion and head-to-head whispering, boiled with disapproval.

Suddenly, one of the conveners of the conference walked up to the microphone and announced in a high-pitched voice: "Comrades, let us now welcome as speaker Chairman Mao's good pupil, Comrade Chen Yonggui."

Before anybody had time to give it much thought, thunderous applause escorted Chen Yonggui to the microphone.

The host's voice was firm when he pronounced "Chairman Mao's good pupil," and although newspapers and rallies had already used the term frequently, nobody had yet called Chen Yonggui that in his presence. Adding the laudatory title "Chairman Mao's good pupil" to Chen Yonggui's name in those days meant to increase his authority and his deterrent clout. It could be considered as a provocative launching signal for conflict.

Some people guessed that Old Chen might announce how to deal with the commanding officer. Others thought that, being surly as he was, Old Chen might rebuke the officer for "not being deep-going and earnest enough." Activists would then seize him and shout, "If you think you can make out by deceiving us, you are dead!"

Consequently some people in the audience had already rolled up their sleeves and were rubbing their hands in anticipation.

Who knows how many were ready for action, or how many provocative speculations Chen Yonggui's speech brought to an abrupt halt? Certainly no one was prepared to hear the following from Chen Yonggui's own mouth: "Comrade Cui Bing made his self-criticism today, and it seems to me that he recognizes where the problems are. What I want to tell you today is that we cannot treat Comrade Cui Bing as a capitalist-roader and attack him wantonly. The sixteen commandments are very explicit when it comes to who is our enemy and who are our friends—this is the question of primary importance for the Revolution. Hey, keeping to the general orientation of the struggle means knowing at whom to aim your spearhead! You ask for an attack? I disagree! Just think about it: Would we have socialism today without the People's Liberation Army? How could army cadres avoid making a few mistakes? When I came back from Beijing the other day with Comrade Cui Bing I was not in favor of traveling by air at all, but I was afraid that somebody would seize him and so I accompanied him on the flight. In a word: What needed to be criticized, he criticized. We can't seize him! And I mean what I say. If you want to seize somebody, seize me!"

The stadium fell into dead silence. Those who were ready to "seize" seemed deflated, staring in amazement as Chen Yonggui took the officer's hand and led him off the stage. The two continued through a corridor of spectators, and into a jeep! Who dared stop "Chairman Mao's good pupil"? Everybody could see clearly that Chen Yonggui treated this commanding officer with an entirely different attitude from the one he reserved for the capitalist-roaders. For several days the Conference had been focusing on attacking Central Shanxi's veteran cadres and "capitalist-roaders," and all the while Chen Yonggui had sat at the rostrum, watching the wanton attacks and not batting an eyelid. Then he made his position perfectly clear.

The above example illustrates a special talent of Chen Yonggui, namely, his ability to make timely use of current theory to accomplish his own practical purpose—something for which one needs a good head, great eloquence, and ingenious skill in dealing with an emergency. This is probably the reason he was able to stand out among other peasant leaders of his time. Looking back, Chen Yonggui's protection of Cui Bing and other cadres was in keeping with Party policy. At the time, however, his actions were based on three simple factors: one, the kindheartedness and sincerity of a peasant; two, the demands of his job; three, the limitations of existing policies.

When Chen Yonggui took control at the County level it was not because he yearned to hold office but rather in order to fulfill the goal of building Xiyang County into a Dazhai-type County, as Premier Zhou Enlai had hoped. In order to achieve this he had to take control of the situation and create a relatively stable environment. This is what the slogan "Learn From Dazhai, Catch Up With Dazhai—You Can't Learn If You Hold No Power" was really about. Only after he assumed power and took control of the situation could he put into practice his theory that "you cannot learn from Dazhai in ease and comfort; you cannot change the face of the country by being smooth and accommodating." Only after that could true learning from Dazhai begin. Rejecting smoothness and accommodation, however, did not mean attacking people at random, it meant standing up for principle, which took a lot more courage.

Speaking of controlling the situation in order to make learning from Dazhai possible, Chen Yonggui carefully increased the range of forces with whom unity could be forged. He was not quick to exclude those who opposed him. After Cui Bing left his post, the Central Shanxi Military Sub-region transferred a commanding officer by the name of Liu Xiujie to take his place. Liu later also assumed the position of Regional Party Committee Secretary for Central Shanxi. Liu Xiujie was a military cadre, so his political inclination, naturally, ran contrary to Chen Yonggui's.[1] But that does not mean that, just because his stance was different, Chen Yonggui did not try to unite with him. On the contrary, he tried to be on friendly terms with him as much as he could, maintaining unity, and thus making possible the emergence of a movement dedicated to learning from Dazhai in the Central Shanxi Region after all.

Sometime between 1968 and 1969, Liu Xiujie brought the Central Shanxi Art Ensemble to Xiyang on tour. Chen Yonggui received them warmly and even invited Liu Xiujie to his house for dinner. In those days Chen Yonggui always referred to Liu Xiujie as Secretary Liu in public, but privately he kept saying "Commander Liu" this and that. During the banquet the two started talking about various problems in Central Shanxi, including the region's "Learn From Dazhai" movement. Their conversation was very straightforward and congenial. Suddenly, Liu Xiujie noticed a little "Red Lantern"-brand radio, then considered an expensive top-grade product, on Chen Yonggui's cupboard.

"You like it?" Chen Yonggui asked smiling. "I bought it for 130 *yuan*. I'll give it to you as a memento."

Liu Xiujie did not try very hard to talk him out of it. In the end he accepted this "gift from the heart."

In the evening, when Commander Liu Xiujie returned from Dazhai to the County guest house, Chen Mingzhu paid him a visit. As Chen Mingzhu entered his room, Liu Xiujie was fiddling with the radio.

1. Of the two opposing factions in Shanxi, one was headed by an army general, Zhang Riqing. Military men in general sided with Zhang against the other faction led by the civilian functionary Lui Geping. (W.H.H.)

Surprised, Chen Mingzhu asked: "Officer, where did you buy that radio?"

"Oh? You want to buy it? It's not for sale. I got it as a gift," said Liu Xiujie laughing, deliberately teasing him.

This would seem to suggest that their relationship was amicable at one time. Unfortunately, in the midst of factional confrontation, in no sense generated by their own will, this changed for the worse later. On some issues the two men could not agree. They even became openly antagonistic. Yet even so, if a union seemed possible, Chen Yonggui, for his part, still wanted peaceful coexistence with his antagonists.

Chen Yonggui advocated a philosophy of struggle, but he also stressed tolerance, so that not a single person he fought against died under lashes or blows instigated by him. I have heard about an incident that occurred after Chen Yonggui took office in Beijing. He was playing poker one night with Chen Xilian, Ji Dengkui, and some other leading cadres from the Central Committee when the phone rang. The caller said that an old cadre from Shanxi Province was critically ill and, since his life was in danger, urgently needed emergency treatment in Beijing. He pleaded with Chen Yonggui to come up with something. The old cadre in question was somebody Chen Yonggui had fought in the past, but at this critical moment of life and death Chen Yonggui never gave it a second thought: He immediately called Zhang Tingfa to find out whether he could have an airplane. As soon as Zhang Tingfa agreed, the plane flew to Shanxi to bring the patient to Beijing. After the patient got well he never once mentioned the criticism and attacks of the past; the only thing on his mind was how Vice-Premier Chen Yonggui saved his life.

This was how Xiyang County, in Chen Yonggui's hands, lived through the "Great Proletarian Cultural Revolution." Chen handled rural affairs in a very flexible manner and achieved, often contrary to expectations, great success.

CHAPTER 20

CONFRONTING HOSTILITY, STIRRING UP CONTROVERSY

Chen Yonggui may have been generous with his opponents, but he still possessed a pragmatic peasant outlook. The moment he felt someone might hurt his basic interests or block his major objectives, he did what he could to make sure that person would not be given the opportunity to do so. That is why many people hated and feared him at the time when factionalism ran rampant in Shanxi. In one case someone even conspired to murder him.

During that period every person, regardless of social status, had his or her own political position. Factional organizations formed among people who held the same political position. As a result, for a long time no one was able to establish peace and social order. In extreme cases of disagreement, husbands and wives whose positions differed lived apart, and fathers and sons who belonged to different factions refused to eat from the same cooking pot. Political position became the touchstone for distinguishing between alleged revolutionaries and the counter-revolutionaries, between alleged true revolutionaries and false ones. Chen Yonggui, being the influential Model Worker that he was, could not avoid being trapped in this general factional trend. What he said and how he dealt with individual issues usually caused discontent among the groups that opposed him. On occasion, they would wrestle the microphone away from him, or even surround and attack him.

Once, as Chen Yonggui and his secretary traveled to a meeting in Taiyuan, the moment they entered the city several armed members of a rebel faction who blocked the way stopped their car. The rebels ordered them to get out. They were quite startled when Chen Yonggui stepped forth. They had no idea that it was Chen they were detaining. This particular rebel group wanted the leadership to put an end to the armed struggle so, whenever they saw a car, they would stop it and demand to know the passengers' attitude toward armed struggle. When they found themselves face-to-face with Chen Yonggui they lost their tongues and let the car proceed. As his car drove off, Chen Yonggui could not suppress his laughter. "These guys sure have a human touch," he commented.

However, things could get a lot tougher, even escalating to the point of threatening lives.

Civilian Administrator Muslim Liu Geping's "Red" faction dominated Xiyang. The neighboring Pingding and Yangquan Counties supported the opposing "United" or "Military Corps" faction of the Long March veteran General Zhang Erqing. The County line was thus also a kind of front line.

One evening as a jeep carrying Chen Yonggui from a meeting in Yangquan sped homeward toward Dazhai a group of people whose identity was far from clear, stopped it as it was about to cross into Xiyang. The nervous driver, his face covered in cold sweat, kept anxiously honking the horn while trying to explain: "This is Old Chen's car. What do you want?"

How was he to know that his words would provoke the hold-up gang into even more aggressive action?

"To stop Old Chen's car, precisely!" came the angry reply. As the man spoke, he pushed his gun inside the jeep and pointed it at Chen Yonggui's forehead.

Bullets don't care whom they shoot. Had they gone past the muzzle of the gun, the outcome would have been obvious. Undaunted Chen stared at the gun. His hand raised a cigarette to his lips. He struck a match, lit the cigarette, and took a deliberately vigorous puff—his way of showing disapproval, even contempt, for the inconvenience.

Chen Yonggui, braving various storms of all kinds from an early age, had seen it all in his lifetime. During the Japanese occupation, when he was planted as a "representative," he went in and out of Japanese blockhouses without losing a heartbeat. In the battle for Yangquan he had charged through a hail of bullets to save the wounded. This time, under the muzzle of a gun, Chen Yonggui's action seemed to come straight out of some movie plot. He sat up straight, stared the gun-wielding intruder in the eye, and flicked out the butt of his cigarette. "Shoot!" he roared, hitting himself in the chest with his right hand. "Right here!"

"Thump."

The gun, already inside the window, fell to the floor of the jeep. Chen Yonggui lit another cigarette. Moving slowly he opened the door, got out of the car, and stared at the group.

"Let's see what you want to do! Whoever has the guts, come forward right now! I'm here, waiting." Chen Yonggui spoke calmly, patiently.

Strange to say, these men who just a moment ago were acting like fierce tigers fresh from the mountain, suddenly stepped back like startled sheep. Keeping an eye on Chen Yonggui, they unwittingly withdrew a few paces. Spurred on by intense factionalism, they had acted on impulse to begin with. But now, so boldly challenged, they suddenly regained their senses and realized that the responsibility for this man's life was too great. He had connections all the way up to the Central Committee. The consequences of any drastic action were impossible to predict. They could think of no adequate response to Chen's challenge. They just entreated with Chen Yonggui under their breath.

"Uncle Chen, this...this...this is not something we actually wanted to do. This...this...this.... Others sent us...us...us...to do this."

That night Chen Yonggui came home alive.

As this story shows, while some people loved Chen, others hated him. His confrontations, however, ran the gamut from near tragedy to something close to farce. This can be illustrated by the response when he chose and wrote the masthead for a local newspaper with the mundane title "Light Chemical and Textile Industry Battlefield Report."

Regarding this incident two things should be made clear: First, the tremendous popularity of model peasants and workers whose support all factions vied to win; and second, the great store all factions put on doing ideological work.

Soon after the beginning of the great catastrophe,[1] China experienced nationwide a phenomenon where everybody tried to woo Model Workers to their side. In order to expand their power and influence and overwhelm their competitors, many mass organizations used every possible means to get the backing of those Model Workers who held their views. On Chen Yonggui's visits to other places, upstart leaders often asked him to write dedications, commemorations and newspaper mastheads. Chen Yonggui could hardly refuse such invitations. He would simply pick up a pen and scribble on paper until he produced something special. Those were the kinds of circumstances in which he produced the newspaper masthead "Light Chemical and Textile Industry Battlefield Report."

The above-named newspaper was the official publication of one so-called Revolutionary Rebel Headquarters. Like all other factions ambitious for Party power they had adopted the following rule: "Before taking political power one must first create favorable public opinion, one must first work hard on the ideological front." The word "battlefield" in the title of this report arose in that context. It referred, not to armed but to polemical battles. So far, all well and good.

On May 1, 1967, the organizers of the national International Labor Day celebrations invited Chen Yonggui to come to Beijing to take part. During the celebration he climbed onto the rostrum at Tiananmen, where Chairman Mao received him. After the manner of a national leader, Chairman Mao firmly shook his hand and said simply: "Salute, Yonggui. Salute!" Excited, Chen Yonggui saluted the Chairman, in return. As this was taken to reflect the Chairman's close affinity with Model Workers, the press, not surprisingly, reported it. What was unusual, however, was that newspapers of all stripes and sizes printed the following in their front-page "Quotations From Chairman Mao" box. The first line said "In Agriculture Learn From Dazhai." The second line said: "Salute, Yonggui. Salute!"

---

1. The author is referring to the Great Proletarian Cultural Revolution.

After this, Chen Yonggui's social status reached dizzying heights. It became almost immeasurable. As a result, people swarmed to this political celebrity of great reputation to make movies, TV programs, newspaper articles and portraits. Some went to his speeches to take a few live snapshots of the man. Others, running into him, struck up a conversation and used the opportunity to shake hands. One often saw various leaders, public security officers, and reporters following him around. Some people even adopted him as "father." Others pretended to be his relatives and fabricated all kinds of rumors. That all this should have happened is perfectly understandable. Who would not want to bask in Chen Yonggui's glory or benefit from association with him!

In the same vein countless demands for his dedications and comments jammed his life.

As a child Chen Yonggui did not receive a day of schooling. He was forty-three when he became formally literate. Needless to say, nobody ever examined his calligraphy. Although this was the case, he could not decline all those earnest invitations to produce occasional writing. It seems that people expected even a word written by him to bring empowerment and good fortune. But after the masthead "Light, Chemical and Textile Industry Battlefield Report" appeared in Chen Yonggui's own handwriting, a public debate immediately followed.

The problem was that the word "battlefield" was written incorrectly. Chen Yonggui had left out one stroke. His flawed calligraphy became the source of many a joke. Everybody who ever read the paper asked "How come the word 'battlefield' is written like that?"

Since there was no such ideograph as "battlefield" the way Chen Yonggui wrote it, should he be asked to correct his calligraphy?

"We can't ask him to do that," many supporters said. "The writing came from the pen of Chairman Mao's good pupil; the way it's written expresses his special character. The aim of the Cultural Revolution is indeed to destroy the old and establish the new. If you can't even write one word without changing a single pen-stroke, wouldn't the Revolution lose all meaning?"

Some people compared Chen Yonggui's masthead writing to Zheng Banqiao's calligraphy. Who in China does not recognize Zheng Banqiao's outstanding calligraphy? When he wrote "South Heaven

Gate" he left out a stroke too. Later generations had to practice their calligraphy by imitating the abbreviated way he wrote it!

Disregarding these "apologists," a debate on Chen's peculiar calligraphy started within the paper itself, then spread to the readership and beyond that to the general public. It went like this: You have a reason for your argument, and I have grounds for mine. At the same time everybody was somewhat cautious, fearing they might arouse the ill will of Chairman Mao's good pupil.

It really should have been a simple matter. When the mistake was discovered, someone should just have reminded Chen Yonggui to correct his error. Chen Yonggui had been asked to and did write mastheads so many times. This one time he made a mistake. That some critics obstinately insisted on making a major issue of it was truly a joke that the era played on people.

When a man is famous, even a puff of smoke from his mouth is savory! His mistakes and weaknesses can end up being lauded as achievements and merits. Wherever Chen Yonggui went, there were always people who commented on the white hand towel tied around his head, on his black peasant jacket, on his peasant shoes made of cloth. It seems as though people thought the white hand towel exemplified some particular virtue of the Chinese nation, as though it stood for China's vast peasantry, as though such symbols rendered China's peasants great, likable, industrious, glorious....

Leaving the word "battlefield" in the newspaper masthead "Light, Chemical and Textile Industry Battlefield Report" the way Chen Yonggui had originally written it seems to have accrued a certain kind of political power to the publishers. But what was this power all about? Nobody can say for sure, and nobody really knows what its implied meaning might be. But one can see from the above incident that the support Model Workers received from the Chairman and the laudatory treatment the Model Workers enjoyed in the public opinion made people almost worship Chen Yonggui.

This pervasive adulation led to serious problems like the time Chen walked out of the theater without greeting the cast. The time was the very beginning of the 1970s, and the atmosphere in Xiyang was very special. Dazhai and Xiyang had become a glowing universe unto themselves.

At the entrance to the Xiyang County Grand Auditorium late one extraordinary night, one could hear human voices seething with excitement, and then bursts of cheers and applause. To the accompaniment of the musical composition "We Navigate the Great Sea Relying on the Helmsman," resounding slogan-shouting punctuated prolonged enthusiastic hand-clapping: Learn from Dazhai!...Salute the people of Dazhai!...Learn from Comrade Chen Yonggui!...Salute Comrade Chen Yonggui!...Long live the spirit of Dazhai!...Long live the victory of Chairman Mao's revolutionary line!...Long live invincible Mao Zedong thought!...Long live the great leader, Chairman Mao! May he live a hundred million years!

This happened during a performance attended by Chen Yonggui.

Back in those days journalists, researchers from different fields, innumerable literary and art organizations, and various celebrities poured into Xiyang and Dazhai. On this particular night, the performers belonged to a Central Shanxi Opera troupe from the provincial capital, and they had just rehearsed the model revolutionary opera *Taking Tiger Mountain by Stratagem*[1] especially for review by the people of Dazhai and Xiyang. Since Dazhai still did not have a ready-made stage, the performance was to take place at the County's Grand Auditorium in Xiyang. You can imagine that they looked upon this chance to pay a visit to and perform in Dazhai and Xiyang as a once-in-a-lifetime honor. If they could just perform for the eyes of Comrade Chen Yonggui, they would not be able to sleep for several nights, yet they would not feel tired either!

The entire country yearned to pay respects to Dazhai and Xiyang, as though they were ancestral temples or shrines full of miracles. Songs spoke of learning from Dazhai and catching up with Xiyang. Meetings and speeches were filled with "Learn from Dazhai, catch up with Xiyang" slogans. No matter where cadres of Dazhai and Xiyang went nationwide, they always received special treatment. Who could miss the marvelous opportunity to have Chen Yonggui personally attend a performance!

---

1. In English this opera has usually been called Taking Tiger Mountain by Strategy; however, strictly speaking, the attackers used a "stratagem," a trick to gain entrance to the bandit redoubt on the mountain. (W.H.H.)

As could have been predicted, the performers were waiting in full dress behind the stage, anticipating the moment when Chen Yonggui would enter the auditorium. Could the old man not walk fast enough to make it on time? Had they mixed something up? They had received the news that afternoon: Chen Yonggui and the people of Dazhai had accepted the invitation to see the performance. So how come, since it was just a few minutes to curtain time, they had still not shown up? The performers were not aware that the people of Dazhai could not stop work early and pack up for the day just because they were going to see a performance. No Commune member, including Chen Yonggui, could leave until dark, regardless of whether they were going to attend a performance, a meeting, or some other type of activity. If there was a special need to waste the daylight hours, this had to be approved and arranged by the Production Brigade Committee.

At around ten o'clock the rumble of a car engine could be heard at the entrance to the auditorium. To the occupants of the vehicle, traveling in from a distance, the sound of applause, bursting the bounds of the auditorium, grew to incredible volume. The spectators clambered to their feet, all eyes turned in the same direction, gazing at the group of people who had just entered. At its head strode the figure most familiar to everybody—Chen Yonggui, with a white towel tied round his head, in contrast to his sun-weathered dark face with its heavy eyebrows and thick lips, beaming above his peasant-style black jacket.

Before the performance started, the announcer made a few simple, incisive opening remarks. He said the opera *Taking Tiger Mountain By Stratagem* was a gift to the people of Dazhai and Xiyang, and that performers hoped to hear their valuable comments. After this prologue, the performance began.

Three hours later, the letters The End appeared on the curtain, but the stage still bustled with unusual noise and excitement. The sound of drum-beating shook the hall while the loudspeaker repeatedly broadcast the music of "We Navigate the Great Sea Relying on the Helmsman."

Rhythmical hand-clapping and high-spirited slogan-shouting followed: Learn from Dazhai!...Salute the people of Dazhai!...Learn from Comrade Chen Yonggui!...Salute Comrade Chen Yonggui!...Long live the spirit of Dazhai!

The show was over and the audience was ready to leave. The show's actors stood neatly arranged on the stage, heroes Yang Zirong and Shao Jianbo in front, the supporting cast behind them, waiting for Chen Yonggui and other leaders to come to the stage to greet them. As Chen Yonggui got up from his seat, all the eyes of the cast focused on him, eagerly awaiting the happy moment. But Chen Yonggui merely glanced at the stage, smiled faintly, turned toward the exit, and followed the stream of spectators as they filed out of the auditorium.

The unexpected move was extremely disappointing for the cast. They had hoped their performance would give them a chance to shake hands with Chen Yonggui and the people of Dazhai, and that they would be able to have a photograph taken with Old Chen. And now....

It is possible that Chen Yonggui had no idea of how they felt. Be that as it may, the show's heroes did not resign themselves to such disappointment. After Chen Yonggui hopped into his jeep, they repeatedly emerged from the human corridor formed by the spectators to run in front of his vehicle, respectfully bowing to him and saluting him, imploring him to reverse his decision to leave.

In all honesty, Chen Yonggui had witnessed many occasions like this. Only a few days before, starting on the fifteenth day of the first lunar month, Xiyang County Town had held a three-day three-night-long Lantern Festival. Every night Chen Yonggui had had to sit on the reviewing stand temporarily put up by the roadside, earnestly reviewing the floats, dragon lanterns, and street performances of all kinds from his vantage ground, and in a most imposing manner at that. On this evening of the opera, sitting in the dead center of the Grand Auditorium, he once again displayed every attribute of a senior official. And when it was over, drained by the day and completely exhausted, he walked out.

That such a thing should have happened does not seem all that strange after all. During that period, just a single move by Chen Yonggui, even his most innocuous utterance, could induce earthshaking consequences. A word from him, if it reached Chairman Mao or Premier Zhou, was much more effective than anybody else's. At the time of the Zhenbao Island Incident the Military Commission of the Central Committee of the Communist Party of China was relieving garrisons of current duty posts throughout the country and shifting them around. By direct order of the Commission the armed forces stationed in Xiyang County were supposed to exchange with the armed forces in Baoding City. However, the head of the armed forces in Xiyang, Jia Huolin, was not willing to leave the County. Not even the Beijing Military Area Command dared take lightly the responsibility for such a decision. Only after Chen Yonggui entered into direct negotiations with the Beijing Area Command did the generals allow Jia Huolin's forces to remain in Xiyang. He was the only military commander in the whole country who was not transferred during the major swap of posts that followed that international incident over Zhenbao.

Theatrical troupes often invited Chen Yonggui to watch them perform. Then the whole country wanted to see what Chen Yonggui had seen. His every word and move were followed with great interest by many people up and down the social scale nationwide, and who knows how many people studied them afterward? Every visitor to Dazhai wanted to see Chen Yonggui, hear him speak, watch him act.

It was, however, impossible to demand of Chen Yonggui that he meet so many people at so many and varied times. Years later, when Party leaders called him to high office in the national capital, it became impossible all together. He shouldered heavy responsibility for all of China's agriculture, every day he had to strain to the utmost to resolve matters of national interest. The demands on him multiplied and left him no time for himself. Despite all this, you could count on Chen Yonggui to make himself available at every crucial moment. He still had to "mount the stage and perform."

His "performance" was particularly vivid when a study group delegated by the Ministry of Agriculture and Forestry came to Dazhai on October 20, 1977. He was working in the fields when they arrived. He deliberately took them up Tigerhead Mountain to the slope that Premier Zhou Enlai had named the "Friendship Slope." There he "put on his show." He first explained to them why he would see them, when he was refusing to see anybody else. "Because you are from the Ministry of Agriculture and Forestry, you are in charge of the agricultural production of the whole nation. How could I not see you? I was afraid that those other disappointed comrades would object, so I picked this spot to receive you."

He went on to say how Minister Sha Feng, when he returned from his trip to Yugoslavia, informed him that in some countries the average per-capita grain production had reached 400 kilograms per *mu*, but he brushed it off by informing Sha Fang in turn, that the average per-capita production in Xiyang County had already reached 400 kilograms per *mu* also and that in Dazhai it already amounted to a ton per person on the average. "Just think," he said, "of what Vice-Premier Deng said at the National Conference on Agriculture. 'If just one-third of all Counties in China became like Dazhai and Xiyang, what kind of increase in grain output would that be?' I didn't figure it up myself, but you can do that when you go back to your offices. You are from the Ministry of Agriculture and Forestry. You should figure it out right away."

All this happened much later when Chen Yonggui carried the burdens of China's whole national agriculture on his back as a Vice-Premier of the State Council.

Returning to the middle sixties, however, which is the subject of this chapter, one might say that as Chen Yonggui's stage expanded the more he was expected to "perform" and the bigger his show became, and the more magical. His "performances" were by no means inferior, even when examined carefully with the benefit of the hindsight. Long before he attained any position outside his home County many people were completely dazzled by his presence on the stage of history. Who knows how many saw in him their champion and Savior?

CHAPTER—21

ACHES AND PAINS OF ADULATION

Chen Yonggui's exemplary views and actions were, however, not entirely without negative consequences, generated not by his and Dazhai's accomplishments as such, but as side effects of their enormous prestige and the adulation that followed in their wake.

Dazhai's entry onto China's political stage drove it far apart from tens of thousands of ordinary villages. Nobody was allowed to play around with or damage its image. The consequences anybody bad-mouthing Dazhai would have to suffer were clear. During the "Agriculture Learn From Dazhai" period, for instance, the East Wind Forestry Center in Xiyang County organized a denunciation rally that lasted for several days, just for the purpose of solving one problem: the alleged "anti-Dazhai" political views of one of the Center's employees.

From the very beginning, Xiyang County took the lead in the national "Agriculture Learn From Dazhai" campaign. After Chen Yonggui's County Revolutionary Committee took over, it started organizing study trips to Dazhai for the workers, peasants and cadres from its various Production Brigades and work units, so they could hear about Dazhai's experiences. After the trips, the work units would gather the participants together to discuss what they had learned from the experience, expose their own shortcomings and compare concrete measures to be taken in learning from Dazhai. The employees of the East Wind Forestry Center discussed Dazhai in pretty much the same way all other work units did, exaggerating the model's miracles and wonders, remarking on how dark and weathered the faces of its peasants were, how big the plots of land had become, how efficient their conveyor lines were and other amazing sights. Then, in the middle of this, of all things, someone obviously insensitive to the timing of his remark, pointed out that the aniseed trees were not growing well.

Aha! Now that was proof of guilt! The benighted critic had deliberately used the pretext of aniseed plant growth to negate Dazhai!

At the time when class struggle dominated the agenda every year, every month and every day, even the most insignificant slight turned into a live target for criticism and denunciation, let alone a slight pertaining to Dazhai, whose fame had spread across the seas!

The man who offered this opinion on aniseed growth, now the target of criticism and denunciation, could not eat during the day and could not sleep at night; he seemed to be having a cold, yet it was not a cold; it seemed like a headache, yet it was not a headache. He had said not more than a sentence of what he really thought, and had run into this kind of outcome; the political climate had brought down on his head a small misfortune. A man from Dazhai who worked for the East Wind Forestry Center finally rescued him.

Jia Jixiang, after he discovered what had happened, said, "He just made a few comments about Dazhai. How could that be treated as being anti-Dazhai? Dazhai welcomes criticism of its shortcomings and mistakes. It simply makes no sense to confuse someone's comments with an anti-Dazhai political stand. This is bound to reflect on the reputation of the 'Learn From Dazhai' campaign."

Without this man from Dazhai, the affair might well have been indefinitely prolonged. A similar problem arising out of an opinion critical of Dazhai occurred at the East Finger People's Commune, Scallion Bed Production Brigade—an advanced work unit when it came to learning from Dazhai. During an inspection of the Commune, County Committee leaders made some remarks about Dazhai's land, but the

Scallion Bed Party Branch Secretary contradicted them with a few qualifying sentences. The County Standing Committee wanted to punish him for his negative attitude toward Dazhai, by expelling him from the Party. In this case, it was Chen Yonggui's son, Chen Mingzhu, who came forward to handle the matter with skill and tact. He made it clear that the Party Branch Secretary had not directed his words against Dazhai. One could not therefore treat them as an expression of anti-Dazhai sentiments.

Even if those were just minor misunderstandings, they are sufficient to explain, when raised to the higher plane of Party principle and class struggle, the pressure the need for political correctness placed on people. Some old cadres said they found it difficult to work in Dazhai, because even the slightest failure to keep pace could easily turn into a serious mistake because it could hurt the image of an advanced Production Brigade.

Chinese people like to worship deities and revere spirits. This is custom handed down by several thousand years of tradition. But treating the Red Flag raised by Chairman Mao Zedong as though it were a deity inevitably caused results that were contrary to expectations.

Let me tell you about another incident that occurred, this time not about, but in, Dazhai.

Around the Grain in Ear[1] time in 1975, due to the negligence of the Production Brigade leader, some fields, in spite of adequate seeding rates, did not produce a good stand of millet sprouts. Unless the Brigade members did some immediate transplanting, Dazhai's yields for that year would be affected, as would its reputation as the Red Flag unit. In view of Dazhai's limited work force, the easiest way out was to mobilize the support of Xiyang County's office workers. In all truth, who among them would have wanted to go? But it was impossible not to go. By about one o'clock in the afternoon the office workers, doing stoop labor transplanting millet seedlings to fill the skips in the rows, were hot, tired and hungry. They really could not carry on any longer. Dazhai Commune members who worked at their side tried to ease their burden.

1. Grain in Ear (Manzhong) is the 9th solar term. It falls before the Summer Solstice.

"You are not used to this kind of work, take a break. We put a great burden on you this morning," they said with sympathy.

The office workers deliberately made light of it and spoke with forced smiles.

"That's OK. It's good for us to exercise!" they said.

At two o'clock in the afternoon the Party Branch Secretary Guo Fenglian finally told the Production Brigade Leader Jia Chengrang: "Tell those office folks to stop. They sit in the office all day long. How do you expect them to take all this? We've had it too!"

Jia Chengrang, in charge of production, was directly responsible for the thin stand of millet seedlings and very much wanted to see the job finished. Nevertheless, he could not tell people to keep working all afternoon.

"Let's go!" he agreed. "I can't keep you people any longer."

The team leaders issued orders to stop work. Dazhai cooks prepared better fare than usual that day, millet gruel with mung beans. However, after a snack and a brief rest, all the visitors still had to go back up the mountain to finish the job.

This type of enhanced, peer-pressure activity arose because Dazhai was the model on the national agricultural front; it was also an example for every trade, profession and line of work. Office workers, factory workers and miners from Xiyang County all went to Dazhai from time to time to take part in labor. Back in those days it wasn't merely a question of transplanting a few *mu* of millet sprouts or planting a few pine seedlings. Contributing labor was seen as a way of making a statement about one's world outlook, as a test of consciousness on the issue of line struggle in the Party, and as a test of one's attitude toward Dazhai and what Dazhai stood for. It was in this kind of political climate that people came in droves every year to plant and harvest, thin and transplant in Dazhai.

Nobody would believe it if I said they did it without complaining. On the other hand, what good was it to complain? It could only invite trouble. This created an invisible pressure. What was the source of this invisible pressure? Was it merely Dazhai and Chen Yonggui?

No. People went not only to Dazhai, it should be remembered, but to all the villages in Dazhai Commune, to other villages in Xiyang

County and to countless villages throughout the country where cadres, students, intellectuals, professionals and off-duty workers went to help out, temper themselves in labor and learn from the peasants. Nevertheless, in Xiyang County, Dazhai generated some special pressure. This may be illustrated by the tree-planting episode that follows.

On a spring day in the 1970s, a group of people who had just finished planting trees came down from the mountain dragging their weary bodies. Without a word they entered the yard of the reception center, sluggishly poured themselves bowls of hot water, pulled cold steamed bread from their satchels, and looked for a quiet corner to relieve the pangs of hunger. Munching on the cold bread warmed by hot water, they were chewing away trying to ignore the aches they felt all over after their hard labor. With the cold bread they swallowed whatever grievances they might have had, which no one dared voice out loud.

Just at this juncture the team leader put on a stern face and asked coldly: "Let's hear your own report. Who was stalling the work up there?"

"What's wrong with this guy?" people thought. "Has somebody shoved some gunpowder down his throat?"

In fact, some County leaders in charge had come that morning to inspect the quality of work and found a patch that had not been planted as specified. They were bent on finding out who was responsible. They could easily have resolved the matter of responsibility but, at a time when people all but automatically raised every incident to a level of higher principle like "class struggle," they suspected that somebody was out of tune with the times and had messed up the tree planting on purpose.

Unearthing no leads, the leaders walked away. They hadn't gone far when one person blurted out a complaint. "They asked for this kind of quality themselves."

Complaining under the red flag planted personally by Chairman Mao was like flying in the face of the will of the people. But the team leader had no intention of going into the matter more deeply, so he pretended he did not hear what had been said.

Someone, however, exercising great political zeal, reported the incident to the higher authorities, without even remembering the name of the leader in question. The higher authorities believed that such an occurrence in Dazhai was no small matter. They were determined to investigate until they cleared up the whole incident. But no matter how much they investigated, they could not get to the bottom of the problem. It was really a question of special circumstances in a special place leading to special results without any special political significance. Yet it dominated the attention of scores of people for days on end.

The truth is that Dazhai's farm work would not have been that affected had all those people not gone there to take part in physical labor. Dazhai people would have gotten the work done efficiently and well. They themselves were not at all harsh with others. They always spoke very politely, with a human touch, as Jia Jincai explained at harvest time.

"We don't care if people are slow, we are only afraid of shoddy work. Stubble should not be too tall. We had a drought this year and are short of millet. The livestock in some Communes have no fodder to eat. So we should try to cut the stalks close to the ground and get all the straw."

So why did those County cadres and office workers feel awkward going to Dazhai to do physical labor? I can think of only one word in answer: Special! People don't take easily to something so special, so fraught with unseen, yet palpable, pressure.

This is what Dazhai's relations with the outside world were like during that special era. On the home front, too, things gradually escalated, guided by the philosophy of struggle. Let me tell you of another incident that happened in Dazhai.

Throughout China it is universally proclaimed that Dazhai citizens love to fight—fight endlessly about anything and everything. Fight, fight, fight, all the way. Fight against heaven and fight against earth, fight against class enemies, fight against capitalism, fight against the bourgeois liberal ideas in one's own head. Whoever doesn't fight, criticize and struggle is in danger of turning revisionist! In those special historical circumstances, it seemed, all the theory and practice in the world needed the example of this miraculous village. And so to "study the theory of the dictatorship of the proletariat," to "solve the problem of bourgeois ideology," and to "place good old cadres in control," all became mottoes of the people of Dazhai.

In the campaign to combat revisionism—the abandonment of revolutionary Marxism—some written material came out that used old Jia Jincai as an example of bourgeois liberalism.[1] The authors felt constrained to solicit the opinions of the people of Dazhai before they put their ideas into an official document for distribution. Jia Jincai's wife, Song Liying, the leader of all the Brigade's women, after reading the material rushed to gather the Party leaders together. As she protested vehemently her face went completely white.

"If they want to circulate the document, let them circulate it! You think I can't go to Beijing? You don't think I can't find Chen Yonggui? I'll ask him, did Jia Jincai cooperate with him back then or did he not! When we first set up the Commune, Old Chen didn't trust anybody else to keep our collective ox but Jia Jincai. And didn't Jia Jincai take it to West Camp to graze and fatten it up so you could squeeze oil out of it? And when Old Chen wanted to rebuild half the village, who split the rocks and cut the stones to build the vaults for all those new cave dwellings? What's the evidence that allows them to trump up charges that Jia Jincai is a bourgeois liberal and a capitalist-roader? If they want to circulate the document, fine. I have something to tell them, indeed!"

It was very unusual to see Song Liying complaining and angry. She had worked for a rich man in her early youth, wiping and scrubbing, suffering day in and day out, and putting up with all kinds of abuse and hardship. As a young woman she led other women into production, setting an example for them in every way. But when it came to this, she got mad! She protested, because the material deliberately blew a few small incidents out of proportion, raising trifles onto a higher plane of principle and Party line. Who could stand to see such trivialities turned into Party-line struggle material?

---

1. "Bourgeois liberalism" or just plain "liberalism" was defined as non-proletarian ideology that put "me first" at the expense of the community and the collective. The Dazhai maxim did not deny the "me," the self, but put "public first, self second" on the grounds that the prosperity of one could only be realized through the prosperity of all. "Libertarianism" might be a better word for what they condemned—thinking only of self, acting only from self-interest, defying discipline, breaking ranks, doing your own thing without regard for others, which when practiced by hundreds of millions in the old society had led to a peasantry dispersed and helpless like a mass of loose sand. (W.H.H.)

This just happened at the time when everybody studied the theory of the dictatorship of the proletariat. Chairman Mao Zedong issued eighteen comments on the theory. He raised the question: "Why did Lenin call for a dictatorship over the capitalist class? We must thoroughly grasp this issue. If we do not thoroughly grasp this issue, we can turn into revisionists." After that, Yao Wenyuan published an article under the title: "About the Social Foundations of Lin Biao's Anti-Party Clique." Then Zhang Chunqiao published his article "About All-Out Dictatorship Over the Capitalist Class." After that various major publications carried numerous pieces written under the pseudonym "Liang Xiao (Two Schools)[1] about restricting the rights of the capitalist class. It goes without saying that Dazhai and Xiyang led the way in this campaign to study theory, offering their concrete experience to the entire nation.

The Deputy Secretary of Xiyang County's Party Committee, Wang Jinzi, who was in charge of the day-to-day affairs, led the charge on the Dazhai Party Branch. In order to bring to light the fact that Dazhai did not live in a political vacuum, he wanted to use the contrast between Chen Yonggui and Jia Jincai to show that the struggle between a revolutionary faction and a liberal or bourgeois democratic faction existed in the Dazhai Party Branch too. There were only two possible examples that one could pull out in order to illustrate this point, and they both occurred before Dazhai became a collective.

The first was the struggle between the Feeble Group of old folks and youngsters, and the Stalwart Group. Actually, both groups were model mutual aid groups in the County. The Stalwart Group lagged behind the Feeble Group not because of any bourgeois-democratic ideology of its leader, Jia Jincai, but because of its mixed-class membership, which included poor peasants, middle peasants, landlords and rich peasants. "When people don't work with one mind, the ghosts blow out the light." The second example had to do with the question: "If they want to get rich quick, the farmers should take up trading themselves." At one time many people suggested that Jia Jincai issue shares, collect money and open a coal pit in order to give the village a chance to get

1. The two schools were Qinghua University and Beijing University where the Gang of Four set up a theoretical research group to bombard the country with their view of class struggle.

rich. At the very beginning Chen Yonggui bought one share, but he later pulled out of the scheme. The conditions back then were such that only manual labor was available to open a coal pit. A score of peasants chiseled and dug for a long time, using up all the subsidy millet they had earned in exchange for labor, and in the end dug out a hole full of water. The venture ended in failure.

Chen Yonggui often talked about these two examples by way of criticizing the concrete substance of capitalism. Not to talk about them would not have been in accord with the political demands of the time. But when Chen Yonggui criticized the Stalwart Group or various alleged "commercial" ventures undertaken by peasants he never so much as hinted at Jia Jincai's name. Whenever he promoted Dazhai in front of outsiders he always spoke of Jia Jincai very highly. Jia Jincai never found any of this objectionable.

When the document we have mentioned openly criticized Jia Jincai by name it was only natural that Song Liying could not stand it. She went to clear the name of her husband, who had gone through a lifetime of trials and tribulations with her. Song Liying held out against the document. But this very trend of political theory studied so earnestly in Xiyang brought criticism of pig-pen capitalism and rabbit-hutch capitalism, imposed restrictions on legitimate household sideline production, and led the way in restricting the small freedoms enjoyed by Commune members throughout the country. When, in the end, people started criticizing the sideline industries in Rear Settlement and East Gully as capitalist sprouts within the collective economy, clearly things had long since gone to ultra-left extremes.[1]

Under the surge of the powerful current of "Dazhai spirit," these few anecdotes merely represent a trickle of nonessential tributaries. The

---

1. If Chen Yonggui had any ultra-left tendencies they showed up in his attitude toward trade and sidelines that he started out thinking of as diversions from the true business of farmers as a class. He always opposed markets because he saw them as hotbeds of speculation, getting something for nothing. He wanted the universal cooperative supply and marketing system to handle that sphere of the economy. Later he came round to supporting productive sidelines as legitimate extensions of collective activity and promoted them vigorously. When I visited Dazhai in 1977, Rear Settlement was under fire, not for making bean noodles (vermicelli) but for cheating the State when selling them at excess levels of moisture. (W.H.H.)

main thrust of Chen Yonggui's years in office in Xiyang was a protracted campaign to build Xiyang County into a Dazhai-type County. Many people had long been saying, "If Xiyang is to catch up with Dazhai, Chen Yonggui should be made Chairman of the County Party Committee."

Now that he had taken over the reins of power he seized the chance to tell Xiyang how to learn from Dazhai using the motto "Agriculture Learn From Dazhai." Thus Chen Yonggui backed away from the great storm of the Cultural Revolution and prepared to concentrate on work at the County level.

CHAPTER 22

XIYANG REPLICATES DAZHAI

Red sun, warm wind, great wave!

While the gunpowder smoke of battle still filled the air in the city of Taiyuan and other places in its vicinity, Chen Yonggui, now Chairman of the Xiyang County Revolutionary Committee, stood on the banks of the surging Jiedu River in Xiyang with several colleagues, contemplating how to tackle the area's barren mountains and unruly rivers in a major way.

Chairman Mao had already put forth the bold slogan, "In Agriculture Learn From Dazhai," and China's vast countryside had stirred in response. Lower Ding Village in Shandong, Sandstone Ravine in Hebei, Jade County and Sheep Shore in Shanxi, and several places in Hunan announced in a great public display of flag-waving, drum-beating and slogan-shouting that they planned to learn from Dazhai and catch up with Dazhai. They engaged in big land construction projects and promoted scientific farming, greatly increasing their grain output.

In Xiyang, however, with few exceptions, most Communes and Brigades only shouted fine slogans without doing anything in practice. To say that you are learning from Dazhai became as commonplace as saying that where the water flows the ground gets wet. Total grain output for the County was a mere 40,000 metric tons, and most Brigade members depended on the grain sold back to them by the State for survival. With the same land and the same conditions, most of the villages in the County managed to produce only about 200 *jin* per *mu* while Dazhai produced over 800. Hence people said that Xiyang, instead of being the first place to enjoy the benefits of proximity to Dazhai just stood idly by in its shadow. According to an old saying, "The lakeside pavilion gets the moonlight first," but Dazhai's neighbors watched passively as the moonlight jumped to the other side of the wall. In the end it was Chen Yonggui who had to tell Xiyang how to learn from Dazhai.

"Those turtles' eggs, they think they'll sweep us away!" exclaimed Chen Yonggui, as his angry gaze swept over the unbridled billows of the Border Block River.

"What do you say? What should we do?" he asked, turning to his subordinates.

"Let's launch a 'Three Battles With Wolf Den Ravine'-style campaign," one of them ventured.

Chen Yonggui did not say what he thought. With an attitude of aloof contempt he took another glance at the river, then took up the challenge of finding a way out.

During his first year in office he had not managed to start any big projects. He had focused on fostering hard, solid work and on a mass movement to create deep, mellow sponge-soil and improve the hillside fields throughout the County. Yet his mind had still been preoccupied with an old script: Learning from Dazhai meant initiating new ideas and big projects. While attending a meeting in Beijing, he called back to say that he had conceived of how to strike at Rake Place and break out of the Zhai Family Bend that meant building a long dike. But there was a piece of good land in Zhai Family Bend that belonged to the East Gate Production Brigade. This Brigade was afraid that with the dike project it would lose land and suffer losses. County representatives talked things over several times without reaching an agreement. So Chen Yonggui turned his attention to the Border Block River Reconstruction Project as the lead task lighting the way to other major transformations of nature. As Chen Yonggui stood on top of a high knoll surveying the river, deep furrows creased his brow. His right hand seemed to be following his train of thought as he pulled out a cigarette and lit it up with a struck match.

"'Three Battles With Wolf Den Ravine'! There we confronted wolves. Here we are dealing with tigers!" he finally said out loud.

The story of "Three Battles With Wolf Den Ravine" is easy to tell. But one has to really immerse oneself in the details in order to fully appreciate Chen Yonggui's ability, wisdom, resourcefulness and boldness of vision. Now, adopting a new perspective, one no longer sees a Chen Yonggui standing in a ravine at Dazhai, but a Chen Yonggui who has planted his feet on the high mountains and big rivers of the whole of Xiyang County. Where should he light the first torch? How should he light it? Chen Yonggui was drawing the blueprint in his head.

Chen Yonggui smoked one cigarette after another. He could hear his colleagues offering suggestions. Somebody proposed they build a multiple-layer dam, another favored the building of a reservoir.

A word here, a phrase there...a hammer here, a crowbar there...all this was music to Chen Yonggui's ears and valuable food for thought. Chen Yonggui pulled out rolled-up cigarettes and offered one to each person. He took one himself and savored it to the end. He then used the glowing butt of the old cigarette to light a new one, which he smoked with great gusto, while thinking in complete silence. Finally, he issued a verdict:

"A river is not so scary. The only thing to be afraid of is our own incompetence. We can't build a dam here like the ones in Wolf Den Ravine. This barrier has to follow the stream—a dike, not a dam. If we block off the flow, we'll be inundating thousands of *mu* of land. So how should the structure be built? The way to do it is to redirect the course of the river with a dike that will confine it to the south side of the valley, then create fields behind the dike on the old flood plain thus protected. Let's have the Water Conservancy Bureau draw a plan, stipulating how deep the base and how wide the top must be to withstand the pounding of the water. We've got cement in the County. As the Premier has said: 'Water is not all that fearful. People can conquer it!'"

The words once spoken stuck like nails hammered into an iron plate. Once the torch was lit, his comrades could see Chen Yonggui's determination rising to meet the challenge. In July 1967, all County cadres above the Production Brigade level gathered at the Grand Auditorium to hear their new Party Secretary's mobilization speech. Chen Yonggui cited examples of Dazhai's great struggle with Wolf Den Ravine, turning it into a place capable of standing up against drought and excessive rain, a place producing high stable yields through scientific farming. He cited the Ravine's production increases year by year as a demonstration of the proposition that human determination can conquer nature.

Observing the manner in which Chen Yonggui smoked up on the rostrum and noting the tone of his voice, a tone that made light of all obstacles, the participants in the meeting gained confidence in their prowess. Chen Yonggui was not disheartened at all by the fact that the South River project could not be started—his faith in bringing the Border Block flow under permanent control remained unshaken. He talked major principles, minor principles, and then went on to announce the County Revolutionary Committee's resolution to "reshape Xiyang's mountains and rivers."[1]

At the beginning of September, 1968, the County Revolutionary Committee staged a mass rally to announce the first stage: a dike and manmade fields along Xiyang's Border Block River. There, after Chen Yonggui delivered a heartening mobilization, he and the other leaders of the County Revolutionary Committee picked up construction tools

---

1. The work undertaken by Chen Yonggui at this point is described hereafter as primarily economic development centered on the creation of new land wrested from the floodplain of Xiyang County's river beds along with other less dramatic but equally effective land reclamation and irrigation projects, all of which amount to expanding productive forces. Actually much more basic and important was the work Chen Yonggui did transforming productive relations, specifically the relations between Party leaders and rank-and-file Brigade members Countywide. By fostering socialist consciousness through education, by promoting to positions of power only those who truly showed commitment to collective development, by insisting on regular, daily productive labor from all village cadres, plus periodic stints at labor from all cadres at whatever level, and other like measures, Chen Yonggui fostered exemplary socialist relations of production in village after village. This in turn unleashed tremendous enthusiasm for production, which enabled one community after another to expand productive forces at top speed. Chen thus realized in a down-to-earth way Mao's Cultural Revolution slogan, "Grasp Revolution, promote production." (W.H.H.)

and led the large contingent of 1,500 public project laborers from Xiyang County's twenty People's Communes to harness the dragon. The plan was to complete the project in two years, but in the end it took only one year and five months to construct the long dike in the middle of the Border Block flood plain. This confined its waters to the southern shore. They built a dike 3,500 meters long, 8 meters high, and 5 meters wide at the base. In the protected area behind it, they built over 2,000 *mu* of fields by carrying in soil from the mountains on the north side.

The project gave a big lift to production. Xiyang County's grain output increased visibly. From a total yield of 40,000 tons in 1966, it rose to 60,000 tons in 1967, only two years after Chen Yonggui took office.

The successful harnessing of the Border Block River made an impact on the entire County. The people of the East Gate Production Brigade no longer feared they would lose their "rice bowl" and stopped worrying and delaying. They went, instead, to the County leadership on their own initiative to approve the beginning of the South River project. This signaled the beginning of big projects: the South River mass campaign, the Zhao Shelter mass campaign, the Qin Mountain Reservoir undertaking and the Water Gorge Reservoir undertaking.

By the time the first spring of the 1970s arrived in Xiyang, Chen Yonggui's big project of leveling hilltops and changing the course of the South River in the County capital was already under way. This project, as previously mentioned, had long been on Chen Yonggui's mind. Every time he went back and forth between Dazhai and the County capital, he had to cross the South River. Seeing its vast flood plain going to waste, he had made a pledge: "If one of these days this falls into my hands, I will move that big mountain, send the River flowing that way, and protect its flood plain to make fields." Once all objections subsided his pledge turned into reality!

He dispatched Wang Fuyuan, a leading member of the County Revolutionary Committee, to the battlefront to direct the project and take part in labor. The project, like the one on the Jiedu River, was originally scheduled for completion within two years but Wang Fuyuan's effort and the hard work of several hundred project laborers completed the dike before the flood season that very year. When Chen Yonggui accompanied the Minister of Agriculture and Forestry, Sha Feng, on his inspection of the project, the latter noticed the extra reinforcement at the base of the dike that increased its width as the pounding of the water increased. Pleased, he patted Wang Fuyuan on the shoulder and pronounced: "If you tell the mountain to lower its peak, it does not dare disobey; if you tell the river to give up its course, it does not dare do otherwise. The power of the masses is limitless."

"We piled rock into the River and increased the efficiency of the manmade dike twentyfold," submitted Wang Fuyuan.

"Good," replied Chen Yonggui. "You led the masses to a great achievement!"

Then they put together four short phrases about the early completion of the project: "We cleared out the Guo Settlement Reservoir above, and silted the Border Block River below. The benevolence of the Dragon King[1] washed out the White Temple Mountain." With these words they presented the project as a gift to the Northern Regional Conference on Agriculture.

During those few years Chen Yonggui thought big and did likewise. He summarily supported the Jiedu People's Commune's Xigubi Production Brigade's project to level off mountains, change the course of rivers and create flatlands without regard for minor details. He encouraged all People's Communes and Production Brigades to have their own new projects. In his words: "The more one does the more one feels like doing, the more one does the more one dares to do, the more one does the better one knows how to do it!"

After a visit to Xiyang, some people from Heshun County were compelled to say: "Xiyang changes the landscape, while we look on amused," and "While Xiyang reconstructs, our two factions fight!"

Xiyang became the battlefront for launching major mass campaigns. Promoters wrote articles about the word "major." Dazhai, which had already turned its land into the high-grade sponge-like soil, started an assault on "water." This brings a story about "water" to mind.

After Premier Zhou Enlai's first visit to Dazhai, when he raised the issue of dependable water supplies with Chen Yonggui, Chen Yonggui

1. The Dragon King is the God of Rain in Chinese mythology.

could not get water off his mind. He built a pond because of water, he constructed a canal because of water. It was because of water, too, that he impetuously hurled a brick to the ground and broke the glass on a table top with his fist. He raved and lectured to a meeting in high-pitched tones of anger until the mood of the whole gathering turned grave, all on account of water that could not be sent up the mountain.

This happened in 1970. Dazhai had become the place of pilgrimage for China's peasants. When spring started turning to summer that particular year, not a single drop of rain fell. A serious drought threatened every field of sprouts on Tigerhead Mountain. Dazhai had a pond, but without an electric hook-up its pump could not deliver water to the uphill side. Despite the situation, visitors, including some foreigners, kept pouring into Dazhai deliberately seeking inspiration from its unique accomplishments.

Walking through the fields with some foreign visitors, Chen Yonggui became more and more upset. When Chen got upset, when he encountered things that made him unhappy, he liked to drink. And the more he drank the more hot-tempered he became. After the visitors left, he drank more than usual, and became unusually irritable. He didn't try to keep his anger hidden from his own people. Cursing, he called them together.

"Look at you! What kind of farmers are you? Are you completely shameless? No water on the hill but you still fucking dare to invite visitors! Pooh!"

He raised his fist and hit it on the office table, smashing its thick glass. This he did while drunk. But when he sobered up he realized he was in the wrong. The following day he brought ten dollars crushed in his fist and handed them to the Brigade accountant: "I'm paying for it! Give me the receipt!"

The glass may have been paid for, but the water still didn't flow up the mountain. That morning Chen Yonggui directed his ill temper at the Brigade Scientific Research Group leader Gao Yuliang: "What are you saying? That the water can't get to the hilltop because there's no electricity? Well! Since when does electricity have feet? It's up to you! It's your job. You think the electricity knows when there's a drought, so it'll take some water uphill for you to irrigate the fields? Huh? Go ask that electricity whether it's got feet or not!"

Young Gao Yuliang could not take this heavy artillery attack for long. He uttered a few words of protest, turned around and disappeared without a trace. Having lectured Gao Yuliang until he drove him away, Chen Yonggui turned to the electrician in the same vein.

Worked up by all this lecturing, Gao Yuliang went around the village venting his pique. In the middle of the night he suddenly decided to do something. He returned to his own house to fetch a flashlight, grabbed a pair of wire-cutting pliers, and went up the mountain surrounded by silence and darkness. It is strange that, while during the day he had pondered and pondered about the problem and could not solve it, in the dead of night it took Gao Yuliang only a few hours of tinkering under the unsteady glow of his flashlight to get the electricity to flow. In the end, having accomplished his mission, his anger subsided. All of a sudden he felt very hungry. But what could he do about his hunger in the middle of the night? Better just rest a bit! And so he stretched out on somebody's grave-mound and went to sleep.

Early the following day, Chen Yonggui went up the mountain himself. He smiled when he saw water coming through the winding canal. He regretted having lectured Gao so relentlessly the previous evening. He intended to thank the young man. The problem was: Gao Yuliang was nowhere to be found. Chen Yonggui returned to the village.

"Where was Yuliang last night?" he asked Yuliang's wife.

"I don't know," the wife seemed puzzled. "I thought he had gone to a meeting."

"Gone the whole black night, and you didn't look for him?" Chen Yonggui smiled. "Aren't you worried he might be gone?"

Gao Yuliang, meantime, was sleeping soundly on top of a nameless dead man.

Lecturing had solved the problem. "Lecturing" was one of the most outstanding abilities of this peasant cadre, Chen Yonggui, whose cultural level (that is to say, reading and writing ability) was rather low. This is how Chen Yonggui operated at Dazhai. This is how he operated in Xiyang. Whenever he encountered a problem of crucial importance he never gave up. He was determined to solve it, and if he could not solve it he lectured and scolded until something changed.

Back in those days Xiyang held a series of meetings and rallies. In addition to the conference of outstanding workers, there was the so-called "gathering of heroes," when cadres awarded citations and red flowers to outstanding people. This took place on the eve of the Lantern Festival in the first month every year. Rectification rallies, self-criticism meetings, and backward Production Brigade gatherings also proliferated, all of them geared toward exposing contradictions and finding out in which areas the County lagged, so that the appropriate course of action could be determined as soon as possible. A motto created at the time went:

Speak of success and achievements
If you want to take off at all,
But fail to expose the problems
And you are bound to fall.

Why did they come up with a slogan like that? Because the situation was pressing enough to demand action.

I recall that around 1969 four People's Communes did not have any projects. Chen Yonggui assembled the Party Committee members from the four Communes in Dazhai and organized a study group for them. "Why is it that all other Communes have projects?" he asked them. "Are you planning to do something?"

Prior to their participation in the study group all those cadres sought to rationalize the lack of projects in their units and defended their positions, but the pressure exerted by the study group was so great that they all, as if on orders from Chen Yonggui, promised to undertake a few projects when they returned home. The beneficial results of the projects undertaken at that time are felt to this day.

During the study group session nobody could escape lecturing and self-criticism. The lecture course shocked the obstinate, well-fed indolence that had taken root over the years, into a state of alertness. People could no longer enjoy the tasty meals spread on their tables or sleep soundly in their cushy quilts. All they could think of each day was how to pass the test of Chen Yonggui's expectations. Chen had a way of dealing with obstinate heads: He lectured them relentlessly, forcing issues onto a higher theoretical plane of Party-line struggle. For those he could not awaken he prescribed "surgery"—cutting them off from positions of power. It is fairly obvious that the experience in Xiyang was not at all what the later criticism and accusations made it out to be: a place where, figuratively speaking, Chen felled trees and chopped off tails, thus threatening socialism itself. Everything he did he set in motion with a clear-cut goal in mind.

The goal was making effective use of compost, water, basic field construction, and scientific farming. This accomplished, the total grain production in Xiyang doubled in just three years, rising from 40,000 metric tons to 80,000 metric tons.[1] Because of this, the Political Bureau of the Party Central Committee adopted Chairman Mao Zedong's motion that the State Council organize an Agricultural Conference of the fourteen northern Provinces in Xiyang. This took place on September 15, 1970. The participants at the Conference subjected the mountains and rivers of Xiyang County to inspection.

This national-level Agricultural Conference was an event of historic significance. At the beginning the Minister of Agriculture, Qian Zhengying, took the chair. But later Ji Dengkui and several other Central Committee leaders arrived to direct it. The participants heard reports from Chen Yonggui and Li Hansuo, who headed the Xiyang County leadership nucleus of the Chinese Communist Party, and then summed up their experiences. Before the meeting the entire Conference visited the Border Block River Project and the South River Project as the most advanced areas in Xiyang's drive to learn from Dazhai. While taking part in physical labor at the South River construction site, Minister Qian Zhengying and some of the participants in the Conference asked Wang Fuyuan for a progress report on his project.

In addition to studying ways of transforming mountains and rivers and increasing grain production, the Conference devoted special attention to the problems encountered in the process of learning from Dazhai and tried to find ways to remove all constraints on production. According to the habitual mode of thinking at the time, this could only be achieved if Xiyang first got a firm grip on class struggle and Party-line

1. Within ten years grain production tripled to 135,000 metric tons.

struggle. It could only be achieved if the proletariat took full control of the leading organs of power. In this context, Chen Yonggui's "lecturing" naturally came to mean that "the people of Dazhai loved to fight, fight endlessly about everything and anything." Incompatible leaders were diagnosed as one of the five categories of misfits in power similar to capitalist-roaders, bourgeois liberals, and unprincipled conformists.

The Conference brought up the name of the well-known old Model Worker Zhang Laotai, as an example of someone who had degenerated morally. Zhang had achieved astonishing results in animal husbandry during the Japanese occupation. This had brought him the honorary title of "The Old Model of the Taihang." Chairman Mao received him after Liberation, and he became quite influential nationwide. By a few years later, however, he had engaged in numerous disputes with people from other areas over his resale of animals for profit. Once the man fell out of favor on this issue, critics added all sorts of misdemeanors to his record, one of the most serious being that he had arbitrarily changed his daughter-in-law's classification from "rich peasant" to "middle peasant," thereby bringing a class enemy into the ranks of the people.

During the Conference the central leadership put Chen Yonggui in charge of this case. Chen investigated with great care. The daughter-in-law, it turned out, had been wrongly classified as a "rich peasant" during the land reform movement. There had been no "rich peasants'" families in her village, but the higher authorities insisted that Zhang Laotai designate one to maintain some class balance. Years later when she married Zhang's son he corrected the injustice, only to be condemned as a "democratic element,"[1] even a "capitalist roader."

After getting to the bottom of all facets of this case Chen Yonggui set Zhang's record straight and removed all the invidious caps from his head. However, the political climate in those days was such that no matter how you corrected or amended the record, you could never really remove such labels as "democratic element" or "capitalist roader" from

1. A "democratic element" was somebody who joined the democratic revolution against feudalism and imperialism, for land reform and national independence, but did not go along with the socialist revolution, which was trying to abolish private ownership of the means of production. (W.H.H.)

the accused. Those cases were only fully resolved at the Third Plenary Session of the Tenth Central Committee in 1978.

Given Zhang Laotai's later behavior it became clear that Chen Yonggui had displayed a brand of commendable daring by clearing up this case. For it was this very maligned Model Worker, Zhang Laotai, who set the tone at the Northern Regional Conference on Agriculture, insisting that the problems in the countryside be solved by taking class struggle and line struggle as the key links while bringing the leadership of capital construction firmly into one's own revolutionary hands.

After the Conference, a new revolutionary upsurge focused on the issue of "the five types of people in power" was set in motion throughout the country, inspiring the slogan "Mass Criticism Inspires Great Drive." The Conference produced a "Summary of the Northern Regional Conference of Fourteen Provinces on Agriculture." The *People's Daily* published an editorial entitled "Agriculture Learns from Dazhai," which pointed out that the Dazhai People's Commune ends with the Dazhai Brigade, but that all of Xiyang County had been transformed into a Dazhai-style County. "If Xiyang can do it, why can't we? If not in a year or two, how about in three? Four or five years should definitely do it!"

The editorial went on: "Delegates at the Conference declared: 'It's the same heaven, the same earth, the same sun, and the same leadership of Chairman Mao! Whatever Dazhai can do, so can we!' This marks the beginning of a new tide of learning from Dazhai, catching up with Xiyang, and major campaigns for the capital construction of farmland, and irrigation and water conservancy projects, that are rapidly being set in motion throughout the Northern Region. Under the compelling force of circumstances which, intolerant of arrogance and complacency, simply push one into action, Chen Yonggui came up with a new formula for moving mountains, filling ravines with soil, and constructing plains for the purpose of mechanization and irrigation."

With the entire nation now learning from Xiyang the political pressure on Chen Yonggui increased geometrically. If Xiyang did not have a new breakthrough, what would all those folks have to learn? There was still only one answer: daring investment in the capital construction of farmland, irrigation and water conservancy projects. To achieve his goal

Chen Yonggui went to conferences and meetings of all sizes, and even published an article in the *Red Flag* Magazine in which he said: "If you just keep spinning around and around in your account books, calculating this and that cost—labor, dynamite, drill rods, what have you—you'll get dizzy from all the calculation, but whatever you calculate will always seem to turn out to be unfeasible. Of course, I am not against accounting. One has to keep accounts, but one must take into account the living human factor when doing so. Count in the enthusiasm of the masses, count in the advantages of collective economy, and above all count in the unrealized potential of all the underutilized labor power of the peasants. Only by taking into account all of that can one properly put a value on the confidence, determination, and enthusiasm of the people."

Around this time Chen Yonggui began looking into the accounting methods of all the People's Communes and Production Brigades under his leadership. There was a ten-mile long[1] Red River in the Red River People's Commune, whose wide flood plain was strewn with rocks. In 1967, the first year of the "In Agriculture Learn from Dazhai" campaign, while the rest of the County worked, Red River's citizens sat around calculating. First they calculated the projected labor cost, second they calculated the necessary investment, third they calculated the estimated profits for that year. Whichever way they calculated the returns on the work seemed uneconomic, so they ended up not doing anything. The following year, while all the other Communes worked full force, they sat around waiting. First they waited for the State to raise funding, second they waited for the County to start a project for them, third they waited for outside assistance, and so again they ended up not doing anything. The third year, while the other Communes achieved even greater results, they still sat around watching. First they watched to see whether the State would pay for the projects of others, second, they watched to see how the other Communes accumulated their funds, third they watched to see whether they could get any interest back on their money, and so they still ended up not doing anything.

In the fourth year the Northern Regional Conference on Agriculture took place, publicizing changes in people, land and grain output in every other Commune. Chen Yonggui went to the Red River

People's Commune in person to pose the question: "You guys did your calculating, did your waiting, and did your watching. What are you planning to do now?"

This finally pushed them into deciding that they, first, needed no investment and, second, wanted no assistance. They worked hard for one year, relying strictly on their own strength, and they built a great 4,800-meter-long dike beside the River and leveled 1700 *mu* of land into good, flat fields, turning into a living example of how to build a Dazhai County. Chen Yonggui talked about their example wherever and whenever he had the opportunity, turning their story into a great news item.

It was Chen Yonggui's brand of calculation and accounting that produced the great sweep and scale of Xiyang's vast endeavor. In ten years of learning from Dazhai, Xiyang invested 140 million *yuan* in the capital construction of farmland and produced 60,000 *mu* of new fields. The County carried out 8,900 projects: It moved over 30 million cubic meters of earth and stone, built over 2,000 Chinese miles of dikes, razed over 1,200 small hilltops, built fields over 170 Chinese miles of vaulted culverts in hitherto untamable gullies, and cut through over 350 cliffs to change the course of rivers. In all, they expanded the land under crops by over 60,000 *mu*, built over 300,000 *mu* of Dazhai-style sponge-soil fields, and increased the area of irrigated land ten times over. Without a doubt, those achievements represent a glorious moment in Xiyang's history.

Judging by his actions and deeds in Xiyang, Chen Yonggui indeed possessed the qualities of a leader. He was a peasant, but then again he was not just an ordinary peasant. He was good at dealing with various complicated issues, revealing an unexpected subtlety, yet acting resolutely in a manner characteristic of peasants. He was also able to raise issues to a theoretical level when the time was right. Certainly he was not well suited for life at the summit, the very vortex of political power and struggle in China. But both the objective and subjective factors combined to lift him into the sphere of high-level policy-making and implementation. Once there he acquitted himself well.

It was during this period that a major change took place in Xiyang County, a technological change that had enormous positive impact on the development of agriculture. Two key players laid the groundwork for this development. One was a very special State leader, the Premier of China, the other a very special peasant, Chen Yonggui.

It all started on May 21, 1965, when Premier Zhou visited Dazhai for the first time. As they stood atop Tigerhead Mountain, Premier Zhou asked Chen Yonggui about the hamlet's use of chemical fertilizers. He then asked about the use of chemical fertilizers by the surrounding Production Brigades. The Premier said: "There's coal in Xiyang. You could set up a chemical fertilizer plant!"

It was a sentence Chen Yonggui could not get out of his mind. It followed him around through many a day and night and many an event. But he was merely a Production Brigade Party Branch Secretary—where did he have the authority to set up a fertilizer plant? The matter was never mentioned again until the time Chen Yonggui rushed to Peking looking for Premier Zhou after the Red Guards made trouble in Dazhai.

When Chen Yonggui came to Beijing in the spring of 1967 for a medical examination, Premier Zhou made a special trip to the hospital to inquire about his health. The visit overwhelmed Chen Yonggui with all sorts of confused feelings.

"The Premier is so busy," he said to himself, "there are so many important national affairs he has to worry about, and I haven't even paid him a visit. Here I am, a simple peasant, and after I've spent just a few days in the hospital he comes to see me!"

He tried to conceal his excitement as best he could, respectfully offering Premier Zhou a seat and preparing to chat with him. As usual, Premier Zhou was up to his ears in work. His secretary had to arrange his guest reception schedule very tightly. This special visit to Chen Yonggui was designed: one, to express his concern; and two, to give him an opportunity to find out how things were at the grass-roots level. The Premier first inquired about Chen Yonggui's illness and the treatment he was receiving, and then went on to ask about the progress of the Cultural Revolution in Shanxi Province. His next question was about the difficulties Chen Yonggui was encountering in managing his County's affairs.

In his later conversations with people, Chen Yonggui said Premier Zhou had asked him about his difficulties. Chen's position was that one should not talk about difficulties in front of a Premier. Premier Zhou Enlai had already shown enough concern and care for Chen Yonggui personally, according him plenty of thoughtful consideration in the way of conferred honors, status, and political treatment. When Chen Yonggui had gone on an official visit to Albania along with a delegation of other Party representatives a few months earlier, it had been upon Premier Zhou's recommendation. How could he talk about difficulties in front of him? Yet, he somehow had to talk about the issues he faced at the time. Finally, he said to Premier Zhou: "The people in Xiyang are dying to use chemical fertilizers. The problem is that there is so little of the stuff in the country, it is very hard to get hold of. We have coal in Xiyang, and we want to make fertilizer—we just need somebody to authorize it."

This was exactly what Premier Zhou had in mind. He had been pondering the direction China's agriculture ought to take. The Ministry of Agriculture and the Chinese Academy of Sciences had just announced that the solution for China's agriculture lay in: one, chemical fertilizers and pesticides; and two, scientific farming. When a few large-scale fertilizer plants appeared in the 1950s, followed by several smaller ones, he had been very pleased. Without much deliberation about Chen Yonggui's request, Premier Zhou made his pronouncement: "How right you are! We are having a meeting to discuss the development plan tomorrow. We can enter your proposal into the State plan. You better go back to write up a report."

Premier Zhou stayed for quite a while, talking to Chen Yonggui about various other subjects. As for the fertilizer plant that Chen Yonggui wanted to set up—that project already had the Premier's approval. When Chen Yonggui returned to Xiyang, he set about making preparations for the plant. On March 24, 1967, the Xiyang County Revolutionary Rebel General Headquarters brought a resolution regarding the preparations for the fertilizer plant, and sent a man to Peking to deliver a written report about it to the Communist Party Central Committee and the State Council. After they sent up their report, Xiyang cadres received no news from Beijing. Just at that time Chen Yonggui decided that he needed a skilled and capable man to take charge of plant construction. After a lot of picking and choosing, he chose Wang Benshan, the leader of City Gate People's Commune. Sometime in April, the Deputy Director of the County Revolutionary Committee, Wang Guike, invited Wang Benshan for a talk and sent him, as Chen Yonggui had suggested, to Beijing to contact Premier Zhou. He was to bring back official authorization for the project.

Invested with the heavy responsibility, Wang Benshan boarded the train from Yangquan to Beijing. All along the way he heard people discussing Dazhai and praising Chen Yonggui. After he got off the train, he moved into the State Planning Commission Guest House to wait for news of the successful completion of his mission. He did harbor a petty wish on this trip—he wanted to see Premier Zhou personally. But Premier Zhou was extremely busy; there was absolutely no opportunity to meet him. It was the Premier's secretary who received Wang Benshan. The secretary told him that the Premier was well aware of his mission. "Just wait," he said.

At the end of May, Wang Benshan went to look up Premier Zhou's secretary again. The secretary informed him that Premier Zhou had already sent his personal approval to Li Fuchun, and instructed him to inquire about it at the State Planning Council. It was as if a heavy burden had fallen off Wang Benshan's shoulders. He rushed off to the Planning Council office. There he saw with his own eyes the five words Premier Zhou had written in ink under the proposal submitted by the Xiyang County Revolutionary Rebel General Headquarters: "Put Li Fuchun in charge." Signed: "Zhou Enlai, May 19, 1967." There was no margin left after the last word of this simple instruction. Below it, Li Fuchun had written his own instruction in ink: "Put Yu Qiuli in charge...." The two instructions stood firm like a rock. That very day the State Planning Council sent down the official document in the form of an urgent dispatch authorizing construction of the Xiyang Chemical Fertilizer Plant.

The Xiyang Chemical Fertilizer Plant was born right there and then!

From this time on, Chen Yonggui took it upon himself to act as the plant's Founding Committee Director. He broke the ground for the plant's builders. Construction work took only one year and two months from the initial preparations to the moment the plant went into production—ten months fewer than originally planned. On December 20, 1968, the chemical fertilizer plant workers announced the good news to Chen Yonggui with drums and gongs. He delivered a moving speech in return. For over twenty years now, from the time it turned out its first nitrates to this day, the plant has supplied agriculture with over 10,000 tons of chemical fertilizer annually, making it possible for the County of Xiyang to increase its grain production to over 130,000 tons.

CHAPTER 23

RECTIFYING CONDUCT

Rectification was the procedure used by the Chinese Communist Party to purify its own ranks and maintain close ties with the common people. It was also the procedure used by Chen Yonggui to educate cadres and dispose of unhealthy tendencies. Amidst a general climate of continuous rectification of the Chinese Communist Party, Chen Yonggui undertook endless rectification campaigns. They were designed to solve a whole range of problems among the ranks of Xiyang County cadres and with the County Standing Committee. For instance: a campaign at the very beginning of the movement to station government cadres and administrative workers in grassroots units; then again in 1973, a rectification campaign against the pursuit of private gain at public expense; in 1974, a campaign to oppose arrogance and shatter complacency; and in 1975, during the Rectification of Youth campaign, a movement that focused on the outlook and working style of young cadres and activists.

Chen Yonggui, in a surprise move, sent peasants out to monitor government operations and industrial production. Under the initial onslaught of information regarding all these various campaigns, my mind could not grasp the thinking behind this. It is only now that I have finally come to realize his true intentions. His decision to place selected peasant representatives in administrative offices and industrial enterprises was his unique way of responding to the policy of stationing government cadres and administrative workers in grass-roots units for firsthand experience. Once, at a mass meeting of administrative workers, he had criticized the cadres by telling them they did not measure up to the peasants. "If a brigade member doesn't show up for work just one morning, he loses two work points. An administrative worker can miss a whole month of work and still be paid his full salary. If a peasant takes a Sunday off, no seed will get planted. Supervision and learning should be mutual. The transfers should work both ways."

Taking into account the urgency of both planting and harvest seasons and the vagaries of weather, Chen Yonggui was very much against the eight-hour workday and Sundays off for peasants, and if not for peasants why for anybody else? His views were a bit extreme, reflecting a brand of genuine peasant consciousness somewhat out of tune with modern industrial society, but his home-grown application of policy did solve a score of serious long-standing problems. The peasant representatives he placed in administrative offices and industrial enterprises were able to crack and solve some hitherto unresolved conflicts and contradictions. In the same spirit, when he mobilized the people to comment on the work of the County Standing Committee, he sincerely wanted them to deal with issues that involved top leadership, not excluding himself. He also asked the county cadres to visit his home to check up on him. If they found any property belonging to the County, he asked that they return it to the public domain. When he returned from Beijing, he went to read the big-character posters put out by the rank and file in order to find out about the level of people's confidence in their leadership. Whatever the problem, he dealt with it as soon as he discovered it. He never left anything unsettled for long. For that reason he was both respected and feared by the county cadres.

The people of Dazhai revered Chen Yonggui as someone who resolved every problem. Even as he tackled his multi-level responsibilities, he never forgot to attend Party Branch meetings on daily life in Dazhai. As China's vast countryside drifted in the great upheaval and lost its orientation in factional strife, while virtual paralysis if not complete breakdown overtook the Party organization (one can only imagine the Party's combat capacity at this time), Party Branch meetings on daily life in Dazhai went on as usual.

Rectification centered, first and foremost, on the Party members and took place mainly at Party Branch meetings, though Chen Yonggui was skillful at turning routine occurrences in daily life into political lessons. In those years the Brigade Party Secretary clashed more than once with Gao Yuliang, the talented Dazhai Scientific Research Group leader. I have already told the story of Chen's conflict with Gao over the electrical hookup for the irrigation pump; as Gao liked to march to his own drummer and often violated community norms in small ways Chen Yonggui found him hard to lead.

Once when Chen Yonggui came back from Beijing he didn't see Gao eating breakfast at the communal mess hall. Some cadres told him they had not seen Gao there for ten days or so, but that he had been leading his team members in the wheat fields. They were raking wheat during the coldest days of the year, following the winter solstice, something no one in Dazhai had done before.

"Raking wheat during the coldest days of the year? I'll see about your raking," muttered Chen. "And also about your absence from the mess hall."

"How come he's not coming to eat?" Chen asked some diners.

"His wife is in confinement, preparing to give birth," someone explained.

When he heard that, Chen Yonggui's facial expression improved somewhat, but he was still upset with Gao Yuliang about the wheat-raking. When Gao did finally show up with this food bowl he asked him, "What do you want to rake wheat for?"

"Wheat raking increases the ground temperature. It helps the wheat grow," Gao Yuliang explained.

Chen Yonggui was startled, because he had not yet heard of such a strange thing.

"What? You mean ground temperature, it, like, grows legs? Him?"

Gao Yuliang did not say a thing. He just went on stuffing food into his mouth with his chopsticks. Chen Yonggui did not seem at all convinced.

"Tell me then, really, how is it that the ground temperature grows legs?" he asked again.

Gao Yuliang had just learned of this phenomenon from an agricultural researcher in Beijing, so he explained: "If you cut off the fine passages in the soil, it reduces water movement, it reduces evaporation, it makes the temperature of the ground go up, it maintains the moisture level."

At the time Chen Yonggui was not ready to accept this explanation, but he noticed later that the wheat in that raked field did take off a little faster in the spring and, in his heart of hearts, he had to admit that Gao was on to something. Like any ordinary peasant, if Chen had not seen it with his own eyes, he would never have believed it. But scientific techniques do not wait for people to straighten out their thinking before they make big advances—that much even Chen Yonggui could understand and accept. He had to admit that he had learned something from Gao Yuliang and he was grateful for it. Even though Chen was publicly recognized at the "agricultural specialist," he felt that a lot of agricultural knowledge was extremely profound, often obscure and not easy to grasp. That is how he felt about agriculture, and that is how he felt about transforming peasant mentality and world outlook. In the long run the latter proved to be the more difficult process by far.

Before very long Chen Yonggui found himself in conflict with Gao Yuliang again. This time Gao was not skipping meals, he was skipping Party Branch meetings, one after the other. When he failed to show up for the third time, Chen Yonggui's heavy eyebrows twisted into a knot and his two cheeks turned white as though covered with frost.

"Go! Tell Gao Yuliang to come! If he doesn't respond, pick him up and carry him over!" said Chen angrily.

Gao Yuliang did not come to the meeting because he was sulking. He received notice while he was eating supper, but he made up his mind to ignore it. As the time for the meeting approached, he told his wife: "If some big shot comes looking for me, tell them they can find me at the Reception Center. If there's no big shot involved, just tell them you don't know where I've gone." And he went off to the Reception Center to "sleep."

Since this was Gao's third absence from a regular Party Branch meeting Chen Yonggui made special note of it. Knowing that Gao

Yuliang was a real "tough cookie," Chen Yonggui was not afraid to be hard on him. They called him once; he didn't show up. They called him twice; he didn't show up. They called him the third time; he had gone "to sleep." The fourth time several people went to press and urge. They twisted him by the arm and grabbed him by the leg: "C'mon! Come to the meeting. It's old Chen's call after all!"

When he finally arrived before the assembled group he didn't even bother to lift his eyelids. He just slumped onto a stool and turned his back on Chen Yonggui and the rest of the assembly.

As usual a dense crown filled the room at the solemn Party Branch meeting on daily life in Dazhai. Except for a few threads of smoke that floated near the ceiling, only an occasional sound of coughing disturbed the air. Some people sat with their heads bent low, others with their eyebrows knit, while a few scrutinized the man in charge of the meeting, searching the expression on his face for a hint as to what was in store. Chen Yonggui sat at the table in front of the assembly hall, scowling.

Pulling that trademark white hand-towel off his head and taking a sip of water, Chen Yonggui said very deliberately: "Some people can't even make it to the Party Branch meeting! Why is that? Huh? Is that the way a Party member behaves? We managed to implore him to come today. Why don't you say something, now that you are here? Speak up! what are you staring at the ceiling for? You think it might fall down on you?"

The assembly sat in perfect silence. Not even a cough disturbed the air. It did not seem that Gao Yuliang was ready to admit defeat. He sat there looking solemn and bided his time. He didn't know what to do with his eyes while Chen criticized him, so he just raised his head and stared at the ceiling. Chen Yonggui felt that his opponent was playing tough, so, playing tough himself, he struck the table with his hand, jolting back into the present those of the assembly who were lost in thought. Ready to name names, he called out in a loud voice: "Yuliang! How many times did you skip the Party Branch meeting?"

"Me? You are asking me? Ttt...twice."

"Skipped the Branch meeting twice! What are we going to do about it?"

"Whatever you say."

"Whatever I say? Huh? You skip the Party Branch meeting twice, you are expelled!" Chen Yonggui struck the table hard with his hand again.

While the sound was still echoing, Gao Yuliang got up and walked toward the door, mumbling along the way, "If you want to expel me fine. Off I go."

His action struck everybody as dumb. Nobody thought that Gao Yuliang had that much guts. Even Chen Yonggui flinched for a moment, but he immediately started turning the situation over in his head. Gao Yuliang did have a temper, all right, but his job performance was consistently good. Although he was brazen enough to contradict the leading group from time to time, he was still able to discharge his duties on his own initiative. Besides there was that matter of the wheat-raking. So when Chen Yonggui saw him leaving the meeting, he rushed to the door and blocked his passage.

"Where do you think you are going?"

Gao Yuliang did not dare leave.

"Don't you want to expel me?" he muttered as they stood face to face.

"Expel? Even if I expel you, you still can't leave. Come back over here and explain yourself."

Gao Yuliang returned to his previous seat, but obdurately remained silent.

Chen Yonggui, his face a steel mask, addressed Gao as well as the entire assembly of the Party members: "If you have something to say, speak out. You shouldn't keep quiet. Keeping quiet is not good. It's wrong to keep it all in. If you let it out, the problem is half-solved."

Chen Yonggui was no longer talking at the top of his lungs. His muted voice now sounded well-intentioned and kind. It was clear that he did not want to "expel," but was rather trying to get to the bottom of the problem and was intent on clearing up the misunderstanding.

Who knows how many similar Party Branch meetings on daily life Chen Yonggui had chaired over the years? Whenever there was a problem, he brought it straight to the meeting and raised a racket over it. He did not mind shouting and wrangling until he was so agitated it seemed he would explode. The moment he solved the problem, however, he relaxed, food tasted sweet once more and sleep came easily. Having solved one squabble, he would move on to another, and each time his voice grew louder. In the course of each such confrontation, the Party members reached a higher level of common understanding. So this time, too, Chen Yonggui adopted his old method and called on people to make themselves heard. His tone, however, was milder than just a few moments ago.

A minute went by without sound.

Two minutes went by. Still no sound.

After some ten minutes, Chen Yonggui's explosive temper flared again. "Bang!" He picked up a teacup and struck it on the table, spattering water all over the place. Waving the cup up and down, he continued to send ripples of water flying. This alarmed everybody in the hall.

"Someone here has things to say, but he's not making a peep. Yuliang, are you going to say something?"

Gao Yuliang hardened his resolve: "No! I'm not going to say a thing."

"And why aren't you going to say a thing?"

Gao Yuliang's manner was just a tough as before, but his voice was low: "If I speak up, someone is bound to get the shakes."

"What? If you speak up someone is bound to get the shakes?"

Here at last was something interesting.

Having found a crack in Gao Yuliang's facade at last, Chen Yonggui took advantage of it with dispatch: "You say that if you speak up, someone is bound to get the shakes. So let them shake then!"

With that Gao Yuliang seemed to lose some heart, but after taking an inch he still reached for a yard. "I'm afraid they'll get sick from too much shaking."

"They'll get sick if I tell you to let them shake? So let them get sick! I'll find them a cure!" Chen Yonggui pressed on, banging on the table again.

When Chen Yonggui took to teaching someone a lesson he had no tact at all. Many people remembered the time he spotted a flock of chickens feasting on grain in the middle of a field. He cursed them out ferociously, "You deadbeats, you! Your mother's—-! Whose chickens are you anyway?" he shouted as the accursed fowl scattered without so much as a cluck or a peep. The moment Chen finished cursing, however, he rushed to pick up the scattered grain, kernel by kernel. Today's meeting was something like that. Lots of kernels lying around to be picked up.

The real problem finally came out in the open. The person causing all the trouble turned out to be the head of the Production Brigade. He had mishandled things and made a mess of several projects. This upset a lot of people and they all objected. But only Gao was willing to make an issue of it. After Chen Yonggui forced the problem into the open and cleared it up, Gao Yuliang held no grudge against Chen or the leader in question. He thanked Chen and announced that he wanted to cooperate with the Brigade leader and help him in his work.

Certainly Gao's talent as a technician and a researcher had something to do with Chen Yonggui's willingness to expend whatever time and energy were necessary to reveal and solve any problems the younger man had. But it wasn't just Gao. He applied the same standards all down the line. He consistently tried to bring out the best in everyone. Hence, though he often provoked resentment, even anger, in the long run he won his compatriots' deep respect and admiration.

Later on, in the winter of 1974, there was another memorable late-night gathering in Dazhai. This time is was not about skipping Party meetings, nor was it about resolving some general problem of outlook or ideology. A serious political struggle was taking place over corruption, and the Production Brigade accountant, Zhao Cuntang, was the target.

Under Chen Yonggui's unified command, a campaign against the decadence of those who seek private gain at public expense was underway in Xiyang County. The campaign drew Dazhai into its turbulent current. Beginning with Jia Chengrang's accountant, Wan Biquing, and others, all through the years, Dazhai's cadres had been impeccable in their handling of collective finances. In that respect, they never left a bad impression with the people and were able to stand up to the ferocious investigations of the "Four Clean" Movement. Only two men, Zhao Cuntang and a certain carpenter, whom I will not name, gave a green light to graft and embezzlement, and soon enough a whole score of problems emerged that aroused public indignation.

Zhao Cuntang was the son of Zhao Xiaohe, who had honorably sacrificed his life for the building of new Dazhai but he turned his back on his father's newly reassured ideals and took off in the opposite direction. During the present meeting, Zhao Cuntang hung his head while trying to account for his behavior A serious interrogation ensued. Chen Yonggui sat in the middle of the gathering, carefully listening to the investigation of the accountant and the speeches of the participants in the meeting. They criticized Zhao Cuntang severely. "We know very well what the problems are. What we want to see is whether you own up to them or try to play tricks on us. Let me tell you: If everything is not clarified here tonight, you won't make it through!"

It was a very cold night, but the temperature at the meeting kept rising. Zhao Cuntang found it unbearable. Chen Yonggui had to weigh everything carefully. For the first time in some thirty years Dazhai's cadres faced a case of economic corruption, and he had to think it through. If the Party disciplined Zhao Cuntang internally it would calm popular indignation. It would also be useful to educate other cadres. In the end Chen Yonggui and his comrades agreed on a temporary suspension from the Party and a warning before the masses for Zhao Cuntang. After Chen Yonggui left Dazhai for Beijing, however, the Party Branch reviewed Zhao's case and rehabilitated him. In the eighties the Brigade members even elected him to serve as their collective's Party Secretary.

In spite of what happened, Zhao Cuntang's attitude toward Chen Yonggui remained warm. He never hit out at Chen when the latter fell from grace and went down under a barrage of abuse. But he never overcame his selfishness either, and soon after he took office new problems emerged.

Since the building of the new village in 1963, Dazhai had based its economy on public ownership, including publicly owned housing. Due to the redistribution of land after 1983 the collective will of the people broke down and the only thing that could be done was to sell housing units to the Brigade members for a price. The quality of the housing, however, was not uniform, and the degree to which units were occupied varied, so that the privatization process was constantly plagued with problems. Those who occupied the good units would not vacate them, while those who could not move into the good units complained. The disputes went on and on.

Those were the circumstances under which Zhao Cuntang, who was then the Party Branch Secretary, stopped taking good care of the members' business. He privately made a secret deal with the County to buy all the vacated good houses and cave dwellings that had belonged to the old collective, then occupy them by force and turn a handsome profit. The people in Dazhai were, to say the least, not pleased with his handling of the situation. It was so obviously different from Chen Yonggui's. People were saying: "Old Chen became Vice-Premier of the State, and yet he never lived better or ate more than we did. But this Zhang Cuntang, he's barefaced with his rotten deals!"

We can see from this that problems easily emerge the moment you relax ideological education. Chen Yonggui's ability to act in exemplary fashion was decided by his farsighted political vision coupled with his capacity for painstaking work. That much everybody in Dazhai could see very clearly after Chen Yonggui stepped down. They learned the lesson thoroughly from the example of several Party Branch Secretaries that followed him.

CHAPTER 24

AT THE VORTEX OF POWER AND CONFLICT

Chen Yonggui might have begun life as an ordinary peasant, but the historical conditions of his time and his extraordinary ability and accomplishments swept him into the vortex of China's political life at the highest level.

After the Conference on Agriculture of the Fourteen Provinces of the Northern Region, the Ninth Party Congress convened in August, 1969, and made Chen Yonggui a member of the Chinese Communist Party Central Committee. He was supposed to represent China's peasants and bring their views to the attention of the Central Committee.

During the Ninth Congress, Chen Yonggui was also chosen to be a member of its presiding body. He sat at the rostrum and addressed the Congress as its keynote speaker. The Second Plenary Session that began on August 23, 1970, on Mount Lushan in Jiangxi, chose him to serve as convener of the North Cinha Group. This made him stand out among other Central Committee members and undoubtedly caused people to regard him with increased respect. Yet, he was basically ignorant of what this Plenary Session was supposed to accomplish. Only after the opening of the session did he find out that the main item on the agenda was the rewriting of the Constitution. He was even less aware that rewriting the Constitution involved a particular important issue: whether or not to establish the post of the President of State. Lin Biao insisted on instituting a State presidency; Chairman Mao opposed it six times. What was the core issue? To Chen Yonggui, as to most other Central committee members, the answer was not at all clear.

When the formal discussion of the draft of the new Constitution began, Chen Boda[1] suddenly showed up at the North China Group's discussion session and took on a pivotal role. He had been elected a member of the Standing Committee of the Political Bureau at the Ninth Congress, and he was commonly known as a scholar of great talent. Naturally, his presence left an impact on the North China Group's discussion session. The members of the North China Group were, however, not able to fathom his intentions. Chen Boda proved to be the scholar he was reputed to be. During the meeting he never raised a straightforward point; instead, he beat around the bush, concocting new theories. For the purpose of establishing the institution of a President of State he first said that Chairman Mao should be elected Head of State. The theoretical basis for this was the theory of "innate genius." During the discussion period, he sat on the sofa, gesticulating joyously as he expounded on the genius of Marx, Engels, Lenin, Stalin and Chairman Mao. Seeing that many people were immature when it came to theory, Chen Boda didn't mince words on this issue.

"Some people oppose the theory of 'innate genius,' he declaimed. "In essence, they oppose the idea that Chairman Mao should become the President of the State."

When Chen Boda thought the moment was ripe he provoked the group into hastily producing a document, the "North China Brief No.

1. Chen Boda had been Mao's secretary. A brilliant intellectual with a radical bent, he was chosen in May, 1966, to serve as the head of the Central Cultural Revolution Group, which included Mao's wife, Jiang Qing, Zhang Chunqiao, and Yao Venyuan, three of the four members of the Gang-of-Four, which later created such havoc with ultra-left policy initiatives. The struggle at Lushan was over the coming succession to Mao's mantle and pitted the Lin Biao Group against the Gang. Chen Boda went out on a limb for Lin and was exposed and denounced by Mao. (W.H.H.)

6." A large contingent of workers, peasants, and soldiers served as members of the Central Committee at that time, and they all felt profound affection for Chairman Mao. Chen Boda's tactics managed to stir up their emotions. They had absolutely no idea that it was Chairman Mao himself who opposed the theory of "innate genius" and the establishment of the post of President of State.

Once he lit the fire Chen Boda took advantage of the situation to throw oil on it. "When Malenkov rose to power he didn't get rid of those who opposed him. If I come to power, I will get rid of the entire opposition." He said, boasting, "If I were General Secretary of the Party, I'd be more powerful than Deng Xiaoping."

Chen Boda's word alerted Chen Yonggui to the complexity of the problem. However, he had no inside information. He thought of Chairman Mao as his benefactor. At the same time, he lacked experience at the highest levels of political life. An intelligent man has to arrive at this own understanding of things by approaching every subject from various angles, so Chen Yonggui maintained his detachment at the meeting and didn't make any unnecessary speeches. The North China Group prepared a list of those who had read the "North China Brief No. 6," and asked all participants to sign it by drawing a circle after their names. Although Chen Yonggui managed to keep a relatively cool head, he was not able to envisage the consequences of that document. When the others drew circles next to their names, he too picked up a pen and cautiously drew a tiny little circle next to his own.

Chen Yonggui sobered up thoroughly when Chairman Mao published a letter under the heading "A Few Opinions of Mine." With a single pertinent remark, the letter exposed Chen Boda's scheming with the North China Group to produce its perverse "Brief No. 6." Mao's letter also negated Chen Boda's theory of "innate genius," saying that with it Chen Boda wanted to blast Mount Lushan flat.

"Even if Mount Lushan were blown flat, I would not be President of State!" Mao wrote.

When Lin Biao realized that the momentum of his drive for power had taken a bad turn, he had no choice but to abandon Chen Boda in order to protect himself. Following Chairman Mao's lead, he, too, announced: "Even if Mount Lushan were blown flat, I would be Vice-President of State!."[1]

Thereupon, the majority of Central Committee members, who had been unaware of the true state of affairs, realized they had been duped. The political cauldron, however, increased Chen Yonggui's awareness, and he joined the subsequent "Criticize Chen Boda" campaign of his own accord.

At this time, the Central Committee issued a document calling on all participants of the Lushan Congress to return to their constituencies and explain what had happened so that the entire party membership might be educated. Chen Yonggui complied. Upon his return to Xiyand, he convened a meeting of a commune Party Committee Secretaries and the Party Branch Secretaries of all units directly subordinate to the County level. They met at the County middle school, where he passed around the Central Committee document and with great sincerity stated in way of self-criticism:

"I was the Deputy Head of the North China Group. I feel a grave responsibility for what happened. Chen Boda is a careerist. He had ulterior motives when he rattled Mount Lushan. I did not report promptly on the situation to the Central Committee, nor did I ask for instructions. I blindly went along for an entire day, and that was a mistake. Chairman Mao's "Few Opinions" gave me a wake-up call: I finally realized how vastly important it is to study and understand Marxism."

Chen Yonggui was decidedly neither a Lin Biao nor a Chen Boda man. After he became famous, he had plenty of opportunity to meet both of them, but he had no contact with either. Moreover in the eyes of those two men, he, Chen Yonggui, did not even exist. Chen Boda could not, however, completely ignore Dazhai. He felt constrained to deal theoretically with Chairman Mao's establishment of Dazhai as the Red Flag standard-bearer in agriculture.

Since, as a member of Political Bureau of the Central Committee, Chen Boda had to endorse Chairman Mao's setting up of the Dazhai model, in March 1966, he participated in the National Learn From

1. Lin Biao's motive for establishing the institution of a presidency was to open up a slot for himself at or next to the summit of the hierarchy. This creates something of a mystery since he was already the heir apparent.

Dazhai On-the-Spot Conference of Twelve Provinces and Municipalities. There he expressed interest in Dazhai's method of work evaluation.

"I have not been to Dazhai, so how do I know that Dazhai has this new method?" he asked. "I heard about it from Zhang Ruifang. When he was engaged in the "Four Clean-ups" campaign he noticed how complicated the system of work evaluation and work point allotment was in most places. He told me that Dazhai had a simple and convenient method: The work was evaluated only once a year, that's all. Now that I know about it I suggest that you all go to Dazhai to learn it. It's the best method, well suited to the conditions of China's countryside. It is the native, homegrown creative experience of the Chinese peasantry.

Warm words!

It was quite normal for Party or State leaders to express their opinions on whatever experience of Dazhai's came to the fore. The truth is, however, that Chen Boda had no energy to spare on studying Dazhai, and was not even interested in its existence, because in his view the one and only model was a Western one. Because of his aloofness regarding Dazhai he even avoided paying it a visit when he passed through Yanquan on his way to Taiyuan, where he had an engagement.

In 1967 he felt no warmth at all for Dazhai's "Iron Girl" Guo Fenglian, who, as Political Instructor of Dazhai's People's Militia, was attending the conference of activists in the "Study of the Works of Chairman Mao," called by a representative of the Beijing Area Military Command. During a film screening one evening Chen Boda deliberately sat next to her and subjected her to a barrage of relentless reproach. During the award ceremony, the representatives of all the other units walked away clutching their presents to the sound of drums and gongs. Only Guo Fenglian was left behind, unable to lift her present and with no one to take notice of it. She left the conference hall sobbing.

As the conference went on and on, Guo Fenglian started feeling that she should not be attending it any longer because she felt wronged and ignored. Chen Yonggui was in Taiyuan at that time, and Guo Fenglian struggled to find a place from which she could call him long distance to tell him that she could no longer take part in the conference. As soon as Chen Yonggui heard what she had to say, he knew all too well what was afoot. He had expected no less from Chen Boda. He told her that she could come back if she could not take it any longer.

Chen Boda's attitude toward Dazhai was expressed at its clearest during the Northern Regional Conference on Agriculture. Having seen the resolution to learn from Dazhai, this man, who never cared for agriculture, took up arms to attack a document that dealt with agriculture. He crossed out the words "Dazhai is a Red Flag personally set up by Chairman Mao" and added his own writing: "Dazhai is an objective existence." He also remarked, as he was crossing out the original: "What does 'setting up' mean?"

Everybody could see what his intentions were.

Later, when Chen Boda started viewing Premier Zhou as a thorn in his side, the extremely close cooperation between Chen Yonggui and Premier Zhou Enlai created an unbridgeable gap between Chen Boda and Chen Yonggui. The gap would only grow with time.

After the Lushan Congress, during a "Criticize Chen Boda and Rectify Incorrect Styles of Work" meeting, Chen Yonggui commented on the scholar-politician's behavior: "It's better he didn't ever go to Dazhai. Had he gone, who knows what kind of poison he would have spread?"

Several Central Committee leaders told Chen Yonggui: "You are wrong. Dazhai is, after all, Dazhai. Whatever he might have said, even if he had visited it, he could never have damaged Dazhai."

That may have been true then, but when others set out to attack Dazhai, their words became lethal weapons.

From the fact that Chen Yonggui survived the real high-level political test at the swirling vortex of the Lushan Congress, one can see the relative foresight and sagacity of this peasant statesman. Many workers and peasants from Hebei and Shanxi who were members of that same Central Committee were easily swayed by Chen Boda and followed him blindly. Chen Yonggui's ability to act independently was one of the important attributes that enabled him to advance to the policy-making level of the Central Committee of the Chinese Communist Party.

CHAPTER—25

DAZHAI RIPPLES REACH THE WEST

As Dazhai's fame increased, so did the number of international friends who wanted to see it. This mountain village in high loess country became an important destination of many a China travel itinerary.

The first foreign friend appeared in Dazhai in 1964 when a guest from Africa set foot on its yellow loess soil. As Chen Mingshu, Chen Yonggui's son, and secretary of the Dazhai Branch of the Communist Youth league, accompanied the visitor on a climb up Tigerhead Mountain, the well-seasoned "Iron Girls" were so dumbfounded by his appearance that they nervously ducked for cover. In order to broaden their horizons, Chen Mingshu called each of them by name to come out and meet the foreign guest and shake hands with him. From then on contacts between the people of Dazhai and foreign visitors were frequent.

From the time that a foreigner crossed Dazhai's threshold for the first time until 1978, some foreigner left a footprint on Dazhai's soil almost daily; 25,478 people of different skin color, different nationality and different creed, came from 134 different countries as members of 2,280 visiting groups. They took back with them fond memories and left behind sincere good wishes. The visits of the foreign guests were facilitated by the state-finance Reception Center, which became responsible for them, while Dazhai Brigade released one Party Branch cadre from other duties to accompany foreign guests, provide explanations, and entertain questions. If a state leader came for a visit, however, Dazhai turned out for the reception in full force.

During those twenty-odd years, twenty foreign leaders above the level of national vice-president or vice-premier came to visit Dazhai. The late President of Mozambique, Samora Moisés Machel, came to Dazhai twice between 1973 and 1976. He exchanged agricultural experiences with Chen Yonggui. Mexico's President Luis Echeverria Alvarez shared notes on raising corn (maize) with the people of Dazhai. He also presented them with orchard-drip-irrigation equipment, and issued a special invitation to Chen Yonggui to visit Mexico.

The Belgian-Chinese authoress Han Suyin, the famous Chinese-American physicists Yang Shenning and Li Zhengdao, the famous American journalist and friend of China Edgar Snow, and many, many others left their footprints, shadows and smiles on Dazhai's rugged landscape.

Of all those who were received in Dazhai, the American friend of the People's Republic of China, William Hinton, left the deepest impression. He established the best relations and the widest contacts of all.

In 1971 Chairman Mao Zedong and Premier Zhou Enlai invited Hinton to come to China. Premier Zhou told him that China had to take the road of self-reliance, arduous struggle and scientific farming. Premier Zhou said Dazhai was a model of all three and recommended that Hinton should concentrate on Dazhai in his quest to understand China, China's agricultural economy and rural society. In high spirits Hinton took his family to Dazhai, where his sister, Joan Hinton, and his brother-in-law, Erwin Engst, their three children and three of Hinton's children stayed for many months.

In the fall of that year Hinton's eighty-year-old mother, Carmelita Hinton, invited by Premier Zhou, brought a group of American young people to China for a work-study tour. They spent a memorable month in Dazhai, talked at length with Chen Yonggui, climbed mountains, moved loess soil, helped bring in the corn harvest and visited capital construction projects throughout Xiyang County.

Between 1971 and 1994 Hinton visited Dazhai many times and, while Chen Yonggui was alive, formed a deep and lasting friendship with him. After Chen was set aside as a national leader, retired to an urban apartment in Beijing, and underwent much unfair and ill-grounded criticism, Hinton tried all possible means and went through every conceivable channel for permission to visit him. When they finally met in 1985 Hinton tried to comfort him, implored him to take good care of himself and encouraged him to defend himself and his life work vigorously. In this last endeavor Hinton promised to help.

At that meeting Chen Yonggui made plans to accompany Hinton on a return trip to Dazhai in the spring of 1986. Sadly, because of Chen Yonggui's untimely death, the two men's wishes never came true. The death did not alter Hinton's plan to revisit Dazhai, however. He did so in 1986 and many times thereafter.

At the height of the "Learn From Dazhai" campaign, not only did foreign visitors go to Dazhai to have a look, but various performing arts groups went there to perform. A visit by the Japanese Haguruma Theatrical Company in September, 1967, left a deep impression.

The Japanese Haguruma Theatrical Company was organized by Japanese revolutionary literary and art workers under the leadership of the Japanese Communist Party. They held high the banner of anti-imperialism and anti-revisionism and supported the thinking of Mao Zedong. This inspired them to make a trip to Dazhai on their visit to the People's Republic of China.

Chen Yonggui welcomed them at a simple reception that served green tea and he talked at some length about class struggle, production and scientific experimentation at Dazhai. His talk was enthusiastically received by the Japanese friends, who took notes and applauded vigorously.

On the day after their arrival in Dazhai, as requested by the Company leader Ms. Long-ko, the members of the Japanese Haguruma Theatrical Company worked in the fields with the people of Dazhai for half a day. The Japanese friends, used to performing on stage, worked till sweat poured down their faces. After work the Company exclaimed emotionally: "The great transformation of Dazhai proves one truth: Once the people of the world master the thought of Mao Zedong, they can turn into a great material force, they can gain great victories!"

She also expressed her intention to arm the Japanese people with Mao Zedong thought upon her return to Japan, and use Mao Zedong thought to push forward the revolutionary struggle of the Japanese people.

That evening, the comrades from the Japanese Haguruma Theatrical Company and Dazhai commune members staged a get-together party where they performed a splendid program eulogizing Chairman Mao Zedong and his teachings. On behalf of the Dazhai Party Branch Committee and all commune members, Chen Yonggui presented the Japanese friends with a color portrait of Chairman Mao and a silk banner inscribed with Chairman Mao's words: "All you need is to combine the simple truths of Marxism and Leninism with the concrete practice of Japan's revolutionary struggle. There can be no doubt as to the victory of the Japanese revolution."

Dazhai, it seemed, was no longer just a simple player in the realm of foreign affairs, but compelled by the currents of the "Cultural Revolution," had already escalated matters to the point of promoting revolution in Japan!

At this time, Premier Chow, taking advantage of the visit of a distinguished foreign head of state to China, decided to visit Dazhai for the third time.

Why would the Premier of the State Council want to visit Dazhai for the third time? This was a question that concerned many public figures from all walks of life, and presented important subject matter for historians.

As the tide of the campaign to learn from Dazhai shaped up nationwide, and just as Dazhai and Xiyang County encountered yet another serious drought, a sensational bit of information was sent out from the national capital, Peking [Beijing].

Ximbua News Agency, Peking, April 23, 1973, cable:

> Mexico's President Luis Echeverria Alvarez and his wife, accompanied by Premier Zhou Enlai, Comrade Deng Yingchao, and Comrade Lin Jiamei, left Peking tonight aboard a special train for a visit to Dazhai.
>
> Traveling on the same train were the following distinguished guests: Mexico's Minister of Foreign Affairs Emilio Auravaz and his wife, Mexico's Ambassador to China Ouniau Andihano Lodi.
>
> At the train station to see them off were: Vice-Premiers of the State Council Li Xiannian and Deng Xiaoping, Minister of Foreign Affairs, Ji Pengfei, and Comrade Xu Hanbing, Deputy Foreign Minister Qiao Guanhua, Minister of Foreign Economic Relations Fang Yi, Chairman of the Peijing Municipal Revolutionary Committee Wu De, and several thousand residents of the capital.
>
> In addition, the honorable guests from Mexico were accompanied by: Minister of Agriculture and Forestry, Yang Ligong, Assistant Foreign Minister Zhang Wenjin, Chinese Ambassador to Mexico Xiong Xianghui and Comrade Chen Xiaohua, Director of the Shenyang Acrobatic Troupe Yin Canzhen with some troupe members.
>
> Diplomatic envoys to China were at the station to see them off.

In just a few minutes the important news had spread within and beyond the Great Wall, to both sides of the Yangtze River. Who knows just how many people sat around their radios talking about it and discussing the event, because this was Premier Zhou's third trip to Dazhai?

On April 23, 1973, Premier Zhou's special train arrived at the Yangquan station at seven o'clock. The asphalt road from Yangquan to

Dazhai that evening resembled a magnificent festival. The villages lining the road were decked out for the occasion and their residents were watching, their heads raised high, hoping to catch a glimpse of the Premier. The fulfillment of this wish would be the greatest honor of their lives! The previous two times the Premier had flown into Dazhai. Nobody wanted to miss this one chance to see him in their midst, passing by, with their own eyes.

A great crowd of people had been bustling about on the main street in front of the Xiyang County Bus Station since early morning. Those in the back finally heard the sound of applause. Then the motorcycles and security vehicles came through, and people started calling each other's attention in whispers: "Look! The Red Flag! Look! The Red Flag! He's here, he's here."

At ten minutes after eight in the morning, Premier Zhou's limousine slowly drove into the village of Dazhai. The ancient hamlet was seething with excitement. School children started dancing the "Welcome, Guests" dance, young village girls were swung to the beat of the "Harvest Song." "Welcome! Welcome! Warmly welcome!" The air reverberated with the sound of the slogan. Premier Zhou, President Echeverria and Chen Yonggui walked at the front of the crowd, smiling, clapping hands, endlessly nodding to the crowd to acknowledge its greetings.

The people of Dazhai noticed Premier Zhou's drawn, emaciated face and his graying hair.

It was a moment engraved especially in the minds of Jia Jincai and Song Liying, an unforgettable memory!

Having emerged from the car, Premier Zhou rested for just a brief moment at the Travel Bureau, then immediately wanted to see the changes that had happened in Dazhai over the years with his own eyes.

After his previous visit to Dazhai, Premier Zhou had discussed the outstanding achievements of Dazhai's transformation of nature with Vice-Premier Chen Yi. He praised Dazhai for having new changes every time he went there. Upon entering the village this time, there were even more smiles on his face than the previous two times.

In the years since he last saw it, Dazhai had again changed greatly—new cave dwellings, new tile-roofed houses, rows of new terraced fields.

Filled with the heroic spirit of self-reliance, Dazhai's arduous struggle had produced great new achievements. All this made Premier Zhou feel very pleased. Along the way he kept talking cheerfully, praising this and that time and again.

"Yonggui," he said with evident satisfaction "I can't recognize Dazhai. What a big change! Your old generation and your young all do such good work!"

The open, flat fields of the manmade plain in the Back Side Draw unfolded in front of Premier Zhou's and President Echeverria's eyes.

"We worked on this one ravine one winter and one spring," Chen Yonggui said to them, "and turned its former twenty *mu* of fields into the present eighty *mu*, increasing the amount of land by sixty *mu*. We gave it a name: the Dazhai Man-Made Plain!"

The red sun hung in the air that day, and a warm wind caressed all faces. Premier Zhou wanted to go up the mountain. The people of Dazhai had prepared a straw hat for him to protect him from the sun, but the Premier thanked them and refused. As the Premier went up the mountain, his body ravaged by illness, his spirits were high and he appeared full of energy and zest. Row upon row, beads of sweat appeared on his pallid forehead. Someone noticed that every so often he secretly gasped for air. Chen Yonggui extended his hand to prop him up a little, but Premier Zhou pushed his hand away.

"Look at you, Old Chen!" he protested. "Isn't the spirit of Dazhai self-reliance and arduous struggle? Dazhai's commune members carry heavy loads up the slopes every day. I want to visit Dazhai in the spirit of Dazhai, walking on my own!"

Observing the Premier's daring spirit, Chen Yonggui quietly withdrew his hand, but his heart ached as he followed him up the slope.

The local Foreign Office cadre was also very concerned about Premier Zhou's health. Wherever the Premier walked, a car followed him. Many people urged the Premier to climb into the car, but his attitude remained firm: No matter what, he just would not sit. He would make sure that the foreign guests were all seated in the car, while he himself continued on foot.

Meandering along the slopes, half way up Tigerhead Mountain, there is a canal. It is the Army and People Canal, which the Brigade and the Commune together had built that year. Now, the bluish-green river water rippled as it flowed through the canal. In the Taihang Mountain region, which experiences drought nine out of of every ten years, water is as precious as gold, silver or pearls. Now with this winding canal that brought water from the Guo Village Reservoir, Dazhai essentially no longer feared drought, however severe.[1] Whenever people looked at this canal, spiraling from the bowels of the mountain, they recalled the first time Premier Zhou climbed Tigerhead Mountain. On that occasion the Premier, his head bent as he looked over field after flat field built on the slopes of the many gullies and ridges, at first had felt very content. After a moment, however, his brow wrinkled as he suddenly thought of a problem.

"How about your water?" he asked Chen Yonggui, who was standing next to him.

"There's enough of it so we don't starve. We have some to wet the compost too," answered Chen Yonggui.

"You better find an adequate water source to irrigate your fields," the Premier warned.

Later that same day, during lunch, as he chewed on a Dazhai-made cornmeal flat pancake, Premier Zhou continued to talk about water conservancy and irrigation. "What will you do if doesn't rain? What will you do if you have three years of severe drought in a row? It did happen in Chinese history! You must find a way to solve the problem of your water source permanently."

And now the peasants of Dazhai had turned Premier Zhou's instruction into concrete action. The sweet water flowed into every mellow sponge-soil field, moistening the parched seedlings. This stirred Premier Zhou to unusual excitement. With vigorous strides he climbed up to the Army and People Pond. Spring was in the air. A gentle breeze caressed his face. He casually unbuttoned his jacket and rested his hands on his waist. He suggested that a collective photograph of all

---

1. Years later, however, the drought was so severe that there was no water even in the Army and People Canal. That was because the County officials, fearing heavy rains that never came, emptied the reservoir to protect the big dam on the river. The prolonged drought that followed kept the water level below the canal's intake gate, so for that season the canal was useless. (W.H.H.)

Dazhai Brigade members, with the terraced fields of Tigerhead Mountain as the backdrop, be taken as a souvenir.

"This will demonstrate the drive and zeal of the people of Dazhai," he suggested.

At his words, the villagers from Dazhai—several hundred of them, young and old—happily surrounded him.

Emotions have the capacity to heighten and concentrate. On this occasion, Premier Zhou stood at the heart of one such moment of intensified emotion. Guo Fengliam and Jia Cunsuo stood on either side of Premier Zhou, supporting him by his arms. Several hundred other Dazhai villagers clustered around him, while the Army and People Pond and the terrace fields formed a unique Dazhai background. Thus the camera recorded an unforgettable moment.

After the picture-taking, Premier Zhou rushed to explain Dazhai's various projects to the foreign guests: the construction of the canal that brings water for irrigation, removing loess heights so the earth can be used to fill gullies and build flat land, the high altitude cableway for transportation. He went on talking for some twenty minutes.

His wife, Elder Sister Deng, interrupted him with a witty comment from the sidelines: "Look at this! The Premier has become a Dazhai guide!" she quipped.

Laughing, Premier Zhou added: "I've been to Dazhai three times. I do know something about it. But if something I say is wrong, I hope Comrade Yonggui will correct me."

Nothing needed correction. Without ever needing to be reminded by his secretary, Premier Zhou was able to tell the complete store of Dazhai, and sum it up with a few major points. Even President Echeverria was awed by the extent of knowledge this Premier of a huge country had about this tiny mountain village.

After a break for rest, Premier Zhou pointed to Five Family Flat and asked Chen Yonggui how long it had taken for those neighboring peasants to change like that.

"Five years," responded Chen Yonggui.

"Why was it backward in the past?" Premier Zhou asked. "They have better soil and more water than Dazhai. Something must be wrong with their leadership."

"It's about the same as Dazhai now," said Chen Yonggui. "If we don't watch it, they will get ahead of us."

"I'd be happy if they got ahead of you," Premier Zhou said. "I'd love it if all kinds of places got ahead of you! You would get ahead again by trying even harder. It would be great if the whole country were like Dazhai."

It was generally hard for the people from Dazhai to follow Premier Zhou's Jiangsu dialect, but this one sentence they heard very clearly and understood very well. Premier Zhou's followed it by addressing the cadres from the Regional Committee for Central Shanxi, Jia Jun and Li Hansuo: "In Xiyang, people have the attitude of: Let the heavens bring drought, we'll go all out! I challenge your troops to learn from Xiyang. Do you have the courage it takes?"

"We have the courage it takes," responded Jia Jun and Li Hansuo.

"Good!" said Premier Zhou. "I'm pressing you to do so. Nothing gets done without some pressure. We are all under pressure!"

Premier Zhou took a brief rest, and went off to climb hills with even more spring in his step. He was a man who refused to stay idle. He talked as he walked, his voice sonorous and forceful. As they strolled past Leech Gulch, he praised Chen Yonggui highly for leaving an "educational field." He also suggested that in the future they turn it into a ravine for education of the young, with slogans "Self-reliance" and "Arduous Struggle" written on the sides. Its purpose would be to teach future generations.

There was a rocky butte in the vicinity of Leech Gulch which, over a long period of time, eroding water had cut deeply into, slicing it in two. Pointing at the gaping cleft, Premier Zhou asked Guo Fenglian: "Little Guo, what do you think is stronger: water or the people?"

"The people are stronger," said Guo Fenglian.

"I say it's the water," said Premier Zhou. "Water can erode that piece of rock into a ditch."

"Water took thousands of years to turn that rock into that shape. People can manage that in just a few days," replied Guo Fenglian.

"Hey, you are right," laughed Premier Zhou. "Young people must be made to understand this kind of argument, Chairman Mao has said, after all, that among all the things in the world, people are the most precious."

"Once you've achieved, what do you have to watch out for?" he asked posing another seminal question.

"The heart of a tiger makes people advance, conceit makes them fall behind," Guo Fenglian answered, laughing.

"Right!" Premier Zhou nodded in approval.

Premier Zhou was very pleased by Guo Fenglian's responses. He urged Dazhai's young generation to forget the past, not to forget the arduous struggle.

During his first two visits to Dazhai, Premier Zhou had shed drops of sweat along the road that leads to Wolf Den Ravine. This time, however, his physical condition did not allow him to go on toward the famous landmark. He could not go himself, but he very much hoped that his wife, Deng Yingchao, would go in his place.

"Are you going to Wolf Den ravine?" he asked her.

Elder Sister Deng said she wanted to go.

"Yes," said Premier Zhou, "coming to Dazhai without going to Wolf Den Ravine doesn't count as coming to Dazhai at all. Go for me, too, please."

On their return to the village, Premier Zhou noticed that some people were walking through a field of standing wheat. He called out to them, asking them not to trample the young wheat seedlings. During the walk back, he explained to the foreign guests how the people of Dazhai intended to achieve mechanization and how they experimented with scientific farming, inspiring repeated exclamations of admiration from the guests.

"He is not just a statesman, he is an expert on farming, too!" they said to each other.

The people of Dazhai invited Premier Zhou and the Mexican guests to the little dining hall for a simple meal of everyday homemade food. Premier Zhou broke one cornmeal steamed bun and one potato in halves. He gave one half of each to Guo Fenglian, keeping the other two halves for himself.

"It's been a while since I've eaten this kind of food. We weren't always able to get it during the war years," he said.

During the banquet, Premier Zhou and Chen Yonggui enjoyed the performance of a Mexican folk song and dance group. President Echeverria especially applauded the Mexican song "Guadalajara," performed by a female member of the Shenyang Acrobatic Troupe.

Shanxi's problem with factionalism was still quite serious at that time. On the day of his visit to Dazhai, Premier Zhou undertook the enormous task of painstaking persuasion and education, to somehow solve the problem of Shanxi factionalism once more. Participants in the events remember that Premier Zhou did not take his midday rest after lunch. Instead he summoned all the cadres in charge of Shanxi provincial and Central Shanxi regional affairs to his room. Half-reclining on the bed, a wool blanket over his legs, he questioned them earnestly about the situation, analyzed the problems, and suggested ways to deal with them.

Because of his concern and care for Chen Yonggui, for the people of Dazhai, and for the situation in Shanxi as a whole, Premier Zhou had criticized Chen Yonggui's shortcomings and mistakes very frankly. In 1968 after he had heard Chen Yonggui's self-critical speech at the meeting held just before the Spring Festival for the purpose of resolving the Shanxi problem, Premier Zhou had made a public statement:

"Comrade Chen Yonggui recently got caught up in factionalism. It's good that he just made self-criticism. We should all learn from this attitude of Comrade Chen Yonggui's."

Owing to Premier Zhou's support and help, Chen Yonggui had been able to make continuous progress since that time. He had held aloof from internal strife, concentrated on production, and could not be held responsible for the impasse that sill plagued the province. Nevertheless there was perhaps a role for him in resolving the matter.

At 4:10 p.m. Premier Zhou bid farewell to Dazhai. All Dazhai Party Branch Committee members went to the Travel Bureau Headquarters to see the Premier and his Mexican guests off, expressing their hopes for another visit.

"Unfortunately, I'm getting old," the Premier told them. "I hope to be able to come again. If my health allows it, however, I will definitely come."

Nobody guessed that this was to be Premier Zhou's eternal parting from the people of Dazhai. When they think about it these days, they all cherish the memory:

"The Premier was so genial with us!"

CHAPTER—26

ASCENDING TO CENTRAL

During the Lushan Congress, Chairman Mao Zedong countered Chen Boda's views by posing a theoretical problem for discussion by the entire Party: Should we uphold the a-priorism of philosophical idealism or the materialist theory of reflection? Is it heroes or or is it slaves, serfs and toilers that make history? He asked that these questions be debated and clarified within the entire Party. He also put forth a resounding slogan: "Read and study conscientiously and get a good grasp of Marxism." On the basis of this theory, he affirmed his own line, which was to depend on and utilize the people's vast talents.

For many years now Chen Yonggui's entry into the Political Bureau and his appointment as Vice-Premier of the State Council have led to much discussion and generated serious controversy. These posts and his fitness for them seem to have become the focal point for evaluating his whole life. Although he was in the very eye of the storm at that time, Chen Yonggui did not seem to recognize how serious his situation was, nor apparently did he fully apprehend the level of complexity of the position history had pushed him into.

After Premier Zhou Enlai's third visit to Dazhai, Party leaders transferred Chen Yonggui to Beijing, giving the public cause for wide-ranging speculation and debate. They transferred Chen Yonggui to Beijing to take part in the study class organized by the Central Committee for the peasants, workers, soldiers and youth that had been elected members of the Central Committee. The class was to last three months. There were twenty-one participants in the study class. The Central Committee assigned twenty cadres, whose specialty was theory, to the task of enhancing the theoretical quality of these new Central Committee members. At that time Chen Yonggui was already a man of sixty, who, having been forced by poverty to herd cattle for others at the age of eight and serve as a hired field hand later on, never had the opportunity to read and study. To be able to sit down and do nothing else but study theory, now that he had become a member of the Central Committee, he saw as his very good fortune.

Nevertheless the study program had one drawback. After Chen Yonggui joined the class in Beijing, Premier Zhou Enlai instructed Yang Dezhong to act as Chen Yonggui's security guard and secretary. After a meeting on one occasion, Chen Yonggui pleaded with Premier Zhou against having a security guard, arguing that nobody dared come near him if he had a guard. He said that he had been given a soldier by the name of Liu to act as his security guard after he became Vice Chairman of the Shanxi Provincial Revolutionary Committee, but that he managed to persuade him to leave. At the time, the daily *Wenhui Bao* gave the case some publicity. Premier Zhou explained to him seriously that contact with the people does not depend on whether or not one has a security guard, but rather on the attitude with which one approaches the people.

"Look," Premier Zhou said, "Chairman Mao has so many guards. Has he lost contact with the people?"

After he joined the study class, Chen Yonggui became somewhat apprehensive of Wang Hongwen,[1] because Wang often exchanged flat-

---

1. Wang Hongwen has often been referred to as a Shanghai worker. However, he really came from Changchun City, Jilin Province, joined the Party in 1956 and became a cadre. He was transferred to a large Shanghai Textile factory to take charge of security and during the Cultural Revolution rose rapidly to become Secretary of the Shanghai Municipal Party Committee and Vice-Chairman of the Revolutionary Committee of Shanghai, from whence he ascended to national prominence. (W.H.H.)

tery and favors with other study class participants. Naturally, Chen Yonggui had no way of telling that Wang Hongwen would develop in the direction and to the extent that he later did, but he never had a taste for his maneuvers and he was not particularly interested in the class, so he looked for an opportunity to visit Premier Zhou and pour out his views to him. Premier Zhou had already perceived the tendency within the group, so his appreciation of Chen Yonggui increased even more, and he told him that he had a head for politics. In view of the fact that the preparations for the Tenth Congress required a lot of work, Premier Zhou arranged for Chen Yonggui to take part in them. This did nothing to diminish Chen's prestige and fame.

Chen Yonggui's status was raised yet another notch by a trip he made around North China in preparation for attending the Tenth Party Congress. Since many people said "Old Chen has never really seen North China" he used the occasion of a Conference on North China Cooperation to take a swing through the whole area, thus enhancing his right to speak.

During this same period of preparation for the coming Congress Premier Zhou added further luster to Chen Yonggui's name by calling on an increasing number of people to go and get to know Dazhai. At that time, groups of old Central Committee senior cadres who had been submitted to investigation during the Cultural Revolution were just being released one after another. Each time a group was released, Premier Zhou went personally to see them, telling them they were "people from the Peach Blossom Spring, who didn't even know there had been a Han dynasty."[1] They had not managed any affairs for so many years, he said, that it was time for them to breathe in some fresh air. He hoped, of course, that they would go to Dazhai to take a look and explore various avenues of development for China's agriculture.

1. An allusion to a famous poem by Tao Yuanming (A.D. 365-427), whose preface to the poem is one of the most influential passages in all of early Chinese prose. It talks about a fisherman from the Taiyuan Era (376-397) of the Chin dynasty who once went up a valley stream and, having lost his way, found himself in a forest of peach trees in bloom, which ended with a spring. He followed the spring through an opening in a rock and emerged in an enchanted land of rich fields, whose inhabitants had never heard of any of the dynasties—Han, Wei or Chin—since their ancestors' flight from the troubled times of the Qin dynasty (221-207 B.C.). Finding this faraway place beyond the Peach Blossom Spring, they never ventured into the world again.

He spent some time talking about this particular matter with Tan Zhenlin.

The Political Bureau of the Central Committee intended to have Chen Yonggui, Wang Hongwen, and other participants in the study class attend the plenary session of the Tenth National Congress of the Communist Party of China even before the study class ended. In the class, therefore, they mainly discussed political reports to the Tenth Congress, and took part in the revising of the Party constitution. They also discussed the issue of quotas for Central Committee membership and alternate membership.

Prior to the Tenth Congress, the Central Committee called a preparatory meeting. The meeting was attended by over one hundred committee members, who focused on the discussion of documents. Directly under their deliberation were the following items: Zhou Enlai's political address, Wang Hongwen's report on the revision of the Party constitution, the draft of the new Party constitution, and Central Committee membership and alternate membership lists.

The Tenth National Congress of the Communist Party of China was officially opened on August 30, 1973. Of the twenty-one peasant, worker, soldier and youth members of the Central Committee study class, twelve were invited to the rostrum and made members of the Congress Presidium. According to the seating arrangement, Chen Yonggui was seated behind Chairman Mao. Chairman Mao presided over the meeting. He seemed to be in good spirits, because the Congress was attended by many representatives of peasants, workers and soldiers, youth representatives, women's representatives, and many old comrades who had been pushed aside and attacked by Lin Biao. During Zhou Enlai's political address to the Congress on behalf of the Political Bureau of the Central Committee, Chairman Mao often interrupted the speech to add a few words. Particularly when the topic of Lin Biao came up, he could not resist throwing out the phrase: "Just before the rain, when the sky is overcast, all the crows are pressed to leave their nest."

After the opening session of the Tenth Congress, Chairman Mao Zedong called the First Plenary Session of the Tenth Congress, which studied the organizational structure of the Central Committee leadership, and announced members of the Political Bureau and the list of candidates for the Standing Committee. On the list of candidates for the Political Bureau, first put forth at the preparatory meeting for the Tenth Congress, was, among others, the name of Chen Yonggui. At the First Plenary Session of the Tenth Congress the list was formally adopted. Principal leaders of the Central Committee participated in all of the small group discussion meetings, achieving unanimous agreement. Everybody knew that Chen Yonggui's educational level was not very high, but everybody endorsed his promotion because of his consistent behavior and contributions to the pioneering work in Dazhai and Xiyang, and because of his political conduct after becoming a member of the Central Committee. His was not an isolated case. A whole group of Central Committee members recruited from the ranks of peasants, workers and soldiers entered the high-level leadership positions within the Central Committee at the same time: Wang Hongwen, Ni Zhifu and Wu Jiaxian among others. This was a concrete expression of Chairman Mao Zedong's philosophy of making use of people's talents. He had already said at the Spring Festival Forum on February 23, 1964:

"All through the ages, the scholars who came in first in the highest imperial examination were never particularly remarkable. Even those who became successful candidates for the highest imperial examination and members of the Imperial Academy were worthless. Only the founder of the Ming dynasty, Emperor Taizu,[1] and his son, Emperor Chengzu,[2] one of whom was illiterate and the other barely literate, were relatively good emperors. Later, during the Jiaqing era of the Ming,[3] when the intellectuals came to power, they were not able to accomplish anything, and the country became difficult to manage. Those who read too much don't make good emperors. Liu Xiu[4] was a great student, Liu Bang[5] was a great blockhead. One should read books, but excessive reading is harmful."

---

1. Reigned from 1368 to 1398.
2. Reigned from 1403 to 1424.
3. Jiaqing was the reign title for the period from 1522-1566.
4. Liu Xiu was the personal name of the Han Emperor Guangwu, who reigned from A.D. 25 to A.D. 57 as the first emperor of the Later Han dynasty.
5. Liu Bang was the founder of the Han dynasty, and he reigned as Emperor Gaozu from 206 B.C. to 195 B.C.

Chairman Mao repeatedly put the idea of depending on the common people into practice during his later years. Time and again he encouraged reliance on the working class and the poor and lower-middle peasants. During the Cultural Revolution he criticized the ideology of "reading books to become an official," advocating instead integration with workers, peasants and soldiers and utilizing the talents of the people.

Chen Yonggui's participation in government and political affairs implemented this line of Chairman Mao's and Premier Zhou's. It was their joint wish that he take an active part in government and political decision-making. His name was on the list of candidates for the Political Bureau which Premier Zhou submitted to Chairman Mao, and Chairman Mao had his final say during the preparatory meeting for the Tenth Congress. For several years prior to that, there had been debates at the decision-making level of the party about whether Chen Yonggui could work for the Central Committee. The majority hoped that Chen Yonggui would come to the Central Committee to work on agriculture, so that he and Dazhai could lead the way in transforming the backward state of China's agriculture.

Chen Yonggui was aware of the above situation, so that he was not taken by surprise when he was chosen to become a member of the Political Bureau. We are already familiar with how, as a peasant delegate to the Ninth Party Congress, he had delivered a representative speech and had acted as one of the conveners of the North China Group meeting during the Second Plenary Session. Before Premier Zhou visited Dazhai for the third time, preparations for the Tenth National Congress of the Communist Party of China had already been completed, and the matter of Chen Yonggui's entry into the Political Bureau had already been weighed and settled.

In a break with tradition, Party leaders kept the concrete content of the Tenth Congress a first-class secret. The one exception: a report on the general spirit of the meeting conveyed by a public communique. This was due to the lesson taught by the Ninth Congress. The Soviet Union had disturbed and assaulted the Ninth Congress as soon as it started, so the Tenth Congress adopted measures to maintain its secrecy, in order to prevent similar Soviet intervention.

After the news of the closing of the Tenth National Congress of the Communist Party of China was broadcast on the radio, the masses back in Xiyang County staged a celebration with drums and gongs on the streets of the County capital. The celebration was really more in honor of Chen Yonggui's appointment to the Political Bureau than about the Tenth Congress as such.

Chen Yonggui returned to Xiyang soon afterward. On September 12th, he gave a report to an assembly of all administrative functionaries at the County level, in which he informed them about the Tenth Party Congress and raised the issue of the future development of Xiyang County.

"There has never been, in China or abroad," he said at one point, "a precedent for the elevation of a peasant representative to a State leadership post. Marx did not resolve this situation, Lenin did not resolve it, Chairman Mao did. This is the result of Chairman Mao's reliance on workers and peasants and his willingness to put them in important positions."

After many setbacks, the Fourth National People's Congress finally met in Peking in January 1975. Chairman Mao had given a clear instruction regarding matters of personnel planning: "The personnel appointments at the Fourth People's Congress will be prepared by Premier Zhou." Nevertheless the situation in China's political circles was rather complicated at the time and great difficulties complicated the convening of the People's Congress. Only Premier Zhou's involvement could settle matters to some degree. But Premier Zhou was very ill as he delivered his "Government Work Report" to the Congress, and continued to be ill as he worked on the arrangements for the election of people to various bodies at the Congress.

Prior to the opening of the Fourth People's Congress, Ni Zhifu ran into Chen Yonggui after a Bureau meeting and, half-jokingly, addressed him: "Old Chen, we'll have to call you Vice-Premier Chen from now on!"

"Look at this guy, this Vice-Premier Chen!" Ji Dengkui and several other leaders also joked.

The Political Bureau had been deliberating on such an appointment for Chen Yonggui for quite some time. In the light of all this, Chen Yonggui was prepared for something important.

At about that time Premier Zhou Enlai requested Chen Yonggui to visit him in the hospital. It was really time he went anyway, since he had not gone to see the Premier for several days. As soon as he sat down on a sofa in the reception room, Chen Yonggui inquired about the Premier's health and learned that, though Zhou's spirits were very high, he was still losing a lot of weight.

"I've asked for you because of the arrangements for the People's Congress," Zhou began. "You should prepare yourself to become a Vice-Premier of the State Council, to promote the spirit of Dazhai to the whole country. What do you say?"

To begin with, Chen Yonggui was stunned, thinking that since he lacked education it would be better not to undertake such a high post.

"Premier, I'm not educated enough. I really am not qualified for it. I think I better not do this Vice-Premier business," he said, greatly agitated.

Premier Zhou's expression changed, suddenly becoming very severe: "Look at you, Yonggui! Are you or aren't you a Party member? If you are, you had better accept the Party's arrangements. The fighting on the Central Committee is so fierce right now—if you don't take part in it, somebody else will have to—so it better be you. The Chairman agrees on this. So do all the other comrades on the Political Bureau. You are a peasant representative...."

Premier Zhou gave him many reasons for accepting. "In the past as well as today, anywhere else as well as in China, talent does not drop from the sky. It springs up from among the people. When the 'Pathbreaker King'[1] entered Peking, did anybody believe he would defeat the Emperor of the Ming? The times produce their heroes!"

Premier Zhou was clearly directing his words against the Gang of Four. If Chen Yonggui did not take charge of agriculture, the Gang

1. The "Pathbreaker King" was a title taken on by the leaders of peasant rebellions at the end of the Ming dynasty, first Gao Yingxiang and, upon his death, Li Zicheng. As Li Zicheng's armies entered Peking in 1644, the last Emperor of the Ming strangled himself, ending the dynasty.

would very likely look for a person of its own choosing to do it. Premier Zhou could not agree to this.

In the end the Premier got his way. Soon after the Congress opened Zhou Enlai announced the appointment of Chen Yonggui as one of eleven Vice-Premiers of the State Council. The list of Vice-Premiers announced that day included, besides Chen Yonggui, the peasants' representative, one Wu Guixian, who was a workers' representative. Everybody raised their hands, applauded for a while, and that was that.

"There was a burst of applause at the Congress and all of a sudden I was a Vice-Premier," Chen put it later in his modest way.

But actually, it seems quite clear, Chen's appointment was by no means a simple matter. Of the eleven Vice-Premiers on the list, Chen Yonggui's name was put in the eighth place, right below Hua Guofeng's.[1] From this, one can deduce the significance of Chen Yonggui's promotion. Its function can be summed up by saying that it added to Mao's contingent in the Central ruling structure, giving Mao and Zhou more leverage in the intense line struggle that dominated the Party at this time. Chen Yonggui's position moved still a few places further forward when the Fifth National People's Congress named him Vice-Premier of the Standing Committee. This resulted from his support for Hua Guofeng in the struggle to smash the Gang of Four.

When simply put, this is how simple it all was, but if one wants to stress the complexity, one would be hard put to say just how complex it was.

From Chen Yonggui's point of view, regardless of how other people saw it or argued it, since the Central Committee had confidence in him, he had to disregard all other considerations and simply do what was asked of him.

"Yonggui, are there any problems?" Premier Zhou frequently asked him.

Were there any problems? Just that he had no education, and could not easily read and evaluate the documents. He often felt like making all kinds of comments on piles of documents he regularly received and

---

1. Hua Guofeng, as is well known, not long thereafter became Mao's successor. (W.H.H.)

read, but he was, in the end, not able to do much of that. Chen Yonggui was not willing to bring up his difficulties in front of Premier Zhou, even when asked.

"Problems there are," he always said. "But with the help of Comrades Hua Guofeng and Ji Dengkui, I, too, can do my job."

The two men he mentioned were the other two appointees to the Political Bureau elevated at the same time as Chen Yonggui.

"Ay-yah, I'm a peasant," he could not refrain from telling people, "and those two are nothing but workers. We are all uncouth folk."

For that reason, he got along very well with them, and their rapport was always very congenial. However, he was rather cautious in his dealings with the other senior cadres whose experience was so different from his own.

When Chen Yonggui first came to Peking, he moved into the Capital West Guest House, and was assigned a secretary, a security guard, and an attendant. All the interior facilities were considered first class at the time. Chen Yonggui, who had been born a peasant, was not at all used to this level of comfort. He complained that living there was too wasteful, and was even very displeased with the attendants for leaving a big ceiling lamp on in the building's staircase, as was the common practice. He called all the attendants to his room, to instruct them not to turn the big light on because it consumed too much electricity. "A small lamp, just so you can see, would be enough," he told them.

After just a few days, Chen Yonggui conceived the idea of moving somewhere else. He brought it up several times with Premier Zhou, pleading with him, and got permission to move later to the Fishing Terrace State Guest House, as arranged by the Central Committee. Several other leaders lived at the Fishing Terrace at that time: the four members of the Gang of Four and Ji Dengkui and Wu Guixian. Each of them occupied a separate multi-storied house with first-class facilities. Chen Yonggui had no taste for this lifestyle, and was truly unwilling to settle there for a long term.

"This is where the foreign guests used to stay," he said. "We can't hang out here forever." He frequently worried about his low level of education, and had a hard time writing his comments on the documents. He was also not used to taking care of the daily business, but he was very willing to "go down" and do some practical work. Consequently, he came up with some ideas. He felt that he had become a member of the Political Bureau in a very particular way, and that he should also be able to dispense his duties in a somewhat particular way: that his own working procedures should correspond to his personal reality. Consequently, he brought up two requests: one, to move out of the Fishing Terrace; two, to implement the "three-thirds system."

Chen Yonggui had an opportunity, on one occasion, to ask Tang Wensheng and Wang Hairong from the Ministry of Foreign Affairs for their views on his requests. After he received their approval, he asked his secretary and a comrade from Xiyang one day in April 1974 to write on his behalf to Chairman Mao and ask for his instructions. In the letter, Chen Yonggui pointed out that he had spent many years in the countryside and was not at all used to city life. The guesthouse gate sentries were strict, too, so it was very difficult for pedestrians to come and go through the gate. It took great effort on the part of his old comrades from the lower levels of the social hierarchy and old Model Workers to come and see him, and he himself was worried that he might lose contact with the outside world, so he pleaded with the Chairman to approve his request to move out of the Fishing Terrace. The letter further said that he was ill-suited for the Central Committee work, and that he hoped to be able to "go down" to encounter some ordinary people and everyday situations, and to take part in some productive labor himself. He would be much more effective conducting fact-finding investigations and instructive type of work than he was issuing orders at the Central Committee.

As a concrete measure, he submitted his "three-thirds system" work plan, according to which he would spend one-third of the time at the selected grass-roots units helping them improve their work and gaining firsthand experience to guide his overall work, he would spend another third of the time running about investigating and gathering information, and the remaining third of the time, he would return to work at the Central Committee. He gave Chairman Mao some additional unrelated constructive suggestions. Chairman Mao was very curious about the letter when it was brought to him, and read it that very night. As soon as he finished reading it at four o'clock in the morning, he picked up his pen and wrote down his comments: "Very well, very well, very well! There are no fish at the Fishing Terrace to be fished. Let the Political Bureau talk it over."

He made a telephone call summoning Chen Yonggui to Zhongnanhai, to find out all the details from him.

On the following day, Chairman Mao attended the meeting of the Political Bureau convened to deal with this matter. They say that he attended very few Political Bureau meetings that year because he became aware of the Gang of Four problem after the Tenth Party Congress. The members of the Gang of Four all lived close to each other at the Fishing Terrace compound. This arrangement was rather convenient for plotting schemes and intrigues. Because of their activities, elements of instability emerged in the Political Bureau and nationwide.

When Chairman Mao entered the Political Bureau meeting room, he first shook hands with Premier Zhou, and then greeted Ye Jianying, Deng Xiaoping and Chen Xilian by shaking their hands too.

"This hand of yours is rather precious," Chairman Mao said cheerfully when he shook that of Chen Yonggui. "One-third in Dazhai, one-third all over the country, one-third at the Central Committee! It doesn't want to be at the Fishing Terrace, because there are no fish to catch there."

At the meeting, Chairman Mao made public Chen Yonggui's letter to him, and officially raised the issue of the Fishing Terrace with no fish to be fished out.

"When Chen Yonggui moves out of the Fishing Terrace," he asked, "what are the rest of you planning to do?"

Nobody at the meeting uttered a word.

"Wu Guixian," Chairman Mao said, turning to the other peasant-worker alternate member preparing to join the Political Bureau, "you move out of the Fishing Terrace, too! As for Chen Yonggui's proposed 'three-thirds system' of work, it is very good. When Chen Yonggui goes down, are you all going to go down too? Descending for fact-finding investigation is a fine tradition of our Party. All Political Bureau members should go down if they can get away."

At that same meeting Chairman Mao brought up criticism of the Gang of Four.

After the meeting, attitudes of the Political Bureau members toward Chen Yonggui varied from one person to another. Most of them looked upon him with approval, especially Ji Dengkui, who had frequent contacts with him.

"You did it again! You've earned the Chairman's praise!" said Ji Dengkui, putting his arm around Chen's shoulders as they left the meeting.

To the Gang of Four, however, Chen Yonggui was simply a thorn. Just one letter from Chen Yonggui had been enough to throw them into confusion. Caught by surprise, they could not prevent Chen Yonggui's action from breaking the tight grip with which they held onto each other's hands. Once Chairman Mao made his position known, it was impossible for them not to move out of the Fishing Terrace. In the evening after the meeting, Jiang Qing charged unannounced into Chen Yonggui's residence and, after barely a few words, launched an attack on him.

"You've got a place to stay. If I leave the Fishing Terrace, where am I going to go?" she protested.

"I have to look for a place myself and get ready to move. I can't take care of anybody else!" Chen Yonggui responded, laughing.

"Isn't there a place for her at Zhongnanhai? Why doesn't she go back there?" he asked his assistants after he saw Jiang Qing off.

And so after that Political Bureau meeting where Chairman Mao passed his verdict, all Political Bureau members who lived at the Fishing Terrace, including the Gang of Four, moved away.

From that time on, Chen Yonggui lived in a single-story house that belonged to the State Management Bureau, on South Street near the Jiaodaokou Road junction area. Although the facilities could not compare with those at the Fishing Terrace, they were not below the level accorded a Vice-Premier. A security guard was assigned to work for him. The arrangement was such that the security guard lived in the front courtyard, while Chen Yonggui lived in the inner courtyard. They set up a Ping-Pong table in the courtyard, to provide recreation for the soldiers. Chen Yonggui's quarters consisted of a reception room and two bedrooms. His secretary, his cook and his driver occupied the remaining rooms. Chen Yonggui had two telephones in his room: one internal and one external. The internal telephone was red. The moment Chen Yonggui picked up the receiver, a voice would ask for instructions: "Awaiting instruction by the senior officer, please."

A carpet, an electric fan and a color television set completed the equipment in the room. Chen Yonggui watched very little television in the evening, because every evening his secretary and the person on duty placed a huge pile of documents on his desk. He was obliged to read them carefully, one by one, and make concrete comments. The reading of documents did not require that much effort, after all, since Chen Yonggui was used to reading books and newspapers and was able to recognize the commonly used Chinese characters or ideograms. If he were not to read them and comment on them all, he would not feel well prepared to speak at the brief head-to-head exchange meeting the following day. But the reading and comments frequently took him a long time, so he would either get up to stretch and take a stroll in the yard or he would watch television for a while to relax his brain.

A set of large-letter print "Selected Works by Chairman Mao" and "Poems by Chairman Mao," occupied a prominent place in Chen Yonggui's day room. The publisher had printed this special edition for senior cadres of the Central Committee out of concern for their eyesight. The furnishings of the rooms for Chen's security guard and cook were complete and each had a telephone at hand. Chen Yonggui had two cars at his disposal: a domestically made Red Flag, and a Datsun imported from Japan.

The cook prepared meals only for Chen Yonggui; he himself ate, along with the driver and the secretary, at the State Council's ordinary mess at Jiaodaokou. Chen Yonggui was used to the homely food of Xiyang, so he brought his cook especially from Xiyang County's Five Family Flat. He often told his visitors that life in his present environment was too restricted, and how much more content he would be with a few days' work in some Peking suburb. But, due to the regulations set by the Security Department in charge of his safety, he was not able to realize this dream.

He always tried to think of something to do in his residence after work, like planting trees and the like. During the few years that he lived there, he planted four apple trees, two pear trees, two grapevines, and two decorative landscaping trees with his own hands. Every summer, the grapevines covered the entire yard with leaves so that it always remained cool and the air was fresh. After Chen Yonggui stepped down from his office and moved away, Xi Zhongxun moved in, and the thing he loved most about this house were the trees in the yard.

"Where one generation plants trees," Xi Zhongxun said of the labor of his predecessor, "those who come after will enjoy the cool."

CHAPTER—27

A LANDSMAN IN BEIJING—CONFLICTS AND CONSUMMATIONS

Public evaluation of Chen Yonggui and the resulting controversy about him have to a great degree focused on whether or not he should have become a Political Bureau member, and whether or not he should have been elected a Vice-Premier of the State Council. Chen Yonggui, who was a model representative of the peasants of new China, felt he could not go beyond leading China's agriculture because of his level of education—in that one respect, he reproached himself for an inherent deficiency.

"When the daughter-in-law returns to her mother-in-law's house, she is not free to do as she wishes. It's all meetings and documents again—never the joy of laboring for a few days and breaking into a good sweat," Chen said frowning every time he returned to Beijing from Dazhai. At such a moment he always hoped to be able to take part in physical labor somewhere for a few days, but the official business he had to undertake as a Vice-Premier never allowed him to engage in it. During the eight years he worked in the capital, the occasions when he could work up a good sweat were very limited.

Though the heavy responsibility for State affairs rested on his shoulders, he could not be too anxious about it. There were all those documents every night that he had to look over, one by one, and write his comments on. If not, what would he do next time the Political Bureau convened a meeting to study problems? Particularly, how would he deal with problems involving agriculture? He received a big pile of documents every day in his office, and his secretary and dispatcher, ever mindful of his difficulties, avoided as much as possible giving him the material that could go without his comments.

Every evening, however, due to some unexpected situation, there would be a document or two that required a few comments from him. More often than not, some word would get him into trouble, and his callous hands would invariably start trembling as he held the pen. On occasions he would summon Jiao Huancheng and Zhang Yinchang to write something for him. There was one time when he got angry because he could not remember how to write the character for "wait." He smoked two cigarettes in a row as he sat there, squeezing the pen in his hand, and still could not remember.

"Will I have to bother them over a single word?" he wondered.

On that particular night he decided not to do it. He would think of it himself, no matter what. He thought about it for about half an hour, still without success. Getting angry, he threw the pen onto the writing desk.

"Damn it! If I can't write it, I'm not going to make any comments," he swore.

Then he walked out into the yard, where he started pacing around the trees he had planted, his arms akimbo. In the reception room, his secretary and the security guard were happily watching television. Huffing and panting with rage, Chen Yonggui entered, threw a cold glance at the television screen, and issued an order.

"How can you think of watching television? Turn it off!"

They were stunned by his behavior, wondering what had happened. Except for the clicking sound of the television being switched off, the reception room became unusually quiet. Everybody was waiting for news of some unfortunate event to fall from his lips, but he held his mouth tightly shut. He took out a cigarette and started fumbling for matches in his pockets. After a few puffs, he sat on the table and issued a second order.

"You stay behind, Yinchang. Deal a hand."

Only then did Zhang Yinchang realize that nothing pressing had happened. Chen Yonggui had simply lost his temper again reading his documents.

Chen Yonggui was not usually given to playing cards. Particularly since he came to Peking, he had lost whatever interest he might have had in that sort of thing. Only when he had guests, particularly important guests like Ji Dengkui or Wu De, when they occasionally got tired of talking, or if they had no official business to discuss, would he end up dealing a hand. Due to his overpowering mentality he never resigned himself to losing, not even in cards. He would not give up until he gained the upper hand. On this occasion, he lost the first game to Zhang Yinchang, and cursed as he shuffled the cards.

"I can't even play cards! Now, that's strange!" he said under his breath.

As he won the second round, his face stretched into a smile.

"Yinchang," he asked grinning, "how do you write 'wait' if you want to say 'wait to deal with it later?'"

"It's the same 'wait' as in 'waiting room,'" Zhang Yinchang answered with a hint of reproof.

"Huh! It's that same character!" Chen Yonggui exclaimed as if struck by a revelation.

He dropped the cards from his hand.

"I'm not playing. Had I known it was that character, I wouldn't have asked you. You guys go on and watch television!"

Happy and calm he returned to his desk.

It was as a result of Mao Zedong's philosophy of utilizing all talents that Chen Yonggui got pushed to the top of the political heap. As soon as Chairman Mao and Premier Zhou placed him in such an important position within the Party and State leadership, however, he displayed a good head for politics and great ability to differentiate between things. This became particularly evident in his relationship with the Gang of Four.

Somewhere between the end of 1973 and the beginning of 1974, the network between Wang Hongwen, Jiang Qing, Zhang Chunqiao and Yao Wenyuan had already formed. Being the youngest of the successors fostered by Mao Zedong, Wang Hongwen was insufferably arrogant. It was inevitable that he should try to further develop his power, and for that he needed props. As the peasant representative in the Political Bureau, Chen Yonggui naturally became his target. Wang Hongwen telephoned to talk to Chen Yonggui, invited instructors in theory to give him lectures, or sent him notices of study sessions in Building 16. Chen Yonggui was dealing with direct commands from a man who was Vice-Chairman of the Communist Party Central Committee, so he could not disobey, but though he found this kind of political climate very disagreeable, he was always hard put to find ways to escape Wang Hongwen's baiting.

Wang Hongwen was in the habit of going to bed late and getting up late, conducting his daily activities between lunch and midnight. During the day he attended meetings and dealt with official business; at night, after he finished commenting on documents, he watched movies. He never got up before ten in the morning. Chen Yonggui, on the other hand, was used to getting up early, but he always napped at noon, and this was the habit that prevented him from keeping in step with Wang Hongwen. What usually happened is that Wang Hongwen would suddenly call up, asking Chen Yonggui to pay him a visit. Chen Yonggui would have to do as he was told, and thus ended up going to Wang Hongwen's residence.

Only rarely did Wang call Chen on serious business. Usually it turned out to be something involving personal relations. Chen Yonggui was always very annoyed when he discovered what he had been called for, because he did not want to participate in personal disputes. Yet, once he was there, he had no way of refusing to do so, so whenever he spoke he would hem and haw. Later on, whenever a call came from Wang Hongwen while he was taking his afternoon nap, Chen Yonggui would hear all the details from his staff members, impatiently turn over, and instruct them to ring him up and say he wasn't in.

Then he would wet his mouth, and prepare to go back to sleep. But, though you can dodge once, you can't dodge fifteen times. If he succeeded in extricating himself from Wang Hongwen's baiting, chances were he could not shake off Jiang Qing's interference. Jiang Qing never telephoned or sent somebody on her behalf. If there was something she wanted, she came right up to see him herself. This is when Chen Yonggui gradually realized how deeply the activities of the Gang of Four were motivated by political ambition.

In 1975, on Chairman Mao Zedong's birthday, Jiang Qing invited twenty-four members of the Political Bureau to Zhongnanhai for drinks. It was nominally a celebration of Chairman Mao's birthday, but Chairman Mao was not present, nor was he informed of the event. Jiang Qing and the "Gang of Four" were very animated at the celebration, so that even Chen Yonggui could see they were harboring hidden intentions. Jiang Qing first proposed a toast for the Chairman's birthday, and then went on to talk about some questions of theory, about the Tang Empress Wu Zetian. Then she suddenly changed the topic, first to General Song Jiang, and then to Lin Biao. Zhang Chunqiao was acting even more strangely, and several times, amidst the clinking of glasses, he and Chen Yonggui started bickering. The reason for their bickering was not entirely clear, but it had something to do with Chen Yonggui's energetic applause during Premier Zhou Enlai's recent speech. Zhang Chunqiao rebuked him for seeking the limelight, and provoked Chen Yonggui's great displeasure. After everybody had plenty to eat and drink, Jiang Qing proposed yet another toast, as a way of showing her ease of mind.

"For the Chairman's happy birthday, I propose that we all drink together. Another toast! Bottoms up!"

Zhang Chunqiao immediately approved her suggestion, but all the other guests had already had too much to drink. Although they did not want to appear disrespectful of Chairman Mao, they hesitated, very reluctant to drink more. On seeing this, Chen Yonggui's temper rose again. He belted out: "OK. This time I'll drink one glass in place of every person here!"

And so he did. He asked the waiter to pour the drinks, and he gulped down twenty-four of them one after the other. He had already had just about enough to drink when Jiang Qing proposed the toast but, as his temper rose, so did his ability to hold liquor: He drank those twenty-four glasses without ever changing expression. Everybody present praised his bravery; even Jiang Qing was stunned by it. When the banquet ended, however, Ji Dengkui was truly concerned for his well-being, worried that something might happen. Chen Yonggui pulled Ji Dengkui into his own car.

"Let's ride in one car, you and me," he said.

As they rode off, Chen Yonggui's tongue loosened and he chattered on and on without any restraint.

"I cracked down this time. Twenty-four glasses! You tell me if I'm a boor! But there was something refined about my boorishness. I took a stand! I dared! Those twenty-four glasses, what do you say?"

"The old conservative blazed a new trail! Bravo!" Ji Dengkui patted him on the shoulder.

"I did it with Zhang Chunqiao again today," said Chen Yonggui. "He scorns me, and I scorn him too! He calls people 'stinky number nine,'[1] and I say he's the real 'stinky number nine' because he stinks nine times, through and over!"

Chen Yonggui talked so much that he forgot to tell the driver to drop Ji Dengkui off at his home. Only when they arrived at Jiaodaokou did Ji Dengkui realize what had happened.

"Hey! Where are you dragging me to! Oh, you!" he protested, laughing.

Chen Yonggui's biggest antagonist during his time in Beijing was Zhang Chunqiao. Chen Yonggui's trip to Nanning shows this particularly clearly.

In the early morning of December 23, 1974, Chen Yonggui and his entourage consisting of Guo Fenglian and Zhao Ergou, Party Secretary of the South Knoll Production Brigade, boarded a plane to attend the Congress of Poor and Lower-Middle Peasants organized by the Zhuang Autonomous Region in Guangxi Province.

1. This refers to the ninth category of objectionable persons. But there was no such official category. The Communist Party named eight categories of enemies starting with landlords and rich peasants and ending with capitalist roaders and bourgeois academic authorities. But the intellectuals, because they were often treated so badly in various re-education campaigns, called themselves the "Stinking Ninth Category," and others took it up. Chairman Mao once jokingly said to an old professor who wanted to quit, "Chiu Lao jiu, bu yao zou!" (Old Stinking Ninth, do not leave us!). (W.H.H.)

When Chen Yonggui's plane landed at Nanning Airport, Chen Yonggui's party went immediately to the provincial Guest House where Chen was received by Xu Shiyou, who was the Chinese Communist Party Central Committee Political Bureau member in charge of the daily operations of the Guangzhou Army, and Wei Guoqing, the other Central Committee Political Bureau member in Nanning, who was currently the Party Secretary of the Guangxi Zhuang Autonomous Region. The three Political Bureau members first held a closed, private meeting. Chen Yonggui was very eager to talk to Xu Shiyou about his conflict with Zhang Chunqiao. Xu Shiyou rose slightly from the sofa and patted himself on the knees. "Nanning is my territory, Old Chen! Feel free to talk about whatever you want!" he assured him.

Chen Yonggui proceeded to tell him how he had locked horns with Zhang Chunqiao, about why he had not visited Zhang Chunqiao when Zhang lay ill in the hospital, and about why he did not want to live at the Fishing Terrace. The more he talked, the more heated up Xu Shiyou became.

"You may be rough and ready, but I'm not exactly that refined either! Zhang Chunqiao puts on his stinky intellectual airs and sticks his hands into everything. Who is he fooling?" asked Xu.

After the private conversation of the three Political Bureau members, Chen Yonggui listened to various reports by other Guangxi leaders. In the evening, Xu Shiyou and Wei Guoqing invited Chen Yonggui for dinner, after which they were to attend an evening of entertainment given by the city of Nanning. Wei Guoqing retreated early on account of his health. Xu Shiyou and Chen Yonggui were both rather fond of drinking and making merry, so they went on with the dinner, clinking their glasses and discussing Zhang Chunqiao and a few others. The waiters who were serving them were afraid they were having too much to drink, and reminded them to be careful not to overdo it.

Xu Shiyou said: "Don't you worry, we can hold a lot!"

Their unwillingness to leave the dinner table delayed the entertainment program prepared by the city of Nanning for two hours.

During that trip to Nanning Chen Yonggui gained the support of Xu Shiyou and Wei Guoqing, and his mood became buoyant. He, Guo Fenglian and South Knoll's Zhao Ergou made a report to the Guangxi

Congress of Poor and Lower-Middle Peasants. They then went to inspect the three Counties that excelled in learning from Dazhai: Wuming, Rongning, and Duan. They gave high marks to Guangxi's irrigation works and land reclamation from the sea. Chen Yonggui's appraisal of the Province still circulates in Guangxi to this day:

"Guangxi is a big granary of socialism: terraces on the hilltops, barns in the foothills. Water conservancy is well developed, too. We've learned a lot here."

The conversation Chen Yonggui had with Xu Shiyou in Nanning was to Chen merely chitchat, no more than an opportunity to give vent to his feelings. He did not reckon that it would come to the attention of higher authorities. However, he underestimated the contradictions of the time.

On New Year's Day in 1975, Chen Yonggui boarded a plane in Guilin and returned to Beijing. That evening, while he studied some documents at Zhongnanhai, he unexpectedly received a call from Premier Zhou, summoning him to the hospital. It was not something Chen Yonggui could have predicted. As soon as he got there, Premier Zhou asked him point-blank:

"Yonggui, you have something against Zhang Chunqiao?"

Chen Yonggui became very nervous. He did not know what disaster might strike or from where. He reported everything that had happened on his southern trip to Premier Zhou. The Premier did not express his views on this matter at that time. He only told him that Xu Shiyou had telegraphed some revelatory material to Chairman Mao, stating that Chen Yonggui had serious complaints about Zhang Chunqiao. Chairman Mao sent the material over to Premier Zhou and the Political Bureau with his comment on it: "To rebuke is not Marxist." From these few brief sentences Chen Yonggui was able to tell Premier Zhou's opinion of Zhang Chunqiao.

"This is what we'll do," Premier Zhou said. "I'll be in the hospital for two more weeks, and when I come out, we'll take care of this problem."

Only then did Chen Yonggui realize that more than just a couple of people had complained about Zhang Chunqiao. Xu Shiyou had used their conversation at the banquet to move against the Gang of Four, which illustrates the essence of the saying: "Though he professes to be a drinker, the wine is not his real interest."

As time went on relations between Chen Yonggui and Zhang Chunqiao became more and more strained. But if Chen fell out with Zhang, he had his differences of opinion with Jiang Qing, too. Although they established a kind of uneasy peace with each other, half of the time he was annoyed with her, and half of the time he smiled at her. She irritated him most when she put forward the slogan: "Criticize Lin Biao, criticize Confucius, criticize the Duke of Zhou," since she used the Duke of Zhou as a pseudonym for Premier Zhou. This didn't sit at all well with Chen, who repeated on many occasions: "Without Premier Zhou there would be no Chen Yonggui."

Chen arranged for Dazhai and Xiyang to use only "Criticize Lin Biao, criticize Confucius," without ever mentioning the "Duke of Zhou." This was one of the reasons Jiang Qing disliked Chen Yonggui. Consequently, he was always uncomfortable after he moved into the Fishing Terrace compound at the end of October, 1974.

After Chairman Mao Zedong pointed out that "there were no fish to be caught at the Fishing Terrace," Wang Hongwen deliberately caught a big fish from the pond behind his house at the Fishing Terrace, and announced to everybody: "Who says there's no fish to catch? I caught a big one!"

But Chen Yonggui still actively negotiated with the State Management Bureau, to look for suitable housing for himself.

After Chen Yonggui's "three-thirds system" of dividing work obligations gained Chairman Mao's approval, although he subjectively wished to spend more time in Dazhai and on the road visiting around the country, this was in reality hard to achieve. During the period from 1974 to 1976, he spent more than half of each year in Beijing, and during the first year of the implementation of his "three-thirds system" he was able to spend only twenty-two days traveling around the country. As it was often difficult for him to return promptly when something suddenly came up at the Central Committee, and because there were all kinds of affairs the State Council left for him to deal with upon his return since it could not stop work altogether while he carried out his "three-thirds system," he attended over two hundred meetings in Beijing each year. Even so, after his colleagues accepted his unique work schedule, Chen Yonggui still spent infinitely more time at the grass-roots level than any other leader, and he was familiar with the situation among ordinary people in much more detail.

At that time, the Gang of Four all too easily cranked up the propaganda machine to criticize the economic determinism of "The Theory of the Primacy of Productive Forces" as the determining factor in historical development.[1] Their thesis was: Had Chen Yonggui not been in charge of agriculture, the level of agricultural production could never have been maintained. This contained a large element of truth, but as soon as those veteran cadres who had just been released and put back to work, and who had all accumulated a certain amount of experience in leadership, grasped production, they were attacked again for bowing to "Productive Forces Theory," as was Chen Yonggui himself. None of them was able to work normally with this new label hanging over their heads.

Chen Yonggui was not afraid. He was not a capitalist-roader, nor was he a "stinky number nine." Moreover, with powerful backing from Chairman Mao and Premier Zhou, nobody dared do a thing to him. At one time, a poster criticizing Chen Yonggui for his alleged adherence to the primacy of productive forces appeared at Qinghua University. Many veteran cadres urged Chen Yonggui to go to the university to take a look, but he brushed it off.

"Ask them to bring it over. I don't have the time!" he said.

He brooked no interference. He was in charge of agriculture, and he would remain in charge.

---

1. Productive forces theory holds that the basic determinant of human history is not politics, not class struggle, but economics, especially the development of the productive forces of society. Hence whatever advances and develops the productive forces advances mankind toward socialism. If, on the other hand, the productive forces have not reached adequate levels and laid down the requisite foundations, it is useless to talk about socialism because conditions are not ripe. This then is a theory of economic determinism that negates the role of human will in history and the dialectical interplay between conscious decisions to transform the conditions of life and the straitjacket imposed on mankind by the conditions of life. Material necessity is one pole of a dichotomy to which voluntarism is the other. Dialectics illuminates the interplay between them, recognizing that, while the material conditions of life determine consciousness, consciousness can also transform the material conditions of life. These are the grounds on which Mao rejected the theory of the primacy of productive forces, which is at the heart of Deng Xiaoping's economic pragmatism—"I don't care whether the cat is black or white, so long as it can catch mice." (W.H.H.)

The Gang of Four was not only using the pretext of criticizing the theory of the primacy of productive forces to create upheaval at the Central Committee, it looked for ways to create disruption wherever it could. During the National Planning Conference in 1976, the Gang of Four kept posing all sorts of objections that revolved around such things as the "Snail Incident" and the question of the "Qingfeng steamship," to the extent that no one could bring the conference to an end. Discussions went on for more than ten days without any results. In the end, it was the Tangshan earthquake that shook the gathering to a close. Chen Yonggui felt extreme aversion to the Gang of Four during this conference.

In the time he worked in Beijing, Chen Yonggui exhibited a dual psychology of intense love and hatred. Relatively well known were his strong feelings for Zhou Enlai. Regardless of how many difficulties he experienced after he came to work at the Central Committee, he never troubled Premier Zhou with them. He often looked for Premier Zhou to report the progress of his work to him, but never to ask for anything.

After Premier Zhou Enlai entered Hospital 301 in 1975, the hospital employed special measures to protect him. Unless there were extraordinary circumstances, nobody was allowed to come to the hospital to visit him. The restriction applied even to Party and State leaders. Having solicited approval from the hospital, Chen Yonggui went to see the Premier. From his sick bed Premier Zhou told Chen Yonggui about the argument that certain times produce their heroes and about Napoleon's philosophy of utilizing the talent and energy of the people. Chen Yonggui experienced a great uplift. As he was about to leave, Premier Zhou shook his hand warmly.

"Yonggui, come whenever you feel like seeing me," he said.

However, when Chen Yonggui went to visit him next time, he was stopped by the sentry at the hospital gate. The reason given was that, as a way to ensure his health, the Central Committee had issued a directive that nobody could go at random to see the Premier.

"Is it possible that I am not allowed to see him even for a moment?" Chen Yonggui said, beside himself with rage.

He had no choice but to get back into his car and return to Jiaodaokou. As soon as he walked through the door, he dialed

Zhongnanhai and asked to talk directly to Premier Zhou's wife, Deng Yingchao. He described his grief at not being able to see the Premier.

"Didn't the Premier say it? You can see him whenever you feel like it!" Deng Yingchao confirmed, and afterward appeared in person to grant Chen Yonggui a "special entry permit pass." The sentry never stopped Chen Yonggui again when he went to the hospital.

On the 8th of January, 1976, just before daybreak, Chen Yonggui's security guard Zhang Yinchang put down the receiver and rushed to knock on Chen Yonggui's door. Chen Yonggui had been attending a Political Bureau meeting at the Great Hall of the People the night before, and had gone to bed very late. Then he could not fall asleep for half the night. He was fast asleep when Zhang Yinchang knocked on the door. He seemed quite unhappy about the disturbance, and he asked with annoyance: "Who is it?"

"Old Chen, there's an emergency," said Zhang Yinchang.

Chen Yonggui finally opened his eyes and told Zhang Yinchang to come in.

Zhang Yinchang informed him that there had been an urgent call from the Central Committee's General Office: The Premier's illness had taken a critical turn. Chen Yonggui was to go immediately to the hospital. Oblivious of everything else, he dressed hastily and anxiously instructed Zhang Yinchang to call the car.

Unfortunately, as luck would have it, his secretary had needed to attend to some urgent business and had taken the driver with him before the crack of dawn.

"Yinchang, where's the car?" asked Chen Yonggui as he came out into the yard.

Zhang Yinchang had to tell him the truth.

"Not before, not later, he has to pick this time to go out!" exclaimed Chen in a fit of frustration.

Chen Yonggui grumbled and moaned and groaned, and after a short while he suddenly remembered the other car: "Yinchang, is the Red Flag here? If it is, *you* drive me there!"

As the nature of his work required, Zhang Yinchang had learned to drive, but he had never driven a Red Flag limousine. He had to explain to Chen Yonggui that he did not dare drive the big clumsy vehicle.

"If you don't dare drive, then carry me on your back!" yelled Chen.

As Chen Yonggui's temper grew, he spoke with less and less sense and tact: A moment later, he corrected his previous "order" and gestured at Zhang Yinchang to press him on: "Hurry to Dianmen. Find out which bus goes to Hospital 301. I'll take the bus!"

Without saying anything, Zhang Yinchang set out to call the State Management Bureau to ask for another car. Just then the driver showed up in the Datsun, bringing the secretary back. When Chen Yonggui spotted the car, his anger subsided.

By the time he got to the hospital, Premier Zhou was already resting in peace, his body placed on the bier. Deng Yingchao and several Political Bureau members were standing around the body, wailing. Chen Yonggui shook hands with Deng Yingchao. Then, as though he had lost his reason, he started thinking about Premier Zhou's three trips to Dazhai and everything else that led to his posting to Beijing, and, as the multitudinous past events poured into his mind, tears started pouring from his eyes.

From the moment of Premier Zhou's death to the memorial ceremony, Chen Yonggui paid his last respects, offered his condolences and participated in mourning events three times. He managed to persevere at first due to his bullheaded will power. Before long, however, he fell ill, was unable to eat or sleep, and had to go to the hospital to be examined. To ensure his quick recovery the Beijing Hospital of Harmonizing Peace assigned a specialist, Dr. Zhang Xiaoqian, to diagnose and treat him, but Chen Yonggui did not stop working. Even when his illness was quite serious, he went on attending meetings, commenting on documents, and taking care of everyday business. Only after Dr. Zhang Xiaoqian completely cured him did he return to Dazhai and Xiyang to make an inspection.

During his time in Beijing, Chen Yonggui did not have many opportunities to see Chairman Mao Zedong. It was always at some meeting, which he would usually attend if the Chairman sent the invitation, but such occasions were very few. Nevertheless, Chen Yonggui's affection for Chairman Mao was extraordinarily deep. The five words, "In agriculture, learn from Dazhai," created a special bond between Mao

Zedong and Chen Yonggui, and made the majority of people view Chen Yonggui with increased respect. After Chairman Mao became seriously ill, Chen Yonggui followed his condition with great solicitude. Day and night, he thought about how important a turn for the better in Chairman Mao's health was for the future of the Party and the destiny of the nation, now that Premier Zhou had passed away. Since he did not have the opportunity to visit the Chairman often during his grave illness, he kept inquiring about the health of the Communist Party leader.

On June 27, 1976, Chairman Mao Zedong's condition took a critical turn, and the Central Committee sent a plane to Shaanxi to bring Wu Guixian back to Peking. Chen Yonggui was doing his grass-roots work in Xiyang, but as soon as he received notification from the Central Committee, he too boarded the plane and returned to Beijing. It was a Sunday, and his security guard Zhang Yinchang, who had remained at Jiaodaokou, took a visitor from Xiyang, Guo Renhe, to see a doctor in the city, then on to the Badaling Hills northwest of Beijing, which the sick man wanted to see before he died. The guard had to lock the house while he was gone and only a few soldiers stood guard at the front gate of the compound. When Chen Yonggui got off the plane at Beijing Airport, no car from Jiaodaokou was there to meet him. The Central Committee had to send another car to take him home. When he arrived at his residence, he could not even get into his own front door. He asked the soldiers where Zhang Yinchang had gone. The soldiers did not know. Chen Yonggui had no place to vent his anger, which stemmed from his concern for Chairman Mao's condition, and so he turned around, got back into the car, and rushed off to Zhongnanhai.

Chen Yonggui spent that night at Chairman Mao's residence, and only after the Chairman's condition stabilized the following day did he go back to Jiaodaokou. Zhang Yinchang was very nervous in the meantime. Having heard that Chen Yonggui had come back, he spent the whole night preparing to answer his boss. But Chen Yonggui was a person whose temper calmed as soon as its cause had vanished, and so, when the two men met the following day, and after Guo Renhe explained the whole story, he never said a word.

At the time of Chairman Mao Zedong's death, Chen Yonggui was in Dazhai accompanying Jiang Qing on an inspection tour. As soon as they received notice of the Chairman's passing from the Central Committee's General Office on September 5, 1976, Chen quickly accompanied Jiang Qing back to Peking. After Chairman Mao's death, Chen Yonggui kept sighing and lost his appetite completely. He stood guard several times, keeping vigil at the Chairman's bier. That was the crucial time of decision in regard to his political fate because the outcome of the struggle between the veteran cadres and the Gang of Four was ultimately closely related to his own destiny.

The aftermath of Chairman Mao Zedong's funeral was the crucial moment in the scramble for power among the highest-level leaders of the Central Committee. For some time around National Day on October 1st there were no meetings of the Political Bureau. The *Guangming Daily* published an editorial under the title "Following an Impromptu Policy," which caught the attention of Hua Guofeng, Ye Jianying and Wang Dongxing, forcing them to adopt some countermeasures.

Only after intensive pondering did Chen Yonggui gain a better understanding of the problem of succession after the death of Chairman Mao Zedong. Once in Dazhai, some associates at the Travel Office asked him, secretly sounding out the tone of his answer, who could become Chairman Mao's successor. He implicitly suggested two men; one of them was Deng Xiaoping.

"When Chairman Mao and Premier Zhou were alive," he later told his associates, "I followed the line of Chairman Mao. Now that Chairman Mao and Premier Zhou have left this world, I'll follow whoever will carry out Chairman Mao's revolutionary line." Consequently, at that crucial period he followed Hua Guofeng, the man who was, without question, his first choice.

After the 1976 National Day, Hua Guofeng gave him a secret order to keep watch on one of the members of the "Gang of Four." Chen Yonggui unflinchingly carried out this duty.

On October 5th in the afternoon Hua Guofeng secretly summoned Chen Yonggui, who instructed his security guard, Zhang Yinchang, to remain at Jiaodaokou and stand by at the telephone. When it rang suddenly, he no sooner picked up the receiver than a voice inquired hastily: "Are you Little Zhang from Chen Yonggui's residence?" Having waited for his affirmation, the voice continued, "This is the office of Director Wang (Wang Dongxing) of the Central Committee's General Office. Please inform your boss of the meeting tonight at Jade Spring Hills."

Zhang Yinchang immediately realized this was not a regular telephone call. The usual practice was for the Secretariat to give notice of all Chinese Communist Party Central Committee meetings. In the case of a State Council meeting, the State Council Office would call. This was the first time that Wang Dongxing's office had called. Besides, Jade Spring Hills was the Central Committee's secondary work address. They would not be going there unless the circumstances were special. Zhang Yinchang's analysis boiled down to two points: one, whatever happens, tonight will mark a turning point; two, something big is afoot at the Central Committee. Consequently, he exercised particular caution.

When Chen Yonggui returned from Hua Guofeng's, he instructed Zhang Yinchang to watch the telephone again. Then he left for Jade Spring Hills. Zhang Yinchang spent the whole night by the telephone, afraid to take off his clothes or go to bed. That was the night when all Political Bureau members with the exception of the Gang of Four, after several days of individual preparations, assembled at Jade Spring Hills to await developments. Hua Guofeng, Ye Jianying and Wang Dongxing instructed Army Unit 834 to arrest the Gang at the Huairen Hall.

Late in the night, the Central Committee's General Office sent a bag of documents to Zhang Yinchang. He usually opened such bags to see whether the documents needed Chen Yonggui's comments. This time, after he opened it, he saw that the documents carried a large caption: "Special Group for the Investigation of the Wang, Zhang, Jiang and Yao Case." Subsequently, Secretary Jiao Huancheng called him from Jade Spring Hills to tell him not to open the documents transferred from the Central Committee. They should be handed over to the driver, Master Tang, and brought directly to Chen Yonggui. When the driver returned to Jiaodaokou soon thereafter to pick up the documents, Zhang Yinchang asked him what was going on. Master Tang still did not know that the Gang of Four had been arrested.

"I've noticed that the cars belonging to Wang Hongwen and others are not there," he said quietly. "I'm afraid something's happened."

Everything became clear on the following day.

That morning Chen Yonggui came back to Jiaodaokou to prepare Zhang Yinchang for a trip to Dazhai and Xiyang. Chen instructed him to take back the news and tell people there to make a clean break with the Gang of Four. As soon as Zhang Yinchang accomplished his mission, he returned to Beijing.

Chen Yonggui was so busy with the struggle to expose and criticize the Gang of Four that he did not go back home to Jiaodaokou for a long time. He finally returned to his residence only when the Second National "In Agriculture Learn From Dazhai" Conference opened in Beijing.

After the crushing of the Gang of Four, Chen Yonggui actively participated in the move to bring Deng Xiaoping back onto the political scene. When the issue of releasing veteran cadres was raised at a Political Bureau meeting, Chen Yonggui stood up.

"If a large group of veteran cadres does not come out, we won't be able to stabilize the situation," he declared. "The sooner they come out, the sooner we'll have stability."

Chen specifically mentioned Deng Xiaoping's name, saying he should be released as quickly as possible. After his speech, Geng Biao first raised his hand to endorse it, and then several other Political Bureau members announced their agreement with Chen Yonggui's opinion.

Swept into the vortex of a complicated political storm, Chen Yonggui displayed a distinct flair for politics, a cool analytical approach and the courage to take resolute action. He was not one to meekly accept orders and follow the current blindly. He was, in the words of Deng Xiaoping, a man who knew how to think.

CHAPTER 28

NOURISHING HOME ROOTS, FENDING OFF FAME

Lofty towers are built from the ground up.

Chen Yonggui's pioneering work, from its earliest beginnings to its grand completion, can be said to have embodied this basic principle.

When he kept returning to Dazhai and Xiyang in the effort to spend one-third of his time working at the grass-roots level, it was precisely for the purpose of consolidating his base among the people so he could offer sound advice to the entire nation and reinforce his "lofty towers" from the bottom up.

Every time Chen Yonggui, the Vice-Premier, showed up in Dazhai, media lenses turned on him, filming footage that showed him leaping from his car, be it the black Red Flag limousine, the gray Shanghai, or some other luxury sedan, and, without ever stopping at his house, rushing up Tigerhead Mountain or entering Wolf Den Ravine as though the soles of his feet were riding on the wind. The video artists would set up the following scenario for him: Chen Yonggui stretches his callused hand, slowly lifts an ear of millet with it, looks to see whether its grains are plump or not, then releases it gently; Chen Yonggui enters a field of emerging corn sprouts, frowns as he squats down to measure the spacing between and within each row with his hands; Chen Yonggui enters a site where a new level terrace is under construction, he points something out to the people who are building up the embankments, he picks up a hammer and breaks a piece of rock.

Those are the vivid images of Vice-Premier Chen Yonggui in the village of Dazhai.

Whether a freezing wind bit to the bone or heavy snow fell on the slopes, Chen Yonggui did the same as all those other brave men and women of steel. In order to turn a small field into a big one, he worked till he dripped with sweat, then sat at the edge of the field eating from his clay pot. At the beginning, the Commune members felt that, as a member of the Political Bureau and Vice-Premier of the State Council, he should not be working like that or eating so much cold frozen food. Chen Yonggui disagreed with this view.

"What kind of model would a Model Worker be who didn't work?"

With these words he prevailed over everybody. At other times, he explained himself thus: "If I didn't come back to work after joining the Central Committee, I would be divorced from practice."

Consequently, all those old stone mason workmates of his secretly admired him. There was nothing they could say.

As Vice-Premier, however, Chen Yonggui was different from those regular farmers. All too often, on account of some event or other, the Red Flag limousine or the Shanghai sedan[1] drove up to the edge of the field. Then Chen Yonggui had to knock the dirt off his shoes, wipe his soiled hands and sit in the car to transact business.

It was the same in Xiyang. He did not really trust the reports he received from the County. In order to get a better grasp of the concrete situation, he applied well the advice of Confucius to "travel around various states."

Once, traveling over hill and dale due east along Zhao Camp Creek, his car came to a stop in front of the main gate of Yan Settlement People's Commune.

As he got out of the car, he was just about to follow the local lead-

1. In Beijing Chen Yonggui had the use of a Japanese Datsun. Apparently in Xiyang the car assigned was a China-built Shanghai sedan. (W.H.H.)

ers into the offices of the Commune, when he heard strident quarreling in a room next door. It sounded like a discussion about grain, so he changed his plan and walked toward the room with the noise.

In that room a Commune-wide meeting for Production Brigade accountants was in progress. One issue had struck a discordant note, causing them all to raise their voices in loud disagreement. These peasants, totally absorbed in their squabble, were completely unprepared for the arrival of a member of the Political Bureau of the Communist Party of China and a Vice-Premier of State to boot. Their voices died away almost instantly. Awed into silence, they watched Chen Yonggui's expression warily. Some broke into a cold sweat.

Realizing the awkwardness of the situation, Chen Yonggui pursed his lips for a moment and then addressed the group: "Go on. Go on with what you were saying just now. Don't be afraid to speak up if you have a problem," he encouraged them.

Silence, a highly unusual brand of silence.

"Weren't you just quarreling about grain? What's wrong with that? Huh?"

One shovel makes the move; two shovels stir the mix. Assuming that Chen Yonggui had already heard snippets of their conversation, a young man took the risk of speaking out of turn and charged ahead with an explanation.

During the great drought of 1973, some villages in Yan Settlement People's Commune did not receive one good ground-soaking rain even in the hottest part of the summer. Their harvests suffered greatly. Chen Yonggui had announced that where production had dropped off sharply, the grain allotment for personal consumption should not be reduced. Still their fall quotas for grain deliveries to the State had not been reduced either. In order to fill the quotas, those villages had to dip into the grain they had stored up collectively for emergencies, and also into the amount allocated for personal consumption. By the beginning of the new Lunar Year, the Commune members all had to work on virtually empty stomachs, which of course affected their morale and their ability to work hard.

The young man who stuck his neck out expected to be given a lecture, perhaps even disciplinary action. He did not expect that, as soon as his words sank in, all the people around him would agree, adding to the tension of the moment.

While Chen Yonggui listened, he deliberated on the problem they were raising. As soon as they were finished, he suggested reviewing the grain balance sheet.

"How many people in your family? How much corn did you get? How much millet? How much grain is for those who work in the fields?"

The more he balanced, the more it became clear that they didn't have enough grain left to feed the people. As he realized the severity of the problem, bumps appeared on his forehead.

By the spring of 1973, most of Xiyang County was suffering from a drought even more severe than the one encountered the year before. The Grain in Ear[1] season had come and gone and there was still no rain. In view of the special situation, where the entire country was learning from Dazhai and catching up with Xiyang, the drought posed a serious menace to Xiyang the model county, on more than one front. The situation demanded immediate drought-prevention measures. During the previous season, 1972, a vigorous anti-drought campaign had achieved excellent results. Once again, Chen Yonggui decided on energetic action. Insisting that the summer planting be carried out as usual, he said: "Let the heavens bring drought; we, the people, will go all out. We'll tramp a thousand *li* for a hundred buckets of water to save one *mu* of seedlings if that's what it takes."

He mobilized several hundred villages—a labor force several hundred thousand strong, and all the motor vehicles and livestock in the County to haul water. He sent the personnel of the entire administration, dependents and all, old men and small children, into the fields to carry water and do the planting. In the end the seeds sprouted. The harvest promised to surpass that of 1972, an unprecedented, outstanding achievement.

Everybody at the time thought this was a tremendous, earthshaking event. They summed it up "Unprecedented drought, unprecedented human effort, unprecedented harvest." Reporters hyped the publicity

1. The 9th solar term.

to some degree, for a little spurring on was what the nation needed. Based on this need, also, the media disclosed Xiyang County's planned grain production and State purchase quota figures, immediately upon the initial victory. However, after the corn sprouted, the Dragon King still kept his sluice gates shut. Unfortunately Chen Yonggui did not pay enough attention to this. He even taunted fate: "Are Heavens trying to test us? I hope they give us another month of drought!"

He had already had the experience: A rain at this particular time, if it was followed by a drought during the hot summer days, would hinder the pollination process. If there was a month of drought first, followed by rain during the hot summer days, the crop would not suffer much at all. It never occurred to him that the weather might act unpredictably, and that his old experience would be put to a new test. When the hot summer days arrived, still no rain fell. Chen Yonggui had no control over the Old Dragon in Heaven; in that respect, he was at a great disadvantage. And so he came to grief. Xiyang suffered a drop in production.

Chen Yonggui and the media had already promised a bumper crop. But when the time came to deliver on the promise in the fall, the discrepancy between actual yields and those planned at the beginning of the year became apparent. This discrepancy was aggravated by windstorms and early frosts that hit the County after the newspapers published the estimated figures. On the heels of the figures come the promise: "Unprecedented drought, unprecedented human effort, unprecedented bumper harvest!"

As for the State purchase quotas, they were determined by the reported figures. The common practice was for various People's Commune Party Secretaries to report production figures to the County Committee every year before the fall purchase, so that State quotas could be fixed. They met at the County Revolutionary Committee dining room.

The first to report was the Party Secretary of City Gate People's Commune, Li Aihu. According to his own recollection, Li Aihu did not report the actual figures at all. He had given it some thought, and decided to report the 1966 totals for the City Gate collective. Although City Gate Commune suffered a severe drought in 1973, due to its members' hard work, its yields for that year were still more than double those for 1966. So he came in with a safely low figure. The second Party secretary, and the third, based their reports on the figures from the first. The County used this data, but the figures were far out of sinc with the actual yields which, in spite of the drought, were very much higher.

Chen Yonggui was not in Xiyang when this meeting took place. When he returned from Beijing and heard about what had happened, he was quite unhappy. Choking with rage, he rebuked the Commune cadres, "You are simply not willing to sell more grain to the State!" he fumed.

He next held a meeting of all Commune Party secretaries at Dazhai's Reception Center, and asked for a second set of reports. Dazhai People's Commune Party Secretary, Qiao Suxiang, reported the first figures this time. He first submitted Dazhai Brigade's figures. His reckoning of the amount of Dazhai grain to be sold to the State was still quite low—100,000 *jin* short of the figure prepared by Chen Yonggui.

Chen flew into a rage again. "I'm prepared to sell 400,000 *jin*. How come you want me to sell 100,000 less?" he asked. Thus Chen Yonggui, concluding that the grass-roots level used the pretext of the drought to under-report yields and sell less of the surplus grain, increased pressure on all the Communes. People say that he "taught Qiao Suxiang a lesson and punished Li Aihu." The truth was, however, that various Commune Party secretaries, under Chen Yonggui's pressure, then turned around and reported figures that were a bit too high, amounting to the total of 240,000,000 *jin*. As winter approached, several old comrades of Chen Yonggui's went to confer with him.

"Old Chen, it seems we have over-reported our yields this year!" they ventured.

"Over-reported? Our report is already on record. What should we do?" Chen said, admitting the problem.

"Don't worry about the record," the old comrades said. "We'll activate the real yield figures and send the report up. Wouldn't that redress the error?"

Chen Yonggui accepted their suggestion and undertook to verify the grain output of the entire County in 1973. He discovered that due to a fall disaster the kernels of corn never properly filled up.

"Oyoyoy! We've got plenty of gunnysacks! We just don't have enough weight to fill them up with!" he sighed.

And so he reported the true yield figure of 210,000,000 *jin* to the Shanxi Provincial Grain Office. These figures, however, never were published.

When the Provincial Grain Office later criticized Xiyang County for falsely reporting its yields, the Office's Director Su Maolin admitted confusion.

"What happened in Xiyang? Their estimated yields for 1973 were too high. We should base everything on the actual yields! I had no idea they gave me false reports!" he protested.

To be fair, had the actual yield figures, once reported and recorded, been made public, this accusation could not have been made. If made it would not have held up. Thus what happened later, the hullabaloo over grain figures, would most likely not have happened.

In any case, at the end of the year there was a grain crisis at Yan Settlement People's Commune, Chen Yonggui's destination that day, and Chen, having entered the room on the side opposite the Commune office, was face to face with it. After Chen Yonggui heard what everybody had to say, he expressed his own conclusion.

"It looks like there's a problem with your yields. You've got no reserves stored up for emergencies. So the more you sell off as surplus, the less you've got to eat. However, let's keep one thing straight, you must take care of your people first!"

Yan Settlement Commune's Party Secretary looked helplessly around. To whom was he to tell his troubles?

"The problem of per capita grain must be solved," continued Chen Yonggui. "Who can learn from Dazhai on an empty stomach? When I go back to the County, I'll check on the public grain."

Chen Yonggui's statement caught everyone at the meeting by surprise. Nobody expected that he would say such a thing. Such comforting words were hard to come by. Hearing them, many people complained that their share of wheat was also much too small.

"If you can't deliver to the State, don't do it," said Chen Yonggui. "We can't leave our people without wheat for New Year's dumplings!"

Chen Yonggui's decision left people feeling that their wishes had been fulfilled.

"Now let's go to that room," the Commune Party Secretary said to Chen Yonggui, pointing to the Commune office.

"What should we go there for?" Chen Yonggui asked, shaking his head. "Are there any rank-and-filers there?"

He had suddenly decided to look into the situation elsewhere, too, and was anxious to leave. After a brief chat with the accountants, whose job was to fiddle with the beads of the abacus, the Commune's cadres and the accountants saw Chen Yonggui off to his car.

Chen Yonggui went back to the County seat to take care of the problem faced by other Commune members who were left with insufficient per capita grain supplies. He recalled grain that had already been purchased and arranged to sell it back. Thus he dealt with the situation properly and skillfully.

One big problem was that back in those years the newspapers got into the habit of reporting grain production output ahead of time. Thus year after year the problem of double accounting would occur. Also, Chen Yonggui and the people at the County level were not careful enough. They often assessed the situation in overly optimistic terms. This practice finally led to a big disaster, which occurred much later, during the period of redress of ultra-leftism. But we will talk about that later.

On another occasion Chen Yonggui's shadow followed him across the County Committee's compound. As he got into the car, his driver stepped on the gas and drove toward the highway. Where were they going? Chen Yonggui said nothing, and the driver never asked. The driver did not think this strange at all; he frequently found out which way to go only once they got on the road. The car descended a slope on the western outskirts of the County capital and arrived at a fork in the road. The driver did not know which way to turn the wheel. As was his habit, he turned his head around asking with his eyes for directions. Chen Yonggui had in fact already made up his mind long ago. As he lay in bed he had been thinking about some problems. He could not limit himself to simply hearing the reports. He had to go to the Communes and take a look for himself. He had not been to West Camp in a long time. He had heard that they were putting on an opera at about that time. What was this opera-going all about? As a result, the driver had no need to turn the wheel of the car. They went straight on, along the road that led west from Xiyang.

This was the period right after the hottest summer days and before the fall harvest season. There was nothing urgent doing in the fields. It was the slack season for farmers, so they hung their hoes on the wall, and looked forward to the rat-a-tat beat of Shanxi opera. In West Camp an opera was indeed in progress. Chen Yonggui's arrival took the leaders of West Camp People's Commune by surprise. Without a worry on their mind, they too had gone to see the performance. They were completely unprepared for Chen Yonggui. Since they were not at their offices, Chen Yonggui went looking for them. When the Shanghai sedan appeared below the stage, the Commune leaders were alarmed. Not only were they singing along at the opera, they were doing some public trading as well. Right next to the stage, they had set up a culled-ox market where old, crippled or sick work oxen were put up for sale.

Chen Yonggui lost his temper. Weeds were growing in the fields, but these farmers hung up their hoes and sang operas! Not that he did not want them to sing, but what about crop production? Will this year's production targets be met? After the crops grow too big, it's hard to use the hoe. If you can't use the big hoe, you have to use the small one; if you can't use the small hoe, you have to dig weeds up with your fingers, and that takes much more effort. In addition they had set up their culled-ox market! If they have old oxen to sell, why don't they sell to the State?[1] Why are they on such good terms with east Hebei, as thick as thieves? Aren't we supposed to be criticizing capitalism within collective economy? What is this, if not a form of capitalism? Those were the issues Chen Yonggui raised to teach West Camp's leaders a lesson. He later arranged to confront them at the County level.

---

1. Chen Yonggui's commitment to collective ownership below and public ownership above was total. He believed that if everyone honestly carried out the delivery arrangements and marketing rules set up by Central everyone would prosper. Hence he insisted on Dazhai and Xiyang doing so. (W.H.H.)

With hindsight, we may conclude that Chen Yonggui perhaps criticized them and dealt with the issue a little too severely. But the level of attention he paid to the field management, the underlying problem here, is rare in China even to this day.

This is the way it has always been: Merit and fault alternate and overlap.

Chen Yonggui paid very close attention to his own power base among the people, caring deeply for all of them. He continuously explored the experiences gained at the base, and very soberly corrected problems as they arose.

In those days, the people of Dazhai endured hard labor. So did most of the people of Xiyang. In winter they leveled the land into larger fields they called plains. In summer they worked on water conservancy projects. Except for the New Year's festival, the Red Lantern Festival and the "August 1st" temple festival, they hardly had any time to catch their breath. But Chen Yonggui suffered along with everybody else; nobody ever complained about that. During the three battles with Wolf Den Ravine he held meetings at night and worked during the day. When everybody sat at home at New Year's playing cards, the shepherds still had to take their flocks up the mountain.

Chen Yonggui climbed up the mountain and took the whips from their hands. "Come on, come on, give it to me. Go home and warm up with your wives. I've already had a chance to enjoy myself today!" he urged.

The shepherds were deeply grateful.

"No, no, no," they kept saying. "That's too much trouble for you."

"When I tell you to celebrate the New Year, you go celebrate the New Year," insisted Chen Yonggui. "How do you herd goats anyway? You make them graze on the hilltops? That's exactly what I'll do, too. I'll make them graze on the hilltops. When you come tomorrow morning, you count them up. I'll pay for any goat that's missing!"

When Chen Yonggui lectured, people often shivered, but for him to come up the mountain and say what he did on New Year's Eve brought tears to the shepherds' eyes! He had the spirit and his own way of showing it! He also had the skills needed to serve the people!

"What makes a mountain potent is not its height but the immortals that inhabit it; what makes a water formidable is not its depth, but the dragons that dwell in it." So goes the saying.

When Chen Yonggui emerged on China's soil, people acted as if he were one such immortal of its mountains and dragon of its waters. Chen Yonggui found this annoying and amusing at the same time.

"I've become a living trademark!" he complained.

During the eight years of his political career at the top, decision-making level, comical happenings kept occurring, which he, as an actor in them, made come to life in an unforgettable and endearing way. Even after his death, right up until today, he continues to enjoy great popularity among the people, while the stories take on some attributes of myth.

In terms of his understanding of and outlook on society and the world one must admit that there existed a considerable distance between him and other members of the Political Bureau. There were many things others could speak about plausibly and at length, while he could hardly put in a single word. He also found it hard to adjust to the lifestyle. People who knew him well could not help making jokes about it.

Right after he walked through the door of the Political Bureau, the Central Committee decided that he, Hua Guofeng, and Ji Dengkui should jointly take charge of agriculture. Ji Dengkui was a man of great charm and wit, and he was quick to make a joke or take a jab at Chen Yonggui, sometimes intentionally and sometimes without thinking. They were having a dinner together one time, when a big fish was brought to the table. Noticing Chen Yonggui's hesitation, Ji Dengkui started to gulp down fish. He was able to spit the stabbing fish bones deftly from his mouth, and continue to swallow big pieces of fish without pausing. As for Chen Yonggui, after each mouthful of fish he had to spit bones many times, while Ji Dengkui urged him on.

"Hurry up! If you don't, we'll finish it off!" he teased.

"I don't really like fish," Chen Yonggui was forced to say, laughing. "From now on, I just won't eat fish at all!"

Ji Dengkui remembered his words, and looked for an opportunity to get back at him. When they had dinner together again, a dish that

Chen Yonggui had never seen before was brought to the table. He took a trial bite and liked the taste very much.

"What's this dish called?" he asked.

"This?" Ji Dengkui immediately jumped in to answer. "This is a special plant from the sea. If you eat it, you can live to be a hundred!"

With that everybody burst into loud laughter.

Chen Yonggui did not care if they laughed. Since he liked the taste, he boldly got down to eating. After the dinner, Ji Dengkui launched his counterattack.

"Say, last time somebody pledged not to eat fish ever again, and now it took him just one meal to eat several thousand of them! Wouldn't you say he went back on his word?"

Chen Yonggui was surprised. There had been no fish on his table!

"Who ate several thousand fish in one meal?" he asked, looking Ji Dengkui in the eye.

"You, our good Old Chen," said Ji Dengkui, stroking his shoulder.

Everybody laughed, but Chen Yonggui was not convinced.

"There were no fish on this table," he said.

"So what was on this plate?" asked Ji Dengkui. "Don't you admit that you ate it?"

Chen Yonggui finally found out, after somebody explained it to him, that "the special plant from the sea" was really a high-quality fish called chum salmon. And so he had to laugh again. The truth was, however, that Chen Yonggui did not much enjoy eating fish.

"No fish or chicken for me! Just give me a scrambled egg," he used to tell his staff.[1]

All this does not quite make him deserve the title "immortal of the mountains, dragon of the waters." Nevertheless, nobody ever denied Chen Yonggui's special status in the broadest sense.

Once Chen Yonggui's "signboard" lit up the public eye, this "living trademark" could be used to "solicit customers." While he was still Party Branch Secretary of Dazhai, the one strong lure that attracted

---

1. Once in Wuxi I ate a meal with Chen Yonggui and Ji Dengkui. The chef served an aromatic dish, dog meat. Chen and I both tried a bite, learned that it was dog meat and refused to eat more. This made us country bumpkins in the eyes of others, but we enjoyed a special boondocks solidarity. (W.H.H.)

tens of thousands of visitors to Dazhai was a chance to see Chen Yonggui. If they did not see him their hearts were not content. Chen Yonggui found this irritating. He feared being tied up by the visitors. As a result, when he was busy, he always hid from the crowds.

On one fall day in the 1970s, he was returning to Dazhai from a County meeting, when he decided to check to what degree the crops had ripened. When he got to the hillside fields half way up Tigerhead Mountain, he noticed a group of several hundred visitors, who were listening to a presentation of Dazhai's experience. The moment they saw a familiar figure in the midst of a millet field, they concluded it must be Chen Yonggui. Consequently, they abandoned the presentation and ran downhill to gather around him. He was quite annoyed at not being able to retreat from the encirclement. But he could not show this feeling to the visitors. Putting on a smile, he shook hands and greeted them. All together, it took him over an hour to "push" them away.

After he moved to Beijing, the Central Committee's Security Bureau was responsible for all his outside movements. They had a system of security protections, which made Chen Yonggui's coming and going very inconvenient. This was the most frequent cause of Chen Yonggui's vexation with his life in Beijing. Each time he felt like going out by himself to take part in labor in the suburbs, circumstances did not allow him to do as he wished. Number one, his official duties were too heavy to find the time; number two, the regulations were too strict to allow him to move freely. Later he did risk going out alone several times and almost got himself into serious trouble. Real life experiences taught him a lesson.

On August 10, 1975, Chen Yonggui finally moved into the house on Jiaodaokou's Fourth Street South. It was arranged by the Central Committee. The house had been the formal residence of an important Qing dynasty's official, Li Hongzhang. Chen Yonggui moved in the morning, and ate his first meal at the new residence at noon.

"In order for the move to be finalized, all we need is the Incantation of the Golden Hoop,"[1] he told his assistant contentedly.

1. The Incantation of the Golden Hoop was used by the monk in the novel Pilgrimage to the West in order to keep the Monkey King under control.

In the absence of the Incantation of the Golden Hoop, Chen Yonggui acted as a runaway wild horse with only one thing on his mind: getting out into the streets to take a look at the world outside. The man in charge of safeguarding his security told him that any such outside movement must first be reported to the Security Bureau.

"Report what?" Chen Yonggui responded in anger. "Don't make so much fuss about nothing."

When he wanted to do something, nobody could talk him out of it. But although he spoke as he did, he was also aware of the precautions he should be taking. His behavior showed it very clearly. After lunch, to guard himself against any eventuality, he underwent a "make-up" transformation. He deliberately put on a black jacket and an old straw hat, which he pulled down over his face to the tip of his brow. Thus dressed like a typical peasant, he strode out of the main gate. Zhang Yinchang and the soldiers assigned to his security were worried, afraid that something might happen if they did not follow him. They did not want to be held responsible if anything went wrong, yet if they followed him, they knew he would get angry again. After a consultation, they decided to follow him and guard him from a certain distance. Entering one of the alleys Chen Yonggui noticed they were following behind. Turning toward them, he flew into a rage: "What are you here for? Go back!" he called out in a rage.

But protecting the senior officer was their duty. They could not give up on him just because he gave them a lecture. And so, while they were being lectured, they paused for a moment, but as soon as Chen Yonggui walked on they followed after him again. When he arrived at a crowded area, Chen Yonggui no longer dared turn his head around lest he reveal his identity, so he just walked straight on. He followed the main road, observing the city scenes and people's state of mind, crossing here and there to look into side streets and alleys.

He noticed a barber shop on Andingmen Avenue, and was immediately attracted to it. After his arrival in Beijing his shaves and haircuts were taken care of by people who came to his room the moment his secretary or security guard made a phone call. After the service, Zhang Yinchang paid the barber according to the fixed price. His clothes were washed and his food prepared the same way. For nine years he had not even been allowed to pick up a razor blade and shave his head. This barber shop specialized in shaving old men. It was just after noon, and there were not many people in the shop. Chen Yonggui entered the shop without making any noise, and took a seat, smoking as he waited for his shave. When his turn came, he planned to chit-chat with the barber and find out the neighborhood news. But as the barber approached him for the shave, he became aware of his identity:

"Why, you are our Vice-Premier Chen, aren't you?" the barber said.

"No, I'm not. You made a mistake," Chen Yonggui laughed, waving his hands.

"No," the barber said, "there's no mistake. You sure are Vice-Premier Chen!"

Zhang Yinchang and the soldiers finally caught up with him at this point. Zhang Yinchang wanted to pay the barber for the shave, but the barber said he did not want anything. After a brief dispute, Zhang Yinchang insisted on leaving the money for the barber. The whole event soon attracted the attention of many people. The number of people who surrounded them to watch grew, as they all wanted to see Vice-Premier Chen with their own eyes. The soldiers, who acted as his security guards, had to restore a semblance of order before they allowed Chen Yonggui to leave. On the way back, his identity was revealed several times, and on every such occasion people encircled him in no time, whether by the dozen or by the hundred. Every time this happened, Chen Yonggui first waved at them and then left in a hurry. With the soldiers maintaining order, it all ended well.

This sort of thing happened many times. On one occasion, after a hot-pot mutton dinner with Ji Dengkui, Wu Guixian and Li Ruishan from Shaanxi at one of Beijing's restaurants, he got into his Red Flag limousine and asked the driver to take him to the Beijing Department Store so he could poke around there. The moment the limousine stopped in front of the store gate and Chen Yonggui jumped out from it, masses of people surrounded him. The security guard had to restore order and clear a path to enable him leave. He never did manage to wander through the store.

When the Central Committee's Security Bureau found out about these incidents and raised the issue of ensuring Chen Yonggui's safety, he finally came to feel that it would not be right for him to go on like that. Thereafter, whenever he really wanted to go out, he gave himself a thorough make-over: he wore a hat, he donned more mysterious clothes, and his soldier guards took off their army uniforms. But he was not able to get much farther than Jiaodaokou and the Dianmen Market. Every time, after he came back from a secret stroll, he sighed.

"I've become a living trademark. I can't go out at all. When the daughter-in-law returns to her mother-in-law's house, she's sure got no freedom!"

CHAPTER—29

FOOTPRINTS ACROSS LANDS AND SEAS

When debating the question of who creates history, in a confused and complicated society people often lose sight of one basic point: Heroes are heroes of the people. Only where there are heroes of the people will you find heroic people. There is no doubt, for instance, that when it comes to Dazhai, Dazhai and Chen Yonggui cannot be separated. First, there was Dazhai, and only then was there a Chen Yonggui. But only once there was a Chen Yonggui in Dazhai, and only because of heroic efforts on his part, did Dazhai become the Dazhai of today. Following the change, Dazhai was no longer merely the Dazhai of its people. The demands of the time turned it into the Dazhai of national significance, while Chen Yonggui became the Chen Yonggui of national significance. Because of this new Dazhai, Chen Yonggui went from village leader to a leader of the nation.

Whether or not one agrees that the road should have been opened to start with, political fortunes opened up the road allowing Chen Yonggui to put his talents to good use.

Year-by-year Chen Yonggui's status and fame rose straight up, increasing his esteem in the eyes of the other deputy leaders on the national level, not to mention the effect on the people below. Li Xiannian was the senior cadre among all State Council Vice-Premiers. It is from him that Chen Yonggui had to ask for a leave of absence whenever he traveled the country or went back home. Chen Yonggui and Li Xiannian got along very well. Every time Chen Yonggui went to Li Xiannian's home to ask for work instructions or simply for a chat, Li Xiannian would ask him to stay for dinner. Consequently, their relationship was not just an ordinary relationship. They were true friends. Chen Yonggui respected Li Xiannian deeply. He was also very open with him.

A story has it that once, after some meeting, the two planned to see a movie together. It was supposed to start at 7.30 PM. At the time scheduled for the beginning of the film Li Xiannian still had not appeared. Chen Yonggui made them hold the show.

"How come the show hasn't started yet?" asked Li Xiannian when he arrived.

"Waiting for you," exclaimed Chen Yonggui.

"Hayah," sighed Li Xiannian. "Why should you wait for me?"

"How would we dare not wait for you?" answered Chen Yonggui, laughing.

Famous people often inspire veneration and admiration in others. In the eyes of these others the good fortune and achievements of their idols seem too high to reach and too deep to fathom. To Chen Yonggui himself, however, his fame felt like Mount Tai weighing on his head.

The proverb says: "If you haven't read their books, you won't know their writing." Chen Yonggui may have been acclaimed as the "expert on agriculture" by Chairman Mao Zedong, but there were definite limitations to his expertise. He could pull off the trick when it came to the loess land of Dazhai and Xiyang County; but managing agriculture on China's nine million six hundred thousand square kilometers was not an easy thing to do! Due to China's size, its geographical and climatic conditions differ widely. Wherever you go, the local Provincial and Regional leaders have worn their official garb for dozens of years, and have been through many a battle and trial. Who will listen to you if you give the unprofessional opinion of an outside dabbler regarding their domestic affairs? In addition, the Chinese people have been influenced by over two thousand years of feudal thinking. Various aspects of this backward thinking cannot be eradicated overnight, certainly not with just a few words. Learning from Dazhai means arduous struggle, self-reliance, hardship and sweat. Can people be convinced to do it?[1]

Chen Yonggui was well aware of all of this. Yet, difficult as it may have been, he still had to do the work. If popularizing Dazhai's experience were not a difficult thing to do, who would need Chen Yonggui? China's agriculture has always been a big problem, there was so much that one had to do if one wanted to increase the output of grain. So Chen Yonggui systematically set out to travel to all parts of the country, within and beyond the Great Wall, north and south of the Yangtze.

After the Tenth Congress of the Communist Party of China in 1973, Chen Yonggui first traveled to inspect the two relatively poor Provinces of Gansu and Shaanxi upon their request and as arranged by the Central Committee. He first went to Gansu, where he studied local conditions and attended the Gansu Provincial "Learn From Dazhai Experience Exchange Conference." In response to a request from the Gansu Provincial Party Committee, Chen Yonggui addressed the Conference on October 3rd. He first talked about the conditions in Dazhai and Xiyang, and then, aiming at problems that other places encountered in learning from Dazhai when they blindly adopted Dazhai's Production Brigade accounting method and when they rigidly emphasized the recall of family plots for private needs, he detailed the actual situation in Dazhai.

When he talked about Dazhai's recall of private plots, Chen Yonggui did not do so in the capacity of a Central Committee leader. Rather, he addressed the Conference as a Party Branch Secretary from Dazhai.

1. The Dazhai example is not a technological one, though it is often presented as such. It is rather an example of transforming ideology as a prelude to transforming society and subsequently nature, an example of transforming productive relations as the key to creating and releasing productive forces, a concrete example of how to "grasp revolution, promote production." Of course Chen Yonggui could not give answers to all the technical problems arising throughout China's vast agricultural hinterland. He didn't have to. His task was to teach people how to take the Dazhai road of socialist politics in command, public interest first, self-interest second, self-reliance and hard struggle, and on this basis seek out the special measures needed to transform their own environment, then mobilize themselves for cooperative efforts to carry these measures out. (W.H.H.)

"We recalled the private plots in 1963, during a flood," he explained. "After a torrential rain, our cave-dwellings caved in and our fields washed away. The Dragon King didn't care whether a plot or a tree was private. When we started reconstructing the fields, turning small plots into big ones, we couldn't leave the job undone just because there was a little private plot here or a private tree there. So we made a decision, we recalled private plots, and in exchange we gave every person an additional 60 *jin* of grain in the fall. We also solved the tobacco smokers' problem collectively by assigning two people exclusively to grow tobacco. Some Commune members complained about the recall of private plots and the 60 *jin* on grain they got to make up for their losses, saying this was like giving eyeglasses to somebody who was blind. What's wrong with giving some extra grain for personal consumption? We even conducted a public opinion poll to resolve the situation. The poll results showed that in 75 of the 80 households both male and female Brigade members were willing to give up their private plots, and that in the remaining 5 the men were willing to do it while the women were not. That really means that only 2.5 households were against the recall. In the end, everybody stated that they did not want the private plots."

At this point in his speech Chen Yonggui's face turned solemn and his attitude cautious.

"We have not yet brought collective interests into full play. If you don't recall people's private plots and you don't recall people's private trees, how can you consolidate and give free rein to the initiative of the Commune members? You can give them sixty *jin* of extra grain if you like, but will those serve any purpose? This is why we have to consider the concrete conditions of each place. We have to find out whether conditions are ripe for abandoning private plots or not. This usually depends on the level of yields in the collective fields. If they are high, who wants to hoe his own strip?"

Chen Yonggui's tone became even more sober when he started talking about the excessive emphasis on accounting in some production units. "Dazhai as an accounting unit has always kept its accounts clear and proper. If you don't pay attention to the consciousness of the masses, to the backbone strength of your unit, and to its unique economic conditions, the nature of accounting in your unit will be out of step. It will become too blind, and that just won't work. And if you haven't managed well with a small accounting unit, how can you manage well by enlarging the unit?"

Having finished his talk about Dazhai and Xiyang, Chen Yonggui went on to present his views on Gansu. He had inspected Jingyuan County, and he now praised the Commune Party Secretary of Han Flat Spring as a man of great resolve and vision. To be able to turn the red sandy soil into fertile fields that could produce two crops a year amounting to a thousand *jin* per *mu* was truly no small deed. With its vast stretches of flat land and with the Yellow River for irrigation, the place had a lot of potential.

After that, Chen started talking about Dingxi. With 80 percent of its territory arid, mountainous, uneven terrain, with its shallow layer of productive topsoil and its abysmal lack of fertilizer, Dingxi had been unable to achieve high yields. These circumstances, he said, made the area suitable for land reconstruction. The place was not as barren as North Hebei's Shashiyu.[1] In Shashiyu people carried soil from great distances to create fields on top of slate. They walked a thousand Chinese miles, carried ten thousand loads of earth, for a field one *mu* in size.

"What you've got here," said Chen Yonggui, "is a layer of soil a thousand meters deep; it won't take that much labor to level some of it. The problem of fuel can be solved, too. If you plant trees, they will grow very fast. You can use wood for fuel, which is infinitely better than burning wheat straw. Who says you can't solve the fuel problem?"

But grain production was not Chen Yonggui's only concern. At the Conference, he also touched upon the question of the over-all development of Gansu Province.

"Let's say that each person can plant three or four *mu* of land," he said. "Over here, all you plant on the four *mu* is grain; over there you have three *mu*, but you plant forage grass for livestock on one, and trees

1. Shashiyu was a village of beggars living in huts on some barren ledges. Inspired by Dazhai, the refugees organized themselves to create fields by carrying in soil from long distances. They even dug a tunnel through the mountain to get at the good soil on the other side. After several years of hard labor they created a model community that did not appear rocky. Acres and acres of solid bedrock had all been covered with soil that grew bountiful crops. (W.H.H.)

on another. Would you be left with no money to spend? If all you plant is grain, all you need is one calamity. If your yields drop, you'll be short of grain. You just might get a higher yield if you plant a smaller area, because your effort would be concentrated; both your fertilizer and your labor force would be concentrated. How could you be left with no money? How can you say that these conditions are not good? All we have in Xiyang are rocky mountains. If we want to plant a tree or make a field, we have to drill into the rocks to make holes for dynamite. We have to blast the hillsides and create hollows to which we carry soil from far away. Only then can we plant something. You don't have to do anything like that here! You've got soil without the explosions—wherever you dig, it's soil. Why can't you plant trees? Why can't you create woodlots? Why can't you solve your fuel problem? And why can't you make compost from straw and increase the organic content of your soil? Plant some forage grass, plant some trees, plant some medicinal herbs. Look, it would be so easy to clear out the land and level your fields!"

Chen Yonggui felt that he had said enough, that he had said all there was to say. There was not much use talking if one didn't get down and do some hard work.

On October 5, 1973, Chen Yonggui went to inspect Shaanxi Province. He delivered a long speech at the conference of cadres organized by the Shaanxi Provincial Committee. He explained the situation in Dazhai and Xiyang by saying that the spirit of Yanan had moved to Xiyang. But as he moved on to comment on the problems in Shaanxi, his tone became even sterner than it had been in Gansu and he made quite a few suggestions. He particularly singled out South Five Top People's Commune for criticism.

"They have very good conditions in South Five Top, both in terms of soil quality and water," he said. "Why don't they level their fields? They should choose a piece of land to work on, depending on the size of their labor force, level it and make a field. Their yields are not likely to drop the following year, in fact, they will most probably increase. If we had conditions like theirs, I don't know how many fields we would have built already. It would be really great if we had such promising natural conditions! We would have turned all the slopes into fields producing high, stable yields."

But, he added, learning from Dazhai was not about talking big, it was all about doing things. He told about how, in 1957, Dazhai's *per-mu* yields were 320 *jin*. In 1958 they were 580 *jin*—an increase of 260 *jin*. When he went to a mobilization meeting in Taiyuan, he was convinced his village would have to be "number one" that time. He never suspected it would not even make the honor roll. Others turned out to be "thousand-*jin* Counties," "ten-thousand-*jin* Communes," and "satellite Production Brigades." The following year, four comrades carried out an investigation and said that all those "thousand-*jin* Counties," ten-thousand-*jin* Communes," and "satellite Production Brigades" were just empty talk.

"That's why talking big is no good," concluded Chen Yonggui. "You have to do the actual work."

During the Conference Chen Yonggui talked about the problem of land consolidation, the merging of private plots, explaining how it had been done in Dazhai and Xiyang but stressing again that conditions had to be right. He also warned that accounting units should not be arbitrarily expanded. He outlined what happened when the level of the accounting unit, and thus of income sharing, was set too high, that is at the Brigade or village level, rather than at the team or village neighborhood level.

"The problems that Comrade Chen Yonggui pointed out do exist here in Shaanxi," Provincial Party Secretary Li Ruishan remarked when Chen finished his speech. "We must use the revolutionary driving force of this East Wind and set off a new upsurge of the 'In Agriculture, Learn From Dazhai' movement. We will also prepare Comrade Chen Yonggui's speech for publication and request that every production team study it, carry out a serious comparative self-examination, work out a plan, and send the Provincial Committee a written report about it."

From that time on, different regions kept requesting, and the Central Committee kept making special arrangements, for Chen Yonggui to visit various Provinces, municipalities and autonomous regions, in order to observe and give speeches. Wherever he went, he publicized the experience of Dazhai and Xiyang and expressed his views on the host locality.

After visiting Gansu and Shaanxi Chen Yonggui undertook an even larger assignment, a request from the Central Committee that he make an inspection tour of the three Northeastern Provinces. He traveled with the heads of two central ministries, Agriculture-Forestry, and Hydraulics-Electricity, and with the head of the State Planning Commission. His party also included outstanding village leaders from Xiyang County.

When Chen Yonggui arrived in the Northeast, the Province of Liaoning was just holding an "In Agriculture Learn From Dazhai" On-the-Spot Conference in Shenyang. Chen Yonggui was there to attend the meeting in person and pass on his valuable experience. He was also there to inspect and instruct. Naturally, his arrival would receive an enthusiastic reception from the leading cadres of Liaoning's Party, political and military establishment. Big posters in the streets carried slogans like "Learn from Dazhai, catch up with Xiyang" and "We warmly welcome Comrade Chen Yonggui's inspection and instruction."

Beginning on January 26, 1974, Chen Yonggui attended the Conference while also leading his group on visits to several Counties, Communes and Production Brigades. On January 29 and 30, Chen Youtang talked about the experience of Xiyang's Rock Flat Production Brigade in learning from Dazhai. Li Suoshou and Zhao Zhiwu gave separate reports on conditions in South Knoll Production Brigade before and after the campaign to learn from Dazhai. Zhang Bin related how Red Water People's Commune waited for three years, observed for three years, calculated for three years, and finally worked for three years on its project. Guo Fenglian, former leader of the "Iron Girls," now Party Secretary of Dazhai,explained the process of Dazhai's growth. In the end, Chen Yonggui delivered his speech.

After the speech, he assembled all cadres above the prefectural Party Committee level for an informal discussion. Wherever Chen Yonggui had gone in Liaoning, he had observed red banners unfurling, as vast numbers of people went ahead with field construction on soil already frozen solid to a depth of three feet. At the meeting, Chen Yonggui affirmed Liaoning's achievements in learning from Dazhai, but he also pointed out some existing problems.

"Isn't this planting of red banners and constructing of fields on the third day of the New Year perhaps just a show for my benefit? Do you usually do this work when the ground is frozen so hard? I am always on the alert for such displays and I insist that nothing be done for show. You have to learn from Dazhai in a genuine, down-to-earth way. You don't build socialism just for the sake of coping with an individual."

After the inspection of Liaoning, Chen Yonggui attended the Jilin Provincial "In Agriculture Learn From Dazhai" On-the-Spot Conference. The meeting was conducted in the same way as the one in Liaoning. The participants listened to presentations by local Model Workers, then the comrades from Dazhai and Xiyang passed on their valuable experiences, and finally Chen Yonggui delivered his speech. During this trip to Jilin, Chen Yonggui particularly emphasized the problems of transforming saline-alkaline soils and soil amelioration.

On February 3, 1974, in the evening, Chen Yonggui's party flew to the Heilongjiang provincial capital, the city of Harbin. Due to the special connection between Daqing and Dazhai, Chen Yonggui only made a brief stopover in Harbin before boarding a train that took him to Daqing city.

There had been no actual association between Daqing and Dazhai, and the two never established any business contacts. For many years, in fact, neither knew very much about the other. Only because of a single slogan uttered by Chairman Mao did the two become brothers under the Red Sun, and their relations become closely coordinated.

In the early morning of the next day, February 5th, Chen Yonggui's train stopped in Daqing. All leading cadres of Daqing's party, political and military establishment approached the train to greet his group. During the morning and afternoon of that same day, Chen Yonggui visited the first oil well at Daqing Oil Field, and then went to see the widow of Daqing's Iron Man Wang Jinxi. Chen Yonggui and Wang Jinxi first laid the foundation of their friendship at the Third National People's Congress. They then got to know each other during the interval between the Third National People's Congress and the Ninth Party Congress. Since numerous occasions arose that threw them together by the time of the Ninth Congress they were true friends who kept no secrets from each other. When Wang Jinxi became ill, Chen Yonggui visited him at the hospital. When Wang Jinxi passed away, Chen Yonggui grieved the passing of a trusted comrade.

When Chen Yonggui walked across the threshold of Mrs. Wang's home during his inspection tour of Daqing, his appearance moved Mrs. Wang deeply. Tears welled in her eyes as she shook his hand and thanked him for coming. Chen Yonggui inquired in great detail about Mrs. Wang's family and her health, prompting her to thank him again. Chen Yonggui told her that China should never forget the spirit of Iron Man Wang Jinxi as it cast off its label as an oil-poor country. Daqing was truly able to forge ahead when conditions allowed it and was able to create conditions for forging ahead where no such conditions already existed, precisely because it stuck to the spirit of Iron Man Wang Jinxi. And so its oil production increased from year to year. Excited, Mrs. Wang said that, when it came to creating conditions for forging ahead, Dazhai did a better job than Daqing.

That evening, Daqing Oil Field held a party in honor of Chen Yonggui, which included a program of entertainment. Chen Yonggui's visit to Daqing ended with mutual encouragement and learning from each other's strong points and weaknesses.

Later, on February 5th, Chen Yonggui officially attended the Heilongjiang Provincial "In Agriculture Learn From Dazhai" On-the-Spot Conference. Having seen how rich the soil in Heilongjiang was, while the grain yields remained relatively low, Chen Yonggui expressed his dissatisfaction to the Conference. "If I could move soil like yours to our place, you would see some real grain production!" he said.

Dressed in a long fleece-lined coat and a leather hat, he faced freezing winds on his various inspection trips, and wherever he went he saw piles of horse dung on the roads that nobody bothered to collect. Since there was not much manure to be seen in the fields, he criticized the local leaders who rode with him in his car: "You folks here sure don't know how to grow crops," he declared. "Not putting any manure on the crops shows how recklessly blind people here are. On the roads alone you could be collecting so much horse dung to use on your fields. Don't you think that would raise your yields?"

"With our soil conditions here, do we still need to use horse manure?" they asked, surprised.

Quite a few people back then said they were not familiar with such a practice. They only gradually came to realize that adding manure, even to their good-quality soil, would still benefit crop growth.

Chen Yonggui later used every opportunity to inspect as many places as possible so as to familiarize himself with agricultural conditions in the whole of China. Most often, he used the occasion of various provincial, municipal and regional on-the-spot "Learn from Dazhai" meetings to popularize the experiences of Dazhai and Xiyang and point out the way for local development. While on an inspection tour of the most remote region of the motherland, Tibet, he noticed that the Tibetan people used a very primitive, backward method to thresh their highland barley. He immediately suggested that they start using the roller-press method, which would increase harvesting efficiency many-fold.

It was then, during the first year of his service as Vice-Premier, that Chen Yonggui, while touring here and there, started contemplating what kind of leader he should be, and the concept of his "three-thirds system" method of work, described earlier, began to form in his mind. But once the State Council approved of his plan, his daily duties at the Central Committee level and the theoretical studies that all Central leaders earnestly engaged in, left him little time to practice it effectively. Before long, "the Shanxi problem" shoved all else aside, occupying all his thoughts and all his anergies. Let me give a brief account of what happened.

On February 9, 1974, just as Chen Yonggui was carefully probing into the problems of agriculture in the great northern wilderness of Heilongjiang, he received an urgent cable from the Central Committee, asking him to return to Beijing that very day. He boarded a special plane that afternoon, and come evening attended a meeting of the Political Bureau at the Great Hall of the People in Tiananmen Square. The central topic of the meeting was "the Shanxi problem." Following a suggestion by Premier Zhou Enlai, the meeting charged Chen Yonggui with finding concrete solutions for problems in Shanxi. The Central Committee intended to have him promptly thrash out the rights and wrongs, and strengthen the unity between two factions that contended in senseless and interminable conflict.

After the meeting, that very same night, Chen Yonggui received a long-distance call that interrupted everything for a pressing family matter. The call was from Xiyang and informed him that his younger brother, raised by his mother in the Yang family of Heshun, but long thought to be dead, was still very much alive and was planning to come to Xiyang to reunite with him. Chen Yonggui had no choice but to shelve Shanxi for the time being and ask Premier Zhou for a leave of absence.

The following morning Chen Yonggui took an official vehicle and returned to Xiyang to entertain his younger brother, born of the same parents. It was the thirteenth day of the Lunar New Year and the area around Heshun and Xiyang suffered a big snowstorm. The mountain ridges were overlain with a pure, silver mantle that made road traffic difficult and dangerous. But, the two families had already agreed to meet on this particular day. A tractor from Heshun carried the entire Yang household to the border with Xiyang County, where Chen Yonggui's driver, Wang Tianbao, met them with a jeep and drove them to Dazhai. The Yangs were not used to riding in cars, so they got carsick and threw up, but they readily endured such suffering in order to meet their renowned, high-placed relative from Dazhai.

Chen Yonggui's household had also been making preparations for several days. They started a big fire in the kitchen to prepare food for the family get-together. When the two brothers saw each other at last, they broke into tears, remembering the old days when their mother had cared for them. After the initial meeting, Chen Yonggui took them to see the lantern display on the streets of the Xiyang County seat. He entrusted his wife, son and daughter with the rest of their visit, while he busied himself with the Shanxi problem and the routine Central Committee duties. On February 12th in the evening he boarded the official vehicle and returned to Beijing.

Back in Beijing, Chen Yonggui listened to many accounts that Shanxi's leaders from various walks of life came to tell. Imbued with the spirit of conciliation mandated by the Central Committee, he then went back to Taiyuan to find a viable solution to the Shanxi problem. He spent almost three months there, holding many meetings, communicating relevant Central Committee directives, and employing various means to guide each of Shanxi's two factions into adopting a realistic, critical attitude toward their own organization and a conciliatory attitude toward the opposition. The war of the two Shanxi factions had raged hot and cold for many years, over many issues, and on a broad scale; it was very difficult to strike proper balance between them quickly. At one point in mid-April 1974, after months of effort, Chen Yonggui got angry and decided to dump the Shanxi problem and let the Central Committee decide what to do about it. On his way back to Beijing, Chen Yonggui did not board an official vehicle as prescribed. Instead, he booked a berth on a regular train and asked for reimbursement when he got back to the Capital. The Security Bureau of the Central Committee promptly reported the incident to its superiors.

On the day after Chen Yonggui's return to Beijing, Premier Zhou invited him to Zhongnanhai, and immediately raised the issue of discipline.

"Comrade Chen Yonggui, why didn't you use the official vehicle to return to Peking? Why didn't you notify the Central Committee? What if something had happened?" he remonstrated.

Chen Yonggui sat on the sofa, with an expression on his face considerably different from the one he used to have when meeting with the Premier. He was low-spirited and dumbstruck, not even in the mood to smoke a cigarette or have a cup of tea. As Premier Zhou aimed his stern gaze at him, he was unable to utter a word for a long time. After turning it over several times in his mind, he finally summoned the confidence to confess his troubles.

"Premier," he said in despair, "it is not that I don't accept the task given me by the Central Committee, but I really can't function on that level. I'm not used to this kind of work. I just can't solve the Shanxi problem."

Premier Zhou's face relaxed a little. He calmed down somewhat and quickly lit a cigarette.

"It is still quite appropriate for you to solve the Shanxi problem," he said gravely. "Just maintain your Party spirit and don't take any factional positions. I'm sure the Shanxi problem can be solved. The Chairman once made a famous remark: 'What's work? Work is struggle!' The resolution of the Shanxi problem depends on whether or not you have the spirit to struggle."

Chen Yonggui felt as though he had been wounded in action, but he did not want to burden the Premier any further. He had no choice but to accept the Premier's directive. The following day he took the official vehicle back to Taiyuan.

It was not until the evening of July 16, 1974, two months later, that the Political Bureau of the Central Committee received leading cadres from Shanxi at the Great Hall of the People. And it was not until the Political Bureau circulated the key points of speeches made by the leading Central Committee cadres during their discussion of the Shanxi problem, that anyone was able to stabilize the situation in Shanxi, the most fractious province of them all.

Chen Yonggui's educational level was not high and he lacked experience in work at the Central Committee level, but he was always able to listen to opinions of the senior comrades and propagate the spirit of Dazhai. Under his care, China's agriculture did develop gradually. During the few years when the "Learn from Dazhai" movement was at its climax, gratifying breakthroughs occurred in Shandong and Hunan, which, relying on learning from Dazhai, transformed impoverished local conditions. Shandong's Yutai County increased its grain production 2.6 times in just eight years, and cadres in Hunan's Xiu County took part in collective labor, turning this practice into a general trend. Chen Yonggui may have been a peasant who could not effectively use his pen, but he possessed an unexpectedly good head, he talked very logically and his summaries were consistently well organized and methodical. People were always convinced by the way he presented an issue. In addition to his most famous axioms such as, "You cannot learn from Dazhai in ease and comfort; you cannot change the face of the country by playing it cool and smooth," and "Learn from Dazhai, catch up with Dazhai; you cannot begin to learn if you hold no power," he also had a dialectical response to natural disasters. When a disaster struck, his instructions to subordinates were: "When it comes to catastrophe those who know what to look for see the potential for strengthening ideology, those who don't know what to look for see the failed crops."

At times he even expressed a certain optimism on the question of misfortune.

"If there is a disaster year after year, you cannot delay fighting it year after year." Thus, in his eyes, you would steel yourself for all eventualities.

In order to accrue good luck in the fight against disasters, he even used literary language to explain them:

"Suffering losses from natural disasters is like paying tuition to the Heavens. Once you've paid it, you are entitled to find out what they can teach you!"

That is how he expressed his basic philosophy that man can conquer nature.

Chen Yonggui was originally assigned to take charge of agriculture, but when the country verged on imminent danger, he had to help the Central Committee deal with other types of work. The big earthquake that struck Tangshan on July 26, 1976, turned into a rigorous test for Chen Yonggui. The earthquake happened soon after the consecutive deaths of Premier Zhou Enlai and Commander-in-Chief Zhu De; Chairman Mao Zedong's illness was at a critical juncture, and the Gang of Four tried to use the confusion to seize power.

Hua Guofeng headed up the group sent by the Central Committee to convey sympathy and solicitude to the people struck by the earthquake, but he was unable to go in person to the disaster area to direct the relief effort and so Chen Yonggui, as his deputy, went to Tangshan to confront the disaster along with the people of Tangshan, to live like everybody else in a tent, and to make concrete decisions regarding the rescue operation. When Chen Yonggui got there, 80 percent of the population of Tangshan had been injured and the number of known deaths had already surpassed 300,000. Chen Yonggui walked around the entire city and inspected the suburbs of Qianan and Yutian before he made a strategic policy decision concerning rescue procedure. Under his direction, earthquake relief and preliminary salvage work were brought to a satisfactory completion after one month.

Those were the footprints left by Chen Yonggui across China. Some of the marks his feet left were sound and strong, but one also sees some twisting and turning tracks here and there. The eight years of life at the top of China's political circles left Chen Yonggui with much joy of success as well as the worry of failure. Be that as it may, when later generations reopen the capsules containing the social records of his time to look for Chen Yonggui, they will, more likely than not, walk away cherishing his memory.

Thunder across the plains.

The white sheep-stomach-weave hand towel from the Taihang Mountain range that created a stir in Peking made astonishing steps across the national border in the mid-1970s and emerged on the territory of Latin America. On that occasion international media gave Chen Yonggui high praise.

In the early morning on March 27, 1975, a special plane that was to fly from Beijing to Mexico already had its suspended doors wide open, waiting for Chen Yonggui and the members of his traveling party to embark. As he stepped up the staircase, waving at the people on the ground, Hua Guofeng, Li Xiannian and other party and state leaders waved back, wishing him a successful trip. Other members of Chen Yonggui's delegation were Vice-Minister of Agriculture and Forestry Xiao Peng; Director of the Department of the Americas of the Ministry of Foreign Affairs, Lin Ping; Permanent Member of the Shanxi Revolutionary Committee and Chairperson of the Xiyang County Dazhai Production Brigade Revolutionary Committee, Guo Fenglian; Deputy Chairman of the Linxian County Revolutionary Committee from Henan Province, Li Zongchang;[1] Chen Yonggui's secretaries, Jiao Huancheng and Li Renpei, and his security guards, Yang Fengxiang and Zhang Yinchang. They were all entrusted by the Party and the people to make a sustained effort toward establishing friendship between China and the people of the Third World. For the first time in his life Chen Yonggui donned a Sun Yatsen-style tunic suit and, as a represen-

1. Li Zongchang was famous for his role in building the Red Flag Canal, which brought water across stupendous mountains and cliffs to Lin County and transformed that whole Honan area. (W.H.H.)

tative of the dignity and prestige of the People's Republic of China, embarked on his second international tour.

The decision to visit Mexico was made in response to repeated invitations from the Mexican President Luis Echeverria Alvarez, after his April 23, 1973 visit to Dazhai. It was the first trip by a Chinese government leader to a Latin American country.

Chen Yonggui knew very well that Mexico exerted great influence among Latin American countries. Echeverria's government held a clear-cut position opposing hegemonism, and played a definite role in uniting Latin America and the Third World in the struggle against hegemony. Friendship between Mexico and China developed rapidly after President Echeverria's trip to China. The purpose of Chen Yonggui's trip was mainly to further develop the friendly relations and cooperation between the two countries. Also, Mexico wanted to benefit from China's international political influence to strengthen its own position, while also drawing on certain experiences from Dazhai to boost its domestic agricultural production and mitigate its internal contradictions. Consequently, Chen Yonggui was amply prepared for the task entrusted to him.

The Chinese government attached high-level importance to the trip. Preparations for it began on March 20, 1975, through a series of eight meetings held at the Capital West Guest House Conference Room. The Ministry of Foreign Affairs conducted special training, examining all aspects of this unusual linking of two continents. The Political Bureau held a meeting at the Great Hall of the People on March 21st, where it approved Chen Yonggui's trip overseas and adopted the "Eight Instructions on the Guiding Principles for All Activities During Vice-Premier Chen Yonggui's Trip to Mexico" prepared by the Ministry of Foreign Affairs of the People's Republic of China.

On the way to Mexico, the plane made brief stops at Tokyo Airport and at Ottawa in Canada, then continued its flight to Mexico City that same afternoon.

The Mexican government staged a grand welcoming ceremony at the airport. When Chen Yonggui stepped from the plane, Mexican President Luis Echeverria Alvarez cheerfully came forward to shake his hand and greet him warmly: "Welcome! Welcome!"

Caiandelo Loweilosa Wade, Mexico's Minister of Hydraulics; Oscar Bulaoaier Aileila, Minister of Agriculture and Animal Husbandry; Alvaro Echeverria, the President's son; and Yao Guang, China's Ambassador to Mexico, were also at the airport to welcome Chen Yonggui.

An orchestra played the national anthems of China and Mexico, and a multi-gun salute was fired. In addition to the people assembled by arrangement of the Mexican government, crowds of town and country folk had poured into the airport. They held Chen Yonggui portraits in their hands and shouted: "Welcome! Welcome!" As Chen Yonggui walked by them, the slogan "Mao Zedong, Chen Yonggui" also emerged amid the general shouts of welcome. Chen Yonggui kept greeting them, waving his hand, nodding his head, smiling. Accompanied by President Echeverria, he reviewed the guard of honor. Then a group of little girls presented all members of Chen Yonggui's delegation with fresh flowers.

Giving expression to the friendship and good will between the people of China and Mexico, Chen Yonggui spoke to the welcoming crowd: "We come here today in response to the kind invitation from the government of Mexico, mainly to learn from the people of Mexico who are our brothers, and to take back your advanced experience and technology so they may flourish in China. We hope this visit will help promote friendship and mutual understanding between the people of our two countries, and that it will bring about the next step in the development of friendly relations and cooperation between China and Mexico."

This was the prevailing atmosphere as Chen Yonggui and his party became high-level guests at Mexico's State Guesthouse.

On March 28th, Chen Yonggui placed a wreath at the Monument of Independence and visited the Museum of Anthropology. At 12.30 PM, he went to the Presidential Palace to pay an official visit to President Echeverria. As the delegation entered the reception hall, President Echeverria happily came forward to greet them, shaking Chen Yonggui's hand as he spoke: "I have been expecting your visit for some time, hoping you would bring us China's and Dazhai's experience!" he said.

"I have come on this visit in order to learn from your country and take your advanced experiences back with me," responded Chen Yonggui.

Chen Yonggui introduced the members of his delegation to the President, and the President shook hands with all of them. When Chen Yonggui introduced Guo Fenglian and Li Zongchang, President Echeverria shook Guo Fenglian's hand most warmly.

"Dazhai's new generation! We are old friends!" he exclaimed.

Picking out Li Zongchang, he said: "You are the boss of the Red Flag Canal! Welcome! Most welcome!"

On March 29th Chen Yonggui, his party and several of his distinguished hosts flew by helicopter to Mexico's major agricultural region in the northwest—the States of Sonora and Sinaloa. When Chen Yonggui's delegation emerged on Sonora's soil, local villagers came out, dressed in national costumes as though it were a festival. They carried Chen Yonggui portraits and played folk music to welcome Vice-Premier Chen. After his visit to Dazhai, President Echeverria had not only reported on his experiences to the Mexican government, he had also shown the movie *Dazhai's Fields* in villages throughout the country. Mexican peasants welcomed the sight of the people of Dazhai organizing collective production and going all out to create land, build irrigation systems, and practice scientific farming. Mexican village heads, too, followed Dazhai's experiences with considerable interest. As a result, land reform activities and a village collectivization movement stirred in vast rural areas of Mexico.

During Chen Yonggui's visit, the leader of the Organization of Villages of the State of Sonora gave a speech welcoming the guests. When he asked the guests to convey his warm regards to Chairman Mao Zedong and Premier Zhou Enlai, the entire audience stood up and applauded enthusiastically.

In view of the request by the Mexican side and the arrangement by the Chinese Government for Chen Yonggui to visit the entire country within a few brief days, land transportation was obviously ruled out. Instead the party boarded a helicopter again and circled over an area more than 300 kilometers in diameter, getting a bird's-eye view of the State of Sonora. The focal point of the tour was water conservancy: three big dams and an irrigation system nestled among the hills. The State financed most of these projects but counted on individual village heads to implement them. Seeing the results, Chen Yonggui praised the fighting spirit of Mexican people.

"Compared to the spirit of Dazhai, we lag far behind," the local leaders kept saying.

On March 31st, Chen Yonggui, moving about by helicopter, visited marshland reclamation projects, modern pig farms and water conservancy projects in several States. He also visited famous cities and pyramids of an ancient civilization. On the evening of April 2nd Ambassador Yao Guang gave a reception in honor of Vice Premier Chen Yonggui's visit to Mexico. On April 3rd in the evening, just before the end of his visit, Chen Yonggui gave a banquet in honor of President Echeverria and his wife. On behalf of the Chinese government, Chen Yonggui presented the Mexican President with a couple of pandas, five tractors and small quantities of improved varieties of rice, soybean, and sorghum seeds. As a personal gift, he gave the President a flower bed. President Echeverria presented Chen Yonggui with a large elephant, improved varieties of corn and soybean seeds, and several drip-irrigation systems for China, of which one was to be given to Dazhai.

During Chen Yonggui's visit, Mexico's official press often carried the news of the visit in large print. A film week, popularizing Dazhai's achievements in transforming barren mountains and unruly rivers through its spirit of self-reliance and arduous struggle was also organized in honor of the occasion. It deeply inspired many Mexican peasants.

According to the prearranged schedule, Chen Yonggui was supposed to end his visit to Mexico on April 4th and return to China. Due to a snowstorm, however, his plane was delayed. Thus he had an opportunity to visit the Mexico City Municipal Industrial Exhibition. It was April 5, 1975, when he finally left Mexico City. As he parted from the crowds that came to the airport to see him off, his portrait appeared again. People waved their hands toward his figure, about to enter the plane, and shouted goodbye repeatedly.

As the plane left the ground, Chen Yonggui dispatched a cable to President Echeverria, expressing heartfelt gratitude for the warm and unstinting hospitality received.

On his way back to China, Chen Yonggui made a brief stop in the Rumanian capital, Bucharest. In the morning he visited several of

Bucharest's new residential districts and cultural facilities. In the evening, G. Ledulescu, a leading Communist and a Vice-Premier and several other Rumanian Party and Government leaders gave a banquet in his honor. On April 7th, Chen Yonggui boarded his plane and flew to Xinjiang, returning finally to Beijing on April 8th. There he was greeted at the airport by Deng Xiaoping, Wu De, Wang Zhen, Li Suwen and other Party and State leaders, who congratulated him on the success of his trip to Mexico.

Back in Peking, Chen Yonggui held a meeting at the Capital West Guest House 1975. Summing up the trip he said: "Our long journey not only strengthened China's cooperation with Mexico and other third-world countries, it also enables us to learn about Mexico's advanced experience with irrigation and water conservancy engineering."

He went on to describe Mexico as "a well-known King of Corn," and reviewed some of Mexico's experience in the cultivation of improved varieties of corn, which he had been able to observe and study at the Mexican Corn Experimental Station.

Successful as the trip was, however, a few negative episodes stained Chen Yonggui's reputation as one adept at polished diplomacy. When his delegation arrived in Mexico City, Ambassador Yao Guang invited everyone to the Embassy, and instructed them to be particularly mindful of what they said and did during the trip. If there was anything they were unsure of and needed to discuss, they should come to the Embassy to talk it over. Chen Yonggui expressed his approval right away, but he really was not careful enough afterward. He was not able to anticipate and forestall various faux-pas made by his delegates and, even in one case, by their leader.

First, every place the delegation went the population greeted it with boundless hospitality. Crowds of people gave them presents, flowers, and even plants. When some members of the delegation could not carry the gifts any longer, they threw some of the plants away right in front of their hosts. Some comrades from the Ministry of Foreign Affairs criticized this as lack of respect for the hosts. When Chen Yonggui found out about this rudeness, he gave them a big lecture at the State Guesthouse.

Even more disturbing was an incident involving foreign currency. According to the rules governing travel abroad, each person received the equivalent of twenty Chinese dollars in foreign currency for the purchase of souvenirs. Ambassador Yao Guang had told Chen Yonggui at the Embassy that Little Guo (meaning Guo Fenglian), Little Jiao (meaning Jiao Huancheng), and Little Zhang (meaning Zhang Yinchang) wanted to buy foreign watches as souvenirs, and that, since Old Chen and he were fellow countrymen (Yao Guang was from Xiyang, too), he would add some money if necessary so they could buy the watches they wanted.

Chen Yonggui did not say what he thought of this in front of Yao Guang, but he could not control his temper later. When they got back to the guesthouse he gathered Guo Fenglian, Jiao Huancheng and Zhang Yinchang together and reprimanded them sternly: "What? You want to use foreign currency to buy yourself wrist watches? Even Premier Zhou wears the Shanghai brand, so why do you have to be so special?"

On this particular question, in terms of setting strict demands on himself and others, Chen Yonggui performed very well. Although he was a Vice-Premier, he did not wear a wrist watch at all; for many years he carried around a pocket watch. The faux pas was: He was not supposed to lose his temper before foreigners in a foreign country, yet he did. Looking very displeased, he kept lecturing Guo Fenglian, Jiao Huancheng and Zhang Yinchang, admonishing them for trying to act special, for not paying attention to what effect this would have on others. Within earshot of the Mexican staff he went on and on, until well after midnight. This lapse of diplomatic protocol on his part later gave rise to slanderous gossip that rippled through elite circles in Beijing. People attributed it to his rustic background.

Being of peasant origin, however, Chen Yonggui was always outspoken and direct. He could not be otherwise. At the same time, he always maintained a simple and thrifty personal style. He did not use foreign currency during his Mexican trip to buy any souvenirs. He just bought a few packs of French cigarettes, which he smoked en route. When he came back to China, he took off the government issue Sun Yatsen-style tunic suit and put on his customary everyday clothing. He did the same in 1976, when he led a delegation to Cambodia. After that trip, too, he took off the Sun Yatsen-style tunic suit and resumed where he had left off—just being himself.

CHAPTER—30

WAS THE VENTURE A SUCCESS?

Chen Yonggui sat in his apartment in the building reserved for senior cadres, sighing as he swallowed mouthfuls of bitter tea: "Back in those days I couldn't resist hitting out in all directions and now I can't avoid drawing fire against myself. I anticipated back then that there would be a day when we reached the end of the rope, but this did not come true the way I imagined it might."

From the Agricultural Conference of the Fourteen Provinces of the Northern Region up to 1978, the higher authorities transferred over thirty cadres out of Xiyang, to push forward the national "Learn from Dazhai" campaign. Opinions on this matter have been widely divergent. The fairest judge of it will, of course, be history. Rumor has it that after Hu Yaobang became General Secretary of the Central Committee of the Communist Party of China, he had an informal chat with Wang Qian during his inspection tour of the city of Chengdu, and this issue came up during their conversation. Wang Qian had been the Provincial Party Committee Secretary of Shanxi from 1974 to 1978 so he was, naturally, quite familiar with the transfers. Yet he felt uneasy talking about it because, he said, the issue would implicate and highlight the "old men."

He was implying that the whole situation had developed in response to the wishes of Chairman Mao Zedong and Premier Zhou Enlai.

Back then, Chairman Mao and Premier Zhou felt that the problem of China's agriculture could be solved by popularizing Dazhai's experience in agriculture as job number one. On one occasion, Premier Zhou told Chen Yonggui that Xiyang should export not only grain but human talent as well. Every relatively good, grass-roots Party Branch Secretary was fit for transfer. Human talent, he said, had to be developed, trained, and made available constantly. Later, during Li Xiannian's second trip to Xiyang, he also brought up the issue of Xiyang's export of human talent. He elaborated on this tentative idea just as he was boarding the railroad car to leave. Throughout the country these proposals of the leaders made themselves felt and resulted in urgent demands on Xiyang. Caught between fine wishes and urgent demands, Chen Yonggui made his experience and the human talent he developed available.

After the 1970 Northern Regional Conference on Agriculture, the Party Secretary of the Grass Gully Production Brigade in Shouyang County, the Model Worker Ji Panhua, made several requests to the Shanxi Provincial Committee and the Regional Committee for Central Shanxi, asking that comrades from Xiyang be sent to help in his work. Shouyang County, with its 800,000 *mu* of land, was twice the size of Xiyang County, but it was unable to increase its harvests and its people still suffered from hunger. Ji Panhua looked for an opportunity during every conference of Model Workers to bring up the matter of outside help with the leadership. The Central Shanxi Regional Party Committee Secretary, Jia Jun, repeated the request to Chen Yonggui. Finally, in 1973, Chen Yonggui agreed to send out some people. Upon approval by Chairman Mao Zedong and the Party Central Committee, several old Xiyang cadres—Zhang Huaiying, Wang Guike, Fan Xifeng and Li Aihu—went to Shouyang County to take charge.

After assuming office in Shouyang, Zhang Huaiying enthusiastically embarked on the promotion of the spirit of Dazhai, and worked hard to eliminate factionalism. Within two years, he managed to unite the two factions that had until then been irreconcilably hostile to each other, on the common ground of learning from Dazhai. He was particularly careful to combine Xiyang's experience in learning from Dazhai with the concrete situation in Shouyang, adapting his working method to local needs and local people. After he started work no unnatural deaths occurred in the County. As a result, the situation in Shouyang changed drastically in just two years: From a grain output of 45,000 metric tons the first year, the grain production rose to 50,000 metric tons by the second year, turning Shouyang from a consumer of State-supplied grain into a grain supplier. The Ministry of Agriculture and Forestry spent two months investigating Shouyang's experience in learning from Xiyang. Hua Guofeng mentioned it six times around that time, giving it his full approval. On September 15, 1975, during the "In Agriculture Learn From Dazhai" National Conference held at the tractor factory in Xiyang, Deng Xiaoping, in talking about Xiyang, brought up Shouyang.

"Xiyang was able to do it, but there is also Shouyang County, which achieved a turnabout in just two years. I have been there. In the past, the place was just like Dazhai, an incredibly poor place. And it turned around in just two years! In some cases it might take three years."

This was how the Central Committee leadership evaluated the work in Shouyang in those days.

After Xiyang's cadres fired the first shot in Shouyang, some leaders at the Central Committee started working on arrangements to send Xiyang's cadres elsewhere to spread Dazhai's experience. During the 1975 "In Agriculture Learn From Dazhai" National Conference, Hua Guofeng visited various parts of Xiyang County. After he saw the site of the new village built by the Rock Flat Production Brigade at Li Family Settlement People's Commune, Hua Guofeng told the Rock Flat Production Brigade Party Branch Secretary, Chen Youtang: "Youtang, you've done the Chens proud! Very proud! How about coming to our place to help us out?"

Based on Hua Guofeng's suggestion, and with the approval of Chen Yonggui and the Shanxi Provincial Party Committee, the Rock Flat Party Branch Secretary, Chen Youtang, and two county-level cadres, Ling Shihuai and Chen Youyuan, transferred out to Hua Guofeng's native County of Jiaocheng to take charge of local affairs. They transformed soil conditions, set up large water conservancy projects, and increased grain yields dramatically.

A transfer with the most resonance, however, was the appointment of Li Suoshou to become Party Secretary of Pingding County.

In 1975, Wang Qian, the Communist Party Secretary of Shanxi Province, first requested that Chen Yonggui transfer the South Knoll Party Secretary, Li Suoshou, to his native Pingding County to help put it on its feet. Chen Yonggui, however, did not approve. When Wang Qian arrived in Xiyang for the national conference on agriculture, he brought up the matter again.

While Chen Yonggui was keeping Wang Qian company at the Little Dining Room of the County Revolutionary Committee Guesthouse, the latter used the opportunity to relate the problems Pingding was having in detail. The County had a population of 240,000 but only 300,000 *mu* of crop land and, in spite of its dense population, agricultural production remained at a standstill for many years. Wang Qian laid out the reasons for Li Suoshou's transfer, and felt he had prevailed on Chen Yonggui, since the latter nodded his head in approval. During the banquet, Wang Qian poured himself a glass of wine, raised it respectfully with both hands, and offered a toast:

"Thank you, Vice-Premier Chen!"

Wang Qian usually addressed Chen Yonggui as "Old Chen" or "Comrade Chen Yonggui," certainly not Vice-Premier Chen. Shocked by the sudden formality, Chen Yonggui felt the "weight" of being called by his official title. He could not help but feel uncomfortable, so he proceeded to call Wang to account for it.

"What? What are you calling me?" protested Chen Yonggui, dismay on his face.

"Oh, I made a mistake. I'm calling you Old Chen."

Wang Qian laughed. Chen Yonggui laughed, too.

Later, Chen Yonggui accompanied the Central Committee leadership on a visit to South Knoll Production Brigade. Just before their departure, he privately left a word with the Brigade's Party Secretary, Li Suoshou: "Get ready to become a County official!"

The sentence left Li Suoshou baffled and anxious. In the evening, he went over to Dazhai to ask Chen Yonggui what it was all about.

"Could I be making up something like that?" Chen asked with a grin.

A few days later, the Provincial Committee sent down Li Suoshou's transfer order, and the Regional Committee Secretary for Central Shanxi, Jia Jun, talked to him formally and took care of the organizational procedures.

This is how Li Suoshou became the County Committee Secretary of Pingding. After he arrived in Pingding, based on the work of his predecessors Guo Cunhua and Qiao Suxiang, with the aid of Qiao Suxiang who remained in the County as the County Committee Deputy Secretary, and through his adoption of some new measures, Pingding achieved extraordinary results. On one hand, Li Suoshou vigorously promoted agricultural production, by advocating hard and honest labor and improvements in scientific farming. He brought about great changes in grain yields and turned Pingding, a perpetual recipient of grain subsidies, into a producer of surplus grain. On the other hand, he put no constraints on Pingding's sideline industrial production. Making the best use of local circumstances, he guided the development of Commune and Production Brigade enterprises, increasing gross income sharply. Given the problem of severe water shortages, he also undertook several large river-diversion projects, so that the hopes of Pingding County, unfulfilled for many years, now came true.

By transforming the face of Pingding, Li Suoshou attracted serious public attention. During the Second National Conference on Agriculture, Li Suoshou was invited to the podium to talk about his experiences. He was planning to read from a speech written for him by somebody else, when Li Xiannian announced how he felt about it.

"You made it all happen by your own true work. Why not tell us about it in your own true words?" suggested Li.

So Li Suoshou talked without a prepared draft. He used vivid examples to illustrate the nature of his work in Pingding. His words reverberated through the Conference. After the Conference, Li Xiannian personally saw to it that a reporter from the *People's Daily* went to Pingding to write a story about Li Suoshou. The result was the well-known long news report "The True Socialist Worker Li Suoshou" carried by the *People's Daily*. Thereafter, two famous Shanxi writers, Ma Feng and Sun Qian, went to live in Pingding for over a month, taking part in all activities including meals and meetings. They wrote the movie script *The New County Committee Secretary*, which later became the award-winning film *Tear Stains*.

After 1978 when Dazhai was criticized for ultra-leftism, Li Suoshou's work was also questioned and crudely attacked on several specious fronts. Li himself was transferred from Pingding and sent to raise chickens in an isolated Xiyang County Brigade, a tragic denouement to a remarkable career.

Xiyang County cadres chalked up great successes in other Counties. They also recorded a failure or two, one of them in Yuci County, near Taiyuan, the Provincial capital.

Around 1976, the Regional Committee Secretary for Central Shanxi, Jia Jun, and his Deputy Secretaries Li Hansuo and Lian Rongde made a special trip to Xiyang to report to Chen Yonggui on the paralysis of the Yuci County organization. They had already changed one crew of leaders with no result. The only way to break out of the standstill was to send someone from Xiyang. They asked the Old West Shelter Party Secretary, Li Wangmao, to take command in Yuci County. The project that Li Wangmao undertook after he became Old West Shelter Party Secretary—cutting through a rock mountain to bring in water—had gained him Chen Yonggui's high esteem. Chen Yonggui was not opposed to sending Li Wangmao to work in Yuci County.

And so Li Wangmao went to transform Yuci County. The work there was complicated by the ideological confusion that pervaded the County. When Li Wangmao arrived, he first took the lead doing physical labor, going so far as to carry buckets in and out of latrines to draw excrement from them. Yet, due to his lack of experience, an insufficient awareness of the degree of difficulty involved, his overly simple work style and a health problem, his performance in Yuci was not outstanding. As a result, he drew more than his fair share of criticism.

In 1978, the Central Committee focused attention on the transfer of cadres from Xiyang once again. Vice-Chairman Ye Jianying, who was studying the relationship between Daqing and Dazhai, initiated the matter.

"We have Dazhai on the surface, and Daqing underground. Can't we combine the two, so that there's a Daqing in Dazhai, and a Dazhai in Daqing?" he asked.

This proposition drew responses from other leading cadres on the Central Committee. On one occasion when Li Xishen[1], who was in charge of the day-to-day work in Xiyang, went to Beijing for a meeting, Li Xiannian invited him, together with Chen Yonggui, to his residence for a cinema show. Li Xishen accepted the invitation and arrived just as Li Xiannian was discussing the issue of Xiyang's cadre transfers with several other senior leaders on the Central Committee. The moment Li Xishen walked through the door, Li Xiannian greeted him.

"No,...oh, here's Li Xishen," he said in the same breath. "That Chen Yonggui of yours is too tight! The whole country wants his people, but he just won't give any away!"

"Chen Yonggui is a conservative," interjected Ji Dengkui. "A diehard! All he knows is how to guard his Xiyang!"

"I can't break down my own power base," laughed Chen Yonggui.

"It's a question of style," said Hua Guofeng in a mild tone of voice.

These top leaders were reaching out to get people from Xiyang because all those famous places in need of help were forcing the issue and making them do it. Dazhai's experience, after all, should be spread by the people from Xiyang County, Dazhai's home.

The period when Chen Yonggui acted as Vice-Premier was the time of most intense struggles between the so-called "Beijing faction" and "Shanghai faction"—that is to say, between the veteran cadres and the Gang-of-Four. The veteran cadres were on relatively intimate terms with Chen Yonggui at the time, and they were also fond of a culinary specialty from Xiyang—the "stretch" or "drawn" noodles. They could not keep from coming to Chen Yonggui's residence at Jiaodaokou for a different-tasting meal. The cook from Xiyang was an expert in this kind of food. He added baking soda and table salt to his dough and kneaded it neither too soft nor to hard, then he doubled and pulled it more times and stretched it into thinner strand than anyone else was able to do.

---

1. Li Xishen, after returning to his home village Five Family Flat, did such a good job in developing production and in capital construction that he was elevated to a County post. Later he was put in charge of the huge "West-Water-East" project to bring water through the mountain from the western slope of Xiyang County to the eastern slope of Xiyang County. (W.H.H.)

Not only did Chen Yonggui have a cook from Xiyang, he was quite a skilled cook himself. His youthful experience in the sesame-seed cake shop served as the basis for his later skill. Ji Dengkui liked to take a few sips with Chen Yonggui before eating the "drawn" noodles. In the midst of the clinking of glasses, he often took a "stab" at Chen Yonggui, accusing him of not allowing any Xiyang cadres to help other regions. He liked to prod him.

"Come on, you old diehard, bottoms up!" taunted Ji Dengkui.

With hands reaching for their cadres from below, and the mobilizing on the part of the leaders, Chen Yonggui, too, was eager to popularize Dazhai's experience. The raw grain that had been cooking for quite some time finally had turned into a steaming rice dish. An order was passed through the top decision-making level of the Central Committee of the Communist Party of China to transfer several people from Xiyang: Wang Jinzi to the Shanxi Provincial level as the Provincial Committee Deputy Secretary; Li Aihu and Fan Xifeng to Shouyang County as the County Committee Secretary and the County Committee Deputy Secretary; the Xiyang-promoted young Commune Secretary Guo Runtang to the foothills of Long White Mountain and the banks of the Songhua River in Heilongjiang Province. After this infusion of new blood into Heilongjiang's blood stream, Heilongjiang truly rose with force and spirit. Seeing the existing problems in the Nanjiang region, after he assumed his new duties there, Fan Xifeng set out the basic measures that were needed if the conditions of the local agricultural production were to be transformed. He took back a detailed report to the Provincial Committee Secretary, Yang Yichen, which received Yang's high praise. Li Aihu[1] was a young Prefectural Party Committee Secretary, whose work at every step revealed his great commanding gifts.

Chen Yonggui routinely saw all Xiyang outgoing cadres before they assumed their new posts. To this day, their tape recordings preserve Chen Yonggui's words, which reveal how heavily his ambition weighed on him.

"All my good men from Xiyang have been transferred out. It may be a good thing, but then again it may turn out to be a bad thing. If one

1. See page 398 for the incident when Li Aihu was chastised by Chen Yonggui for under-reporting grain yields. (W.H.H.)

day they should be ousted from their new positions, I wouldn't be surprised if people start saying that Chen Yonggui's hands had been extended too far, grabbing for too much power beyond Xiyang. Speaking of power: Mine is not negligible. I'm a Vice-Premier! But should a time like that come, a time of repudiation and ousting, that very power and influence will become a crime! If you want to go, fine, but do a good job. Don't make it possible for them to drive you out. I have great confidence in you, yet I feel worried at the same time. I'm afraid they'll send you packing!"

Coincidences, if one can use that word in this case, do happen. Chen Yonggui's words turned out to be prophetic. The transfer of so many cadres weakened Xiyang's backbone. Work in the home County suffered, and the cadres who had been transferred elsewhere were exposed in the end to undeserved reproach, demotion, suspension and banishment to the "cow sheds" of the boondocks.[1]

As the tide of history changed, this group of vigorous cadres that had been sent out from Xiyang was washed back, as shoddy goods diverted from export to domestic consumption, by an irresistible political ebb tide. For a while, some people ridiculed them, some found fault with them, some sympathized with them, while others simply sighed. History has proven that whether they rose or fell, floated or sank, their course always followed the undulations, the twists and turns, of Chen Yonggui's own career. Their reputation suffered the same fate as did Chen's. Whether their merits were real or fake will become evident once the tide reaches its nadir and begins to reverse itself. The fresh red fruit that they cultivated will then be appraised strictly on the basis of people's contrasting points of view. Some people may say it was sweet, others that it was bitter. Yet it is very hard to draw a clear line between the sweet and the bitter while the tide is running out.

---

1. During the Cultural Revolution, cadres transferred to the countryside to do manual work alongside the peasants were said to have been sent to the "cow shed." The practice did not end with that movement. The reform targeted large numbers of socialist road activists in office and sent them down to the "cow sheds" to raise pigs, graze sheep and herd cattle. The so-called "Literature of the Wounded" has been strangely silent on this subject. What's bad for the goose is apparently not bad for the gander. (W.H.H.)

As for Chen Yonggui's initiatives, at the end of the seventies when he came under attack, he was criticized for ultra-left extremism, particularly as exemplified by his pioneering labor allocation arrangements. These grew out of his prime goal in life, which was to advance toward Communism. Throughout his career, everything he did was based on two main principles that served the ultimate goal: Do things collectively and strive for scale. Implementing such principles, however, involved a process, a set of stages and modes of transition from one stage to another. Thus Chen Yonggui became particularly interested in the problems of transition and transitional forms of organization like his "special teams" that concentrated some of the labor power of small accounting units (production teams) to carry out large projects that laid a material base for larger accounting units (Production Brigades, or even township-sized Communes).[1] These teams created the necessary conditions for a transition from smaller to larger or, as collectivists saw it, from lower to higher.

Higher levels of organization mean higher levels of accounting units. The history of changes in accounting unit size in Xiyang is quite complicated. Beginning in the late 1950s, the whole County made the transition from elementary agricultural Producers' Cooperatives to advanced agricultural Producers' Cooperatives, setting up accounting units on the basis of individual natural villages. This later became known as "Production Brigade accounting." The Sixteen Village Regulations, later issued by the Central Committee, brought about a general reduction in the size of accounting units to the team level. This became known as "production team accounting." But at the time when Xiyang County cut back all of its accounting units to the team level, the

---

1. Special teams enabled a community organized in relatively small units to undertake large projects that were otherwise beyond their capacity. They were a transitional form that bridged the gap between small accounting units before conditions had been created to merge the units into one. In Chen's view these transfers of labor power were qualitatively different from the arbitrary transfers of property—grain, pigs, pumps, tractors, buildings—to units at higher levels that were part of the content of the abusive, ultra-left "Communist wind." Chen's special teams did not transfer existing wealth, they created new wealth at higher levels of organization. (W.H.H.)

Shanxi Provincial Government approved Dazhai as a place suited to Brigade or village scale accounting and allowed that to continue.[1]

In the spring of 1965, the County Committee Secretary, Yuan Yaoxian, suggested establishing a Dazhai Joint Commune, which would combine unified political leadership with separate economic arrangements. Dazhai formed a Joint Commune with Five Family Flat, Gao Family Ridge, Gold Rock Slope and Gold Gully, and established a General Party Branch Committee with Chen Yonggui acting as General Branch Secretary. In 1967, after Chen Yonggui took charge of the day-to-day operations in Xiyang County, many people suggested that the entire County make a second transition to Production Brigade accounting. The topic was raised by the South Gate Production Brigade and several other Brigades during Chen Yonggui's trip to Wang Camp People's Commune to resolve a factional dispute there.

While Chen Yonggui was sitting with Wang Camp peasants on an earth embankment, smoking and having a heart-to-heart talk, he gave them the following advice: "Certain conditions are needed for any transition to a higher level of accounting. At present, we still can't raise the grain output of the County high enough. We can't solve the problem of feeding all our Commune members, many of whom are working on virtually empty stomachs. The County has borrowed 20,000,000 *jin* of grain from the State. With this kind of economic base, how can you make the transition?"

But, after one year of hard work, the grain production in the County increased 40 percent. Having solicited opinions from various leaders in the County, Chen Yonggui announced that grain borrowing by Commune members in the County would no longer be necessary. Thus the entire County could make the transition to Production Brigade accounting.

When it came to making the transition to Communes as the basic accounting units, things were much more difficult. At the beginning of the 1970s, City Gate Commune was the first to merge agricultural production and sideline industrial production into a single account. But

1. The whole exercise was somewhat academic since the entire village of Dazhai was no bigger than an average team in most villages elsewhere. (W.H.H.)

there were too many disputes over trifles. The Commune even had to intervene to start up a platform truck. Gradually the accounting slipped back once again to the Production Brigade level.

Since Communism and the realization of Chairman Mao's idea of People's Communes, "larger in size and collective in nature," was the ultimate goal on Chen Yonggui's mind, he was eager to test more advanced arrangements in practice. Hua Guofeng raised the issue of transition in his speech at the First National Conference on Agriculture in April, 1975. That same year, Chen Yonggui wrote a report on the transition from team accounting to Brigade accounting. Chairman Mao Zedong commented on it immediately, but no method for carrying it out was ever discussed at the Conference of Eleven Provincial and Municipal Committee Secretaries chaired by Deng Xiaoping, because the Gang-of-Four rose in revolt during the Conference.

In 1976, by way of popularizing Yugoslavian experience with "agro-industrial combines" based on the joint management of agricultural production, industrial processing and marketing, Chen Yonggui, never one to give up, suggested that Commune-level accounting be tried out in Xiyang. The County Committee decided that the trial should be carried out by the Dazhai People's Commune on account of its relatively favorable conditions. Preparations took place over a period of two years, during 1976 and 1977, and the experiment officially started in 1978. In terms of agricultural production, the new system did not fundamentally upset the previous method of carrying on production and allocating income, but now all property had to be appraised and all expenditures approved by the Commune Committee.

Judging by the material I was able to see, it is very hard to analyze whether the new accounting method benefited grain production itself in terms of increasing yields, because unpredictable catastrophes occurred during each year of the transitional period. An additional negative influence was exerted by account-cooking and false reports on yields before the transitional period began. In terms of capital construction, the concentration of land made possible by merging accounting units very much favored the creation of new fields. Ever since the early 1950s, for instance, Five Family Flat had claimed a portion of Dazhai's land, but the formal creation of the joint Commune solved the problem. An exchange enabled Five Family Flat to return the land to Dazhai. Only then was Dazhai in a position to harness Wolf Den Ravine.

When held together too rigidly, however, the Commune system prevented the initiative of individual villages from coming into full play. Even seeing a film became subject to approval by the Commune. The people at the grass roots lost a lot of initiative. In terms of the development of sideline industrial production, however, the transitional period was truly the time when the foundations for small town- and village-owned enterprises were laid. Within three years, the average personal income grew by 34 Chinese dollars. During that period Chen Yonggui, too, felt the need for Commune and Brigade enterprises (that is, the present "small-town and village enterprises"). Using local corncobs, the residue from ear corn shelled by hand or small machine, he set up a furfural factory, which is today part of the Dazhai Country Chemical Group, famous throughout the Province.

Conventional wisdom has it that all these strivings for scale and collectivity resulted from Chen Yonggui's peasant consciousness, peasant idealism and peasant ways.[1] But I am not sure how this period, from the time when transitional labor allocation arrangements were criticized to the establishment of the rural agro-industrial combined enterprises that

1. The Gang of Four notwithstanding, the development of productive forces is no doubt the motive force propelling human history forward. Where Mao differed from Liu and Deng was not on the primacy of the productive forces, but on the character of the productive relations—the systems of ownership, forms of accumulation, patterns of distribution—needed to expand the productive forces of China after land reform. Mao strove to create socialist relations of production as the liberating framework for burgeoning productive forces, particularly the labor enthusiasm of hundreds of millions of working people for constructing a nonpolarized society. Liu and Deng, in contrast, castigating Mao's initiatives as "Utopian," "dogmatic," and "political," raised a pragmatic "black cat-white cat" banner: forget isms, what's good is what works. Under cover of this conventional wisdom they pushed free market reforms every bit as "political" as Mao's, but aimed in an undeclared opposite direction. Their goal: capitalist relations of production. Socialism, they promised, would materialize as a matter of course, by evolution, no revolution needed, once the productive forces reached a certain level. Mao characterized this view as "economic determinism," a mechanical distortion of the "Theory of Productive Forces" that obscures the interdependence of the forces and relationships of production, negates the role of superstructure, of culture, of human consciousness and human will in history, asserting only the unchallenged supremacy of material necessity. (W.H.H.)

one finds in Dazhai Commune today, should be judged. Were Chen's initiatives, after all, successful ventures, or failures? They were, it seems, something that history had in store, and the transition nurtured by Chen Yonggui played itself out with an air of inevitability until stranded high and dry when the collective tide ebbed away.

CHAPTER 31

JIANG QING UPSETS DAZHAI

A big red parasol offered a cooling screen to the public figure on whom all gazes were fixed. Dozens of people were clustered on the four sides of the parasol. Two big red horses and two big white horses had accompanied the dignitary on her trip. Her entourage included an enormous truck packed with the clear water she used for her meals, the commode she used to empty her bowels, the flowers and plants she used to adjust the air she breathed. All this was quite out of the ordinary—imposing in its pomp, and redolent of power and might. Jiang Qing, the wife of Chairman Mao and a leading political figure, came to Dazhai at the beginning of September, 1975.

Having just been informed of Jiang Qing's impending visit, leading members of the Dazhai Party Branch Committee bustled about preparing according to her instructions her living quarters and report material. To have Jiang Qing present in person was truly a rare occasion. On the eve of her trip, she had examined, with Zhang Chunqiao, Wang Hongwen and Yao Wenyuan, the ways in which to deal with the situation she was about to face.

"Come tomorrow," she said, "I will be in Dazhai, mobilizing public opinion."

The people of Dazhai had absolutely no idea concerning Jiang Qing's intentions. But they were very happy that "Comrade" Jiang Qing was coming to make a personal inspection. Consequently, the leading members of the Party Branch Committee enthusiastically went to the Yangquan train station to meet her, and people gathered at the entrance to the village to form a welcoming corridor.

Chen Yonggui had been in Beijing working on preparations for the National "In Agriculture Learn From Dazhai" Conference when he heard that Jiang Qing was going to Dazhai. He had rushed back to the village to receive her.

Jiang Qing first went to Small Gold Settlement, near Tianjin, and then quite unexpectedly showed up in Dazhai, never letting Chen Yonggui know beforehand what her schedule would be. Around that time, Small Gold Settlement had become Jiang Qing's spot, her favorite "Arts" village—a place where everybody, regardless of sex or age, could compose poetry, and a place that many people wanted to visit. But Chen Yonggui had no interest in such things and had never set foot in that Brigade. Deng Xiaoping later criticized Jiang Qing's behavior as "learning the trivial, while ignoring the main issue," which only deepened the contradiction between the "Gang of Four" and the veteran cadres of Deng's group. Some distance between Chen Yonggui and Jiang Qing was inevitable. Such were the circumstances when Jiang Qing showed up in Xiyang County.

As she entered Dazhai village, Jiang Qing posted three demands: There would be no blasting within a radius of thirty Chinese miles; there would be no horn-honking or other loud noises in the vicinity; the cave dwellings that she and her entourage were to occupy should be connected.

No blasting within thirty miles? That meant that several Communes would have to halt their irrigation and water conservancy projects. No horn-honking in the vicinity? That meant that regular bus service to High Tower, White Lamb Ravine, Wind Stage and Water Gap could not be maintained. All caves at the Reception Center were lined with laid-up cut stone. If openings were to be made in them, what would happen to safety standards? When the director of the Travel Office, Zhai Baojin, received Jiang Qing's requests, he immediately asked Chen Yonggui for instructions.

"Connect the caves? We'll have to blast them with dynamite!" he protested.

Jiang Qing was not pleased at all when she found out her wishes could not be carried out.

"If you can't do it, then build me a few new connected caves," she retorted like a spoiled child.

"For a project like that I'll have to ask the Central Committee for instructions!" Chen Yonggui answered to her face.

Jiang Qing was not happy at all but, as she had no way of controlling Chen Yonggui, she had to shut her mouth. Chen Yonggui was put into a difficult position by Jiang Qing's requests: Could he afford not to respond to the demands of such an important personality? I have been told by some Dazhai residents that, although Chen Yonggui did not like it, he did, in the end, somehow find a way to connect the caves.

What exactly did Jiang Qing want to accomplish with her trip to Dazhai? At the time, nobody in Dazhai was able to fathom her intentions. They only knew from careful observation that she, after arriving in Dazhai, did not: one, listen to reports by Dazhai's cadres, and two, familiarize herself with the concrete situation in the village. I have heard that she made the following announcements in front of Dazhai's cadres:

"I have come on behalf of the Great Leader, Chairman Mao."

"I want to turn Dazhai into a 'spot.'"[1]

In Beijing she had pushed her way in to Chairman Mao's presence and asked for ten cents, then turned around and made various swift arrangements before rushing off to Dazhai. Nobody in Dazhai understood what she had up her sleeve. Only after the smashing of the Gang of Four did people realize that she wanted to grab this "spot" in the limelight to reinforce her own prestige and power.

---

1. A "spot" in this context means a "squat spot," a community where a cadre settles down to live and work and learn, as preparation for drawing conclusions about the current situation in the area, and by analogy the region or even the whole country. (W.H.H.)

The people of Dazhai may not have known the real situation at the time, but Chen Yonggui must have been aware of it. Quite clearly, he knew the organizational affiliations of individuals within the Political Bureau, but he was not at liberty to disclose them.

Jiang Qing came secretly and left in a hurry. Her first trip to Dazhai was not publicly announced, but she later made a big public statement about it. When she came to Dazhai for the second time, she was even more daring and even more surreptitious. She still did not listen to local reports and did not look over any detailed local material. She busied herself all day criticizing the Duke of Zhou and striking back at the "rightist tendency to reverse her verdicts."

The second time around Jiang Qing went up the mountain, accompanied by Guo Fenglian. After the climb, she suddenly remembered the oil sand-beans she had left in Dazhai on her previous visit. She was curious about their growth.

The oil sand-bean is a kind of plant that can be processed into cooking oil. It is very rare in China. Perhaps because of some neglected special significance of the bean, Jiang Qing wanted it buried in Dazhai's soil. After her first departure, the local residents had planted some of it experimentally in the vegetable garden, treating it as a "curio" plant. On her second visit, Guo Fenglian took Jiang Qing to the field where the oil sand-bean was growing, albeit very unevenly. Seeing its miserable appearance, Jiang Qing pulled a long face.

"What have you done to it? Huh?" she scolded. "You've turned my hopes into soap bubbles! I've given you such good seed, and you've planted it to turn into this! This, truly...."

Shaking her head, she lectured Guo Fenglian and a few others who were with her until no one could stand it any longer. They explained to her that, in order to make the soil more suited for the cultivation of the oil sand-bean they had mixed two tractor-cart loads of sand with the soil on one half of the field! The trouble was that Dazhai was located in a high-altitude, cold, red clay region, quite different from her native Shandong and therefore unsuitable for the cultivation of this type of crop.

Jiang Qing did not listen to them at all. She grabbed a grub hoe with both hands and struck the field with it several times. Then the words that flew out of her mouth made her sound like a quarrelsome old hag: "You've been too careless abusing the oil sand-bean like this. You haven't taken me, Jiang Qing, seriously!" she complained bitterly.

As the people of Dazhai remember, Jiang Qing was dressed very neatly and her manners and movements were quite quick. She would often disappear in a wink and alight somewhere else, as if carried on the wind. This time, after recovering her composure, she personally demonstrated how to dig a deep trench behind the row of oil sand-beans. This emboldened the villagers to make a comment.

"This will increase the land temperature, Your Excellency. The sun will dry up the moisture from the roots. Your oil sand-beans are likely to dry up and die!"

Jiang Qing stopped in her tracks, looking perturbed. She stood transfixed in front of the villagers, as though realizing how naive she had been. But how could she so easily acknowledge her naivete? She would simply have to have the final say, in order to save her precious face. However, since she couldn't think of a convincing retort, she decided to bide her time.

Actually it was not the first trench Jiang Qing had dug in Dazhai, and she resolved to use it to have the last word.

Meanwhile, after she had finished with her inspection of the oil sand-beans, Jiang Qing decided to take a look at Dazhai's corn. From what I understand, the following happened after she made her way into the corn field to relieve herself.

The corn grew very well that year in Dazhai. A big ear of corn was in the making on every stalk. Little ears were even forming down below. Jiang Qing's eyes sized up the little ears, and her face turned livid.

"You call this an experimental field?" she yelled, her thready voice at dressing-down pitch. "Huh! With ears of corn this small?"

Pointing a finger at Guo Fenglian, she continued: "You simply won't listen to me! You listen to Deng Xiaoping! You are arrogant, you are backward!"

While she exercised her right to criticize, she also decided to take action. She walked into the field and started breaking off the corn tassels, one by one. Her action at first stupefied Guo Fenglian and Gao Yuliang. They allowed her to continue through several rows before they realized she wasn't going to stop. Then they rushed forward to dissuade her.

"Your Excellency, the corn is just in the silk, it's flowering right now. If you break the tassels off, how will it pollinate? There will be a big drop in grain output! Besides, this is the field where we are crossing two types of corn. If you break off the tassels, we'll never be able to produce the new hybrid variety!"

After the explanation, Jiang Qing started to doubt her own action. Like one who has just sobered up and finds no interest in her previous drunken behavior, she silently circled several stalks of corn, then walked from the field.

After every unwise and disgraceful act Jiang Qing looked for a soothing remedy. Suddenly she remembered the trench she had dug with her own hands a year earlier. During both of her trips to Dazhai, she had requested only the company of Guo Fenglian. Chen Yonggui could join them only if especially asked. Without such request, he was usually not in evidence. On this second visit, she asked Guo Fenglian to accompany her to the trench. Unfortunately, since the trench no longer existed, the moment was fraught with tension.

Jiang Qing's trench-digging activity had quite a history: Even before her first trip to Dazhai, the village had decided to build a pig farm in the lowest terraced field at the foot of Tigerhead Mountain. When she arrived a few days later, she toured the mountain on horseback and selected that very spot to dig a military-style slit trench. She bound a towel around her head and put a pair of white gloves on her hands. These were supposed to make her look like a farmer! She picked up a shovel and dug it in a few times before assuming a tired look, then spoke to the few employees at her side.

"Would the experienced workers kindly take my photograph?" she asked. "It will be published in the Internal Reference News Bulletin, do you mind?"

She had made herself up that way only for this photograph.

So when Jiang Qing asked to see the slit trench she had dug during her previous visit, Guo Fenglian could no longer conceal the truth. Guo informed her that, after study by the Party Branch, the Commune had designated the site for a mechanized pig farm. Before Guo Fenglian could finish explaining, Jiang Qing covered her ears with her hands, and charged at her:

"I'm not going to argue with you!" she shouted, fixing her eyes on Guo Fenglian so fiercely that the young Party Secretary broke into a cold sweat and began to quiver.

"Do you know why I've come here? Huh?" demanded Jiang Qing. "I've come to fight revisionism! You destroyed my trench, without even telling me about it! Why did you want to build a pig farm there? Who told you to do it?"

Under this all-out attack, Guo Fenglian did not dare make a sound.

"You don't want to say who it is, but I know it anyway!" As Jiang Qing's temper rose so did her voice. "You haven't got the guts! You listen to Deng Xiaoping, but you won't listen to me, Jiang Qing! You should make a thorough self-criticism, Little Guo."

It was clear that Jiang Qing had targeted Chen Yonggui. The reason was that Chen Yonggui favored her opponents on the Central Committee, and Jiang Qing was well aware of it. Although there were no divisions on the issue of Dazhai among the members of the Gang of Four, which included Jiang Qing, when it came to Chen Yonggui personally, each side was on guard against the other.

The truth is that after Jiang Qing had left Dazhai the first time, nobody there had given the matter of the trench much thought. Since nobody had anticipated that she would come back, they had used her trench site as part of the foundation for the pig barn. That moment of carelessness brought down on them a great disaster because Jiang Qing came again!

While Jiang Qing vented her anger on Guo Fenglian, one of the bodyguards, in an attempt to rescue his Party Secretary from her predicament, ran back to the village to look for Chen Yonggui.

"What can she do about the trench?" retorted Chen Yonggui, showing his aversion for Jiang Qing.

He did not take any interest in the whole episode. But Jiang Qing wouldn't leave Guo Fenglian alone. She continued berating her as the car drove back to the village. Before they got there little Guo broke into tears.

On another occasion Guo Fenglian accompanied Jiang Qing into the mountains on horseback. During the outing, Jiang Qing mentioned that she wanted to invite the people of Dazhai to watch a movie with her.

When Her Excellency watches a movie, how can Dazhai's cadres refuse to keep her company? In order to come on time for this "special" occasion, none of them dared have their dinner. Who would want to be responsible for holding up such an important event? Once there, however, they waited and waited. Their stomachs rumbled, but there was no sign of Jiang Qing. What happened? Nobody knew for sure. All they could do was to sit and wait, keeping watch at the gate of the Reception Center.

After a long time, a message came from inside. Her Excellency was asleep! So, in order to keep Jiang Qing company at the movie, Dazhai's cadres had given up their evening meal. Now they had to swallow their discomfort without a grumble. The Central Dignitary's traveling companions explained to them how to react.

"This is just how Her Excellency's temper is. When you are angry just don't say a word. All will be forgotten!"

Jiang Qing woke up. She swaggered out of the Reception Center, strutted about putting on airs, and sat down on a chair right in the middle of the conference room.

The grand new auditorium was located on a high hill to the south of the village, overlooking Dazhai. It had already received several dozen State dignitaries and served as the stage for numerous report sessions and performances given for visiting Central Committee senior cadres. This time, Jiang Qing's presence was somehow coquettish. The Party Branch Secretary, Guo Fenglian, and several girls from Dazhai were at her side. Dazhai's burly men were all seated at the back. Before the film projection, Jiang Qing had to make a few opening remarks:

"Comrades," she began. "I have asked you here today to see a film because I want you to understand a few principles, understand a bit of science. Why have I asked Little Guo to sit in front? Because she is a woman! Women deserve to occupy a superior place. In the future, humanity will enter into matriarchal society, that is to say, women will hold power. I urge you to change your own family names. You should use your mother's family name."

People were baffled by her speech, not understanding why they should change their family names from father's to mother's name.

A peculiar science education film appeared on the silver screen, but Jiang Qing was not really paying much attention to the footage. She moved her lips ever so slightly, and the attentive bodyguard immediately knew that she was sweating. Afraid that the special guest might feel neglected, the bodyguard very cautiously brought out a hot towel prepared well in advance and lifted her legs up. She comfortably closed her eyes. The people in her entourage were used to this; they had learned to do the things that pleased her. The people of Dazhai were used only to communing with crops and stones. They did not know how to treat anybody with such special courtesy. This could make outsiders feel rather unhappy.

There were times when Jiang Qing did not lose her temper. She was quite satisfied when she saw Xiyang County's Central Shanxi Opera Troupe rehearse the revolutionary model opera *The Azalea Mountain*. She began her life as a film actress and, after she became involved in political life, she was still mainly in charge of the arts nationally. When she came to Dazhai, she was supposed to see a local Xiyang theatrical production. After the rehearsal the first-time actress who played the role of Ke Xiang became famous in Xiyang County. Jiang Qing showed great interest in her after she saw her perform. She climbed onto the stage to meet the actors and directed the young actress through gesticulation. This made an entry of great interest in the history of Xiyang's Central Shanxi Opera Troupe. It was without precedent to perform before so exalted a personage.

One evening, people from Jiang Qing's entourage called the village asking for Guo Fenglian. They said Her Excellency needed Guo's help and that she should immediately come to the Reception Center. Guo Fenglian had just returned from the fields after a day of labor. Even the hair on her head was wet with sweat. She hurried anxiously to the Reception Center, only to discover that Jiang Qing had already gone out.

"Jiang Qing has gone?" she exclaimed, incredulous.

With sweat soaking her entire body and her heart beating wildly, Guo Fenglian must have felt an awful despair at that moment. She could find no trace of Jiang Qing, and had no way of telling what kind of trouble was about to engulf her. At that moment, Guo Fenglian thought of looking for Chen Yonggui. In case something big was brewing, how would she justify herself to him if she didn't?

"Jiang Qing is at the Supply and Marketing Cooperative," someone said just as Guo was worrying about what to do.

If this was true, Jiang Qing had been roving in front of the Cooperative's counter since she finished her dinner! Guo Fenglian rushed to the store, planning to accompany Jiang Qing back to her quarters, but she did not have enough courage to speak up.

Before long Chen Yonggui, puffing on his cigarette, also showed up in front of the Cooperative. As soon as he heard about Jiang Qing's activity, he had begun to worry that she might be giving a very hard time to the Coop's sales clerk.

A big crowd had gathered in and around the store, surrounding Jiang Qing, listening to her unremitting pontificating and watching her enraptured moves. This kind of attention was not something with which she was unfamiliar. In the past few days, she had assembled over eighty personalities from the art world to talk to them individually. She focused on name-calling and condemnation, but listened respectfully as a local poet, Zhang Yongmei, recited a flattering poem she had written: "Following Jiang Qing, We Will Fight Forever."

Jiang Qing then turned to the salesclerk behind the counter and asked: "Do you use your father's or your mother's surname?"

"My father's," replied the clerk.

This reply displeased Jiang Qing. With a tone that was reprimanding she offered guidance: "In matriarchal societies women hold power. When we reach Communism, there will be an Empress. Why do you take your father's surname and not your mother's? You must change that in the future."

The salesclerk just stared at her blankly, unable to respond with courtesy. He just hemmed and hawed, to express that he got it!

Jiang Qing turned around to discover that Chen Yonggui had arrived. She proceeded to question him, sounding quite fragile and delicate for once.

"Yonggui, do you use your father's surname or your mother's surname?"

"Father's," answered Chen Yonggui.

"Why don't you use your mother's surname?" Jiang Qing pursued.

Chen Yonggui was not used to this kind of interrogation even if it was from one of China's most unique people. He could not bear the sight of her, yet he was not able to deal with her the way he did with the people in Dazhai, by banging on the table, staring at them, smashing bricks into pieces, or patiently talking reason. He just managed to produce an unnatural smile on that pig-iron face of his, while he forced himself to nod a few times and utter a few grunts in response.

To express human sympathy, Chen Yonggui wanted to prepare a simple evening meal for Jiang Qing. Jiang Qing accepted the invitation and came to his house for dinner. Chen Yonggui's wife, Song Yuling, prepared Xiyang's famous millet-flour pancakes especially for the occasion. Since she had just about finished all preparations, the meal was set to proceed smoothly. But the moment Jiang Qing sat down at the table, she announced that she wanted to sleep, and her nursing staff helped her into Chen Yonggui's bedroom to lie down. As the evening progressed it was not clear whether she was awake or not, so no one dared disturb her. Sleep, of course, is a kind of enjoyment, too. But this particular "sleep" of Jiang Qing's was hard to understand. Chen Yonggui was very unhappy about it, but it was not appropriate for him to say anything.

Heavens can turn stormy and unstable without warning; people's fortunes can turn to misfortunes overnight. Jiang Qing had not anticipated when she came to Dazhai for the second time that she would only spend a miserable few days there. At 11 AM on September 5th, an urgent cable arrived from the Central Committee. It informed Jiang Qing that the Chairman's illness had taken a serious turn and that she should return to Beijing as soon as possible. Jiang Qing was more familiar with the condition of Chairman Mao's health than anyone else, yet she did not appear anxious at all. She followed her usual routine in getting dressed and making herself up, and then she sat down to play cards with her entourage. It was 5 PM that afternoon before she leisurely left Dazhai for the north.

Various celebrities have left impressions of their personalities and character with the inhabitants of the high loess slopes of Tigerhead

Mountain, among them that of Premier Zhou, and many other senior cadres of the Central Committee. Some of the impressions clashed and fought each other, yet remained behind to be quietly weighed in the minds of the people of Dazhai. To a man and woman, however, the people will tell you they still have a headache when they think of Jiang Qing. Chen Yonggui's wife, Song Yuling, remembers wanting to have a picture taken with Jiang Qing at the time of her visit, but Chen Yonggui would not agree to it.

"What do you want that picture for?" he asked her.

The question seemed quite mysterious to her at the time, but she finally understood what it was all about after the Gang of Four was smashed.

CHAPTER 32

POPULARIZING "DAZHAI-STYLE COUNTIES"

September 15, 1975 arrived. It was a day that motivated and revitalized Chen Yonggui, but it also put pressure on him. Because of the distinction that his pioneering work had brought to Dazhai and Xiyang, the Party Central Committee had decided to hold the "In Agriculture, Learn From Dazhai" National Conference on location, in Xiyang, in Chen Yonggui's home County.

Chairman Mao Zedong himself had proposed the Conference. Adopting his proposal, the Political Bureau passed a resolution that determined the scope and time for the Conference. The two Vice-Premiers who were in charge of agriculture nationally, Hua Guofeng and Chen Yonggui, spent a long time making preparations. Hu Qiaomu was in charge of drafting the report that Hua Guofeng was to read. Hua Guofeng was very pleased with the draft, commending the author on the quality of writing and his ability to get to the heart of the matter.

"I was inspired by the spirit of Dazhai," Hu Qiaomu responded.

The drafting of various materials on Dazhai and Xiyang, including the reports to be given by Xiyang County Party Committee Deputy

Secretaries Wang Jinzi and Guo Fenglian, was assigned to the journalist Song Shayin and his group of writers. Song Shayin had enough confidence and literary talent, rather uncommon among typical journalists, to be able to produce all the materials needed for the Conference within a short period of twenty days. He often stayed up working until two or three in the morning and, once he had handed in the Conference material, needed to be hospitalized, due to excessive fatigue.

All the chief leading cadres of China's 2,300 Counties, including all leaders of agricultural work above the County level, amounting to a total of over 3,700 people, were supposed to attend the gathering. Where was a small County town like Xiyang to find an auditorium big enough to hold the 3,700 participants? It just happened that Xiyang Tractor Factory was about to open, and there was a huge workshop where the machinery had not yet been installed. It was decided that the Conference would take place in this workshop. The organizers issued small stools to all participants, making seating conditions rather hard but still bearable. Organizing food and lodging for so many thousands posed a considerable additional problem for the small County town. Leaders from Shanxi Province, the Central Shanxi Region and Xiyang County all worked to set up appropriate arrangements. They lodged a good number of participants in factories and enterprises as far as four miles out of town.

Hua Guofeng arrived in Xiyang ahead of time to inspect the progress of preparations for the Conference. He stayed at the Number Two Hostel. Chen Yonggui had already returned to Dazhai to receive Jiang Qing on her visit. Deng Xiaoping, who was then in charge of the day-to-day operations of the Central Committee, and Political Bureau members Yao Wenyuan and Wu Guixian flew in on September 15th just before the opening. Hua Guofeng chaired the Conference, while Chen Yonggui delivered the inauguration speech.

Chen Yonggui's presence undoubtedly provided the center of attention. His status at this Conference was decided by his astounding pioneering undertaking in agriculture. But the person that people followed with equal if not more interest was Deng Xiaoping, who was scheduled to deliver a speech on behalf of the Central Committee. It was Deng

Xiaoping's first public appearance after he resumed work in 1975,[1] and many old cadres were looking forward to hearing him speak. When Hua Guofeng announced Deng Xiaoping's speech, the entire assembly broke into thunderous applause. Deng Xiaoping raised his hand several times in an attempt to stop it, but the applause just grew even bigger, and many people in the audience rose to their feet. Several people who attended the Conference told me that many participants started crying, taken aback by the sudden realization of just how many old veteran cadres had been senselessly overthrown. After the applause subsided, Deng Xiaoping started his speech without ever looking at the prepared draft.

"I am essentially a layman when it comes to agriculture," he began. "The true experts here are Comrade Chen Yonggui and Comrade Hua Guofeng. The success of this Conference rests squarely with Comrade Yonggui, Comrade Guofeng, and all the other comrades sitting here with us today who have been working in agriculture for many years. You should all use this Conference to lead the way in spreading the 'Learn from Dazhai' mass movement to every corner of the land."

Deng Xiaoping went on to talk about propitious and pressing circumstances. At that very moment, he said, some areas were already pulling the country backward. He seriously criticized Guizhou and Sichuan Provinces.

"I am from Sichuan myself," he said. "This is precisely the state of affairs in Sichuan. Sichuan is falling behind. Furthermore, Sichuan is not alone. Other Provinces suffer from the same condition to varying degrees."

Then Deng turned to the topic of emphasis, Learning from Dazhai.

"Dazhai has a vast accumulation of grain," he said. "Xiyang has a vast accumulation of grain. That's why we have a problem of genuine learning from them, in contrast to phony learning, and learning that is

---

1. Deng Xiaoping was set aside as a capitalist roader soon after the Cultural Revolution began but Mao brought him back to work in 1975 when Premier Zhou Enlai became too ill to carry the burden of his office. In 1975 Deng Xiaoping served as acting Premier but was set aside again after the first Tiananmen Incident in 1976. He returned to work for the third time in 1977 after the death of Mao Zedong and the arrest of the Gang of Four. (W.H.H.)

half-true half-false." He went on to explain this in some detail: "Learning from Dazhai, I beg you all to make note, is not only the question of grain yields. One has to study the concrete policies adopted by Dazhai and Xiyang."

His speech emphasized Dazhai's method of work evaluation and work point allotment. He called on the entire nation to learn from and draw on this experience.[1]

Those who were attentive enough to this speech of Deng Xiaoping heard nuances suggesting certain parameters of China's political scene that called for examination and analysis. The rostrum of the Conference seated Deng Xiaoping and Hua Guofeng, but also Jiang Qing and Yao Wenyuan. The four, in fact, formed two fronts. When Deng Xiaoping first started his speech, Jiang Qing interjected that Chairman Mao himself had sent Deputy Chairman Deng to join the Conference. After Deng Xiaoping said a few more words, Jiang Qing interjected again with condescension, as if she were the hostess and he a guest of questionable legitimacy, that Chairman Mao had wanted Deputy Chairman Deng to say a few words at the Conference.

Deng Xiaoping reviewed the overall conditions of China's agriculture, praised Dazhai's and Xiyang's spirit of fighting against heaven and earth and finally said: "If just one-third of the Counties in China were like Dazhai and Xiyang, we would not have enough space to store all the grain."

That was the period of most intense struggle between Deng Xiaoping and Jiang Qing. Jiang Qing was not scheduled to talk at the Conference's opening ceremony but she staged a surprise attack, asking to say a few words. She was well aware of the Central Committee's decision that provincial, municipal and regional first secretaries should not attend the Conference, yet she said that various provincial first secretaries were not attending the Conference because they did not take agriculture seriously. She did not say much about the topic at hand, but immediately changed her tone and turned to the issue of the political campaign to criticize the classical novel *The Water Margin* that was just

1. Deng was not known for praising Dazhai or for urging people to study the Dazhai experience. Presumably at this Conference he was boxed in and had to give praise while reserving a different opinion. (W.H.H.)

being launched at that time. She said that the crucial point of *The Water Margin* was to make Chao Gai (the real hero) into a mere figurehead.

"There are people in the Central Committee right now who are making Chairman Mao into a mere figurehead," she said.

The participants at the Conference did not necessarily realize at whom Jiang Qing was aiming her attack, but people like Deng Xiaoping, Hua Guofeng, Chen Yonggui and Yao Wenyuan most certainly knew. That is why Hua Guofeng did not go along with Jiang Qing's request to have the draft of her speech printed, or to have its recorded tape broadcast on the radio. He promptly informed the Central Committee, and through Central reported the whole incident to Chairman Mao Zedong himself. When Chairman Mao heard about Jiang Qing's remarks he said: "What nonsense! That's quite beside the point!" He gave his clear instructions: "Don't distribute the draft, don't broadcast the recording, don't print the speech."

Chairman Mao sent the instructions to Hua Guofeng and Hua complied. He didn't replay the tape of Jiang Qing's speech at the Conference or distribute a written draft to the delegates. He also arranged through Wang Qian, the Provincial Party Secretary, that the speech would not be broadcast in Shanxi Province either.

Jiang Qing's presumptuous usurpation of the host's role and the confusion she created caused Deng Xiaoping some discontent. After the opening ceremony, Deng Xiaoping, responding to a request from Chen Yonggui, went to Dazhai to stay over. He was planning to stay the night, which he had not had the opportunity to do on his only previous visit, but by some unlucky coincidence he ran into Jiang Qing there. Rather than share the Guest House with her, he walked around a while, climbed the mountain, and left.

After the opening ceremony of the National Conference, the delegates visited key Communes, Production Brigades, and irrigation and water conservancy capital construction projects in Dazhai and Xiyang, and then went on to Beijing to continue the Conference.

When the Conference resumed in the capital, Hua Guofeng made his "Motivate the entire Party, go in for agriculture in a big way, struggle to popularize Dazhai Style Counties" report. The text was divided into five sections: "Popularizing Dazhai-Style Counties is the combat mission for our entire Party," "In the building of Dazhai-Style Counties, the County Committee is the key," "Conduct thoroughgoing education on the basic political line of the Party," etc. The emphasis was on County Committees as the key. This brought forth six criteria for the successful establishment of a Dazhai-Style County: (1) the existence of a united and militant core within the County Committee leadership, which resolutely executes the Party line and Party policy; (2) the established preponderance of poor and lower-middle peasants capable of waging determined struggle against capitalist activities and carrying out effective supervision and reform of the class enemy; (3) the capacity to maintain County, Commune and Production Brigade-level cadre participation in collective productive labor, as Xiyang County had long done; (4) rapid progress and sizable results in the capital construction of farmland, mechanization of agriculture and scientific farming; (5) continuous expansion and strengthening of the collective economy, with production and income of the poor Communes and Production Brigades catching up or surpassing the current levels of average local Communes and Brigades; (6) comprehensive development of agriculture, forestry, animal husbandry, fisheries and sideline enterprises, with increased production, increased numbers, significant contributions to the State, and gradual improvement in the living conditions of the Commune members.[1]

In a section entitled "Conduct thoroughgoing education on the basic political line of the party," Hua Guofeng raised four issues pertaining to the strengthening and development of the collective economy that needed to be properly and carefully solved: (1) overcome the drain on labor power brought about by individual farmers who work outside the collective economy (2) organize the scattered craftsmen who work on their own; (3) return private plots and reclaimed wasteland in excess of the amount stipulated by Party policy for individual Commune members' use to the collective (4) cor-

1. This emphasis on comprehensive community development was always a basic part of Mao's program. It is important to take note of it here because when the "reformers" toppled Chen Yonggui and discarded the Dazhai model they charged that Mao and Dazhai cared only about grain and rashly sacrificed everything for grain. (W.H.H.)

rect the tendency to waste public assets and neglect accumulation in the process of distribution.

This report had been approved after discussion by the Political Bureau of the Central Committee. Right after the report Jiang Qing expressed her dissatisfaction: "This report, to put it mildly, is revisionist!" she pronounced, pointing at Hua Guofeng and Chen Yonggui.

The two leaders declined to comment on Jiang Qing's attack. The only thing Hua Guofeng did after he read his report was to send it to Chairman Mao for checking and approval. On the evening Chairman Mao read the report, he marked it with just one word, "Read." Then, behind the heading on the document he added, "Wage five years of arduous struggle, motivate the entire Party, go in for agriculture in a big way." He asked that the text be circulated as Central Committee Document No. 21 (1975 Issue). The Central Committee transmitted it to various grass roots organizations nationwide.

When it came to putting into effect the conclusions of the "In Agriculture, Learn From Dazhai" National Conference, a serious split occurred between the Gang of Four on one side and Deng Xiaoping and Hua Guofeng on the other. This was first revealed on the issue of propaganda. All large publications in the country at the time propagated the spirit of the National Conference on Agriculture. The *Red Flag* magazine listed all the items on the Conference's agenda. As Yao Wenyuan examined the list, he saw an item that he crossed out with his pen.

"Don't print it," he said. "I don't want to keep printing that same old stuff," he added.

Several days later, he sent his instructions down to the *People's Daily*:

"Don't print things just because they are about Dazhai. You should also be more prudent with the Daqing propaganda."

Yao Wenyuan had attended the National Conference on Agriculture, too, and he knew very well what Chairman Mao's intention had been. After the Conference, he behaved with relative detachment, at least outwardly, but his attitude toward the Conference was nevertheless plainly evident.

After the National Conference on Agriculture, the Gang of Four first used the movement to criticize the Chinese classic, *Water Margin* to strike at Deng Xiaoping. They later moved on to criticize the use of his well-known "three directives" as the guiding principle. In the end, after the upheaval at Tiananmen, they forced him to step down.

Zhang Chunqiao expressed his profound dissatisfaction with the issues outlined in two sections of the report: "Conduct thoroughgoing education on the basic political line of the party," and, "In the building of Dazhai-Style Counties, the County Committee is the key."

"Isn't the Provincial Committee a key, too? How about the Central Committee?" Zhang asked pointedly.

He said that the consolidation of the party organization and the rectification of incorrect styles of work were "learning in form only," and that dispatching work teams was none other than "a refurbished version of the reactionary capitalist class line and a peach-garden experience." In April 1976, Hua Guofeng, who was then in charge of the operation of the Central Committee, was preparing to send out a circular to affirm the Central Committee Document No. 21, Year 1975, and affirm that conducting thoroughgoing education on the basic political line of the Party in the countryside, consolidation of the Party organization, rectification of the incorrect styles of work, and dispatching work teams were all correct.

Zhang Chunqiao, however, was still not satisfied. He offered his opinion rather belligerently at a meeting of the Political Bureau: "Who knows whether education on the basic political line of the Party is correct or not? Perhaps the reactionary political line forces work team members out, so they cannot rebel in their offices, organizations and institutions." He also said: "We cannot keep deploying based on the Central Committee Document No. 21. The situation has changed!"

Because of his action, the meeting was unable to formulate a resolution, and so the documents were not circulated.

During May and June 1975, the State Council decided that the Ministry of Agriculture should organize an on-the-spot Conference on planting, harvesting and field management in the north, and an on-the-spot Conference on rice production in the south. The Central Committee entrusted Chen Yonggui to convey to these Conferences Chairman Mao Zedong's important instructions regarding the Socialist Education Movement, which reaffirmed that the Central Committee

Document No. 21 should be conscientiously put into effect, and stressed his support for the work of Party committees on all levels. Some people from Shanghai and Suzhou said that Chen Yonggui could not represent the Party Central Committee because his speeches expressed "out-and-out, the theory of the primary importance of the productive forces." They used this method to indirectly criticize Deng Xiaoping's "theory of the primary importance of the productive forces." This is why the spirit of The First "In Agriculture, Learn From Dazhai" National Conference, although it played a certain role, did not completely prevail. After the defeat of the Gang of Four, when Party leaders criticized the Gang on various fronts, they used all these episodes as concrete evidence of the Gang's anti-Dazhai position.

Two months after the break-up of the Gang of Four, on Hua Guofeng's suggestion, the Central Committee's Political Bureau passed a resolution to hold The Second "In Agriculture, Learn From Dazhai" National Conference in Beijing. Hua Guofeng chaired the Conference, and Chen Yonggui made a report entitled "Thoroughly criticize the Gang of Four. Launch a new upsurge in the movement to popularize 'Dazhai Style Counties.'" The Conference raised five rallying cries, including "Celebrate the Great Historic Victory," and "Raise the Red Banner Proclaiming 'In Agriculture, Learn From Dazhai' Even Higher." It criticized the Gang of Four, affirmed the positive momentum gained in the entire country since The First "In Agriculture, Learn From Dazhai" National Conference, and further reiterated the importance of creating "Dazhai Style Counties."

When this Conference pushed Chen Yonggui onto an even higher plane, it called yet more attention to this originator of Dazhai, and confirmed him as a Chen Yonggui of national significance. Reflecting this new status, Chen Yonggui announced the rapid emergence of agricultural development in Shandong, Jiangsu, Anhui, and other provinces since The First "In Agriculture, Learn From Dazhai" National Conference. He brought up concrete examples: "Grain production in Shandong increased by 5,400,000 metric tons between 1974 and 1975; this year, again, it rose by 5,500,000 metric tons. There are also many Counties that were subjected to serious interference by the Gang of

Four, yet they held against the interference, resolutely put into effect Central Committee Document No. 21, and achieved new results through their unflinching commitment to learning from Dazhai."

Following the directive Chairman Mao had issued before his death, that China accomplish mechanization of its agriculture by 1980, Chen Yonggui again brought up the issue accelerating the pace of farm mechanization. He commended Hebei, Shandong, Guangxi, Jiangsu, Hunan and Anhui on the state of "the five small industrial enterprises," announcing that by 1975, 90 percent of the People's Communes and 60 percent of all Production Brigades in the country had already set up enterprises, for a national total of over 800,000 units. His call, in fact, was the driving force behind the later industrialization of China's countryside.

Chen Yonggui first set up several enterprises in Dazhai People's Commune. After that, several coastal regions like Shandong and Jiangsu laid sound foundations for the establishment of Production Brigade enterprises. On top of that, under the policy of economic revival, which came into effect after the Third Plenary Session, the present integrated systems of agriculture, industry and marketing developed. Gao Court Township's East Street Village in Huolu County, Hebei Province, had been a poor village with an average per-capita annual income of seventy Chinese dollars. While continuing to produce grain, they developed a local welding-rod plant into a titanium steel factory, the likes of which was very rare in China. This village ended up producing 45 percent of the national titanium steel output, and the average per-capita income in the village rose to 1,200 Chinese dollars.

In discussing these successes one must remember how the motivating force behind "the five small industrial enterprises" combined with later policies. Just before the end of the Plenary Session, the newly appointed Chairman of the Communist Party of China, Hua Guofeng, especially invited Guo Fenglian, Li Xishen, who was then the Deputy Secretary in charge of operations at the Xiyang County Committee, and Chen Yonggui to a banquet. He discussed with them the situation in the battle against the Gang of Four and the ways for Dazhai and Xiyang to forge ahead in the new circumstances.

"At present," Hua said, "although Chairman Mao has passed away, the Gang of Four has been toppled and we can concentrate our energy on learning from Daqing and from Dazhai." During the banquet, Li Xishen announced in front of his table that in 1977 Xiyang County's grain yield reached 150,000 metric tons.

"Good! That's the right kind of spirit!" exclaimed Hua Guofeng, slapping himself happily on the knees. He raised his glass and congratulated Dazhai and Xiyang on their continuous progress.

This was the most concrete expression of Chen Yonggui's lifelong ideological commitment to collective economy and the "large in size, collective in nature" principle. Not only did Mao Zedong, Zhou Enlai and Hua Guofeng give it their approval, not only did two Political Bureaus of the Central Committee adopt it, Chen Yonggui was able, on behalf of the Central Committee, to personally impress his agenda on the various departments of the Central Committee itself and on various departments of Party organizations on other levels as their foremost duty. His call took pride of place over all others.

After Chen Yonggui became a member of China's highest group of leaders, he carried out his ideas with outstanding success. That he, as a peasant, gained the confidence of the Communist Party leadership through tireless battles on big issues and through numerous political movements, marked him as a man and a leader of exceptional quality.

CHAPTER 33

WEST-WATER-EAST

Perhaps Chen Yonggui's greatest material achievement was planning and carrying out the magnificent "West-Water-East" project. With this engineering feat the peasants of Xiyang cut an 18.5-kilometer-long tunnel through Zhanling Mountain and built dams and aqueducts to bring surplus water from Zhanling's western drainage basin into the heart of Xiyang County, enough water to irrigate five townships, supply the needs of many new coal mines, and replenish the reservoirs of Xiyang County Town.

Stories regarding Xiyang's water diversion project kept emerging, one after the other, and have been circulating for over ten years now. They have not yet faded away into the endless flow of history. Even though the water was never diverted to the ideal location envisaged by Chen Yonggui, two townships out of five have been receiving water from the project for years and the deep artificial lake at the eastern terminus has become a famous "scenic spot" that people enjoy so much they forget to go home. After the precipitous fall of the Red Flag of Dazhai, just about all the foreign guests and celebrities who visited Dazhai asked to be taken to the water diversion project to see what was so unusual about it.

When it comes to Xiyang's irrigation and water conservancy works, it was not Chen Yonggui who first dreamed them up. For many years, decades and centuries, under numerous dynasties, Xiyang's population had had its fill of suffering from water shortage and torment by drought. In the Ninth Year of the Republic,[1] Xiyang experienced a particularly severe drought. All the crops withered away, and thousands of people died from hunger. Were it not for the spirit that made Xiyang's populace "carry a hundred buckets of water from the distance of a thousand miles to irrigate one *mu* of land" during the severe drought of 1972 and 1973, people would have been in danger of starving to death again. Fifteen of Xiyang's twenty People's Communes experienced severe water shortages at this time. During the drought season, over one hundred Production Brigades had to travel over hill and dale in search of drinking water. When first hit by the spring drought, members of the Silver Hollow People's Commune had to cross a mountain over 1,000 meters high and walk over 30 Chinese miles to bring water from Peach Net and Yellow Cliff. The scramble for water in the movie *The Old Well* is an authentic depiction of the situation in Xiyang. There is a jingle in Xiyang County that says:

> My well has dried,
> I can't find a bride.

The story of Xiyang's quest for water is more fascinating than a good novel.

In order to solve the water shortage in the 1950s, the County Committee had already led the masses in the construction of several water reservoirs, designed to ease the water problem for part of the region. The people of Xiyang composed a folk song about those water conservancy projects:

> Five water reservoirs,
> Two higher, three lower.
> Here we raise fish,

1. 1920.

There generate power.
Irrigation water flows
North, East, South and West.
Ten thousand crop acres
All do their best.

The five water reservoirs were never completed, but the song expressed the heartfelt wishes of the people of Xiyang. When compiling Xiyang County annals during the Qing dynasty, Xiyang's successful candidate in the highest imperial examination, Li Guangyu, used a sentence from the Shanxi general annals to pass a verdict on Xiyang: "Not suitable for canal construction." Yet, after just a few years under the Communist Party rule, Xiyang was bringing its farmland rapidly under home-built irrigation.

For many years after Chen Yonggui stepped onto the political stage the word "water" kept harassing him. He could not get Premier Zhou's questions, "What are you going to do if you have a big three-year drought? What are you going to do if you have a big ten-year drought?" off his mind. In Xiyang nine out of ten years were dry. Grasping the issue of water was a big thing. After the Conference on Agriculture of the Fourteen Provinces of the Northern Region, he braved a mighty storm to go down to Ding Ravine, and climb up to Sheep Fold Ridge. He asked for technical personnel from the Department of Irrigation and Water Conservancy to find an adequate source of water. In the end they determined that diverting the Su River, located west of Xiyang, was the solution. There was a big mountain blocking the Su River from this intended course. The only way to deal with that was to drill an 18.5-kilometer tunnel through the mountain.

Former Xiyang County Magistrate Gao Xiubao remembers that people already had gone out prospecting and drawing plans for this project in the 1960s. But nobody dared make the final decision due to its relatively large scope and cost. The grandiose project, therefore, remained on the drawing board. For these very same reasons the County Standing Committee, when it met to discuss Chen Yonggui's proposal, did not accept it. The project was too difficult and vast. The Committee was afraid that it would never get finished.

During the opening of the National "In Agriculture Learn From Dazhai" Conference Chen Yonggui made his decision: The eyes of the entire nation were turned on Xiyang; if Xiyang retained the status quo, wouldn't it in fact be falling behind? Lin County was able to come up with the Red Flag Canal; why shouldn't Xiyang County be able to undertake this water diversion project?

And that is the beginning of the story of water diversion in Xiyang. This became the prototype for all rumors and hearsay that emerged in the 1980s from the water diversion tunnel. Xiyang had a total of 400,000 *mu* of land. When it started the "Learn From Dazhai" movement, it already had 40,000 *mu* of irrigated fields. At the meeting of the County Standing Committee, Chen Yonggui laid down his decision: With the completion of the water diversion project, the County would develop irrigation on 100,000 *mu* (17,000 acres) of its land!

No less than 100,000 *mu* under irrigation! That was the brilliant plan conceived by Chen Yonggui!

And as this new conception was about to unfold on Sheep Fold Mountain (a sprawling summit scarcely noticed by anybody until then), strangers began pouring in—water conservancy specialists with their surveying instruments and leaders from the Shanxi Water Conservancy Bureau. News that senior Central Committee leaders supported this water diversion project suddenly reached the mountain. The experts' plans quickly encompassed the whole of Xiyang's landscape: 50,000,000 Chinese dollars in investment; a Home Nest Water Reservoir storing 60,000,000 cubic meters of water to the west of Sheep Fold Mountain; an 180-kilometer-long main canal, 18.5 kilometers of which would be a tunnel chiseled through the mountain—a tunnel that rivaled in length, if not in diameter, the Mont Blanc tunnel from Italy to France—and several hundred kilometers of distribution canals—a world-class project!

After the Xiyang water diversion project plans came out, the Sheep Fold Mountain construction site started to resound with the rumble of explosions, the coming and going of vehicles raising clouds of dust, the sounds of steamrollers, earth-moving machines and the "Learn From Dazhai" song. One could hear the intense racket of competing air hammers. County Committee leaders came to work on the spot. Propaganda departments came to agitate. Support units of the

Yangquan Mining Bureau and officers and men of the People's Liberation Army joined in opening the tunnel. The terminus of this "voyage" was 100,000 *mu* of irrigated fields.

One might say that without Dazhai to serve as the foundation stone and without Vice-Premier Chen's big name and fame, the blueprint for this kind of water diversion project would never have been drawn up. Indeed, all those scholars, celebrities and brave international explorers have been lured to the project only because of Dazhai's uniquely astonishing record. In order to gain their own perspective on the real facts about the water diversion project, they have been prepared to pay any price and disregard all obstacles to come to the location and take a look for themselves. Regardless of its measure of success and failure the project can never be wiped from the annals of the earth.

After the Xiyang water diversion project got off the ground, an expert from the provincial capital Taiyuan showed up in Chong Family Ridge, which is located just below Sheep Fold Mountain. He was none other than the Deputy Director of the Provincial Water Conservancy Bureau, Liu Xitian. He was accompanied on his inspection by Li Xishen, the Deputy Secretary of the Xiyang County Committee in charge of the day-to-day operations.

Due to his concern and support for Xiyang, Deputy Director Liu Xitian wanted to gain a genuine understanding of the hydrography of each place he visited, and he raised objections and made suggestions with warmth and enthusiasm wherever he discovered problems. In one place, the Commune members had built two power stations both competing for water on the same stream without storing up any reserve. Liu Xitian observed this, took out his calculator and started figuring. When he was done, his face turned grave.

"Old Li, you must square this account! Look, the flow of water is not very large, yet you are losing 20,000,000 cubic meters of water this way! You are losing two Guo Settlement Reservoirs[1] worth of water! How about building a water reservoir instead?"

Li Xishen gave the expert's suggestion much careful consideration, whereupon he assigned the County Water Conservancy Bureau's tech-

1. Guo Settlement Reservoir was a large reservoir further south in the County. (W.H.H.)

nician Gao Qixiang to make a survey and start drawing plans. There was already a small water reservoir below Chong Family Ridge—the Xing Settlement Reservoir, with a capacity of 3,000,000 cubic meters. In order to add the 20,000,000 cubic meters needed to store all the runoff, they prepared to build a big 30,000,000 cubic meter reservoir. But the survey showed that the existing location could only store 10,000,000 cubic meters. In order to build a big reservoir with a capacity of 30,000,000 cubic meters, they would have to build an enormous dam behind which the impounded water would reach all the way to Xing Settlement. Xing Settlement was hard put to hide its anxiety over future inundation. Chen Yonggui was the only person who could make the final decision in the matter.

The on-the-spot meeting called to decide on the location of the future Gate Mountain Reservoir took place at Anping People's Commune's Xing Settlement Production Brigade in the winter of 1976. County Committee leaders working at the location and outside experts all assembled at the simple facility, and anxiously awaited Chen Yonggui's vital input. Chen Yonggui asked for a special leave of absence from the Central Committee in order to return to Xiyang for this meeting. Although his expression looked rather aloof when he appeared at the meeting, he did not make any declarations or issue any orders right away, but suggested talking things over.

"I've come back to discuss this with you," said Chen. "Aside from the few government and Party leaders here, all other participants in the meeting are experts and engineers. Some are from the Central Institute for Geological Planning, some are from the Institute for Coal Planning, others from the Institute for Water Conservancy Planning. We have eighty people here. I plan to give you my opinion, and I want all of you to give me yours. This way, we'll have over eighty opinions! In my view, the spot originally chosen for the dam is not safe, but we have to consider the people of this village, too. Why not simply move the entire village of Xing Settlement, so that we can move the dam back? Any other possibility means spending much more money!"

As soon as Chen Yonggui expressed his view, Liu Xitian raised both hands in endorsement. Following his example, all the experts present expressed their support while bringing up some complementary opinions.

Before long, the Shanxi Provincial Committee, too, expressed its concurrence with the proposal. The final plan took shape soon thereafter.

In the spring of 1977, after Liu Xitian had inspected Pingding County's water conservation project, he saw construction plans for Xiyang's Gate Mountain Reservoir. He said that Xiyang should emulate Pingding's experience in dam construction and build the dam first, then construct a road and an aqueduct on top of it, so that three purposes might be achieved with one stroke. This would be pleasing to the eye, and would turn the location into a scenic spot.

In June 1977, the Chief Engineer at the Central Department of Hydropower, a man by the name of He, went to Xiyang and made a very important proposal: If they were to follow Pingding's example and build a concrete dam, problems would very likely arise with the hoisting equipment. Furthermore, given Xiyang's topography, there was a danger of water seepage. It would be safer to build a rock-filled bituminous dam like the one in Shaanxi, which also had an aqueduct and a road on top of it.

The final decision went the Chief Engineer's way.

Subsequently, with the exception of the County Committee Standing Committee member Jia Huolin, who remained on duty, the entire Committee went to work at the construction site. There they slept on the ground and ate corn meal with the common people. Working alongside the mobilized peasants, they directed the project, cutting into the mountain and splitting rocks. Various County institutions, factories and mines continued their regular operations, while transferring several thousand of their employees to work on cutting into the mountain, splitting rocks, and building the stone dam. The entire Anping plain swarmed with a sea of humanity and an incessant stream of draft animals and vehicles, who began work with sun's rising, and stopped when the moon came out. Nobody felt that there was anything strange about this, nobody felt the work was too hard. Their hearts looked with hope at the prospect of water, at the prospect of 100,000 *mu* of irrigated fields. Through publicity accorded it by the journalists at the urging of the leaders, the outstanding achievements at the Gate Mountain Reservoir became famous throughout Shanxi and throughout the country.

During the summer of 1977, the Central Department of Hydropower sent another expert to the project. He very conscientiously undertook a rather thorough inspection of the entire water diversion scheme. His conclusion was that both the source of water for and the geographical features of the Settlement Nest Reservoir were inadequate, and that the only way to go about it was to divert the Horse Stable River from Heshun County. The Xiyang Water Conservancy Department also suggested bringing the Horse Stable water in. In the process, the intended reservoir with the capacity of 60,000,000 cubic meters of water became a reservoir with the capacity of 130,000,000 cubic meters, and its location was moved to the village of Sunshine. The tentative plan was rather astonishing. Even Li Xishen did not dare express his support or disagreement lightly. What was he to do? He decided to leave it to Chen Yonggui's commanding ability and boldness of vision.

The word from Li Xishen reached Chen Yonggui's residence in Peking. Chen answered by telephone: "You must find out whether there is a scientific basis for this suggestion. Call people in to make a survey and draft a budget, so we can see whether it's feasible or not."

Before long, the plan for the reconstruction of the Reservoir received vigorous support from the Shanxi Provincial Committee. Provincial Committee Secretaries Wang Qian and Wang Tingdong went to the construction site for an on-the-spot investigation. They concluded the enlargement of the Reservoir would not only increase its water storage capacity but also mitigate the dangers of floods for the Central Shanxi plains, which would mean killing two birds with one stone. Rumor has it that the Shanxi Provincial Committee had yet another calculation: The construction of water reservoirs with capacity under 100,000,000 cubic meters was usually the responsibility of the Province where they were located; the construction of water reservoirs with capacity over 100,000,000 cubic meters was usually the responsibility of the Central Government. If the water diversion project could get the support of the Central Government, who would raise any objections to that?

When the matter came to Chen Yonggui's attention, he had even less reason to object. Those 100,000 *mu* of irrigated fields were his main objective; if that could be realized his mind would be at ease.

Before long, this world-class engineering project received support from Li Xiannian, Yu Qiuli and other Central Committee leaders. It was put on the list of State projects.

Around this time Li Xishen, who was in charge of the day-to-day operations at the Xiyang County Committee, went to Beijing to attend a meeting on agriculture. Qian Zhengying, the nation's Minister of Hydroenergy, was also at the meeting. The moment Qian Zhengying saw Li Xishen, he wasted no pleasantries before embarking on the topic of water: "I've seen Xiyang's water control projects. They're worthy of the Great Yu![1] You fellows have plenty of spunk when it comes to water control! If you dare do it, I dare support it! I'll give you three specialized units5 to help you out, all right?"

"Even if my project were bigger, it couldn't use the force of three specialized units!" protested Li Xishen, startled. "I thank Minister Qian and the leadership for the kindness, but I really could not find a way to employ three specialized units. I don't even think I will need one specialized unit."

At this time Chen Yonggui interrupted his regular work to return to Xiyang for an inspection. Wherever he went he was followed by reporters, photographers, and Provincial, Regional and County leaders. Everybody wanted to find out about the water diversion project on the spot and share in the credit from association with it. The water project became something to be passed around with general approval, and Chen Yonggui's fame increased even more with it. The Central Committee decided that this would be the project ceremonially dedicated at the Third National "In Agriculture Learn From Dazhai" Conference in 1980!

The water diversion project became "a pearl in the palm" of Xiyang!

Most exciting was the progress made in driving the long tunnel under Zhanling Mountain. To speed up the work, drilling, blasting and clearing began not just at the two ends of the tunnel but right across the middle at eight more faces opened up by driving four 45-degree off-

---

1. Yu, the reputed founder of the Xia Dynasty (c. 21-16th century B.C.), who came to the throne because of his ability to control floods through construction of canals.

vertical shafts down to the axis of the tunnel from selected spots close to the trans-mountain highway up above.

Thus large numbers of "tunnel hogs" with crash helmets, goggles and face masks could attack the rock at ten places simultaneously. Those at the eight faces in the middle moved away from each other toward the crews approaching from the neighboring shafts as fast as they could blast loose and move rock. Each shaft boasted equipment sufficient for a small coal mine: Down one side a set of cut-rock steps leading to the bowels of the earth, in the middle a track made of wooden ties and steel rails, at the top a power-driven winch, and riding the track, going down empty and coming up loaded, small ore cars each of which carried several tons of broken rock at a loading. Down in the rapidly lengthening tube the tunnel hogs pushed new track east and west as fast as the rock came out.

Night and day ear-shattering noise enveloped these shafts and the two extremities of the tunnel. It came from the large air compressors running constantly to power the jackhammers down below, from the diesel-engine-driven generators supplying needed electricity, from the winches that whined and squealed as the heavily laden cars came up, and from the roar of the rock falling as new loads of scree tumbled down the embankments toward the road.

If the sound was deafening above ground, it was even more so below where the jackhammers worked up a racket fit for the Devil's kitchen without a moment's rest except for those intervals when the firing crews loaded dynamite, lit fuses and set off the blasts, and the work crews cleared enough space to start drilling again. Peasant volunteers from the six Xiyang Communes slated to get water from the project manned most of the crews, but they worked side by side with a scattering of skilled hard-rock miners from the Yangquan Mining Bureau and electricians and mechanics from Xiyang County Town and Yangquan City as well, not to mention specialists from the Army.[1] Engineers and technicians kept running back and forth while teams of cooks and cooks' helpers made corn meal dumplings and boiled cabbage in huge steam-

1. These specialized units were mechanized earth-moving contingents that included fully manned bulldozers, scrapers, power shovels and trucks. (W.H.H.)

ing woks under makeshift roofs of mud and straw. The people of Xiyang County had never seen such lively scenes before, scenes in which someone from almost every family in at least half the County took part.

The engineers soon proved they knew their stuff. The ten tunnel shafts driven in from the ten faces all met and matched up within a few centimeters of allowable error and before the year was out the tunnel pierced Sheep Fold Mountain from one side to the other. Even though Central authorities stopped the whole project dead, as is described in Chapter 38, enough water ran out of the mountain itself into the tunnel and on to the east to supply all year round two of the six Communes originally included in the project.

Several leaders assembled in the Conference Room at the Xiyang County Revolutionary Committee Guest House—Vice-Premier of the State Council Chen Yonggui, Provincial Committee Secretaries Wang Qian and Wang Tingdong, Regional Committee Secretary Li Hansuo, Xiyang County Committee Deputy Secretary Li Xishen, Dazhai Production Brigade Party Branch Secretary Guo Fenglian, to name a few. The first speaker, Li Hansuo raised the question of preparations for the ceremonial dedication of the water diversion project at the Third National "In Agriculture Learn From Dazhai" Conference. As soon as he began to speak, Wang Qian got up from his seat and started to wave his hands in front of his subordinates, using rather stern language: "Can we really get the water here by the Third National 'In Agriculture Learn From Dazhai' Conference in 1980? If not, what are all those leaders from all over the country going to look at? Li Xishen, I ask you to concentrate very hard when you consider this question. This water diversion project is not only a Xiyang issue, it's already become a national issue. It has to be considered at the Provincial level and at the Regional level, too. Li Hansuo, you have to figure out what to do at the Regional level. Guo Fenglian has to deal with it on Dazhai level. As for the question of accommodation for the Congress participants, you don't have to worry about that, I'll take care of that. I've already said it, but let me make it perfectly clear: If anybody makes a mistake, you'll have to account for it to the Central Government! Well, I'm sure you know about that, since Vice-Premier Chen is here!"

Li Xishen was the first person to find problems raised by Wang Qian's orders hard to crack: "Secretary Wang," said Li Xisheng, somewhat daunted by the difficulties facing him, "I will carry out the duties you have bestowed on me to the letter, but I will have problems with the labor force, timing, lodging, etc. Considering only the mobilization of an adequate labor force, completion by 1980 is problematic. Not to mention that we cannot do some of the very particular engineering projects right away. That's why we don't dare start work on the Main South Canal."

Wang Qian smiled, spoke a few words of encouragement, but did not budge from his position at all.

The water diversion project affected leaders on all levels, from the Central down to the County, the Communes, Brigades and teams. They were all willing to contribute their energy and hard labor to the project. The former County Magistrate, Gao Xiubao, told me that every time he went to the Provincial level to have some part of the project or funding approved, every single Provincial leader acted on his own initiative. He gave me the example of one Jia Chunzhi, a one-time Director of the Provincial Planning Commission, who later became the Deputy Governor of the Province. Old Gao told me that every time he went to look for him, he called a meeting immediately to study the problem and make a decision. On one occasion, Jia Chunzhi told Gao Xiubao: "If you have any problems just come and ask!"

"Ask whom?" asked Gao Xiubao.

Jia Chunzhi tapped himself on the chest: "Ask Old Jia."

CHAPTER 34

UNDER TIGERHEAD MOUNTAIN DAQING MEETS DAZHAI

As I was revising this particular chapter, I heard a popular song from afar:

> We, the young,
> Gather today
> In boats rocked
> By a gentle breeze.

It echoes the ardent sentiments of young people as they encounter one another, but it is a far cry from the encounter of the two red banners on the production front that waved over China in 1977. That year the two banner bearers met in the shadow of Tigerhead Mountain—not a gathering of youth but a joining together of old battlefield veterans, friends who had long been apart. It was an encounter that expressed the wishes Mao Zedong left behind at his death; it was an encounter that strengthened the alliance of workers and peasants in their common goal of building a new society.

The recently held National "In Industry Learn From Daqing" Conference, with Hua Guofeng, Ye Jianying and Li Xiannian mutually affirming the position of Daqing and Dazhai as the two red banners of the country, served as a forerunner for the face-to-face meeting in Xiyang. After Dazhai and Daqing had both sent representatives to the National Conference on Daqing, the first response of the representatives from Daqing was to stage this visit in person to their counterpart model unit in Shanxi. Thus they set up an encounter of historic significance!

When the Daqing representatives set out from Beijing, Chen Yonggui rushed back from the Capital to be on hand to greet the oil workers from the Northeast. The members of the Dazhai Branch Committee went to the Yangquan train station to wait for them. Among the representatives of Daqing were several leaders in charge of front-line management such as Song Zhenming, the ten "Great Pacesetters" of Daqing like Qu Qinghua and his colleagues, the Deputy Director of the No. 1202 Drilling Crew, Yin Wenzhu and the Director of the No. 1205 Drilling Crew, Wu Xiang Dong, famous from the days when Iron Man Wang was still alive and led them in the field. They brought with them the warmth of friendship, more valuable than ten thousand taels of gold and sat down side by side with their hosts from Dazhai to encourage each other and learn from each other.

Over the past twenty years, the trekking of more than 7,000,000 Chinese visitors and more than 20,000 foreign visitors had left a spacious road that circled the slopes of Dazhai's gullies and ridges. But when Chen Yonggui led the representatives from Daqing up Kang Family Ridge, he took a precipitous, bumpy, narrow winding trail. As they climbed, there were times where there was not enough space to place both feet firmly on the ground, and they had to use their hands to hold onto the earth. One of the members of the climbing party at first thought Chen Yonggui had turned off the main road onto this trail because he had some business to take care off, but when he saw him starting to climb the slope, he reminded him: "Old Chen, that's an impossible path!"

People familiar with Chen Yonggui know how riveting his eyes could be. He did not have to say a word, it was enough to be subjected to just one of his glances. This comrade got quite nervous when Chen Yonggui gave him a look. But Chen Yonggui turned his gaze back from the man and planted it on the visitors from Daqing. "That's exactly the kind of path we want to take." Emphasizing the significance of the route he went on, "Both Daqing and Dazhai have emerged from difficult roads!"

There was no need for further explanation. Everybody understood what he meant. And so they all started climbing the narrow winding path to which he had led them.

This move of Chen Yonggui's was again misconstrued by a Commune member who was working in the orchard nearby. Putting down his tools, he yelled at the group: "Hey, take it easy over there! That's an impossible path!"

Chen Yonggui did not give him one of his looks; he just cracked a meaningful smile. "No visitor has ever taken this path. With our comrades from Daqing, we'll be the first ones."

You don't have to beat hard to sound a gong; the representatives from Daqing knew all too well what kind of road this was! Who knows how many such roads Daqing and Dazhai had taken since the 1950s! The choice of the little winding path indeed carried profound significance. It brought out many disquieting associations in the minds of people from Daqing and Dazhai: Both places had emerged in the 1950s and followed the Communist Party's path of self-reliance and arduous struggle onto the road of socialist construction of industry and agriculture in China. Ah, how many heroic and moving stories remained imprinted in their memories! As the representatives from Daqing followed Chen Yonggui into the orchard, they could not suppress their excitement at the sight of ridges and gullies filled with various fruit trees in bloom.

"Wonderful!" they exclaimed. "This is a true fruit-blossom mountain! It's beyond imagination how the people of Dazhai managed to turn the bare hills of Old Tigerhead into this cornucopia of blooming fruit trees!"

Amidst praise from the visitors from Daqing, Chen Yonggui decided to bring into play his role as Vice-Premier. Using modesty typical of a good host he said: "The people of Daqing have contributed to this orchard, too! Didn't your Iron Man Wang use to say: 'When the conditions exist, go ahead; when they don't exist, then create them and go ahead!' We were inspired by the spirit of Iron Man Wang when we created conditions where there had been none before and turned the flanks of Tigerhead into orchards in bloom. Comrade Wang told us a truth. We understood through our own experience: If you really want to change something it is not that hard, the question is whether you are determined, whether you do it or not. Are you the doer, or the looker? Are you self-reliant, or do you ask for help? If you speak of self-reliance and arduous struggle, but you want material and money before you start doing things, then you are a far cry from the spirit of Iron Man Wang! Some people keep asking to this very day how much money did the State invest in Dazhai after all? These are the people that have never believed in self-reliance and that have never taken the masses into account!"

The representatives from Daqing followed by saying: "That's right! How can we build a country, how can we make China prosperous and strong without the spirit of arduous struggle?"

Dazhai and Xiyang organized social evenings and informal discussions for the representatives from Daqing. They all received wide coverage by the press. Some papers broke new ground in the style of reporting on the encounter between the people of Daqing and Dazhai, in order to make it more lively for the readers. One report, entitled "One Hero Shakes the Other Hero's Hand," wrote: "As the people of Daqing shook hands with the people of Dazhai, their hearts were flooding with warmth; no words could adequately express the feeling that those were the kind of hands that heroes love to shake."

The news story continued: "As the people of Daqing shook hands with Guo Fenglian, they could feel the calluses on her palms and fingers. Yet those were the hands that were creating the future. "As the people of Daqing shook hands with Liang Bianliang, his palm was as hard as a rock and the back of his hand as rough as soil. Yet those were hands working energetically for socialism...."

Many more paragraphs on various people's hands followed.

After all this attention to hands, the article went on to report on what kind of hardships these heroes had experienced in the old society. Their depiction in "One Hero Shakes the Other Hero's Hand" was intended to stir sympathy among their readers, but it also served to represent the effect Daqing and Dazhai had in China and abroad in those days. In order to make breakthroughs in socialist industry and agriculture in China, in order to use the experience of selected units to promote work in the entire country, the Chinese Communist Party and Mao Zedong frequently took to setting up models and examples. This was an old tradition in the Party's style of work.

On the day of the Daqing delegation's arrival, Dazhai Production Brigade and the Xiyang County Committee of the Communist Party of China staged a welcoming rally, with speeches by Guo Fenglian, Li Xishen and Song Zhenming, and exchanges of autographed albums with symbolic significance. Chen Yonggui accompanied the delegation on a tour of the key projects in Dazhai, South Knoll and Xiyang. On May 31, 1977, Chen Yonggui took the delegation to visit the just-opened Yellow Cliff Distillery. Upon Chen Yonggui's suggestion, the Xiyang County Revolutionary Committee decided to change the distillery's name to "Pioneer Factory." At the beginning of June, Chen Yonggui took Daqing delegation to see the water diversion "West-Water-East." The road to the project passed by the County's Dazhai Nitrogenous Fertilizer Plant, a factory personally authorized by Premier Zhou Enlai. The workers at the plant were hoping that Chen Yonggui and the delegates from Daqing would pay them a visit. As Chen Yonggui led the delegation back from the water diversion project all the workers assembled at the entrance to the plant, beating gongs and drums. Chen Yonggui stopped his car and he and the Daqing delegates riding with him jumped out. The plant's General Branch Secretary, Zhao Xingyuan, who had just attended the National "In Industry Learn From Daqing" Conference, stepped forward.

Chen Yonggui asked him: "Has your fertilizer plant yet been reorganized on the model of the Daqing enterprise?"

"We are working on it," said Zhao Xingyuan.

"Good," said Chen Yonggui. "When you set up a Daqing-type enterprise, I'll bring a delegation to visit you."

Chen Yonggui shook hands with Zhao Xingyuan and the workers who were lined up to welcome him, and waved goodbye.[1]

---

1. The author Qin Huailu was a maintenance worker in this plant and personally took part in this welcome to the Daqing delegation. (W.H.H.)

At the end of their visit to Dazhai, as the members of the Daqing delegation took leave of Tigerhead Mountain, tears welled up in their eyes. The friendly encounter had been a complete success.

A true friendship lasts forever. Even after they took leave of Tigerhead Mountain, the people from Daqing continued to recall Dazhai with deep nostalgia. Even after Dazhai's precipitous fall, Daqing's workers continued to sympathize with Dazhai. When in 1989 Xiyang County experienced some difficulties in purchasing oil, cadres thought of peddling Dazhai's old influence in Daqing to buy oil. They asked Guo Fenglian to go to Daqing. When the Director of the County Petroleum Department and Guo Fenglian arrived in Daqing and when Daqing's leaders found out the purpose of their visit, they were very straightforward: "Did Xiyang think about Dazhai's connections to buy oil when it criticized Chen and all his works? If Dazhai were here to buy oil, we would give it. If it's Xiyang, we wouldn't give it even if we had it! That's how we are in Daqing. We keep things in proportion when redressing leftist mistakes." Thus Daqing drove home its indignation at Xiyang for joining in the general condemnation by throwing stones at Dazhai after it had fallen down and out of favor.

On June 17, 1977, another two sets of hands, separated by the distance of a thousand miles, clasped each other under Tigerhead Mountain. One belonged to the hosts in Dazhai, the other to the fighters of the "Hard-Boned Sixth Company," a model army unit of the Beijing-Nanjing Military Area Command.

A white-haired general, Liao Hansheng, political officer of the Nanjing army, accompanied the famous "Hard-Boned" unit.

Liao Hansheng had fought in bloody battles alongside folks in Shanxi for eight years during the War of Resistance Against Japan. His arrival caused an upsurge of emotion in people waiting to greet the visitors! He said repeatedly, "I have eaten Shanxi's millet. Its color is like gold. Its flavor gushes out when you put it in your mouth, just killing you with that savory taste."

This brought joyous laughter from the welcoming crowd.

On June 17th, the 1,500 people assembled at the auditorium greeted the soldiers and their commanders. To their surprise a second white-haired general appeared on the podium: The Political Officer of the Peking Military Area Command, Qin Jiwei. When Qin Jiwei's name was called out, the old peasants of Xiyang recalled how brilliant and formidable the young General Qin had been thirty years ago. He had left footprints all over Xiyang's landscape as he fought the aggressor in bloody battles day after day, month after month; spent shells from his rifles had left a trail behind them in the old forests and on the tortuous mountains that stretch from east to west across the County. The sound of his forceful commands had swept across the yellow cliffs and valleys.

When the Shanxi Provincial Committee Secretary at the time, Wang Daren, introduced him by saying, "This is 'Commander Qin' of the Taihang Mountain region of thirty years ago," applause exploded like the sound of beans being fried at high temperature. Through thunderous applause the old liberation army base at the core of the Taihang was venting its intense feeling for its past history. Political Commissar Qin patted the hair at his temple and sighed that he was now old. Then he uttered from the bottom of his heart: "It's Dazhai that's drawn me back!"

This one sentence again stirred the emotions of those thousand and some people in the auditorium, and the atmosphere again changed back from serious to animated.

At that time the Central Committee had already placed the "Hard-Boned Sixth Company" in the same position as Daqing and Dazhai—a national model unit. Everybody knew about the dedicated, work-prone "Hard-Boned Sixth."

In order to strengthen the friendship between the People's Liberation Army and Dazhai, the soldiers of the company pitched tents in the "educational ravine" and helped the people of Dazhai build dams, construct fields and create little plains for several weeks. The people of Dazhai have not forgotten the beads of sweat that the People's Liberation Army men shed on Dazhai's land while sharing comfort and hardship with them. They left behind numerous marks that prove that "the army and the people go together like fish and water." From "The Army and the People Canal" and the "Peasant Support Pond" to their pitched-tent camp, the People's Liberation Army had hoisted its sails high on the broad river of "learning from Dazhai."

Local people have never denied the friendship and support for Dazhai given by the Peoples Liberation Army. Yet during the era of redressing ultra-left mistakes, some people used this army support to negate Dazhai's self-reliance. This view must surely be seen as too prejudiced! Viewing a political concordance solely in economic terms will only leave too shallow and simplified a version of history, reducing it to the most callow level of conventional wisdom and Philistinism.

CHAPTER — 35

A MARSHAL AND A GENERAL DROP BY

The wider and farther the magma of the "In Agriculture, Learn From Dazhai" movement flowed, the higher Tigerhead Mountain rose on the horizon. The fame of its symbolic loftiness already surpassed that of the fabled Five Mountains,[1] so that an ever greater number of top-level leaders came to visit. They felt they would experience profound regret if they failed to see it with their own eyes. This is precisely the feeling that compelled Ye Jianying and Wang Dongxing to go to Dazhai.

Vice-Chairmen Ye Jianying and Wang Dongxing visited Dazhai and Xiyang from September 11th to September 15th of 1977, in the company of Chen Yonggui, other Central leaders and Xiyang County cadres.

The Brigade Committee entrusted two outstanding Dazhai women, Guo Fenglian and Song Liying to show the Party notables around. A number of provincial and regional leaders, both civilian and military joined the tour, the most prominent among them Dazhai's old friend, Wang Qian, Party Secretary of Shanxi.

1. The Five Mountains: Taishan, Hengshan (in Hunan), Huashan, Hengshan (in Shanxi), Songshan.

September 11th was a particularly fine, sunny day, as though specially arranged for the two Vice-Chairmen's visit. A bright, warm sun shone down. No breath of wind stirred. The corn on the ridges and in the gullies of Dazhai and Xiyang was beginning to ripen and the sorghum tops looked like a sea of red brooms. Although the area had experienced an extremely violent windstorm just as autumn began[1] the crops were doing very well. Chen Yonggui had returned to Dazhai a few days earlier and, taking in the vast panorama of bumper crops on all the ridges, in all the gullies on and below the mountains, he happily recited to the County cadres:

> The weight of corn
> So heavy in the ear,
> Loads the mountain
> With all that it can bear.
> Pendant panicles of millet,
> As far as the eye can roam,
> Affirm a bumper crop
> For us to carry home.

In honor of Ye Jianying's and Wang Dongxing's visit, the villagers of Dazhai swept their streets and yards clean while the townsfolk decorated Xiyang County Town splendidly for the festive occasion. As far as Join Up Ridge they also swept the road leading from Dazhai to Yangquan so clean that it resembled a city street, and as the final touch they neatly whitewashed the lower trunks of the Beijing poplars that lined the two sides of the road.

During the Eleventh Party Congress, Ye Jianying had said in front of Guo Fenglian: "I have to go to Dazhai, very soon." Thus when Chen Yonggui returned to Xiyang at the end of August to survey the windstorm damage, Guo Fenglian entrusted him with a letter for Ye Jianying that contained an official invitation to visit Dazhai. As soon as Ye Jianying received the letter, he called Chen Yonggui to his place, warm-

1. The Beginning of autumn is equivalent to the 13th solar term.

ly invited him to sit on the sofa and pressed him to have a Zhonghua brand cigarette. There was only one topic he wanted to discuss: his intended visit to the Model Brigade. As for the time and the itinerary, he left it all to Dazhai to arrange. Since Wang Dongxing had long planned a visit, in the end they went to Dazhai together, alighting at Yangquan station in the early evening of September 11th.

The car engines of the welcoming group started up. Guo Fenglian and Ye Jianying were seated in the same Red Flag limousine. Chen Yonggui took a seat in the car behind.

"Which way is Dazhai?" Ye Jianying asked.

"Southeast of Yangquan," replied Guo Fenglian.

"I have been to Shanxi, but I have never come to this part," said Ye Jianying, speaking with a heavy Cantonese accent. "This time I've come to learn from Dazhai."

During the rest of the journey he inquired in detail about the situation in the village.

The Red Flag limousine entered the territory of Pingding County at dusk. Guo Fenglian told Ye Jianying about the changes Pingding experienced after Li Suoshou became its County Committee Secretary, and after the County started learning from Dazhai. Watching the crops on both sides of the Pingding highway, Ye Jianying said with obvious emotion, "It's different. The moment you enter Shanxi, it's different. The corn is planted very densely here."

The Red Flag limousine drove up to the bridge over the Gate Road Ravine. Ye Jianying noticed crops growing luxuriantly on the immense expanse of the reclaimed flood plain there. The sight moved him greatly.

"This river bed used to be very wide before, didn't it?" he asked.

"Very wide," answered Guo Fenglian. "They built that dike to confine the river to one side and created fields."

The darkness enveloping the highway from Yangquan to Xiyang delivered the Red Flag Limousine to the Dazhai Reception Center. Dazhai's cadres were gathered in two rows, forming a welcoming corridor. Ye Jianying and Wang Dongxing stepped from their cars and shook hands with everyone.

The Dazhai Guest House staff had prepared the room for Ye Jianying well in advance. His wife, Ye Xiangzhen, noticed that they had set up a soft bed for him. As he had trouble turning in bed on account of his age, she wanted to ask the reception center to bring a different one. Seated on a sofa, Ye Jianying shook his head: "Don't bother the people of Dazhai with it. I came to Dazhai to learn, to exercise, and to rest, but not to inconvenience anyone," he said, turning to the employees of the center who hovered about, anticipating his every wish.

Wang Dongxing showed the same spirit. On September 12th in the morning, after he got up, he saw the attendants busily cleaning the room. "I'm a fit man!" he protested. "I should be doing some physical work, you know! At the very least, let me clean the room and wash the floors with you."

The attendants politely refused his services.

That morning, Ye Jianying and Wang Dongxing picked apples in front of Liang Bianliang's house and prepared to visit homes of some Dazhai Commune members.

"Where's your home, Yonggui? Where's your home?" Ye Jianying asked Chen.

The peasant Vice-Premier pointed to the southwest.

Ye Jianying and Wang Dongxing arrived at Chen Yonggui's house as Chen's wife, Song Yuling, was bringing several babies from the village nursery to greet the two leaders. They entered Chen Yonggui's one-story house, No. 88. Everybody sat around a small round table. Chen Yonggui's little son Chen Mingliang and his grandson Chen Xingfu came up to their father to sit with him.

Wang Dongxing looked at Chen Mingliang, and then pointed at Chen Xingfu: "He is bigger!"

"My grandson is older than my son!" said Chen Yonggui, nodding his head and laughing.

Amidst laughter, all the members of Chen Yonggui's family had a photograph taken with the two Party and State leaders. Wang Dongxing wanted to see Chen Yonggui's inner chambers.

"Oh! It's very small!" he exclaimed when he saw the bedroom: "The bed is small, too!"

After the visit with Chen Yonggui's family, the two notables followed Chen Yonggui to the house of Jia Jincai and Song Liying. As soon as Ye Jianying entered, he called out: "Jia Jincai?"

"He's gone to the field. Gone to work," answered Song Liying, busy with cooking.

"Yielding to the worthy one?" said Ye Jianying with a wry grin.

Ye Xiangzhen, not understanding the meaning, said: "Are you messing the Mandarin duck[1] score?"

"Jia Jincai and Song Liying are a married couple," explained Li Xishen, who thought that Ye Jianying was asking whether the two were husband and wife.

Ye Jianying laughed, but repeated his question: "Yielding to the worthy one?"

"Right! Right! He's the one who yielded to the worthy one," somebody who had solved the riddle called out.

Chen Yonggui, getting the point, immediately replied: "He yielded his post to me."

Ye Jianying was finally satisfied. He nodded his head.

Ye Jianying and Wang Dongxing went on to visit Guo Fenglian. There was a framed photograph of Premier Zhou holding Xiaojun[2] on her wall. Chen Yonggui pointed at the photograph and told Ye Jianying: "My son, Mingliang, was a bit upset when this photo was taken because the Premier held Xiaojun and did not hold him. I told him the Premier would come again. It never occurred to me the Premier would no longer be with us."

Ye Jianying and Wang Dongxing fell silent. Everybody in the room fell silent too. It was as if each person was inwardly expressing his or her grief over Premier Zhou's death.

After a moment of silence, Ye Jianying gave Chen Yonggui the presents he had prepared earlier—a box of candy, a box of apples and a bottle of liquor. Accepting the gifts, Chen Yonggui said: "I thank Vice-President Ye!"

Ye Jianying then gave identical presents to Guo Fenglian, who shook his hand as she thanked him in like manner.

After they left Guo Fenglian's home in the company of Chen Yonggui, Ye Jianying and Wang Dongxing drove in a car up the moun-

1. Mandarin ducks stand for an affectionate couple.
2. Presumably, Xiaojun was Guo Fenglian's little son.

tain to the "Peasant Support Pond." Ye Jianying was already well aware of the story of the pond. He was very much moved by the grand vista that unfolded there and he told his host, "Yonggui, Hong Kong is an island of some four million people. They depend entirely on Heaven for their drinking water. When it rains, they don't let a drop leak away."

He used this example to encourage Dazhai and point out most emphatically the bright future of large-scale water conservation efforts.

After the "Peasant Support Pond," Ye Jianying and Wang Dongxing visited Chen Yonggui's experimental field. Chen Yonggui explained how at that field they were now planting 4,000 plants on each *mu* of land, as opposed to the 1,600 to 2,000 planted in the past. Chen Yonggui strode out into the field and stripped an ear of corn, showing the golden splendor of its kernels. Ye Jianying joined him and, while Chen Yonggui gesticulated, said: "Break it off! Break it off!"

The master photographer who followed them around saw this as a scene that would make a wonderful memento. Ye Jianying was happy to pose for him, holding a corn stalk with one hand and pointing at Chen Yonggui with the other: "You stand over there. You stand over there!" The photographer's lens snapped as Ye Jianying and Chen Yonggui broke off the corncob together, leaving to history a colorful record of their affinity.

When Ye Jianying and Wang Dongxing came back from the mountain, they were invited to see a song and dance program prepared by Dazhai's young propaganda team. Ye Jianying had been having problems getting around, but he categorically refused to be supported as he walked toward the auditorium. His vigorous strides stirred those who were watching him. Wang Dongxing, who walked behind him, started singing in time to Ye Jianying's steps: "Valiantly and spiritedly, we bestrode the Yalu River!" This stirred an outburst of laughter.

People say that Huang Zhong,[1] at eighty, refused to give in to old age. Everybody felt that Dazhai somehow rejuvenated Ye Jianying. His aids observed that he was much more energetic. Dazhai's intense regenerative powers had worked their magic on him. On September 13th in the afternoon, Ye Jianying climbed into his car one more time to go up

1. An old General from the Three Kingdoms period, also known as "Old Huang Zhong."

Tigerhead Mountain and visit Dazhai Commune's Great Tiger Ranch. The first thing he saw at the ranch was a poem written by ranch employees and displayed on a wall as part of their wall newspaper.

As Marshal Ye climbed
Tigerhead Mountain,
Mountain flowers bloomed
Red in bright array.
Clear voices of the people,
Soaring high in song,
Lit up our ranch girls' faces,
Joyful for this day!

Having read the poem, Ye Jianying recited four lines off the top of his head in response:

As I look down from
Tiger Mountain's top,
I see endless terraces
Green with crop.

Chen Yonggui laughed, and everybody clapped hands as a sign of appreciation.

During his stay at Dazhai, Ye Jianying forgot fatigue. From the 13th to the 15th of September, he read almost a hundred thousand words worth of material, visited South Knoll Production Brigade, the Guo Settlement flood-control reservoir, the Dazhai Exhibition Hall, and the location where Jiang Qing dug her notorious trench.

"In Gansu Province," Chen Yonggui told him, "there is 'a Dazhai County' but people there still go out to beg for food!"

"How can that be called 'a Dazhai County'?" asked Ye Jianying. "We have to give them some concrete help to solve their problems."

On September 15th Wang Dongxing went to visit Rock Flat Production Brigade. Chen Yonggui told him about Rock Flat's Party Secretary, Chen Youtang. Wang Dongxing immediately asked: "Where has this Chen Youtang been transferred to?"

"To Jiaocheng," answered Chen Yonggui. "He went to transform the mountains and the rivers of Hua Guofeng's Jiaocheng. He went to bring Wenshui River water to Jiaocheng's parched land."

"Did his family go with him when he went to Jiaocheng?" asked Wang.

"No, it didn't," replied the new Party Branch Secretary of Rock Flat, Zhang Guixiang. "He still even gets his work points here at our Production Brigade. This is where he gets his grain, too."

"Aha!" exclaimed Wang Dongxing. "You are subsidizing the manufacture of cadres! How about turning out still more people with ability here in Dazhai and Xiyang?"

"We've transferred some twenty or thirty people from here," responded Chen Yonggui, "and people still accuse us of not being willing to give up our cadres. We've been picked clean."

"And people still complain to superiors about it!" added the Provincial Committee Secretary of Shanxi, Wang Qian.

"Somebody has even tried to complain about me!" added Chen Yonggui, laughing.

"You should go to the national level next time! Carry the spirit of Dazhai to the entire nation!" said Wang, gesturing with his hands to emphasize his point.

Ye Jianying did not go to Rock Flat that day. He concentrated his energy on writing poetry. According to his aids and attendants, Ye Jianying spent several days hammering out just one poem. By the 14th in the afternoon he was not feeling well. He had a slight fever, yet he continued to sit at his desk working on revisions. He went on until late that night, and again continued at 6 A.M. on the 15th. As he advanced in age, this great Marshal, who once commanded powerful armies on the battlefield, became fascinated with poetry-writing and was determined to leave a poem under the Red Banner set up by Chairman Mao Zedong himself.

At noon on the 15th Ye Jianying brought his poem out under a low apple tree in front of his room, No. 6. He placed the poem in Guo Fenglian's hands and asked her to read it aloud. Chen Yonggui joined them there. The three of them sat together, and Chen Yonggui listened as Guo Fenglian read the verses. When she finished, Ye Jianying said: "Comrade Yonggui, revise it for me!"

"Thank you, Vice-Chairman Ye," responded Chen Yonggui, "but I couldn't revise it! Don't revise it! It's very good the way it is!"

"I will give it to you when I write it out with brush and ink," said Ye Jianying.

The title of the poem was "A Poetic Narration on Learning From Dazhai." Marshal Ye introduced it as follows: "From September 11th to September 15, 1977, I went with comrades Dongxing and Yonggui to learn from Dazhai. I was truly dazzled by so many things that I could not take them all in at once. I request to submit this poem as a record of my feelings.

"Comrades Dongxing and Yonggui, please make corrections...."

After Wang Dongxing returned from his visit to Rock Flat at noon, he also presented Dazhai with a dedication, which began with "Learning From the People of Dazhai," and continued:

> In Dazhai determination is high
> Great rivers submit to command.
> "Conquer disaster" is the people's cry.
> Their laughter pervades the land.

When Wang Dongxing began writing his "Learning From the People of Dazhai," Chen Yonggui told him: "It would be better not to write a thing like that!"

Wang Dongxing put down his pen, slightly irritated, and retorted, "Yonggui! I have a sincere desire to learn from Dazhai, I am not making anything up. While the Chairman was still alive, he used to tell me quite frequently: 'Dazhai is a very fine place. We should learn from it.' Chairman Mao was not able to come in his lifetime, on account of his advanced age and a heavy work-load. He is no longer with us, but we still wanted to come. I and Vice-Chairman Ye came this time, saw it with our own eyes and, you might say, we've fulfilled Chairman Mao's last wish. I have a sincere desire to learn from Dazhai. Wouldn't it be great if China's entire countryside could be molded after Dazhai! Like

Comrade Deng Xiaoping said: 'If just one-third of the countryside reached Dazhai's level, we would have no place to store all the grain!' That's why I have to write like this."

Fighting to suppress tears, Chen Yonggui said: "You have my approval to write that sentence. Dazhai does not belong to me. It belongs to the Party, to the entire nation."

Wang Dongxing laughed and, picking up his pen, said: "Now you are talking! That's precisely the position of the Political Bureau."

This rather emotional exchange, to me, clearly showed the Communist Party Central Committee's feelings about Dazhai and Chen Yonggui. Or, to reduce it to a more basic level, it showed the feelings of surviving Communist Party members for Chairman Mao Zedong. It is precisely due to such passionate feelings that the position of Dazhai continued to rise, increasing the gap between Dazhai's experience and the reality of the rest of China.

At three o'clock in the afternoon, as Ye Jianying and Wang Dongxing were about to leave Dazhai, the members of Dazhai's Party Branch Committee, Dazhai Commune members, County, Regional and Provincial leaders, and all the employees gathered in the Reception Center courtyard to see them off, wishing them a triumphant trip back.

When the limousines arrived at the Yangquan train station, Ye Jianying and Wang Dongxing stepped forward to shake hands with Guo Fenglian, Song Liying, Li Xishen, and the others who had come to see them off. They parted from each one individually. Ye Jianying called for his secretary and asked him to give Guo Fenglian a commemorative badge of Chairman Mao's Memorial Hall. He also gave Guo Fenglian his telephone number. Chen Yonggui and Wang Qian went on to accompany the departing guests all the way to Taiyuan. When Dazhai and Xiyang cadres asked Ye Jianying to come again in 1980 for the Third National "In Agriculture Learn From Dazhai" Conference, Ye Jianying replied with tears in his eyes: "I'll come again! I'll come again!"

"I'll come with him," Wang Dongxing said. "I'm coming for sure. I'm still young and healthy, I have no problems eating, sleeping or running around. Everybody is likely to come in 1980 for the meeting: Chairman Hua, Vice-Chairman Deng, Vice-Chairman Li."

"We'll let you make the future arrangements for our stay," he said, thinking about the age of Chairman Hua Guofeng and several other Vice-Chairmen. "Chairman Hua is in good health, so you can drag us all over the place. We'll come for sure in 1980, for the meeting."

The train-station bell announced the departure of the train. As the wheels began to turn, people aboard and on the ground said goodbyes, keeping in their hearts emotions difficult to express in words.

Under alleged "leftist" influence, the Communist Party Central Committee's appraisal of Dazhai's experience reached an unprecedented height, assigning to Dazhai the role of the model for continuing the revolution under the dictatorship of the proletariat, and turning it into the model for the future of China's countryside. The learning from Dazhai's experience up and down the country was not allowed to get out of step. In a political environment where "one simply had to forge ahead, compelled by the force of circumstances," Chen Yonggui outlined Dazhai's and Xiyang's experience in four sentences: mass criticism of revisionism, mass struggle against capitalism, mass effort for socialism, mass longing for communism. As a result, Dazhai and Xiyang approached the realm of absolutes.

From the First National "In Agriculture Learn From Dazhai" Conference to the Third Plenary Session of the Eleventh Congress of the Communist Party of China, an increasing number of people on all levels intensified their learning from Dazhai. The press reported every word and move from Dazhai. The *Red Flag* magazine continuously published featured pieces on Dazhai. Not only agriculture, but industry, commerce, finance, culture, education, health, civil administration, youth, women and every other trade and profession were supposed to set Dazhai as their example. Dazhai's cadres attended meetings of the Central Government and went everywhere to pass on their valuable experiences. It seems they simply had to go everywhere in China, and even abroad. Several of Dazhai's main leaders concurrently held other leadership positions, ranging from alternate member of the Central Committee at the top, to Party Branch Committee member at the bottom, simultaneously shouldering many responsibilities. Who could have foreseen that before long they would fall all the way from Ninth Heaven to Ninth Hell?

PART THREE

THE DISAVOWAL OF CHEN YONGGUI

CHAPTER—36

CHEN YONGGUI CAST ADRIFT

During the second half of 1978, Party theorists launched a big debate about the criteria of truth. The debate soon gained great momentum and waxed broad in scope. It touched upon many issues, but it directed its spearhead at Chairman Mao Zedong's theory of continuing the Revolution under the conditions of the dictatorship of the proletariat. China stood at the starting point of a new phase, pressed into examining its entire past from a new point of view.

To begin with, Dazhai had been upheld as a model of socialist collectivization, but its evolution into the standard-bearer for the entire nation coincided with the extraordinary era of the Cultural Revolution, so that its experience inevitably entered the orbit of Mao's continuing Revolution and took on a tinge of the ultra-leftism with which its detractors stamped the whole theory. Consequently, as the critics started rethinking the path of development for China's whole economy, including agriculture, they began, within certain limits at first, to reevaluate Dazhai's experiences, its various endless battles and struggles and some of its other concrete problems, and came up finally with an appraisal that was the exact opposite of the one made by Mao

Zedong and Zhou Enlai, and the one made by Marshal Ye Jianying just a year earlier, which had urged everyone to study Dazhai and "Learn its present. Learn its future." Before they were done they had thoroughly repudiated Dazhai as a fraud, a new kind of State-pampered Potemkin Village that no one need take seriously.

From this time on, Dazhai's, Xiyang's and Chen Yonggui's reputations declined precipitously. The decline had nothing to do with the merits of the case. Their reputations declined because they were systematically destroyed in Party councils, in the media, in the universities and schools and everywhere that the ideological reversal and the policy turnabout assumed command.

In December 1978, the Third Plenary Session of the Eleventh Congress of the Communist Party of China convened in Beijing. The Congress put great emphasis on shifting the focal point of Party work and wrenched the guiding ideology of the Party as a whole into an enormous sea change that negated the earlier theory of class struggle as the guiding principle. Chen Yonggui had his own views on this issue, but he was extremely supportive of the new emphasis on building the economy, so he endorsed the Congress's resolution by raising his hand. During the Congress some people presented different opinions regarding Dazhai and the Dazhai problem, and some of these even caused violent reactions. Chen's thinking on the subject could have been critical, but he remained silent.

After the Congress, Chen Yonggui was not in the mood to remain in Beijing, so he returned to his home base in Dazhai and Xiyang County.

Chen Yonggui's Shanghai brand sedan, loaded with his unspoken feelings of dejection and depression, arrived in the village he called home. As he got out of the car, this master of Dazhai, typically, did not go first to his own house. Putting aside his depressed feelings, he walked toward the dam-bedecked and terraced mountain. With every step his eyes traveled in all directions, sizing up the scene.

The newly built little plain at Back Side Draw was seething with activity just as before. Clouds of dust flew through the air as grub hoes and shovels turned and glinted in an earth- transforming dance. Bulldozers came rumbling, as though asking for instructions from him!

Chen Yonggui was already over sixty years old, but his step was as agile as ever. His manner was composed and his expression cool, although he felt inside as though he had tipped over a bottle of magnolia vine extract and was unable to cope with its fumes.

"Old Chen, you are back," came a sound of greeting from a young man with a shovel.

"Hm," Chen Yonggui nodded solemnly. The young man had nothing else to say, so Chen turned his dark face back toward the plain. Observing with cool detachment, Chen Yonggui could not detect anything unusual.

"Brother Jin! You've just come back, and not a moment of rest!"

Chen Yonggui had been used to this form of familiar address used by peasants, which was a bit more cordial when used to address elders. After he went to work for the Central Committee, many people had changed "Brother Jin" to "Old Chen." But there were still some of his old work mates who found it difficult to alter their habits and they went on calling him by his nickname. When he had got together with these trusted comrades in the past he always appeared calm, but this time his face looked as though a storm had crossed it. His intimates had no idea what was behind the change.

Liang Bianliang, Song Liying and several Dazhai Party branch members crowded around him, but they did not seem to have much to say. Heedless of the condition of the ground under him Chen Yonggui simply sat down, took out a pack of cigarettes and lit one up. As soon as he put the pack on the ground, some of those surrounding him sat down too, while others squatted. As was the custom, they all took cigarettes out of the pack, put them in their mouths, and stared furtively at Chen Yonggui's troubled face. Several months had passed since Old Chen's last visit to the village. Getting to see him was a rare opportunity. These cadres and rank-and-file Brigade members had many things on their minds, but as soon as they saw his serious expression they decided it was not the right time to bring up too many issues.

"How many days have you been at it?" Chen Yonggui started his serious inquiry.

The Party Branch members answered him disjointedly.

"Is it easy to break up the frozen layer of ground?"

The Party Branch members made a simple report.

Chen Yonggui stole a somewhat resentful gaze in the direction of the bulldozer. The members all dispersed at the same time to continue with their work. Chen Yonggui remained standing in one corner of the field and waved at the bulldozer operator. The bulldozer started pushing a mountain of yellow earth toward him with added power.

From the time Dazhai established mutual aid teams to that very moment, Chen Yonggui had left numerous footprints on the slopes of the area's many ridges and ravines. He was quite skilled in all manner of farm work, including plowing, embankment construction and weeding with a hoe. As for the work in the village, he used appropriate measures to deal with all issues, regardless of how small they might appear. He never left anything unresolved. Although people could no longer see either the white hand towel tied around his head or the long-stemmed pipe dangling from his neck, his habit of participating in physical labor remained unchanged. At times he would leap out of his car and rush into the field to harvest millet, on other occasions he would join in building terrace-retaining walls. Even after he had become Vice-Premier, he still continued to eat in the fields. If he had to attend a meeting in town, he would not leave *the* fields until the Brigade members had finished their day's work. Undoubtedly, his behavior served as a model for the people. This was the real, historical Chen Yonggui.

The triumphantly advancing bulldozer swept rippling earth in the direction indicated by Chen Yonggui's hand, a hand that seemed to be making the bulldozer work with extra power!

Chen Yonggui's return propped up the villagers' morale. In the past few months the number of visitors to Dazhai had dwindled. Unable to detect which way the wind was blowing, they were confused by random bits of information that reached them. They urgently needed to thrash everything out so that the truth could emerge. Most important, they wanted to know whether they themselves had made any mistakes. In the end, some people were unable to hold themselves back until the meeting scheduled for the evening. They quietly surrounded Chen Yonggui again.

"Old Chen, haven't you just attended the Third Plenary Session? What was it all about?" the Brigade members asked.

"The circular will come down later. As for the broad issues, the newspapers have already reported on those," Chen Yonggui answered sounding very matter-of-fact, if a little defensive.

"How did the people at the Conference treat us?"

"How could they treat us? They are treating us like they've always treated us!"

Chen Yonggui's voice now began to sound more annoyed. His mouth would not divulge any information, but his face revealed disquiet.

Chen Yonggui's hand kept signaling to the bulldozer, and the bulldozer kept advancing triumphantly, enlarging the area of the little plain, foot by foot, yard by yard.

After the Third Plenary Session, Chen Yonggui began to hear all sorts of criticism from everywhere. It weighed heavily on his mind and inevitably started to influence his speech and his behavior.

At the beginning of 1979, the County Committee of the Communist Party of Xiyang called a Conference of Party representatives to elect a new County leadership team. Chen Yonggui made a special trip from Beijing to Xiyang to take part. According to the agenda, he was scheduled to deliver the opening address. The more heavily things weighed on his mind, the more he thought about the late Mao Zedong and Zhou Enlai. When he uttered his first words, therefore, he suggested that the meeting remember with heartfelt grief the passing of the great leader and teacher Chairman Mao, as well as of Chairman Mao's close comrade-in-arms Premier Zhou, and of Commander-in-Chief Zhu De. Then he urged that those who sacrificed their lives for the transformation of Xiyang's old, backward image be remembered with deep sadness. After he made the suggestion he was overcome with sorrow, and tears started rolling down his face. Losing control, he began weeping bitterly. Finally, controlling his emotions, he used the opening address to talk about the significance of the recent Party Congress, and he stressed the need for determined implementation of the resolutions of the Third Plenary Session, the need for a shift in the focal point of all work, the need for continued commitment to learning from Dazhai and the establishment of high-standard Dazhai-type Counties, and the need to continue their good work in Xiyang County.

Chen Yonggui said what he said because, despite the great shift in the guiding ideology of the Party, the Congress session had not specifically negated the idea of learning from Dazhai and he expected the work of popularizing Dazhai-type Counties to go on. The Conference elected Chen Yonggui to the post of Communist Party Secretary of Xiyang County, but it was very obvious after the Congress that Chen Yonggui fell short of the new demands and that he was falling out of step.

The implementation of the spirit of the Third Plenary Session in Xiyang County involved many issues. In the past, the recall of private plots, the closing of country fair market trading, and the transition to Production Brigade accounting units had all been widely publicized local experiences. The new call for the transfer of private plots back to individual use and the opening of country fair market trading was causing great ideological confusion in the county. Many people were calling it a capitalist restoration or a concrete expression of revisionism. As the originator of the Dazhai experience, Chen Yonggui, in particular, was not able to take to the new direction easily, overnight. The ideological conflict resulted in inaction, so that for a long time Xiyang did not open market trading at its country fairs and did not return private plots, thus demonstrating serious disaffection with the thrust of Central Committee decisions. As the reform trend gathered momentum the leading cadres in the County organized a meeting at Dazhai's Travel Office. There Chen Yonggui expressed the following view:

"If you have to release private plots, release them! I was the one who raised my hand at the Third Plenary Session. If the release turns out to be wrong, it won't be your responsibility."

And yet, despite what he said, there were still many People's communes in the County who did not distribute private plots because of their own ideological opposition. It wasn't until the second half of 1979 that the County finally started implementing the Seventeen Resolutions, including the establishment of private plots and open markets for trading.

The most recently promulgated "individual responsibility system" in agricultural production was an attack on Chen Yonggui's philosophy of collective agriculture, which over the years had became embodied in the slogan "large in size and collective in nature." When it came to the implementation of the spirit of the Third Plenary Session, Chen Yonggui remained very cautious. He did not force any decisions; rather, he solicited opinions from the County Standing Committee several times, listening to their views. Li Xishen, Gao Xiubao and some others proposed a "triple management" system. They would execute production contracts on the household level for the isolated houses and shanties in the hills, and their family production would be the basis for distributing family income. They would execute production contracts at the group level for regular Production Brigades, making groups still responsible for joint production planning and compensation. They would retain the Production Brigade accounting system for advanced Production Brigades.

Chen Yonggui endorsed the proposal at the meeting of the County Standing Committee. Once the Committee adopted this proposal between 1980 and 1982 it gradually put the "triple management" system into practice. Chen Yonggui made some adjustments in Dazhai's mode of production, allowing for the independent management of three sidelines in agriculture. These he organized into three teams: the forestry team, the machinery team, and the soy sauce and vinegar workshop. Thus he made the teams responsible for operating sidelines and the Production Brigade responsible for keeping sideline accounts. He gave the teams duties as well as cash awards. Chen Yonggui also stated at the meeting that the responsibilities of Production Brigade management were too heavy and that they should be divided among the teams—the smaller the share, the easier its management would be.

Chen Yonggui was not at all familiar with the "household production contract system" that had just emerged elsewhere in the country. He expressed disagreement with one such experience in Anhui Province at a meeting reported by newspapers, maintaining that it was not appropriate for Xiyang. He was even less satisfied with the public evaluation of Mao Zedong at that time, saying that it was grossly unfair. He definitely could not get used to the reproach some people aimed at Chairman Mao Zedong. He said that the spirit of the Third Plenary Session should not be implemented at the cost of distorting Chairman Mao's image. In the face of the new central task of shifting the focal point—the emphasis—of all party work from class struggle to building the economy, Chen Yonggui's alleged "leftist" ideology remained very strong. Dazhai's and Xiyang's Red Flag in the field of national agriculture now became a stumbling block in local attempts to change the focal point of work—in a word, to shift from "politics in command" to "developing production" period.

Because of this, a section of the public started to feel resentment toward Chen Yonggui. The media raised various issues: the validity of Xiyang's grain yield figures, the irrationality of its project allocations meaning alleged excessive investment in water conservancy—especially in "West-Water-East"—its conceit and arrogance, and even the legitimacy of its vaunted self-reliance. Since such opinions constituted a personal attack on Chen Yonggui, he, above all others, was extremely mindful of these issues. He made a long distance telephone call and summoned County Committee Deputy Secretary Li Xishen, Regional Committee Secretary Li Hansuo, and Song Shayin, who was in charge of the media and public opinion work, to Beijing, making all the arrangements for their trip.

"The reporters say that our grain yield figures are dishonest, that our project allocation is not rational, that we are conceited and arrogant, that we have not done the best-quality work and that we restrict the liberties of our Commune members," he told them. "Xishen, find an appropriate occasion to inform the leaders involved. As for the grain yields, you should all check the figures one more time when you get back. We must clarify any double account keeping. However, we have not had any nominal sales of grain to the State in recent years, we have not undersold by even one pound. You should make this known as well."

Many Central Committee leaders were extremely concerned about the proper handling of the Dazhai and Xiyang problem. When the issue of grain yields came up in their conversation, several Vice-Premiers told Li Xishen, "If there has been a mistake, you should correct it on your own initiative. If you do it by yourselves, everything will be fine. You won't even lose your advanced unit status." Consequently, in December 1979, Guo Fenglian even attended the National Citation Conference of Model Workers and Advanced Collectives, where she received a State Council

Award. As many as 116 groups of foreign visitors, numbering 2,256 individuals, still came to Dazhai that year and 4,205 Chinese visitors as well.

When Li Xishen returned to Xiyang from Beijing, the Shanxi Provincial Committee of the Communist Party of China called the Third Plenary Session of its Seventh Congress. Chen Yonggui telephoned again to ask Li Xishen to clarify the situation and account for it to the Provincial authorities. The Third Plenary Session of Shanxi's Seventh Congress convened at the end of 1979. During the session, the Central Shanxi Regional Group discussed Dazhai grain yields, with participation from Regional leaders and *Shanxi Daily* reporters. On behalf of the Xiyang County Committee, Li Xishen reported to the Plenary Session on his own investigation of grain yields and double account keeping in Xiyang. After his speech, Provincial and Regional Committee leaders commended Xiyang for its willingness to clear up its own problems, saying that this was the right attitude. On the afternoon after the investigation, the *Shanxi Daily* carried Li Xishen's report.

When I conducted my own research I wanted to hear Li Xishen's opinions from his own mouth.

"We didn't think there was a problem with it back then at all," old Li said as he heaved a deep sigh. "We came out with a plan at the beginning of each year and we estimated the yield every year before the harvest. Journalists published the estimated figures for publicity and propaganda purposes. At the end of the year, the real yields were frequently quite different from the estimated yields. Much of it was due to natural disasters like windstorms, hail and frost, which occur frequently in the fall. "For instance, at the time when I was in charge, I went on a trip to the United States on June 28, 1978. Just as I was leaving, reports of the estimated yields came out in the press. When I came back, several People's Communes like High Tower, White Lamb Gully, and Zhan Mountain had been hit by frost, while several others had been pounded by hail, reducing the projected yield by 15,000 metric tons. BUT the newspapers had already published the figures, so we were obliged to sell the grain to the State according to those published figures. I didn't think this was a problem at the time, but it has turned out to be an immense issue now."

Just a few months after the newspapers revealed Xiyang's incorrect yield reporting, the *People's Daily* carried the editorial: "We Cannot Afford Another Folly Like the Water Diversion Project," and the *Shanxi Daily* came out with the piece "Dazhai's Departure from the Spirit of Dazhai." Party leaders dispatched cadres to make repeated criticisms of Dazhai's experience, labeling it "one of the gospels," and launching personal attacks on Chen Yonggui, whom the press criticized, without mentioning his name, as "the leading cadre of Xiyang," "the autocrat" and the "feudal patriarch."

"Hooh! It's easier to avoid being eaten up by a tiger than being devoured by men!" said Chen Yonggui with a deep sigh after he saw such criticism.

On one occasion when Chen Yonggui returned to Dazhai from Beijing, several chief leaders of the County Party Committee went to visit him in an attempt to console him.

"Hooh! We're treated as feudal patriarchs now!" said Chen Yonggui, heaving another deep sigh.

They say that after this, in order to protect his feelings, some of the Central Committee leaders made an agreement:

"Don't give the material that deals with this to Old Chen, he'll be less upset if he doesn't see it."

CHAPTER — 37

DENUNCIATIONS LARGE AND SMALL

Some Central Committee members wanted to protect Chen Yonggui's feelings, but how could anyone protect Chen Yonggui from the avalanche of reproach that descended on his head after the Third Plenary Session of the Eleventh Central Committee?

The media, in all its forms, now subjected Dazhai, and with it Chen Yonggui, to a barrage of reproof, rebuke and castigation that covered everything about the Brigade and its past from eating frozen food while working in the fields, which was true but was now ridiculed instead of praised, to surviving on State aid, which was untrue but made into a damaging case by an atrocious warping and reconstructing of all facts and figures.

People often judge history from the standpoint of practicality, using common sense alone to judge specific happenings. During the reforms of the 1980s, rural areas put into effect the system of single family unit production and accounting, thereby negating the collective campaigns to control water and rebuild and transform hillsides. Thereafter many people unequivocally labeled these collective activities "ultra-left," "reckless," "foolish," and the like. They carried this tendency to extremes to the point where some people even went so far as to vilify the peasants of Dazhai for eating frozen food. Various newspapers, large and small, drummed up the charges, thus further distorting the story of Dazhai's three battles with Wolf Den Ravine. Defiling these battles as the "least glorious page" in Dazhai's history became an habitual practice with certain journalists and commentators. They forgot that history does not develop according to the blueprint that humans design in the quiet of their studies. Rather it takes shape under the pressure of various natural and social forces and often has no choice but to take this or that circuitous route.

If we are to speak of the "dialectics" of eating frozen food, we must first know something about the historical circumstances the people of Dazhai encountered and about the objectives of their struggle after they organized their Cooperative.

The truth of the matter is the media have evaluated the issue of eating frozen food very differently at different times. During the "Learn From Dazhai" period journalists eulogized eating "frozen food" as a symbol of the people's fighting spirit. When Dazhai came under attack for following an "ultra-left" line, the media used "frozen food" as proof that Dazhai and Chen Yonggui made outrageous demands on peasant builders. At the extreme end, the tongues let loose were shouting: "To liberate the peasants from slave labor, we must first criticize the "ultra-left" extremes of Dazhai!"

Liang Bianliang, who used carrying poles and baskets made of steel that year in Wolf Den Ravine, recalled those days for me. "The people of Dazhai never wanted to eat frozen food. However, it was just like being at war, they had no choice. Land building projects must be executed on time. They are seasonal and have to be rushed. If the job in Wolf Den Ravine was not completed during the first winter, the land could not be planted the following year. Worse than that, all work done could be washed away. The layout of the area, the way the flood waters came down, dictated that a major concentrated effort had to be made the very first winter. The most suitable time for gully work is just after the harvest before the ground freezes. Then it's still easy to move rocks and dig soil. Labor is much more efficient then than after the ground freezes to a depth of three feet.[1] The problem is, this kind of ideal time is limited. It's even more limited after the ground freezes. Once you break through the crust you have to keep going. That means you have to eat right at the edge of the field. Men start work very early. Women bring the food to the edge of the field as soon as they finish cooking it. In cold weather like that, after the long walk to the fields, the food can't help but get cold. A thin layer of ice sometimes forms on top of the porridge. I can't believe anyone could turn this into a fault on our part."

In later years Dazhai's critics turned into a crime the organizing of work in such a way that people ended up eating frozen food into a crime, but back then it served its purpose. In one winter of construction, the peasants of Dazhai constructed 38 stone terraces and created over 20 *mu* (four acres) of "man-made plains."

One day in Wolf Den Ravine Zhang Huaiying, then Party Secretary of Xiyang County, ate frozen food along with the peasant-builders. He told Chen Yonggui not to worry about the criticisms he was hearing. "Frozen food can cool you off," he said. "Certain journalists may not be able to stomach it, but I can."

What Zhang Huaiying said that day to comfort Chen Yonggui unexpectedly came back to haunt him. Barely a few years later, a leading cadre berated him,"We can't allow the peasants to eat at the edge of fields during the autumn harvest!"

"Eating at the field's edge during the busy harvest season is an age-old practice," replied Zhang Huaiying. "If you don't do a rush job, how are you going to harvest the grain?"

Reasonable as it was, the opinion only made him suspect as "extreme."

When he discussed this period of history with Chen Yonggui years later, he concluded: "When I fall from favor, I'm afraid it's going to be worse than eating frozen food at the edge of the field...." The conversation of the two men reflected their acceptance of hard struggle for the common good. But the reality of hard struggle was not something that most nonpeasants could readily accept. Nobody treated the idea itself

1. Three chi in the text. One chi (commonly also chih) equals 1.0936 English feet.

as suspect, but genuinely engaging in hard struggle was not an easy thing to do.

"Who doesn't want to eat well? If you serve frozen food side by side with hot noodles, of course the people of Dazhai will pick the hot noodles. But where is the hot food going to come from on a freezing day in a snow-covered field?"

This was Chen Yonggui's own evaluation of the frozen food issue.

I later had an opportunity to talk to Jia Jincai. Dazhai's history of that time could in many ways be said to be also the personal history of Jia Jincai. It had by no means been erased from his memory by age. This is how he explained the frozen food episode to me:

"The sky had sent down snow. But the first thing in the morning I went to the quarry anyway to cut stone. The people in charge of delivering food to the construction site, when they got out of bed, noticed that I had gone off to work, so they showed up at the quarry bearing food. They called me to eat right away, but when I took the lid off the clay pot, a thin layer of ice had already formed on the porridge that had just been cooked. Jia Chengxian spoke for us all when he suggested that we light up a fire and heat up the food—but where could we find any firewood with that thick cover of snow on the ground? Let's face it, on a day like that, who cares whether it's frozen or not? After you eat it, it gets warmed up in your stomach anyway! That's not the first or the last time I ate that kind of food."

I was moved by the old hero's words. I began to feel that all other speech in the world sounded frivolous. During the "Learn From Dazhai" movement, some newspapers used the example of frozen food to commend Dazhai. There was even a song that went: "Frozen food is sweet, frozen food tastes good...." Later, when it came time to charge "ultra-leftism," the same newspapers used the same example to attack and satirize Dazhai. Today, Chen Yonggui has already passed away, but Jia Jincai is still going strong despite his old age.

Old Jia later spoke with a sigh when I brought up these divergent attitudes.

"People's mouths have a hundred lives," he said. "When they are good, they turn you into a deep fried cruller; when they're bad, you're no more than dog shit."

The people of Dazhai themselves have never made frozen food sound like a mouth-watering delicacy. The example of their "frozen food eating" should only be used to illustrate how they confronted relentless fate with unrelenting will.

When all is said and done, however, politics can be merciless.

Imagine this winter scene: While work progresses on Wolf Den Ravine the Dazhai coop members go out to work at dawn. The cold wind stings their faces relentlessly. The pallid sun climbs listlessly over the top of Tigerhead Mountain. One after another, clay pots suddenly appear around the base of the new dam. They contain abundant servings of rapidly cooling food. Nearby, Chen Yonggui carries a large stone with both hands and places it on top of the dam. After he arranges the stone to his satisfaction he seems to realize what is on everybody's mind. He issues his instructions: "Let's eat! If anyone's food is frozen, let's build a fire and warm it up. We must be careful not to ruin our stomachs. The comrades who took part in the meeting last night haven't slept at all. If they honestly can't take it any more, they may look for a cozy nook on the sunny slope and take a nap. One way or another though, we must accomplish our task for the day. After we are done, we'll all get a full night's sleep. We'll hold off the next meeting until tomorrow night."

When he finishes he personally passes out the clay pots to each member of the Coop. Hot and sweating from work, how can they possibly feel the food is too cold? At this particular moment every day, many feel as though Chen Yonggui himself radiates some sort of body-warming emanation.

This is the story of how the people of Dazhai fell to eating frozen food. It is also the story of how Chen Yonggui led the members of Dazhai Cooperative into a bitter struggle with nature. Every trace of frozen food that the people of Dazhai once ate is now gone, but the stone dams they built while feeding on the frozen food have withstood numerous severe trials. They now stand as historical monuments, stone memorials to the perseverance of man.

"We should erect a monument to the builders," some people once suggested back then.

Jia Jincai laughed the suggestion off.

"Aren't these rows of terraces and dams monument enough in themselves?" Jia asked.

Apparently they are not.

The critics did not stop at complaining about "frozen food." They launched an attack on the whole idea of farmland capital construction and kept escalating the damaging scope of their denunciations over the years.

The achievements were there for all to see and were publicly recognized—they were a reality that could not be denied even at the height of the campaign to criticize Dazhai. But, after ten years went by, a book out of Henan, *The Rise and Fall of the Red Flag of Dazhai*, negated those great achievements all over again. This is how the book evaluated Xiyang's farmland capital construction and irrigation and water conservancy projects:

"Xiyang carried on great mass campaigns year after year: The more they engaged in farmland capital construction projects the more numerous and the greater in scope the projects became. Their basic purpose was really to keep the peasantry under control in a stockade where they could only commune with earth, draining all their wit and strength ceaselessly moving piles of yellow earth back and forth."

This kind of conclusion was confusing to hundreds of thousands of peasants. What peasants work at is precisely the planting of fields. If they don't have any land they can't plant or harvest any grain. If they don't harvest any grain, they go hungry. Is it possible that they committed a crime by getting involved in a few farmland capital construction projects to increase their harvest?

What people find even harder to understand is the following: Chen Yonggui confronted the cadres and people of Red Water Commune because of their policy: One, calculate; two, wait; and three, watch. He pressed them to go ahead and do something. The book *The Rise and Fall of the Red Flag of Dazhai*, compares Xiyang County's farmland capital construction drive with the agricultural practices of the United States and France. The book says: "In the United States it takes, on the average, less than half a man-hour to grow one *mu* of wheat; in France it takes 1.7 man-hours. But in Xiyang it takes around 288 man-hours to achieve the same result. How can a closed society with an economic structure of equalitarianism that stifles the people's initiative, how can asceticism of the 'purest' kind which disregards incentives and recklessly runs counter to all natural laws, how can such a society advance into socialism?" The book's conclusion regarding Xiyang's farmland capital construction is that "it destroyed the healthy development of agricultural production" and that it was "an extremely bitter lesson."[1]

Those who know people engaged in crop production see such comments as a cruel joke. When an outsider evaluates Chinese agriculture he can easily lose contact with reality and talk nonsense. The book did not consider the existing natural conditions and level of scientific knowledge and technology in the United States and France, and did not look at the reality of Xiyang County. Is it appropriate to pillory Xiyang people with foreign examples? It is only because Xiyang is located in a bleak and barren mountain area of high summits and steep slopes, where conditions are extremely harsh, that Chen Yonggui led the people of Xiyang into unprecedented battles to transform nature and increase grain output. Gross yields in the County went from 40,000 metric tons to 130,000 metric tons in just a few years. This is a fact nobody can deny. In order to achieve this stupendous goal, Chen Yonggui had to use all his talent and energy and mobilize all the talents and energies of his peasant compatriots. Can it be that somebody would rather have the peasants build jeweled palaces in elf-land hills[2] than construct fields and build soil here and now in earthbound China?

For ten years Xiyang learned from Dazhai, turning hilltops, gullies and the flood plains of rivers into fertile farm land. They added 60,000 *mu* to the crop land of the County, and built over 300,000 *mu* of organically rich Dazhai sponge soil. In the process they also increased the size

1. The venality and cynicism of this attack can only be fully appreciated if one is armed with knowledge of what happened later. "Reformers" used United States and French agriculture to ridicule Dazhai, then turned around and liquidated the scale of Chinese agriculture with family contracts on minuscule plots that made most viable mechanization impossible. Chen Yonggui was creating mountain fields that machines could work. The "reform" turned great level plains into noodle strips that peasants could only work with hoes. (W.H.H.)

2. "Elf land hills" are something like the Chinese equivalent of "cloud-cuckoo land." (W.H.H.)

of their fields precisely in order to create conditions for the mechanization and modernization of agriculture, confident that, through the efforts of this and several future generations, Xiyang too could reach advanced world standards of labor productivity. It does not take much effort or imagination to see how ridiculous and preposterous, not to mention dishonest and cynical, the arguments of this *Rise and Fall* book are. As a negative example, the book shows all the more clearly how unusual and outstanding was the man Chen Yonggui and how great were his achievements.

The key to the whole effort of such co-authors as Li Guoqing and Yang Yuci, Sin Qitai and Xiong Zhiyong, articles such as "Dazhai's Departure From the Spirit of Dazhai" and books such as *The Rise and Fall of the Red Flag of Dazhai* is exactly the outstanding nature of the man, Chen Yonggui, and the greatness of his achievements. Since the collective road no longer suited people at the pinnacle of power, their media journeymen moved from denigrating Chen Yonggui's achievements to assassinating his character. They revived a whole series of slanders and calumnies such as the charge that Chen Yonggui came to Dazhai, not as a poor-peasant famine refugee, but as a runaway landlord; the charge that he served as a real, not a bogus, Japanese puppet; the charge that he nefariously usurped Jia Jincai's position as Party Secretary; the charge that he intimidated Li Shunda and forced him off the Provincial Party Committee, and the charge that he covered up the crimes of his second wife's divorced husband for personal advantage.

In spite of the fact that Central Authorities had already cleared Chen Yonggui's name of the many slanders and rumors that his detractors circulated after his career came under attack, in 1982 the Secretary of the Communist Party of the Central Shanxi Region attended a Youth League Congress in Xiyang County Town and charged, all over again out of the blue, that Chen Yonggui was a runaway landlord from Shandong. No wonder Chen Yonggui's son Chen Mingzhu rushed to the County Guest House to confront that regional functionary and demand proof. Local officials who looked into the matter never unearthed a single fact to back up the Secretary's contention.

Landlord origin was not in itself a cause for attack. Zhou Enlai, after all, was of landlord origin, as were many outstanding Communists. The damage, in the case of Chen Yonggui, did not arise from any truth, but from the possibility of a cover-up from a man posing as a poor peasant's child when he had really been born a landlord. Such fraudulent posturing would constitute a severe violation of Party norms and provide justification for punishment, even expulsion.

If myths about Chen Yonggui's "bad" class origin and deceitful cover-up found many takers in the reform period, so too did recurring myths about Chen collaborating with the Japanese. These made him out to be not a national hero, but a traitor to the nation.

When Chen Yonggui took power as Party Secretary of Xiyang County he himself drew back from factionalism and pulled the whole County out of factional contention insofar as that was possible. This alienated the Deputy Party Secretary of Shanxi Province, an equal colleague of Chen's on the Provincial Party Committee, who had close ties to one side, and set the two leaders at lasting loggerheads. Some time later this Provincial Deputy Secretary made an inspection tour of Xiyang County. At the Dazhai Exhibition Center he saw mention of a 1943 incident when Chen Yonggui, carrying out his duties as a bogus representative, delivered grain to the Japanese. Chen's rival immediately seized on this to claim that Chen was a real puppet, not a bogus one. He then spread this story far and wide. Sun Jiaji, former Political Officer of the Beijing Public Communications Brigade, who had been Regional Chief in 1943, refuted this charge thoroughly, but this did not squelch the rumor or silence its author once it became politically advantageous to defame Chen Yonggui.

Concerning Jia Jincai's yielding his position to Chen Yonggui, the 1990 book, *The Rise and Fall of the Red Flag of Dazhai*, turns the incident completely around and accuses Chen of slandering Jia as a man soft on landlords and rich peasants, to the point where the calumny so damaged Jia's reputation that the villagers shunned and isolated him. Unable to do any work, communing only with cows, he quit in disgust in favor of Chen Yonggui.

"What yielding to the worthier person?" the authors quote Jia as saying. "I just couldn't do my job any more. I didn't have his skill. I couldn't outdo him. So I just let him have my job."

After this passage caught my eye, I went to look for Jia Jincai to double-check the facts one more time. Jia Jincai fanned out his hands in disbelief and sighed, "Look, if you sleep long enough, you'll wet the bed! When did I ever say such words about Chen Yonggui, that I couldn't outdo him?" Here he paused for emphasis. "I let him become Secretary. I urged him three times to take over. This I will never deny."

Distorting the plain words of living participants in past events—all in order to serve one's own purposes—this, indeed, is what the main skill of *The Rise and Fall of the Red Flag of Dazhai* is all about.

Critics also attributed to Li Shunda the information that Chen Yonggui had intimidated him and driven him off the Provincial Party Committee. The slanders on this point were so heavy that Chen Yonggui told many people that he truly couldn't take it any more.

"How can they say that I intimidated Li Shunda?" Chen asked, still angry. "I was learning from him. When he was dropped from the Provincial Party Committee's Standing Committee, that had nothing to do with me! The two factions in Shanxi were leaning heavily on me. They were leaning on him too, so they bent our relationship all out of shape. What was I supposed to do?"

"Nothing happened between Old Chen and me," Li Shunda said at an enlarged meeting of the Political Bureau convened by the Central Authorities to solve the Shanxi problem in 1974. "I have no idea why all these stories started popping up, but I know they did nothing to bring us together after factionalism pushed us apart."

One rumor that I haven't seen in writing but one that has been circulating verbally in Xiyang County and Shanxi since Chen Yonggui suffered eclipse concerns the divorced husband of Chen's second wife. Factional opponents accused this man, who was a high-school teacher, of raping one of his students. The local court tried and sentenced him to a long prison term. His wife, unable to face public scorn as the spouse of a rapist and a convict, divorced him. Later she married Chen Yonggui, bringing with her to Dazhai her small son, whom Chen Yonggui adopted.

After a few years, investigations into factional injustice in Shanxi proved conclusively that the teacher had not raped his student. The case was a frame-up. The local authorities wanted to clear the man's name and restore him to his job but they realized that this might be embarrassing to Chen Yonggui. Chen had, after all, married an innocent man's wife and had adopted his child. They sent someone to see him and sound out his reaction. Chen Yonggui supported the investigators' conclusions, no matter how embarrassing they were to him personally. The man was innocent. They should clear his name and give him back his job. And so, by mutual agreement, they settled the case.

But Chen Yonggui's detractors made something quite different out of the affair. Chen, they charged, had used his great power and influence to institute an investigation in order to cover up and bury the crime committed by the school teacher whose former wife Chen had married. The sole purpose of this action was to give his adopted son a clean record as the offspring of an honorable citizen, not the spawn of a criminal. Thus they added another big black blotch to Chen Yonggui's record, not to mention carrying one factional dispute in Shanxi to a new level.

Oh the storms and tribulations of our society! Do they have to be so complicated?

CHAPTER—38

WEST-WATER-EAST SMASHED

The fate of the great water diversion project in Xiyang County inevitably intertwined with the changing situation in the country. This largest and most ambitious of Chen Yonggui's projects, bringing westward flowing water eastward, right through a massive mountain, could not avoid becoming the target of the most vehement criticism. By 1980 the media was bent on "driving" the project down from Ninth Heaven straight into Ninth Hell. The *People's Daily* published an editorial on June 15, 1980, under the title "The Folly of Water Diversion Projects Like This Should Never Be Repeated." The wording was unyielding and the attitude unequivocal; it expressed devastating censure, amounting to total denial:

> The Water Diversion Project in Shanxi's Xiyang County, which has gone on for four or five years with the number of invested man-days approaching the figure of 5,000,000 and the cost already reaching 90,000,000 Chinese dollars, has finally been abandoned. This has been an extremely painful lesson about

construction of water conservancy works, something worth pondering for all of us.

For the past two years the project has been consuming one-tenth of all water conservancy funds in the province of Shanxi. With its requisition of manpower, including Xiyang County's public project laborers from various People's Communes and Production Brigades; cadres, workers, and teachers from offices, factories, mines, enterprises, utility companies and public service units; mine workers from the Yangquan Mining Bureau; and officers and men from the People's Liberation Army Corps of Engineers, one can say with certainty that no expense and no human or financial resource was spared on this project. Based on estimates, every mu of irrigated land would have cost over 1,000 Chinese dollars if the entire project were completed.[1]

For a very long time in the past we were cutting down everything in sight because we only wanted to plant grain, right? We neglected questions of the quality of soil, topography, customary production practices, technological capability and similar concrete conditions—all for the singular emphasis on grain production. What ought to have been a forest was not a forest, the land suitable for animal grazing was not given to animals to graze, where there should have been orchards we planted no orchards, the land fit to be turned into fisheries was not turned into fisheries. Not only did we not develop the potential of the land, we forced people into hardship and tended to produce

1. These figures charge the whole cost of the project to agriculture. Actually the water was much in demand for opening new coal mines in Xiyang since Yangquan mines were almost exhausted. Also Xiyang County Town with 30,000 residents, needed water urgently. Costs should have been shared three ways. The labor charges are also controversial. If one figures labor at one yuan a day, many a Dazhai mu cost 2,000 yuan in labor alone. But what was the opportunity cost of such slack season labor? Most Chinese peasants are drastically underemployed in the winter months, so labor costs should be adjusted accordingly. (W.H.H.)

shortages. This erroneous "single strike" policy was reflected in the capital construction of farmland. The most obvious aspect of it everywhere was insistence on the creation of uniform "irrigated fields" from dry land, the insistence on "man-made plains," "level fields," "mellow-soil fields," and the insistence on "connecting disjointed fields into big strips of land" that could be cultivated like gardens. Enormous manpower and bundles of money were wasted on the moving of yellow loess with minimal gains. Not only were there no gains; we destroyed the ecological balance and left the legacy of trouble to our children and grandchildren.

Our country is still very poor; for a rather long time we have been unable to come up with large sums of money to invest in agriculture. We cannot afford to make ineffective investment; even with effective investment we have to make careful calculations and strict budgeting. We cannot afford to invest one thousand Chinese dollars to create one mu of irrigated land as we did with Xiyang's "water diversion" project, even if we were to evaluate it as partially rational, which would mean disregarding the fact that the project itself was inequitable because it actually seized other people's water to irrigate Xiyang's fields. We cannot afford to build irrigated fields even at one-half of that price, namely at 500 Chinese dollars per mu. If we use that method to develop our agriculture, the more we work at it the poorer we will become.

Xiyang's "water diversion" project was ridden with malpractice, despite great objections by its technical personnel. Why was it possible to just say "let's do it" and then do it, and go on with it for several years? Why did three full years go by after the smashing of the "Gang of Four" before it was stopped? A very important lesson from this experience is the feudal family-style rule of some comrades in the leadership. There are

> some comrades among our leaders who, once they become "big shots," want to issue orders to everybody, direct everybody and control everything based on their personal likes and dislikes, although they have absolutely no knowledge of science and technology, and are moreover unwilling to listen to expert opinion. And then, no matter how high up or how low down in the hierarchy you go, there are always some comrades who flatter them and who protect them. Even when their positions are clearly absurd, they are continuously praised and their wishes are carried out without hesitation or delay....

At the same time this editorial came out, a reporter for the Xinhua News Agency filed an important news item which read: "Enormous investment and small gain, a waste of money and manpower: Xiyang's 'Water Diversion' Project is put on hold."

Before the editorial and this news item came out, the construction site of Xiyang's "Water Diversion" Project was still reverberating with sounds of hammers, explosions, competition, vehicles running back and forth in endless cycles, cranes and forklifts shaking heaven and earth. And then the ice-cold downpour descended from the heavens, drowning the fires of the whole record-shattering effort. Work stopped. Popular feeling cooled off.

After receiving an urgent telegram from higher authorities to stop work the directors at the Project Headquarters turned pale. They telephoned Provincial leaders imploring that they be allowed to complete work on two almost finished parts of the project. They had all but completed work on the Xing Settlement Reservoir, and had just put in place the form work for the Peace Mountain Aqueduct. They really could not stop work right there and then. Could not the higher authorities in charge postpone their stop-work decision by a few days? If not, economic losses would be unbearable! The answer came back that because of the articles already published in the press the work had to be terminated at all cost; there was no time to consider economic losses. When I went to research the issue, many people felt certain that the decision was purely political. Halting the project was a political necessity for consolidating the decisions of the Third Plenary Session of the Eleventh Central Committee.

Those who did not understand the situation did not believe at the outset that an entire project which was just rounding off would be stopped just because of one newspaper article. Even some journalists did not believe it. I found some people who had worked for the Project Headquarters, and the old County Committee leaders Li Xishen and Gao Xiubao, who were working for the County Water Conservancy Bureau at that time. I found these and many others who truly deeply regretted what had happened.

After the authorities, brooking no delay, forced work to stop on the water diversion project, even greater hailstorms descended from the Heavens: article after article, condemnation after condemnation criticized this engineering marvel as evidence of the most evil crimes. The water diversion project did not end up as any "pearl" ceremonially presented to the Third National "In Agriculture Learn From Dazhai" Conference. Following the changing political situation, it was driven instead into Ninth Hell. Some public opinion organs even went so far as to suggest that the chief person responsible (meaning Chen Yonggui) should be charged with criminal responsibility.

In view of the new thrust of politics I do not know how ultimately to evaluate the project. Neither do I know what history will conclude about it in the future. One thing I have come to understand, however, is that after the torpedoing of the primary water diversion project, West-Water-East, the majority of the 800 various water conservancy sub-projects that had been undertaken in Xiyang during the ten years of learning from Dazhai fell into ruin. Countless water conservancy installations came to a premature end, and even some of the other water conservancy projects that were well known nationwide suffered. Today, years later, we can see quite clearly that ideology begat this kind of folly. The excuse sounded reasonable, of course. "We must cut back costs to stimulate production."

"If I had put the money that was used only for water conservancy projects into agriculture and other things," a policy maker of the time once said, "we would have had tangible improvements a long time ago."

What he really meant was that he would not stand for water conservancy in any form.

Because of the criticism that bundles of money were wasted on moving yellow loess with minimal gains, because of the negative attitude toward the "irrigated fields created from dry land," the "man-made plains," the "level fields," and the "sponge soil fields," because of the assertion that "we destroyed the ecological balance and left the legacy of trouble to our children and grandchildren," and because of the investment in agriculture that was continuously cut on the grounds that "we cannot afford it," the new power holders allowed farmland and water conservancy capital construction to slide. Bundles of money were wasted on buildings and halls and fancy limousines, while production fell victim to a vicious circle of cutbacks. No wonder agriculture today constitutes a social problem difficult to crack.

Nevertheless, the practice of the past ten years and the rethinking of earlier experiences confirm that there were indeed some problems with the water diversion project. The irrational distribution and extravagant display criticized by the article in fact existed to a certain extent. Although Chen Yonggui has passed away, we who are still alive must draw lessons from these problems. Despite all this, however, Xiyang's water diversion project should be regarded as a milestone in the history of the development of Xiyang County, of Shanxi and of China. We need to affirm it as precious!

After the work on the water diversion project stopped and the sound of its criticism faded away, Shanxi Provincial Committee Secretary Huo Shilian went to Xiyang to talk to the then already deposed Li Xishen. Having inquired about Li Xishen's health and state of mind, Huo Shilian asked him with a smile: "Xishen, how did the water diversion project come about?"

Li Xishen told him about the original project proposal, the surveys and the construction itself, and then added: "Secretary Huo, why have you come to Shanxi if not to do a good job for Shanxi? Old Chen was also thinking about the future of Xiyang! If people above were giving him money, why shouldn't he have done it? If we were given more money, we would have opened the Main South Canal, too!"

Huo Shilian was all smiles as he listened. He wanted to know how Li Xishen felt about other things. Li Xishen said that he could not accept the criticism published in the press. Huo Shilian consoled him:

"It's simply a propaganda gambit. No conclusive decisions about the case have been made at the top," he concluded. But if no high-level body has drawn any conclusions, holding off making them as the years drag by has been as devastating as any condemnation. Lack of action is a form of wrecking too, and one well known to bureaucracies world wide.

Although the water diversion project drew an avalanche of criticism as "a folly," "a high-handed scheme" and "a waste of money and manpower," Xiyang's veteran cadres and the people of Xiyang still cherish the memory of it to this day. Its abandonment was a sore point that Chen Yonggui could not get off his mind while he still lived. Tormented by merciless illness, Chen Yonggui had tears in his eyes when he told Li Xishen, who had come to visit him: "Xishen, I will not be able to see water delivered through the water diversion project. After I die, if you get a chance, you must request that the leadership revive the project. All that government money should not be spent for nothing."

As he recalled Chen Yonggui's words, Li Xishen said that Old Chen's voice had been alarmingly weak, but his determination was unflinching and his meaning clear.

The scrapping of the water diversion project caused various reactions in society at large. A ten-year-long period of actual testing through use has shown that this project, at one time called "a folly," "a high-handed project" and "a waste of money and manpower," was after all something that the people of Xiyang needed, and something that the people of Shouyang and other Counties needed very much as well. Isn't abandoning a project just because of a few newspaper articles an even greater folly? This was not only a loss for Xiyang, but also a great loss of government funds. According to some directors of the water diversion project, if the work had not been stopped that year, striking the iron while it was hot could have completed it in its entirety at an additional cost of only 20,000,000 Chinese dollars. To reopen it now would need at least 50,000,000 Chinese dollars of additional funding.

After the government abandoned the project the Provincial Water Conservation Bureau's construction team had to leave, much of the construction equipment had to be moved away, and huge quantities of construction material were irrevocably lost.[1] Since the tunnel had already been cut through the mountain, and there only remained some final touches to be put on the Gate Mountain Reservoir, after 1984 the government earmarked special funds several times to round off the work at Gate Mountain. The reservoir has already filled with water, and it has solved the problem of water supply for several factories and drinking water storage for the three rural townships of Quiet Peace, City Gate and Li Family Settlement.

"When we visit the graves to burn paper money honoring the dead," the peasants of Li Family Settlement say, "we must first offer some to Old Chen."

But although people show great interest in the foundation of the impounding structure on the western flank of Zhang Mountain, the Dragon Gate Reservoir, it remains nothing but an historical exhibit because in the present circumstances there is no way to revive this project. Even when special funds are earmarked from above, they are withheld on account of divergent political views. Rumor has it that one year the highest levels of the Provincial administration earmarked 4,000,000 Chinese dollars for water conservancy work in Xiyang County, but a Deputy Commissioner for the Central Shanxi Region simply erased it from the record in order to make a clean break with Dazhai. Thus the work that Xiyang should have undertaken could not proceed, no western drainage basin water can reach the tunnel intake, and the only water that flows out the other end, as of now, is spring water from inside Zhan Ridge itself. But since the tunnel is, after all, almost 19 kilometers long, this is no small amount.

With this particular issue in mind I paid a visit to the veteran leaders who had been struggling with the water diversion project in the past, in order to ask them their opinions on the shut-down. I first found Li Xishen.

---

1. It is my understanding that the mechanized construction units that the Province assigned, over Li Xishen's objections, stood idle for three years, machines, manpower and all, after the project stopped. The depreciation of the machines alone came to a huge sum, as did the workers' wages. (W.H.H.)

"To this very day," Li said, "I believe that the water diversion project was a blessing for Xiyang. However, as I look over the past from my present vantage point today, I can also see the problems inherent in the project. But I don't think one should totally deny the whole undertaking, I don't think it should have been shut down just because some mistakes were made, particularly as it was just beginning to get somewhere. With a complete shut-down like that, the heaviest losses, after all, were suffered by the government."

He sighed with disappointment as he spoke, and looked quite despondent.

I also looked for the one-time General Director of the water diversion project, Gao Xiubao. When I found him, he was watching television with his grandson in his arms. When I asked him whether the water diversion project had been a "high-handed project" and "a waste of money and manpower," he said: "People have very lively tongues. Let them say whatever they want to say!"

When I asked him to talk about his views anyway he burst out angrily, "Water has come to Xiyang. People have stored it up. How can you call that high-handed? As for the waste of money and manpower, I don't know. But let me ask you something. Was the Red Flag Canal a waste of money and manpower? Was Pingding's water diversion a waste of money and manpower? Doing any water conservancy project can always be called a waste of money and manpower. Does that mean that none will be done in the future?"

Wanting to hear as many opinions as possible, I went to look for the former water conservancy specialist at the water diversion project, Qu Runsheng, who is now Director of the County Water Conservancy Bureau. I asked him whether the newspaper's charge that the water diversion project had been "high-handed" had any grounds at all?

"There is some ground, in fact," Director Qu said. "Transferring the Bright Sun Production Brigade from Shouyang to Xiyang in order to build the Dragon Gate Reservoir was somewhat high-handed. I wouldn't say that for the rest of the project, however."

His opinions seem to be basically no different from those of the other two veteran cadres. Bright Sun Production Brigade was transferred back to Xiyang because the Dragon Gate Water Reservoir was being constructed on Bright Sun Production Brigade's territory. That seems understandable. I felt that the Director's views were the most objective, the most practical, and the most forthcoming.

"Old Qu," I asked him again, "the papers have said that as soon as the water diversion project got off the ground, it cut off 20 percent of the water from the Su River, so that all the water conservancy installations on the lower reaches of that west-flowing river had to be scrapped. Is there any truth in this?"

"Just look at the map," Director Qu answered. "Xiyang is located on the upper reaches of the Su River. Look at the entire length of the river. Look at its length on the territory of Xiyang. Could a dam in our County account for 20 percent of the water flow? How could it cause the scrapping of conservancy installations on the lower reaches?"

Enough is enough! No wonder there has been such a strong reaction to the shutdown of the water diversion project. What the articles have written is not fair! If you look at the project from a political point of view, it obviously had to be tailored to a certain set of demands. Certain individuals shut it down regardless of whether it met the demands or not, simply because they had to subordinate it to their new policies. One might say that without Dazhai and Chen Yonggui, Xiyang could never have developed a water diversion project on such a broad scale, and the government would never have committed so much funding to it. Yet, it must also be said that the water diversion project was the only way to solve the problem of water shortage in Xiyang.

I have found out at the County Water Conservancy Bureau that, due to the opening of a new underground coal mine, the water level in Xiyang will drop even more in the future. When the mine is opened it will be impossible to solve even the problem of drinking water for many Brigades in Xiyang County and for Xiyang County Town itself, let alone talk about creating irrigated fields. If other solutions to the problem are to be found, they will require even more investment than the water diversion project, and it will be even harder to find the money to spend on them. Water is the biggest crisis facing the people of Xiyang. It is a public issue requiring a most urgent solution. The only way open to Xiyang County is still to divert surplus water from West to East.

Being a natural resource, water is owned by the State. Water conservancy projects are State property, and should, as such, be protected by the State. A high-level command torpedoed Xiyang's water diversion project ten years ago. Its achievements and errors, its rights and wrongs, are already passing through the sluices of history. The public will be able to find the right answer. When that happens, people will extol these famous lines from a poem of Chairman Mao Zedong:

> Wait until
> Bright mountain flowers
> Come into full bloom.
> Their smiles
> Will come from within.

CHAPTER—39

DAZHAI A WARD OF THE STATE?

The most basic, most serious and most damaging charge against Chen Yonggui and Dazhai was that the Dazhai model was an economic fraud, not an exercise in self-reliance but a sinkhole for State funds. The charge that Dazhai succeeded only with massive State aid was a most unjust falsehood, one that Chen Yonggui could not tolerate right up until the day he died. It remains one of the most important issues over which the yellow-loess hill folk of Dazhai cry out in protest to this day. I have been compelled to examine it very carefully, since it is crucial to answering the question of whether the history of Dazhai is to be defined as positive or negative. Seeking an answer I moved into a mountainside cave-dwelling, so long and at the same time so narrow on the inside that its inner space resembled a railroad car buried in a butte. Here is what I frequently heard from the lips of the people of Dazhai themselves: "Every household in Dazhai thus owes the State 10,000 Chinese dollars! The more you guys write about it the more our debt grows! When is this account going to be cleared?"

Everybody was saying the same thing. I heard the story almost as many times as there are crows on Tigerhead Mountain.

At first, my head was spinning and I was confused, unable to figure out what was behind all these rumors. It seemed as though Chen Yonggui's grim, dignified face implored my righteous indignation by darting discontented glances at me from the official portrait put out by the Central Committee after his death. My blood pressure rose, and for the first time I felt the weight of dealing with this whole affair, but I had no way of evading it. After dinner, I went to pay a visit to Liang Bianliang, taking the question with me. Liang Bianliang was very constrained, treating me at first as he did all the other reporters: No invitation to sit down, no offer of tea, just some random snorts and grunts. Later, presumably noticing my sincerity but still full of indignation, he handed me a little stool and asked me to have a seat. Then he poured out all his bitterness, and I found out how this slander got started.

I was just beginning to research Chen Yonggui's lifelong endeavors at that time, and had not yet thoroughly grasped all the issues involved. I was not sure how to regard the assertion that "every *jin* of grain that Dazhai sold to the State amounted to a State subsidy of 22 Chinese cents," and that State assistance to Dazhai amounted to 10,000 Chinese dollars per household on the average. Furthermore, I had no idea where all this invidious information came from.

Finally one day I set my eyes on an article entitled "Dazhai's Departure From the Spirit of Dazhai," which had been well mauled by the tongues of Dazhai. The *Shanxi Daily* published it on October 17, 1980, on the first and third page. Its authors were the famous muckrakers of the reform era, Li Guoqing and Yang Yuyin. Now years have passed since they concocted "Dazhai's Departure From the Spirit of Dazhai," but the effects produced by the article are still clearly visible. All these years, that article has been providing spiritual food for those who wish to attack, humiliate and negate Dazhai. As recently as June 1990, the Henan People's Publishing House issued *The Rise and Fall of the Red Flag of Dazhai*. This polemic, which, as we have seen, badmouthed Dazhai's farmland capital construction, by no means stopped there. It completely contradicted Chairman Mao Zedong's slogan "In Agriculture, Learn from Dazhai," completely canceled out Premier Zhou Enlai's proclamations regarding the spirit of Dazhai, and concluded, on the basis of the article "Dazhai's Departure From the Spirit of Dazhai," that Dazhai "was a model which the government built by piling on loads of money."

In 1980 when the *Shanxi Daily* published the Departure article, radio stations, the press, magazines—the whole media panoply—locally and in other regions, picked it up, it became the most sensational topic of the day. Millions of baffled readers shook their heads: How could it be that the government spent almost a million Chinese dollars to prop up a place that official propaganda touted as the very model of self-reliance? If it shocked people at home, the article also left an extremely bad impression abroad. Following the new official polity, many foreign journalists also turned Dazhai into a model of government assistance. The British biographer Claire Hollingsworth concluded that Dazhai "was propped up by government investment." In May 1991, a friend from Japan came to Dazhai to find out for himself whether or not Dazhai received unwarranted assistance through government aid and investment. Unable to see Guo Fenglian, the visitor kept inquiring from his escorting guide, "Guo Fenglian is locked up in prison, isn't she?" The questions persisted until he finally saw Guo Fenglian face to face.

In view of all this, I came to realize the critical importance of clarifying right from wrong, both domestically and abroad. The ongoing injustice compelled me to throw aside considerations of personal comfort and safety and plunge headlong into the vortex of this Dazhai issue. I felt a compulsion to unravel its mystery and have engaged single-mindedly in this quest for almost a decade.

The information revealed in the original, close to ten thousand word long, article, "Dazhai's Departure from the Spirit of Dazhai," diverged so obviously from the limited material that I had previously checked out, that I was forced to undertake much more prolonged and meticulous research than I originally thought necessary. In order to answer conclusively the damaging content and devastating figures published in the *Shanxi Daily*, I had to review many years of press clippings, search through archives, visit offices and bureaus, track down bank records and commercial receipts, and interview scores of people from the lowest to the highest, anyone and everyone who had been involved in a meaningful way with the saga of Dazhai.

For the sake of brevity I will hereafter refer to the article, "Dazhai's Departure from the Spirit of Dazhai" as Departure.

After a brief, incisive introduction, Departure said: "The question that now presents itself keenly to the people is: What should our new understanding of Dazhai be? How should we evaluate Dazhai's experience? This is not only a question of the way we should look at a given model, but a question that relates directly to the choice of road we take in modernizing China's agriculture, and as such it has caused widespread concern and debate."

By posing the question in this way, the authors of Departure had indeed touched upon the crux of the issue. Why were so many celebrities and noteworthy individuals running off to Dazhai to engage in analysis and inquiry into the growth of that extraordinary Brigade? Was it just for the sake of Dazhai itself? Or was it, indeed, because of Dazhai's relationship to the question of what road our country's agriculture should take if it was to modernize? Of course, it was the latter.

In order to show Dazhai as a false model created by State assistance, which the authors asserted it to be, Departure goes through great pains to revamp and warp the following concrete examples:

1. Dazhai's "Army and People Canal" and "Unity Ravine Aqueduct."

> Departure made the following public pronouncement:
> The "Army and People Canal" was built with government investment, through a joint loan to several Production Brigades in the area (the total loan amount was 83,000 Chinese dollars; Dazhai's loan amounted to 23,200 Chinese dollars, which has not been paid back to this day) and through their shared labor, with the help of the People's Liberation Army. Of the six water cisterns, five (three large, two small) were built by County and Commune expert teams and administrative cadres; only one small cistern was built by Dazhai Production Brigade itself....As for the "Unity Ravine Aqueduct"—this is a reservoir and water diversion project built

> entirely by county and commune expert teams with government investment. Not counting this project, just for the "Army and People Canal" and the five water cisterns linked to it, the County and the Commune put in 70,000-80,000 man-days of labor and invested 202,900 Chinese dollars.

This issue was the first calumny I picked up in my attempt to clarify the Dazhai question. Departure states that the "Army and People Canal" was built with government investment, "and that the 'Unity Ravine Aqueduct' was built entirely with government investment," but after making these two claims the authors make no further statement on the amount or source of this government investment. If they had evidence, why didn't they present it? Their reluctance on this score casts doubt on their whole exposition.

Responding to the above accusations, Liang Bianliang, Song Liying and Jia Jincai, who sat in a row in front of me, replied: "We did not receive a cent of government investment for the construction of the 'Army and People Canal.' You can look into that yourself. Where is there any such evidence?" When the topic switched to the water-conservancy loan, Liang Bianliang spoke with dead earnestness: "This we did have, but that was a standard loan for investment in the construction of water conservancy works. We paid it back."

I followed this clue to Dazhai Township Credit Cooperative, where I verified it with a leader there. The manager confirmed that up to 1978 Dazhai Production Brigade was never late with its loan payments to the Credit Cooperative. After that, what was left of the claim published in Departure?

As for Departure's statement that several Production Brigades in the area built water cisterns through shared labor, I went to Gold Gully Production Brigade, which is located directly behind Tigerhead Mountain, to find its former Secretary Zhao Yinquan, an old friend of Chen Yonggui. I asked him to give me a detailed account of how those cisterns were built.

"We helped build a cistern in Dazhai," said Old Zhao after thinking a moment. "That was so we could use it to send water on to Gold

Gully Production Brigade. It served as a way station. These cisterns were joint ventures because the scheme was a joint project servicing several villages."

Finally, as I carried on with investigation into People's Liberation Army aid to cistern and canal construction, I came to understand the whole issue more deeply. Liang Bianliang and Guo Fenglian explained the matter to me in detail.

"Why the name 'Army and People Canal'? And why the name 'Peasant Support Cistern'?" Liang Bianliang asked. "There's a reason behind it! Back then, when Chairman Mao came out with his slogan 'In Agriculture, Learn From Dazhai,' we had already begun to dig the 'Peasant Support Cistern,' and the 'Army and People Canal' was already half finished. Neither project was yet completed. I remember, we lined the 'Army and People Canal' with plastic sheets to prevent water from seeping out when we let it through to the other villages. Just around that time Army comrades came for field training. When they saw what we were doing, the senior officers took Chen Yonggui by the hand and said that they simply had to do some work for him—that they would be very unhappy if he did not let them. This is why the projects got named the 'Peasant Support Cistern' and the 'Army and People Canal.' Outsiders gave us some help but it was spur-of-the-moment and irregular."

Liang Bianliang went on to say: "These Departure guys didn't 'expose' enough. We've still got a 'National Unity and Friendship Ravine'! How explain that? As we worked rebuilding our fields in North Zhao Gully after the flood of 1963, a delegation came for a visit—a delegation of representatives of our country's thirty-seven national minorities, including Tibetans, Uigurs, and Zhuangs. When they saw what was going on they just picked up tools and began to work without ever saying a word. They worked for the better part of a day. That's why we named the ravine the 'Unity Ravine.' That's the kind of assistance we got!"

Guo Fenglian added that in regard to Army aid in the cistern construction, some of those leaders who had made the decision to help were still around. "When they came to visit recently, they made an interesting remark. 'Why did Premier Zhou, during his third visit to

Dazhai, want to have a souvenir picture taken with all of Dazhai's Commune members right next to the Peasant Support Cistern? Why did he want to use the 'Army and People Canal as the backdrop?' This was, in fact, an act of great political significance celebrating self-reliant progress, but people have now turned white into black and stood all the facts on their head."

The situation with the "Unity Ravine Aqueduct" is even more absurd. Strictly speaking, this was a Dazhai People's Commune project, undertaken by the Commune. So how is it that it has been laid on Dazhai Production Brigade's shoulders alone? It started as a project that would benefit the entire Commune by bringing water from Yang Family Slope Reservoir to more than ten Production Brigades of the Commune. But in order to back its assertion that the government assisted Dazhai, Departure dropped nine of them from the joint venture. No one knows where Departure got the figure of 202,900 Chinese dollars. The people of Dazhai themselves are quite baffled by it.

2. Dazhai's high-altitude cableway.

Departure states: "Those responsible for Dazhai's high-altitude conveyor cableway say that it was built with funds they raised themselves and through reliance on their own labor, while it was in fact built with major help from the Yangquan Mining Bureau and Yangquan Agricultural Machinery Plant, administered by the Second Light Industry Bureau. These units dispatched over twenty workers who labored for three to four months putting in over 2,000 man-days, and provided gratuitously a considerable amount of equipment and material, such as electrical motors, pneumatic drills, and steel cables imported from Japan, suffering a loss of 41,670 Chinese dollars."

In regard to this project Liang Bianliang explained the whole situation to me. Back in those days, he said, Dazhai Commune members hauled manure up the slopes using shoulder poles. All visitors to Dazhai frowned at this. He often used to hear visitors' comments, as they walked by: "These folks here have too hard of a time of it. Why don't they try to do something about it?" When he went to the Reception Center to meet visitors one day, several of them offered him a suggestion: "It's too tiring to carry manure on those shoulder poles up the mountain, and it's not very efficient either. The best thing to do would be to build a high-altitude cableway. This would greatly lighten the burden of physical labor." Liang Bianliang had never heard of such a thing, but it became a reality soon enough.

At this point in his story, Liang Bianliang provided me with a lead: "Shengbing from the Agricultural Machinery Plant was one of the people who personally took part in the building of the cableway. Perhaps you better look him up to check on this information."

Subsequently, I found this Wang Shengbing at the County Agricultural Machinery Plant. Old Wang Shengbing had already turned sixty. He kept saying that he was too old, that he was unable to find use for his skills. He yearned very much for the old days.

"Back then," he recalled, "our country encouraged industry to aid agriculture, and my job was specifically to support agriculture. I visited just about every village in Xiyang County and did away with a lot of hard labor by introducing agricultural machinery. In February, 1967, our plant was preoccupied with the problem of mechanizing Dazhai and we called a meeting to discuss this. Through democratic election, the Party members voted to have me travel to Dazhai to solve the problem of mechanization there. It was because I had a good command of machinery, electrical work, bench work and welding—conditions for the job other people could not fulfill. After I got to Dazhai, I moved into the Reception Center and had my work cut out for me. I installed an electric mill and an electric roller-husker—machines needed almost daily in ordinary life. Later, in consultation with Chen Yonggui and Liang Bianliang, we decided to install several high-altitude cableways: in Wolf Den Ravine, on Kang Family Ridge, and at Peace Slope. I have been visited by journalists before and praised in the press for my achievements in mechanizing Dazhai. With Dazhai Brigade members doing the leg work and the heavy lifting, I, the lone technician, installed seven high-altitude cableways between 1967 and 1972, and created a network of cableways on Tigerhead Mountain. This greatly reduced the need for heavy physical labor.

"As for workers coming from Yangquan, that's true. Some workers came. I had some problems with my equipment, and I had to borrow winches from the Yangquan Mining Bureau. I asked Old Chen and Old Liang to allow me to call for assistance from the Bureau. As soon as my

Yangquan mates heard that it was a question of helping Dazhai, they said they would be happy to come. I only asked for several qualified workers, but they came, a score or more, together with their foremen, and stayed to work under my direction for quite a few days. After they left, a dozen or so people still stayed behind to work with me for another period of time. In the end, they left me to continue the job by myself.

"As for those assertions published by the *Shanxi Daily* about steel cables imported from Japan and other expensive equipment, they are completely groundless. Those cables were discarded by the coal mine after they had been replaced and were no longer needed. The mine treated them as waste and sold them for 5 cents a *jin* to anybody who wished to buy them. I drove a truck with Liang Bianliang to the Yangquan Mining Bureau, and we hauled over five tons of steel cables, about 500 *yuan* worth, in one load. Liang Bianliang paid for them by check. Some of those cables were from Japan, but they were the same thing, they were worn and no longer in use underground. Dazhai obtained them through barter. The Mining Bureau was experiencing some problems with the distribution of daily provisions to its employees, so Dazhai supplied them with grain and bean flour noodles (vermicelli), while Yangquan helped Dazhai get the steel cables it needed. Both solved their problems this way. We also bought some towing cables and other material from the Goods and Materials Bureau. I paid for them by check, according to their original price."

This shows that the authors of Departure were somewhat careless in preparing their piece. They didn't even bother to look for any of the participants in the events they described. I have absolutely no idea where they dug up that figure of 41,670 Chinese dollars in government investment.

3. The funding of the agricultural mechanization pilot project.

Departure states: "Dazhai's sprinkle irrigation and drip irrigation projects were built with 166,217 Chinese dollars allocated by the government to fund the agricultural mechanization pilot project, with another 150,000 Chinese dollars invested by the County Water Conservancy Bureau, and with assistance from technical personnel especially assigned by the government. In addition to the discarded machinery reported as worthless, the machinery obtained at depreciated value and the cost of the partially returned material, the net amount used on Dazhai's sprinkle irrigation and drip irrigation projects was 103,456 Chinese dollars."

Also: "The people responsible for the agricultural mechanization of Dazhai have said that 'of course we ourselves bought the ninety-some pieces of machinery of twenty-some different types that belong to the entire Production Brigade.' Actually, most of them were bought with the government funding for the agricultural mechanization pilot project, at a total expense of 361,315 Chinese dollars (this includes the 68,138 Chinese dollars spent on the building of the mechanized pig farm). In addition to the cost of pilot program personnel and discarded, depreciated and removed machinery, the cost of free transfer and servicing expenses for Dazhai's machinery, spare-parts and capital construction equipment came to 234,471 Chinese dollars."

This clearly shows that the authors of the Departure got overly "heated," so to speak.

So heated that they confused sprinkle irrigation with drip irrigation. You could say that sprinkle irrigation was one of the agricultural mechanization pilot projects, but the drip irrigation equipment in Dazhai's apple orchard was a special gift from Mexican President Echeverria to Chen Yonggui. How can that be considered government assistance? It is not logical at all to count a gift from a foreign president as government assistance. As Guo Fenglian recalls, the Mexican President sent three sets of this equipment to China: one went to Hunan, another to Beijing's Miyun Reservoir, and one to Dazhai. After Chen Yonggui received the gift, he asked Premier Zhou for instructions. Wouldn't it be more appropriate if the government set a price on it and Dazhai paid for it? he asked. Premier Zhou explained that this was a matter of political significance, not a question of trade. "Use it in your production now. We will even have to preserve it later for its precious historical value. It is not something you can set a price on."

I also found out about other aspects of the irrigation project from people who had been involved with it back then: the veteran cadre in charge of the agricultural mechanization pilot project, Wang Benshan; the man in charge of the mechanized water conservancy, Li Guanbin; and a third person who had been in charge of the funding.

In 1974, the Central Committee held a national conference on agricultural mechanization in Xiyang, in order to draw a concrete plan for the mechanization of China's agriculture by 1980, as called for by Chairman Mao. That same year, the Chinese Academy of Agricultural Mechanization Sciences made detailed preparations for a key pilot project, called the Agricultural Mechanization of the Northern Han Nationality Mountain Area: Dazhai Experimental Group. This Academy reportedly set up other similar experimental units in Shaoshan in Hunan Province and Yanan in Shanxi Province. The Leading Group for Agricultural Mechanization at the Shanxi Revolutionary Committee decided which of the provincial, regional, and County level work units in the industrial, transportation and scientific sphere that dealt with farm machinery and water conservancy were to form the Dazhai Agricultural Mechanization Experimental Group.

The group arrived in Dazhai in May 1974. Comrades from the central government's No. 1 Ministry of Machinery also took part. The Chinese Academy of Agricultural Mechanization Sciences provided 500,000 Chinese dollars for an investment fund, disbursing it in stages through a separate account especially set up for the purpose at the County Agricultural Mechanization Bureau. It never had any economic ties with Dazhai itself. There was no such thing as government investment in Dazhai, as claimed by Departure. The figure given by the article is patently untrue.

The project undertook to introduce machinery prototypes suitable for use in mountainous areas and to develop small-scale farm machine tools and implements suitable for farming in mountainous areas. Dazhai only provided some land for the experiment. If the units that provided land for the experiment incurred losses, they could claim compensation. Those were the conditions under which the comrades from the Dazhai Agricultural Mechanization Experimental Group began their work. Liang Bianliang remembers that, having been informed of the project, he could not put his mind to rest. The Group's chief leader, who was also the head of the Provincial Agricultural Mechanization Bureau, Qin Juli, told him: "I want to find out whether we can mechanize the mountainous areas after all."

Wang Benshan told me that he had thought at the time that Dazhai had to be chosen for the pilot project, because its field size was relatively appropriate compared to others in the mountainous Xiyang County area, and because it was the national red-flag standard-bearer in agriculture. What place was better suited for the project?

Guo Fenglian telephoned Chen Yonggui in Peking to ask for his instructions and to inform him of other Committee members' opinions. Chen Yonggui's response at the time was that this issue required careful consideration, because of its possible impact on Dazhai's self-reliance if it did not work out. "I'll come back to look into it," he added. When he got to Dazhai, comrades from the experimental group explained to him that the funding of the project had absolutely nothing to do with Dazhai, that the project would simply use some Dazhai land and would in no way have consequences for Dazhai's claim of self-reliance.

After repeated reassurances from the experimental group, Chen Yonggui concluded that there was no harm in letting the agricultural mechanization pilot project use a piece of Dazhai's land. By a Committee decision, Liang Bianliang was put in charge of selecting the land and providing the services of blacksmiths and carpenters, but he did not participate in other work of the experimental group.

After the experiment, the experimental group gave Dazhai preferential treatment by selling it machines and implements suitable for use on mountainous terrain at reduced prices. A comrade from the County Agricultural Mechanization Bureau arranged the transfer of property and took charge of accounts. He determined each price individually, according to the length of time in use and the wear and tear on each piece of equipment. For instance, he turned a submersible pump over to Dazhai at its original price because it was new and had never been used. On the other hand, he sold a hot-air drier at 20 percent of its original price because it had already been in use for two years. I found some material that shows that this same comrade sold the sprinkle irrigation equipment installed in two locations, Kang Family Ridge and Basking Snake Rock, at different prices. He transferred the one in Basking Snake Rock at 90 percent of the original price, while, due to the degree of its previous use, he sold the one in Kang Family Ridge for 60 percent of the original price.

Over eighty pieces of agricultural machinery and equipment were involved in the experiment. The Group discarded part of them as worthless, then took them away. Twenty-six had proved successful in the experiment. The Group priced them according to the degree of use and transferred them to Dazhai. The material confirms that the original price of the twenty-six pieces of equipment, including tractors, four-wheel vehicles, cranes, threshing machines, under-water pumps and pulverizers was 45,003.94 Chinese dollars, while their depreciated price was 16,856 Chinese dollars. My investigation shows that Dazhai paid everything up and cleared its account with the County Agricultural Mechanization Bureau on August 30, 1977.

The material also confirms that, as part of Dazhai's experimental sprinkle irrigation project, the experimental group installed 2,024 meters of sprinkler lines in Kang Family Ridge at the original cost of 26,573 Chinese dollars. These the Bureau transferred at a depreciated value of 17,143.8 Chinese dollars. Another 1,426 meters of sprinkler lines at Basking Snake Rock transferred at a depreciated value of 11,120.4 Chinese dollars. The total depreciated value of the two sprinkling systems was 28,264.2 Chinese dollars. My investigation has shown that Dazhai paid everything up and cleared its account with the County Agricultural Mechanization Bureau on December 15, 1977. Judging from this, both Chen Yonggui and Dazhai on the one hand and the Experimental Group and the Mechanization Bureau on the other were quite careful and serious when it came to determining the depreciated value of transferred machinery. Both sides handled the issue rather well.

As for the issue of "free transfer" and "servicing of Dazhai's agriculture" raised by the Departure article, I specifically posed the following question to Wang Benshan: "Was there ever such a thing as free transfer and servicing of Dazhai's agriculture?"

"The successful experimental equipment and pipelines were all transferred at the depreciated value," Wang Benshan said. "There was absolutely no such thing as free transfer, and there was never any question of servicing Dazhai's agriculture."

"It's a question of how one sees government assistance," other members of the experimental group told me. "There are always two sides to everything. Dazhai may have received assistance from the government, but then all those technical research personnel assigned were not there to assist Dazhai but rather to benefit the agriculture of the entire northern dry region. It is wrong to deny government assistance, but it is even more wrong to claim that Dazhai was built on government investment and assistance. We shouldn't praise somebody to the skies when things are fine, and retreat completely when there is a problem, going so far as to step on people's faces. This will certainly not benefit the development of China's agriculture."

The above was said in response to the distortions written by the authors of Departure. Is there anything else one can say to induce them to cool-off their heads?

4. Did Dazhai plant mulberry trees and cultivate silkworms?

Departure states: "Dazhai's fruit orchards and the mulberry trees planted to cultivate silkworms were also obtained through free government assistance or bought with government money. In 1976, for instance, the Provincial Bureau for Agriculture assisted Dazhai with over 300,000 free mulberry shoots and a sum of 80,000 Chinese dollars to build a silkworm culture facility."

When I inquired about this from Song Liying and several other veteran Committee members, they all roared with laughter.

"When did Dazhai plant mulberry trees to raise silkworms? The devil must be beating them on the lip to come up with nonsense like that," they protested in unison.

According to the material that came into my possession, this is the truth of the matter: It was the Big Tiger Ranch at Dazhai's People's Commune that planted the mulberry trees to raise silkworms. As part of the effort Big Tiger Ranch did use a piece of Dazhai land to plant a part of its mulberry trees.[1] The authors of Departure did not bother to do any research at all. They simply made things up at random. Thus their unrestrained newspaper fabrications produced yet another grave inconsistency.

5. A question of simple data regarding scientific research.

---

1. Big Tiger Ranch was on top of Tigerhead Mountain on Commune land that bordered that of the Dazhai Brigade. The Commune, as stated before, comprised twenty-three villages and invested on their behalf in projects beyond the power of any individual village. (W.H.H.)

In trying to prove government assistance to Dazhai, Departure deliberately circulated the following information: "Since 1975, government funds allocated to Dazhai for various scientific research have amounted to 57,049 Chinese dollars."

People in Dazhai say that this is worthy of the "crooked monk who cannot recite a true sutra." At the peak of Dazhai hype, there were almost as many people of all kinds doing research in Dazhai as there are fleas on a cat. From the Central Government level to the County level, every scientific research institute and every academic institution concerned with life sciences wanted a piece of the action. Could one call the expenses they incurred while in Dazhai assistance to Dazhai? By that logic, an advanced unit could never have research personnel of any kind pursuing research projects on its territory.

6. Several miscellaneous items.

Departure stated: "The government and several national defense factories assisted Dazhai with electric lines, electric bill subsidies, explosives, and fuses set aside for it to the amount of 22,940 Chinese dollars."

This is what I found out about the question of electric lines: In 1963, after a devastating flood in Dazhai, people at all levels of authority, from the central to the local, came to Dazhai to express their sympathy. They wanted to give assistance to Dazhai, but Chen Yonggui thanked them all and refused. On one occasion, as Zhang Rong, then Deputy County Committee Secretary accompanied Chen Yonggui to Taiyuan to submit a report, he once again sought his opinion: "What might be the difficulties you still have now?"

"To tell you the truth," Chen Yonggui said, "I don't need help from above for anything right now, but I have one problem. I don't have electricity. If we could get electricity, we could greatly increase the speed of home repairs and reoccupy our cave-dwellings much faster."

Zheng Rong reported this to the Provincial authorities. Later, when a Deputy Director of the Central Government Planning Committee heard about it, he suggested to the Shanxi authorities that, if they felt there was a problem with this, the Central Government would help solve it. That query, had, in fact, put Shanxi on the spot, so Shanxi took the initiative to solve the problem of electric lines for Dazhai.

In order to bring electricity to Dazhai, the line had to pass two other Production Brigades, Liu Settlement and Five Family Flat. How could one possibly omit those two brigades? Wouldn't that be like cutting oneself off from the masses? Consequently, Dazhai received electricity together with Liu Settlement and Five Family Flat. As for the cost of the line, Li Xishen told me the builders calculated the charges according to government regulations, which stipulated that the State was responsible for the high-voltage lines while the local people's collectives had to take care of the low-voltage lines.

When I was checking this material, a cadre of the County Water Conservancy Bureau, Li Guoqing, offered the following detail: In the second half of 1973, Dazhai owed the County Water Conservancy Bureau 3,900 Chinese dollars in water and electric fees. The Director of the County Water Conservancy Bureau at that time, Wang Shengguo, consulted with his Deputy Qu Runsheng, and they decided that it was really rather unseemly to bring the debt up with the folks in Dazhai. They decided to use some of the Bureau's available funds to write it off. They informed Li Guoqing, who was then working with the County Production Group, of their decision. They did not think the whole thing was a big deal. Nobody imagined that the affair might bring down a major disaster on them.

"We are in trouble, partner!" the Bureau's Deputy Director Qu Runsheng told Li Guoqing one day. "Liang Bianliang showed up at the door, trying to find out who wrote off that electric bill, as though Dazhai had no money to pay for it."

Li Guoqing became quite nervous about this, too. He had not expected Dazhai to pursue the matter. He could not think of a way to deal with the situation right then. When they went to the Post and Telecommunications Bureau to report on the situation to the County Committee Chairman, Zhao Mancang, who was attending a meeting there, Zhao Mancang relieved them of responsibility by saying he would explain to Dazhai that it was he who had arranged a temporary loan for them. The following day, Liang Bianliang came with a check to clear the account at the County Water Conservancy Bureau. Remembering this, Li Guoqing was deeply moved.

"The folks in Dazhai would not stand for any unpaid-up accounts," Li said. "If they had a dependent mentality, they could have just not mentioned those 3,900 Chinese dollars in electric fees. It is precisely because they would not tolerate a bad name that they got so upset about what happened." This incident confirms that Dazhai was not at all the way Departure described it as dependent on government assistance for everything.

As for the explosives, I have seen a document about it, and when I checked the information with Liang Bianliang he confirmed that my information was factual. Both Dazhai and Xiyang were in the midst of a vigorous campaign for the capital construction of farmland. In order to create little "plains" out of small terraced fields in the gullies and on the ridges, they needed explosives. Chen Yonggui had heard there was a chemical factory that every year disposed of its reject explosives deep in the mountains, and he considered it a pity that they wasted the explosives like that. Why not use them for the capital construction of farmland? Back then, this sort of thing fell into the range of security issues to be kept secret, so Chen Yonggui demanded that the matter be kept secret and that the defective explosives be used with proper care. Having considered the matter carefully, the Shanxi Military Area Command charged the head of the Central Shanxi Military Subarea and Xiyang County Armed Forces, Jia Huolin, with the delivery of explosives and fuses to Dazhai and with helping to create plains through hill-razing and gully-filling. After the factory moved the explosives and fuses to Dazhai, for security reasons, the manager sent several types of specialists to Dazhai to provide technical assistance and ensure safe explosions. One can say that the above actions constitute government assistance, but it does not seem fair to criticize this kind of government assistance as free-loading or any sort of crime.

Speaking of assistance to Dazhai, it existed before 1964, too. I made a thorough investigation and saw some material relating to then Minister of Agriculture Liao Luyan's inspection trip to Dazhai in May 1964. He prepared material entitled "The Situation Regarding Outside Assistance to Dazhai." He mentioned, for example, that a certain factory gave it a portable steam engine, a certain unit gave it a few water pipes, and cited a limited number of similar instances. Minister Liao knew about them, so did Premier Zhou and Chairman Mao. However, these great men did not deny Dazhai's self-reliance on account of the limited outside assistance that Dazhai received. On the contrary, they set it up as the red-banner standard-bearer of self-reliance and arduous struggle on the national agricultural battlefront.

From what I know, Dazhai was receiving assistance from above even at the peak of Dazhai hype. The mulberry seedlings that Departure brought up were precisely one such instance. I was told by several village secretaries that many Production Brigades were planting trees at that time, and in some instances they did not pay the Ministry of Forestry for the tree seedlings. Such cases were limited in number though. Since Dazhai occupied the highest, most respected, special place, exalted by the entire nation, it is quite natural that the Provincial, District, and County Forestry Departments would give it some tree seedlings to help with the afforestation of its mountains and riverbanks. As to which of the tree seedlings Dazhai paid for and which it did not, it is hard to find out now because both Jia Chengfu, who was in charge of forestry in Dazhai, and Zhao Suheng, the accountant at that time, have passed away.

When it comes to the issue of various County administrative cadres, factory workers and miners doing physical labor in Dazhai, this is truly something that should not be on the table. Those were the days when the Party widely promoted cadre participation in collective productive labor and Chairman Mao singled out Xiyang County as an example of cadre participation in labor. We are not talking about Dazhai alone. Which Production Brigade in Xiyang County has not benefited from cadre labor? This phenomenon of cadres, workers and all manner of employees coming in droves to Dazhai to work in the fields and/or plant trees was a special consequence of that special era. Cadre participation in physical labor is indeed a good thing but, due to the political climate of that time, people often trundled all over the place by the hundreds and thousands to engage in labor for the sake of appearances, and the effects of this practice were not very good. That the personnel who did all the trundling grumbled at times is understandable, too. It would not be amiss to draw a lesson from this experience.

As to the question of how one should view the assistance Dazhai received, I may as well use the words of the authors of Departure themselves: "Of course, it is only proper that the government should extend some financial and material assistance to the People's Communes and Production Brigades in the countryside; this is not in contradiction to encouraging them to develop a spirit of self-reliance and arduous struggle. One cannot say that by receiving some government assistance they are not self-reliant and do not struggle arduously."

However, this is not what the Departure writers wanted to say. The purpose of these phrases was to provide window dressing for quite the opposite reasoning. That is why after this brief opening statement the authors immediately gave their writing brush a twist and, as though following its distorted shape, wrote:

"Without the massive assistance of numerous government departments on the Provincial, District, and County level, relying strictly on its own manpower and financial resources, Dazhai would never be what it is today and Tigerhead Mountain could never have been transformed into its present shape. The facts provide ample evidence that Dazhai indeed departed from its past pioneering spirit of self-reliance, thus negating itself."

This is how Departure defined Dazhai. In order to reinforce their barefaced lies, the authors of the article published some very non-objective, startling data: "Just the above-mentioned instances of financial and material assistance amount to a total of 844,565 Chinese dollars. If we take it that Dazhai has 83 households, i.e., 480 individuals, according to the 1976 and 1977 census, each household received over 10,000 Chinese dollars and each individual over 1,750 Chinese dollars on the average."

And: "If we calculate the aforementioned government assistance, it turns out that, in addition to the cost determined by the fixed price of grain, the government subsidized every *jin* of grain sold to it by Dazhai by 22 cents."

All the odd and even numbers are there; the figures are perfectly clear. That one sentence just nails it!

What effect could publishing this argument about government assistance and the figures of 844,565 Chinese dollars in total, over

10,000 Chinese dollars on the average per household, and 22 cents of subsidy for every *jin* of grain have ten years later? Let us not talk about factual inconsistencies for the moment; let us just look over the figures provided by Departure.

The figure of 844,565 Chinese dollars is grossly exaggerated; the total, by their own calculation, comes to only 639,030 Chinese dollars. This alone goes to show how hot-headed the authors are. Now, if we want to talk about State investment in agriculture, it has decreased significantly in recent years and China's grain yields have been fluctuating below what they used to be. This relates directly to the issue under discussion here: Making calculations based on government investment in agriculture and the grain that agriculture provides for the State in order to level accusations at Dazhai is, historically speaking, untenable. Dazhai surpassed all others in grain deliveries to the State long before the State took any notice of Dazhai. The political tides of that time demanded the establishment of a pilot project, and many people jumped on the bandwagon by turning the pilot into a "model," extolling it as a "model," and by extending the hand of friendship to the "model" that appeared, which brought in its wake a host of problems not easy to keep in balance.

Later, of course, a new conjunction of powerful forces likewise demanded and generated the later criticism of the model as "ultra-left," and so, many people, especially careerists and "movement specialists," again climbed on the bandwagon. What is hard to understand, however, is why so many people, who habitually make a complete turnabout from absolute approval to absolute denial, why do they, when they pick up their pens to write, always attack somebody else, with never a word of self-criticism?

Here is what Liang Bianliang had to say about State aid: "If we asked for money back then, we could have taken in, not just hundreds of thousands, but millions of dollars. There would have always been somebody willing to give it. But we could not ask for it. Even when they gave it, we didn't want it. We didn't take it. We were serious about self-reliance."

And this is what was on Chen Yonggui's mind just before he died. When Dazhai's old members, Liang Bianliang, Guo Fenglian and Song

Liying went to see him, his weak voice crossed his barely moving lips to talk about it. Chen Yonggui's strained and anguished final words may serve as his legacy to mankind: "Dazhai was not made with government money, the adulation of journalists or any boosting by State leaders. The painstaking and systematic effort of its people created Dazhai."

After Departure defined Dazhai theoretically and in terms of numbers, it proceeded to add insult to injury: "In all those years, Dazhai's demands on the government and the government's assistance to Dazhai really went overboard. In this respect Dazhai was truly one of its kind; others could only watch it and sigh. That representative from Dazhai adopted an extremely dishonest attitude: on the one hand, he flatly denied government assistance to Dazhai; on the other, he kept lecturing people to learn the so-called 'spirit of self-reliance and arduous struggle' from Dazhai. All that deceptive talk in fact ridiculed the true spirit of self-reliance and arduous struggle."

Departure adopted highly irregular methods when it launched its total offensive against Dazhai. According to Dazhai residents, several journalists, when writing about the issue of home construction in Dazhai, used their clout to invite several stonemasons from the Third Ford People's Commune village of Guo Family Settlement to the Reception Center in Dazhai, to induce them to testify that Dazhai hired their labor at below the going rate. The people of Dazhai were extremely grateful to the Guo Family Settlement stonemasons for their forthright attitude. Even though the journalists applied great pressure, the stonemasons stuck to their story: "Dazhai's workpoint share in those days was 1.5 Chinese dollars; our workpoint share at the time was only 90 cents. For several years around that time, laborers from other villages in Xiyang were also getting 1.5 Chinese dollars in Yangquan, but they had to pay for their own food and drink. We were given free food and drink while we worked on the cave-dwellings in Dazhai; that was certainly most attractive!"

Despite this, Departure grossly slandered home construction in Dazhai when it claimed that the model Brigade took advantage of hired labor from outside.

A lie, in the end, is a lie—sooner or later people are bound to see through it. Although "Dazhai's Departure From the Spirit of Dazhai" came out with tremendous fanfare and had great influence, the passage of time and later developments gradually began to reveal its falsehoods. Reporter Liu Dan launched the first critical attack on Departure in Guangzhou's *The Contemporary* in January 1988. Other papers, like *Yellow River*, *Shanxi Branch Reconstructs*, *Shanxi Youth*, *Central Shanxi Daily*, *Literary Gazette*, and the like, used different means to reveal how "Dazhai's Departure From the Spirit of Dazhai" made serious departures from historical realities. Unfortunately, to this day the case has not been settled. It has become, instead, even more complicated and malicious.

Liang Bianliang, Guo Fenglian and numerous other senior residents of Dazhai who have been wronged, keep bringing the question up. They challenge and try to enlighten the various journalists who go to Dazhai to research stories, but the whole truth has still not come out. Chen Yonggui, now eternally asleep on Tigerhead Mountain, and the earthbound peasants who are still hacking at the gullies and pounding on the ridges of Dazhai, can only find consolation in the famous Buddhist saying:

> He contained in his big belly
> All that could be endured in this world.
> His kind face smiled at whatever there was
> To smile at under heaven.

CHAPTER — 40

HOLDING TOGETHER EVEN WHEN APART

In 1980, as the unprincipled barrage of reproach came down, Chen Yonggui was unable to continue working. He stayed at home all day contemplating events from the past or receiving visitors who came to see him. At times he felt depressed sitting at home, so he climbed mountains all by himself or went wandering around the fields. He would come to a certain spot and remember how, during a drought one year, he had dug into the plough pan to press seeds into the moist soil; he would go on to another field and remember the fight he had had with someone over the dikes they were building that winter; or he would climb to a hilltop and remember how angry he had become when somebody cut down a pine tree there.

During that period of their lives, Chen Yonggui's wife, Song Yuling, his pampered little son Chen Mingliang, and his grandson Chen Xingfu reached a nadir in their emotional lives. They conversed out of habit with people who came to their door, but they had very little to tell them. It was as though their everyday lives had lost all meaning. When Chen Yonggui decided to return to Beijing, they were overwhelmed with feelings of disappointment and lost hope. As to Chen's future direction, his dismal prospects, they could not but resign themselves to sharing his fate.

Now Chen Yonggui was about to leave his native soil, which he had spent so many years transforming, remolding and bringing under cultivation. A continuous stream of visitors came to see him. Some were from Dazhai, some from Xiyang, and some were rare visitors from faraway places whom he had not seen in years. Some expressed their respects, some merely sighed, and some secretly wiped away their tears of grief over the imminent parting. The usually gregarious Dazhai Commune member Jia Jiusheng somehow fell silent in front of the sallow-faced Chen Yonggui, suddenly unable to say a single word. Only one bitter tear rolled from his burning eyes, falling almost audibly onto his soiled jacket.

After a time of endless bustle and excitement, Dazhai now sank into a melancholy state of indifference and solitude. Criticized by the press, devalued at meetings, its past experiences negated, Dazhai found itself in the predicament where even its old revolutionary utterances were criticized time and again. The newspaper article "Dazhai's Departure From the Spirit of Dazhai" had reduced its stupendous accomplishments to a by-product of state assistance. Being a resident of Dazhai, Jia Jiusheng silently sighed over this tragedy and the predicament of Dazhai's old captain, who had led the arduous struggle for so many years.

Some thirty years earlier, Jia Jiusheng stood in opposition to Chen Yonggui. He had been a member of the "Stalwart" mutual-aid group. Unwilling to admit defeat, he stuck with his group and kept working, but in the end he still lost the battle against the "Feebles." Jia Jiusheng had also been the most active of the people who advocated opening a coal pit through collectively held stock shares. Active though he may have been, the pit never materialized. Nevertheless, after the establishment of agricultural cooperatives, Jia Jiusheng always worked with Chen Yonggui. Both men were good with crops and in the field. "No discord, no concord," you might say. After some ten years of discord, the two had developed a deep affection for each other.

Of course, however deep this affection may have been, Jia Jiusheng still knew perfectly well Chen Yonggui's temper and lack of tact when he lectured people. One morning several people wanted to ask Chen Yonggui for instructions in a particular matter, but they did not dare go up to him because he had given them a good scolding the night before. Of his own accord, the jovial Jia Jiusheng came forward.

"What are you afraid of? Huh?" he asked boldly. "He's not a tiger! If he lectures you, just bear with it!" And he stormed off to look for Chen Yonggui.

Chen Yonggui was sitting by himself at the edge of his brick-bed kang, with his face buried in his hands. Only after looking at him carefully did Jia Jiusheng realize that Chen Yonggui was sobbing. He did not need to ask why. Chen Yonggui was atoning for the sharp scolding he had dished out the night before! Chen Yonggui would pound on tables and toss teacups during meetings, but when he got up the following morning and reflected on such outbursts he always grew repentant. Jia Jiusheng did not immediately bring up the question of work instructions. Instead, he gently comforted him: "What are you crying about? What's been done's been done. Nobody's marking it down against you!"

Chen Yonggui looked up and pulled him down to sit next to him. Taking a deep breath, he asked: "Tell me, was what I said last night to the point or not?"

Jia Jiusheng had only one way of dealing with Chen Yonggui, which was to offer him well-meaning advice. He was the person who could guess Chen Yonggui's moods better than anyone else.

When Jia Jiusheng told me about all this, he was lying on his sickbed. "Old Jia," I asked him, "how come everybody was afraid of Chen Yonggui's lecturing except you?"

"It's like when a doctor takes your pulse," Jia replied. "He's got to take it right! If you made a mistake, you had to avoid at all cost coming in front of him. Only when you figured out how to remedy your mistake was he able to suppress his temper. If you'd made no mistakes and he lectured you, you just had to stand up to him stubbornly. If you were as pig-headed and obstinate as he was, he would eventually soften up. He was not an ill-intentioned person, and he never held grudges against people. That's why I was not afraid of him!"

How much easier it was for Jia Jiusheng to deal with Chen Yonggui that morning when he found him at home crying!

As Chen Yonggui was about to leave Dazhai, Jia Jiusheng went to pay him a visit. He crossed his doorstep, and found a place to sit down. Without greeting him, Chen Yonggui, who was lying on the kang, pushed an open pack of cigarettes toward him. The meaning was clear!

"Will you be able to come back for a visit after you leave?"

The question was loaded with emotion, but the tone was carefully measured. It also carried with it much hope.

Chen Yonggui appeared suddenly vulnerable as he emitted a long huffing sound. "Who knows?" he sighed.

Jia Jiusheng sighed silently in response. It seemed to him that Chen Yonggui had already lost control of the rudder as his career slipped away.

People are probably all like that in comparable situations. Nobody else can even guess what lonely, miserable, tragic feelings overtook Chen Yonggui when he started sliding downhill. He no longer attended meetings. He did not even go out to walk around. His mental burden grew at unchecked speed. When people came to see him, he greeted them with a vague expression of welcome, but he did not have much to say. When he could not think an issue through, he was in the habit of taking out a newspaper and reading articles that were critical of him, looking for the ways people were analyzing "that former leading cadre of the Xiyang County Committee."

Jia Jiusheng smoked with Chen Yonggui, and gradually struck up a conversation. Tears started rolling from their eyes as they exchanged reminiscences.

To this day Jia Jiusheng blames his sons for not buying a wreath for Chen Yonggui when his ashes returned for eternal rest in Dazhai. He himself, still weak and frail, was just coming out of the hospital.

"A lot of people sent wreaths for Old Chen," he told me, sighing. "But those two little sons of mine could not even accomplish a thing like that. A cat should take care of mice, a man should take care of his house. Those two sons of mine are already in their twenties and thirties, yet they could not even take care of a thing like that!"

All those interesting incidents that happened during the period when Chen Yonggui was preparing to leave Dazhai will never be entered into the record, but they remain vivid in the memory of Dazhai's residents. The story I like best is the one about a trip that Chen Yonggui and Jia Jincai took together.

Having been together through thick and thin for several decades, Jia Jincai and Chen Yonggui enjoyed a spirit of unusual and easy cordiality. The two had had some differences in the past, but they were never jealous of each other and they never complained about each other. They were always understanding and reasonable.

As Chen Yonggui bade his eternal farewell to Dazhai and Xiyang, a thought suddenly appeared in his mind: He wanted to make a tour of all his favorite places by car. He grabbed Jia Jincai, who had come to see him: "Jincai, come with me! I'm afraid this will be the last time for us to ride together!"

The last time? Or was it maybe the first time? Although the two had struggled and endured together for many decades, Chen Yonggui often rode to other places for meetings, inspections, or in search of solutions, while Jia Jincai stayed back in the village splitting rocks. Although his sun had already set behind the western mountains, Chen Yonggui continued to enjoy the privilege of having a car and a driver. So of course Jia Jincai was more than happy to have the opportunity to get out of the village and take the proffered ride!

The wheels started spinning, leaving the village of Dazhai behind, pulverizing their chatter along the way, and with that chatter the regrets over the several-year-old "grand plan for a great undertaking" as well as, thank the mountain sprites, Chen Yonggui's depression.

"We'll go wherever the road takes us. It'll drive our cares away." Chen Yonggui's face squeezed out a smile as he spoke to Jia Jincai, who sat behind him. Jia smiled ever so slightly in response, unable to find words to express what was on his mind.

The car wheels climbed up the Golden Rocks Slope, and went down the Rainbow Bridge Pass, continuing to roll in the direction of Fengju. As they traveled, they tossed away their depression, and their conversation, growing animated, brought smiles to their faces.

Chen Yonggui took a puff on his cigarette, then continued his lively exchange with Jia Jincai: "Jincai, do you still remember what the connection is between Rainbow Bridge Pass and our Dazhai?"

"It's not something I've looked into like you have," Jia Jincai answered, "but I do remember what the elders used to say about it. Rainbow Bridge Pass is a gap in the mountains that used to be guarded by soldiers, and Dazhai was responsible for training and maintaining them, right?"

"Our elders could never forget it. It was something that happened over a thousand years ago." Chen Yonggui laughed.

At this point the car had already made the turn toward Fengju, and arrived at the Chuankou intersection.

"But that doesn't mean that we in Xiyang should be looked down upon!" Chen Yonggui continued. "We've produced a few great men in history! Jincai, this is Wind Gap People's Commune, Spring Mouth Production Brigade. Do you know who was born here?"

"I couldn't say," said Jia, caught off guard.

"The great Number One Scholar of outstanding promise for the dynasty!" said Chen Yonggui.

He was talking about the famous Jin Dynasty Number One Scholar, Yang Yongyi[1] who served as minister under several emperors. To this very day, the site of the terrace built to honor his achievement when he placed first in the Imperial Academy examination had been preserved in his native village of Chuankou. Chen Yonggui, however, could not recall his name.

The road to High Tower passed through Wind Gap first, and then through more than ten villages that belonged to the Zhao Camp People's Commune. Chen Yonggui was casting a very familiar gaze over the fields that lay on the two sides of the road. The flood plain of the dry riverbed at Zhao Camp had been built into field upon field of fertile farmland, covered now with a dark green expanse of corn and sorghum. The corn and sorghum had changed the look of the river bed completely. In the old society, this was a poor place with grain yields

1. Jin was the "Golden Dynasty" (1115-1234). One of the Tartar Dynasties that ruled China's North, while the Southern Song ruled the South. Overpowered by the Mongols.

barely reaching 100 *jin* per *mu*. Now, the yields had increased ten times. As the movement to learn from Dazhai gradually deepened, reservoirs, dams, high pressure irrigation pumps and the like have all appeared in the valley. Xiyang became a treasured land of endless innovation that produced enormous quantities of surplus grain.

"What a great place! This is really a great place! No wonder people call the Zhao Camp flat 'The Valley of Grain'!" Jia Jincai said excitedly.

Chen Yonggui was feeling very good for a change. "It's not only grain! They produce good people here, too! Haven't you heard of the Ming Dynasty Minister Qiao, whose post would equal that of a Minister of Organization or Minister of Defense today. He protected four or five emperors!"

Chen Yonggui was referring to Qiao Yu, who was born in South Cross Mountain, a village that was now a part of the Zhao Camp Commune. Due to his outstanding literary and artistic talent, he served the Dynasty as the Secretary of Official Personnel Affairs, wielding great power over personnel matters. When he was demoted, he became very influential in the history of Shanxi, a history the people of Xiyang are particularly familiar with.

"Still, his office was not as high as yours," teased Jia Jincai. "We've never had a Vice-Premier in the history of Xiyang before!"

"I'm nothing, really," Chen Yonggui retorted. "We haven't had an Emperor yet in Xiyang. But wasn't one of the political entities during the Warring States Period the State of Fei Zi in Jingyang? Its supreme ruler was called King Kuei! His domain was not large, but still it was larger than the territory of Xiyang today. The State lasted for about one hundred and thirty years. I haven't even been Vice-Premier for ten years! What a difference!" Chen Yonggui sighed as he spoke: "I've courted a lot of trouble, being a member of the Political Bureau and Vice-Premier for the past eight years. How do you think I performed? Some people say that the Water Ravine Reservoir is like a sieve. I wasn't prepared for it to be filled with water at that time! There were hardly a few *mu* of good land in the whole Zhao Camp Valley. What was more important, securing land or securing water? We blocked the river to one side in order to construct fields! If that reservoir can basically hold some water at all, that's already not bad!"

The gently disposed Jia Jincai may not have been to many places but he, too, had an opinion about such a major issue of right and wrong.

"People talk too much," he volunteered. "When something is good, it's more fragrant than a twisted doughnut right out of the hot pan; when it's bad, it stinks worse than dogshit. We've seen plenty of this in Dazhai during the past few decades!"

"A tall tree catches the wind," said Chen Tonggui, passing Jia a cigarette. "Being in high position, I was open to attack. You can't stop people talking about you when you become famous. If I've made mistakes, they should be examined by the Central Committee. Even Chairman Mao made mistakes, so how could we be that correct? But when a wave sweeps across the lake, the clear water becomes turbid. Even building dams and dikes and constructing fields becomes an issue, stressing grain production and water conservancy becomes an issue, educating people becomes an issue, exclaiming 'Standing on Tigerhead Mountain, I look on Tiananmen' becomes an issue, even...."

Chen Yonggui, who had not had a chance to complain to anybody for quite some time, used this opportunity to spill out all his pain. Jia Jincai had been wanting to ask him about the situation at the Central Committee for several days, but he did not dare open his mouth. Now, Chen Yonggui spread everything in front of him. Jia Jincai understood perfectly well and paid close attention.

The car crossed the Zhao Camp Valley and, accelerating uphill along the highway to High Tower, managed to climb up a difficult stretch of the road.

High Tower is the largest village in Xiyang County, with a long history, vast stretches of fertile soil, and rich folklore. During the War of Resistance Against Japan, the village was the seat of the East Xiyang County Government. A Ming Dynasty Attendant at the Ministry of War, Zhao Fu, was born here. He took part in suppressing Li Zicheng's rebellious army, but was not as famous as Yang Yongyi or Qiao Yu. Naturally, Chen Yonggui and Jia Jincai discussed him too as they drove by.

When Chen Yonggui had come to visit High Tower in the past, there were always people waiting for him at the Commune main gate. It goes without saying that the Commune leadership would always report to him on the most recent developments, and then take him around to hear his comments. This time, Chen Yonggui was free to do as he pleased. He had not planned the visit. When he entered the village, nobody paid any attention. He was not in the mood to stop in High Tower, so he turned around right away and went back in the direction of Xiyang County Town. Very few people in High Tower even knew that he had come.

There is a big hillside in the High Tower area covered with pines. As they drove past it, Chen Yonggui told the driver to stop the car. He wanted to get out. The dark green pines and emerald cypress trees were beckoning.

Chen Yonggui stood under a pine tree, taking in the scenery up and down the hill, and released a long groan. He was very familiar with the place. He distinctly remembered the look of the few pines that lined the highway. Today, however, the place felt strangely unfamiliar. Jia Jincai does not remember exactly what Chen Yonggui talked about at that particular spot, but the memory of the emotions Chen Yonggui's body language conveyed remains vivid in his mind.

The air was very fresh. The mountain wind stirred the green pine branches. The scent and the motion helped dispel Chen Yonggui's worries.

"Jincai, let's go up there to sit for a while!" Chen said, pulling Jia Jincai closer.

As he spoke he handed him another cigarette.

Jia Jincai, who had resolved to give up smoking, could not refuse Chen Yonggui's kindness. He followed him up the pine- covered hillside.

"Jincai, didn't you always use to say that those who are like bears are better than those who are like dragons? The two of us fit into the category 'from an exchange of blows friendship grows.' Let's agree on one thing today: If I die first, you send me a flower wreath; if you die first, I'll send you one. All right?"

The skin-and-bones Jia Jincai slowly took a long hesitant drag on his cigarette before replying, "Huh. Huhuh. Yes, of course."

"I could already see from the time we first set up the mutual-aid groups that my ten sentences did not measure up to even one of Chen Yonggui's," Jia Jincai said when he told me about this incident. "The moment he moved his lips, you had to do as he said even if you didn't like it, that's how convincing he was. But when he got into trouble, then the issue of whether he was right or wrong became magnified."

Jia Jincai then told me an even more interesting story. After Chen Yonggui climbed the pine-clad hillside that day he stood around hesitantly for a while. Then his face broke into a grin as he suddenly walked up to Jia Jincai and sat down behind him back-to-back, pressing closely against him.

"Jincai, can you guess what this is all about?" Chen asked.

The stolid Jia Jincai had no idea what the answer was, so he simply smiled foolishly. To this very day Jia Jincai has not been able to figure out what that back-to-back lean-in was supposed to signify.

It had never occurred to him that Dazhai, with hundreds of millions of eyes observing it carefully, would sink so far overnight. It never occurred to him that Chen Yonggui, whom he had once recommended three times for office before he became famous, would fall into such deep disgrace.

In the winter of 1985 Jia Jincai was invited to Beijing to appear in a documentary film. He kept thinking about one major event after the filming, which was to visit Chen Yonggui at the hospital. The hospital was under special protection, and the entrance gate was strictly guarded. One could not just simply go in. Jia Jincai entrusted his son-in-law with procuring him an entry pass for the hospital through Chen Yonggui's daughter Chen Minghua, and only then was he able to see Chen Yonggui. Gravely ill, Chen Yonggui was no longer able to talk, so the two men could only communicate their emotions through tears.

After Chen Yonggui died, Jia Jincai did not get an appropriate opportunity to mourn his death. Only when Chen Yonggui's ashes returned to Dazhai did Jia Jincai, no longer able to do manual labor, take out twenty Chinese dollars to buy a decent flower-bedecked wreath, fulfilling the promise he had given Chen Yonggui on the pine hillside in High Tower.

•

Back then everybody in the village knew that Chen Yonggui was about to leave for Beijing. But which day would it be? Chen Yonggui remained silent about it. A few days after he took Jia Jincai to Gaoluo to distract himself, Chen Yonggui called Guo Fenglian, Liang Bianliang and Song Liying to take a walk across Dazhai's ridges and ravines with him, remembering the old days as they went. He told them he would leave that evening, on the night train. There was no other way for him to leave, since otherwise people from the County and even beyond would gather to see him off and they would all be crying. This way, by the time the car stopped in front of his house to pick him up, most people were already sound asleep. Chen Yonggui shook hands with the few friends who knew about his departure. After he got into the car, he heard Jia Jiusheng sobbing "Good bye!" Chen Yonggui jumped out of the car again and, with tears in his eyes, waved everybody away: "Go home! All right, all right, go home!"

And he was gone. The sound of his car gradually died away in the distance. Those who had assembled to see him off secretly wiped away their tears. Zhao Cuntang and several other young people sighed: "The golden casket is broken, but no part of it is missing. I doubt that we will ever see another man like that under this big willow tree of ours."

CHAPTER 41

DRIFTING IN BEIJING

When Chen Yonggui left Dazhai, he took his wife Song Yuling, his little son Chen Mingliang and his grandson Chen Xingfu with him. The people from Dazhai kept inquiring about where he lived, what he did every day, and what his life was like. They also tried to find out whether the Central Committee treated him well or not. They heard that the Central Committee undertook a thorough investigation of him, but that he was allowed to continue living at his Vice-Presidential residence at Jiaodaokou. But Chen Yonggui, they were told, said that if he no longer held the position he should no longer be using the residence and, on his own request, moved to an apartment in Block 22 of the high government cadres' apartment complex. They did not know whether this information was correct or not.

Chen Yonggui had been making mistakes all his life. He made errors in his work. But his actions after he moved to Beijing, and after he was removed from office, revealed the attitudes and qualities of the peasant statesman he had become. After he had joined the Political Bureau and became Vice-Premier, he was supposed to transfer his residence registration and do the paperwork needed for changing his official occupation to "cadre" (functionary). But he said: "What should I change that for? I don't want to depart from the peasants!" So although he had become Vice-Premier of the State Council, his feet remained in Dazhai, where he continued to earn, register and be paid for his work points. The State only provided him with some living allowances.

Not only that, whenever he had returned to Dazhai from Beijing he did not allow security guards to do sentry duty for him. He also could not help getting upset with receptionists who held doors for him: "What are you holding that door for? To separate me from the masses?" But it was their job to hold doors for all those leaders who poured in to submit reports and receive instructions, and for all the visitors and dignitaries that arrived from all quarters to see him. Even if Chen Yonggui were to split himself into ten, he could not manage to open doors for them all! His receptionists were put in a difficult position: damned if you do, damned if you don't.

So when Dazhai fell from grace and the stunned Chen Yonggui returned to Beijing, the first question he had to face was where to live? It was the second half of 1980, and the mass media were harshly criticizing Dazhai for ultra-leftism. At the end of 1980, however, the Central Committee circulated Document No. 83, which contained the Shanxi Provincial Committee's investigative report with its relatively fair appraisal of Dazhai. As for the Central Committee's attitude toward Chen Yonggui personally, the intention all along was to protect him. His treatment and privileges remained unchanged, and his residence remained on the Vice-Presidential level at Jiaodaokou.

But Chen Yonggui expressed a contrary opinion to the State Management Bureau: "If I'm not a Vice-Premier, why should I be living at Jiaodaokou? I've always been prepared for either the top or the bottom level!"

He asked many times to be allowed to move out of Jiaodaokou and have his security guard protection revoked. The State Management Bureau leaders did not meet his requests right away, being mindful of the international impression a sudden downgrading would make, but they did agree to give half of his courtyard residence to someone else while he remained in the alternate half. Chen Yonggui did not agree to this, saying that even so he would still be treated specially. The State

Management Bureau then found him a house at Lumicang. After he looked at it, Chen Yonggui shook his head, saying that this courtyard was just about as big as the one at Jiaodaokou. The Bureau then decided to have him live in Block 22, just east of Mushudi on the south side of Fuxingmenwai Ave, which is an extension of Changganjie, Beijing's main thoroughfare. This was a block reserved for high government cadres. Meeting the requirement for ministerial level treatment, the Bureau assigned him to Apartment 23, Entrance 5, which consisted of several rooms on the twelfth floor.

After he saw the apartment, Chen Yonggui agreed. He asked his secretary to move him before the New Year, but due to the secretary's busy schedule and New Year celebrations this did not happen until after the Spring Festival. After the move, some of Chen Yonggui's privileges remained unchanged. He was, for instance, the only person in Block 22 to enjoy special accommodations. While in office, he had had two cars at his disposal: a Red Flag limousine for official business and a Datsun for everyday use. He returned the Red Flag limo when he was relieved of office, explaining that it consumed too much gas, but retained the Datsun for personal use. In order to cut down on gas consumption, he did not use the Datsun very much. He often went out on foot to take care of his business. His son, relatives and friends were thus even less inclined to use the car. His driver ended up receiving frequent Gas Saving Awards.

Just a few months after being relieved of office, Chen Yonggui had dismissed his cook. He and his wife took care of the cooking themselves, and he even said that it was easier this way to eat whatever he felt like. At the time of his move, the State Management Bureau had agreed to let him take with him all the furnishings from the Jiaodaokou residence, but Chen Yonggui wanted to take only what he really needed, since the apartment had built-in wall closets and cabinets and there was not enough space for many things. Consequently, he only took items in everyday use, such as beds, carpets, the old TV set, the filing cabinet for documents, and so on. Everything else remained at the old residence.

After he lost his official position, he received 200 Chinese dollars a month in salary, which left him in a rather strained financial situation. He occasionally encountered someone who protested that his salary was too low for his expenses.

"I get whatever is set by the policy," he replied. "That's how much I eat. I don't want to beg for anything from the higher-ups."

Chen Yonggui became a true citizen of Beijing. He had to get used to the various habits of city dwellers. Every morning at dawn the old residents of the capital practiced *taijiquan*, exercises placing great expectations for a long life on benefits from this practice. At that time of day people practicing *taijiquan* appeared under the trees of the city's parks, avenues, and on the banks of the Soonly River, and their lives seemed as steady and worry-free as though they were living in a jeweled palace in the hills of the immortals.

Chen Yonggui was used to getting up early. For several decades, spring, summer, autumn or winter, he had spent tens of thousands of dawns and dusks building a solid strong body by wielding hoes and pickaxes in the remote mountain area. He was truly not quite accustomed to life in the multi-storied, luxurious and extremely comfortable apartment building for high-ranking cadres. At the beginning, he went out to walk as soon as he got out of bed, to stretch his legs and catch a breath of the fresh morning air. In the course of time, as he watched the people practicing *taijiquan*, he began to envy them and was seized by a sudden inspiration to try the exercise himself.

It is actually hard for people used to working with sledge hammers and grub hoes to adjust their bodies to the acrobatics of the city folks. At first Chen Yonggui just walked around with his hands propped at his hips. Then he got used to swinging his arms around as he walked or ran. As days went on, however, he started yearning for his life in Dazhai,and he raised his arms and began swaying them in the motion used in field construction. As he was swaying in this movement one time, an old man grabbed him by his arms. Turning around, he recognized Old Man Wang, whom he frequently came across on the street. He did not know his personal name. They called each other "Old Man."

"Ayah! You healthy old man," exclaimed Old Man Wang. "What kind of boxing routine is that?"

"This is, hmm.... This is farmer's boxing!" said Chen Yonggui laughing. He exchanged a cigarette with Old Man Wang. "This is how I used to plant. I'm not boasting. When I was a few years younger, I could cover several *mu* of land like this!"

"When in the mountain, depend on the mountain; when near water, depend on water!" Old Man Wang advised him. "You are now in Beijing, you should do as we do! Here's the deal: I'll be the master, you be my disciple. I'll take you in for one week."

Move by move, the old man taught Chen Yonggui how to do *taiji-quan*. But after just a few sessions, Chen Yonggui lost interest in it.

"No, no, no. When I do this boxing of yours, I don't spend enough energy. Let's switch around: I'll be the master, and you be my disciple! I'll take you in for one week, and teach you how to do my farmer's boxing!" he said, turning the tables.

After he moved to the apartment building for high-level cadres, Chen Yonggui never quite felt like himself. Closed in by the four walls, all he could see was the telephone, the television, the electric light, the automatic elevator. How interesting could that be? He could not sit still. He was constantly trying to find some chore with which to occupy himself. He read newspapers, grew potted flowers, listened to the news.

Observant people noticed that Chen Yonggui's smoking took on a fixed pattern. When he finished smoking one cigarette, he could not bring himself to throw out the butt: He would dig out the tobacco with his finger before he went on to smoke another cigarette. After he became Vice-Premier, he continued to smoke the Sanqi cigarettes out of habit, but he also started smoking the Zhonghua, and some other high-quality brands. After he was relieved of his office, he had to take stock of the family resources when it came to smoking and drinking, so he replaced the Zhonghua brand with the Da Qianmen brand and the like. Those were the days when his mind revolved around the cigarette that he held in his closed mouth even while he read newspapers, tended to his flowers or listened to the news.

As the days went on, he grew depressed doing these same things over and over, and he was very happy to receive folks from back home and acquaintances who came to see him. He also gladly went to the No. 34 Supply Station located right next to Block 22 of the apartment complex or to the open market for a stroll. While in office, wherever he went he constantly wanted to engage in physical labor; after his political reversal, he was not in the right state of mind to go back to Dazhai because of the people in Xiyang and Dazhai who had attacked him when he was down. Yet, while he remained physically in Peking, his heart was still in Dazhai. Since he could not turn into reality all his hopes and plans for Dazhai, he kept seeing those hopes and plans in his dreams.

Several times he woke up in the morning telling his wife: "Ayah! I don't work during the day, but there I was last night, in my dreams back in the village planting, telling everybody what to do, how to plant in moist soil, how to plant in dried-up soil, how to plant in warm soil, how to plant in cold soil!"

Although he had just gone through a big political purge, he remained the same as any peasant who subsisted on the yellow loess soil—unable to wean himself from the need for physical labor no matter where he went. The political climate, however, deprived him of the power to engage in physical labor, so all he could do was stroll about the open market in the capital, looking for a home to go back to.

Chen Yonggui's spirits always picked up when he led hometown visitors to the free market in Beijing, holding his straw hat with one hand and resting the other on his waist. He escorted all the guests from Xiyang and Dazhai, showing them around. At the free market, he was always interested in fruits, gourds, vegetables and farm produce, listened to the sellers advertising their curios and antiques, and followed with interest the bargaining and haggling over prices. When he quietly compared the present situation with the years when the open markets were closed because the sole emphasis was on grain production, he had to admit that things were much more lively now, and that this was, after all, good.

"Life in Beijing is not bad, after all," a visitor from Xiyang once exclaimed looking over the wares at an antique stall. "You've got everything here."

"Yeah, it's true. It's a fine place to live. Only, damn it, there's never enough money. If I don't go out I get bored just sitting at home, but the moment I get out I spend too much money. I can't take it, really!"

One time he took a hometown friend from the Public Security Department to the market. As they approached a stall, they saw a group of people surrounding a pile of crockery casseroles and haggling over their price with the owner. Chen Yonggui watched for a while and then, beside himself with rage, interceded in support of the buyer: "What kind of crockery is this?" Chen yelled. "It's much worse than the kind we make in the countryside!"

Just like any other peasant, Chen was outspoken in dealing with everything, regardless of the situation.

Those were the days when Chen Yonggui liked to go out by himself. After he moved into the apartment building, he had done away with his security guard, his secretary, and his cook. Only his driver, Tang Zhanxin, and the little Datsun sedan still remained in his service. Master Tang came to Block 22 every morning to see whether Chen Yonggui needed to go out on any business. This honest and kind driver had been assigned to him by the Army the moment he came to Beijing, and remained in his service continuously for many years. During his last few years, Chen Yonggui liked to pour his heart out to his old driver.

"How long before you die, Master Tang?" Chen Yonggui once asked him in a moment of excitement during one of their conversations.

Master Tang thought the question both funny and annoying: "You may be involved with my life otherwise, but whether and when I live or die is none of your business! Yama, the King of Hell, will decide when my time comes!" But this is not what he told Chen Yonggui. Beating around the bush, he answered: "I can't figure out when I'll die. It's not up to me!"

"I'm not looking forward to your death," Chen Yonggui said laughing. "I just remembered the other drivers who had worked for me. There were three drivers at one time, and now only you are left. I just wanted to make a deal with you, that you continue to drive for me while I'm still alive. When it comes time for me to die, your age will be just right for retirement. What do you say?"

Chen Yonggui meant his words to be witty and funny. He had been recalling with nostalgia his past drivers. When he worked in Xiyang, he had had a driver by the name of Wang Tianbao, who had fallen ill and died a few years before. His driver from the time when he worked on the Provincial level had also died recently. Both drivers had been good comrades and had good rapport with him. But in terms of the length of time and the depth of friendship, nobody had been quite like this Tang

Zhanxin in Beijing. He did not talk very much, but he was a person of great integrity—someone Chen Yonggui trusted and could rely on.

On one occasion Tang Zhanxin drove Chen Yonggui to the office complex to take care of some business. When Chen Yonggui got out of the car, he told him: "Master Tang, there's no need for you to go around with me this morning. Why don't you go back home and help your wife make dumplings? There's no need for you to pick me up at noon either. I can get back by myself."

Without responding, Master Tang drove away, but at noon, just as Chen Yonggui was about to board a bus for his apartment complex, a car stopped right next to him. Master Tang jumped out of the car.

"How come you are here again?" asked Chen Yonggui in surprise.

He shouldn't have been surprised. Ever since Chen Yonggui had dismissed his secretary and his security guard, Master Tang had served not only as his driver; he also took care of his safety and everything else. Although Chen Yonggui had sent him home that morning to make dumplings, Tang did not feel very comfortable about that. What if something were to happen to Old Chen and there was nobody around? From Chen Yonggui's point of view, however, the more he was able to go to crowded places by himself, the more enthusiastic about it he became.

The Central Committee had been very concerned about Chen Yonggui ever since he moved permanently to Peking. After the Party's Twelfth Congress, Deng Xiaoping, having inquired about Chen Yonggui's state of mind and living conditions, invited him for a personal meeting. As soon as Chen Yonggui entered his reception room, Deng Xiaoping greeted him warmly and invited him to sit down. Knowing how fond of smoking Chen Yonggui was, Deng Xiaoping instructed his assistant: "Bring two packs of the Panda brand!" After that, the two men sat on the sofa and started formal talks. Deng inquired about his health, living conditions and frame of mind. He urged him to study hard and take good care of his health and not to burden himself psychologically because he had not been elected by the Twelfth Congress. Chen Yonggui poured out much of what was on his mind.

When they touched upon the topic of Chen Yonggui's relationship with the Gang of Four, Deng Xiaoping said: "Old Chen, you are not one of the Gang of Four's people. The Central Committee knows this perfectly well. Be assured that as long as I'm alive and well, you won't be implicated with the Gang of Four."

As they talked about the situation in Dazhai and Xiyang, Deng Xiaoping said: "Don't hesitate to let us know what you think. On specific issues, look for Zhong Xun. He'll take everything into consideration."

Chen Yonggui was very content after his meeting with Deng Xiaoping. He told several people afterward that the conversation with Deng Xiaoping had cheered him up.

Around that time, the then General Secretary of the Central Committee, Hu Yaobang, also met with him. He told him that he was a man of great merit, and he should not allow some past events to threaten his health. He also told him not to give in to mental pressure because he had been dismissed from his State and Party posts. He specifically informed him that Comrade Li Xiannian had spoken very fairly on his behalf, about the irrigation and water conservancy capital construction, for instance. Chen Yonggui requested that the General Secretary clarify the question of his status and his past work. Hu Yaobang said that Dazhai was good, all right, but that policy had changed and it was no longer a suitable model. Deng Xiaoping and Hu Yaobang talked to him about many things, and Chen Yonggui on his part opened his mind and analyzed himself. He was able to take philosophically his dismissal from the Political Bureau and the loss of his Vice-Premiership. As he repeatedly told people, he had been psychologically prepared for it for quite some time.

Many stories about Chen Yonggui still circulate among the citizenry of Beijing: about his street strolling, visits to the open market, shopping trips, and the like. People say that Chen Yonggui frequently went out to shop for food after he lost his posts. The State Management Bureau had set up the No. 34 Special Supply Station in the apartment complex for high cadres especially to provide vegetables for the high-ranking leaders. Why should they have to worry about getting their food? But Chen Yonggui was different. He went out and made rounds of shops and stalls, feeling that, since he had nothing else to bring home, at the very least he could bring a few pounds of vegetables.

There was a time when a long line had formed in front of a vegetable stall. Everybody was in a hurry to buy some vegetables. When Chen Yonggui saw the situation, he dutifully took up his place in line, waiting his turn. But somebody recognized him right away, and people started shouting, "Elder Chen is buying food!" and "Uncle Chen is buying food!" so that the people in front of him made room to let him buy ahead of them. Chen Yonggui smiled and waved his hands, saying he wanted to wait in line like everybody else. Finally, the people in front of the line started calling him, too, to hurry up, and so he was pushed and pulled to the front of the line, for once enjoying "special privileges."

Beijing residents say that in his late years Chen Yonggui handled his relationship with the people of the city and with the Central Committee leadership exceptionally well. The better the relationship was handled the better people came to understand his role, including his errors, in the "Cultural Revolution." This may also be one of the reasons that people still cherish his memory to this day.

After Chen Yonggui left Dazhai, the people of Dazhai paid him a great deal of solicitude and thought of him even more kindly than before. The cadres and masses from the village kept going to Peking to pay him a visit. Dazhai's old and new cadres like Liang Bianliang, Song Liying, Jia Jincai, Gao Yuliang, Zhao Suheng, and Zhao Cuntang all went to visit him, with Liang Bianliang making the trip almost annually. Consequently, Chen Yonggui's home was often full of guests. Their consumption of grain and vegetables was quite high, but Chen Yonggui, oblivious to this, accorded everybody proper treatment.

"Next time when somebody comes, they should telephone me first at home, so I can send the car to meet them at the station. We've got a car, you know!" he enjoined his guests.

When Gao Yuliang went to visit Chen Yonggui, Chen Yonggui accorded him the same proper treatment. He treated him for lunch, and then dragged him to the elevator: "Let's go! We've still got some time to while away. Let's take a walk outside."

As the two took the elevator down and walked into the bustling street, they brushed past the masses of people coming and going around them. Disregarding all this activity in the street, Chen Yonggui pulled his countryman close to him: "Yuliang, tell me something. What is it that I did wrong after all? Whatever it is, tell me! I want to know."

Chen Yonggui was well aware of the public opinion. After a period of painful self-reflection, he was eager to hear different opinions. Gao Yuliang seldom heard him seek the opinion of others so sincerely, but as he observed Chen Yonggui now, he felt much closer to him than in the past. When they were children, Gao Yuliang and Guo Fenglian called Chen Yonggui "uncle," but as Chen Yonggui's fame grew and since even his sponsors among the top country leaders were calling him "Old Chen," Gao Yuliang changed the way he addressed him to "Old Chen" as well. As they toured the streets now, Gao Yuliang thought about the old days and he unwittingly called him "uncle" again.

"If you ask me," Gao replied, "you took too many duties upon yourself. You were minding the business of the Central Committee, you were minding the business of the Region, when it came to our village your word was always listened to. How could you possibly take care of all that without a hitch? Some experiences were successful in our village, but they didn't work elsewhere! How could every profession and line of work learn from Dazhai, as the slogan called for during those years? There are not that many things one can learn from our village after all!"[1]

"You are right. I've been getting the worst of it during the past few years. When the people above cried, 'Ninety-nine,' I delivered 'one hundred and one.'" Chen Yonggui's voice was high-pitched due to his excitement, and he gesticulated to stress his point. "I've read the Central Committee Document No. 83 many times, and I think that it's more or less acceptable. The Central Committee has assumed responsibility for problems that occurred in the Learn from Dazhai campaign, but I'm responsible for it too. Whatever was my responsibility, I don't

---

1. Again, we are treated to the notion that Dazhai's role was simply technical or agricultural, rather than political and ideological. What the whole country had to learn from Dazhai was its proletarian world outlook, its "public first, self second" stance, its commitment to collective prosperity and "self reliance and hard struggle" as opposed to the go-it-alone, "enrich yourself" Philistinism that replaced it. Young Gao missed the point completely, as it seems author Qin also does. (W.H.H.)

push it onto the higher-ups. Huh! The attacks have been coming from all directions these past few years, and too many people have been offended. Now the push has come to shove and those folks are ready to strike back. In the past all I thought about was how whatever Dazhai could do, the entire country could do for sure, too. Now I've finally brought myself to recognize that there is a serious problem with uneducated folks like me, because we cannot see through things. Huh! I was illiterate until the age of forty-three! That's hard to deal with. If I were younger, I'd go to college for a few years!"

If Chen Yonggui could accept the Central Committee Document No. 83, passed in 1980, so could the people of Dazhai. Before the document was approved, Dazhai's and Chen Yonggui's social position were in a sorry plight. Once the document circulated through the nation, media criticism of Dazhai more or less stopped, and the days of intense misery were over. When Vice-Premier Wan Li went on a tour of inspection to Shanxi some time later, in 1984, he said that the issue of Dazhai should never be mentioned again. He also said that Dazhai's three soil-deepening techniques and the sponge soil building were the right thing to do.[1] This gradually brought about a fair-minded evaluation of Dazhai.

Since the Central Committee dealt with the issue of Dazhai and learning from Dazhai impartially, Chen Yonggui became increasingly introspective about the past. As a result, he told Gao Yuliang during their walk through the city streets: "There was nothing wrong with our promotion of self-reliance and arduous struggle in the past, but we should rethink some of the concrete measures we took. Some people were particularly rigid in work and income distribution, breaking down the principle of payment according to work performed. This was not suitable for most other places, and we have to gradually recognize and admit this. I used to frown upon the administration's eight-hour work-days and Sundays, not taking into consideration that those were the freedoms won by the workers after the French Revolution in their

1. Wan Li proves to be as ignorant as Gao Yuliang. Major questions of ideology, goals and policy—the Socialist Road, versus the Capitalist Road—are being debated, questions in regard to which the Dazhai experience is seminal, and Wan Li reduces the experience to soil amelioration techniques! (W.H.H.)

struggle against the capitalists. Yah! I've become old. In the future, when you do something, you should use the advantages to offset the weaknesses. Carry forward my strong points but don't perpetuate my shortcomings!"

CHAPTER — 42

AT THE EAST END STATE FARM

As the second year of Chen Yonggui's forced retirement wore on, the millstone around his neck gradually became lighter, but he felt less and less comfortable with growing flowers, reading newspapers and strolling about the open market. Is it possible, he thought, that despite my shortcomings and mistakes, the Communist Party has not been nurturing me for all those years just so State money can be wasted on my salary? He called on others to come up with some ideas, while he tried to devise a solution.

In the end, he came up with a new idea. He had been running into Han Kai, a journalist who lived in his building, quite frequently. Han Kai helped him at the time he was trying to find a solution to his situation. Han Kai wrote a report on Chen Yonggui's behalf to the Central Committee, in which he said that he wanted to be useful to the Party while he was still alive, and he pleaded with the Central Committee to find some concrete work for him. The Party Central Committee evaluated Chen Yonggui's report in 1983, and gave him the position of consultant to Beijing's East End State Farm.

The media had not suddenly disappeared from the scene, leaving him alone. On the contrary, somebody was always following his tracks. There were very few people, however, who knew about his appointment to Beijing's East End State Farm or his activities there.

"Ling...ling...ling," the telephone rang in Apartment No. 23, Entrance 5, Block 22, of the Fuwai Apartment Complex. Chen Yonggui, who had just been straightening corn flowers on his balcony adjacent to the living room, sighing and complaining, "Why do you only bloom, why don't you bear fruit?" heard the ringing and out of habit stopped what he was doing to answer it.

"Hello! Where? Ah, Old Zhang!"

The call came from the East End State Farm Office Manager and the Farm Enterprises Party Branch Secretary Zhang Derun, informing him of a Party Branch meeting that afternoon concerning day-to-day activities at the farm. The news dispelled Chen Yonggui's gloom, giving way to a feeling of happiness. Since he had started working at the farm a year ago, every time he was informed of a meeting at the farm, he attended without fail. He had not gone to the farm in the past month, so he was going to take advantage of the routine Branch meeting to pay his monthly party membership dues and find out what was going on at the farm.

After he acknowledged receiving Zhan Derun's information, however, he knitted his brow, because the State Management Bureau had called him the night before for a document-reading session that was to take place that same afternoon. For a while after he had lost his position, the documents were sent to him directly from above, so that he could read them by himself. At some point later on, however, the Bureau changed this practice and invited all the old comrades to the Bureau every time a document was to be circulated, and had it read to them collectively. Chen Yonggui had been attending those meetings without fail, too. But now that the two meetings were scheduled for the same afternoon, which one was he to attend? Out of habit, Chen Yonggui lit up a cigarette and, propping his hands on his waist, started pacing about on the living room carpet trying to decide what to do.

After lunch, at a little after 1 P.M., his driver Tang Zhanxin rang the bell at the Chen's residence. As usual, Chen Yonggui briefly greeted

Master Tang at the door, took the last drag on his cigarette, and finished drinking his freshly brewed tea, before following him into the elevator and down to his car.

The Datsun drove straight to the east following Fuxing Avenue. It arrived at the intersection at the bottom of the western yellow city wall, and just as Master Tang was preparing to change direction Chen Yonggui said decisively: “Don’t turn! We are going to the farm!”

Master Tang did not say anything, just maintained his accustomed silence. Until that moment he had thought they were going for the document-reading that afternoon. This was an entirely new agenda.

“I told you this morning that I was going to read documents,” said Chen Yonggui, noticing driver Tang’s confusion. “But I went back on my word at noon because the farm is holding a Party Branch meeting on day-to-day activities. Both things are happening the same afternoon, so I can either float at the top listening to documents or go down to the grass-roots level to see what is going on. You tell me, Master, what should I do: float at the top or go down? If you think I should float at the top, just switch the ‘channel’and drag me to the State Management Bureau!”

Master Tang was well used to Chen Yonggui’s jokes, so he laughed and shook his head, stepping on the gas as he continued in the direction of Dongzhimen along the road leading to Tongwang Airport, following the route of bus No. 359.

No longer a Vice-Premier with a post that brought him in touch with the people, Chen Yonggui became a frequent traveler on this asphalt road. Every single event and detail at the East End State Farm now affected him.

The East End State Farm, which was also called Peace Farm, had never attracted much attention among the populace of Beijing, let alone nationwide. After Chen Yonggui took up his position at the farm, however, its reputation gradually grew. The old man watched the scenery through his car window, recalling the full story of the events that had led to his becoming a consultant at Eastland: Han Kai, the journalist, had been sitting on the sofa in his living room when Chen Yonggui brought out a large apple and put it on the tea table next to him.

"Try it," Chen Yonggui urged. "See how tasty our Dazhai apples are!"

Han Kai did not refuse. Chewing on the apple as he engaged in small talk, Chen Yonggui's voice choked after a few sentences, as though he was about to break into tears.

"Han Kai, can you help me?" he asked. As he spoke, he patted himself on the chest: "I feel so oppressed in here. I can't take it any more! I can probably live another three to five years, maybe even longer. You tell me: Does it seem proper to you that I should be at home every day growing flowers, reading newspapers, staring at the TV screen?"

Han Kai asked how he could help him.

"I have only one thing in mind," Chen Yonggui continued. "Don't you know my defect by now? I can do anything, I don't care what it is. But when it comes to this," he moved his hand as though he were writing, "it's a nightmare!"

Han Kai immediately understood what was troubling Chen Yonggui. Right then and there he wrote his persuasive report on Chen's behalf, asking that he be assigned to some legitimate work.

Not long after they sent the report in, the Central Committee transferred it to the State Bureau for Agricultural Assignments. The department in charge called him to find out what kind of assignment he would find appropriate.

"How about if we leave you in the Central Administration Office as a consultant?" they suggested.

"No," responded Chen Yonggui. "I want to work on the grass-roots level. I want to do something concrete."

A few days later the department called again. They had arranged another high position in the bureaucracy and wanted to hear his opinion about it. Chen Yonggui shook his head again: "I'm not going there. I'm not going there. I'm not fit for administrative work. I want to go to the grass-roots level. A farm would be the best."

In the end Chen Yonggui chose Beijing's East End State Farm, where he could serve as a consultant. The farm was not far from Beijing City proper. Chen Yonggui had visited it in the past, when he conducted inspections in his previous capacity. He was relatively familiar with the affairs of the enterprises there.

Chen's idea to seek Han Kai's intervention had paid off, and now the old man could put his intelligence and experience to work for East End State Farm.

When the news of his new appointment reached the farm, it immediately created a sensation. His name attracted the attention of every person employed there, and a number of amusing anecdotes began to circulate. The farm's leaders were rather happy when they heard the news. They prepared a small suite for Chen Yonggui equipped with office furniture, a washroom with a toilet.

The first time Chen Yonggui went to work at the farm, he had made up his mind: There should be no major disturbance created on his behalf. He hoped everybody would go on with their farm work. Master Tang was to drive him quietly into the farm courtyard, whereupon he would look for the farm's leaders, so as to receive their assignment to him. When his car stopped in the main courtyard, however, a large group of people had already assembled there to shake hands, greet him, welcome him. Overcome by their hospitality, Chen Yonggui thanked them from his heart, smiled, nodded, and waved to everybody.

The farm's leaders led Chen Yonggui into the reception room, where they staged a little welcoming ceremony for him. Party Committee Secretary Liu Bingliang, Farm Director Zhou Weixin, Office Manager Zhang Derun, the one-time Party Committee Secretary who was now retired to the position of a consultant, Zhang Shida, were all at the meeting. During the meeting, Chen Yonggui explained what his plans for work at the farm were, and he expressed hope that the comrades would understand his frame of mind. The leaders stated that Uncle Chen's arrival was indeed a rare occasion, and they hoped that he would give them some instructions about the operations already under way. During the meeting, Liu Bingliang specifically entrusted Zhao Jianzuo from the Reception Center with receiving and accompanying Chen Yonggui and, as protocol required, received his temporary Party organization credentials, enrolling him in the Party Branch of the farm enterprise where he was to take part in Party activities.

After the meeting, the leadership invited Chen Yonggui to a simple banquet. After the meal, Chen Yonggui formally received his assignments from Manager Zhang Derun. As he shook Zhang Derun's hand,

Chen Yonggui said: "Old Zhang, you are the Party Branch Secretary, and I am just an ordinary Party member under your leadership. From now on, I will pay you my Party membership dues on time and I will report on my work to the Party Branch. Please let me know every time the Party Branch holds a meeting on day-to-day activities, because I definitely want to participate!"

Chen Yonggui was more than ten years older than Zhang Derun. As for their qualifications and past service, Zhang Derun was a career cadre, while Chen Yonggui started as a Model Worker of national renown and went on to hold important posts in the Party and State bureaucracy. But Zhang Derun did not at all regard Chen Yonggui as different on account of these disparities. He treated him exactly the same as he did all the other Party members. When Chen Yonggui addressed him as "Old Zhang," he acquiesced, but Chen Yonggui himself preferred to be called by his name, "Comrade Chen Yonggui." Those were the circumstances in which Zhang Derun accepted the "ordinary Party member" who rode in a luxury sedan.

In the above manner Chen Yonggui opened a new chapter in his sadly restricted life.

On the day the Branch met to discuss daily activities Chen Yonggui got out of the car in the farm courtyard. He was greeted by Zhao Jianzuo, who saw him to Party Branch Secretary Zhang Derun's office. Zhang Derun was in the middle of a discussion with Director Guo Jingen of the farm dairy. When the latter saw Chen Yonggui at the door, he walked up to him to shake hands warmly. The dairy had been praised as an advanced unit both by the National Trade Union Organization of China and by the City of Beijing. After Chen Yonggui started working for the farm, he often went there to inquire about it and had therefore had extensive contacts with its Director, Guo Jingen. As they met this time, they did not digress very far from the topics they usually discussed. But since the Party meeting on day-to-day activities was just about to begin, Chen Yonggui had to interrupt the conversation to pay Zhang Derun his Party membership dues for that month. Zhang Derun recorded the transaction and announced: "Comrade Chen Yonggui, it's time! Let's go to the meeting!"

Zhang Derun escorted Chen Yonggui to the meeting room, where the full Party Branch membership was already in attendance, waiting. As Chen Yonggui entered, people shook his hand and greeted him; some invited him to sit next to them. Over the years, Chen Yonggui had become used to ordering people about during meetings. During his years in Dazhai, at every meeting, he always sat in the most prominent seat, overlooking everybody from a certain vantage point. His position was quite different now. When he participated in the Party Branch meetings, he always sat together with all the other Party members, passing cigarettes around with those who sat around him, and drinking tea. He felt very happy, in fact. "I'm flexible," he used to say. "Only the general who can act as a foot soldier is a true general." As the Party members discussed this and that with him Zhang Derun announced the beginning of the meeting. The subject of the meeting, he said, would be the discussion of people's views about the responsibility system in village production, and a brief survey of their own most recent work. After the announcement, the audience fell into a brief silence, which usually preceded the firing of the first shot. Zhang Derun's gaze fell on Chen Yonggui: "Comrade Chen Yonggui, could you tell us your opinion?"

Chen Yonggui took a drag on his cigarette, smiling modestly at Zhang Derun: "Let's have other comrades talk first. It's all within the Party, it doesn't matter if we say something wrong."

As a result Zhang Derun called on somebody else to speak.

After a while, the Party members became embroiled in a lively debate. Everybody examined the current policy from a different angle, as it affected their work on the farm. As Chen Yonggui listened, he reflected on the past year he had spent working there. Although he had come out from the city only once or twice a month, he had managed to visit quite a few of its operations. He noticed that the ground at the State-operated animal-feed plant was not level, and suggested that comrades from the Farm Machinery Station straighten it out. He visited the Weiguo Pig Farm with its ten thousand pigs and suggested ways to make their breeding more economical.

He received an invitation to visit the Oil Processing Plant and accepted it right away. When he came up to the gate of the plant, however, he shook his head and, refusing to go in, asked for his driver to take him back. The leaders at the plant asked him what was wrong, and he told them without beating around the bush: "Whether I go or not makes no difference. You still have these tall weeds at the plant's gate. How much better can it be inside?"

This affected the plant workers very much. They looked for reasons for the neglected condition of their factory and found those at fault. After they dug up the weeds, they improved conditions inside the production facilities and even built a fish pond outside. For this Zhang Derun had praised Chen Yonggui at one of the previous Party Branch meetings. Chen Yonggui, however, engaged in a bit of self-criticism.

"I didn't behave too well toward the comrades at the oil pressing plant," he said, apologizing for his abrupt withdrawal.

After everybody discussed standard social issues, Zhang Derun again tried to induce Chen Yonggui to talk: "Comrade Chen Yonggui, it's time for your opinion!"

Chen Yonggui smiled again and finally moved to speak. Having heard others, he felt he had an over-all view of the situation. "First of all," he said, "unity with the Central Committee should be maintained as units implement the responsibility system on the agricultural battlefront. Generally speaking there should not be any contention over it. If looked at concretely, however, some places have the tendency to act too abruptly when they introduce the household responsibility system. They lack ideological preparation and suitable conditions. A big question remains whether places like that can undertake regular capital construction of the fields. What is even more grave, some places are unable to protect collective property or carry out public accumulation. Some public facilities have been greatly damaged. Such units are having great difficulty even in developing basic reproduction. They depend on the State, but the State cannot assume the responsibility either. Sooner or later, natural and man-made calamities are bound to occur...."

As soon as Chen Yonggui spoke, the Party members started interjecting their own words, and the temperature at the meeting rose several degrees. In their minds, they generally acknowledged Chen Yonggui's level of understanding and the fact that he thought differently from the average person. Since meeting was about to dissolve, everybody started saying whatever came to their minds, without much restraint. At this point Zhang Derun showed considerable wit as he tried to coax weighty words from Chen Yonggui's mouth.

"Comrade Chen Yonggui, could you report to the Party Branch something about your work in Dazhai and at the Central Committee?"

Chen Yonggui grasped another cigarette butt and answered with humor: "I should be reporting on my work from that period to the Central Committee! Hahaha!"

"Nobody can pick the lock on Comrade Chen Yonggui's past," said Zhang Derun, intrigued.

During his assignment to the East End State Farm, Chen Yonggui did some truly fine work for the farm. Whenever foreign guests came to the farm, they always asked for Chen Yonggui. As long as he was around, the foreign guests showed much more initiative in their business negotiations. The Xiyang Guest House wanted to open up a bakery. Through Chen Yonggui's contacts, a specialist from East End State Farm volunteered to help. As a result of his expertise, the pastry they produced in Xiyang could never keep up with the demands of the marketplace. Every time Chen Yonggui showed up at the farm, the farm's employees asked him to their homes and invited him for drinks. He never refused. After the last Party Branch meeting, a female Communist Party member from the bakery by the name of Chen Tianping said to him when she saw him: "Uncle Chen, come to visit us at home, would you?"

Chen Yonggui immediately obliged and went to her house for some tea.

At that time many people in China as well as abroad wrote letters asking about Chen Yonggui's activities at East End. In some cases, letters asked for his technical advice. Unexpectedly, soon thereafter, this agricultural expert of great repute vanished from the East End State Farm without a trace.

CHAPTER 43

A CHAIN SMOKER FALLS ILL

Chen Yonggui, recently referred to as the "healthy old man," fell ill. Chen Yonggui never surrendered to illness. He didn't look like a sick man this time either. People watched him take the elevator down and saw him walk down the road as briskly as ever, propping one hand on his waist while holding a straw hat in the other. Who would believe he was ill?

He was ill, nevertheless. At first he felt tightness in the chest and shortness of breath. He also lost his normal appetite. Later, his cheeks became sallow, he ate visibly less, and he coughed frequently, spitting phlegm.

While still healthy, he always liked to go out. But who was he, after all? How would people receive him? He had a hard time dealing with this issue. The year before he died he was planning to go back to Dazhai with William Hinton for a visit, but he did not see his wish fulfilled before he passed away.

After his illness became more severe, be began treating it as a cold at Fuxing Hospital, which was located right behind his apartment complex. Although doctors examined and treated him with the best of care, after half a month his condition did not improve. Chen Yonggui thought it strange. Can it be that a cold does not get cured after all this time? His family and his driver urged him to go to Beijing Hospital for a checkup, but Chen Yonggui had a hard time with that.

"People took all this trouble with me at this hospital. Would it be all right if I just walked away?" he asked.

"Your medical files have always been held at the Beijing Hospital!" Master Tang reminded him.

Chen Yonggui hesitated. According to the previous arrangement, he was supposed to go for medical treatment to Beijing Hospital, but in the given circumstances he still felt he should ask the Central Committee for permission to do so. He sent his request to the Central Committee General Office, which approved it and made the necessary arrangements to have him admitted to the hospital, devoted especially to high cadres.

The morning before he entered Beijing Hospital, Chen Yonggui still walked to Ganjia Street to buy food. He bought two pounds of chicken eggs and some vegetables, and boarded a bus home to cook lunch. The bus was very crowded when he got on, so he could not find a place to sit down. When the passengers realized that Chen Yonggui was squeezed with them on the same bus, they vied with each other to give him a seat, and struck up a lively exchange. Nobody knew that this was the last time they would see him.

When Chen Yonggui finally entered Beijing Hospital, the hospital's Director Wu had already left for the summer retreat at Beidaihe with the Central Committee leaders in order to oversee their rest. The hospital telephoned Beidaihe. Director Wu immediately called back, personally informing Chen Yonggui that he would be back at the hospital the following morning at 8 AM to examine him. At exactly 8 AM the following day Director Wu entered Chen Yonggui's sickroom to begin the examination procedure.

Chen Yonggui was a complicated man, and his illness was, likewise, a thorny affair. Director Wu and other physicians in charge examined Chen Yonggui for a whole month, but were still hard put to diagnose his illness. One day, Director Wu told Chen Yonggui, half-joking and half-searching for an answer: "Old Chen! You sure are a strange man, and so is your illness. I haven't been able to find out what's wrong with you for a whole month! How can that be?"

"If you can't find it, don't look for it," laughed Chen Yonggui.

"How can I not look for it?" said Director Wu.

After a great effort by the Director and other doctors at the hospital, and after examining his internal organs with various diagnostic instruments, they finally found a lump at the back of his chest. Laboratory tests of tissue samples showed lung cancer. The hospital quickly decided to operate on him, for which they needed a signature of family consent.

"Forget it, I'll sign it," said Chen Yonggui.

"We can't do that," explained Director Wu. "Who'll be responsible if something happens?"

"I'll be responsible if something happens," Chen Yonggui said, laughing. "Or get Mingliang to sign it!"

The hospital did not agree. The rules required that the oldest son act as guarantor and sign papers of consent with the hospital. Master Tang called Xiyang long distance in the name of the Central Committee General Office, asking that Chen Mingzhu come at once to Peking. The sudden phone call badly frightened Chen Mingzhu. He only found out what it was all about when he got to the hospital. Once there he took care of all the formalities required and Chen Yonggui went in for his first surgery.

On the 15th day of the eighth month of the Chinese lunar calendar in 1985, Chen Yonggui's sons and daughters all came to Peking from Xiyang to see their father. Chen Yonggui asked for permission from the physician in charge to leave the hospital to spend the Moon Festival with his children at home. The physician in charge refused on account of the serious nature of his condition, but he smiled and comforted him.

"Elder Chen, there will be many other occasions!"

"You can't fool me about my illness," Chen Yonggui said with a sigh. "This will be my last Moon Festival. You better let me go home!"

Chen Yonggui pleaded so anxiously and persistently that the hospital finally allowed him to go home for the traditional meal of dumplings. He returned to the hospital that same evening.

At the very end of that year Chen Yonggui's condition improved. Aware of it, he asked the hospital's Director Wu to let him go home for the traditional New Year's get-together with his family. Hospital rules did not allow patients in his condition to go home, but Director Wu, out of special consideration for Chen Yonggui, called a hospital staff meeting, which approved his home leave under two conditions: one, he was not allowed to drink; two, he was not to go outside. Chen Yonggui said that he had stopped drinking a long time ago, but he asked to be allowed to have one shot of liquor for the New Year season. The hospital approved his request, and so Chen Yonggui sent off the last Spring Festival of his life with half a glass of white lightning made from sorghum. During the New Year's Eve his young son Chen Mingliang, an inquisitive boy, played with firecrackers, while the heavy-hearted Chen Mingzhu kept asking him to stop. Chen Yonggui, not wanting to disappoint the child, said that he could go on. Mingliang happily resumed his game, while Mingzhu withdrew to a corner where he secretly cried because it was obvious that the child still did not understand at all how ill Chen Yonggui was.

Chen Yonggui went home on the 28th of the last month of the lunar year. On the 20th of the first month of the New Year he returned to the hospital. As he was leaving home he told his wife and his driver: "I won't be coming back after this. I won't be coming back."

The news of Chen Yonggui's hospitalization spread through Beijing and reached Dazhai and Xiyang. His relatives of all ages from back home kept coming to see him. Cadres and ordinary folk from Dazhai and Xiyang kept coming to see him. People from the East End State Farm kept coming to see him. There was a period when illness destroyed Chen Yonggui's appetite. He only felt like eating watermelon. It was the coldest time of winter, and it was very hard to find any watermelons on the market. East End State Farm's Zhang Derun and several other leaders combed half the city without finding any trace of watermelon. Party Secretary Liu Bingliang was not convinced: Could it be that in a great city like Beijing there was not a single watermelon to be found?

On the following day Liu personally led a watermelon-shopping crew on an expedition to various city markets, and in the end they bought a watermelon that satisfied Chen Yonggui's deep craving. In a show of affection for Chen Yonggui, a stream of Central Committee leaders kept coming to the hospital, too, to extend their greetings. Hu Qili, Bo Yibo, Yu Qiuli, Hao Jianxiu, and other Central Committee dignitaries repeatedly passed the hospital gate, bringing the Party Central Committee's profound concern for Chen Yonggui and greetings from other leaders. After Yu Qiuli's and Song Zhenmin's visit, people named it "Daqing visits Dazhai." When Hao Jianxiu, who usually addressed Chen Yonggui as "Uncle Chen," visited him, people called it "workers visit peasants."

Many people in Shanxi looked for an opportunity to visit Beijing as soon as they heard of Chen Yonggui's hospitalization. When Ma Feng and Sun Quian, two famous Shanxi authors who had deep feelings for Dazhai, came they started talking about the past. As they recounted how they had spoken fairly about Dazhai during the period when the media accused the village of taking an ultra-left road, the conversation grew longer and longer. When Niu Guiying, a female Shanxi Opera star who was retired on account of old age, and the famous female singer Guo Lanying visited Chen Yonggui, he already spoke with great difficulty, but he still wanted to talk about the folk opera *The White-Haired Girl*[1] and about meeting with Ding Guoxian at the Third Plenary Session. As he talked with the two women, he forgot his illness and his fatigue because he was seeing them for the last time and he wanted to talk to his heart's content with folks from his mountain homeland.

Dazhai Party Branch Secretary Song Liying, several cadres from Xiyang, Chen Yonggui's wife, son, daughter, daughter-in-law, grandson, and leaders-in-charge from the Central Committee Management Bureau and the State Council Management Bureau stood around Chen Yonggui's hospital bed. The illness had taken away that typical Chen Yonggui disposition, his trademark for dozens of years. His eyes receded behind their lids and his cheeks stuck to the bones beneath. After a coughing spell that was hard to endure, Chen Yonggui breathed with difficulty, while his son and daughter tried to prop him up in bed to relieve his pain. But no matter how hard they tried, there was no escape

1. The White-Haired Girl is a famous modern opera from the days of land reform, very popular still throughout Shanxi and elsewhere in China. (WHH)

from the suffering caused by the illness. His eyes, deep buried in their sockets, strained to see Song Liying's tear-stained face. He could only dimly make out the State leaders standing next to his bed. It looked as though Chen Yonggui had many things he wanted to say, but the cancer cells had long disabled his vocal cords. His lips moved and, by paying close attention, those around him could make out that he was repeating two sentences: "I didn't run them into debt. I didn't drag the country into debt!"

It was obvious that those two sentences had been putting an enormous psychological pressure on him for a long time. It seemed he had been carrying Mount Tai on his head for ages. When he had left Dazhai, the Dazhai Production Brigade still had a collective accumulation of 170,000 Chinese dollars and several hundred thousand *jin* of grain in its storehouse. This is a fact that the people of Dazhai have generally acknowledged all along. Moreover, the common people in Dazhai like to compare the economic conditions of the time when Chen Yonggui was in charge with the present, saying that now all the collective property is subsidized and the Brigade has borrowed 2,000,000 Chinese dollars from the State. The two sentences Chen Yonggui was uttering on his deathbed were aimed at that notorious article "Dazhai's Departure From the Spirit of Dazhai" published on October 17, 1980, in the *Shanxi Daily*. The influence on public opinion of its statement about State support for Dazhai could still be felt throughout society. The article provided inspiration and negative source material to the authors of *The Rise and Fall of the Red Flag of Dazhai*, who tried, with their invidious tract, to revive all the calumnies piled up by others. Between them these two publications have even had serious consequences abroad.[1]

There were so many things that Chen Yonggui wanted to tell people who came to see him as he lay stretched on his hospital bed. There was

1. Without these two books the outrageous attack on Mao's whole rural policy contained in Chinese Village, Socialist State by Friedman, Selden, and Pickowicz, could never have been launched. The three American authors follow every twist and turn of the original polemics, and especially the slander that under socialism only massive State aid can bring prosperity to any rural community. Self-reliance they say, parroting their Chinese forerunners, is a fraud. (W.H.H.)

so much bitterness he wanted to spill out. As words came to his tongue, however, he swallowed them down. His most frequent words were: "If I lived four more years, Mingliang would be graduating, Xingfu would be getting married! But I don't even have four months to live!"

Later: "This kid's fate is bad. He can't depend on me!" he said, pointing to his little son Mingliang. And, pointing at Mingliang and his mother, "I'm throwing these two at your mercy," he said to leaders who came to see him. "Take good care of them! If you don't, I'll be cursing you in death just as much as I have cursed in life. I was tough alive, so you better believe I'll be tough dead!"

"You too!" he said, pointing at his old driver, Master Tang. "Don't let it turn out to be: 'I like you while you are alive; when you die, I kiss you goodbye!' I'll be after you when I die, too!"

To this very day an emotional yet significant utterance of Chen Yonggui's circulates among the old cadres in Xiyang: "I can't tell who's good and who's bad!" It was something he told Zhang Huaiying when he visited him at Beijing Hospital. After Chen Yonggui entered the hospital, he particularly missed Dazhai's and Xiyang's old cadres, and among them especially Zhang Huaiying. When his daughter-in-law, Jia Chengtang, was about to leave Beijing for Xiyang, he instructed her specifically to ask Zhang Huaiying to come to see him soon.

This brought Zhang Huaiying to Beijing for a third visit to Chen at the hospital.

There is a famous literary allusion about the profound friendship between Guang Zhong and Bao Shuya, whose fortunes changed contrarily during the Warring States period. The allegory is quite appropriate in the case of Chen Yonggui and Zhang Huaiying. Zhang Huaiying first served as Chen Yonggui's superior; then Chen Yonggui became Zhang Huaiying's superior and comrade-in-arms. The friendship between the two was quite unusual, surviving extraordinary vicissitudes during its long history.

When Zhang Huaiying, responding to the special request, came to see Chen Yonggui, Chen was holding off his fate and had been able to regain his faculty of speech to some degree. After a few words he started crying, broken-hearted, holding firmly onto his friend's hand. He thanked him for coming yet another time to see him, and expressed sadness at his own destiny. Zhang Huaiying consoled him: "Don't be sad! You've known the joy of achievement and the pain of defeat, you've had happy experiences and absorbed sorrowful lessons. Just think about it: You once toiled for the rich, hawked sesame seed cakes, and lived from hand to mouth. No matter which way you look at it, you've broken even!"

His words made Chen Yonggui feel truly happy. "Hey, you're right! How come you haven't told me that before?" he exclaimed.

And so the two men started talking.

"Comrade Huaiying," said Chen Yonggui, taking a deep breath and pouring out his heart, "I've lived my entire life without being able to tell good people from bad! I never knew the good from the bad!" His words were obviously an attempt at self-examination in front of Zhang Huaiying. The latter accepted it in silence, shaking his head, sensing that the conversation was making Chen Yonggui too excited. It was not true that Chen Yonggui had never been able to judge the true colors of people. Zhang Huaiying himself had witnessed Chen Yonggui's level of understanding and his foresight in dealing with such issues. He comforted Chen Yonggui and urged him not to think too much, to take care of himself.

"No. Since you are here," Chen replied, "I want you to analyze objectively the road the two of us have taken."

Chen Yonggui then mentioned the few people in Xiyang and Dazhai who had vilified him while he was down and, as he talked, he choked on tears.

While still a player on China's political stage, Chen Yonggui had predicted that he might suffer any number of fates. Consequently, he did not necessarily think highly of the people who kept flattering him, inflating his ego and taking cues from him. Nevertheless, as his status grew, he was not able to see through all those under him too clearly. He was only able to draw firm conclusions about them after both he and they had been tested by tumultuous events.

In truth, due to Dazhai's lofty reputation, and especially after he became Vice-Premier, Chen Yonggui heard very little criticism. People were afraid to raise any objections lest these be confused with ambivalence toward Dazhai, and they were afraid to speak to him directly. Such circumstances frequently breed unhealthy results. Chen Yonggui's true mistake was in employing a few people who seemed to be good workers but whose characters were less than admirable. The common people did not trust them very much, but nevertheless suffered from the adverse effects of their actions. There were times when these lieutenants messed things up to a fare-the-well, then pushed the blame onto Chen Yonggui. Yet he always carefully considered every opinion and objection that he heard.

In 1974, Xiyang planned to build a stadium, but when the County applied for approval from the Shanxi Provincial authorities, Wang Qian, the Party Secretary of Shanxi, stalled the project. When Chen Yonggui heard of this on his return to Xiyang, not only did he not blame Wang Qian, he even criticized the County leadership.

"You can't just ask the government for money whenever you feel like it!" Chen said. "Wang Qian stopped the stadium project. He did not consult with me before making his decision, but I approve of the veto. If you ask for money these days, you'll get it even if you say it's for the devil to climb a tree. What I'm afraid of is that you won't be able to come down once you climb up. Doing projects that benefit production is fine, but it's better if we don't build a stadium. We shouldn't be inviting trouble upon ourselves."

Two years later, the County applied to the Province again, and the Province supplied funds for the stadium. Because of this matter Chen Yonggui summoned Li Xishen to Beijing to tell him that some people objected to the loan.

"We had better act sensibly," he said. "Although the Province has approved funding, I think we better reject it!"

As soon as Li Xishen returned to Xiyang, he returned the loan to the Province. On the following day, reporters wrote about it and praised his action. To this day some people blame and resent Chen Yonggui for that.

"If only Old Chen had been a bit more relenting in those days, we would have a stadium now," they complained.

On the occasion of the Chinese Lunar New Year one year, Xiyang's Beiguan Production Brigade Party Branch Secretary Song Zhibao walked to Dazhai to see Chen Yonggui. He showed anger from the moment he entered the door. Chen Yonggui invited him to sit down but he refused. Chen Yonggui asked him what was the matter. Holding back his real grievance Song Zhibao answered:

"Old Chen, I've brought my party membership card with me. I want to complain!"

Chen Yonggui felt that he had better not get angry too, so he calmly knit his brow: "Well, nobody will dare expel you. Speak up," Chen said.

Once Song Zhibao broke the ice, he let it all out: "We work on field construction projects all day long, building, building, building. But more than half the land in Xiyang is in Second Slope. If we don't get to work on those Second Slope fields, there is no way we are going to increase grain production significantly."

Song Zhibao went on to cite many examples of neglect of the fields in Second Slope, forcing Chen Yonggui to confront the gravity of the situation. Chen Yonggui completely accepted Song Zhibao's position, demonstrating that when he was presented a reasonable case he was not hard to win over.

When Chen Yonggui said, in the midst of his illness, "I have not been able to distinguish between good and bad people," he was referring to those people who, after Dazhai had fallen from heaven, spoke unfairly and with bias, irresponsibly published unsavory material under assumed names, acted without conscience and renounced all personal responsibility. They sided with the media in its total repudiation of Xiyang and Dazhai, sinking so low as to pass on personal insults, and doing other dubious things they should not have done. Undoubtedly, this was like stabbing the old man, who had devoted his entire life's energy to the struggle against the barren mountains and unruly rivers, right through his heart.

His utterance, however, if taken literally, held yet another level of meaning. How could it be said that he had never recognized, sought out or supported good people? It decidedly did not apply to Zhang Huaiying, who had fostered him and helped him all along. Chen Yonggui at the very end confirmed what an honest and upright man Zhang Huaiying was, a man who did not easily swing with the tides. This means that Chen Yonggui, after all, could tell who was good and who was bad.

To this day it is not fully known what Chen Yonggui and Zhang Huaiying talked about during their three meetings in the hospital room, but a few cadres and family members heard bits and pieces of the conversation here and there. As he looked back on his entire life from his sickbed, Chen Yonggui focused on the events that had occurred during the Cultural Revolution.

"I was in the wrong when it came to the denunciation of our Provincial leaders," Chen Yonggui said as he remembered the indignities inflicted on so many of Shanxi's veteran cadres. "The Central Committee said to topple them, and so I let the denunciations unfold below. The denunciations that engulfed Xiyang in the fall of 1967 were the work of the Provincial Revolutionary Committee and the Provincial Military Command. I thought about whether to let the denunciations spread to Xiyang over and over again. I've made self-criticism on account of these events at the Provincial level, and I've felt all along that I was in the wrong."

Even in illness, Chen Yonggui was able to reflect back on his role in the Cultural Revolution and criticize himself. However, no matter what he did, he was not able to undo the slander and libel directed against himself by other people. On his sickbed his moaning was periodically interspersed with agonized shouts about the article "Dazhai's Departure from the Spirit of Dazhai," about the water diversion project, about his past, about grain production in Xiyang.

What Chen Yonggui hoped for was justice, a fair judgment by history. If time allowed, he was prepared to wait for that justice. But time was running out.

Chen Yonggui's family waited at home on the evening of March 25, 1986, while his eldest son Chen Mingzhu remained at the hospital. After discussing this with his father, Chen Mingzhu had his sister Minghua's husband Youming stay to watch over the sick man. Chen Yonggui slept that night. He even slept soundly. Chen Mingzhu thought his father's ability to sleep indicated a big turn for the better, but the doctors were quite clear about the real advance of his illness.

Various instruments were ready at the bedside and doctors and nurses were constantly on call. If they left the room at all, the sound of a bell would summon them immediately. In the morning of the following day Chen Yonggui's condition visibly worsened, to the point where all rescue measures became ineffective. This went on until 8:35 PM when the doctor announced with a sigh: "Inform the Central Committee General Office to make arrangements for the funeral." Chen Yonggui thus quietly left this world, without attracting any major public attention.

CHAPTER 44

A CANCER DEATH CALLS FORTH MASS SORROW

As was the case with so many other remarkable people with ideals and integrity in China, death, rather than removing Chen Yonggui from public consciousness, induced an even more widespread interest. Numerous people inquired about his death, numerous people missed him, and many, many others were prepared to pay whatever it cost to see his body one last time. The Xinhua News Agency carried the news domestically, calling him a model worker of national fame and evaluating his entire life with rather high marks.

Before he died, Chen Yonggui had asked that there be no memorial service after his death and no big ceremony. He just requested that after cremation his ashes be taken back to Dazhai for burial by his children. He did not want to be buried in Wolf Den Ravine because he could not cast off the traditional peasant belief in geomancy. He claimed that Wolf Den Ravine was an inauspicious site. But events did not conform entirely to Chen Yonggui's wishes. Several leaders from the central administration, Dazhai and Xiyang leaders, and representatives of the East End State Farm showed up to bid farewell to his remains, and even papers in Hong Kong and Macao reported the event.

During the farewell ceremony at Babaoshan an unexpected individual showed up. Hua Guofeng arrived in a special car to take part in memorial services. That morning, Hua Guofeng had telephoned Chen Yonggui's family to find out whether any important Central Committee leaders were attending the ceremony. He decided to go on his own initiative. People from the Central Committee Management Bureau and the State Council Management Bureau were there. So were the representatives from Dazhai, Xiyang and the East End State Farm, as well as the celebrated author from Shanxi, Ma Feng. Li Yiqing, the first person to bring Dazhai's achievements to the attention of the central, decision-making level of China's leadership, did not come because he was no longer mobile, but his wife Lu Qing attended in his place with tears streaming down her face.

An elegiac couplet attracted much attention at the ceremony. It read:

> His righteous energy shapes a rainbow arch.
> We offer tears of sorrow to his sterling spirit.
> The revered hero has passed into history.
> His annals will light the way for future generations.

These lines appeared in a photograph published by a Hong Kong newspaper. Its author, Han Shouwen, was a retired cadre from the People's Liberation Army Logistics Institute, whose friendship with Chen Yonggui ran deep. In order to express his grief over his friend's death he had not closed his eyes for several nights. In the end he produced the above lines modeled on a famous poem by Zheng Banqiao. The couplet was written in tears, one could say.

Han Shiuwen's poem might better have reflected the genius of gruff old Chen Yonggui if written thus:

> His righteous energy forged a rainbow arch.
> We offer tears of sorrow for his rock firm spirit.
> The bluff journeyman hammered his way into history
> Pounding cracks for future generations to smash through.

From the early morning, April 4, 1986 was an unusual day in Xiyang and Dazhai.

Peasants lined the road leading from Yangquan to Xiyang, conversing, asking questions, trying to keep their eyes on the road, impatiently waiting for the passing of the remains of the only peasant in Chinese history to have become Vice-Premier.

This peasant's ashes were about to be returned to his native soil.

No one had published anything in the papers, broadcast any news or circulated any information in an internal Party document. Who knows where the people heard and confirmed that Chen Yonggui was returning to the village that day?

Yet, overwhelmed by painful memories, the people of Xiyang County and the village of Dazhai opened their hearts to receive the spirit of Chen Yonggui, the man who had struggled on their behalf for so many decades.

Chen Yonggui's old driver, Master Tang, drove his little old sedan draped in black gauze, while tears welled in the corners of his eyes like strings of pearls. Crushing under its wheels the tears of many others along the road, the car slowly pulled into Dazhai. Master Tang had been in extremely low spirits for a number of days. To make sure that nothing went wrong, the Army provided him with an assistant for the journey.

In the County town spectators filled the street, along with all types of vehicles, colorful flower wreaths, and journalists with flash bulbs at the ready in search of hot stories.

Strings of small firecrackers exploded from Jiepai Ridge in Xiyang to send Chen Yonggui off. Their crude, deep banging shook the heavens, the mountains, the valleys, and the traffic on the road. The people of Dazhai claim they alone spent three or four hundred Chinese dollars just on firecrackers for the occasion.

Lamenting and sobbing, sobbing and lamenting, the sounds merging one into the other, people crowded all the way from Liu Settlement Junction to Dazhai to commemorate.

This was a spontaneous manifestation.

The people of Dazhai had built a spirit shed for Chen Yonggui the day before, but later, for reasons unknown, they quietly pulled it down.

This resulted in even more wailing due to grief that could not be expressed.

Dazhai's cadres and leaders from the Central, the Provincial, the County and the Regional level walked solemnly amidst the crowd of people, escorting Chen Yonggui's ashes into the village. His son Chen Mingzhu carried the urn through the street, stopping at each family home, in every corner and every field. Amidst the sound of the band playing and the incessant firecracker explosions, he led the procession to the spot where the ashes were to be laid to rest, to an open grave pit on Tigerhead Mountain that had been prepared well in advance. He sprinkled a portion of the ashes on Dazhai's land; the remainder were mixed in one urn, to join the ashes of his first wife, Li Huni.

Before Chen Yonggui's ashes entered the village, Dazhai had held a simple memorial ceremony. Liang Bianliang presided over the affair while Gao Yuliang delivered the memorial speech following closely the contents of the obituary published by the Xinhua News Agency. The Xinhua obituary had been approved by the Central Committee, and its evaluation of Chen Yonggui was generally accepted nationwide. After the memorial ceremony, Liang Bianliang and Gao Yuliang followed the crowds up the mountain to attend Chen Yonggui's burial.

"Stop blowing! STOP BLOWING!" Liang Bianliang screamed suddenly. "You are irritating the dead! You are irritating the dead!"

Nobody knows why.

His enraged tearful outburst pierced the sound of the wind instrument ensemble playing traditional, mournful funeral music. Halfway through the sentence he had struggled for a moment and then collapsed to the ground unconscious. He was in a state of shock. He came to only the following day after treatment at the hospital. When I visited him researching my book, I asked him why he had been affected like that. Sitting on a kitchen stool, Old Liang sighed.

"Hooh! It was really difficult arranging everything at that time. Many of the things that happened were enraging. We didn't even get the use of a car to receive his ashes."

Based on what Old Liang told me, I infer the following: When Chen Yonggui assumed power, everybody exalted him; when he lost power, everybody committed to careerism pushed him away! Just like in the proverb, "Close to eyes, close to hearts. When one departs, there's no feeling left." This is an inherent traditional concept of the Chinese people, or at any rate, of traditional officialdom.

The entire burial of the ashes was just this simple, and just this complicated at the same time. After the burial, the assembled crowds dispersed, the wailing sound of wind instruments and the heart-wrenching firecracker noises ceased. The sound of sobbing and wailing faded away, leaving only the countless wreaths at the grave and the chaotic debris of exploded firecracker scraps all over the ground nearby. Numerous hard footprints engraved on Dazhai's soil remained as a record of people's fond memories. They also were left to receive Chen Yonggui's gratitude to those who had buried him if that was part of their world view.

> We remember today!
> We remember in our hearts!

Using artistic dialectics of sorts, famous writer Zhang Kejia demonstrated the value of human life and death in our society in his poem "Some people." Not only did Chen Yonggui not fade from people's memory after he was put to rest eternally on Tigerhead Mountain, more than ever before he came to embody a special kind of life. A certain longing for him continued to circle through the minds of the people of Dazhai, as well as through the various sinews and channels of society. Thinking of him, people frequently shed tears over what others might call minor details.

According to custom, on the third day after the burial of Chen Yonggui's ashes, third-day mourning rites were performed for him. Chen Yonggui's sons Chen Mingzhu and Chen Mingshan, daughter Chen Minghua, daughters-in-law Jia Chengtang and Zhang Runming, clad in black gauze and weeping bitterly, ascended Tigerhead Mountain to sweep their father's grave.[1] His old fellow villagers, who had been struggling through thick and thin with him over several decades, also

1. Sweeping of the grave is the traditional Chinese way of paying respects to a dead person.

climbed the mountain, driven by their tears. When they saw the wreaths and firecracker residue at the grave site, they suddenly felt they were hearing Chen Yonggui's endless lecturing at a typical meeting.

Chen Yonggui had been in the habit of attempting to consolidate and rectify Dazhai's cadres and Party members at the end of each year. This was the occasion when Party members often heard his famous remark: "It's only the rank-and-file who can't get rich, there are never leaders who can't get rich. When the rank-and-file share what they have, if each household gives you just one bowl of food you've already got more than you can eat."

This remark became the motto of Dazhai's Party members and cadres, and as a consequence legends of the "absolutely honest accountant" Jia Chengrang, and the upright and uncorrupt cadres like Jia Jincai, Song Liying and Liang Bianliang emerged. Chen Yonggui was even more strict with himself. As they swept his grave, Song Liying told Chen Yonggui's children about the time he had refused to accept an allowance.

The Production Brigade held a general meeting of all its members one winter evening to announce the final state of the ledger and the amount of cash payments due at the end of the year. When Chen Yonggui's name came up, the accountant read out the statement of his daily labor dividends, grain allotment and deductions, and made the following announcement: "The Production Brigade Party Branch Committee has decided, after some examination of the circumstances, to give Old Chen an allowance of 40 Chinese dollars as compensation for his high outside expenses."

"What allowance are you talking about?" protested Chen Yonggui, who had been sitting on a square stool next to the rostrum. He got angry the instant he heard the announcement.

"You often go on field trips and have additional expenses because of that. Forty dollars is not much. It's the Brigade's decision," several Party Branch members said.

"No way," Chen Yonggui refused categorically, as he took a last puff on his almost extinguished cigarette. "I should be getting my allowance from only one place, wherever that might be. Once I get it, I shouldn't be getting it from anyplace else!"

Over the years, Chen Yonggui often held concurrent posts at Central, Provincial, Regional and County levels, and leaders at various levels contemplated giving him additional allowances. From the very beginning, Chen Yonggui considered the issue carefully and insisted that he should be given only one allowance. Since he was still registered as a permanent resident of Dazhai, the questions of his allotments and cash dividends were all taken care of on Dazhai's books.

The allowance Chen received as Vice-Premier from the Central Government, and the special subsidies given to all model workers on the Provincial level, covered the economic burden of his traveling and living elsewhere. He refused everything else. Chen Yonggui got upset at the mere mention of any extra allowance.

"I can't become a landlord! I can't be getting something for nothing!" he protested. "Other places are paying my expenses outside. So long as I don't lose money, it's fine. What are you giving me that for?"

Comforting voices rose from all over the meeting hall, urging him to take the money, saying it was just a small symbolic gesture. "You always have guests. Buy a few packs of cigarettes and treat them to a few smokes! The Production Brigade was taking into account your special needs!"

"No way!" insisted Chen Yonggui. "No matter how you justify it, I'm not going to take it! I can't become the new landlord! Since you've already taken this money out, why don't you buy yourselves some cigarettes? If you don't want to smoke, fine! Let me stew, then, that's all!"

A smile appeared on his face as he spoke.

As for Chen Yonggui's special needs, there were quite a few of them. He usually had too many guests, so that the wheat flour he received as his standard allotment from his Production Brigade was not sufficient to feed them. Consequently, Chen Yonggui once brought the issue up just before the end of a Party Branch meeting.

"I have one personal suggestion that I would like everybody to think over. How about if my workpoints were computed in wheat? There's no need to give me corn. I have all these guests all the time, so there's never enough white flour. If I could get my work points' worth in wheat, out of consideration for this special situation, I would not have to ask people to buy wheat flour."

That is how small Chen Yonggui's request was, a mere trifle. Yet, small as it was, the Party Branch Committee continued to give him corn just as before, out of who knows what considerations. When they heard this story at their father's grave, Chen Yonggui's children could do nothing but sigh.

"Dad, oh, dad!" they moaned. "Powerful and famous as you were out there, you could have just winked at the Grain Bureau, and all the grain you wanted would have been sent to your door!" Who knows whether Chen Yonggui, in his eternal sleep below ground, could hear them?

An old friend of Chen Yonggui's came for the grave-sweeping—someone who had matured right in front of his eyes, Li Xishen. In the early 1970s, Li Xishen was the Party Branch Secretary of Five Family Flat. Five Family Flat planted some rice experimentally one year and reaped a bumper harvest. Each Brigade member received 20 *jin* of rice. In way of reporting the good news to Chen Yonggui, Li Xishen brought him 20 *jin* of rice, too. Chen Yonggui had seen the rice grow out of the yellow loess in Five Family Flat and was very happy about that, but he firmly refused to accept Li Xishen's gift.

"By planting rice in Five Family Flat," Chen said, "you fellows have put yourselves well ahead of Dazhai. Dazhai is planning to do it, too. As for the 20 *jin*, you better take it back. If I take 20 from you, then 20 from him, I'll soon turn into a landlord!"

Chen Yonggui was very insistent, but so was Li Xishen, who refused to take it back. He kept explaining that his village had specifically sent its own home-grown rice over for tasting. Stubbornly, Li Xishen left the rice behind, but after his departure Chen Yonggui had someone take it back to Five Family Flat and sent word to Li Xishen that he had kept just a small quantity for tasting and was returning the rest. Although the whole thing was not a big deal, it remains imbedded in Li Xishen's memory to this day.

Facing Chen Yonggui's grave that day, Li Xishen respectfully placed a cigarette on it as an offering, mumbling to himself: "Old Chen, you are someone who's been a Vice-Premier, but how rich did you ever get? You should see some of these cadres today! All it takes is to become a director of a company that employs just over ten people, but they ride in luxury cars and they smoke these fancy Asma cigarettes!"

Chen Yonggui was a heavy smoker in his day, but fancy cigarettes like the Asma brand were a novelty to him. While he held office in Beijing his security guard, Zhang Yinchang, also served as his orderly. Items like "purchase of Sanqi brand cigarettes for Chen Yonggui" often showed up among Zhang Yinchang's living expense bills. These cigarettes cost less than 40 Chinese cents per packet. They were Chen's preferred brand because his income was always rather limited and he could not indulge himself. According to Central Committee regulations, people like Chen Yonggui, who fell into the category of subsidized cadres, received a living-expense allowance of only two Chinese dollars per day. He needed money every day for food, tea, laundry, and other incidentals so his budget was very tight. Whether in Beijing or somewhere else on a tour of inspection, Chen Yonggui always had to follow the procedures set by regulations for every eating and lodging expense.

On this account, he always told Zhang Yinchang when they got to some place: "You must square my accounts with everybody! Follow the regulations! We can't make any exceptions just because I'm a Vice-Premier! If I bite off more than I can chew right now, the chewing will get even more difficult in the future!"

After one of his inspections of Guizhou Province, just before he boarded the plane for departure, some Guizhou Provincial Committee leaders placed a case of Maotai liquor on board and told Zhang Yinchang: "This is a present for Vice-Premier Chen. Don't tell him anything right away, wait till you get to Beijing." But as they disembarked in Beijing, as soon as Zhang Yinchang mentioned the case of Maotai, Chen Yonggui got angry.

"How could you just bring it back like that? You should have paid for it!" Zhang Yinchang had to pay Guizhou before they settled the matter and put it behind them.

Real life is never as perfect and pure as a fairy tale. Every step Chen Yonggui made in life left mud on the soles of his shoes. Nobody regarded him as absolutely stain-proof. In his lifetime he did receive some simple gifts on occasion, for sentimental reasons or out of courtesy. When it came to gifts from foreign visitors, however, most of them were sent to the departments in charge of foreign affairs and the reception of foreign visitors. Chen was able to place strict demands on himself from the beginning to the end, and to refuse to accept things except in very special circumstances. Even after he withdrew from public life and moved to the high-level government cadre apartment complex in Beijing, he still refused to accept presents when his countrymen came to visit him. Once the Director of Dazhai's furfural factory, Li Jixiang, visited him and brought along a few pints of sesame oil. The sesame oil was a special product of Xiyang which was not easy to buy on the market.

"In the future, just come," said the annoyed Chen Yonggui. "I don't want you to be bringing this and that, and this goes for all visitors from back home. The Central Committee has just held the Twelfth Congress and announced full rectification of the party within three years. I've heard that the campaign will surpass even the one held in Yanan! I've steered clear of economic incentives and benefits all my life, I don't want my name to be sullied by some gift just before I die! You remember what I used to say? It's easy for the leaders to get rich. It's making the common people rich that's darn hard!"

This was a concrete expression of the old generation's honesty in performing official duties. Had the Communist Party of China from the onset behaved in the same way as the bureaucracy of the old society, giving in to corruption, ripping off wealth and cutting itself off from the people, how could it have ever established the People's Republic of China? How would ordinary folk ever have come to sing the song, "Heaven is Great! Earth is Great! But not as Great as the Kindness of the Party!"?

Chen Yonggui's face and figure will not again appear in this world, but the stories he left behind will not be easily erased from human recollection. Like a gentle wind, at times they stir people's memories and longings, at other times they stir people's dreams. And the more this is so, the more disturbed the people of Dazhai and Xiyang become because the more they look back on the past, the more they reflect on the reality of the present.

CHAPTER—45

SURVIVORS COMPOSE AN ELEGY

Dazhai's precipitous decline came as if overnight. The teeming crowds of visitors disappeared. The tune of "Learn from Dazhai; Catch Up with Dazhai" was forgotten. Tigerhead Mountain and Wolf Den Ravine, which in the past seethed with excitement, became desolate and dreary! The newspapers that in the past had most consistently carried the banner headline "Learn From Dazhai, Catch up with Xiyang" all of a sudden turned around and attacked, serving as public instruments for vitriolic criticism of Dazhai's alleged "ultra-leftism." Chen Yonggui, whose image once shook all China and whose fame spread throughout the world, went from bad to worse, from smoke to oblivion. He had acquired an entirely different status in the eyes of the public and, after suffering a most difficult and painful twilight retirement, went to his death disgraced.

The new movement to criticize and rectify "leftist" mistakes that surfaced in the "In Agriculture, Learn From Dazhai" campaign did not adopt a measured approach, summarizing the experiences and examining the lessons of learning from Dazhai. Rather, it arbitrarily made unwarranted accusations against Chen Yonggui, including "exposés" of an allegedly lurid personal life. This was a perfect replay of an age-old common pastime in Chinese civilization: When a wall is about to collapse, everybody gives it a push.

Only after society filed Chen Yonggui's annals in the archives of history did bold souls fish his "question" out of the dry well of time and start clearing up some of the factual truths.

Society's assessment of Chen Yonggui resembled the waters of the Songxi River. When a flood crest nears they sweep down in a surging tide, looking as though they could swallow the whole wide world. But after the crest goes by they subside to a flow so gentle that people, at their leisure, can enjoy a good swim.

After 1984, some of the things that were sound about Dazhai became debatable again, and people once again weighed the rights and wrongs of Chen Yonggui's achievements. After his inspection of Qiliying in Henan, Li Kiannan, the late President of State, pointed out that in the future agricultural development would still have to base itself on the principle of self-reliance and the spirit of arduous struggle, and it would follow the road of collectivism. He, in fact, reaffirmed the Dazhai spirit.

With the lapse of time, the relationship between the Dazhai spirit and China's entire agricultural development induced people to reconsider and impelled party leadership on all levels to reformulate their attitudes toward the Dazhai issue. At the end of July 1989, after an inspection of Dazhai, Li Ligong, Secretary of the Party Committee of Shanxi Province, enthusiastically commented that "the Dazhai spirit should be transmitted from generation to generation." All major papers in Shanxi publicized his statement. At the beginning of September 1990, Wang Senhao, Governor of Shanxi, went to the old liberated area in the Taihang Mountain range to conduct some on-the-spot business. After hearing reports from Dazhai's cadres when he visited Dazhai, he said: "Dazhai's spirit of profound patriotism and love for the collective, of self-reliance and ardent struggle, that was once advanced by Premier Zhou, is correct. Moreover, it has an immediate practical significance for the present as well. The past "leftist" mistakes of the "Learn From Dazhai Movement" had nothing to do with the Dazhai masses. Dazhai's experiences in the capital construction of irrigation and water conservancy projects are very valuable; they should be popularized."

The descent of the Red Flag of Dazhai from the Ninth Heaven to the Ninth Hell made the serious consequences of this extraordinary phenomenon, its damage to their own work all too obvious to the cadres and masses of Xiyang. Consequently, after ten years of drifting along with the tide, propagation of the Dazhai spirit revived in Xiyang County. At a meeting of the People's Congress in 1990, County Magistrate Wang Guining in his "Government Work Report," raised the issue of the need for renewed popularization of the Dazhai spirit in Xiyang. The County then reentered it as a Congress Resolution. Amidst this new irresistible tide in Xiyang, at the Tenth Party Congress held in the County on October 18, 1990, County Committee Secretary Gao Qixiang advanced the following thesis:

> The fame of our County's village of Dazhai spread through the world as early as the 1960s. This was due to its heroic undertakings and outstanding achievements in controlling the mountains and rivers and transforming nature through self-reliance and arduous struggle. Its successes made it into the advanced model for the entire nation on the agricultural battle front. In his incisive summary, Premier Zhou Enlai gave the Dazhai spirit his highest evaluation and full approval. We have turned a new page in history now, but as we look back in an attempt to realistically reappraise Dazhai, it is not difficult to see that self-reliance and arduous struggle were the pillars of its sudden rise, that they were the indestructible, true, vital quintessence of the Dazhai spirit. This sort of spirit nurtured and trained a whole generation in Dazhai, and encouraged the two hundred thousand or so people of Xiyang to wage an unprecedented struggle to lift themselves from the state of poverty and blankness.

Without a doubt, under the new historic conditions of reform and openness, this commendable spirit will yet inspire us to strive without respite to create new results and attain ever greater achievements. The lessons of Dazhai's self-reliance and arduous struggle are plentiful; the enthusiasm of the people of Dazhai for difficult pioneering undertakings, the perseverance with which Dazhai's cadres continued to take part in physical labor and their style of maintaining close relationship with the masses, their character of patriotism and love for the collective are all components of this spirit.... We propose that the tradition of self-reliance and arduous struggle be carried on and that in no circumstances should it be limited just to the agricultural battlefront or just to the area of capital construction for irrigation and water conservancy. It should unfold in every trade and industry, in every aspect of every line of work at all stations in our society. We should let it become our psychological weapon in surmounting difficulties and develop it as our internal motivating force.

After the Party Congress, posters exclaiming "Carry on the Dazhai Spirit" kept cropping out all over Xiyang County, and the capital construction of farmland gained a momentum surpassing by far that of earlier years. Following the constant change in political climate, people could gradually see a favorable turn in Dazhai's fate. In April 1991, the new County Committee Secretary, Fu Yiyuan, took office. After a conscientious investigation he quickly realized that, if he wanted to make a breakthrough, he would first have to adopt a clear attitude on the issue of Dazhai and on Xiyang's learning from Dazhai. As this presented itself as an unavoidable issue, Fu Yiyuan used the occasion of a meeting of cadres above the County Deputy level, held in July of that year, to present a long report on the propagation of the Dazhai spirit. In the report he appraised the Dazhai spirit as a national spirit, needed not only in the early 1960s but also in the new era of reform and openness of the 1990s. While propagating the spirit of Dazhai, he differentiated between the Dazhai spirit and some "leftist" mistakes that occurred during the period of learning from Dazhai.

This report evoked strong repercussions in Xiyang, becoming for a time the hottest topic of street gossip and debate. Many of the veteran cadres, who had waged valiant struggles during the "In Agriculture, Learn From Dazhai" campaign, broke into tears as they regained ease of mind. Dazhai's and Xiyang County's propaganda departments and cultural bureaus mobilized their resources to propagate the Dazhai spirit. They put together a Dazhai exhibition in a very short time, and reopened the old Dazhai Exhibition Hall that had been closed for over ten years. County Committee Secretary Fu Yiyuan and County Magistrate Wang Guining personally arrived on the day of the opening to cut the ribbon at the ceremony. After the opening, throughout the day, domestic and foreign guests toured the Exhibition Hall. The event was covered by the *Central Shanxi Daily* and *Shanxi Daily* in print, and by the Shanxi Television Station in its broadcasts.

In August 1991, the Party Branch Secretary of the Theater Company of Shanxi, Peng Yi, traveled to Dazhai and Xiyang to give a talk. Both Dazhai Brigade and Xiyang City gave him a warm and friendly reception. He used the term "the heroic people of Dazhai and the heroic people of Xiyang" in his address, and he summed up by saying that he and his troupe members matured as the result of learning from Dazhai. All this was entirely different from the tenor of public opinion ten years earlier.

After a spell of unfair lashing, the media and the literary and art circles gradually liberated their true feelings toward Dazhai and Chen Yonggui. In 1982, China News Agency reporter Han Kai wrote a report entitled "Chen Yonggui at Home" for the Hong Kong press. In the report he wrote that Chen Yonggui, when asked about his views on Chinese agriculture, expressed his satisfaction with the current responsibility system in agricultural production and then, upon brief contemplation, added: "China is so large, with its 800,000,000 peasants. If we depended on the State for investment, the money would be gone in no time. Collective accumulation is very limited, too. In the end, we still have to turn to the spirit of arduous struggle and self-reliance: The fish makes use of the water, the water makes use of the fish; this is mutual aid...."

Back in those days many people abroad were relatively concerned about Chen Yonggui's fate. This article caused a strong reaction overseas. Overseas Chinese in the Philippines immediately published the article saying: "We are glad to hear that Chen Yonggui is safe and sound on the mainland." Obviously, numerous people recalled Chen Yonggui with fondness. Not long after his death in 1986, the *Shanxi Youth* published a piece of reportage "Chen Yonggui's Spirit Returns to Dazhai." The magazine sold out as soon as it came off the press.

I would like to mention here a female reporter for Canton's paper *The Contemporary* by the name of Liu Dan, whom cadres of Dazhai's International Travel Office met in the fall of 1987. The purpose of Liu Dan's travel to Dazhai this time was not investigative reporting along the lines of the great discussions about the changes in Dazhai after the Third Plenary Session, re-reinforced with comparisons of Dazhai before the Congress, or the provocative airing of criticisms of Dazhai's "leftism" that implied that everything now was better than in the past.

No! First of all, she revealed the irregularities in reporting on Dazhai. As instructed by the leadership of her paper before the trip, she tracked down Liang Bianliang, Song Liying, Guo Fenglian and a few other comrades in Dazhai and, showing great sensitivity, found out what their feelings were. She also took the trouble to visit Party Branch Secretary Gao Yuliang, where she discovered that the people of Dazhai felt strong moral indignation over the article "Dazhai's Departure From the Spirit of Dazhai. After she returned to the Travel Office and sat alone in her room, she broke into tears, keenly aware that every individual had a story that was hard to tell.

The Contemporary published her literary record of actual events on January 26, 1988, under the title "From the Fiery-Red Dream to the Lush-Green Reality," which received wide public attention. The opening sentence of her piece read:

> After I accepted the assignment to visit Dazhai, the newspaper leadership said, "The aim of your trip is to track down the sources, find out the things that the readers want to know about Dazhai, and write them up."
>
> Later, she wrote with passion:
>
> As I faced Tigerhead Mountain, the man-made plains, the railroad-car-like cave-dwellings half-buried in the hills, the dead and the living, the rich and the poor people of Dazhai, I was compelled to ponder deeply, and to reflect. I have seen many weddings and funerals, many happy and many tragic events, to the point where

> my heart has armed itself with a hardened, callous layer that no ordinary emotion can penetrate. Who would have thought that Dazhai could reach and move so deeply the tough cords at the bottom of my heart? It suddenly occurs to me to change just one word in that famous dispatch that Caesar sent back to Rome, Veni, vidi, vici, and to send a telegram to my paper with a simple message that expresses my state of mind: "I've come, I've seen, I...."

Piercing the truth with a single pertinent remark, the piece went on to expose the unfair conclusion that "the State subsidized by 22 Chinese cents every *jin* of Dazhai's grain." After its original publication, four other magazines like Red *Cliff* and *Creative Nonfiction* carried this literary record of actual events. Similar pieces continued to appear in Hong Kong and domestic magazines. After the third anniversary of Chen Yonggui's death, the sixth issue of *The Branch Reconstructs*, a publication sponsored by the Shanxi Provincial Committee of the Communist Party of China, carried a piece entitled "Chen Yonggui's Testament, Recorded During His Last Interview," which gave Chen Yonggui a high evaluation. It generated powerful reverberations.

Recently articles about Dazhai and Chen Yonggui have been appearing constantly in magazines like *Shanxi Youth*, *Liaoning Literature and Art*, *The Age of Civilization*, and the like. The articles have exposed many of the issues, like the question of the State aid to Dazhai, that the people of Dazhai have been castigating some of the media for unfair propaganda in the past. In 1990, the Central Broadcasting Station and the Xinhua News Agency published internally the information that Xiyang was once again raising high the name of Dazhai.

On April 25, 1991, *The Economic Daily* published an article entitled "The Village of Fanggan Explains What Is Worth Keeping and What Should Be Thrown Out." The article stated that, when the reporter visited this village with the average per capita annual income of 3,800 Chinese dollars and asked the villagers how they achieved such remarkable development, they answered with an astonishing sentence: "We never stopped learning from Dazhai." Because of this, the reporter described the unfair conduct of the media circles toward Dazhai as "throwing the baby out with the bath water."

During that same period Shanghai's *Literature and Art Gazette* published reportage by Gu Xusheng entitled "Dazhai People Yesterday and Today." Writing about extraordinary actions taken in criticizing Dazhai, the article said: "That same year, the meritorious and highly capable Li Suoshou was sent back to Xiyang, along with the whole group of cadres that had been promoted together with him: Zhang Huaiying from Shouyang County, Li Xishen from Xiyang County, Chen Youtang from Jiaocheng County, Li Qimao from the city of Yuci. Some of them were sent to rural townships, others were sent to the village grass-roots level, while still others went into early retirement."

Gu Xushang added: "Liang Bianliang smacked his lips as he dragged on his cigarette, breaking into a cough every so often. He said that during the first few years of the 1980s everybody found fault with and made unwarranted charges against Dazhai, spreading all manner of errors and falsehoods. They brought to light everything from the general direction followed to what goes on behind the scenes, they criticized everything from the general Party line to people's private secrets; even the old hero Jia Jincai, who was pushing seventy, started cursing at people who were pointing accusing fingers at his back. Chen Yonggui and Guo Fenglian became targets of public criticism."

The article took an impartial position, examining history from today's perspective: "It has been confirmed that the Central Shanxi Region is Number One in Shanxi when it comes to grain, and that Xiyang leads the way in the Central Shanxi Region. It must be said that the basis for this has been the great capital construction of farmland undertaken during the 'In Agriculture, Learn from Dazhai' campaign. When the Party Branch Secretary of Daqiuzhuang, which is located within the Tianjin municipal area, came to observe Dazhai, he told Guo Fenglian: 'Daqiuzhuang has been developing sideline industries in the past few years, but it can still not depart from the agricultural basis built during the years of learning from Dazhai.' The masses in Shuimotou say: 'We've cut a tunnel through the mountain and changed the course of the river. We've added trade to our agriculture, forestry, animal husbandry and sideline industries. It is all because of the inspiration to work hard that we got during those years of learning from Dazhai.'"

"The other year Dazhai Village Branch Secretary Jia Chenglin visited Shandong to study the commodity economy of nine county towns. Every single leader from the nine counties told him the same thing: 'Our economic foundation is still the base we built during those years of learning from Dazhai.'"

The reportage also revealed the concern of some Central Committee leaders for the Dazhai issue: "On January 14th of this year Elder Sister Kang Keqing received Guo Fenglian at her Peking residence. As they were about to part, Elder Sister Kang said: 'Chen Yonggui was a good comrade. I remember the people of Dazhai with great fondness. As soon as I recover from this illness, I really want to go back to Dazhai to take a look.'"

This shows that although Chen Yonggui had passed away, his image was not forgotten. Posterity was singing him a belated song of praise.

In addition to the attention given to Chen Yonggui in the domestic media, the deceased peasant leader did not fade from the memory of international press circles either. On the Chinese Lunar New Year's Eve in 1986, Dazhai Travel Agency met two reporters from the Japanese Asahi Shimbun. They came because of a book that had been published in Eastern Europe, publicizing the present status of Dazhai in China and the conditions in Dazhai after the Third Plenary Session. According to Chinese tradition, all institutions are closed on the last day of the last month of the lunar year, and all the peasants are busy shopping for the Spring Festival. The sudden arrival of foreign guests elicited a great deal of attention from the County government. In spite of the holiday, local functionaries made careful preparations for their reception.

After the Japanese reporters arrived, Party Branch Secretary Gao Yuliang first gave them a talk. He explained the change in Dazhai's circumstances after the Third Plenary Session of the Eleventh National Congress of the Communist Party of China. Afterward, Liang Bianliang and several veteran cadres spoke about Dazhai's history, with particular emphasis on important events that occurred in Chen Yonggui's lifetime. With the exception of the meeting with Gao Yuliang, local cadres successfully kept outside closed doors those individuals from Central Government institutions who accompanied the reporters during their visit. Perhaps there was an unspoken purpose in that!

The reporters gave a special banquet for the old couple, Jia Jincai and Song Liying. They rarely had an opportunity to meet with an old married couple of this sort, where the age difference was over twenty years. On the table, along with various sumptuous local foods, the reporters placed a bottle of special liquor distilled in Fenyang that they had brought from Beijing. Through an interpreter, the reporters proceeded to talk with Jia Jincai, who was almost eighty, asking about his personal history, his family and his living conditions. Due to his advanced age, Old Jia's memory was noticeably weakening, so Song Liying answered many of the questions in his place. After the banquet, the reporters gave the Fenyang liquor bottle with the liquor that remained to the old couple as a souvenir. To this very day, the bottle, still half full, remains in their home.

This is the way the river of history flows: There is the main stream, but there are also turbid counter-currents. As the public's understanding of Dazhai continuously enlarges, the media keep clarifying the question of Dazhai and Chen Yonggui. Nevertheless, there are still people who stand in the opposing camp, confounding right and wrong, confusing black and white, maintaining and even increasing the criticism of Chen Yonggui and the Dazhai spirit of ten years ago. The book written by Sun Qitai and Xiong Zhiyong in 1990, *The Rise and Fall of the Red Flag of Dazhai*, which I have already mentioned in previous chapters, is precisely one such negative example. At its core, the story of the rise of the red banner of Chen Yonggui and Dazhai, is used as a vehicle to criticize and negate Mao Zedong's and Zhou Enlai's philosophy of agriculture espoused after the founding of the People's Republic. It uses a false theory of "collectivization, communization, Dazhaization" to defile the "In Agriculture, Learn From Dazhai" movement as Mao Zedong's second "siege of the cities by the countryside" and his misguided campaign to build "Utopia."

The book completely disregards the great achievements of the thirty-year-long development of agriculture after the establishment of the

People's Republic. Flaunting the banner of a critique of "leftism," it openly criticizes Mao Zedong and secretly repudiates Zhou Enlai. It uses an extremely prejudiced attitude to deride various Party committees that had fostered Dazhai and supported Chen Yonggui, without granting them a single redeeming feature. The readers of my book will have noticed, perhaps, that no writer used Chen Yonggui's name when the media criticized Dazhai ten years ago. They used instead such euphemisms as "the former leading cadre of the Xiyang County Committee." But the authors of this book not only blame Chen Yonggui by name; they fill their tome with a blend of sheer fabrications, half-truths, and unfair warped evaluations.

As pointed out earlier in this volume the book, so recently published in Henan, criticizes Dazhai's and Xiyang's capital construction of farmland as "an indulgence in fantasy" and its transformation of the conditions of production in agriculture as "an endless moving of yellow earth." Similar nonsense can be seen throughout the book. Even more unfair is the book's conclusion about "State aid to Dazhai," which Dazhai and Chen Yonggui could never accept. Without clarifying facts, the authors merely intensify the statements of the *Shanxi Daily*'s Departure article. They do not bother to check out any of the data with the parties or people concerned. My repeated investigation has revealed that the data in the book do not match the records, that they are basically inconsistent with the facts. In a word, the data are a fraud in their own right. Public opinion has concluded that this book uses the standpoint of "bourgeois liberalism" to evaluate Dazhai and Chen Yonggui, and that sooner or later it will be punished by history.

As time goes on, things are constantly tested and verified in practice. Eventually the correct defeats the false, the truth prevails over the lies. In the long run both domestic and foreign media will undoubtedly set Chen Yonggui's story, too, on the right track.

CHAPTER—46

"HIS MERITS TOP TIGERHEAD MOUNTAIN AND ENVELOP THE EARTH"

When Chen Yonggui passed away, Tigerhead Mountain and Wolf Den Ravine wept, drenching the village of Dazhai and its surroundings with bitter tears. Discussions and disputes among the people of Dazhai on how to give expression to their heartfelt grief started immediately. The opinions and requests varied, but everybody's common wish was to build a memorial for Old Chen that would be of lasting significance. They finally reached an agreement: They would erect a stone stele for him, regardless of cost!

Before Chen Yonggui's ashes came back to Dazhai to rest, Liang Bianliang and several members of the older generation spent an entire day halfway up Tigerhhead Mountain busily pounding away at bedrock to dig out his grave. Why would they want to dig the grave into this hard, sharp-edged ledge? Because every time Chen Yonggui took foreign visitors up the mountain, he always went to sit on the same rock outcrop and commented with a sigh: "Bury me here after I die, so I can stand a bit taller and see a bit farther!"

He used to say with a laugh, "When I say 'Standing on Tigerhead Mountain I gaze toward Tiananmen, embracing all of China,' it is precisely because I want to stand a bit taller and see a bit farther. Can you really see Tiananmen from Tigerhead Mountain? Who would believe that?"

In order to respect Chen Yonggui's last wish, the people of Dazhai would have placed his grave there on that ledge no matter what, even if it were twice as hard to dig.

Dazhai's cadres had no time to waste in making preparations for the erection of the stele. First they went to Shijiazhuang to make contacts for the cutting of the stone and they worked on sorting out the text to be engraved on it. Then they organized Dazhai labor to build a road up the mountain so the stele could be carried up. After that they invited craftsmen to build the coffin pit.[1] This went on for over two years. During this time, all those good-hearted residents of Dazhai kept waiting, kept expecting, kept vehemently demanding, all in the hope that the two black stone tablets, one on each side of the stele, which would symbolize Chen Yonggui's entire life could be erected on the spot halfway up Tigerhead Mountain as soon as possible, adding grace to Old Chen's grave.

In his hospital room in Beijing Chen Yonggui had voiced his wishes regarding the activities to follow his death. But there was no way he could have anticipated the major actions that his comrades-in-arms back home were undertaking on his behalf. The things that he did anticipate were a memorial service, flower wreaths, various restrained memorial activities. Consequently, he repeatedly instructed his family and the cadres from Dazhai who were coming to visit him not to hold a memorial service after his death, not to organize any kind of activity. He wanted to avoid needlessly spending people's money. Putting up a few wreaths would be quite enough, he maintained, since they wouldn't take up too much good land. Under the new responsibility system the village had allocated use rights to all the land, so taking up somebody's allotment would create a problem. "Even if they don't say it out

1. This pit, minute in scale, resembles in design any and all of the famous Ming Tombs in Beijing—a stone masonry-reinforced cylindrical mound, an encircling moat and, outside that, a parallel encircling wall holding back, on the uphill side, the detritus of the mountain slope. It resonates a distinctly imperial flavor, symbolic, no doubt of the high regard his fellow townsmen all held for Chen Yonggui. (W.H.H.)

loud, they'll still blame me in their hearts," warned Chen Yonggui. "So you better not do anything!"

"Not do anything, not do anything...." Who knows, maybe his relatives told him they would not do anything. Maybe the village cadres verbally agreed not do anything either. But even had they really not wanted to do anything, this would hardly have passed muster with the people. And now the cadres were counting on their fingers, over two years in time, all the distance they covered to build the grave and erect the stele, all the expenditure of labor and money. But the people of Dazhai did not regret any of it. This was something that all the villagers wanted and demanded!

In the summer of 1988, after craftsmen laid in place a flight of steps leading to Chen Yonggui's grave, they at last set up the final memorial, the stone tablets. On the front of the stele several large ideographs declared "Eternal glory to Comrade Chen Yonggui." On the back side the inscription said, "His merits top Tigerhead Mountain and Envelop the Earth." In addition to the large inscriptions, the text in smaller ideographs noted that the stele was built by the people of Dazhai. The rest consisted of excerpts from Xinhua Agency's obituary. The grave, one could call it a tomb, a skillfully fashioned cylinder of well-cut, finely fitted granite blocks, was topped by a mound of earth. Embedded in the face of the stone cylinder was a black stone tablet, the size of a man, which said simply: "Chen Yonggui's grave." On the two ends of the enclosing wall, so reminiscent of a Ming Tomb as it circled three quarters of the way around the cylindrical grave itself, creating a moatlike passageway around it, sat two sculptured stone tigers, symbolic guardians of Tigerhead Mountain. They looked out on the stunning view of myriad terraces and endless mountains that so transfixed Chen Yonggui as he gazed northward striving to raise Tiananmen over the horizon, at least in his imagination.

After more than two years, more than seven hundred torn calendar pages after Chen's death, the people of Dazhai selected July 15, 1988, the anniversary of the death of the great Song dynasty patriot and General Yang Ye, to erect Chen Yonggui's stele and stage the unveiling rites. In view of the fact that Chen Yonggui was still a controversial figure in China at that time and that the Central Committee had not yet made an unequivocal conclusion either affirming him or repudiating him, the Xiyang County Committee and Xiyang People's Government dodged the occasion. The Village Party Branch invited them, but they made no official response. This had its propitious side, it gave the people of Dazhai complete freedom. The Dazhai Township Party Committee and the Township People's Government, because they were on Dazhai's side, had already sent flower wreaths for Chen Yonggui earlier. They now dispatched representatives to take part in the unveiling ceremony. Except for the invitation given to the County, Dazhai had not notified anyone else. They were afraid they might cause trouble for the people if they informed them of the event. Besides, Dazhai is a small village facing many economic difficulties. If too many people were to come, it would be difficult to treat them all with due courtesy.

They never imagined, however, that this event would bring several hundred influential individuals from all walks of life, who came to take part of their own accord. The Political Director of Beijing Municipality's Jiaotong Production Brigade, Song Jiajia, came; the old Xiyang County Party Committee Secretary from the 1950s, Zhang Huaiying came; the former Pingding County Committee Secretary, Li Suoshou, reputed to be "socialism's man of action," came and with them many others. A heavy stream of people and vehicles arriving from dawn to dusk reinforced the notables. Two hundred wreaths lined up in rows all but concealed the grave as they overflowed and piled up on the pine-clad slope above.

At 10 AM, the band started playing funeral music, as its members slowly walked the road from the village of Dazhai around and up the mountain all the way to the memorial site. Along the way, the air was filled with the sound of exploding firecrackers. The people of Dazhai had been going up to the grave all morning in droves to burn paper money and express their grief. By the time the unveiling ceremony started, there were already more than five hundred people there. The old hero Jia Jincai, who by that time had some difficulty walking, rode up Tigerhead Mountain in a car. Liang Bianliang and Dazhai's cadres walked up in the procession behind the band.

The head of the Dazhai Village Committee, Jia Chenglin, hosted the unveiling ceremony. He presented the life of Chen Yonggui basically as it had been evaluated in the Xinhua Agency's obituary, together with the alterations, slightly in Chen's favor, that had been made by the Central Committee after an investigation. This supreme body had added the word "famous" in front of "national model worker," and had inserted the phrase "He was Vice-Premier of the State Council from 1975 to 1980" in the text. At the end they appended the following: "Comrade Chen Yonggui wholeheartedly supported the principles, the line and the policies of the party after the Third Plenary Session of the Eleventh Party Congress." This visibly enhanced the official evaluation of Chen Yonggui. People, however, were free to draw their own conclusions.

Gao Yuliang spoke during the ceremony on behalf of the Dazhai Party Branch Committee, making an even more careful appraisal of Chen Yonggui, and calling on the people of Dazhai to continue to hold high the great banner of "self-reliance and arduous struggle" and build an even better Dazhai of today.

When it came time for a family representative to speak, Chen Mingzhu bowed to all the guests and thanked the guests, the Dazhai Party Branch and the village of Dazhai for erecting the stele for his father. Chen Mingzhu's voice choked with sobs as grief overwhelmed him. Zhang Huaiying and Song Jiajia were both moved to tears.

It is too bad that no modern equipment recorded this historic moment. Two journalists from the Central Television Station, who had just set foot in Dazhai, heard about the ceremony only after it was over. They expressed their disappointment to the County Committee Communications Group Director Jiao Huizhen.

"Too late! It's too late now!" they bemoaned. "Such a valuable piece of news! Too bad we didn't make it on time!"

After the ceremony Zhang Huaiying, Song Jiajia, Li Suoshou, and Guo Fenglian encircled the stele and had their photograph taken as a memento.

The imposing stone stele that looks down on Dazhai from half the way up Tigerhead Mountain has been receiving cigarettes, cakes, fruit, and canned goods from numerous visitors who come to pay their respects and make their offerings at the steps leading to the base of the stele. Countless white silver coins have been stuck on top of the stone above the tablet that reads "Chen Yonggui's Grave." The cigarettes, the cakes, the fruit, the cans, and the white silver coins act as repositories for the best and kindest in people's hearts and souls, for their dear memories and their unexpressed hopes.

So many visitors who come from long distances on official business to Xiyang disregard their travel fatigue and climb Tigerhead Mountain because of Chen Yonggui's memorial tablet, and tomb. They want to see it with their own eyes. So many journalists who come to Xiyang to cover stories also want to take a trip to Tigerhead Mountain to dig up some fresh information. In the past two years, highly placed functionaries have also constantly climbed the mountain to visit the now famous site and find out about the situation in Dazhai.

The manager of Dazhai's Travel Office had one unusual visitor who seemed to be spoiling for trouble. As soon as he walked through the doors of the Travel Office, he requested that the manager take him to Chen Yonggui's grave site. The manager prepared the register and turned to inform him of the way, when the visitor got angry: "What is wrong with you people here? What's the big deal? I just want to trouble you with one visit, and I'm paying you 30 dollars for it!" The manager thought the tone of the man did not sound right. Then he poked his head out of the door and saw a luxury sedan parked there. Who was this visitor after all? It remains a mystery to this day.

Since Chen Yonggui's death, some foreign visitors have come every year to Dazhai from thousands of miles away. They too want to visit Chen Yonggui's grave and it always leaves a lasting impression on them. William Hinton, an old friend of Chen Yonggui, with whom Chen Yonggui was planning to revisit Dazhai while he was still alive, could now only come to say farewell at the grave. But Dazhai did not fade from Hinton's memory on account of Chen Yonggui's premature death. He has used several occasions when he comes to inspect a mechanization project in Zhangzhuang and Wanggungzhuang, some hundred miles away, to stop in Dazhai, call on his old friends, have a chat with them, and then make on-the-spot investigations of several places with successful collective economies in Xiyang County—places like Beinangou and Zhaozhuang. Many foreign visitors to Dazhai inquire about the whereabouts of some of Dazhai's old-timers and about their current circumstances, showing as much interest and concern for them as ever.

Kawakami Kozai once said: "The deceased is like a man of the moment!" As the time passes, people in high positions keep mentioning Chen Yonggui. From old cadres and leaders that he once nurtured with painstaking care to foreign students who have read about his exploits, they keep coming to Dazhai to inspect it long after Chen Yonggui has gone. After they have toured Dazhai and paid their respects at Chen Yonggui's grave, and after they have witnessed the present condition of the slopes, the terraces and the fields on the many ridges and in the many ravines on Tigerhead Mountain, they sit down to talk with Dazhai's and Xiyang's cadres. Almost always they express their hope that Dazhai will continue to hold high the great banner of self-reliance and arduous struggle so as to keep breaking a new path for mankind.

China today still cares for Chen Yonggui.

Chen Yonggui belongs not only to China but to the whole world.

After Chen Yonggui's sun had set behind the western mountains, during the time when he was placed in a cozy nest in Beijing through arrangements made by the Central Committee, many people in Dazhai and Xiyang hoped that he would go back to take a look. His visitors could not help but bring it up, the moment they walked through his door: "Old Chen, when are you coming back to Dazhai to take a look?"

Chen Yonggui always put on a smile: "I'm waiting for the people to forget me before I go back!"

But as he was a contemporary peasant representative, the embodiment of China's peasantry after the establishment of New China, there was no way the people would forget him, there was no way the society would forsake him. His legacy to the society will be carried on by future generations, the glory that radiates from his body will still reflect on Mother Earth in the future. As the constant reappraisal of history proceeds, Chen Yonggui's image keeps getting ever more distinct, ever stronger.

When the enveloping mist has lifted, history will have crystallized the immutable Chen Yonggui.

POSTSCRIPT

THE DAZHAI SPIRIT LIVES

"In Agriculture, Learn From Dazhai!" As soon as these five ordinary, common words passed over the Great Leader's lips they turned into a trend, they began to radiate magnificent brilliance, they displayed enormous power, they produced social effects. They affected and continue to affect this generation of a new age.

As I meticulously sorted through Chen Yonggui's heritage, I happened to visit Gaoqian, the East Street Party Branch Secretary from Huolu County in Hebei Province, the Director of the Rural Agricultural, Industrial and Trade Combine, and the all-China Model Worker Zhang Yinzhou. His had been a poor village, dependent on State-supplied grain for food and on loans for livelihood. The average per capita annual income there was 70 Chinese dollars. After Gaoqian became the Party Branch Secretary there, the village worked hard for a few years in the spirit of "relying on arduous struggle." It increased the average grain yield to 1,000 *jin* per *mu*. The common accumulation reached 8,000,000 Chinese dollars, and the average per capita annual income rose to 1,300 Chinese dollars. After the Third Plenary Session, he summed up the experiences and lessons of the movement to learn from Dazhai and started developing industry on the agricultural base the village had consolidated. The community set up seventeen rural enterprises, with an annual output value of 20,000,000 Chinese dollars. Their main product, ilmenite, constitutes 45 percent of all the ilmenite produced in China. In the sphere of agricultural production, they introduced reforms based on his unified system, without letting go of involvement in agricultural production as stipulated by the household responsibility system. They created a neighborhood production responsibility system, maintaining their grain yields above 1000 *jin* per *mu*, and established mechanized tillage on all the land of the village. These measures attracted attention from the State Council.

The village of North-South Gully, Li Family Settlement Township, Xiyang County, also inspired me greatly. This was one of the places that continued with collective production after Xiyang basically implemented the household responsibility system. Learning the lesson of the inflexibility of excessive centralization, and avoiding the drawbacks of the excessive fragmentation of the household responsibility system enabled North-South Gully to institute a payment-for-product household contract system. The members have achieved a progressive increase in grain yields of 5-10 percent annually, and have carried on continuous capital construction of farmland throughout the years. Due to their adherence to collective production, their sideline industries experienced astonishing development, with their average per capita annual income reaching double that in comparable areas.

Many places in Shandong and Henan, too, have embarked on a new road of rural collectivization and industrialization relying on the Dazhai spirit. When asked by visitors from Dazhai and Xiyang to account for their experience, they say that in their development, before anything else, they have relied on the Dazhai spirit and collective effort.

Regardless of the age, the concepts of "self-reliance and arduous struggle" both "large in scale and collective in form" stand on undefeated ground. In the past, following the political drift of one man, power holders torpedoed so many positive things without arousing protest. This in no way benefits our present and future growth.

Conversely, an examination of Dazhai's successes and failures that seeks the truth from facts arising from Chen Yonggui's lifetime experience, opens up an unimpeded channel for the development of China's agriculture and greatly contributes to it.

EDITOR'S AFTERWORD

Chen Yonggui was a good farmer and a good engineer. He invented and developed many practices that transformed dry land farming in North China. Outstanding among them was the creation of "Dazhai Sponge Soil" and the gully-stabilizing horizontal "Arched Stone Dam." For this reason there is a tendency, even in this book, to reduce Chen's achievements to the realm of technology. In Chapter 41, Political Bureau member Li Xiannian is quoted as saying that Chen's work in irrigation and water-conserving capital construction was good. Since nobody was condemning Chen Yonggui's technical innovations while the powers that be went after his political essence hammer and tongs, this amounts to damning with faint praise. Viewing Chen's contribution as technical also leads to such one-sided views as that expressed by the young Dazhai cadre Gao Yuliang who, after Chen's forced retirement, tried to reassure him by saying, "You took too many duties upon yourself. How could you possibly take care of all that (Central, Regional and Village affairs) without a hitch? Some experiences were successful in our village, but they didn't work elsewhere! How could every profession and kind of work learn from Dazhai, as the slogan called for during those years? There are not many things one can learn from our village after all."

To reduce Chen's achievements to a few advanced farm technologies is to miss the main point of his life work, which was congenitally ideological and political. The goal of any revolution must be to create "new" men and women, people with a new attitude, new goals, new moral principles, and a new world outlook. The shift from feudalism to capitalism, which took several hundred years to effect, created in erstwhile feudal Europe and in less-encrusted North America, new bourgeois men and women who, in the heyday of the rise of their class, tended to question everything. They were agnostics, rationalists, even atheists who pioneered a tremendous liberation of thought and spirit, laid the foundations of modern science, broke feudal barriers to trade and commerce and ushered in a great new era of economic, political, social and moral development. In the end, it seems, what they introduced, dynamic and productive as it was, and inspiring as its "all men are created equal" and "one man, one vote" rhetoric remains, turned out to be another form of rapidly polarizing class society dominated by an elite who learned to expropriate from wage labor a higher percentage of surplus value as private profit than feudal lords ever extracted from serfs as land rents, or slave owners ever gleaned in products and services from slaves.

In this century the maturing of capitalism brought the prospect of socialism onto the agenda of mankind. Socialism, to succeed, must in its turn create a brand of "new" men and women imbued with working people's ideology and dedicated to ending exploitation of all kinds, once and for all. It is no longer sufficient just to substitute one kind of expropriation for another. To usher in such a sea change, great pioneers of proletarian ideology—"One for all and all for one," "public first, self second"—are needed.[1]

1. In the feudal era, to name just one aspect of the "new" thinking, one could mention the entrepreneurial spirit of those pioneers who believed in saving to invest rather than saving to hoard. They created a climate that condemned misers as morally abject, subversive and evil, when a scant hundred years earlier kings, princes, barons and bishops all hoarded wealth as a matter of course and were praised to the skies for the treasures they accumulated. (W.H.H.)

Ordinarily they will not arise full blown but must be developed and tempered by long experience of disciplined wage labor and protracted struggles to build solidarity among the dispossessed. The thing that is so remarkable about Chen Yonggui is that he seems to have sprung forth full blown as a proletarian, dedicating himself at a very early age to *da gong, wu sz* (all for public, no thought of self). The Dazhai slogan *xian gong, hou sz* (public first, self second) is the basic outlook required of a rank-and-file socialist citizen who is aware that the welfare of each individual is dependent first and foremost on the welfare of the community of which he or she is a part. Such a citizen will therefore strive for a reasonable balance between his or her personal interests and those of the community as a whole but, when serious conflict arises between these, will put community first. "All for public, no thought of self" is a more demanding criterion of unconditional service, Such is the basic outlook required of a Communist, a member of the vanguard who can lead the way forward by force of dedicated example. This latter attitude Chen Yonggui cultivated seriously as his own, while urging ordinary folk to adopt and practice the former.

There were circumstances surrounding Chen Yonggui's early life that were certainly special and may have laid a foundation for his selfless attitude. Clearly, other people in similar circumstances have reacted in diametrically opposite ways. Chen was, to all intents and purposes, orphaned at the age of six when his father died. He was already living with two widowed old ladies, who later adopted him as their own, but he never took their name and was treated as an interloper by a Dazhai community dominated by family heads named Jia. It was the same name the widows who sheltered him carried from birth. The widows' property was not his, nor was he, by community custom, in line to inherit any of it, which is one reason the community ostracized him. The Jias of Dazhai were fearful that he would, one way or another, seize Jia family property.

Chen Yonggui worked the land for the two women, their daughter and the daughter's daughter-in-law, all of them also eventually widowed, and did odd jobs for others. He later became a long-term hired laborer for a local landlord, but never, prior to land reform, did he own any property himself or expect to own any. He was thus, in a deeply petty-bourgeois community of small holders, by status at least, a birthright proletarian. This could have made him, but for some reason did not make him, ruthlessly selfish. Just the opposite. All his life he had the deepest feelings of sympathy for the underdog. These showed up most vividly when, in the early sixties, victims of crop failure showed up to steal corn out of Dazhai's fields. Chen's response was most unusual, as is made clear in Chapter 10.

The seminal test of Chen Yonggui's character and outlook took place much earlier, however, right after land reform, when Mao Zedong called on the peasants to get organized. Chen Yonggui never assumed that he could prosper by going it alone. He was very much in favor of getting organized, but he faced a difficult choice. A group of able-bodied males formed the first mutual aid group in Dazhai, the Stalwarts, and since Chen was most well known as a hard and skillful worker, they wanted very much for him to join. On the other hand, a group of childless old folks and parentless orphans also wanted to organize for farming and asked him for his help.

Which way was he to go? In the end, to the surprise of everyone, Chen joined the feeble discards of the community. Many of the youngsters had lost their parents in the war. Their fathers, wartime comrades-in-arms of Chen Yonggui's, had died at the hands of the Japanese. He could not in good conscience refuse to help them. And so he chose to go with the Feeble Group, counting on the skills of the old and the enthusiasm and growing strength of the young to outproduce the Stalwarts at their own game. At the start most people thought him crazy, but he proved them all wrong when his group harvested the best crops of all and went on to serve as the foundation for what later became a village-wide producers' cooperative.

Choosing to go with the Feeble Group was remarkable in itself, but perhaps even more remarkable was Chen Yonggui's vision of a cooperative commonwealth of China that stretched North and South from border to border and from the seas of the East to the deserts of the West. When he stood on Tigerhead Mountain, he said he could see Tiananmen, the central square in Beijing. People laughed at this but Chen used it as a graphic symbol for keeping the welfare of the whole in view, while still looking after the home folks on the loess-laden flanks of Tigerhead. Thus when, in the interests of stable prices and an "ever normal granary," the State took control over the grain trade nationwide, Chen supported the move wholeheartedly and strove to fulfill, or over-fulfill Dazhai's quota of State deliveries every year. And thus also, when unprecedented flood disaster struck, Chen mobilized his compatriots to refuse aid in favor of restoring fields and homes themselves, so that public funds and material goods could all go to communities less prosperous than his own.

When, in hard times, other peasants of nearby villages raised prices to profiteer in the market with bread and cakes from their surplus flour, Chen Yonggui went so far as to mobilize Dazhai peasants to continue selling at State-decreed prices, thus undercutting the widespread price-gouging and bringing curses of "spoilsport" down on their heads.

Where did such remarkable vision and far farsightedness come from? Why did Chen Yonggui possess it? If he wasn't born with it, what impelled him to cultivate it as his own? That is a difficult question to answer. What was even more remarkable in the light of his world outlook, which indeed included concern for the working people of the whole world, was his ability to inspire others to adopt the same ideology. While he personally led Dazhai Brigade and Xiyang County, he developed in his own and neighboring villages at least two score men and women who shared his point of view so fully they became outstanding proletarian leaders in their own right, two score and more who practiced "all for public, no thought of self" themselves while teaching others to put "public first, self second." In due course Chen Yonggui and his proteges mobilized thousands, even tens of thousands of rank-and-file people to put their faith in community solidarity and work together for common prosperity.

Wherever people truly studied Dazhai enthusiasm rose, the pace of development quickened and outstanding achievements in production, the transformation of nature, community building, and the extension of social services (medical care, education, cultural activities) followed one after the other.

The existing forces of production were everywhere more or less equal. The land, of course, varied in its fertility, but usually where it was poorer people had more of it to till. The tools, the implements, the draft animals, the technology inherited from the old society, and the vast pool of labor power constantly renewed and expanding—these were universal factors.

The relations of production, likewise, were also everywhere more or less the same. Once the working peasants completed land reform through the expropriation of the landlords and rich peasants and, urged on by the Communist Party, pooled their land to create a system of collective assets and shared income based on work performed, the relations between people at the point of production (relations characterized by a new ownership system, new production processes, and new principles of distribution) seemed also, on the surface, very much the same.

Why then did some villages do so much better than others? Why did Dazhai take off economically? Why, once Chen Yonggui came to power in the county, did Dazhai's neighboring villages also take off? Why were so many Dazhai people able to take the lead in distant communities and reproduce, far from home, replicas of the successes they had left behind?

The answer lies in the way in which they applied the political lessons learned from Chen Yonggui and Dazhai; in the way in which they deepened and enriched the framework of collective ownership with socialist consciousness, commitment and behavior on the part of a transformed group of leaders that above all; and fundamentally, transformed what, under the new arrangements, mattered most—the relations between leaders and led.

Throughout the Chinese countryside local Party members assumed the role of a leading core. Party leaders, claiming to represent worker and laboring peasant interests, held decisive power, took responsibility and, for better or worse, made policy, administered affairs, and set the example in word and deed for every sphere of community life.

Thus, in addition to an egalitarian ownership, production and distribution system, the sphere of productive relations had to include, if it was to be socialist, the question of an equitable relationship between the leading core and the rank-and-file—a relationship absolutely crucial to the success or failure of any community. A fair and honest leading core dedicated to community progress could successfully mobilize people for cooperative effort that, once launched, generated its own momentum and achieved astonishing results. A venal leading core devoted to self-advancement, favor seeking and influence peddling, could drag people into an apathy that generated despair and, in the long run, conditions approximating a squalid feudal fief where lord and serf alike existed in stalemated, stagnant tension.

What Chen Yonggui did was set a selfless example himself, in part by doing his regular share of productive labor and insisting that all cadres do the same. On that solid foundation he worked tirelessly, through serial rectification meetings and self-and-mutual criticism sessions, to teach socialist ethics and world outlook to others. He was able to impart to many of those around him his own profound faith in collective action, in the power of people working together to unleash a force far greater than the sum of its parts. While doing so he cultivated and promoted those who showed the most commitment and promise. In case after case the startling results in production and community building provided their own justification and inspiration for further progress and development.

Chen Yonggui's Dazhai was the most successful example in rural China of the implementation of Mao's slogan "Grasp revolution, promote production." Wherever people followed the true spirit of Dazhai and not some outward form (like building Dazhai-style cave homes or duplicating Dazhai arched dams) yields rose, silviculture, fisheries and animal husbandry prospered, industries took root and grew, health care education and culture flourished.

This was the essence of Dazhai and the reason Mao Zedong called on the peasants of the whole nation to "Study Dazhai." New technologies were a fruit of the Dazhai spirit, not the Dazhai spirit itself. Without working together for the common good no community could create "Dazhai Sponge Soil," because to do it, in the conditions of the fifties, meant first, carrying all the corn stalks to centrally designated areas where water was available all winter; second, chopping these stalks fine with stalk chopping knives (later diesel or electric powered silage choppers), mixing them with earth, night soil, animal manure and if possible some fertilizer, then piling them in long piles to ferment; third, keeping them wet with water to maintain bacterial action and turning them periodically for even fermentation; fourth, carrying the seasoned compost back up and out to the terraced fields and incorporating it deeply so as to transform the soil to a depth of a foot or more.

Corn production based on this process required 240 or more man hours per *mu* (one-sixth of an acre), diesel or electric power, manure, fertilizer and night soil, constant attention and the will to carry it through. Few families could contemplate doing such a project alone, but any community dedicated to cooperation could organize such compost production and make it well worth while. The yields on Dazhai sponge soil in the dry, drought-prone loess slopes of the Taihang Mountains amounted to 140 bushels of dry shelled corn per acre, year after year. This is a yield that American farmers are glad to get. The State of Illinois in the best of years rarely averages over a hundred bushels to the acre.

So great was Chen Yonggui's influence, that not only did Dazhai achieve these kinds of yields but after Chen took over as Party Secretary of Xiyang County, village after village in the County also began achieving or even surpassing these yields. In the early 1980s before the land was re-divided, I traveled to Dazhai with a young woman who worked out of Taiyuan, Shanxi, for the All China Association for Friendship With Foreign Countries. The reformers had already begun their attack on Dazhai, denigrating Chen and the village as a fraud. When we came over the mountain into Xiyang County the whole countryside, which had been suffering the same drought as the Counties all around it, was blooming with green, vigorous, pollinating corn, a most marvelous demonstration of peasant farming at its best. The young lady gasped in amazement.

"But I thought Dazhai was all false," she said.

"Now you'll have to figure out for yourself who and what is false," I answered.

Depending primarily on the former poor and hired peasants, uniting with all willing middle peasants, taking collective spirit seriously, putting public first, self second, using self-reliance and struggling hard, that was what made Dazhai so special, and that's what Chen Yonggui meant by putting politics in command. If the politics, starting with the class alliance and ending with collective will, were sound and firm the technology followed in due course.

The horizontal arched dams in Wolf Den Ravine that Chen Yonggui invented were another example of technology that only a community united as one could put into practice. Chen thought of the idea after gully-busting rainstorms had washed out the rich terraces in the ravine bottom twice. To build dams like that in the short time available between the autumn harvest and the onset of winter demanded the concerted effort of all available labor power, both male and female. It required many mutually dependent teams—a team in the quarry cutting stone, a team on the mountain transporting stone, a team in the gully digging down for firm foundations, a team in the gully laying stone, other teams blasting loess earth on the ridges and moving it, by all means available, into the hollow behind the rising dam—a collective project if there ever was one.

Chen Yonggui solved the technical problems posed by the conditions on Tigerhead Mountain in Shanxi. When, as Vice-Premier, he became responsible for the development of agriculture in the whole country, he didn't need to know offhand solutions to the technical problems posed by rice paddies in the lower Yangtze valley, or desert oases in Xinjiang. What these places needed him for was political mobilization, the Dazhai spirit, mobilizing the former poor-and-hired as the core, drawing in the middle peasants, putting "public first, self second," practicing "self-reliance and hard struggle." If the communities mobilized in that way with that spirit, they could discover for themselves what to do with their environment. In the case of Wuxi, near Taihu Lake in Kiangsu Province, the key task was rebuilding the countryside so that channels supplying water for the paddies and channels draining water away ran under a single road network linking all fields. Making one space serve three functions—human access, water supply and water removal—was a brilliant solution to a difficult problem that saved large amounts of land for crops and greatly simplified their care. But only fully mobilized communities willing to invest enormous quantities of labor could do what Wuxi villages did on a vast scale.

With Dazhai-style mobilization and Dazhai spirit every community could realize its full development potential in the form of an open-ended ascending production spiral. Not only could local communities rationalize crop-raising, they could pursue all-around development by going in for orchards and forests, livestock and fisheries and beyond that into nonfarm sidelines including industries both labor intensive and high tech. Far from pursuing grain production to the exclusion of all else as detractors charged, Dazhai developed an all-around economy that included evergreens on Tigerhead Mountain's higher slopes, apple trees on the broad Kang Family Ridge, walnuts and persimmons wherever they would grow, a bean noodle factory that produced market vermicelli plus by-product feeds that greatly expanded pig raising in Backside Draw, a laboratory producing antibiotic medicines, a bauxite mine (worked for a time only), two coal mines, and a furfural factory transforming Xiyang's abundant corncobs into a valuable industrial chemical (this at the County seat). Dazhai also encouraged others to do the same. By 1975 there were already over 800,000 Dazhai-inspired industrial enterprises at the village level in China. In later years, including the years since Deng's "reforms," the number grew to many millions. The proponents of "Reform" like to claim credit for this whole trend. That claim is patently untrue.

Through no fault of his own or of Dazhai's, Chen Yonggui occupied a vital niche at the very core of Chinese politics in the era, so recently concluded (only temporarily, for sure), of antagonistic confrontation between the socialist road and the capitalist road. Mao Zedong chose Dazhai as the model for the socialist road in the Chinese countryside. He also saw it as a model that could provide a firm base for socialist development in general, the foundation for a universal socialist economy in China. The Liu-Deng clique came to power, with a totally contrary view of China's development overall, and of China's rural development in particular. New policy makers could not, however, reverse course without first tearing Dazhai's image apart and replacing it with another—a privatized, free-market, capital-intensive image presented by such a village as the now notorious Dachiuzhuang.[1] For this reason the details of the attack on, and the

1. Dachiuzhuang came to grief two years ago when its leader ordered beatings of subordinates that ended in their deaths and then mounted armed resistance against the police sent to investigate the incidents. During later investigations he also bribed high officials for details of his impending indictment and obtained a copy of everything, including his arrest warrant, before anybody came to arrest him. (W.H.H.)

defense of, Chen Yonggui and Dazhai have indispensable value for illuminating what the political struggle in China has all been about in the latter half of the twentieth century. Through exploration of the Dazhai story one can approach an understanding of Chinese politics as a whole. Dazhai can serve as that "sparrow" mentioned by Mao, which on dissection reveals the truth about all "sparrows," and beyond that, the whole "avian realm."

Unfortunately, although author Qin Huailu opens the door to this crucial enlightenment, he never actually walks through it. He never comes to grips with the essence of the whole matter —why Dazhai and Chen Yonggui rose so high and so fast, and why Dazhai and Chen Yonggui fell so hard and so far. It must be admitted, however, that he does better with the former than with the latter question. Qin talks about the seminal article already mentioned, "Dazhai's Departure From the Spirit of Dazhai" and then asks how one article in the press could bring down something as solid, as meaningful and as outstanding as Chen Yonggui and Dazhai; bring down something, furthermore, that had so much support from prestigious officials at all levels from Chairman Mao Zedong and Zhou Enlai to local County and Commune functionaries. Qin expends what may seem like an unreasonable proportion of his text on details of the support and encouragement China's most important Communist Party and State leaders gave to Dazhai over many years, all of which, it seems, came to naught after one critical attack in a provincial paper.

Astute readers will conclude, of course, that Dazhai was not done in by any article in the press. It was not the media that "reversed the case" on Chen Yonggui and Dazhai. For many years before 1980 Liu Shaoqi and Deng Xiaoping considered Mao's designated peasant hero and his thriving collective community a bone in their throat, a thorn in their side. As early as the middle sixties they were looking for ways to bring both down—witness the intense attack launched against Dazhai by Liu-inspired and directed work teams during the Socialist Education Movement described in Chapter 13. Witness also the small but revealing incident that happened in 1971 when my mother took a group of American high-school students to China as guests of Premier Zhou. High foreign ministry officials did their best, including all manner of unprincipled maneuvers, to pry the group out of Dazhai weeks before the month's stay that the Premier had approved for this visit had expired. They only failed because Dazhai's women's leader, Song Liying, absolutely refused to go along.

Once the Liu clique came to power in late 1978 (without Liu, who died in 1969, a medically neglected victim of the Cultural Revolution) its leaders set the stage for destroying Dazhai through a media offensive. This took some time to get off the ground, then struck hard with that notorious October, 1980, article by journalists Li Guoqing and Yang Yuyan, "Dazhai's Departure From the Spirit of Dazhai."

The Departure article, however, was only one facet of the multi-layered offensive launched by Deng and his cohorts as they laid the groundwork for their 1980 *coup de grace*. There were many other facets, one of which directly involved me. Since Deng wanted Chen Yonggui out of Central Councils, and wanted both Chen and Dazhai thoroughly discredited, he used every avenue of attack available. One of them was to make invidious comparisons between Dazhai's labor-intensive methods of crop production and the mechanized methods practiced in Europe and North America. Holding up the latter as models, Deng's media minions asked, "How can Chen Yonggui lead China toward modernization when his methods require 288 man-hours to raise one *mu* of wheat, while in the United States less than one hour is sufficient and in France less than 1 ½ hours suffice?"

To nail down such facts and make them vivid, and thereby effective against the very popular peasant Vice-Premier, Chen Yonggui, behind-the-scenes persons of influence put me on national television two or three times in 1978 to tell how I raised 1,800 *mu* (300 acres of corn) singlehandedly in Pennsylvania and still had time to do agricultural consulting work in China. At that time I was particularly interested in establishing some objective criteria for measuring China's agricultural modernization, and it seemed to me that the most basic measure had to be labor productivity, particularly since the institutions of the Chinese agricultural establishment (the ministries, the colleges, the academies, and the extension services) tended to ignore this completely in their push for high yields without regard for the stepped-up intensity or duration of the labor required.

I knew Chen Yonggui well and I admired him, Dazhai and by extension Xiyang County immensely. I traveled through much of China with Chen Yonggui and Ji Dengkuei as a participant in a 1978 National Capital Construction Conference tour. En route we exchanged compatible views on scores of subjects and issues, though we never could agree on no-till, to which I was committed, as the future farming system. Chen was all for tillage, intensive, careful tillage. In the absence of practical demonstrations, no amount of talk about no-till could change his mind.

When we returned from the trip I found I was scheduled to speak about labor productivity to the whole nation once again on TV. It never occurred to me that the reason I was up there talking about this was that Mao's enemies, the anti-collective, pro-privatization clique, could use Western labor efficiency on the land to make Chen Yonggui look bad. It wasn't long, however, before they shocked me into awareness by attacking Chen and Dazhai on exactly these grounds. After that they pursued the matter for a whole decade as the 1990 anti-Dazhai slander, *The Rise and Fall of the Red Flag of Dazhai* makes clear. (See Chapter 37.)

The "reformers'" real attitude toward labor productivity was specious, however. Having discredited Dazhai by this and scores of other methods, they then turned around and carried out the atomization of China's farmland by means of the family contracts of the "Responsibility System." Because it turned large fields into small noodle strips only one, two and not more than a few meters wide, this reform made raising labor productivity with mechanization virtually impossible. Meanwhile, Chen Yonggui and the people of Dazhai (up to the moment in 1983 when local officialdom forced them into breaking up their collective) were busy turning small fields into big ones to create conditions for mechanization. In the light of this, the media attack, in which I inadvertently played an unsuspecting but nevertheless shameful, ground-breaking role, was both venal and cynical.

A second example demonstrating not merely neglect but even contempt for productivity occurred in Long Bow Village, Changzhi City, Shanxi, where, beginning in 1977 I worked with Wang Jinhong, the Brigade Party Secretary, to mechanize the bulk of the corn crop. Using China-made machines supplemented with foreign prototypes already available in Shanxi, we successfully mechanized all fifteen of the operations required for field corn production, while simultaneously cutting costs and raising yields. With our set of equipment twelve people were able to raise 1,200 *mu* of corn and get twice the yield previously obtained by hand methods. Measured in grain produced per man this was a fortyfold increase in productivity.

In the fall of 1982 the local authorities insisted on breaking up Long Bow's land and dividing it as noodle strips among all the families in the village. This "reform" smashed the mechanization, idled two-thirds of the equipment (the machines sit rusting to this day in the machinery yard), and sent labor productivity into a tailspin—from a hundred *mu* tilled per laborer to 5 *mu*. At this point China's leading ideologist of agrarian "reform," Mr. Du Rensheng, sent a team of cadres down from Beijing to prove that Long Bow's mechanization was no good anyway, that Long Bow reported false yields, false outlays and false profits and that therefore nothing was lost by breaking up the most promising example of peasant-style mechanization so far realized in China.

All this by way of demonstrating that it was not the media or the journalists, as such, that did Chen Yonggui and Dazhai in. It was the "reform" itself. The achievements of Dazhai and of Xiyang and the many other Counties that followed Dazhai to prosperity, outstanding as they were, were incompatible with the goals of the "reform." The slogans endorsed by Deng Xiaoping: "Enrich Yourselves" and "Some Must Get Rich First" were incompatible with Dazhai's core slogans: "Public First, Self Second" and "Self-reliance and Hard Struggle." Subsequent developments have conclusively demonstrated that the fundamental objective of the "reform" was to convert land-sharing members of collectives into propertyless proletarians with nothing to call their own except their two hands and nothing to sell but their labor power—i.e., the goal of the reform was to turn labor into a commodity like any other on the market and thus lay the foundations for capitalism.

Since this goal was not and is not in the long-range interest of the majority of peasants, Deng and colleagues set about trying to prove that, all evidence to the contrary, collective agriculture was a dead end and provided peasants with no way out. To do this they had to destroy Chen Yonggui's reputation and that of Dazhai along with it. They had to convince the whole nation that Dazhai was a fraud, and in this they succeeded in the main, although, as Abraham Lincoln said so long ago, "You can fool all of the people some of the time and some of the people all of the time, but you can't fool all of the people all of the time," an aphorism clearly demonstrated by the skepticism displayed by Qin Huailu.

It is not clear to me whether author Qin Huailu understands what has been laid out above. Certainly he does not make it very clear in this volume. But there may be good reasons for that lack of clarity. The simplest is that he didn't understand the main parameters of the ongoing political struggle himself, which seems unlikely. Another is that he knew very well what was behind the smashing of Dazhai, but in the political climate created by Deng Xiaoping he couldn't afford to spell everything out openly. He could best serve the cause of Chen Yonggui and Dazhai by explaining the good work they had done, and by recounting the encouraging words and the many visits of prestigious old revolutionary cadres from Premier Zhou Enlai to Marshal Ye Jianying who supported the whole project, thus laying a strong foundation for understanding and sympathizing with Dazhai without provoking the wrath of those in power.

There are some grounds for thinking that the latter explanation is valid, but there are other indications in Qin's text which seem to illustrate an inadequate grasp of the antagonistic nature of the ongoing class struggle in China since the completion of the New Democratic phase of the revolution in 1949.

In the later nineteenth and early twentieth centuries three mountains pressed down on the heads of the Chinese people. These were imperialism, bureaucratic capitalism and feudalism. The victory of the Peoples Liberation Army over the compradore regime of Chiang Kai-shek (Jiang Jieshih) ended the domination of the first—imperialism. The subsequent expropriation and nationalization of the assets of China's Four Families, and other bureaucratic capitalists, finished off the second—bureaucratic capitalism. Between 1946 and 1953 when the organized peasants broke up the power of the landlords and rich peasants by means of thorough and universal land reform, they removed the last of these mountains—feudalism.

So far so good! But what would happen next? Clearly China faced a great transition, but a transition to what? Chairman Mao said the next step was to build socialism. With socialism on the agenda the principal internal contradiction would shift from that of the Chinese people versus the landlord class, to that of the Chinese people versus the capitalist class, at that time an uneasy ally of the workers and peasants because of the anti-imperialist content of the Revolution. Henceforth the main content of national politics would be supervision over and restriction of the capitalist class by a government representing a core alliance of workers and peasants and with added support from the important stratum of free professionals. Handled carefully, a potential antagonistic contradiction could be resolved peacefully with an eventual buy-out of big entrepreneurial capital by the government, while small capital units could save themselves by merging to form cooperatives along lines pioneered by peasants.

Though Mao's program won strong support from the masses of workers, peasants and free professionals he never won full consensus for it in the nation or even inside the Communist Party. Within the Party a clique grew up around Liu Shaoqi and Deng Xiaoping that favored a long period of undisturbed mixed economy that would allow for the rapid development of the capitalist class, a parallel free market economy in the countryside that would generate a rich peasant class and, as has been demonstrated by history, the eventual flowering of full-fledged capitalism, which would, in the view of its advocates, serve as a necessary stage for the development of productive forces prior to any talk or action relating to socialism. Maoists view this as fleshed-out "theory of the primacy of productive forces" or more simply, just plain "productive forces theory," always a hotly debated topic among Marxists.

Thus a long internal struggle began at the core of the Communist Party, including its highest levels. Over time and through bitter experience, Mao began to see this struggle not as a divergence between cliques supporting two different roads to socialism but as a struggle between a headquarters representing working class forces committed to socialism on the one hand and a headquarters dominated by "Party people in authority taking the capitalist road," and committed to capitalism, on the other. This developing contradiction was fundamentally antagonistic.

Having failed to check the capitalist roaders by all ordinary means, Mao launched the Cultural Revolution as one final mass effort that, through mobilizing the whole people, could bring the conflict to a head and assure victory for the working class and socialism—a bold, unprecedented and perilous move.

Qin Huailu calls the Cultural Revolution "the great disaster" and of course it did, in the long run, lead to disaster for millions of ordinary people, for Mao and for socialism. But what Qin Huailu apparently did not see was the antagonistic nature of and the complexity of the struggle, particularly the way in which the bourgeois headquarters shifted tactics from "Right" to "Ultra-left," both forms posing equal dangers to socialist progress. Qin tends to see the contest, at least as it matured, as one between the "old cadres" and the super radical Gang of Four. He shows no appreciation of the three-way struggle that actually developed, no appreciation of the powerful hold on power and policy exercised by the "rightist" old cadres, the "capitalist roaders" grouped around Liu when he still lived, then around Deng after the latter inherited the mantle of opposition leader.

Puzzled by the fact that in the Socialist Education Movement a pair of diametrically opposed policy documents came down directly from the Central Committee, one of which proved viable and "correct" while the other led patently to disaster and was "erroneous"; and realizing clearly that it was Mao's "correct" document that supported and saved the old peasant cadres at the grass roots, many of whom were on the verge of suicide while others had already killed themselves, Qin writes, "If one takes the position that Chairman Mao, so solicitous of all the old cadres at the grass roots, represented the correct line, then why did the 'Great Proletarian Cultural Revolution' that he himself set in motion later hurt so many old cadres?"

Qin Huailu either failed to realize, or hesitated to express, that the choice was never simply one between "old cadres" and the Gang, but very much a three-way struggle between Mao's headquarters and its steady, operative socialist line and alternating Right and Left attacks on Mao's line from Deng Xiaoping's headquarters on the one hand, and similar attacks usually Left in form but Right in essence from Jiang Qin and her clique on the other. Throughout the history of the Chinese revolution, at every crucial stage of development, similar three- sided struggles took place, with Mao's line, once he established his leadership, under constant attack from both Right and Left deviations, as they were labeled in the movement.

During the Cultural Revolution, while many important players shifted allegiance, sometimes more than once, and many coalitions of "strange bedfellows" came and went, those who sided more or less consistently with Liu Shaoqi and Deng Xiaoping, were Po Yipo, Peng Jen, Tan Jenlin, Marshal Ho Long, Lu Dingyi, Ye Jianying, and many other prestigious old cadres. Siding with Mao were Zhou Enlai, Hua Guofeng, Ji Deng Kuei, and Chen Yonggui. Up to a certain point this list should include Lin Biao, Chen Boda and the Gang of Four. The turning point came when personal ambition spun these protagonists off into extreme sectors of left field where they pursued other variants of opposition. Much steadier was the corps of committed Maoist activists, old and new, who held posts at all levels throughout the country. These were matched, however, by a similar corps of Liu-Deng activists, many of whom held equal or superior positions of power nationwide.

This book of Qin Huailu's does not describe any three-way struggle, nor does it go into any depth in regard to class struggle during the transition to socialism. Whenever class struggle comes up Qin speaks immediately of landlords and rich peasants, the class enemies of an earlier period, without apparently recognizing that the principal contradiction of Chinese society itself had shifted away from feudalism to capitalism, and without apparently appreciating what a fearful specter the transition to socialism raises in the hearts and minds of the elite of this world, including, not surprisingly, entrenched bureaucrats. On the other hand it was just this transition and the opposition it engendered that became Mao's greatest concern, the target of his most intense study, and the area where he made his greatest contribution to socialist theory and practice.

Qin said: "The Cultural Revolution was a product of the theory of continuous revolution." This implies stupendous voluntaristic power on Mao's part, since if this upheaval was the product of a theory then it was created by the man who formulated the theory. I think it fair to say that the Cultural Revolution was not the product of any theory, but was the result of a congenital clash between contending class forces for the heart, the soul and the future of China. It was a necessary product of the attempted transition to socialism which the victory of the New Democratic Revolution over imperialism, feudalism and bureaucratic capitalism brought onto the agenda of Chinese history in the second half of the twentieth century. Powerful forces and potent leaders who didn't want socialism blocked the way and eventually prevailed, but not without a titanic struggle. Unfortunately for socialism, during the Cultural Revolution the real struggle was masked and confused by debilitating factionalism that served the opposition well, whether or not anyone willed it. Counter-revolution won the first round of battle in this struggle, but because it is not the product of a theory but a process generated by history itself, and by new classes on the stage of Chinese history—the working class and a collectively tempered peasantry—more battles are surely on the way.

If Qin did not understand the essence and the parameters of the new class struggle very well, neither, it seems, did Chen Yonggui. After Mao died and the new Central leaders replaced Hua Guofeng, they repudiated Chen Yonggui, removed him from office and forced him into limbo. He kept asking himself and those who sympathized with him what he had done wrong. He never seemed to grasp that he was a victim, one of the most important victims, of that stage of the class struggle. He had such faith in the Communist Party as a whole that he seemed unable to imagine that the Communist Party could split, could change color at the top, could fall into the hands of "capitalist roaders" who would, in turn, repudiate him, repudiate Dazhai and repudiate the finest achievements of socialist construction. He kept examining his own past, his own record, to see where he had gone wrong. If he had grasped the real situation in its totality he would not have fallen into introspection and self-criticism, but would have girded himself for a fight, focused his energies and consciously renewed the struggle that had dominated most of his life. His fate would not then have been so tragic. No matter what happened to him he could have died at peace with himself.

Of course there is the possibility that Chen Yonggui was not so blind to what had happened to him as Qin describes. He, like Qin, had to survive in a supremely hostile environment both in and outside of the Communist Party. Once Deng and his group took over, they ruthlessly purged the Party of Maoists wherever they found them, removed Regional, County and Commune-level cadres from their posts wholesale and sent them to rusticate by tending livestock in remote villages. Most of Chen's core Xiyang County group who had gone out to develop other parts of the country suffered punishment of this kind. The rhetoric was all "forget the class struggle, let's get on with economic construction" but the action was all political, aimed at suppressing any and all conscious socialist opposition and dismantling any and all socialist components of the super-structure. In such a situation, developing and activating a viable opposition strategy was no simple or easy matter. If Chen Yonggui had a resistance strategy he was not at liberty to pursue it publicly. There may be dimensions to his struggle about which we are not and cannot easily become aware.

Science fiction space travelers scour the universe looking for new civilizations, but in the farthest reaches of space they never seem to find any social phenomena that transcend the elite-dominated configurations so redundant in human history—violent tribalisms, intolerable slavocracies, oriental despotisms, stagnant feudal fiefs, rapacious monopolists, or outright fascist bullies—either these or "end of history" idealizations of America's polarized and crisis-ridden democracy. This reflects, of course, not the paucity of the universe but the paucity of the bourgeois imagination. For while this esoteric intellectual search went forward something truly new in history arose in China—the peasant innovator, Chen Yonggui, and the new social construct, Dazhai—a man and a community dedicated to "public first, self second," "self-reliance and hard struggle" whose members transformed both themselves and their environment to build, amidst most unfavorable surroundings, a prosperous, shared life with an innate open-ended potential for growth and improvement.

The Dazhai phenomena genuinely stirred the imagination of China and the world. Deservedly so, for the man and the community exemplified the best, most mature and viable example of what the world working class movement, with its roots in German philosophy, French rationalism, British trade union building and Utopian socialist dreaming could produce. Here was no Utopian construct but rather a sweat-stained, mud-spattered working example of what ordinary, earthbound people could do if they accepted a few practical equalitarian principles and, depending on their own talents and the resources they found around them, worked hard to transform all the parameters of their economic, social and political life.

Of course the latent entrepreneurial bourgeois and budding comprador types operating throughout the superstructure of Chinese society, backed up by the would-be rich peasants scattered throughout the rural base, hated what they saw at Dazhai. Dazhai's success threatened to block the road to the exploitation of wage labor. The rapid development of China during thirty years of socialist construction had demonstrated the astonishing potential of the national economy. The would-be bourgeoisie could see that by reverting to a more traditional property ownership system and, through a normal process of attrition, by turning labor into a commodity, China could generate and support, as envied India already did, scores of millions of coupon-clipping, stock-speculating, profit-hogging entrepreneurial upstarts who enjoyed all the perks of modern Western life, while the compradore types at the top, by cutting the foreign multinationals in on a slice of the proceeds, could actually move into world class positions of wealth and power far beyond the dreams of previous generations of Chinese.

Meanwhile, the vast majority of the working population, in their hundreds of millions, would barely be able to maintain a degrading subsistence existence. Who cared? There would always be more room at the top for those who were brazen enough, skillful enough, and ruthless enough to claw their way up. That was the natural, normal way of the world. It was all in accord with fundamental economic laws of development which Dazhai ignored, violated and turned upside down, contradicting in its immature, idealistic folly the essence of human nature itself.

One could feel the anti-Dazhai fear and hatred in the hearts of those Foreign Ministry officials who tried to pull my mother's group out of Dazhai in 1971, one could feel that same hatred in the heart of that privatization ideologue, Du Rensheng, whom I met and clashed with after he helped smash Long Bow's successful mechanization initiative in 1983, and one could feel that same hatred in the hearts of those Ministry of Agriculture cadres who constantly threw roadblocks in the path of the mechanization project launched at my initiative by the United Nations Food and Agriculture Organization in 1990, a project that required scale in village agriculture and thus new forms of collective organization. It is a hatred that causes people possessed by it to stop at nothing, to ignore any fact, to tell any lie, to violate any regulation of government or norm of human behavior in order to wreak havoc on and destroy successful community cooperation.

In 1971, in order to force my mother's group out of Dazhai, the Foreign Ministry officials tried to break up her American Youth Group from below, mobilizing black against white, nonrelatives against relatives to win a majority vote to leave, moves that violated the very principle of international solidarity and hospitality. With similar venality, in the early eighties the "reform" group stopped Xiyang's West-Water-East project dead in its tracks in the last stages of its completion, after the expenditure of tens of millions of *yuan* and tens of thousands of man-days of peasant labor. The officials cut off their noses to spite their faces, or as the Chinese say, picked up a rock only to drop it on their own feet—anything to hit back at Chen Yonggui, Dazhai and Xiyang.

What is the source of this hatred? I have asked that question many times since encountering the phenomenon and have given it much thought. It stems, I think, from the same source as the gut hatred most Chinese landlords harbored for the Chinese Communist Party. If the Party won a victory it would mean land reform, the end of land rents and the end of the landlords, not as individuals, but as an exploiting class. For it was clear to all, including the landlords, that land rent collectors cannot get along without laboring peasants, but laboring peasants can get along very well without land rents or the landlords who collect them. By the same token, at the end of the twentieth century, in spite of the collapse of the first socialist experiments worldwide, the bourgeoisie and would-be bourgeoisie are now faced with a similar reality. Capitalists cannot get along without wage workers, but working people, including working peasants, can get along very well without capitalists. Chen Yonggui and Dazhai proved that and that's why Dazhai engendered such fierce opposition.

There you have the nub of the problem and it means, I predict, that we are facing a wild twenty-first century, full of alarums, upheavals, struggles and deep, indispensable change!